Training in Integrated Relational Psychotherapy

Barbara Poletti • Giorgio A. Tasca
Luca Pievani • Angelo Compare
Editors

Training in Integrated Relational Psychotherapy

An Evidence-Based Approach

Editors
Barbara Poletti
Department of Oncology
and Hemato-Oncology
University of Milan
Milano, Italy

Department of Neurology and Laboratory
of Neuroscience
IRCCS Istituto Auxologico Italiano
Milan, Italy

Luca Pievani
Scuola di Psicoterapia Integrata
Bergamo, Italy

Giorgio A. Tasca
School of Psychology
University of Ottawa
Ottawa, ON, Canada

Angelo Compare
Department of Human and Social Science
University of Bergamo
Bergamo, Italy

ISBN 978-3-031-71903-5   ISBN 978-3-031-71904-2 (eBook)
https://doi.org/10.1007/978-3-031-71904-2

© The Editor(s) (if applicable) and The Author(s), under exclusive license to Springer Nature Switzerland AG 2024

This work is subject to copyright. All rights are solely and exclusively licensed by the Publisher, whether the whole or part of the material is concerned, specifically the rights of translation, reprinting, reuse of illustrations, recitation, broadcasting, reproduction on microfilms or in any other physical way, and transmission or information storage and retrieval, electronic adaptation, computer software, or by similar or dissimilar methodology now known or hereafter developed.
The use of general descriptive names, registered names, trademarks, service marks, etc. in this publication does not imply, even in the absence of a specific statement, that such names are exempt from the relevant protective laws and regulations and therefore free for general use.
The publisher, the authors and the editors are safe to assume that the advice and information in this book are believed to be true and accurate at the date of publication. Neither the publisher nor the authors or the editors give a warranty, expressed or implied, with respect to the material contained herein or for any errors or omissions that may have been made. The publisher remains neutral with regard to jurisdictional claims in published maps and institutional affiliations.

This Springer imprint is published by the registered company Springer Nature Switzerland AG
The registered company address is: Gewerbestrasse 11, 6330 Cham, Switzerland

If disposing of this product, please recycle the paper.

Foreword

Every mental health professional, it seems, recognizes the central and curative nature of the therapeutic relationship. They know this truth in their bones from undergoing a successful course of personal treatment, from conducting psychotherapy, and from reviewing the empirical research. Whether conceived as a precondition of patient change or as a process of change, the psychotherapy relationship proves essential.

This recognition of the powerful centrality of the therapist-patient relationship has been accompanied by two profound ironies. The first is that, until recently, we did not know which components of the therapy relationship proved effective. Colleagues and I have rectified this gap in multiple editions of the meta-analysis-fueled *Psychotherapy Relationships That Work*. The second irony is that, until this book, we did not know how to successfully train clinicians in these demonstrably effective relational behaviors (for a welcome exception, see societyforpsychotherapy.org/teaching-learning-evidence-based-relationships).

Training in Integrated Relational Psychotherapy: An Evidence-based Approach marks a crucial milestone in the maturation of learning and teaching evidence-based relationships. The four talented editors have gathered an impressive collection of chapters that address the broad foundations of the topic. Following introductions to the integrative approach and relational case formulation, the authors address patient motivation and their contributions to the relationship (a lacuna in most works on therapy relationships). The core of the book describes effective methods of imparting skills in the therapy relationship (e.g., repairing alliance ruptures, teaching interpersonal skills, promoting experiential development and self-awareness). That leads to advancing competence-based training in relational skills throughout psychotherapy education. The next section then examines how integrative relational principles are manifested and taught in several leading systems of psychotherapy.

The final section of this compendium features personalizing psychotherapy, which is the second goal (and second volume) of our *Psychotherapy Relationships That Work*. One can behave responsively with clients in a multitude of efficacious ways, including the three presented here: stepped care, patient feedback/routine outcome monitoring, and patient preferences. So much cutting-edge research distilled for our training and clinical use.

The future of psychotherapy portends the integration of the interpersonal and the instrumental, of the relational and the technical, in the tradition of evidence-based practice personalized to the individual patient. I am honored to introduce this future-leaning treasure. Enjoy and learn from it, friends.

Department of Psychology John C. Norcross
University of Scranton
Scranton, USA

Foreword

It is rare to read a book that delivers on its promise, and *Training in Integrated Relational Psychotherapy: An Evidence-Based Approach* is an exception to this rule. Here the academic, researcher, and clinician enter into an exploration of evidence-based approaches and their implementation in the training, application, and the evaluation of psychotherapy. This book deftly meets the needs for the experienced or the newly initiated psychotherapy researcher, clinician, and academic.

The four expert editors succinctly create a choir of international authors who thoughtfully and methodically express their individual scientific perspectives in a collective voice. Readers are immediately introduced to the historical underpinnings of evidence-based psychotherapy and engage in a compassionate and steadfast exploration of common factors, the therapeutic alliance, patient assessment, the customization, and evaluation of treatment and the training of psychotherapists.

Training in Integrated Relational Psychotherapy: An Evidence-Based Approach is an apt dissemination of the integrated approaches and reflects the mission and purpose of the Society for the Exploration of Psychotherapy Integration (SEPI). The book's content and tone is equivalent to attending one of SEPI's annual international conferences. The editors expertly include chapters that explore a variety of theoretical approaches, clinical practice, and diverse methods of inquiry. The readers learn how to solidify their ability to assess and formulate cases and deepen their knowledge in motivation, attachment, and meaning making. Similar to an experiential psychotherapist, the editors bring theory, research, and practice to life by including a focus on the training of a psychotherapist and how to enrich the interplay between therapist and patient. The reader develops a deeper understanding of the essential role of a therapist in the therapeutic process and the necessity of patient feedback and direction.

Like SEPI, *Training in Integrated Relational Psychotherapy: An Evidence-Based Approach* brings clinicians, academics, and researchers together in collaboration and enables clinicians to learn and utilize the finding of evidence-based research, and for researchers to learn from the observations of clinicians working with the issues that arise in the practice of psychotherapy and the training of a psychotherapist.

This book meets the needs of the psychotherapy enthusiast and advances their understanding of evidence-based approaches. After reading this book, the reader can feel confident in their understanding of best practices. *Training in Integrated Relational Psychotherapy: An Evidence-Based Approach* is an excellent addition for anyone engaged in the field of psychotherapy.

Harvard Medical School
President Elect for 2026, Society for the
Exploration of Psychotherapy Integration,
Boston, MA, USA

Kristin A. R. Osborn

Contents

Part I The Integrated Approach in Psychotherapy

Towards an Integrated Approach to Evidence-Based Practice
in Psychotherapy... 3
Angelo Compare and Antonino La Tona

Part II The Formulation of the Clinical Case in the Integrated EBP Approach

Case Formulation: Developing a Shared Understanding of the Patient's
Relational World... 25
Giorgio A. Tasca and Barbara Poletti

Part III Understanding Patient Functioning: Motivational Systems, Attachment, and Meaning Organizations

Motivational Systems for the Understanding of Patient's Functioning... 47
Camilla Pozzi and Francesco Greco

The Postrationalist Perspective: Personal Meaning Organisations
(PMO) and Their Functioning.................................. 71
Daniela Merigliano

The Assessment of Attachment for Case Formulation............... 103
Patricia M. Crittenden, Giuliana Florit, Andrea Landini, and Susan
J. Spieker

Part IV Training in the Therapeutic Relationship

Alliance Ruptures and Repairs..................................... 141
Laura E. Captari and Catherine F. Eubanks

The Therapeutic Relationship as an Attachment Relationship: The Role of Epistemic Trust 167
Alessandro Talia

Mentalization in the Therapeutic Relationship 179
Paula Ravitz and Giorgio A. Tasca

The Role of Trauma in the Therapeutic Relationship 195
Luca Pievani, Cristina Mapelli, and Isabel Fernandez

Training Therapists in Common Interpersonal Skills 233
Tao Lin and Timothy Anderson

iCAST: Possible Steps Toward the Integration of Nonverbal Signals into Psychotherapeutic Practice 245
Fabian T. Ramseyer

Part V The Therapist's Experiential Training and Self-Awareness Development

Personal Experiential Training Within the Integrated Psychotherapy Pathway 261
Monica Bononi, Silvia Busti Ceccarelli, Emilia Martino, and Martina Manzoni

The Path of Self-Awareness Development and the Role of the Co-trainer 279
Laura Carelli, Cristina Morrone, and Mara Zanni

Part VI Evidence-Based Techniques

Interweaving Techniques and Therapeutic Relationship for the Treatment of Personality Disorders 307
Antonella Centonze, Tiziana Passarella, Raffaele Popolo, Paolo Ottavi, and Giancarlo Dimaggio

Attachment-Based Family Therapy: Theory, Clinical Model, and Training 329
Guy Diamond, Suzanne Levy, and Brianna Brennan

Trauma Resolution: A Healing Journey Through EMDR Therapy 343
Isabel Fernandez, Eugenio Gallina, and Roger Solomon

Dialectical Behavior Therapy (DBT) 379
Cesare Maffei

CBT-E: Addressing Eating Disorder Psychopathology with Cognitive Behavioral Strategies and Procedures 397
Riccardo Dalle Grave, Simona Calugi, and Selvaggia Sermattei

Dynamic-Relational Treatment of Pernicious Personality: Working with Perfectionism. 417
Paul L. Hewitt, Anna Kristen, Samuel F. Mikail, and Gordon L. Flett

ACT and SchemaTherapy 445
Luca Altieri, Valeria Monaco, and Stefano Stefanini

Integrating Sexology into Evidence-Based Psychotherapy Practice 477
Francesca Cavallo, Gianpaolo Salvatore, and Andrea Lenzi

Part VII Personalization of the Treatment

Stepped Care Model in Integrated Evidence-Based Practice Relational Psychotherapy. 501
Angelo Compare, Barbara Poletti, Luca Pievani, Jacopo Stringo, and Antonino La Tona

Using Patient Feedback in Psychotherapy and Training 521
Katie Aafjes-van Doorn

Using Patient Preferences to Customise Therapy 537
Antonino La Tona, Agostino Brugnera, Jacopo Stringo, and Mick Cooper

Index. 553

Part I
The Integrated Approach in Psychotherapy

Towards an Integrated Approach to Evidence-Based Practice in Psychotherapy

Angelo Compare and Antonino La Tona

1 Research in Psychotherapy: The Role of Common Factors

Psychotherapy as an instrument of treatment has historically found it difficult to fully fit into the panorama of health promotion-oriented professions, as it deals with factors that cannot easily be quantified and analysed in classical scientific terms. An example of this long-standing debate relates to the diatribe about the empirical evidence of psychotherapy results, the incipit of which can be traced back to the article/provocation by Eysenck (1952), which spanned the history of psychotherapy in the second half of the twentieth century. Ever since the very first theoretical conceptualisations of applied psychology articulated by Lightner Witmer (McReynolds, 1997), who established the first psychological clinic in 1896, clinical psychologists have been uniquely associated with a scientific approach to patient care. Witmer has repeatedly pointed out that 'pure and applied sciences are advancing on a single front. What delays the progress of one, delays the progress of the other; what favours one, favours the other' (McReynolds, 1997, p. 249). As early as 1947, the idea that young psychologists should be trained bilaterally, both as scientists/researchers and as health professionals, became a functional policy of the American Psychological Association (APA) (Hilgard et al., 1947). Early mental health professionals such as Thorne (1947) emphasised the importance of scientific and functional methodologies with which to combine, in their clinical practice, the application of the experimental approach to the individual case and to their own experience.

To build a bridge between research and practice in clinical psychology, psychotherapy researchers have increasingly focused their attention over the past 40 years on studies of the effectiveness and efficiency of different therapeutic treatments. In this delicate and fascinating field of mental health research, two approaches are

A. Compare · A. La Tona (✉)
Department of Human and Social Sciences, University of Bergamo, Bergamo, Italy
e-mail: antonino.latona@unibg.it

especially prevalent among researchers and clinicians. On the one hand, there has been the development of so-called 'empirically supported treatments', which are based on randomised controlled clinical trials (RCTs) aimed at establishing the efficacy of a specific treatment for a specific clinical disorder and the weight of therapeutic/technical factors specific to a treatment model (Westen et al., 2004). On the other hand, there has been the emergence of studies related to the 'common factors' perspective, aimed at confirming the so-called 'Dodo verdict' (Luborsky, 1995)—the substantial equivalence of effectiveness of different psychotherapies. The difference between these two approaches is linked to the presence of different epistemological and conceptual foundations regarding psychotherapy and research. One factor that has historically contributed to widening the gap between research and clinical practice is 'the popularity of theoretical paradigms that embrace epistemologies based on personal experience rather than controlled data' (Herbert, 2003). The APA Society of Clinical Psychology's Committee on Science and Practice emphasised the importance of identifying, studying and disseminating therapies supported by empirical evidence. The official starting date for this approach in psychotherapy was 1995, when the APA's 'Task Force on Promotion and Dissemination of Psychological Procedures of Division 12 (Clinical Psychology)' identified 'a number of psychological interventions considered to be empirically validated treatments, later called *empirically supported treatments (ESTs)*' (Herbert, 2003) or *empirically validated treatments*. This interest in promoting the importance of ESTs probably goes back to the broader movement, which originated in Great Britain, initially called *Evidence-Based Medicine (EBM)* (Sackett, 1997). In a 1995 report, the task force outlined the criteria for selecting an EST and reported a preliminary list of 25 selected treatments, which reached 71 in 1998 (Chambless & Ollendick, 2001). In accordance with APA guidelines, many projects have been developed to disseminate the evidence-based (EB) approach in the field of mental health, although often, the results of this effort have not had any real impact in the clinical-professional field. Therapists working with patients on a daily basis in routine care settings remain predominantly sceptical of the results obtained from highly controlled RCT studies, in which patients are rigidly selected according to specific symptom-diagnostic characteristics and therapists strictly follow highly standardised treatment protocol models (Del Corno & Lo Coco, 2018). In routine clinical practice, therapists are increasingly confronted with clinical situations characterised by very multifaceted diagnostic pictures that hardly fit into the rigid classifications of psychiatry diagnostic manuals (Rossi Monti, 2012). It is important to emphasise, however, that the psychotherapist is not prejudicially opposed to empirical research but calls for it to answer questions deemed useful and/or essential in the management of his or her daily practice. An example is the *survey* conducted in Canada by Tasca et al. (2015), which showed that the topics of understanding the mechanisms of change in psychotherapy, the components of the therapeutic relationship and the effective methods of training therapists who are able to genuinely treat patients are considered central topics for 'useful' research for the practitioner. In recent decades, a strategy has become widespread to foster greater integration between research and clinic, capable of building a bridge between two necessarily communicating realities. Professional awareness has emerged that the enriching dialogue between research and clinical practice can be based on research that starts from therapeutic practice and is able to elaborate work proposals that are highly relevant to the clinician (Levy et al., 2015).

Historically, EB research has aimed to examine whether therapeutic treatment is effective in curing patients. Practice-based research, on the other hand, tries to assess whether a specific therapeutic relationship, based on the characteristics of the therapist, the patient and their relational encounter, can be helpful in overcoming the problems a subject presents (Lo Coco, 2021). In the early 2000s, the *Evidence-Based Practices (EBPs) Project* was developed to increase patient access to empirically supported interventions (Mueser et al., 2003). Specifically, the EBP project aimed to improve access through the development of standardised intervention 'packages' created in collaboration with different actors, including clinicians, patients, family members, therapy supervisors and mental health project managers. More recently, the EBP approach has signalled the need to move towards greater personalisation of treatment. Norcross and Wampold (2018) pointed out that research supports how no therapeutic treatment works for all patients and what works with one patient may not be indicated for another. A therapist is inclined to modify their therapeutic approach with their patient, depending on the patient's needs. Furthermore, therapists who are most effective with their patients are able to be responsive and flexible in the therapeutic relationship with a specific patient and at different points in time with the same patient (Norcross & Wampold, 2018). As early as the 1990s, psychotherapy research tended to shift its cognitive focus to the mechanisms of change that were put in place to facilitate the patient's recovery rather than the effectiveness of treatments. Lambert and Bergin (1992) described a number of therapeutic factors as the main elements associated with patient improvement in psychotherapy: extra-therapeutic factors, common/relational factors, expectation/placebo, therapeutic techniques and the therapist's person. As summarised well by Duncan (2002), Miller et al. (1997) extended the use of the term *common factor* from its original meaning of non-specific or relational factor to include four specific factors: the client (40%), the therapeutic relationship (30%), the placebo (15%) and the technique (15%). The percentages of influence given in brackets in the previous sentence were provided by Assay and Lambert (1999). Although there is general agreement about the relevance of these four process areas, 'the specific factors within each of these categories vary considerably in type and number, with "limited apparent agreement"' (Grencavage & Norcross, 1990) among researchers.

First, the possible and concrete action of client-related factors is closely linked to the particular type of epistemology (and its underlying techniques) typical of each clinical-therapeutic approach. Thus, to allow patients to make the main contribution to change in psychotherapy (Duncan, 2002), the selected approach must give them the role of leading actors in the therapeutic process itself. This is only possible by conveying to them the idea of being at the centre of a process of possible improvement—the therapeutic space is not so much configured as a relationship between an 'expert' therapist, who suggests to the client how to solve their problems, but as a dialogical process capable of activating the client's internal and relational resources, which will be the guide to change. Not all approaches convey this idea to patients, especially if the underlying epistemology is more deterministic rather than constructivist-oriented. Thus, if the medical model characterises the theoretical underpinnings of a particular approach, the patient will not feel like the 'heroic client' (Duncan, 2002) but only an object subject to the action of external factors, such as medication or the skill experience of a psychotherapist or 'guru'. At the same time, to allow the relationship factor to play a transformative role in psychotherapy, the therapist must construct a particular bond with the goal of changing a client's dysfunctional situation. The use of direct or indirect communication, a one-down or one-up position, open or closed questions, short aphorisms or long restructurings, suggestions or rationality in the prescription of homework, etc., can quickly meet therapeutic goals, but to select the best type of communication and relationship, in accordance with the specific patient and the different steps of psychotherapy, the flexible use of therapeutic techniques is necessary. From this point of view, a therapist's *responsiveness* construct has become increasingly relevant (Stiles & Horvath, 2017). For example, it has been shown that in psychodynamic therapies, better results are achieved with patients when the therapist does not rigidly follow his or her own treatment model but employs *adherence flexibility* to meet the patient's characteristics (Owen & Hilsenroth, 2014). Further evidence has shown the importance of the therapist being flexible in their therapeutic approach to manage ruptures and repairs in the alliance (Safran et al., 2000) and to adapt to the patient's characteristics (level of motivation, interpersonal style and self-esteem) (Høglend et al., 2011).

Concerning placebo-related factors, hopes and expectations, Duncan (2002) noted that clients' awareness of being cured is not the only element that can make the placebo component effective for significant therapeutic improvement; for placebo to work, 'an assessment of the credibility of the therapist and related techniques' (Duncan, 2002) is also required. Regarding technique and model factors, Assay and Lambert (1999) defined them as beliefs and procedures unique to each specific treatment. Technique and model factors are not the last and least relevant to the therapeutic process, but they are a key element since, as indicated earlier, they heavily influence the realisation of the effect of the other common factors. Recently, a review by Mulder et al. (2017), entitled *Common* versus *specific factors in psychotherapy: opening the black box*, tried to synthesise the available evidence on this issue. Mulder et al. (2017) began by pointing out an apparently contradictory fact: there is both evidence supporting the fact that different psychotherapies work 'in the same way' (i.e. produce effects of entirely comparable dimensions and evidence of superiority of certain specific psychotherapies over others, at least for certain disorders). In essence, there is enough data to argue that psychotherapies work on the basis of 'common factors', from which they would derive roughly the same efficacy, and that there are specific differences related to specific treatment factors. Not only do both positions seem theoretically plausible, but there is also sufficient data to confirm both positions. As pointed out several times (Mulder et al., 2017), this dichotomy of positions is, by no means, new; indeed, one could cite a famous debate between Rogers and Skinner (1956) (fathers of behaviourism and 'client-based therapy'), in which the latter argued that specific learning components activate specific changes, while the former argued that a genuine, healthy therapeutic relationship was 'necessary and sufficient'. Does this dichotomy, in light of the evidence supporting both positions, still make sense? Or, for the benefit of the advancement of this fascinating field, is it possible (as much as necessary) to overcome it? Perhaps, in line with the evidence mentioned above, the differences between these positions are less relevant in practice than they appear in theory. Rogers and Skinner (1956) pointed out that there seems to be a mutual recognition by theorists of the two poles of the relevance of 'the other side'. Proponents of 'specific factors' recognise the importance of non-specific factors, such as patient involvement, optimism and active and explicit collaboration, in achieving clear and shared goals. Conversely, 'common factors' theorists recognise how, in some very specific clinical contexts, such as phobic anxiety disorders, interventions that are not at all 'common' but rather very limited/specific, such as exposing the patient to the phobic stimulus, are necessary. Furthermore, a key point Mulder et al. (2017) emphasised is that 'common factors' are no longer considered a generic container: when we talk about common factors, we are not talking about an 'anything goes' but rather about interventions that, although 'common' to different psychotherapies, are quite specific in their function and that might possess their own distinct curative power. In essence, the debate on the dichotomy of common versus specific factors seems today to be more of a distraction from the 'simple' and only question that should be asked: 'What are the mechanisms that produce an effect in psychotherapy?' (Goldfried, 2019).

In conclusion, it is important to emphasise that some of the most important methodological criticisms of Luborsky's Dodo verdict have been pointed out by supporters of the EST approach (Chambless & Ollendick, 2001): 'Luborsky's (1995) conclusion that there are no significant differences in the efficacy of different psychotherapies should be reconsidered for the following reasons: (a) errors in data analysis, (b) exclusion of many types of patients from the trial (e.g. adolescents and teenagers), (c) incomplete generalisation of comparisons between therapies that have never been carried out and (d) erroneous assumption that the average difference between all treatments considered with all problems can be taken as the difference between any two types of treatment for a specific disorder. Concern for patients' well-being requires psychologists to be wary of accepting Dodo's verdict (Chambless & Ollendick, 2001).

2 Integration in Psychotherapy: Models

Since its inception, integration in psychotherapy has been characterised by dissatisfaction with specialist approaches and a desire to look beyond the boundaries of one's own school/theory to see what can be learnt and how patients can benefit from other forms of scientific behaviour change.

The first example appears at the 1932 APA congress, where psychiatrist French (1933) drew parallels between psychodynamic and Pavlovian conditioning processes, particularly between repression and extinction. The paper was published in proceedings, together with comments (French, 1933). Similarly, Kubie (1934) proposed that certain aspects of the same psychoanalytic technique could be explained in terms of the conditioned reflex. A first integration strategy emerges here: assume that different schools have called similar, if not the same, processes by different names and explore the similarities.

In 1936, Sol Rosenzweig (Wampold & Imel, 2017) went beyond this position in what is a famous article that speaks from the very title of *common factors*, arguing that the effectiveness of various therapeutic approaches according to him had more to do with their common elements than with the theoretical explanations on which they were based. It was in this article that the even more famous Dodo verdict, a true slogan of the integrationist movement, was quoted. The verdict was, in fact, the subtitle of the article: 'At last the Dodo said, "Everybody has won and all must *have* prizes"'. Rosenzweig did not just launch the idea of common factors but proposed three specific ones: (a) the personality of the therapist, (b) 'interpretations' (i.e. active interventions) and (c) synergy between target aspects of different orientations (Wampold & Imel, 2017). Here, however, a first difficulty emerges: Is it possible to have different views on common factors? Can the 'common' factors be uncommon? The answer is overwhelmingly positive, and, in fact, of the three classes of factors identified by Rosenzweig, perhaps only the first class will converge into the nonspecific common factors of today—nonspecific *factors in the sense that they are not part of any theoretical orientation but are present although not theorised and considered common to all orientations* (Tracey et al., 2003). These tend to be future relational factors. The second class contains specific but differently named interventions in the various orientations (French, 1933), while the third class proposes a further integrative strategy, the analysis of synergies (i.e. the existence of different and specific interventions that then interact mutually reinforcingly). Thus, there are three different ideas of integration: common interventions not envisaged by theory and thus non-specific, common interventions envisaged by theory but named differently and finally interactions between specific and objectively different interventions. For a while, the second strategy prevailed (i.e. the idea that therapists do similar things by naming them differently). Woodworth (1958) introduced another argument that explained the dissatisfaction of clinicians and encouraged them to look for the solution in integration: no one *psychotherapeutic approach seemed powerful enough to overpower the others in terms of effectiveness*—'no one [school] is good enough'. The fact that circumscribing psychic experience within a single theoretical–interpretive framework risked making psychotherapy ascientific insofar as it was inclined to select natural phenomena (in this case, the presence of unconscious and behavioural determinism) on the basis of a cultural rather than a scientific choice. Therefore, the risk is that of adapting the individual to the theory and not the other way around, generating artefacts in the experience of the therapeutic relationship. One of the most interesting topics in recent years in the field of psychotherapy research has concerned the issue of the treatability of patients, especially those with personality disorders (Stone, 2007). Emphasis has been placed on a range of characteristics pertaining not only to the patient that are independent of psychopathology and refer to character, temperamental, environmental or cultural factors but also on how these aspects are combined with the same factors belonging to the therapist. It highlights how the psychotherapeutic experience develops within a relational dimension that is not only communicative (i.e. the information that the patient and therapist exchange) but also how the characteristics of both come into play within this relational dimension.

The following question then arises: What role does psychotherapy play in this scenario? The psychotherapist in turn is a user of this evolution, and the current challenge for integrated psychotherapy also lies in the need to establish a more appropriate balance between clinical epistemology and cultural and social change. From this point of view, the new challenge therefore lies in the need to understand whether psychotherapy should adapt to this new mode of communication and thus use new relational codes or whether psychotherapy can represent a dimension in which what it poses as therapeutic is the re-establishment of a narrative of the individual's experience through a now faded verbal code. The asynchrony between change and adaptation that undermines the configuration of the linearity of evolutionary time thus also concerns psychotherapy. These questions impose, more than ever before in the history of psychology, a reflection on the sense of an integrated approach that more accurately qualifies the function of the common factors of efficacy in relation to their transtheoretical configuration by conferring on verbal functions, in a future that does not seem far off, the role of a further common factor of therapeutic efficacy.

3 The Evidence-Based Practice Integrated Approach to Psychotherapy

Psychotherapy integration is characterised by dissatisfaction with single-model approaches and a concomitant desire to look beyond the boundaries of the school to see how patients can benefit from other ways of conducting psychotherapy (Norcross & Goldfried, 2005). Through this theoretical perspective, an attempt is made to tailor psychological treatments and therapeutic relationships to the specific and varied needs of individual patients, as defined by a multitude of diagnostic and, in particular, transdiagnostic considerations. Psychotherapy must take into account the individual differences and social and cultural characteristics of patients. The clinical reality is that no single psychotherapy proves effective for all patients and situations (Norcross & Lambert, 2018). It is not easy to answer the question that the scientific community has been asking for decades about the possibility of giving rise to a transtheoretical form of psychotherapy that focuses essentially on the experience of the therapeutic relationship, which we recall *is considered the most important common factor of efficacy* and all those variables that characterise the clinical process (Norcross & Goldfried, 2005).

This is the driving force behind integration, flexibility, and instrumental and functional adaptation to the patient's needs. This is also clear by making analogies with other clinical areas. For example, would you entrust your health to a doctor who prescribes the same treatment to every patient without analysing the person in front of them or the type of pathology? Or, to make an educational analogy, would you reward educators who employed the same pedagogical method (say, a frontal lecture) for each educational session? Or would you entrust your child to a childminder who provided the same response (say, a nondirective attitude or reprimand) to every child and every misbehaviour? 'The answer is most probably no.' Patients in psychotherapy do not deserve less consideration. It is as difficult as ever to challenge a heterogeneous and functional approach, as exemplified by the possibilities introduced by integration in psychotherapy. After all, who can seriously challenge the idea that psychological treatment must be tailored to the specific needs of the patient? The integrated psychotherapy model draws from research on therapy processes and outcomes rather than from idiosyncratic theory or ideological syncretism. The number of psychotherapists who identify their orientation with the integrated approach is steadily growing, yet there are still few psychotherapy training programmes that include the development of an integrated practice.

Boswell et al. (2010), from Pennsylvania State University, highlighted the main elements of integrated psychotherapy and specified how it can be learnt during training and clinical supervision. The approach proposed by Boswell et al. (2010) is based on assimilative integration and common factors. They attempt to identify common therapeutic factors and principles of change that are transversal to the various approaches and, starting from a main reference orientation, assimilate techniques from other orientations (Boswell et al., 2010). For example, starting from a humanistic approach, compatible cognitive–behavioural techniques can be integrated while remaining within the theoretical framework of the orientation. According to Boswell et al. (2010), facilitating the process of change can be considered the core competence of psychotherapy. Goldfried (1980) identified five common factors that represent five specific processes of change:

- promote an expectation of the usefulness of the treatment pathway
- establish an optimal therapeutic alliance
- facilitate patient awareness
- provide corrective experiences
- promote a continuous reality check

These processes can be promoted in different ways and with different levels of effectiveness by different orientations. Each approach generally focuses more on some processes and less on others. For example, Rogerian techniques can stimulate a strong alliance (Castonguay & Beutler, 2006), whereas the use of homework, typical of behavioural therapy but alien to Rogerian therapy, can provide a corrective experience. Furthermore, clinical research shows that there may be techniques that are functional for a given patient–therapist pair but ineffective for another.

According to the authors, therefore, the core competence of the integrated approach therapist concerns the understanding of change within and outside one's primary frame of reference, combined with knowledge of a broad clinical repertoire (Castonguay & Beutler, 2006). A competent integrated approach therapist is aware of the change process they are facilitating and of the client's characteristics that influence the choice of techniques to use. For example, a client with a high level of interpersonal conflict might not benefit from a cognitive technique, such as Socratic dialogue, but might respond well to a humanistic technique, such as empathic reflection. It is important, therefore, that the practitioner recognises these issues and is up-to-date and informed about the clinical evidence found in research, so as to adapt the techniques and therapeutic modalities to the client with whom he or she is in relationship (Prochaska & Norcross, 2018).

4 The Role of the Therapeutic Alliance

In light of what has been described, the ability to establish a good therapeutic alliance is an essential element for an integrated approach therapist, given the importance recognised to this factor by various theoretical orientations and scientific studies (Flückiger et al., 2018). The alliance should not only be promoted but also be constantly evaluated. A therapist must be able to recognise and cope with inevitable ruptures in the relationship by utilising the contributions made by different approaches. It is also important for a therapist with an integrated approach to be able to formulate a diagnosis, conceptualise the clinical case and plan treatment within a multidimensional approach. The therapist's attention must not stop at the symptom but at everything that can be useful for successful treatment. The foundations of the application of the various techniques are based firstly on an approach centred on EBPs and then on the therapeutic relationship, with the clinical objective of increasing the patient's awareness of functioning patterns in the self-other relationship, particularly those of a maladaptive type, and learning to read the subjective meanings of emotional, cognitive and behavioural experience. It is fundamental for a future therapist to experience specific skills that will allow them to develop an effective therapeutic relationship that fosters a high therapeutic alliance, making the clinician capable of intervening precisely and effectively in all those situations in which there is a risk of 'breaking the alliance'.

Integrated psychotherapy is a 'transversal' model of therapy that uses different theories and tools (cognitive, behavioural, systemic, psychocorporeal, psychodynamic and emotion-focused) in relation to the evidence in the scientific literature (EBP), providing tools for the therapist to better intervene strategically in each individual case and not applying a single model to different situations or clinical problems. Thus, without a functional technique, a therapist will find it difficult to build a relationship, communication and strategy oriented towards change. In light of the above, it is important to emphasise that *technique is important, but it is not everything*. In particular, during a young therapist's training, learning a specific set of techniques, and adherence to them, is a key point, but through years of experience, the technique has to change in accordance with each therapist's personal style. Only through personal evolution can techniques be changed and improved, allowing the therapeutic process to be more efficient. We must also consider that some steps of psychotherapy are more related to 'tailor-made' applications of personal insights and perceptions (also with a percentage of 'mystery' and unexplained and unresolved issues) rather than the repetition of well-learnt techniques. Wampold (2015) argued that the factors that most influence the effectiveness of psychotherapies are related to certain typically human characteristics (which he refers to as the 'humanistic component' of psychotherapy):

1. the tendency to attribute meaning to the world (through interpretation, explanation, attribution of a causal link, mentalisation of self and others, and organisation of experience in the form of a narrative);
2. the tendency to influence and be influenced by others (i.e. to live in relation to other people, to act on them and to be subject to social influence);
3. the tendency to change over time through:

    (a) a meaningful relationship (particularly attachment bonds, such as that between parents and children, between partners within a couple bond and between psychotherapist and patient);
    (b) the creation of expectations (which explains the great influence of suggestion, the placebo effect and rituals in the therapeutic field);
    (c) the acquirement of a new capacity (mastery) (i.e. developing a sense of self-efficacy and control over events, particularly internal ones related to emotional reactions such as fear, anger, anxiety and depression).

With regard to the therapeutic relationship, as already mentioned, the *Working Alliance* or *Therapeutic Alliance* construct has emerged as a transversal element in various psychotherapeutic approaches. Various scholars have endeavoured to operationalise this concept, distinguishing within it various dimensions and developing specific psychometric instruments for its evaluation. The construct of a therapeutic alliance refers to the collaboration and bond between the patient and therapist, which is considered one of the most important common factors in psychotherapies. A now accepted research finding is that the relationship between therapeutic alliance and positive therapy outcomes has been demonstrated (Horvath et al., 1993). The most recent meta-analysis on alliance (Flückiger et al., 2018) confirmed (including 295 studies and more than 30,000 patients) that alliance is an important element in predicting patient change in therapy beyond the theoretical reference model. Furthermore, it has been shown that an improvement in the therapeutic alliance predicts patient improvement in subsequent sessions (Zilcha-Mano, 2017).

In general, it is clear from the research data that the particular combination of the characteristics of the therapist's and the patient's attachment significantly influences the quality of the relationship, the therapeutic process and the outcome of the treatment, but the ways in which this interaction is expressed remain to be clarified. The attachment bond between therapist and patient, moreover, should not be understood in a static way but as a dynamic process that changes over time on the basis of the patient's different needs. An effective caring relationship tends to be organised in at least three different moments (Mallinckrodt et al., 2005):

1. a first phase (corresponding to the first sessions) of initial agreement by the therapist with the patient's attachment model (acceptance of the role unconsciously assigned to him/her by the patient and gratification of his/her expectations). For example, assuming a more rational attitude with distant patients and greater flexibility and emotional participation with anxious ones (accepting slight violations of the *setting*, additional sessions or shifting appointments, letters and messages, etc.);
2. a second phase (when the attachment relationship is established and offers a sufficient secure basis) in which the patient's distorted and defensive representations can be gradually analysed by confronting him with his contradictions and helping him to question himself;
3. a third phase of psychological reorganisation of the patient with the development of a new, more balanced and adaptive view of himself and his problems.

In summary, we could say that therapists who are more confident and display better empathic and interpersonal skills can develop a stronger and more lasting working alliance with their patients and are better able to conduct short- and long-term therapy by adapting to the personal needs of different patients. The clinician is also interested in knowing how to handle clinical situations in which a positive alliance with the patient does not develop. Research on alliance breakdowns and repairs has shown that the interpersonal signs of a weak alliance are not necessarily predictors of a negative therapy outcome. Thus, it does not appear to be the negative quality of the alliance per se that is predictive of a worse outcome but rather the poor ability of the patient–therapist dyad to manage alliance processes by intervening to repair episodes of rupture during the session (Eubanks et al., 2018). In the model of alliance ruptures and repairs (Safran et al., 2000), great emphasis is placed on the therapist's ability to deal constructively with difficult situations during the session. In this model, it is recognised that it is important for a therapist to be able to identify the behavioural and interpersonal signs or 'markers' of alliance breakdown, but the therapeutic element lies in the ways he or she deals with elements of tension in the session when faced with the recognition in the patient of negative feelings towards the therapy or the therapist (Muran & Eubanks, 2021).

Hentschel (2005) pointed out that a problematic aspect of empirical studies investigating alliance is their tendency to view the construct as a treatment strategy and a predictor of therapeutic outcome—if the therapist is instructed, for example, on methods to increase the level of alliance, and is then asked to evaluate the alliance, this can lead to contamination of the results. The use of neutral observers or the creation of counterintuitive studies is therefore recommended. However, the majority of the available studies are based on self-report alliance questionnaires. To overcome this important methodological limitation, we now have at our disposal important tools for assessing therapeutic alliance processes from the coding of psychotherapy session transcripts, such as the 3RS (Muran & Eubanks, 2021) and the IVAT (Colli et al., 2019).

Finally, it is important to remember that in addition to the therapeutic alliance, other processual elements are associated with the outcome of psychotherapy (Norcross & Lambert, 2018), referring to the quality of the clinical relationship and the characteristics of the therapist rather than to aspects inherent to the technique, for example, empathic skills, sharing goals with the patient, taking a positive and assertive attitude (i.e. being able to effectively express one's emotions and opinions without prevaricating the patient) and being consistent and authentic in the actual relationship.

5 The Role of Evidence-Based Techniques According to the Type of Problem Presented by the Patient

Introduced in Italy in the 1990s, EBM was hailed as the methodology that made it possible to move away from a highly inhomogeneous and fragmented clinical practice without precise points of reference and towards an EB clinical practice based on validated methodologies. However, this perspective, aimed at ensuring EB clinical practice, raised a number of criticisms and objections. First, it could be objected that in medicine, it is not possible to refer only to evidence of efficacy, precisely because this is not an exact science but a clinical one, and many times, an individual's experience may be worth more than evidence of the efficacy of a treatment. Evidence is also obtained by 'measuring' treatments and outcomes, and not everything is measurable in the social health field. The starting point is the realisation that every social and health worker has probably grown up within a traditional paradigm, according to which clinical practice is based on personal observations and pathogenic hypotheses are often conjectural. EBP proposes a paradigm according to which the practitioner's observations can be integrated with the scientific evidence available by systematically interrogating the data available in the literature. This reasoning becomes more problematic when it comes to psychotherapy, outcomes, efficacy and the therapeutic process (Del Corno & Lo Coco, 2018).

A correct evaluation of the effects of psychotherapy implies regular *follow-up* activity and the conduction of empirical RCTs that confirm the efficacy of the treatment according to an *EB* model that offers valid results that can be generalised to the scientific community. From this perspective, it is necessary to carry out research on *efficacy* (to experimentally demonstrate that a treatment acts on a specific disorder excluding the influence of other factors), on *effectiveness* (to evaluate the outcome of psychotherapies as they are practised in the concrete reality of routine clinical contexts) and on *efficiency* (to evaluate the efficiency of the treatment in terms of cost-benefit and real applicability).

Criticism in recent decades regarding the inherent problematic nature of scientific studies on the outcomes of psychological interventions has led to the emergence of practice-based research within the scientific community (Margison et al., 2000). A combination of factors, such as the rising costs of mental health care and the deteriorating economic situation, led to policy measures that resulted in a restriction of the number of reimbursable therapies so that the role of EB techniques is particularly functional with a view to primary and secondary prevention of increasing psychological distress. The psychologist or psychotherapist who works using

EB techniques is able to formulate clear and theoretically consistent clinical case conceptualisations, assess the patient's pathology as well as clinically relevant strengths, understand complex patient presentations and make accurate diagnostic judgments. Clinical experience also involves the competence to identify and help patients recognise psychological processes that contribute to distress or dysfunction. Treatment planning involves setting treatment goals and tasks that take into account the individual patient, the nature of the patient's problems and concerns, the likely prognosis and expected benefits of treatment and available resources. Treatment goals are developed in collaboration with the patient and consider the worldview and sociocultural context of the patient and their family. The choice of treatment strategies requires knowledge of the interventions and research that supports their effectiveness, as well as relevant research to match interventions to patients (Castonguay & Beutler, 2006). Clinical competence (EB) also requires knowledge of psychopathology, treatment process and patient attitudes, values and context, including cultural context, which may influence the selection and implementation of effective treatment strategies. Therefore, therapeutic skills and flexibility require knowledge and competence in the delivery of psychological interventions and the ability to tailor treatment to a particular case. Flexibility manifests itself in the tact, timing, pace and framing of interventions, maintaining an effective balance between consistency of interventions and responsiveness to patient feedback and attention to recognised and unrecognised meanings, beliefs and emotions.

Clinical competence also involves monitoring the patient's progress (and changes in the patient's circumstances, e.g. loss of work and serious illness) that may suggest the need to adjust treatment (De Jong, 2012).

Over the past decade, treatment outcome monitoring (ROM) has proven to be an effective tool for reducing the dropout rate of patients in therapy (Lutz et al., 2021). Continuous monitoring of patient improvement over the course of sessions has been associated with feedback provided to therapists about their patient's condition. In summary, research can help a therapist monitor their patient's progress and be aware of any worsening. If progress is not progressing adequately, the therapist will need to modify therapeutic strategies or address problematic aspects of treatment (e.g. problems in the therapeutic relationship or in the implementation of treatment goals) as appropriate. If insufficient progress remains an unresolved problem, the therapist will consider alternative diagnoses and formulations, consultations, supervision or referral. In the meta-analysis by Shimokawa et al. (2010), it was seen that this method of ROM and feedback to the therapist is particularly useful for patients at risk of therapeutic failure (e.g. presenting significant deterioration during the course of treatment). The average patient at risk of failure in the feedback condition achieved 70% better results than patients at risk in the control condition without feedback to therapists.

Clinical EB experience can therefore enable clinical psychologists and therapists to tailor interventions and construct a therapeutic environment that respects the patient's worldview, values, preferences, abilities and other characteristics, centring the problem from a personalised care perspective (De Jong, 2012).

6 Customisation Based on Patient Preferences and Needs

Over the past 15 years, feedback and personalisation interventions based on patient preferences and needs have had a significant impact on the field of psychotherapy research and have demonstrated their potential to improve treatment outcomes, especially for patients with an increased risk of dropout (De Jong, 2012). We know from Norcross and Goldfried's (2005) research that there is no universal treatment that works for all patients; what works for one patient may not work for another. Paul's (1967) iconic question (*Which treatment, by whom, is most effective for this individual with that specific problem?*) is effective in describing what non-specific factors may represent and what weight the research-based model of integrated psychotherapy may have.

For this reason, it is necessary to tailor a treatment focused on personalisation based on the patient's preferences and needs to the transdiagnostic characteristics of the individual patient in a specific context. A meta-analysis by Swift and Wampold (2018) of more than 16,000 patients compared the outcome of patients with personal preference matching vs. non-matching, finding greater treatment effectiveness with patients who had expressed a preference for the treatment model (or therapist). Moreover, patients receiving treatment that did not take into account their preferences were almost twice as likely to drop out of therapy.

With a view to customising to the patient's preferences, it is important to focus on the following:

- what works for specific patients and for different people with different problems
- adaptation, responsiveness, customisation and tuning
- creation of a new therapy for each patient
- *customisation* of the patient's case according to the research evidence

Research on the relationship between client preferences and psychotherapy outcomes has provided strong support for clinical assessments. Normative data on 'what works for whom' (Fonagy et al., 2005) provide essential guides to effective practice. However, psychological services are more likely to be effective when they respond to a patient's specific problems, strengths, personality, sociocultural context and preferences. EBP involves consideration of a patient's values, religious beliefs, worldviews, goals and preferences for treatment with the psychologist's experience and understanding of available research (Norcross & Wampold, 2018).

Several questions frame the current debates on the role of patient characteristics in EBP. One concerns the extent to which cross-diagnostic patient characteristics, such as personality traits or trait constellations, moderate the impact of empirically tested interventions. The question concerns the extent to which social factors and cultural differences require different forms of treatment or, conversely, the extent to which interventions extensively tested in majority populations can be readily adapted for patients with different ethnic or sociocultural backgrounds. Another question concerns the maximisation of the extent to which widely used interventions adequately take developmental considerations into account, both for children and adolescents (Hawley & Weisz, 2002) and for the elderly. A third question concerns the extent to which variable clinical manifestations, such as comorbidity and polysymptomatic presentations, moderate the impact of interventions. Underlying all these questions is the issue of how best to approach the treatment of patients whose characteristics (e.g. gender, gender identity, ethnicity, race, social class, disability status and sexual orientation) and symptoms (e.g. comorbidity) may differ from those of the samples studied in the research. This is a matter of active discussion in the field, and there is a growing research focus on the generalisability and transportability of psychological interventions.

Available data indicate that a variety of patient-related variables influence outcomes, many of which are cross-diagnostic characteristics such as functional status, readiness for change and level of social support (Norcross & Goldfried, 2005). Other patient characteristics are essential to consider when forming and maintaining a treatment relationship and implementing specific interventions. These include but are not limited to (a) variations in problem or disorder presentation, aetiology, symptoms or concomitant syndromes and behaviour, (b) chronological age, developmental status, developmental history and life stage, (c) sociocultural and family factors (e.g. gender, gender identity, ethnicity, race, social class, religion, disability status, family structure and sexual orientation), (d) current environmental context, stressors (e.g. unemployment and recent life events) and social factors (e.g. institutional racism and health care disparities) and (e) personal preferences, values and treatment-related preferences (e.g. goals, beliefs, worldviews and treatment expectations).

It is precisely for this reason that 'the integration of the best available research with clinical expertise in the context of the patient's characteristics, culture and preferences' (Norcross & Lambert, 2018) turns out to be a necessity that, when scientifically structured, can represent a good psychotherapeutic process, guaranteeing effective and functional outcomes for the individual patient and his biopsycho-social complexity.

7 Putting the Patients and Their Problems at the Centre of Clinical Practice

Today, the patient is increasingly empowered to take on behaviours aimed at protecting and enhancing *health to* increase his or her knowledge of what is on offer and to acquire better lifestyles. Clinical psychologists, therefore, should acquire a clear orientation towards the patient who is to be followed, assisted, cared for and informed. It is essential to acquire the patients' point of view, to listen to them and communicate with them, to make them active and participate in every single phase of the service process, to propose solutions that contribute to improving their service experience and their care pathway and to make a significant contribution to the optimal match between supply and demand. In light of the above, it is clear that clinical psychologists can integrate techniques and characteristics and must deal with the individual person to make the complex choices necessary to conceptualise, prioritise and treat multiple symptoms, which often have manifestations and etiopathogenesis that vary from patient to patient. It is important to know the person who has the disorder in addition to knowing the disorder the person has.

Clinical decisions should be made in collaboration with the patient based on the best clinically relevant evidence, taking into account the likely costs, benefits, resources and options available. It is the treating clinical psychologist who makes the final judgment on a particular intervention or treatment plan. The involvement of an active and informed patient is generally crucial to the success of psychological services. Placing the patient of his or her problems at the centre of the treatment pathway determines the applicability of the research findings in relation to the personalisation of treatment. The application of research evidence to a given patient always involves probabilistic inferences; therefore, continuous monitoring of the patient's progress and adjustment of treatment (as needed) are essential for EBP.

In conclusion, psychotherapy, the therapeutic process, the outcomes and the relationship are clinical dimensions that must be analysed in a 'complex' and multi-perspective way, so as to highlight limits, possibilities and new needs due to the bio-psycho-social change we are experiencing. There is no therapy that is 'the same' as any other, just as each symptomology is characterised differently depending on the 'person' who manifests it. Precisely for this reason, a competent integrated approach therapist who uses practices and techniques (EB) must be aware of the process of change they are facilitating, of the client's characteristics that influence the choice of techniques to be used and of the modalities and possibilities provided by psychotherapy monitoring and feedback in therapy (Fig. 1).

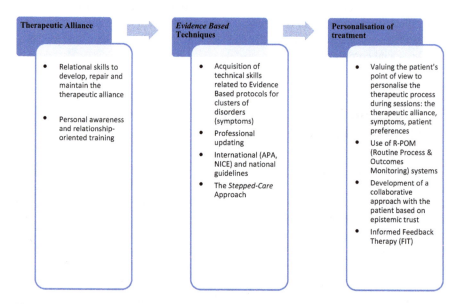

Fig. 1 The pillars of integrated psychotherapy based on evidence-based practice

References

Assay, T. P., & Lambert, M. J. (1999). The empirical case for common factors in therapy: Quantitative findings. In M. A. Hubble, B. L. Duncan, & S. D. Miller (Eds.), *The heart & soul of change – What works in therapy*. American Psychological Association.

Boswell, J. F., Nelson, D., Nordberg, S., McAleavey, A., & Castonguay, L. G. (2010). Competency in integrative psychotherapy: Perspectives on training and supervision. *Psychotherapy: Theory, Research, Practice, Training, 47*(1), 3. https://doi.org/10.1037/a0018848

Castonguay, L. G., & Beutler, L. E. (2006). Principles of therapeutic change: A task force on participants, relationships, and techniques factors. *Journal of Clinical Psychology, 62*(6), 631–638. https://doi.org/10.1002/jclp.20256

Chambless, D. L., & Ollendick, T. H. (2001). Empirically supported psychological interventions: Controversies and evidence. *Annual Review of Psychology, 52*(1), 685–716. https://doi.org/10.1146/annurev.psych.52.1.685

Colli, A., Gentile, D., Condino, V., & Lingiardi, V. (2019). Assessing alliance ruptures and resolutions: Reliability and validity of the Collaborative Interactions Scale-revised version. *Psychotherapy Research, 29*(3), 279–292. https://doi.org/10.1080/10503307.2017.1414331

De Jong, K. (2012). *A chance for change: Building an outcome monitoring feedback system for outpatient mental health care*. Leiden University.

Del Corno, F., & Lo Coco, G. (2018). *Disegni di ricerca in psicologia clinica: Metodi quantitativi, qualitativi e misti*. Edizioni Franco Angeli.

Duncan, B. L. (2002). The legacy of Saul Rosenzweig: The profundity of the dodo bird. *Journal of Psychotherapy Integration, 12*(1), 32–57. https://doi.org/10.1037/1053-0479.12.1.32

Eubanks, C. F., Muran, J. C., & Safran, J. D. (2018). Alliance rupture repair: A meta-analysis. *Psychotherapy, 55*(4), 508–519. https://doi.org/10.1037/pst0000185

Eysenck, H. J. (1952). The effects of psychotherapy: An evaluation. *Journal of Consulting Psychology, 16*(5), 319–324. https://psycnet.apa.org/doi/10.1037/h0063633

Flückiger, C., Del Re, A. C., Wampold, B. E., & Horvath, A. O. (2018). The alliance in adult psychotherapy: A meta-analytic synthesis. *Psychotherapy (Chicago, Ill.), 55*(4), 316–340. https://doi.org/10.1037/pst0000172

Fonagy, P., Roth, A., & Higgitt, A. (2005). Psychodynamic psychotherapies: Evidence-based practice and clinical wisdom. *Bulletin of the Menninger Clinic, 69*(1), 1–58.

French, T. M. (1933). Interrelations between psychoanalysis and the experimental work of Pavlov. *American Journal of Psychiatry, 89*(6), 1165–1203. https://doi.org/10.1176/ajp.89.6.1165

Goldfried, M. R. (1980). Toward the delineation of therapeutic change principles. *American Psychologist, 35*(11), 991. https://doi.org/10.1037/0003-066x.35.11.991

Goldfried, M. R. (2019). Obtaining consensus in psychotherapy: What holds us back? *American Psychologist, 74*(4), 484–496. https://doi.org/10.1037/amp0000365

Grencavage, L. M., & Norcross, J. C. (1990). Where are the commonalities among the therapeutic common factors? *Professional Psychology: Research and Practice, 21*(5), 372–378. https://doi.org/10.1037/0735-7028.21.5.372

Hawley, K. M., & Weisz, J. R. (2002). Increasing the relevance of evidence-based treatment review to practitioners and consumers. *Clinical Psychology: Science and Practice, 9*, 225–230. https://doi.org/10.1093/clipsy.9.2.225

Hentschel, U. (2005). Therapeutic alliance: The best synthesizer of social influences on the therapeutic situation? On links to other constructs, determinants of its effectiveness, and its role for research in psychotherapy in general. *Psychotherapy Research, 15*(1–2), 9–23. https://doi.org/10.1080/10503300512331327001

Herbert, J. D. (2003). The science and practice of empirically supported treatments. *Behavior Modification, 27*(3), 412–430. https://doi.org/10.1177/0145445503027003008

Hilgard, E. R., Kelly, E., Luckey, B., Sanford, R., Shaffer, L., & Shakow, D. (1947). Recommended graduate training program in clinical psychology. *American Psychologist, 2*, 539–558. https://doi.org/10.1037/h0058236

Høglend, P., Hersoug, A., & Bøgwald, K. (2011). Effects of transference work in the context of therapeutic alliance and quality of object relations. *Journal of Consulting and Clinical Psychology, 79*(5), 697–706. https://doi.org/10.1037/a0024863

Horvath, A., Gaston, L., & Luborsky, L. (1993). The therapeutic alliance and its measures. In *Psychodynamic treatment research: A handbook for clinical practice* (pp. 247–273). Basic Books.

Kubie, L. S. (1934). Relation of the conditioned reflex to psychoanalytic technic. *Archives of Neurology and Psychiatry, 32*(6), 1137–1142. https://doi.org/10.1001/archneurpsyc.1934.02250120014002

Lambert, M. J., & Bergin, A. E. (1992). Achievements and limitations of psychotherapy research. In *History of psychotherapy: A century of change* (pp. 360–390). American Psychological Association. https://doi.org/10.1037/10110-010

Levy, R. A., Ablon, J. S., & Kachele, H. (2015). *La Psicoterapia Psicodinamica basata sulla Ricerca*. Raffaello Cortina Editore.

Lo Coco, G. (2021). L'efficacia dei trattamenti psicoterapeutici: per una ricerca basata sulla pratica clinica. *Ricerca Psicoanalitica, 32*(2), 403–417. https://doi.org/10.4081/rp.2021.261

Luborsky, L. (1995). Are common factors across different psychotherapies the main explanation for the Dodo Bird verdict that "Everyone has won so all shall have prizes"? *Clinical Psychology: Science and Practice, 2*, 106–109. https://doi.org/10.1111/j.1468-2850.1995.tb00033.x

Lutz, W., De Jong, K., Rubel, J. A., & Delgadillo, J. (2021). Measuring, predicting, and tracking change in psychotherapy. In M. Barkham, W. Lutz, & L. G. Castonguay (Eds.), *Bergin and Garfield's handbook of psychotherapy and behavior change* (7th ed.). Wiley.

Mallinckrodt, B., Porter, M., & Kivlighan, D. (2005). Client attachment to therapist, depth of in-session exploration, and object relations in brief psychotherapy. *Psychotherapy: Theory, Research, Practice, Training, 42*(1), 85. https://doi.org/10.1037/0033-3204.42.1.85

Margison, F. R., Barkham, M., Evans, C., McGrath, G., Clark, J. M., Audin, K., & Connell, J. (2000). Measurement and psychotherapy: Evidence-based practice and practice-based evidence. *The British Journal of Psychiatry, 177*(2), 123–130. https://doi.org/10.1192/bjp.177.2.123

McReynolds, P. (1997). *Lightner Witmer: His life and times*. American Psychological Association.

Miller, S. D., Duncan, B. L., & Hubble, M. A. (1997). *Escape from babel: Toward a unifying language for psychotherapy practice* (Vol. 32). W W Norton & Co Inc.

Mueser, K. T., Torrey, W. C., Lynde, D., Singer, P., & Drake, R. (2003). Implementing evidence-based practices for people with severe mental illness. *Behavior Modification, 27*(3), 387–411. https://doi.org/10.1176/appi.ps.52.1.45

Mulder, R., Murray, G., & Rucklidge, J. (2017). Common versus specific factors in psychotherapy: Opening the black box. *The Lancet Psychiatry, 4*(12), 953–962. https://doi.org/10.1016/S2215-0366(17)30100-1

Muran, J. C., & Eubanks, C. F. (2021). *Il terapeuta sotto pressione. Riparare le rotture dell'alleanza terapeutica*. Raffaello Cortina.

Norcross, J. C., & Goldfried, M. R. (2005). *Handbook of psychotherapy integration*. Oxford University Press.

Norcross, J. C., & Lambert, M. J. (2018). *Psychotherapy relationships that work* (Vol. 55). Educational Publishing Foundation.

Norcross, J. C., & Wampold, B. E. (2018). A new therapy for each patient: Evidence-based relationships and responsiveness. *Journal of Clinical Psychology, 74*(11), 1889–1906. https://doi.org/10.1002/jclp.22678

Owen, J., & Hilsenroth, M. J. (2014). Treatment adherence: The importance of therapist flexibility in relation to therapy outcomes. *Journal of Counseling Psychology, 61*(2), 280–288. https://doi.org/10.1037/a0035753

Paul, G. L. (1967). Strategy of outcome research in psychotherapy. *Journal of Consulting Psychology, 31*(2), 109–118. https://doi.org/10.1037/h0024436

Prochaska, J. O., & Norcross, J. C. (2018). *Systems of psychotherapy: A transtheoretical analysis* (9th ed.). Oxford University Press.

Rogers, C. R., & Skinner, B. F. (1956). Some issues concerning the control of human behavior. *Science, 124*(3231), 1057–1066. https://doi.org/10.1126/science.124.3231.1057

Rossi Monti, M. (2012). *Psicopatologia del presente: Crisi della nosografia e nuove forme della clinica*. Edizioni Franco Angeli.

Sackett, D. L. (1997). *Evidence-based medicine*. Paper presented at the Seminars in perinatology.

Safran, J. D., Muran, C. J., & Savi, E. (2000). *Teoria e pratica dell'alleanza terapeutica*. Laterza Editore.

Shimokawa, K., Lambert, M. J., & Smart, D. W. (2010). Enhancing treatment outcome of patients at risk of treatment failure: Meta-analytic and mega-analytic review of a psychotherapy quality assurance system. *Journal of Consulting and Clinical Psychology, 78*(3), 298–311. https://doi.org/10.1037/a0019247

Stiles, W. B., & Horvath, A. O. (2017). Appropriate responsiveness as a contribution to therapist effects. In *How and why are some therapists better than others?: Understanding therapist effects* (pp. 71–84). American Psychological Association.

Stone, M. H. (2007). *Personality-disordered patients: Treatable and untreatable*. American Psychiatric Association Publishing.

Swift, J. K., & Wampold, B. E. (2018). Inclusion and exclusion strategies for conducting meta-analyses. *Psychotherapy Research, 28*(3), 356–366. https://doi.org/10.1080/10503307.2017.1405169

Tasca, G. A., Sylvestre, J., Balfour, L., Chyurlia, L., Evans, J., & Fortin-Langelier, B. (2015). What clinicians want: Findings from a psychotherapy practice research network survey. *Psychotherapy (Chicago, Ill.), 52*(1), 1–11. https://doi.org/10.1037/a0038252

Thorne, F. C. (1947). The clinical method in science. *American Psychologist, 2*(5), 159. https://doi.org/10.1037/h0060157

Tracey, T., Lichtenberg, J. W., Goodyear, R. K., Claiborn, C. D., & Wampold, B. E. (2003). Concept mapping of therapeutic common factors. *Psychotherapy Research, 13*(4), 401–413. https://doi.org/10.1093/ptr/kpg041

Wampold, B. E. (2015). How important are the common factors in psychotherapy? An update. *World Psychiatry, 14*(3), 270–277. https://doi.org/10.1002/wps.20238

Wampold, B. E., & Imel, Z. E. (2017). *Il grande dibattito in psicoterapia: l'evidenza della ricerca scientifica avanzata applicata alla clinica*. Sovera Edizioni.

Westen, D., Novotny, C. M., & Thompson-Brenner, H. (2004). The empirical status of empirically supported psychotherapies: Assumptions, findings, and reporting in controlled clinical trials. *Psychological Bulletin, 130*(4), 631–663. https://doi.org/10.1037/0033-2909.130.4.631

Woodworth, R. S. (1958). *Dynamics of behavior*. Henry Holt and Company.

Zilcha-Mano, S. (2017). Is the alliance really therapeutic? Revisiting this question in light of recent methodological advances. *American Psychologist, 72*(4), 311–325. https://doi.org/10.1037/a0040435

Part II
The Formulation of the Clinical Case in the Integrated EBP Approach

Case Formulation: Developing a Shared Understanding of the Patient's Relational World

Giorgio A. Tasca and Barbara Poletti

1 Introduction

In this chapter, we outline a case formulation approach to understanding patients in integrative psychotherapy. Such an approach allows the clinician to develop a shared understanding of the patient's interpersonal world to inform a treatment plan and focus. Randomized controlled trials of psychotherapy test treatments that are standardized rather than individualized to patient problems (Persons, 1991). But psychotherapy as practiced in the real world is a personalized process that is specific to the individual characteristics of each patient. The model we describe in this chapter is based on attachment and psychodynamic theories that illustrate the factors that underlie problems in living that patients experience. Fundamentally, this is a transdiagnostic and integrative approach to case formulation that understands the unique factors that underlie each individual's problems. That is, we argue that symptoms and diagnoses based on the Diagnostic and Statistical Manual of Mental Disorders (DSM-5, APA, 2013) and the International Classification of Diseases (ICD-10; WHO, 1992) provide only a surface level understanding of patients and so are limited in their capacity to guide treatments. The underlying aspects that cause or maintain problems in living have their roots in the patient's attachment history that affects current relationships and capacities to adaptively manage negative affect (Hewitt et al., 2017; Tasca et al., 2021).

G. A. Tasca (✉)
School of Psychology, University of Ottawa, Ottawa, ON, Canada

B. Poletti
Department of Oncology and Hemato-Oncology, University of Milan, Milano, Italy

Department of Neurology and Laboratory of Neuroscience, IRCCS Istituto Auxologico Italiano, Milan, Italy

Case Example: Joel
In this chapter, we present a running case example of Joel, a fictional patient who also appears in the book *Achieving Psychotherapy Effectiveness* (Leszcz et al., 2015) and in the chapter on mentalizing by Ravitz & Tasca in this volume. Joel is a 42-year-old married man who recently separated from his wife, Sara. Joel and his wife have a 3-year-old daughter, Charlotte. Joel loves his daughter, but his wife has custody of Charlotte, and Joel is resentful because he feels that Sara "controls" his access to his daughter. Joel came to therapy reluctantly—he felt that he had to do so to appease his wife in order to see his daughter, which makes him even more resentful and angry. His goal for therapy is to placate his wife and see his daughter, but his wife's goal for Joel's therapy is for him to be less angry. In his work as a supervisor of a shipping and receiving department, Joel is hostile and critical of his subordinates. He described having to "use the whip" with his subordinates so that they are more productive. He has no close friendships, and he is not close to his siblings. Joel described a childhood in which his father, who had problems with alcohol, physically and verbally abused Joel. His father terrorized the family and often criticized and humiliated Joel, calling him a "loser" and a "creep." His mother was likely frightened and submissive in that environment. His mother often tried to maintain the peace in the household. However, she was she not emotionally available to Joel. Joel learned quickly that authority figures were critical and attacking toward him, that he needed to protect himself from others, be self-sufficient, and that he had to be very vigilant about what was occurring around him in order to maintain some sense of security. This made him highly sensitive to perceived criticism. In his adult relationships, others often experienced him as cut off from his emotions, and angry and intimidating. His anger was likely a means of protecting himself from his expectations of others as hostile and critical. Further, he internalized a sense of himself as a "loser," that is, his self-concept was extremely negative which furthered his need to protect himself from situations in which this negative self-concept might be reinforced by hostile and controlling others.

2 Attachment Theory

The foundation of our case formulation approach is attachment theory. Attachment theory is one of the most important theories of human behavior, relationships, and emotion regulation (Mikulincer & Shaver, 2019). John Bowlby (1969) originally developed attachment theory, which Mary Ainsworth further elaborated in her work with infants (Ainsworth et al., 1978). Mary Main (Main & Hesse, 1992) extended attachment theory to adult functioning. Infants are born into the world with attachment behaviors (crying, cooing, reaching, eye gaze, crawling) that are meant to keep attachment figures close and ensure survival in the early years. Repeated interactions between attachment figures and children over time are encoded in the implicit memory system of the child and develop into internal working models of attachment (Bretherton & Mulholland, 2008). Through attachment experiences (repeated interactions with attachment figures), children develop internal representations of care and expectations of others that provide self-regulating and self-comforting functions (Zilberstein, 2014). These internal working models are the templates for organized attachment behaviours that affect a range of human functioning in children and adults such as affect regulation, relationship quality, narrative coherence (i.e., coherent and relevant narratives of attachment relationships), and capacity to mentalize (i.e., to understand the self and others' behaviors in terms of mental states such as desires, needs, intentions, thoughts, and feelings). Mentalizing is a particularly important capacity in order to make sense of one's relational world and to empathize with the self and others. The chapter by Talia and colleagues in this volume provides a deeper treatment of attachment theory, and the chapter by Ravitz and Tasca in this volume provides more information about mentalizing.

One can categorize organized attachment behaviors as secure or insecure, and the latter can be further sub-characterized as dismissing or preoccupied. Main and Solomon (1990) also described a disorganized pattern of attachment. Individuals with *secure* attachments have a positive view of self and others. During childhood they experienced attachment figures as "good enough" (Winnicott, 1973), that is, their parents were typically available and responsive. Securely attached adults are capable of receiving and giving love and care, they expect others to be available in times of distress, they have adaptive means of regulating their emotions, their narrative of attachment relationships is clear and coherent, and they are capable of mentalizing.

Those with *preoccupied* mental states tend to have a positive view of others but a negative view of self. Their childhood attachment relationships might have been characterized by inconsistent caregiving in which parents were sometime available and others times not available, resulting in the child excessively signaling their attachment needs by crying or remaining upset even when soothed. Adults with preoccupied attachments are highly concerned about loss or abandonment in relationships, and their emotion regulation is maladaptive in that emotions tend to remain high and easily activated. Their preoccupation with relationship loss and their activated emotions interferes with narrative coherence and their capacity to mentalize or reflect on their own or others mental states.

Those with *dismissing* attachment styles tend to have a positive view of self but a negative view of others. Attachment figures in childhood were often neglectful or unavailable, and the child learned to downplay displays of need. Dismissing adults minimize or disregard the importance of relationships, and so they are overly self-sufficient. Their emotions tend to be low key and sometimes dismissed to the point of not having an adequate understanding of their own feelings. Their narrative of attachment relationships is impoverished, and as a result they struggle with mentalizing as they have a difficult time with understanding their own and others' mental states.

Finally, those with a *disorganized attachment* have a negative view of self and of others. Their early attachment experiences are often fearful because these individuals may have experienced trauma or other childhood adversity. Adults with disorganized attachments both fear and are needy of relationships and intimacy. Their emotions tend to be either overwhelming or dissociated. Their narrative is confused when talking about trauma, which greatly inhibits their capacity to reflect (mentalize) on their own and others' mental states.

> **Therapist Worksheet: Assessing Attachment in Adults**
>
> 1. Ask about and listen for the patient's relationship episodes. What are the important relationships in the patient's life? Ask about details regarding a recent interaction that was positive or negative. What were the sequence of events? How did the patient feel? What were the patient's wishes and intentions for the interaction? What is the patient's understanding of the other person's intentions? How did the interaction turn out and why?
> 2. In order to assess the *narrative coherence* of attachment, listen for clear, complete, relevant, and logical responses to questions like the following: Who raised you? Provide me with a few adjectives to describe your relationship with your mother/father when you were a child? Provide some examples to illustrate why you chose these adjectives to describe your childhood relationship with your mother/father? When you were upset or hurt as a child what would you do? What did your parent do when you were upset or hurt? If the patient provides few examples from childhood or does not remember examples from childhood, consider this a marker of *dismissing attachment*. If the patient is distracted or derailed in their responses due to anger toward attachment figures, then consider this a marker for *preoccupied attachment*.
> 3. Assess for *disorganized attachment* with questions like the following: "Were you ever frightened as a child? Did you experience any adverse or traumatic experiences?" If the patient is overwhelmed by their emotions while answering these questions, or cannot maintain narrative coherence (e.g., is overwhelmed by emotion), or shows signs of dissociation (e.g., loses track of the original question or of the context of the interview), then consider this a marker of *disorganized attachment*.
> 4. Ask questions regarding the patient's capacity to *mentalizing*: How do your childhood experiences affect you now as an adult? Why do you think your parents behaved the way they did during your childhood? If the patient's responses do not consider mental states of the self and others (e.g., "I don't know" or "That is just the way they were."), or if the responses are too certain of others' mental states (e.g., "I know that she was trying to undermine me"), then consider this as a marker of limited mentalizing and, therefore, insecure attachment.
> 5. Use valid and reliable measures of attachment: (a) The Experiences in Close Relationships Scale—12 (ECR-12; Brugnera et al., 2019) or the (b) Relationship Questionnaire (RQ; Bartholomew & Horowitz, 1991).

3 Patient Attachment and Therapist Interpersonal Stance

Research suggests that attachment insecurity and the accompanying deficits in mentalizing are associated with higher levels psychopathology (Bakermans-Kranenburg & van IJzendoorn, 2009; Bateman & Fonagy, 2006; Maxwell et al., 2018; Tasca & Balfour, 2014). Patients with preoccupied attachments tend to do better in therapy in which there is a steady increase in the therapeutic alliance over time (Tasca et al., 2006). Presumably these patients need to experience the closeness and security inherent in a positive alliance in order to improve. Conversely, patients with dismissing attachments might have a greater propensity to drop out of treatment, especially if the treatment is too demanding of them in terms of interpersonal intimacy (Gallagher et al., 2014; Tasca & Balfour, 2014).

These research findings suggest differing interpersonal stances that therapists can take to improve outcomes for patients with different attachment styles (see Tasca & Balfour, 2014). Psychotherapists may experience attachment *preoccupied* patients as overwhelming and needy (Leszcz et al., 2015). Therapists must keep in mind that these patients' behaviors are a result of their attachment history that required hyper-signalling to attachment figures in order to get their needs met. Their emotions and concerns about relationship loss may make it difficult for them to mentalize. Such patients may benefit from taking a more ego-observing stance to their emotions and relational problems, rather than remaining in an emotionally activated state and preoccupied about their relationships. That is, therapists may help patients with preoccupied attachment to step back from their emotional experiences and to use their cognitive capacities to understand their relationships and themselves better.

On the other hand, psychotherapists may experience those with *dismissing* attachments as aloof and distant. It is challenging for therapists to keep in mind that these individuals downplay emotional needs because of their attachment history in which muted expressions of emotions and behaviors were most adaptive. Therapists must try to engage patients with dismissing attachments carefully by not demanding that the patient express emotions too early in therapy. Therapists must appreciate that while patients with dismissing attachments appear emotionally disengaged, these patients nevertheless may have physiological responses to stressors even if they are not capable of describing or expressing their emotions.

As indicated, those with *disorganized* attachments may have widely inconsistent and extreme approaches to relationships and emotions that may leave clinicians feeling confused or overwhelmed. These patients had frightening early experiences that resulted in inconsistent and extreme means of experiencing emotions. Their emotional and physiological experiences may be hyper-aroused or hypo-aroused in some instances (Ogden & Minton, 2000), both of which interferes with their capacity to mentalize. A therapist's task with such individuals is to help them stay within a zone of optimal arousal. If the patient is hyper-aroused (emotionally overwhelmed), then the therapist must work to lower the arousal by using their tone of voice and pacing of subject matter to slow the patient down, provide empathy and support, and perhaps help the patient focus on concrete details of daily activities. If the patient is hypo-aroused (detached or dissociated), then the therapist must work to heighten the patient's arousal by helping the patient to ground themselves in the moment, asking the patient to pay attention to bodily sensations, ask about the patient's emotions, or be curious about what is in the patient's mind.

> **Therapist Worksheet: Treatment Goals and Therapist Interpersonal Stances for Each Attachment Style**
>
> 1. *Preoccupied attachment*: help to reduce the patient's fears of abandonment by remaining consistent and empathic, downregulate the patient's emotions by focusing on thoughts, reduce the disruption of emotions on the patient's narrative coherence by slowing the patient down and pacing, mentalize the patient by encouraging reflection of their own and others' intentions.
> 2. *Dismissing attachment*: help to increase the patient's emotional connection to others by focusing on here and now of therapeutic relationship, help the patient reduce defenses against affect by focusing on the patient's feelings, increase a coherent narrative by helping the client to appreciate the links between past events and their current circumstances, help the patient to reflect on their own and others' internal experiences that underlie behaviors.
> 3. *Disorganized attachment*: help the patient to remain in the optimal zone of arousal—increase arousal when patient is hypo-aroused (focus on bodily sensations, ask about what is in their mind) or decrease arousal when hyper-aroused (grounding in the moment and discuss concrete topics, talk about thoughts and not feelings), reduce disorganization caused by trauma by slowly developing a coherent narrative of the trauma, help the patient appreciate the role of abuse on their affective states and their capacity to reflect.

Case Example: Joel's Attachment State of Mind

Joel is uncomfortable getting close to others, has problems trusting others, and finds it difficult to allow himself to depend on others. He gets uncomfortable when anyone wants to get close to him or be more intimate with him. Joel did not receive much positive nurturing from his parents—his father was critical and abusive and his mother was emotionally unavailable. When asked about his childhood experiences, Joel remembered the abuse generally, but did not describe any instances or details. His memories of his mother were very vague, and he could not remember any instances in which she interacted with him in a meaningful way. He claimed to have none or only vague childhood memories before age 12.

The therapist hypothesized that Joel had a *dismissing attachment*, but ther were also disorganized mental states caused by the abuse that Joel experienced. In the first session of therapy, Joel was certain that the therapist was going to conclude that Joel should not have access to his daughter. Joel also assumed the therapist was going to say something to humiliate him, and so Joel was very guarded and defensive with the therapist. Joel's narrative hinted at a very negative self-concept when he described feeling like "shit," and worried that the therapist would conclude that he was a "loser." Joel actively pushed the therapist away with his hostility, and he tried to control the session by telling the therapist "I won't let you ask those kinds of questions." The therapist did not respond with counter-hostility or dominating behaviors, instead he maintained a neutral inquisitive stance, and empathically reflected Joel's concerns about the outcome of the therapy sessions. Importantly, the therapist considered Joel's dismissing attachment style, and so the therapist did not require Joel to express his emotions, instead the therapist tried to disconfirm Joel's expectations of authority figures as hostile by making his own motivations clear and by validating Joel's concerns as understandable. The therapist also helped Joel to mentalize with regard to others by asking Joel to consider the motivations and feelings of important figures in his life, like his wife.

4   The Case Formulation Model

The model we use for a case formulation is based on Malan's (1979) Triangle of Conflict and Triangle of Persons. Hewitt et al. (2017) and Tasca et al.' (2021) re-imagining of Malan's (1979) model represents the interplay of *intrapersonal* dynamics (attachment needs, affect/anxiety, and defense mechanisms) in the Triangle of Adaptation and *interpersonal* dynamics (the consistency of interpersonal patterns across past relationships, current relationships, and therapeutic relationships) in the Triangle of Object Relations (Fig. 1). Hewitt et al.' (2017) and Tasca et al.' (2021) model incorporates a contemporary attachment approach by

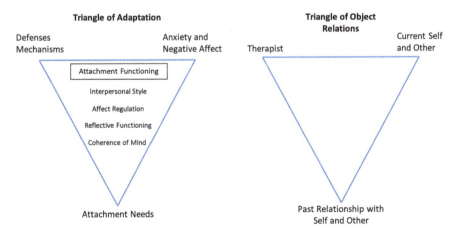

Fig. 1 Triangle of Adaptation from an attachment perspective. (Adapted from Tasca and Balfour (2014))

putting attachment needs at the apex of the Triangle of Adaptation (Fig. 1). The intrapersonal and interpersonal dynamics illustrated by this model develop over time and are simultaneously determined by and define attachment functions (interpersonal style, affect regulation, reflective functioning, and coherence of mind).

In the Triangle of Adaptation, attachment needs are the basic and historically earlier developments that drive the rest of the model. Attachment needs of someone who is *preoccupied* with regard to attachments tend to include needs that are relational in nature (i.e., needs for closeness, security, sexual desire, and intimacy). Attachment needs of someone who is *dismissing* in their attachments tend to be more self-definitional in nature (i.e., needs for self-assertion, self-pride, and self-care). One with *disorganized* attachment related to trauma may have extreme attachment needs for security and safety, and they may fluctuate between relational and self-definition attachment needs in an inconsistent manner.

The key aspect of the Triangle of Adaptation is that the patient's attachment needs often were unmet by attachment figures, or the patient's expressions of their needs were punished or humiliated by attachment figures. As a result, whenever the patient experiences or wishes to express an attachment need currently in their adult life, they may automatically experience anxiety or negative affect (e.g., fear, panic, shame, guilt, contempt, anger). To cope with or manage the negative affect, people develop defense mechanisms, which are unconscious means of mitigating anxiety and negative affect (Perry & Hoglend, 1998). Defense mechanisms vary from being adaptive (altruism, self-reflection, humour, suppression) to maladaptive (acting out, passive aggression, denial, projection). Research indicates that maladaptive defensive functioning is related to greater psychopathology and to poorer outcomes in psychotherapy (Perry & Bond, 2012). Table 1 provides a list of defense mechanisms from adaptive to maladaptive.

Table 1 Defense levels and examples of individual defenses

Level	Example defense	Description
7. High adaptive	Altruism	Neutralizes an anxious situation by an act of goodwill to another
	Humour	Finds a funny aspect of a difficult situation to help self/other endure it
	Sublimation	Converts an unacceptable impulse to an acceptable form
	Suppression	Consciously and temporarily forces feelings/thoughts from awareness
	Self-observation	Dealing with emotional conflict by reflecting on own feelings, thoughts
	Isolation of affect	Recalling a painful event without experiencing the associated emotion
6. Obsessional	Intellectualization	Uses abstract thinking to minimize emotional discomfort
	Undoing	Negates or makes amends for unacceptable thoughts/feelings

(continued)

Case Formulation: Developing a Shared Understanding of the Patient's Relational World   33

Table 1 (continued)

Level	Example defense	Description
5. Other neurotic	Displacement	Transfers feelings/responses from an appropriate person to a less threatening person
	Reaction formation	Substitutes actual thoughts and behaviors for their opposite
	Repression	Removes unpleasant wishes/thoughts from consciousness, but the emotions remain
	Omnipotence	Responds to emotional conflict by acting superior to others
4. Minor image distortion	Idealization	Grossly exaggerates positive qualities of self or others
	Devaluation	Grossly exaggerates negative qualities of self or others
3. Disavowal	Rationalization	Illogical justification of one's behaviors or feelings
	Projection	Attributes unacceptable characteristics in self to others
	Denial	Completely unable to acknowledge unpleasant reality/thoughts/feelings
2. Major image distortion	Projective identification	Must protect self from bad others
	Splitting	People are only either good or bad
1. Action	Help-rejecting complaining	Elicits help but then rejects it
	Passive-aggression	Indirectly expresses anger
	Acting out	Is driven to act out impulsively

Adapted from the Defense Mechanisms Rating Scale (Perry, 1990)

As the Triangle of Adaptation (Fig. 1) suggests, attachment needs, negative affect, and defense mechanisms are determined by and simultaneously affect attachment functioning. For example, consistent use of maladaptive defense mechanisms like denial (i.e., a failure to acknowledge one's own thoughts and impulses) or projection (i.e., misattributing one's own feelings and impulses to others) will severely limit one's capacity to mentalize (consider behaviors in terms of one's own and others mental states), will interfere with a coherent attachment narrative (not remember or be overwhelmed by attachment memories), and reduce the quality of interpersonal relationships (blame others, too passive in relationships, dominate others).

Case Example: Joel's Case Formulation with the Two Triangles

Let us consider a case formulation for Joel based on the Two Triangles (Fig. 2). Recall that Joel likely has a dismissing attachment style (i.e., he downplays the importance of relationships and he diminishes his experience and expression of feelings). And he also has elements of a disorganized state of mind with regard to trauma (i.e., he sometimes experiences high levels of humiliation and self-loathing, and anger toward others). As a child, his normal attachment needs for and expressions of self-pride or self-assertion were met with verbal and physical abuse by his

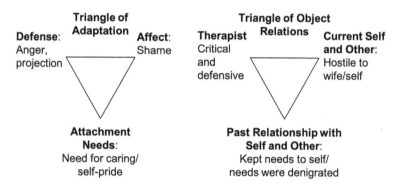

Fig. 2 Joel: Triangle of Adaptation and object relations

> **Therapist Worksheet: Identify Elements of the Triangle of Adaptation**
>
> 1. *Attachment Needs*: Assess the predominant attachment needs of the individual by asking them to describe a relationship episode that includes details of important interactions with significant people in their current lives. Ask the patient what was going through their mind during the interaction and what they wished from the other. Attachment needs may not be consciously accessible or defended against, and so the therapist must listen for attachment-related themes (e.g., needs for closeness, intimacy, security, self-assertion, self-pride).
> 2. *Affect/Anxiety*: Focus on the patient's narrative of a relationship episode, ask the patient about the feelings or other affects that arise when they consider their attachment needs. Were they worried, ashamed, afraid, anxious, panicked? Remember that these affects may be disconnected from the attachment needs, and so when a patient speaks of anxiety or shame, consider which attachment need may be related to the affect.
> 3. *Defense Mechanism*: Ask how the patient manages their anxiety, fear, shame. Probe for the nature of the defense mechanism (e.g., does the patient turn anger inward or outward, do they blame others, do they minimize or put it out of their mind, do they intellectualize?). Remember that defenses occur automatically and that the patient may not link the defense mechanism to a negative affective experience.

father. His mother was largely unavailable for security and caring—and so these normally occurring attachment needs of Joel's were rarely if ever met and were sometimes punished. The therapist got a hint of Joel's *attachment needs* when Joel referred to himself as a "loser," when he worried that the therapist would come to the same conclusion, and when his only expectation of the therapist was not that Joel would receive caring and empathy, but rather that the therapist would be critical and humiliating. The main *affects* that emerged from Joel's narrative included an underlying sense of shame and humiliation. That is, any time that his attachment needs for self-pride or for caring might surface he automatically re-experienced the shame and humiliation that he experienced during his childhood. For example, when the therapist suggested to Joel that perhaps therapy could be helpful to him (an expression of caring), Joel's response was to predict that the therapist would inevitably come to the conclusion that Joel was a "loser." Joel used a range of *defense mechanisms* to manage his underlying sense of shame and humiliation. Most of these defenses were geared toward minimizing his feelings and externalizing his self-punitive experience of shame. For example, he blamed his wife for controlling him by withholding access to his daughter. This is a form of defensive anger in which the focus is placed on the other person and their motives rather than on his own internal experiences. In terms of defense mechanisms, he used projection (that others were angry, not him), projective identification (that he had to protect himself from others' anger), and denial (that the abuse he experienced had no impact on him currently).

Joel's intrapersonal dynamics illustrated in the Triangle of Adaptation had an impact on his current attachment functioning (Fig. 2). His close relationships, with his wife for example, were characterized by anger and conflict. He tried to dominate his wife, and she retaliated by restricting his access to his daughter. His affect regulation was poor. That is, his maladaptive defenses were not adequate to contain negative affect. His tendency to project his anger, for example, led to further conflicts with his wife. Joel's mentalizing deficits were characterized by a focus on external factors and others rather than on his own internal experiences. This diminished his capacity for empathy, to understand his wife's motives, and to appreciate his therapist's intentions. Not surprisingly, he had limited capacity for narrative coherence in that he could not make sense of his current problems in the context of his attachment history. As indicated in the Triangle of Object Relations, he was critical of himself, hostile to his wife, and critical and defensive towards his therapist.

5 Communicate the Case Formulation with the Patient

One of the key tasks for a therapist when developing a case formulation is to communicate the formulation with the patient. This should be an iterative process in which the therapist begins by sharing their impressions of the patient's attachment history and attachment functioning (interpersonal style, affect regulation, coherence of mind, and reflective functioning) with the patient. The patient's responses and feedback to this process can help the therapist to modify or adjust the formulation. Here is a narrative that the therapist might share with Joel, for example, that reflects Joel's dismissing attachment state of mind: *"Given what you said about your upbringing I can understand that you are weary of me and my intentions. People who were supposed to take care of you didn't, or they were hostile and controlling toward you. I can see how not showing what you think and feel to others was the safest thing to do—you learned that from the very beginning. However, it looks like your expectation of others may be causing you problems now, especially in your relationship with your wife.*" This formulation speaks to Joel's difficulty with mentalizing ("weary of my intentions") and his avoidance of affect as an adaptive response in the past ("not showing what you feel was the safest thing to do") that is no longer adaptive ("causing you problems now").

The therapist also might develop and share aspects of Joel's Triangle of Adaptation with Joel. "*From what you've said, every time you needed help or support from your mother, she simply couldn't provide it. And the few times that you wanted your father to be proud of you, he only dismissed or humiliated you. Those experiences must have been painful for you. I get the sense that you internalized these messages—I heard you refer to yourself as a 'loser' and you expected me to do the same. I can imagine that you learned quickly not to feel any pride or not to ask for caring. So, you minimize or avoid these feelings and needs. It makes sense that when someone does express interest or care for you, like you wife or perhaps me, you don't trust it* (defense). *You expect others to neglect or humiliate you, and this makes you angry.*" This narrative of the case formulation identified Joel's attachment needs ("needed help or support..., wanted your father to be proud of you"), and how these needs were neglected or punished which led to negative affects related to humiliation ("...must have been painful for you"). To manage this, Joel engages in several defense mechanisms ("...minimize...you don't trust it... makes you angry").

6 Use the Case Formulation to Guide Treatment

As indicated above, an assessment of a patient's attachment style could help the clinician to adjust their interpersonal stances and approaches to a patient. The *Therapist Worksheet* (above) describes each attachment style and provides a guide to therapists on how to develop treatment goals and on interpersonal stances that work best for each patient. In this section of the chapter, we discuss which aspect of the Triangle of Adaptation (attachment needs, affect/anxiety, or defenses) to focus on based on an assessment of the patient's level of mental functioning as outlined in the Psychodynamic Diagnostic Manual (PDM-2; McWilliams & Shedler, 2017).

Assess Level of Mental Functioning First, it is important that therapists assess the overall level of mental functioning of the patient (Table 2) in order to decide on which aspect of the Triangle of Adaptation to focus. People at a *healthy level of mental functioning* generally are adaptive in terms of affect regulation, emotional range and control, and ability to mentalize. They tend to be resilient and have flexible coping strategies. Their identity is coherent, and they feel that they have a purpose or meaning in their lives. Such individuals are not likely to seek therapy unless there is an acute crisis or stressor.

Those at a *neurotic level of mental functioning* generally experience minimal or mild impairments in mental capacities. They tend to respond to stress with some rigidity in coping styles, their defense mechanisms are not optimal but do not result in a distortion of reality, their relationship problems tend to be specific or circumscribed and not generalized to all relationships, and they can tolerate negative emotions without becoming impulsive. Their sense of identity is relatively coherent, they can observe themselves and others from multiple perspectives (i.e., they can mentalize), and their self-esteem may be mildly impaired.

People with a *borderline level of mental functioning* are susceptible to disorganization caused by high levels of overwhelming affect. Their coping is moderately to severely compromised, and so they may be impulsive with intense episodes of anger, anxiety, or depression. They tend to have recurring problems with intimate, social, and work relationships.

Their impulsivity may lead to problem behaviors including gambling, sexual acting out, binge eating, substance abuse, and self-harm. Their defense mechanisms tend to be in the less adaptive range (Table 1). They have a sense of self that is often disorganized, and so their identity may not be coherent and their self may not be sufficiently differentiated from others. McWilliams and Shedler (2017) make an important distinction between higher and lower levels of mental functioning among those with a borderline personality organization (see Table 2).

Those at the *psychotic level of mental functioning* tend to have severe deficits in most or all capacities of mental functioning, including problems with reality testing and disturbed perception. Some with severe personality pathology may report delusional thinking, inability to separate one's own thoughts and feelings from others, or the conviction that their own attributions about others are correct regardless of the reality or evidence.

Triangle of Adaptation: Focus on Affect/Anxiety For those patients at a *healthy or neurotic level of functioning* who experience optimal functioning or mild impairment (Table 2), therapists can focus treatment on the affect/anxiety pole of the Triangle of Adaptation (McCullough, 2003). These patients have the capacity to tolerate strong emotions in therapy, and so helping them to experience their feelings more fully will help them to validate their attachment needs. Patients may have problems with certain adaptive feelings associated with attachment needs, like grief, anger, or feelings about the self. If that is the case, then therapists can help patients to pay attention to their feelings and identify attachment needs that underlie the feelings. Defenses may arise automatically in the patient during this work (e.g., the patient may diminish their needs or intellectualize rather than feel their emotions). But the objective is exposure to the feared attachment needs and the affect/anxiety that arises from those needs.

The therapist is most helpful when verbally labeling the affect, encouraging the patient to physically feel the emotion, and perhaps asking the patient to imagine acting on the emotion in fantasy. The goal of therapy for patients at the healthy or neurotic level of functioning is to express their attachment needs adaptively without anxiety or inhibiting affects. During this work, therapists must always assess the patient's level of anxiety and capacity to experience their emotions. If the patient's level of arousal becomes too high, then the therapist must help the patient to calm themselves and offer support and validation.

Table 2 Levels of mental functioning

Level of mental functioning	Description	Triangle of Adaptation
Healthy		Focus on affect/ anxiety
Healthy/ optimal	Optimal or very good functioning in all or most mental capacities, with modest, expectable variations in flexibility and adaptation across contexts	
Neurotic		
Good/ appropriate	Appropriate level of mental functioning with some specific areas of difficulties. These difficulties can reflect conflicts or challenges related to specific life situations or events	
Mild impairment	Mild constrictions and areas of inflexibility in some domains of mental functioning, implying rigidity and impairment in areas such as self-esteem regulation, impulse and affect regulation, defensive functioning, and self-observing capacities	
Borderline (higher level)		Focus on defenses
Moderate impairment	Moderate constriction and areas of inflexibilities in most or almost most domains of mental functioning, affecting quality and stability of relationships, sense of identity, and range of affects tolerated	
Borderline (lower level)		Focus on self or other aspects of attachment needs
Major impairment	Major constriction and alteration in almost all domains of mental functioning (e.g., tendency toward fragmentation and difficulty in self-object differentiation), along with limitation in experience of feelings and/or thoughts in major life areas (i.e., work, love, play)	
Significant deficits	Significant deficits in most domains of mental functioning, along with problems in the organization and/or integration-differentiation of self and objects	
Psychotic		
Severe deficits	Major and severe deficits in almost all domains of mental functioning, with impaired reality testing; fragmentation and/or difficulties in self-object differentiation; disturbed perception, integration, regulation of affect and thought; deficits in one or more basic mental functions (e.g., perception, integration, motor, memory, regulation, judgment)	

Adapted from McWilliams and Shedler (2017)

Triangle of Adaptation: Focus on Defenses For patients with a *higher level of borderline mental functioning* who have moderate deficits (Table 2), therapists may focus the work on modifying the patient's less adaptive defenses (McCullough, 2003). First, therapists can help patients to recognize their defenses. This might involve therapists gently pointing out the defense (e.g., "I noticed that you smiled when you described that painful experience"), speculating about what is being defended against (e.g., "I imagine that was a very difficult loss and that you would want to minimize the pain or not think about it."), validating the defense (e.g., "It makes sense to me that you would want not to feel the pain in order to keep caring for your children."), and perhaps provide a context for the defense (e.g., "Given what you said about your mother's depression when you were a child, it seems that you have always had to be the strong one.").

A useful technique in modifying defenses is for therapists to help the patient to identify the costs and benefits of a defense (e.g., "Ok, so smiling when you might feel hurt helps to keep you upbeat. What are some of the costs that come with doing that?"). Therapists must remember that modifying defenses may leave the patient vulnerable to negative affect and shame, and so it is critical to have a strong therapeutic alliance. As with any other aspect of the work, therapists must continually monitor the patient's level of anxiety and discomfort and slow down or reduce the focus on defenses should the patient begin to feel overwhelmed.

Triangle of Adaptation: Focus on Attachment Needs (Self and Other) For those patients who are at the *lower level of borderline mental functioning* or at the *psychotic level of mental functioning* who experience major to severe deficits (Table 2), therapists should focus on the attachment needs pole of the Triangle of Adaptation. However, the therapy should be slower paced that is practical, supportive in nature, and skills-oriented. The goal of therapy might be to develop a more positive self-image or a better connection to others. Regarding the patient's self, therapists might help the patient to be more compassionate with themselves, teach the patient about more adaptive interpersonal behaviors (e.g., assertiveness), and support the patient to try new behaviors by taking small tolerable steps. The therapist may accomplish this by encouraging the patient to mentalize (e.g., "How do you think I am seeing you right now?… I'll tell you what I'm thinking."). Regarding connection to others, therapists might help the patient to have a better understanding of others' intentions, develop more adaptive perspective on relationships (not too dependent on others or too critical of others), and develop greater capacity for trust (e.g., "Can you put yourself in his shoes for a moment, and try to understand why he is upset?").

The development and maintenance of the therapeutic alliance is key to working with patients with borderline level of mental functioning, and in many cases the continual experience of and repair of alliance ruptures is the central feature of the therapy. Much of the work is accomplished by the therapist encouraging a mentalizing stance in the patient about the therapeutic relationship (e.g., "What do you think I feel about you being mad at me?… Is there anything I have done to make you feel that way?… Actually, I am thinking…"). Therapists must keep in mind that any self-disclosure must be done judiciously and carefully, always with the patient's therapeutic goals in mind, and never as a countertransference enactment.

Case Example: Joel's Capacity to Mentalize
Joel is likely functioning at the lower borderline level characterized by major impairment in mental functioning (Table 2). He has important deficits in his capacity to trust others, his defenses are maladaptive (projection and projective identification), and his view of self is extremely critical. He believed that the therapist was going to humiliate him and recommend that Joel not have custody of his daughter. The fundamental challenge for the therapist in working with Joel was to establish a therapeutic alliance—in fact, repairing alliance ruptures was an ongoing aspect of

the work in the early stages of the therapy. The therapist's main interventions focused on helping Joel to mentalize. That is, the therapist took a non-expert stance of curiosity, used judicious self-disclosure to help Joel understand his intentions, asked Joel to consider his wife's intentions, and validated the need for Joel's defensiveness without necessarily agreeing with his defensive behaviours or views of others. This following exchange was characteristic of their early meetings:

Joel: I know what's coming. Do your worst. You're going to tell me that I'm screwed up. I'm going to appease my wife by coming here, and maybe she'll calm down.

Therapist: I know you see me as part of the problem, but I'd like to see if I can be part of the solution (Therapist attempts to establish a therapeutic alliance by identifying a common goal).

Joel: I know what you're thinking (Joel is overly certain in "knowing" what is in the mind of the therapist, indicating a deficit in mentalizing).

Therapist: Let me tell you what I am thinking. (Therapist self discloses as a means of helping Joel to mentalize). *I'm thinking that you are scared of losing your daughter, you are hurt, and you are angry. And those feelings make sense to me.* (Therapist validates Joel's feelings).

Therapist Worksheet: Use the Case Formulation to Find a Therapy Focus

1. Assess the patient's level of mental functioning (Table 2; and McWilliams & Shedler, 2017) and use that assessment to determine what aspects to focus on in the Triangle of Adaptation.
2. Patients with *healthy or neurotic level of mental functioning*: Focus on the affects/anxiety pole of the Triangle of Adaptation. Help the patient experience their feelings more fully and identify their attachment needs. Verbally label the patient's affects, encourage the patient to physically feel the emotion, and ask the patient to imagine acting on the emotion in fantasy.
3. Patients with *high level of borderline mental functioning*: Focus on the defenses pole of the Triangle of Adaptation. Help patients to recognize their defenses by gently pointing them out, speculate about what is being defended against, and validate reasons for the defense. Point out the costs and benefits of the defense for the client as a means of encouraging them to modify or relinquish the defense.
4. Patients with *low borderline level or psychotic level mental functioning*: Focus on the Attachment Needs pole of the Triangle of Adaptation. Regarding the self: help the patient to be more compassionate with themselves, teach the patient about more adaptive interpersonal behaviors, and support the patient to try new behaviors by taking small tolerable steps. Regarding connection to others: help the patient to have a better understanding of others' intentions, develop more adaptive perspective on relationships, and develop greater capacity for trust. Continually work on developing and repairing the therapeutic alliance as this will be a central aspect of the therapy. Help the patient to mentalize by realistically considering their own intentions and those of others, including the therapist. Therapy tends to be practical, concrete, and skills-oriented.

7 Conclusion

An integrative transdiagnostic case formulation is key to develop an individualized treatment goal and plan for each patient. Clinicians can use assessment tools to evaluate attachment, like the ECR-12 (Brugnera et al., 2019) and the Relationship Questionnaire (Bartholomew & Horowitz, 1991). Therapists can use the DMRS (Table 1) to assess level and quality of defense mechanisms (Perry, 1990), and the PDM-2 is a useful resource to assess the levels of mental functioning (Table 2; McWilliams & Shedler, 2017). An important aspect of psychotherapy is for therapists and patients to have a shared understanding of the patient's problems and relational world that are a manifestation of intrapersonal and interpersonal dynamics as illustrated in the Triangle of Adaptation and Triangle of Person (Fig. 1). The integrative case formulation helps the therapist to understand the patient, to inform therapist interpersonal stances toward the patient, and to define the targets of therapy.

Chapter Review Questions

Exercise 1 Read the following statements that a patient might say. Which attachment style is best represented by each of the statements?

Secure   Preoccupied   Dismissing   Disorganized

1. I have to rely on myself, others aren't going to be there for me. _____
2. I'm worried that he will leave me. I ask him for reassurance all the time, and I think it's getting annoyed with me. _____
3. I don't know how I feel about it. It really doesn't matter how I feel. _____
4. My parents weren't perfect, but they did the best they could. _____
5. I can't talk about the assault. If I do, I will lose control.... What was your question? _____
6. I get so angry that she left me and how she won't return any of my text messages. _____

Exercise 2 Underline and identify the elements of the Triangle of Adaptation (*Attachment Needs; Affects/Anxiety; Defense*) in the following patient narrative.

"She spent a lot of money on the trip, and I'm worried that we can't afford it. I need her to act responsibly for me and the children. I kept thinking 'if you really loved me and the kids, you wouldn't do that'. I wish I could just tell her to get a refund, but then I'd feel guilty for depriving her and the kids—who am I to place such restrictions on them? So, I just stopped talking to her. We barely talked this morning and she and I just went to work. Then at work one of my employees made a mistake and it annoyed me, but I felt guilty for being annoyed, so I didn't say anything about it. I ended up fixing it myself. It's so hard to find dependable people. By the afternoon I was so upset that I ordered a bunch of food, and binged in the car."

Exercise 3 Which of the levels from the Defense Mechanisms Rating Scale are best characterized by each of these patient statements. Use Table 1 as a reference:

High Adaptive; *Obsessional*; *Other Neurotic*; *Minor Image Distortion*; *Disavowal*; *Major Image Distortion*; *Action*

1. I was angry at my boss, but I took it out on my wife when I got home.
2. You are the best therapist I have ever worked with.
3. How do I feel about losing my job? In the context of what is going on with the global economy, fluctuations in the bond markets, and systemic social problems, it was inevitable.
4. It's her fault that I lost my temper. She shouldn't have said that.
5. I need to put it out of my mind for now so that I can do this school assignment.
6. She is such an angel and I can't believe that she's dating that evil man.
7. They wouldn't let me use the computer, so I threw a glass against the wall.

Exercise 4 Below are descriptions of four patients. Rate their level of mental functioning using the descriptions in Table 2 (i.e., *Healthy, Neurotic, Borderline, Psychotic*).

1. Roberto is a father of two and married to Kelly for 12 years. They had difficulty in their marriage several years ago, but they received marriage counselling and their relationship is a little better. He works at a bank, but he has not been promoted, and this affects his self-esteem. He meets his only long-term friend for drinks about once a month. Every few months he experiences low mood and difficulty sleeping, but after a week or so the symptoms improve.
2. Giuseppe regularly thinks about suicide since his wife left him several years ago. He binge drinks on the weekend. He lost his job last year and is still unemployed. He has no close friends, and he does communicate with his family members. He spends his days at home, alone, surfing the internet.
3. Chiara is a university student who has good friends since grade school. She is dating Helen and describes the relationship as close and supportive. Clara reports occasional arguments with her mother since Clara left for university, but they seem to remain close despite the conflict. Clara reports some anxiety before exams, but she is managing well.
4. Maria is 35 years old and recently broke up with a boyfriend which was very stressful for her. Her longest romantic relationship lasted only a few months. She is dissatisfied with her work as a part time waitress. She cannot afford to live on her own, and so is living with roommates, with whom she often argues. She has student debt that she does not intend to repay, and she did not complete her university degree. Maria has panic attacks about once a week during which she cannot leave her home or go to work.

Chapter Review Answers

Exercise 1 1. Dismissing; 2. Preoccupied; 3. Dismissing; 4. Secure; 5. Preoccupied; 6. Fearful/Disorganized

Exercise 2 *She spent a lot of money on the trip, and I'm worried that we can't afford it. <u>I need her to act responsibly for me and the children</u>* (Attachment Needs). *<u>I kept thinking "if you really loved me and the kids, you wouldn't do that"</u>* (Attachment Needs). *I wish I could just tell her to get a refund, <u>but then I'd feel guilty for depriving her and the kids</u>* (Affect/Anxiety)—*who am I to place such restrictions on them? So, <u>I just stopped talking to her. We barely talked this morning</u>* (Defense) *and she and I just went to work. Then at work one of my employees made a mistake and it annoyed me, but I felt guilty for being annoyed, so <u>I didn't say anything about it. I ended up fixing it myself</u>* (Defense). *<u>It's so hard to find dependable people</u>* (Attachment Needs). *By afternoon I was so upset that I ordered a bunch of food, and <u>I binged in the car</u>* (Defense).

Exercise 3 1. Other Neurotic (Displacement); 2. Minor Image Distortion (Idealization); 3. Obsessional (Intellectualization); 4. Disavowal (Rationalization); 5. High Adaptive (Suppression)

Exercise 4 1. Neurotic; 2. Borderline; 3. Healthy; 4. Borderline.

References

Ainsworth, M. D. S., Blehar, M. C., Waters, E., & Wall, S. (1978). *Patterns of attachment: A psychological study of the strange situation*. Erlbaum.

American Psychiatric Association. (2013). *Diagnostic and statistical manual of mental disorders* (5th ed.). American Psychiatric Association Press.

Bakermans-Kranenburg, M. J., & van IJzendoorn, M. H. (2009). The first 10,000 Adult Attachment Interviews: Distributions of adult attachment representations in clinical and non-clinical groups. *Attachment & Human Development, 11*, 223–263.

Bartholomew, K., & Horowitz, L. (1991). Attachment styles among young adults: A test of a four-category model. *Journal of Personality and Social Psychology, 61*, 226–244.

Bateman, A., & Fonagy, P. (2006). *Mentalization-based treatment for borderline personality disorder: A practical guide*. OUP.

Bowlby, J. (1969). *Attachment and loss, Vol. I: Attachment*. Basic Books.

Bretherton, I., & Mulholland, K. A. (2008). Internal working models in attachment relationships: Elaborating a central construct in attachment theory. In J. Cassidy & P. R. Shaver (Eds.), *Handbook of attachment: Theory, research, and clinical applications* (pp. 102–127). Guilford Press.

Brugnera, A., Zarbo, C., Farina, B., Picardi, A., Greco, A., Coco, G. L., et al. (2019). Psychometric properties of the Italian version of the Experience in Close Relationship Scale 12 (ECR-12): An exploratory structural equation modeling study. *Research in Psychotherapy: Psychopathology, Process, and Outcome, 22*(3), 392.

Gallagher, M. E., Tasca, G. A., Ritchie, K., Balfour, L., & Bissada, H. (2014). Attachment anxiety moderates the relationship between growth in group cohesion and treatment outcomes in Group Psychodynamic Interpersonal Psychotherapy for women with binge eating disorder. *Group Dynamics: Theory, Research, and Practice, 18*(1), 38.

Hewitt, P. L., Flett, G. L., & Mikail, S. F. (2017). *Perfectionism: A relational approach to conceptualization, assessment, and treatment*. Guilford Press.

Leszcz, M., Pain, C., Hunter, J., Maunder, R., & Ravitz, P. (2015). *Achieving psychotherapy effectiveness*. Norton.

Main, M., & Hesse, E. (1992). Disorganized/disoriented infant behavior in the Strange Situation, lapses of monitoring of reasoning and discourse during the parent's Adult Attachment Interview, and dissociative states. In M. Ammaniti & D. Stern (Eds.), *Attaccamento e psicoanalisi*. Gius, Laterza & Figli.

Main, M., & Solomon, J. (1990). Procedures for identifying infants as disorganized/disoriented during the Ainsworth Strange Situation. In M. T. Greenberg, D. Cicchetti, & E. M. Cummings (Eds.), *Attachment in the preschool years: Theory, research, and intervention* (pp. 121–160). University of Chicago Press.

Malan, D. H. (1979). *Individual psychotherapy and the science of psychodynamics*. Butterworth.

Maxwell, H., Tasca, G. A., Grenon, R., Faye, M., Ritchie, K., Bissada, H., & Balfour, L. (2018). Change in attachment dimensions in women with binge-eating disorder following group psychodynamic interpersonal psychotherapy. *Psychotherapy Research, 28*(6), 887–901.

McCullough, L. (Ed.). (2003). *Treating affect phobia: A manual for short-term dynamic psychotherapy*. Guilford Press.

McWilliams, N., & Shedler, J. (2017). Personality syndromes: P axis. In V. Lingiardi & N. McWilliams (Eds.), *Psychodynamic diagnostic manual* (2nd ed., pp. 15–67). Guilford Press.

Mikulincer, M., & Shaver, P. R. (2019). Attachment orientations and emotion regulation. *Current Opinion in Psychology, 25*, 6–10.

Ogden, P., & Minton, K. (2000). Sensorimotor psychotherapy: One method for processing traumatic memory. *Traumatology, 6*(3), 149–173.

Perry, J. C. (1990). *Defense mechanisms rating scales* (5th ed.). The Cambridge Hospital.

Perry, J. C., & Bond, M. (2012). Change in defense mechanisms during long-term dynamic psychotherapy and five-year outcome. *American Journal of Psychiatry, 169*, 916–925.

Perry, J. C., & Hoglend, P. E. R. (1998). Convergent and discriminant validity of overall defensive functioning. *The Journal of Nervous and Mental Disease, 186*(9), 529–535.

Persons, J. B. (1991). Psychotherapy outcome studies do not accurately represent current models of psychotherapy: A proposed remedy. *American Psychologist, 46*(2), 99–106.

Tasca, G. A., & Balfour, L. (2014). Eating disorders and attachment: A contemporary psychodynamic perspective. *Psychodynamic Psychiatry, 42*(2), 257.

Tasca, G. A., Ritchie, K., Conrad, G., Balfour, L., Gayton, J., Lybanon, V., & Bissada, H. (2006). Attachment scales predict outcome in a randomized controlled trial of two group therapies for binge eating disorder: An aptitude by treatment interaction. *Psychotherapy Research, 16*(1), 106–121.

Tasca, G. A., Mikail, S. F., & Hewitt, P. S. (2021). *Group psychodynamic-interpersonal psychotherapy*. American Psychological Association Press.

Winnicott, D. W. (1973). *The child, the family, and the outside world*. Penguin.

World Health Organization. (1992). *The ICD-10 classification of mental and behavioural disorders: Clinical descriptions and diagnostic guidelines*. World Health Organization.

Zilberstein, K. (2014). The use and limitations of attachment theory in child psychotherapy. *Psychotherapy, 51*(1), 93–103.

Part III
Understanding Patient Functioning: Motivational Systems, Attachment, and Meaning Organizations

Motivational Systems for the Understanding of Patient's Functioning

Camilla Pozzi and Francesco Greco

1 Motivational Systems: Description and Development

According to the perspective of evolutionary psychology, the human being is equipped with inborn, evolutionarily determined psychobiological systems of behaviour regulation that regulate specific sequences of emotions and behaviours aimed at achieving an adaptive goal (Liotti et al., 2017). The authors who have studied them refer to these psychological systems of regulation or control with the term "motivational systems (MSs)" or alternatively "emotional or affective systems", to indicate how the study of human motivation is intrinsically connected to the study of emotions (Panksepp et al., 2015; Liotti et al., 2017; Gilbert, 1989). In this chapter, we will refer to them as motivational systems, by virtue of a greater centrality of motivation as a factor in understanding the functioning of the human being. In fact, as we will come to understand throughout this chapter, motivational systems guide and orient the subjective experience and the emergence of emotions, as well as provide directionality to behaviours. It is therefore crucial for all mental health professionals to know how these systems operate in the mind of every human being, regardless of the theoretical approach. The evolutionary ethological approach, in fact, offers the possibility of adopting a perspective free from any psychotherapeutic theory and the closest possible to the basic research in neuroscience (Panksepp et al., 2015).

C. Pozzi
Private Practitioner, Bologna, Italy

F. Greco (✉)
Private Practitioner, Bologna, Italy

Private Practitioner, Specialist Outpatient, Program of Eating Disorders, AUSL Modena, Modena, Italy

The Evolutionary Theory of Motivation (ETM) (Liotti et al., 2017), to which we mainly refer here, is one of the developments of the very rich contributions to the study of motivation in an evolutionary perspective. Nevertheless, it finds numerous points of contact, integration, and overlap with the theories elaborated in this framework by other authors, thus responding to our need to integrate evolutionary knowledge into clinical practice.

Before delving into the description of the characteristics of the most relevant MSs, we proceed to a brief review of the contributions that have influenced the study of human motivation in an evolutionary perspective—besides contributing to the development of ETM—and which seem to us relevant for the purposes of our discourse.

1.1 Contributions to the Study of Human Motivation in an Evolutionary Perspective

Historically, the first contribution to the study of human motivation in an evolutionary ethological framework was made by Charles Darwin with the volume *The Expression of the Emotions in Man and Animals* (Darwin, 1872). His thesis holds that every single fundamental emotion has an innate and universal basis and is at the same time only a component of a more complex motivational system, aimed at the pursuit of a specific and evolutionarily founded goal. However, only in the centuries that followed did studies by other authors provide empirical support for his thesis. These studies include the contribution of Paul Ekman, who offered a substantial contribution in support of Darwinian theories with his famous studies on the facial expressions of emotions and the review of numerous researches carried out over the years (Ekman, 1973). He could observe that, regardless of the culture of belonging, there was a surprising agreement in the recognition of the facial expressions of emotions: individuals from different cultural backgrounds, who among them had never had any contact or interaction, recognised the facial expressions of emotions based on universal expressive patterns. Ekman's primary emotions include fear, sadness, anger, disgust, surprise, and joy. Ekman's studies, while supporting evolutionary theories, do not neglect the relevance of cultural and social variables to the expression of emotions. Emotional experience, in fact, is inextricably linked to social relations and therefore is affected by the rules learnt during the socialisation process, showing a certain degree of social relativism (Barone, 2007). Ekman (Ekman & Friesen, 2003) talks about so-called display rules, meaning all those modifications that allow the individual to show appropriate behaviour from an emotional point of view. Therefore, acknowledging the situational value of emotions entails understanding that all emotions, including the basic ones with biological, genetically determined substrates, have a specific meaning that is highly contextualised and dependent on social relations—conventions imposed on the authentic expressions of emotion. According to Ekman, these cultural factors—rules of accentuation, attenuation, neutralisation, and simulation—enable an individual to exhibit appropriate behaviour from an emotional perspective; however, they cannot completely eliminate the existence and functionality of the primary emotional process; at most they modulate or prohibit their expression.

John Bowlby, father of the Attachment Theory (Bowlby, 1969, pp. 73, 80), conceptualised the attachment system, which is undoubtedly one of the most studied since his contribution, as one of the motivational systems—or systems for organising behaviour towards an objective with evolutionary value. Integrating data from ethology and evolutionary biology with psychoanalytic theories, he defines attachment as an innate and universal psychobiological system that organises and regulates behaviour (of attachment) and mental states towards the fulfilment of a purpose (care, comfort, and protection). This allows the organism to maintain or achieve a homeostatic condition when experiencing physical or mental pain or prolonged loneliness.

Later, Paul Gilbert (1989) theorised the existence of social mentalities by defining them as "the organisation of different psychological skills and modalities—for example, attention, thinking and tendency to action—guided by motivation to secure particular types of social relationship" (Gilbert & Petrocchi, 2012, p. 28). He distinguishes four social mentalities, corresponding, as we will see, to four of the interpersonal motivational systems (IMSs) described by ETM; these are attachment, caregiving, social ranking, and cooperation, all activated in accordance with the biosocial purpose that each person automatically and innately aspires to achieve.

Much more recently, Panksepp has made a significant contribution in this direction. Based on data from significant neuroscientific research, he has supported both the Darwinian thesis and the numerous ethological observations (Lorenz, 1974, 1989), according to which there are systems of organisation and control over the genesis of primary emotions. In his monumental book *Archaeology of the Mind*, the author describes the existence of seven emotional/motivational systems. These systems arise from the oldest and deepest parts of the brain and organise different emotions (and the corresponding motor actions) in typical sequences for every objective that is evolutionarily significant (Panksepp et al., 2015). This indicates that specific neuronal circuits can be identified in the activation of these organisational systems, rather than in the development of particular emotions. Based on the emotion or the behaviour that most characterises the functioning, Panksepp describes these basic affective systems as follows: RESEARCH—corresponding to the exploratory system, ANGER—corresponding to the competitive/ranking system, FEAR—corresponding to the system of defence, CARE—corresponding to the caregiving system, SEXUAL DESIRE—corresponding to sexual-mating system, PANIC—corresponding to the attachment system, and PLAY—corresponding to social play. As we will see later, these systems overlap in a fairly clear way with those elaborated by Giovanni Liotti and his team in the Evolutionary Theory of Motivation (Liotti et al., 2017).

1.2 The Evolutionary Theory of Motivation and Interpersonal Motivational Systems (IMSs)

As we discussed earlier, we can consider MSs as innate dispositions that are activated in the interaction with the environment, be it social or interpersonal, regulating subjective experiences, emotions, thoughts, and physical sensations outside of conscious awareness. The fact that MSs evolved well before consciousness in other species implies that they can operate outside of it, but it is true that in the human being the activation of a single MS can manifest itself to the conscious experience, determining the emergence of sensations, specific emotions, thoughts, and behaviours. Motivational systems therefore operate outside of consciousness and reside in the oldest areas of our brain, which is why we share most of them with other animal species, except for one more recent evolutionary motivational system—that of intersubjectivity—to which we will return later.

In the field of the Evolutionary Theory of Motivation (ETM), some authors, belonging to a fringe of Italian cognitivism, have developed a neo-Jacksonian conception of motivational architecture. Drawing on MacLean's triune brain theory (MacLean, 1990), these authors have identified three hierarchical levels in which the motivational systems are placed: the most archaic level, identifiable as the brainstem system; the second level, of the limbic system and the archipallium; and the third level, evolutionarily more recent, of the human neocortex. In this hierarchical perspective, each system is able to transmit inhibitory or excitatory signals in a top-down flow to the systems afferent to the hierarchically lower levels. These last can then transmit information in a bottom-up stream to the hierarchically superior systems that can process such signals with greater flexibility (Fig. 1).

Among the MSs belonging to the lowest level (reptilian motivations), we find those systems that we share with all the other animals: homeostatic regulation system (physiological regulation), the system of reptilian sexuality (without the

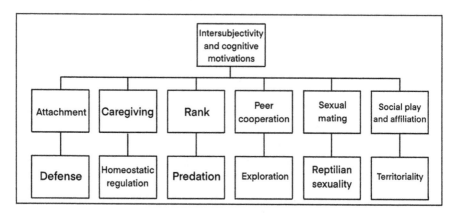

Fig. 1 Introduction to an overview of motivational architecture as understood in ETM. (Transcribed and adapted from Liotti et al. (2017))

formation of a sexual couple), the system of territoriality (defence of the habitat, den, or nest), the predatory system (aggressiveness aimed at obtaining food), the exploratory system (exploration of the environment functional to the achievement of the goals of other SM), and the defence system, which will be examined later.

At the second level, there are the interpersonal motivational systems (limbic motivations) that regulate the social interaction in mammals and that are activated in the "interpersonal encounter": attachment (seeking protection and care), caregiving (offering care), ranking MS (definition of the dominance rank), sexual bond (stable sexual mating), cooperation (joint focus on a common goal), social play (exercise of other ways without pursuit of a specific goal), and affiliation (belonging to the social group).

On the third level, we find the motivational system of intersubjectivity, which is typically exclusive to the human species and differentiates us from all other animals as it allows us to build narratives to give meaning to experience. The motivational system of intersubjectivity promotes metacognitive functions, that is, the understanding of our and others' mental states (such as intentions and emotions). We will dedicate a deepening to some of these systems, as they are essential to understand the psychological functioning of human beings.

Although the concept of hierarchy cannot fully explain the genesis of MSs (for a closer look, we refer to Liotti et al., 2017), all motivational systems—the most archaic and the most recent—have evolved in accordance with the principles of survival and adaptation to the environment; they are therefore intrinsically aimed at achieving specific goals. In other words, each motivational system responds to an objective evolutionarily relevant to the survival of the species rather than that of the individual. Each motivational system, as we shall see later, contains rules for activation and deactivation based on the achievement of specific goals. One example among the most ancient systems is the system of defence, which is aimed at protecting the individual from environmental dangers or hazards. It is triggered when such threats or hazards are encountered and deactivated when the goal of self-protection is achieved or the danger disappears.

Another characteristic that needs to be emphasised is that MSs are activated by the individual's exposure to internal or external stimuli, physiological alterations, or interactions with others. In other words, the activation of MS can be defined as "context-dependent". For example, the existence of an environmental threat indicates the context in which a perfectly working system of defence should always activate; similarly, the homeostatic system should react to stimuli such as hunger, thirst, and cold; in the same way, if a child shows signs of suffering, it is possible—and desirable—that the caregiving system is activated, resulting in a series of complex emotions and behaviours. In this latest example, it is less likely—and indicative of some problem—for the competitive/ranking system to be activated, as we will see later. Moreover, the same emotions can emerge in correspondence with different motivational systems and assume different meanings based on the motivation active at that particular moment. For example, guilt is an emotion that can emerge both within the caregiving system—when one feels guilty of not providing proper care—as well as within the cooperative system—when one fails to cooperate or reneges on the agreement with the other person and causes harm. Without the ambition to summarise here the Evolutionary Theory of Motivation (for which we refer to Liotti et al., 2017), we limit ourselves to reviewing the main characteristics of some of the most useful motivational systems in understanding the psychological functioning of the human being.

- *Systems of Defence*

As we have mentioned, the defence system, belonging to the motivations of the lower level, is activated in response to signs of environmental danger and is typically shown through behavioural responses such as freezing, attacking, fleeing, or fake death. Porges' Polyvagal Theory (Porges, 2001, 2007) offers us the possibility to understand the neurophysiological mechanisms behind the activation of these behavioural responses. When confronted with a threat to our survival—a predator's attack, or in today's world, any minor event such as a physical attack or an environmental catastrophe—our bodies react automatically and unconsciously; thus, we experience an initial moment of freezing and tonic immobility, which is mediated by the activation of the sympathetic nervous system. This first reaction to danger allows one to be less visible to the "predator" in the first place, and in the second place, to quickly—and automatically—choose the best option between fighting and fleeing—reactions that are also mediated by the sympathetic nervous system. When neither attack nor flight represent effective responses to defuse the threat, our parasympathetic nervous system, particularly the dorsal nucleus of the vagus nerve, activates by mediating a response known as fake death. Unlike tonic immobility mediated by the sympathetic system, fake death consists of hypotonic immobility—vasovagal syncope, dissociative responses—and represents in a way the extrema ratio of the defence system. Emotions typically involved in the system of defence are alert—in freezing, fear—in fleeing, destructive anger aimed at annihilating the aggressor—in attacking, and extreme impotence—in fake death.

The system of defence, which is common to all animals, gives rise to the system of attachment in mammals, as the presence of an environmental threat might trigger the search for an attachment figure who can provide protection from the threat; in other words, the attachment system is able to deactivate the defence system—except for the case of disorganised attachment. However, the defence system is not only activated in high-risk situations—when it is functional and extremely important—but it can lead to a sort of short circuit even in the absence of any actual physical danger, in those situations involving intense anxiety or post-traumatic conditions.

- *The Attachment System*

When we experience physical or mental pain, suffering, fear, or conditions of prolonged loneliness, the attachment system is innately and automatically activated in us human beings, just like in all mammals (Bowlby, 1969, 1988; Liotti, 2001). The aim of the attachment system is to obtain protection by the attachment figure—in the child—and by the most significant figures (for example, a partner)—in adulthood; the system is deactivated when this goal is attained. The behavioural and emotional sequence that we observe during its activation typically consists in approaching and clinging to the attachment figure; if the goal is achieved, the individual experiences joy, comfort, and safety. At that point it is possible to activate the exploratory system, which allows to separate from the attachment figure and therefore to experience a "safe autonomy". Otherwise, that is, if the behavioural responses do not result in protection by the attachment figure, the subject first experiences fear, then anger (in the form of protest) sadness, and finally emotional detachment.

As self-consciousness develops and grows, the activation of the attachment system becomes less rapid than in childhood; nevertheless, echoing Bowlby's words, we must remember that the attachment system is activated "from cradle to grave", understanding it is therefore essential/crucial for adult psychotherapy. As we will see, the fact that the attachment system is activated in adults has significant implications for the understanding of the patients who come to us. Starting from the child's initial attachment experiences, internal working models (IWM) are structured; these are internalised procedural representations that predict how the other person will respond to the need for care, in other words, they are models of *self-with-others* (Liotti, 2001). While in mammalian cousins the activation and deactivation of the attachment system are aimed exclusively at the restoration of protection, in humans they assume a double role:

They guarantee protection whenever the mind/brain senses danger; they contribute to the formation of meanings on the outcomes of these moments of request for help and response to the call for help in time—the internal working models. When the first experiences of a request for protection encounter prolonged and repeated failures during the development, in the mind of the child first, and of the adult then—in fact, from the cradle to the grave—peculiar internal working models are established; these, as we will see, will be insecure, affectively connoted, and have an impact on the relational functioning of the person.

- *The Caregiving System*

The caregiving system is complementary to the attachment system in interpersonal relationships when pain signals and requests for help are sent by a conspecific—often belonging to the same social group, but not exclusively. From a behavioural perspective, the activation of the caregiving system involves/consists of taking care, offering comfort, and helping the other person; the goal is the restoration of safety and the cessation of their painful state. The system is characterised by a range of emotions: solicitude, also connoted by anxiety; compassion; tenderness, with a protective purpose; anger, when the other person does something to put oneself in danger; guilt, when you cannot protect them; impotence, when you cannot protect them (Liotti et al., 2017). We often witness a "hypertrophy" of the caregiving system in those people who exhibit compulsive caregiving as a strategy of adaptation that heavily influences interpersonal relationships.

- *The Competitive/Ranking System*

From an evolutionary perspective, for all mammals, the competitive or ranking system is activated in order to define a dominance or submission hierarchy through ritualised displays of aggressiveness. The innate and unconscious activation of the competitive MS entails sending signals of aggressiveness in order to obtain signals of surrender or submission in response, that serve as the rule for the deactivation of the competitive MS in both individuals that interact. The stimuli that activate the competitive MS are signals of challenge from a conspecific, the perception of judgement, ridicule, or guilt, or the threat of a limited resource, which for humans, unlike other mammals, can be more abstract; that is, for example, receiving admiration or recognition of personal value, or protecting a psychological boundary. It is therefore clear that when an individual activates the competitive system in the dominant subroutine, the symmetrical activation of the same motivational system occurs in a submissive or dominant subroutine.

The emotions that typically come into play in the dominant subroutine are anger—accompanied by threatening behaviour distinct from the anger experienced by the caregiver—fear—when the subject notices the possible superiority of the other—or pride and contempt—when the other person emits signals of surrender and the subject emerges as the "winner". In the submissive subroutine, in conjunction with the emission of signals of surrender, emotions such as shame, humiliation, fear of judgement, envy, and sadness arise—all emotions related to recognising the superiority of the other.

While in the competitive system the aggressiveness is ritualised, meaning that it is addressed to one conspecific but not aimed at their annihilation, in the predatory system/behaviour—from which the competitive MS derives—the aggressiveness is addressed to members of other species considered as food. The emotion of contempt for the defeated in the competitive system evolved from the emotion of disgust, present in the predatory system, which inhibits the consumption of potentially harmful food. The study of competitive motivation also allows us to distinguish the nature of two social emotions that represent a source of considerable suffering and that emerge within two different motivational systems: guilt and shame; while guilt, defined as "the perception of having done something wrong or harmful", is an emotion associated with a caregiving motivation, shame, defined as "the pervasive perception of being wrong", can frequently arise when a competitive motivation is at play (Gilbert & Petrocchi, 2012).

As we will see later (see paragraph 3), in psychopathology, we frequently witness a stiffening of the psychological functioning on issues related to competitive motivation, as it happens for the other motivational systems.

- *The Cooperative System*

In humans and other mammals, motivation for cooperation is activated when there is a goal to be achieved that is not perceived as a limited resource—as in agonistic behaviour—but as a goal that could be more easily achieved by collaborating with one or more individuals in the social group of belonging. While for the other animal species the achievement of the purpose determines the cessation of the cooperative behaviour, in the human being the activation of the cooperative behaviour is repeated much more easily in time. The emotions that emerge from the cooperative system upon reaching the goal are joy, loyalty, and trust, while failure to achieve the goal results in guilt, remorse, distrust, and even hatred towards the other person, as a result, for example, of them breaking the pact of trust. As we will see later, the cooperative system is an essential element in the construction of therapeutic alliances (Liotti & Monticelli, 2014).

- *The Intersubjective Meaning System*

At the last hierarchical level, that of the neocortex, there is a higher-level motivation, unique to *Homo sapiens*, which we name "intersubjectivity", a motivational space within which it is possible to access metacognitive and mentalisation skills (Liotti et al., 2017). In ETM, the intersubjective system would exercise a regulatory function over lower-level systems, but the abnormal activation of the underlying systems can cause intersubjectivity to dissolve. The intersubjective motivation is of paramount significance for psychotherapeutic work and for the construction of the therapeutic alliance, as it highlights a fundamental need of the human being: establishing a deep intimacy, at least with another human being (Salvatore, 2023).

The intersubjective motivation is the one that allows the possibility of experiencing a deep "intimacy" with the other (Stern, 2004; Meares, 2000; Salvatore, 2023), opposed to what happens, for example, with the attachment behaviour, which serves to obtain protection from danger and a safe base from which to explore, more than an actual intimate connection. This need, which, like attachment, is present from birth, allows for processes of co-regulation that are crucial in the early stages of life, and its satisfaction allows for the continuity of the internal experience and therefore the development of an identity and a sense of self-cohesion and coherence.

2 Interpersonal Motivational Systems, Psychopathology and Therapeutic Alliance

2.1 IMSs in the Interpersonal Functioning of the Patient and Understanding of Psychopathology

As mentioned before, interpersonal MSs are based on innate tendencies and should not be rigid and inflexible but rather alternate between activation and deactivation according to the relational context. They, however, are shaped by memories of what has happened in the individual's history, and their functioning develops peculiar individual variations due to the effect of learnt elements (Bowlby, 1969). In animals, the functioning of MSs is exclusively pertinent to biological life, made of primary needs and motivational urges to satisfy them; on the contrary, in humans, the motivational functioning is significantly influenced by the ability—unique of this species—to give meaning to everything that occurs in the environment: the search for meaning that has always guided man in the discovery of himself and the world (Tomasello, 2014). Our perception of the environment, in fact, is linked to the meaning we give to things that happen in our lives. Our minds build a coherent history of who we are, on the basis of the precocious experiences of intersubjective sharing of our needs and desires—linked to interpersonal MS. We subsequently try, more or less consciously, to remain consistent with this history throughout our lives. As a result, it is possible that the activation of our MSs is influenced by both environmental stimuli (elements of context) and how we perceive these stimuli based on the meanings we assign to experience (elements of meaning). When a person does not have enough positive early experiences of intersubjective tuning, motivational systems may become decontextualised, rigid, or confused.

If, for example, an individual has built a prediction—based on their history—that the other is almost always abusive and devaluing, the ranking MS may take action even if the context does not involve competition or border protection. In this case, we would have a fully functional motivational system whose activation is influenced by the interpretation of the context.

Regarding the attachment system: while it performs its functions in recalling the adult's protection, the child processes meanings about himself, others, and the relationships between these parts (the IWM) throughout time. These meanings, in turn, will make a significant contribution to the individual's sense of self, even if the person has different relational experiences as an adult than he did with his attachment figures. Early attachment experiences provide an internal operating model that guides the subject's relational behaviour in adulthood. According to the Attachment Theory (Bowlby, 1969, 1973, 1980) people who have had a secure attachment experience consider other people as helpful and caring and their own selves as lovable and deserving of care, but in therapy, we rarely meet people who have followed a similar path. Those with avoidant attachment tend to perceive others as unavailable and rejecting or hostile, while they view themselves as undeserving of love, forcing them to rely solely on themselves. Those with insecure ambivalent attachment tend to regard others as unpredictable and unreliable, while they construct an image of themselves as loveable yet fragile and non-autonomous. If, for example, the episodes reported by the patient frequently involve the activation of the competitive system—situations in which the person feels challenged or fears the judgement of others, regardless of contextual stimuli—it is possible to hypothesise that their ranking system is particularly responsive because it is influenced by IWM-oriented (Internal Working Model) expectations that others will devalue and humiliate them.

Let's look at some examples of how hyperactivation, inhibition, or stiffening of motivational systems can be a relevant aspect for understanding the patient's functioning in relation to experiences of early attachment. When someone's need for comfort is consistently ignored or rejected (Avoidant attachment), they may internalise the implicit scheme that "if I show suffering or ask for comfort, then the other person will be unavailable or refuse me, so I better resort to a forced autonomy". Because the other is portrayed as unavailable and rejecting, it is possible to structure a strategy aimed at autonomy and self-sufficiency, with an inhibition of the activation of the attachment system and attachment behaviours, an overactivation of the exploratory system, and a stiffening on other motivational systems more practicable, such as the agonistic system (or, in other cases, the caregiving or sexual MS).

Or, if the person has experienced closeness and comfort in an incoherent and inconsistent way, feeling uncertain about the stability of the secure base, it is possible that they have structured within themselves the implicit expectation "if I express my need for autonomy, then I will lose the care and love of the other person" (ambivalent attachment). When there is a healthy desire for exploration, the individual represents oneself as vulnerable and the other person as inconsistent in providing protection; therefore, a great effort is needed to establish proximity in a relationship by using control strategies. In many cases, particularly when the person is experiencing pain, there is an over-activation of the attachment system and attachment behaviours (such as persistently expressing pain, asking for aid, etc.), as well as an inhibition of the exploratory motivational system; in these situations, it is possible that other motivational systems will stiffen in addition to the hyperactivation of the attachment system. For instance, if the child's attachment needs have been repeatedly violated and they only experience warmth and connection when they exhibit performative behaviours, it is possible that they will internalise the belief that "I am worthy of love and appreciation only if I am good, the best", so we can witness a hyperactivation of the competitive system.

Therefore, from a clinical perspective, the understanding of the consequences of disorganised attachment allows us to better comprehend the functioning of many of the patients who have experienced developmental trauma throughout their lives (Herman, 1992). Unfortunately, for these individuals, the figure that should have been a source of protection and comfort was also a source of danger due to mistreatment, abuse, neglect, or violence. Consequently, dissociated and incompatible IWM developed (Liotti & Farina, 2011), causing the defence and attachment systems to activate simultaneously. In these patients, as adults, we see the simultaneous activation of the defence system and the attachment system when they experience suffering conditions, which has important implications for psychotherapy (for a more in-depth study of the topic see Liotti & Farina, 2011).

Although most of the research focused on the attachment system, it is reasonable to assume that the first life experiences regulated by other ISMs, give rise to memory structures and expectations, similar to IWMs, which can influence the subsequent expression of those IMSs in adult life (Liotti & Monticelli, 2008). IMSs in fact are activated and deactivated by environmental stimuli and regulated—or rather, dysregulated—by dysfunctional interpersonal schemes and by problematic interpersonal cycles of the patient (Monticelli & Liotti, 2021; Safran & Segal, 1993; Semerari, 1999). While normal operation implies the harmonic activation of interpersonal MS, psychopathology can be represented as the result of the non-harmonic and rigid activation of the interpersonal motivational systems that represent the epiphenomenon of the patient's problematic interpersonal cycles and dysfunctional interpersonal patterns (Safran & Segal, 1993; Semerari, 1999; Monticelli & Liotti, 2021)

A frequently observed phenomenon, particularly in the field of personality disorders—but not only—is the structuring, in adults, of coping strategies that rely on the rigid and stereotypical activation of specific motivational systems with characteristics that we could define as "compensatory". When we talk about coping strategies, we mean those modalities that, despite the enormous costs to which they can expose us in the present life, in the past served as adaptive strategies in the relationship with the reference figures; in other words, they were "useful" to survival. In adults, the development of dysfunctional interpersonal or IWM patterns may involve the establishment of coping strategies—considered as unconscious and automatic survival behaviours—such as perfectionism, avoidance, and self-sufficiency, to name a few examples.

According to ETM and its subsequent developments (Monticelli & Glauser, 2022; Liotti, 2011; Liotti & Farina, 2011), there is a connection between some serious personality disorders—e.g. avoidant, dependent, borderline, narcissistic, and histrionic— disorganised attachment stories, hypertrophic motivational systems, and what are defined as "controlling strategies". According to this perspective, controlling strategies—defined as punitive or caregiving—consist in the hyperactivation of motivational systems with a vicarious function—that is, competitive and caregiving MSs—capable of deactivating the (disorganised) attachment system associated with pain and intense fear. Because IWMs that regulate the vicarious IMSs are more cohesive and organised than those that regulate disorganised attachment in subjects with trauma and unprocessed grief, controlling strategies thus allow for a stabilisation and greater ability to integrate.

This perspective suggests that, in the most severe cases of avoidant, dependent, histrionic, borderline, or narcissistic personality disorder, the adoption of controlling strategies may be the most effective strategy to stabilise relationships, and especially one's own mental states. For instance, we frequently see patients who repeatedly adopt caregiving behaviours even when the circumstance doesn't require it, in an attempt to preserve a solid and consistent sense of self; this could be the case of Gregory, a 56-year-old man whose relational exchanges are centred on a compulsive caregiving behaviour, high levels of guilt, and obsessive-compulsive and dependent personality traits. Gregory's mother suffered severe depression when he was a child, so he had to take care of her and give up his attachment needs—with an inversion of the attachment relationship. He learnt that the only useful strategy to obtain a minimum of security in the relationship—and a positive response to the need for intersubjectivity—is to sacrifice one's own needs and take care of the other person.

Similarly, we can observe individuals who show a rigid activation of a competitive motivation in the dominance subroutine; for example, in those cases of narcissistic personality disorder, in its overt variant. Alternatively, intense and unregulated feelings of shame, complacency, and hypersensitivity to judgement are manifestations of the hyperactivation of the competitive system in the submissive subroutine. These symptoms are present in narcissistic personality, but also in the case of borderline personality, in which a deep generalised shame—connected to the hyperactivation of the competitive MS, vicariant of the attachment MS—may involve a rigid complacent behaviour in order to free oneself from the critical judgement of the others; this results in a subsequent loss of awareness of one's own needs and the identity diffusion, typical of this clinical condition (Monticelli & Glauser, 2022; Liotti, 1999).

The relationship between IMSs and psychopathology is also explanatory to other clinical forms of psychopathology, such as social anxiety, depression, and eating disorders. According to ETM (Liotti, 1994/2005), in the case of social anxiety, an increased sensitivity to shame would both indicate and be reinforced by the expression of the uncontrolled activation of the competitive system in the submissive subroutine. According to this perspective, these patients' strong propensity to pervasively activate the agonistic system in the submissive subroutine represents the core of the pathology.

Some authors have made interesting contributions to our understanding of depressive disorders by referring to ETM; this perspective suggests that activating the competitive system is the only way to address the painful experience of feeling unloveable, which resides in IWMs of the individual suffering from depression. In the implicit and non-declarable nucleus of the cognitive "depressive" organisation (Guidano & Liotti, 1983), we find the themes of loss and defeat, which, according to the authors, could be organised in this way: "If I am good and I achieve the goal that's so important for my attachment figures—I am the best in school, I win the race, I take care of my mother—I will get attention and closeness. So, I must commit as much as possible, and devote all of my efforts to achieving success" (Onofri & Tombolini, 2003, p. 6). The emotional loss would thus be counterbalanced, in an entirely unconscious manner, by a strenuous effort to achieve success and avoid failure in the performance field. However, the implicit belief that "all this trouble is not enough to gain love" in the depressive episode is concretised in the experiences of defeat, of little personal value, inadequacy, abulia, and anhedonia typical of defeat in the submissive subroutine of the competitive MS.

According to Monticelli and Glauser (2022), dysregulation of the competitive MS, accompanied by emotion dysregulation and shame, is a risk factor for the development of body image disorders in adolescence and late adolescence. This would play a critical role in the onset and maintenance of eating disorders, by reinforcing feelings of inadequacy and personal discomfort.

2.2 IMSs in Clinical Dialogue: Implications for the Therapeutic Alliance

Understanding how the patient behaves on a motivational level is, as we have seen so far, a very useful source of information for understanding the patient's interpersonal functioning and psychopathology, allowing us to make informed decisions in psychotherapy. However, we can only obtain this knowledge through observation of what happens in the clinical dialogue.

Two observable aspects can be distinguished:

- The first involves the activation of the patient's IMSs as they report and describe them in their explicit narrations of events, speaking of themselves and their difficulties within the dialogue with the therapist—diachronic aspects;
- The second takes form in the immediacy of the present moment of the clinical dialogue, which can be considered as a distinct interpersonal context in which

the therapist and patient are two subjects who move on specific motivational registers in their reciprocal interaction—synchronic aspects.

Observing IMSs in the diachronic aspects of clinical dialogue concerns the therapist's ability to recognise the activation of IMSs in the patient's narrative, through the shared exploration of critical episodes that the patient reports. The synchronic aspects of the dialogue, on the other hand, allow us to learn about what is happening in the present moment—the here and now—of the clinical dialogue.

The research group of Liotti, Fassone, and Monticelli, in this regard, has developed a tool for the analysis and coding of IMSs within the clinical dialogue (AIMIT, Liotti & Monticelli, 2008), through the analysis of session transcripts (for an in-depth study, please refer to their volume, Liotti & Monticelli, 2008).

For our purposes, it is enough to know that what happens in the therapeutic dialogue can be summarised as follows: The patient reports an episode in which a certain ISM is active, but in the moment when they tell it they can be motivated by the same IMS or by a different one. For instance, when a patient with anger dysregulation tells us about an episode in which they were very angry with their boss—competitive motivation—they may do so with an active attachment motivation, showing suffering and therefore seeking our care and comfort; or they may act with an active competitive motivation in the submissive subroutine, feeling ashamed for their anger outburst and fearing our judgement; or in the dominant subroutine, more or less subtly criticising us about the fact that the therapy is not working; or they can tell us about the same episode with a cooperative motivation that allows a shared exploration of the episode in order to find a shared meaning. As previously stated, when one member of the dyad activates a particular IMS, the other member simultaneously and unconsciously activates a symmetrical or complementary IMS. Because of this, the therapist in the previous example should be able to observe the IMS active within themselves, exhibiting cooperative, competitive, or caregiving behaviours in response to the patient's relational modality. Obviously, what has been previously said would be partial because the therapist participates in the clinical dialogue with their own story, interpersonal patterns, and vulnerability, but this limited space would not allow us to explore a topic as broad as this. However, it is important to reflect, albeit briefly, on the role that IMSs can play in the therapeutic alliance construction, as well as the importance of the therapist's ability to resort to what is known as "inner discipline" (Safran & Segal, 1993; Dimaggio & Semerari, 2003).

As many studies demonstrate, the therapeutic alliance is the non-specific factor most predictive of psychotherapy success, as it is a clinical and theoretical aspect of great importance (for a recent meta-analysis, see Horvath et al., 2011). According to the evolutionary cognitive perspective, the therapeutic alliance is possible when therapist and patient cooperate in the pursuit of shared goals in an effective climate of trust and respect, in other words, when both are motivated by a cooperative MS. Working in the field of cooperative motivation, rather than other interpersonal motivational systems, provides fertile ground in the therapeutic dyad to access a higher-level motivation exclusive to *Homo sapiens*: the intersubjective motivation, a motivational space that allows access to metacognitive and mentalisation skills.

When an attachment behaviour burdened with insecure or disorganised IWMs is triggered in the patient during a session, it can easily become a threat to the therapeutic alliance: for instance, if the therapist responds by activating the caregiving system, this might result in interpersonal dysfunctional cycles; these are characterised by the activation of memories and problematic behaviours related to the attachment system, with the activation in the patient of insecure or disorganised IWMs.

When you leave the solid and welcoming ground of the cooperative system to move to other insidious and less secure systems, such as the attachment system, caregiving system, ranking system, or sexual motivation, you lose the possibility of accessing the construction and elaboration of shared meanings, and it becomes easy to encounter breakdowns in the therapeutic alliance, remaining involved in problematic interpersonal cycles (Liotti, 2001; Dimaggio & Semerari, 2003; Greco et al., 2016). Dealing with such situations is never simple for the therapist, and it is probably one of the most difficult challenges to handle. The therapist's responsibility is to restore the relationship to a state of cooperation and equality, because only in this dimension can the patient experience a meaningful change. In these cases, the escape from the interpersonal dysfunctional cycles and thus the possibility of bringing the relationship back on a cooperative level, is made possible by the therapist's exercise of inner discipline; only this way, the patient can be provided with a different way of interacting with the others (Dimaggio & Semerari, 2003).

The Inner Discipline is a mental attitude, a set of management strategies of problematic emotional experiences that are activated in the therapist—for example, anger, impotence, guilt, mental pain, shame, pleasure in being appreciated or cared for by the patient—in response to a behaviour of the patient—for example, the activation of attachment, ranking, caregiving, sexual MSs. In such cases, the therapist must become aware that the patient's behaviour has struck a sensitive chord that needs to be properly addressed, in order to avoid the activation of harmful interpersonal processes for therapy (Safran & Segal, 1993).

3 Clinical Case: The Case of Amy

- *First Encounter*

Amy is a friendly and mild-mannered 43-year-old woman who works in public administration and lives alone. She has been in a relationship with a man her age for some years and describes it as very complicated.

At the time of the first psychological interview, she complains of prominent depressive symptoms, such as frequent crying, lack of energy, great difficulty going to work every day, and a sense of despair.

During her first interview, Amy cries, continually apologising for her condition:

A: (cries) I am sorry doctor, I should not be seen in these conditions; I am unable to handle myself!

Since the first steps, we can grasp the motivational aspects that characterise the communication: "I am unable to handle myself" suggests how Amy is being pushed in this moment by her ranking MS, in the submissive subroutine.

T: I can guess this is a very difficult time for you, so you don't have to apologise.
A: You're very kind, but I should stop doing that!

The therapist demonstrates empathy, attempting to convey the possibility of a suspension of judgement, but Amy is still very attached to self-criticism. We will later understand, how for her, the self-criticism is not only linked to the specific context but to her general functioning.

T: What should you stop doing, Amy? What do you mean?
A: I should stop whining like a child and start to work to get out of this situation.

It's still too early for Amy to leave the comfort-zone of self-devaluation, so her raking MS remains active: "I should stop whining like a child".

T: Okay, Amy, I understand that this situation is not acceptable to you. I have a proposal for you: how about working together to try to figure out exactly what "this situation" is like?

The therapist begins to implicitly propose a shift of the active IMS, from a ranking MS to a cooperative MS: "*I have a proposition for you: how about working together*". In the dialogue that follows, we can see the patient's resistance to a change in her motivational structure.

A: Ah, there's little to understand, I'm a crybaby who can't handle herself...
T: However, I can see you are suffering. Are you aware of the reason? Do you have any notion of what's causing you to suffer?
A: My whole life makes no sense! I don't want to get out of bed in the morning; I don't want to see anyone; I just want to disappear.
T: (…) Amy, does it make sense for you to have some meetings to better understand the situation?

- Assessment

During the interviews, it was possible to assess a severe depressive symptomatology, which the patient had previously experienced in a weaker form. Amy had somehow lost the will to do everything she used to do. She still had the job, but she feared that this escalation of sadness and unmotivated crying would lead her to lose it shortly afterwards.

Amy reported thoughts characterised by a lack of meaning in life and despair. She cried every morning when she woke up, and she said she felt like she was trapped in a black hole with no escape.

From an interpersonal point of view, Amy showed a consistent framework of difficulties in communicating her needs and desires to anyone, accompanied by the feeling that expressing her opinion to others would lead them to leave and/or judge her negatively; she also felt that she could never escape the demands of others, even when they were clearly unbalanced against her.

From a descriptive diagnostic approach, the presence of major depressive disorder and dependent personality disorder (DSM-5; APA, 2013) was detected. The explanatory diagnosis, moreover, tells us of a functioning based on the ranking MS in the submissive subroutine, associated with a caregiving behaviour that is close to compulsive oblativity (Bowlby, 1983). Although depressive symptomatology was predominant at the time of the evaluation, a more accurate reconstruction of the patient's functioning revealed that the personological characteristics were the foundation of it.

- *Biographical Information and Affective Story*

Amy comes from a traditional family in southern Italy, very attentive to traditions and family ties. Being the only girl and having an older brother, she grows up with the clear understanding that her desires are unimportant and that asking others to meet her needs is seen as selfish behaviour. Convinced by the belief that the most important thing is that others are happy and satisfied, she spends her childhood and adolescence staying in the shadows, trying strenuously to create as little annoyance as possible in order not to attract the anger of others, under penalty of disapproval and threat of abandonment.

During her university period, Amy moves to a large university town in northern Italy, where she lives a life of sacrifice and few opportunities. In the same period, she suffers the loss of her father, an event that, in addition to bringing great suffering, exacerbates her already strong sense of responsibility and guilt, a circumstance for which the university ended perfectly in time. Immediately after the end of the university studies and with the beginning of the first job, she meets Paul, with whom she begins dating.

Following an initial phase, the relationship grows closer, and Amy starts to feel more connected emotionally. Regrettably, Paul shifts between unstable jobs, expressing his inability to commit to long-term obligations in both his professional and personal lives; he exhibits a self-centred personality almost immediately, setting an asymmetrical relationship that puts Amy in a position to look after him and satisfy his desires. Amy was not unfamiliar with this situation, and upon hearing Paul's explicit request for care, she instantly proceeded to gratify all of his desires. Thus begins a love story centred almost entirely on interpersonal dependency (commonly known as affective dependency).

- *A few months later*

A: *We've been together for 8 years but he has no intention of taking the next step in this relationship. I would feel the need to grow from this point of view, move in together and try to create a family, but Paul doesn't want to know. He says he thinks we're fine…*

T: *Mmm, I imagine the disagreements on what to do in the future are causing you a lot of grief. Is that it?*

The therapist tries to always ask Amy's opinion about what she has understood or imagines she has understood. If the goal is to shift the motivational structure to the cooperative MS, then it becomes necessary to proceed with shared knowledge and feedback.

A: *Absolutely; I feel trapped. If I insist on this point, I'm afraid he'll leave me; if I don't, I will always be unhappy. Either way, my life will be a failure!*
T: *So Amy, if I understand you correctly, do you feel that by pursuing your needs and desires you will end up being alone and unhappy?*
A: *Well, we could say that...*
T: *Do you have this feeling in other areas of your life?*
A: *All the time!*
T: *Would you like to give me some examples? It may help us to better understand the emotions, thoughts and behaviours that are activated in front of certain situations.*

The therapist proposes to Amy a shared exploration of her own mental state with respect to the critical situation, with the goal of building a perspective that can be observed by both.

A: *At work for example; if colleagues ask me a favour, I simply cannot say no. I don't know, a shift change or an extra task. It is the rule ...*
T: *In these scenarios, what risks would you consider if you said "no"?*
A: *Well, someone might be offended.*
T: *Yes, it's a possibility... But then what would happen?*
A: *Mmm, I don't know; I just don't see that as a possibility.*
T: *Now we are here, you and I; let's try together to observe what thoughts, emotions and feelings emerge if we imagine that you say no to a colleague who asks you yet another favour. I want to specify that today our goal is not to change your modus operandi, but only to get to know it better. Let's imagine the scene.*

In this passage, it is noticed how the therapist tries to carry out two procedures in parallel:

1. T tries to explore the basic belief through laddering; what is Amy's expectation if she were to keep the line and say no? This would be important for observing the patient's representations and understanding what terminal purposes she is protecting by avoiding saying no and asserting her needs.
2. Amy's fear of even considering this option is evident to the T, so he works in parallel on the therapeutic alliance through the solicitation of the cooperative MS: *"let's try **together** to observe what thoughts, emotions and sensations emerge if we imagine that...";* *"today **our** goal is not to change your modus operandi, but only to get to know it better".*

By doing so, the T tries to build a shared place of observation of her mental state, putting Amy safe from what scares her most.

A: *I imagine the other person might get offended, never talk to me again and convince others that I am not a good person to keep close.*

T: Do you think that this refusal could ruin the other person's representation of you and consequently influence others?
A: Yes, maybe it's that...
T: Okay, what scenario do you imagine in that case?
A: I don't know, I would risk being alone maybe.

After a few steps Amy expresses her ultimate purpose to protect: not to be alone.

T: I understand Amy. So, if you imagine yourself refusing a request, you fear that others may think that you are not good and consequently move away, to solve this risk you tend to accept most of the requests, is that so?
A: Yes, it is.
T: This strategy, however, costs you the feeling of being trapped, as you said, is that right?
A: That's right...
T: Well, then if it's okay for you in the next meetings we will focus on this dilemma in order to better understand how it works and evaluate together any intervention.
A: All right, it seems like a good idea...

In this last passage, we can observe how the T tries to share with Amy what he has understood of her psychic functioning, offering her a feeling of clarity about what often upsets her. Finally, he suggests that they work together to better understand the dilemma and, eventually, take into account possible alternatives. Compared to the beginning, the last exchanges show a less frequent activation of the ranking MS, which translates into less self-criticism and judgement in favour of a better openness to discussion and a possibility to delve deeper into her own mental processes.

According to ETM, when the therapist actively engages in a collaborative motivation with the patient, there is a greater propensity to shared exploration, resulting in improved metacognitive skills and increased sense of security in the patient. For some time, Amy will work in therapy on the ability to monitor her mental states, maintaining a critical distance from them, through imaginative and self-monitoring techniques such as ABC (Ellis, 1962). Such work has always had as a foundation the attempt to maintain a collaborative motivation.

- *Commitment*

Once one has improved their self-monitoring skills and gained, at least in part, a critical distance from their mental states, they often need to move on to a phase of action: a change in some of the coping mechanisms that people use to avoid the painful experience (sometimes such mechanisms coincide with symptomatology). These phases are very delicate because acting differently from one's own coping strategy can sometimes be frightening, which is why the relational aspects in therapy—especially the therapeutic alliance—become crucial.

In Amy's case, coping behaviour consisted primarily of generalised complacency and perfectionism, both of which are incredibly effective strategies if the goal is to avoid external criticism and subsequent abandonment. As agreed at the beginning of the journey, after a few months of work, the T proposes to Amy that she start exploring the possibilities of behaving differently than the ways described above.

T: Amy, I've noticed that your ability to monitor what happens to you with a little more critical distance has improved a lot over the last period. Your ABC clearly indicates this, do you agree?

A: Yes, actually I seem to be more aware of what worries me, but I still have a lot of fear.

T: Of course, I believe that better understanding the way we function is necessary to see clearly, which is already something, but it is not always enough to produce changes and therefore better master our fears. That's obviously what I can tell you based on my knowledge; what are your thoughts?

In this way, the T provides the patient with the technical knowledge required to move forward, but most importantly, he pauses to ask the patient for her opinion, ensuring that the collaborative climate established from the start is never broken.

A: Well, I understand that if I want to feel better, I need to change something in the facts, but I'm terrified, and I'm not sure if I want to deal with all of this, even though we mentioned it from the start.

In this step, you can notice the risk of breaking the therapeutic alliance. Although Amy understands the importance of putting in place new coping mechanisms, she doesn't feel ready to do so.

T: Okay, Amy. I understand very well that you are afraid of this. Let me make you a proposition: as we stated at the beginning of the journey, our goal is to make you more autonomous in your choices and less fearful of the opinions/reactions of others, do you agree?

A: Yes, that's right.

T: Well, after a first phase in theory we should now try something different from the usual, such as saying "no" on occasion. However, it is equally important that you feel at least a little more confident about starting. What do you think if we reflected/brainstormed together about what would make you feel safer in a situation that typically puts you at a disadvantage?

A: Yes, but how?

T: Well, for example I thought we could start this phase right here! From the therapeutic space. We could use this place and this relationship to take the first steps towards a new coping strategy. What do you think, can you do it?

A: Mhh, like how?

T: We could imagine hypothetical situations, for example, or we could think of putting them on stage, as in a role-playing game.

A: Like a theatre?

T: Yes, but the focus is on experience rather than performance.

A: Doctor, I'm too ashamed to do this kind of thing, I feel stupid.

Amy finds it difficult to even simulate such an interaction; in fact, the mere thought of it activates her ranking system again, bringing back the fear of being judged and the embarrassment of exposing herself.

T: Amy, I already knew that asking you would put you in a difficult situation. We've been working together for a few months now, but I did it to keep up with our therapeutic goals. Therefore, I suggest that we start working on it and stop every time you feel that this shame becomes too annoying, maybe by doing an ABC together. What do you think? In this way we could work gradually on coping and at the same time reflect on what is going on inside of you, without rush but with commitment.

A: Well, then I think we will stop often... (smiles).

T: It doesn't matter, Amy, we're not here to run, we're here to build. When you build you go calmly so that everything built can withstand the necessary time. So, welcome to Amy's theatrical workshop... (smiles).

The therapist attempts to provide a safe relational space based on peer collaboration for Amy while staying loyal to her goals. In fact, although very scared, Amy has an extreme need to work on her coping skills to identify the parts of her life that have caused her to experience severe depressive episodes thus far.

The patient began an assertive training in which she progressively developed the ability to master her painful mental states and put her needs on a par with others. Two years later, Amy generated such a profound change in her sense of self that she now felt worthy. The increase in her self-monitoring and her tolerance of painful emotions, combined with a sense of mastery and self-efficacy, led to an improvement in her self-confidence. Amy subsequently ended her relationship with Paul and committed/dedicated herself to new experiences, such as travelling and spending her money on herself.

References

American Psychiatric Association. (2013). *Manuale diagnostico e statistico dei disturbi mentali. Quinta edizione: DSM-5*. Tr. It. Raffaello Cortina.

Barone, L. (2007). *Emozioni e sviluppo. Percorsi tipici e atipici*. Carocci.

Bowlby, J. (1969). *Attaccamento e perdita* (Vol. I). Bollati Boringhieri, 1972.

Bowlby, J. (1973). *Attaccamento e perdita* (Vol. II). Bollati Boringhieri, 1975.

Bowlby, J. (1980). *Attaccamento e perdita* (Vol. III). Bollati Boringhieri, 1983.

Bowlby, J. (1988). *Una Base Sicura: Applicazioni Cliniche della Teoria dell'Attaccamento*. Tr. It. Raffaello Cortina, 1989. (Original work published 1988: *A secure base: Clinical applications of attachment theory*).

Darwin, C. (1872). The expressions of the emotions in man and animals. John Murray

Dimaggio, G., & Semerari, A. (Eds.). (2003). *I disturbi di personalità. Modelli e trattamento. Stati mentali, metarappresentazione, cicli interpersonali*. Laterza.

Ekman, P. (1973). Cross-cultural studies of facial expression. In *Darwin and facial expression: A century of research in review* (pp. 169–222). Academic Press.

Ekman, P., & Friesen, W. V. (2003). *Unmasking the face: A guide to recognizing emotions from facial clues* (Vol. 10). Ishk.
Ellis, A. (1962). *Reason and emotion in psychotherapy*. Citadel.
Gilbert, P. (1989). *Human nature and suffering*. Erlbaum.
Gilbert, P., & Petrocchi, N. (2012). *La terapia focalizzata sulla compassione. Caratteristiche distintive*. FrancoAngeli.
Greco, F., Pozzi, C., & Gremigni, P. (2016). *La dissociazione. Fenomenologia clinica, sviluppi psicopatologici e implicazioni per la psicoterapia*. Maddali e Bruni.
Guidano, V., & Liotti, G. (1983). *Processi cognitivi e disregolazione emotiva. Un approccio strutturale alla psicoterapia*. Tr. It. Apertamenteweb, 2018.
Herman, J. L. (1992). Complex PTSD: A syndrome in survivors of prolonged and repeated trauma. *Journal of Traumatic Stress, 5*(3), 377–391.
Horvath, A. O., Del Re, A. C., Flückiger, C., & Symonds, D. (2011). Alliance in individual psychotherapy. *Psychotherapy, 48*(1), 9.
Liotti, G. (1994/2005). *La dimensione interpersonale della coscienza*. Carocci.
Liotti, G. (1999). Il nucleo del disturbo borderline di personalità: un'ipotesi integrativa. *Psicoterapia, 5*(16/17), 53–65.
Liotti, G. (2001). *Le opere della coscienza: Psicopatologia e psicoterapia nella prospettiva cognitivo-evoluzionista*. R. Cortina.
Liotti, G. (2011). Attachment disorganization and the controlling strategies: An illustration of the contributions of attachment theory to developmental psychopathology and to psychotherapy integration. *Journal of Psychotherapy Integration, 21*(3), 232.
Liotti, G., & Farina, B. (2011). *Sviluppi traumatici*. Raffaello Cortina.
Liotti, G., & Monticelli, F. (2008). *I sistemi motivazionali nel dialogo clinico*. Raffaello Cortina.
Liotti, G., & Monticelli, F. (Eds.). (2014). *Teoria e clinica dell'alleanza terapeutica. una prospettiva cognitivo-evoluzionista*. Raffaello Cortina.
Liotti, G., Fassone, G., & Monticelli, F. (2017). *L'evoluzione delle emozioni e dei sistemi motivazionali*. Raffaello Cortina.
Lorenz, K. (1974). *L'altra faccia dello specchio*. Adelphi, 1991.
Lorenz, K. (1989). *L'anello di re Salomone*. Adelphi, 1989.
MacLean, P. D. (1990). *The triune brain in evolution. Role in paleocerebral functions*. Plenum New York Press.
Meares, R. (2000). *Intimacy and alienation: Memory, trauma and personal being*. Psychology Press.
Monticelli, F., & Glauser, N. (2022). La terapia dei disturbi legati alla disregolazione della vergogna. *Quaderni di Psicoterapia Cognitiva*, (51), 72–90. (ISSN 1127-6347, ISSNe 2281-6046).
Monticelli, F., & Liotti, M. (2021). Motivational monitoring: How to identify ruptures and impasses and enhance interpersonal attunement. *Journal of Contemporary Psychotherapy, 51*(2), 97–108.
Onofri, A., & Tombolini, L. (2003). La prospettiva cognitivo-evoluzionista, i sistemi motivazionali interpersonali e la psicoterapia cognitiva dei disturbi dell'umore. *Psicobiettivo, 1–16*
Panksepp, J., Biven, L., Alcaro, A., & Clarici, A. (2015). *Archeologia della mente: origini neuroevolutive delle emozioni umane*. R. Cortina.
Porges, S. W. (2001). The polyvagal theory: Phylogenetic substrates of a social nervous system. *International Journal of Psychophysiology: Official Journal of the International Organization of Psychophysiology, 42*(2), 123–146.
Porges, S. W. (2007). The polyvagal perspective. *Biological Psychology, 74*(2), 116–143.
Safran, J. D., & Segal, Z. V. (1993). *Il processo interpersonale nella terapia cognitiva* (Vol. 85). Feltrinelli.
Salvatore, G. (2023). *La vergogna del terapeuta. Da nucleo di sofferenza a fattore di cura*. Raffaello Cortina.

Semerari, A. (Ed.). (1999). *Psicoterapia cognitiva del paziente grave. Metacognizione e relazione terapeutica.* Raffaello Cortina.

Stern, D. N. (2004). The present moment in psychotherapy and everyday life (Tr. It.). In *Il momento presente. In psicoterapia e nella vita quotidiana.* Raffaello Cortina, 2005.

Tomasello, M. (2014). The ultra-social animal. *European Journal of Social Psychology, 44*(3), 187–194.

The Postrationalist Perspective: Personal Meaning Organisations (PMO) and Their Functioning

Daniela Merigliano

1 The Model

The viewpoint from which we move in the analysis we are about to embark on, the postrationalist model, takes its course from an epistemological approach that conceives of reality as a continuous, multidirectional, multi-layered flow of emotional and cognitive processes in constant unfolding in which the individual, as observer, imposes his own personal order in experiencing and knowing (Maturana & Varela, 1985, 1987).

Starting from Humberto Maturana's (1978) evolutionary *or natural epistemology*, we intend to refer to the application of evolutionary aspects to the study of cognitive mechanisms with a methodology that is concerned with investigating knowledge processes, treated as an emergent faculty of biological and adaptive trends. This property has developed on a par with other aspects of life and as such is to be regarded as a biological as well as psychological process. We must introduce here the concept of *autopoiesis* (reproduction, self-production), understood as a continuous generative process of self-renewal through which perturbations from interaction with the external world are transformed into progressively more complex and integrated levels of personal identity and self-awareness (Maturana & Varela, 1985, 1987). A complex cognitive system is *organisationally closed* because it admits no alternatives to its experiential order, which corresponds to the *personal meaning* on which the continuity and coherence of its sense of self are based. However, such a system is also *autonomous* since it does not require anything other than constant referentiality to itself. And, again, it is *open* to exchange with the external environment. In essence, then, we can say that an individual cognitive

---

D. Merigliano (✉)
Società Italiana Terapia Comportamentale e Cognitiva (SITCC), Rome, Italy

Cognitive Postrationalist Psychology Laboratorio Roma, Rome, Italy

system corresponds to a *self-organising self-referential system* insofar as cognitive processes play an absolutely central role in the construction of that ordering of reality that we commonly refer to as *personal experience*. It is like saying that *'every life is a point of view of the universe'* (Ortega y Gasset, 1994, p. 134), meaning that *'all knowledge is knowledge from a given point of view'* (ibid.).

Here, then, we come to the premises useful for understanding the narrative form of the individual's identity. We need to recall the concept of *personal meaning*, which is the foundational element defining the type of systemic coherence to which each *organisation of personal meaning* is bound during its life cycle. Personal meaning represents the design processuality in a constant ordering of networks of variously interrelated significant events, which brings forth an experience of the self and the world (*'I'*) specifically recognisable as the unity and continuity of the self over time (*'Me'*) (Guidano, 1991, 1992).

We therefore return to the concepts of *multidirectionality* and *multileveledness of* emotional and cognitive processes that flow in a continuous unfolding to which the individual, as observer, imposes a personal order on his experience of himself and reality (Maturana & Varela, 1985, 1987).

The multimodal aspect is due to the fact that we must conceive of knowledge as not only cognitive but also emotional, sensory, perceptual, coenesthetic and procedural. The multi-level aspect is explained by the fact that the emergence of language and its progressive articulation means that experience takes place constantly, simultaneously, on a dual level:

- *That of immediate experience*, which is not tied to intentionality, flows on its own, continuously and incessantly.
- *That of the conscious self-image* that is always one step behind the immediate experience, because it must continually reorder and refer to itself the moment-by-moment occurrence that has meanwhile already moved on (Guidano, 1988).

In his studies, Guidano then clarified these aspects by adding the concept of *sameness*, understood as the set of stable characteristics of the personality, which represents the sense of continuity and is characterised by the so-called *emotional traits* (recurrent patterns of emotional activation, which are always the same), and the concept of *hypseity*, that is, the set of *emotional episodes* that in turn depend on the emotional traits themselves. These concepts, derived from Ricoeur's thought, are best explained by the author: *'The true nature of narrative identity ... is only revealed in the dialectic of hypseity and sameness. In this sense, the latter represents the main contribution of narrative theory to the constitution of the self...'* (Ricoeur, 1988 (2016, Ital. ed., pp. 231–232)). The *emotional episodes* or *stirrings* that make up ipseity are discordant patterns of the flow of experience that give a sense of discontinuity, however brief. Emotional episodes present peculiar characteristics: the emotion that is triggered is very intense, the moods are vivid and multiple in a precipitous succession, they are accompanied by related imaginative scenarios, they are sudden, apparently non-derivable, and at the end of their occurrence, an emotional reverberation remains for a variable duration of time.

In the process of ordering the experiential data, following this paradigm, then each individual is the bearer of a *Meaning* that allows him or her to recognise and refer to each immediate experience of self and the world. This systemic invariant represents the expression of a process of self-organisation through which the individual structures a sense of personal continuity and consistency over time (sense of self-conscious self-image). This implies that personal meaning stands as a foundational, unique and invariant element that defines the type of systemic coherence to which each *personal meaning organisation* is bound during its life cycle. This determines the proactive, projectual processuality in a constant rearrangement of networks of variously interrelated significant events, which develops an experience of self and the world ('I') peculiarly recognisable as the unity and continuity of one's self over time ('Me') (Mead, 1934; Guidano, 1992). We thus refer to an ontological perspective for which to *exist* is to *know*, and emotions are forms of knowledge insofar as they correspond to that immediate ordering of reality that we perceive as *given* in the flow of our praxis of living. All knowledge inevitably reflects the specific self-referential constraints from which a given cognitive system structures its experience (Guidano, 1988, p. 88). As Bennett reminds us, there can be no knowledge without emotion. We may consider ourselves aware of something, but until we have felt its essence, its power, it is not our domain (1988).

The experiential data, hitherto experienced as pre-constituted objective realities, once brought into sharper focus, are referred to oneself and integrated, becoming part of one's identity narrative, enriching it. Narrative identity unfolds in a processual manner in the constant dialectic between the I who experiences and the Me who explains and evaluates the experience (Mead, 1934). On the basis of these concepts, it is good to remember that in psychotherapy a change is achieved when the Me's evaluation of the I changes, following a careful focusing of the experienced or ongoing experiences. According to Ricoeur (1995, 2016), through language we make sense of experience, thereby constructing our narrative identity, which remains unique and unrepeatable thanks to the constant dialectic between the Narrator Self that explains and evaluates and the Protagonist Self that experiences.

Maturana's belief that *everything happens in language* highlights how the consciousness we have today, which is the central element of our experience of ourselves and the world, would not exist without language (1978, 1993, p. 11). The human need for language is also linked to the fact that it gives us the structuring of time. We humans constantly perceive reality in narrative terms; we are always within a present that comes from a past and goes towards a future. Even putting an event into a sequence that has a beginning, an unfolding and an end always takes place within a temporary segmentation. Here, then, is how in human beings, for the first time, experience begins to unfold and flow simultaneously on the two levels we have described: a first level that is the one we share with all the animals on the planet and which is the level of immediate experience; and a second, simultaneous level that pertains to the ordering that this immediate experience has, through the sequential structures that language offers (Guidano, 1998). In essence, this typically *human* characteristic is none other than *thematic language*, which consists in having the capacity to structure experiencing in a sequence that always has a beginning, an unfolding and an end, and yet this sequence belongs to a particular order in which all the data of lived or vicarious experience are conceptualised by language (Guidano, 1998). Thus, we can say that human beings tell stories in order to be in relationships with others, and they tell stories to themselves in order to reorder the experience they are going through, attributing it to themselves with that particular and specific way of meaning that is *their own personal one*. In the practice of *storytelling*, the construction of one's own meanings takes place, and language, the unique property of human primates, is the instrument through which experience is organised in narrative form. Sequencing the events and the experiences related to them involves assembling the different emotional activations taking place, reorganising the experience itself and giving it meaning, and attributing to it meanings that, continually revised and updated, enrich and expand the narrative plot of that certain life story (Guidano, 1998). The data integrated within the personal narrative allow a harmony of functioning. Data that otherwise remain outside the personal narrative, not fitting into one's own narrative plot, express the discrepancy through psychopathological symptoms. In therapy, one works on the emergence of a discrepant emotional activation for which the Narrator Self can no longer explain the ongoing experience of the Protagonist Self: the internal coherence of the system is threatened, hence the emergence of symptoms and thus the need to reorganise the discrepancy that has occurred.

Let us conclude this first part of our analysis by reiterating, in Mauro Ceruti's words, how in the perspective of complex systems, knowledge processes are treated as emergent properties of biological systems: '… *the system considered, among the stimuli that come to it from the environment, selects those that are admissible and those that are not, those that can be integrated in the cycles that define its organisation (and therefore its identity as a living being) and those that cannot be integrated*' (1989, p. 93).

2 Personal Meaning Organisations

On the path we are following towards understanding the functioning of the harmonious and the pathological human being, we move *from symptom to meaning* in the investigation of the different ways of elaborating personal meaning. We thus arrive at a reconstruction of a *specific life theme* that represents the narrative unfolding of personal meaning throughout the life span. We are aided in this endeavour by a *descriptive psychopathology* that classifies the abnormal experiences as they are reported by the patient and which are observable by his behaviour. We thus deal with what is observable and shareable. And we then make use of *explanatory psychopathology* that creates hypotheses about the coherence and meaning of a pathological event. The explanatory approach deals with everything that belongs to the subjective experience. This is why we resort to such an indispensable tool for the recognition of a subjectivity directly expressed in its systemic invariant, the ordering principle of experience: personal meaning.

If, as mentioned earlier, we consider the individual as an expression of a self-organised process, through which a sense of uniqueness, continuity and personal consistency over time is structured, in the encounter with the patient's reality we need to consider:

- the type of Personal Meaning Organisation by which is meant the *'set of processes underlying the elaboration of a personal meaning for which, while experiencing numerous transformations, an individual retains his or her sense of personal uniqueness and historical continuity'* (Guidano, 1988, p. 12).
- the quality of the dimensions of the elaboration of experience, belonging to *narrative or syntagmatic thinking* (Bruner, 1988, 1991, 1992), in a *continuum of* expression of this process in the various organisations of meaning, i.e. the capacity for abstraction, integration, flexibility, the degree of metacognition, generativity and the level of global articulation of one's experience.

Having considered the two variables and learned the problem brought, we can set up the psychotherapy work with our patient.

2.1 The Four Personal Meaning Organisations (PMO)

According to the postrationalist approach, the great variability of psychological and psychopathological manifestations found through clinical observation can be represented by a limited number of invariant patterns of organisational closure. Such patterns produce a wide range of cognitive, emotional and motor modalities that can reorder specific discrepant emotional oscillations (Guidano & Liotti, 1983).

In this perspective, Vittorio Guidano (1988, 1992) identified four dimensions of personal meaning:

- depressive organisation (DEP)
- the phobic organisation (FOB)
- the psychogenic eating disorder (PED) type organisation
- obsessive organisation (OSS)

Organisations of personal meaning, which cannot be defined simply by their association with a specific type of disorder, are to be understood as processual entities characterised by specific ways of articulating one's immediate experience, of explaining and referring to oneself this experience, and this can also be seen in asymptomatic subjects. Despite the fact that the nomenclature attributed to the four organisations evokes a pathological characterisation, the symptomatology underlying the various systemic invariants only sometimes becomes apparent, in the event of decompensation, showing the expected nosographic picture (Reda, 1986; Merigliano, 2019b).

Normally, an identity pathway that is harmonious develops according to a non-pathological itinerary in continuous evolution according to an orthogenetic progression. Considering emotionally disruptive events that pose as activators of discrepant emergencies, the individuals most vulnerable to these would typically be those whose mode of elaborating their own meaning is characterised by excessive concreteness or poor integration skills, rigidity and non-generativity (Picardi & Mannino, 2001; Merigliano, 2019a, b).

In order to fully understand identity dynamics, let us consider at this point specific dimensions of the self: the *inwardness* and *outwardness* that Guidano identified in the last period of his studies (2010). In the attachment process, these dimensions allow for the stabilisation of an organisation of personal meaning. We distinguish the former as based on a focus from within, *inwardness*, in which the individual directs the construction of identity on inwardness and the maintenance of a sense of self. It is as if to say that the system tends to transform the external environment in order to adapt it to internal activations. In the process of focusing from the outside, *outward*, the subject organises the construction of his or her identity on attunement to an external reference. In this case, the attitude is focused on grasping discrepancies from the set of constructed relationships. There is a tendency to modify one's internal world in order to modulate it on the outside (Lewis, 1992, 1994; Guidano, 2010; Garger & Guild, 1984).

A second front to bear in mind when analysing the identity functioning of the four organisations of meaning is *field dependence*, which, recalling Witkins' (1949) studies of the late 1940s, distinguishes people into two groups: the *field-dependent* and the *field-independent*. In their approach to reality, the former shows a marked sensitivity to the context and its signals in an overall predominantly interpersonal mode, while the second group, the field-independent, moves their way of experiencing by displaying a distinctly cognitive attitude, less oriented towards analogical, emotional aspects, in a more logical-analytical approach, which keeps itself independent of the field in which it finds itself (Guidano, 2010).

We will see later how the four PMOs perform in this respect.

Lastly, it is worth considering that in addition to the four main organisations of meaning, defined as *'pure'*, in clinical practice we increasingly find *'mixed'* organisations precisely because in the various stages of development the reciprocity modes that steer identity development in one direction are not constantly and uniquely established (Reda, 1986).

Personal Meaning Organisation Type PED

In the Psychogenic Eating Disorder (PED) type of Organisation of Meaning there is an emotional recursive oscillation, in which a vague self-perception alternates with the unavoidable need to refer to the outside world in order to derive a clear, stable and defined sense of self. The PED subject experiences a continuous personal unreliability in decoding his own internal states. Never trusting his own internal emotional reading capacity, he finds himself looking to the judgement of others for his own sense of self. It is as if our patient affirms: 'I *feel as* I *think the other sees me…*'. Typical are the behaviours of avoidance and avoidance of confrontation with the outside world on pain of feeling criticised or devalued. This mode finds its origin in an attachment with characteristics of ambiguity, type A4/C, in which the child is constantly anticipated and redefined in its internal states by the parent (Crittenden, 1994, 1997). Here, emotions are never clear and defined. From the second year of age, the child focuses mainly on what we call *'self-conscious emotions'* that require the intervention of a cognitive appraisal in order to be activated: guilt, disgust, embarrassment, shame, and again emptiness, vagueness, indefiniteness, intrusiveness, disappointment, inconsistency and inadequacy (Lewis, 1992, 1994; Guidano, 2010). Attention to purely bodily aspects such as the sense of hunger, satiety, and motility makes it possible to keep within manageable limits those discrepant emotional oscillations that would otherwise be difficult to control. Focusing on such control of physical aspects and image, favours a more stable perception of oneself in the immediate future and, in the meantime, allows attention to be diverted from the emergence of feelings of inconsistency, inadequacy and failure, becoming *a diversionary activity* in this sense effective.

The two styles of attribution of *internal* or *external* causation underlie two distinct typologies with contrasting characteristics.

In an *external attributive style*, the anorexic pattern is expressed. Here one observes active controlling behaviour that contains the emergence of emotions of failure, incapacity and non-recognition, favouring a distance from the other perceived as intrusive and deceptive. In this active type of functioning, these subjects often appear accelerated.

Conversely, in an *internal attributive style*, with a bulimic and/or obese pattern, the strategic mode that contains within manageable limits the critical emotional oscillations of vagueness, emptiness and inadequacy consists in considering oneself the reason for failures, fiascos and disappointments, or rather, circumscribed aspects of one's being such as an ungainly body because it is ugly or fat and a personal unattractiveness. The motor and visceral patterns are passive.

This PMO has an *outward-looking* approach to reality and a *field-dependent* interpersonal mode.

Other peculiar aspects of this specific type of functioning can be accompanied by the onset of variously expressed eating disorders. Disorders of the sexual sphere are frequently observed in both males and females, correlated with experiences of non-confrontation and non-exposure. Attitudes of defiance, opposition and transgression underlie pathological conduct concerning gambling, kleptomania, theft. In the most severe cases, one may even witness self-harming behaviour. Physical pain helps to '*feel*', patients tell us, for whom their own internal state is often undecidable (sense of emptiness, 'I do *not perceive myself, I have no sense of me*').

A tendency to maximise one's own performance correlated with high expectations of oneself in order to guarantee the subject an expectation of an optimal result from which to derive a sense of a capable, competent, effective self. Often this is correlated with avoidance and renunciation of confrontation for fear of failure, not feeling equal to the test. In general, the attitude of perfectionism in a maximal way guarantees positive judgements on one's own performance or on oneself in general, which confirm an adequate and appreciable self-perception. It is a bit like saying that '*to feel normal I have to be special ...*'.

In this context, should the '*character*' that one has built up over the course of an existence prove to be fictitious, inconsistent and disappointing in relation to the expectations sown, the subject may not be able to bear the severe sense of failure, and so the clinical picture may result in suicide attempts or outright suicides sustained by a perception of oneself as a braggart, an impostor because of the *bluff that* others will learn of.

An imbalance in this PMO can be observed predominantly in situations in which the individual finds himself exposed to perceived inadequate handling of the confrontation, feeling involved in expectations that he cannot meet. Critical may become those conditions in which he/she feels that his/her responsibility in the relationship or in an endeavour is increased or, again, in circumstances in which the person has failed or, conversely, has achieved unexpected success, convinced that he/she will not subsequently be able to sustain the expectations created around him/her. The areas affected can be all those in which the person moves (emotional, family, work, social). Another important eventuality that may lead to a decompensation is when the PED subject becomes severely disillusioned with an affectively significant figure such as a parent or partner, due to a progressive change in the other's image in a pejorative sense.

Personal Meaning Organisation Phobic

Panic attack disorder, acute anxiety state, generalised alarm, agoraphobia, claustrophobia, hypochondria and specific phobias are the *descriptive* psychopathological presentations that in the *explanatory* reading proper to the postrationalist model represent a possible expression of the functioning of the PMO FOB. Syndromes and symptoms of this kind are posited as a form that a self-referential, concrete way of articulating and reorganising experience takes in order to maintain its own internal coherence. The *panic crisis* event, therefore, signals to us a disruption of systemic coherence patterns due to a non-generative reorganisation process of the system: a discrepant datum is not decoded nor integrated into the personal narrative plot that sustains identity coherence. This means, as described, that the narrator self can no longer explain the protagonist experiencing self. And thus, the symptom appears as a possible expression of that certain personal meaning, in this case the Phobic one, in a system, that at this point, has decompensated. In order to reconstruct the dynamics of decompensation, it is necessary to refer to an enlarged sphere of life cycle phases, reconstructing *how* that specific personal meaning is articulated and *how one* arrives at the psychopathological manifestation *panic attack*, which expresses *one of the* possible ways of elaborating the experience in the organisation of phobic meaning.

In this PMO, the interferences that occurred during development on the exploratory behaviour and on the search for autonomy seem to favour the formation of a personal meaning that is organised within a recursive oscillation rhythmically spent between the need for protection from a reality perceived as hostile and threatening, and the need for freedom and absolute autonomy in this same reality (Guidano,

1988). This mechanism develops through an indirect limitation of the child's autonomous exploratory attitude, through an overprotective parental attitude or even through the parents' unwillingness to act as a secure base for the child's exploration (Guidano, 1992).

The individual with PMO FOB is structured as an *inward* type system, i.e. from internal reference plots it grasps the sense of continuity and *field-dependent* mainly in a spatial sense.

The decompensation dynamic in this case provides that in a system in which attachment and exploration are conceived as antithetical and not complementary, as in fact they are, there is a marked sensitivity to events experienced as threatening, dangerous, constricting and unprotective. Fear and non-control are the primary recognised emotional experiences. The attachment pattern is of the anxious type, attachment C, in which the caregiver shows constant instability and unpredictability to the emotional access by the child. In a *coercive* attachment style, we find *active coercive* children who, due to the constant attention they receive, show a high perception of being loved and would never accept to go down a level. Then there are the *passive coercive*, who may draw their parents' attention with disarming attitudes or physical symptoms. Both categories, active and passive, can develop in a person with phobic significance; they can present themselves at different points in development, for example the active category in childhood and the passive category in adolescence (Guidano, 2007).

In an *overprotective attachment*, a condition of decompensation can occur in:

- situations that prompt discrepant experiences between emancipation and autonomy on the one hand and the possibility of maintaining the bond on the other.
- conditions in which the perception of excessive physical, concrete or emotional closeness by the significant figure may produce feelings of closure, constraint and loss of freedom.
- conditions relating to the establishment or breaking of an emotional bond.
- occasions when one perceives an increase in responsibility, commitment or involvement in one of the areas of life, whether sentimental, professional, etc.

The related symptomatology is generally of a *constrictive* type (panic attacks with air hunger, suffocation, chest oppression, tachycardia). In this case, the sense of one's own autonomy and personal freedom is perceived as threatened, evoking an experience of non-control, constraint, cage or trap.

In a *non-secure base type of attachment in* which the significant figures do not lend themselves to constant and reliable access, the most frequent conditions of decompensation concern all those situations in which a distancing from the significant figure is perceived, whether it be physical-spatial, emotional or cognitive. Typical complaints in this case are a lack *of protection* with a sense of being lost, dizziness and leg weakness. Here, the possibility of feeling constantly protected and cared for is perceived to be in danger. In both cases, all situations in which the subject experiences a sense of *loss of control* can produce decompensation.

Obsessive Personal Meaning Organisation

The core constituent invariant of the obsessive system concerns a constant uncontrollability of one's own existential condition whereby the individual experiences constant uncertainty about a perception of self as positive and simultaneously as despicable, since there is invariably no possibility of achieving a unified sense of self. In a typically *ambivalent* attachment, the behaviour of the caregiver is constantly perceived as having two diametrically opposed meanings at the same time, as carrying a double message (welcome-distance, helpfulness-rejection). The typical family climate in this case is permeated by a high potential for emotional activation without, however, providing the right support on the possible keys to interpreting the emotions themselves. A clear prevalence of verbal-analytical modalities is observed to the detriment of analogical ones. The dichotomous experience of the self leads to a continuous active search for a sense of personal unity that is implemented with analytical control modalities that contain sudden and critical emotional oscillations between antithetical and irreconcilable tones. Such an eventuality, if it occurred, would threaten the possibility of a stably unified and integrated self-perception. In this communicative climate, emotions in the sense that they '*must not be felt*' appear banned, and there is a clear prevalence of focus on discipline, rigour, and norms. This ambivalent pattern, if pushed to the point of serious functioning with paradoxical and conflicting demands on the child, can result in the phenomenon of *double attachment in* which the child is placed in the paralysing condition of having to decide or choose the undecidable, that is, neither one nor the other of the two options posed by the parent. The attachment pattern is of the A3/C type. A continuous sense of uncertainty and doubt is experienced, the prevailing emotion is shame in the sense of complete contempt for oneself in a total negative perception of oneself. And again, guilt and disgust. In the constant need to achieve that unified sense of one's being, the *all-or-nothing* mode works by guaranteeing either a completely positive or completely negative experience of self. On the other hand, in a condition where emotional experience is banished, there is no possibility of recognising and discriminating intermediate categories, as no capacity for emotional differentiation is present. It is almost constant a selective inattention to emerging experiences that in most cases are not attributed to oneself but rather to the outside. As mentioned, there is a need to adhere to an order of abstract rules of a religious, ethical, moral and legal type. The system is *outward* in the sense that subjects with OSP OSS derive from external frames of reference the perception of their own continuity of self. It is like saying that they focus on themselves from the outside. In emotional recognition, there is a prevalence of what Michael Lewis defines as '*self-conscious emotions*' such as shame, embarrassment, disgust and guilt, which require cognitive mediation to activate (1992, 1994). The obsessive subject is defined as '*field independent*' (Witkin, 1949) in that he does not appear to be influenced by the *field*, in the sense that if he is presented with a problem to solve, he disassembles to reconstruct the given context for himself and then initiates the resolution procedure. He brings into play an impersonal approach to otherness that he conceives as *non-human* but still *cognitive*: a *testing hypothesis approach*. Reality, approached in terms of thought and understanding, in an absolute primacy of the *verbal* and a purely analytical approach, is treated with a prevalence of *digital* communication, as emotional communication is practically absent. Typical symptoms, which again are posed as diversionary activities, attempt the control and management of highly emotive and therefore difficult to decode situations, which are thus not focused on at all. Emotions concerning uncertainty or ambiguity, anger or sexual activation are frequent factors of decompensation. Experiencing anger or sexual activation automatically produces the perception of self as despicable or dirty, which the patient often cannot even attribute to himself, alternatively activating symptoms such as intrusive ideas or images, doubts and rituals. Meticulousness and the attitude of doubt arise from the constant need to differentiate positive from negative aspects. This is the phenomenon of *under-inclusion, whereby to* a reality that is always broken down into details, systematic doubt is applied in order to achieve definitive certainty. We can recognise two styles of attribution of causality in this organisation:

- The obsessive who feels himself to be the complete repository of certainty, has an *external* attributive style, in the sense that everything depends on the external world that is despicable and hostile.
- When one loses this certainty, one engages in a desperate attempt to seek confirmation of one's despicability and unworthiness. Here, attribution is totally *internal* and the mode of doubt at all costs prevails in the constant demand for reassurance and confirmation of one's worthiness/unworthiness.

The decompensation *dynamic* in obsessive OSP occurs in any situation in which it is difficult to decode conflicting emotional emergencies that generate uncertainty about a perception of oneself as positive, or, on the contrary, despicable. Such disturbing, but unfocused and therefore unrecognised activations can lead to decompensation as the cause of the uncontrollability of one's existential condition. Critical, abrupt oscillations between antithetical and irreconcilable emotional tones jeopardise the possibility of a unified and integrated self-perception. The only guarantee of managing such uncontrollability and ambivalence is given, as described, by implementing a continuous search for certainty and control with the best known modality, which is the analytical and cognitive one.

In an internal coherence in which the sense of personal unity depends on the perception of absolute control over oneself, all conditions that are highly emotive and therefore difficult to manage, can lead to discrepancies to the point of actual system breakdown.

In such conditions, decompensation occurs more frequently:

- in building, maintaining and closing emotional ties
- in all matters of responsibility and compliance with ethical standards
- in the management of sexual activation and anger

The typical symptoms (meticulousness, fussiness, rituals, doubts, intrusive ideas or images, etc.) once reconstructed, turn out to be the only possibility the patient currently has to cope with discrepant activations that he cannot decode and refer to, becoming *effective* diversionary activities. This happens because control can be exercised by actively excluding emotions, fantasies, images, impulses, putting into practice distracting actions that on clinical observation appear in the form of *obsessive symptoms* (Guidano, 1988, 1992; Merigliano, 2013).

Depressive Personal Meaning Organisation

A Depressive Personal Meaning Organisation is structured by a Type A attachment style. Attachment patterns of this type, avoidant, are characterised by the child's inhibition of emotional expressions in order to ensure proximity with caregivers perceived to be unable to accept them, because they are rejecting or directly absent, without provoking their estrangement or worse, rejection or maltreatment (Crittenden, 1994, p. 97). A type A attachment in which one recognises as a basic emotional oscillation a recursive alternation of Despair/Rage will give rise to a Depressive type of Personal Meaning Organisation whose narrative nuclei will be centred on experiences of unworthiness, unlovability and loneliness, correlated with relational themes such as loss, abandonment and rejection. In general, the pervasive experience of self consists in perceiving oneself as never being able to achieve a stable emotional attachment, despite continuous effort. This generates a sense of unworthiness and unlovability to which one relates one's negativity and inability to relate. These subjects tend to focus from within (*Inward* mode) and *do not* appear *dependent on the external field* in their mode of functioning (*Field Independent*) (Witkin, 1949).

The reconstruction of the decompensation dynamic must consider that the system can be put into crisis by all those situations that produce a subjective experience of loss referable to the uncontrollability of one's own negativity. Every discrepant emotional emergency concerning the theme of the inevitability of loss and loneliness can cause a decompensation in this type of Organisation of Meaning. Emotions such as anger and despair, which, on the other hand, are prevalent, are generally difficult to manage. Attachment patterns that favour the processing of an experience of loss can be found in cases in which:

- there was an early loss of one of the parents or a significant change in the image of the parents in a negative sense
- there has been a prolonged or final separation from them
- a relationship is established in which continual threats of abandonment or withholding of affection results in an ongoing experience of loss and rejection
- an inversion of the caregiver-child role occurs whereby the latter has to take care of the parent

As an adult, critical phases occur in the case of:

- separation or death of the significant figure
- labour or economic failure

- forced changes such as that of the house, for example, perceived as loss, or the approach of middle-life (sense of one's own worthlessness)
- situations of personal success in the various areas (sense of low value of the achieved goal and loneliness) (Guidano, 1998, 1999; Merigliano, 2019a, b)

Considering the characteristic and prevalent aspects in Depressive functioning, these subjects may show specific and peculiar modes, tendencies and experiences among which are

- a rather common feeling of repugnance for one's origins, accompanied by an experience of profound shame at the idea of belonging to the same gene pool as one's parents, deplorable in every way.
- The need to impose a titanic effort on oneself to sustain *impossible feats* in order to secure a semblance of affective fitness that is otherwise unattainable. The theme of a pronounced sensitivity and intolerance to *effort* is typical of this PMO who, in order to be able to withstand a conspicuous expenditure of energy, must give himself a precise meaning, preferably one with affective-emotional connotations.
- Constantly experiencing that existence coincides with *struggle*, with having to fight for everything. This is indeed constraint, but it also becomes the structuring essence of functioning in its innermost substance.
- a pervasive perception of extraneousness and exclusion from the world in which one feels '*other* than', foreign and not belonging, due to personal negativity.
- The commonly experienced condition of loneliness and inability to ask for support or help, produces a functioning marked by *self-sufficiency and self-management in autonomy*, where often loneliness rather than suffered is pursued as a goal and possibility.
- The search for a reality that is extraordinary and different from the ordinary one that is perceived as ephemeral, transient and '*timeless*'.
- The theme of *loss* in this PMO presents itself as an ordering factor in the experience of self and the reality that is oriented and determined by it, but also as a constraint that connotes and limits up to the psychopathological expression of such experiencing.
- The presence of the typical mechanism of *emotional disconnection* enables the individual thus organised to keep particularly emotionally activating aspects out of focus, which thus remain in the background.
- Very often DEP subjects, in order to protect themselves from a desperate experience of loss, tend not to recognise a personal involvement in relationships with significant affective figures, attributing it to purely contingent circumstances. They also tend to limit their expansiveness towards their partner and children as a further protection against their own *dangerous* emotional investment in the other, as they always perceive the end, the loss of this inherent in the bond.
- Generally, such individuals end non-significant relationships, while more often they are abandoned by their partners in important ones, following multiple tests

of the other aimed at ensuring that they are accepted by them precisely because of those aspects of negativity that attest and confirm personal unlovability.
- More precociously than the other PMOs, they approach the sexual sphere and more often have promiscuous conduct in which more than others may incur situations of mistreatment suffered. This happens because of the pervasive perception of unlovability that leads the subject to submit even to unwelcome conduct on the part of the partner in order to ensure affective closeness. It is as if the DEP subject felt he or she had to '*pay*' in some way for the closeness, the bond, the affective interest of the other, not deserving it.
- Every meaningful bond is based on the vital need on the part of the DEP subject for the other to *adhere to his or her* specific themes and to choose him or her exclusively for precisely those *negative* traits that alienate others. As described, the need and demand for this leads these persons to impose on their partners burdensome tests that confirm this adherence to themselves precisely because of those unpleasant traits that characterise them.
- Since there is a constant marked difficulty in processing the *loss*, PMO DEP subjects peculiarly show a failure to *process grief*, keeping it stuck. Especially in conditions of closure of a romantic relationship, they tend to isolate themselves after the loss of a loved one to the extent that they never change their image of the other, remaining stuck in the pervasive experience of loss, loneliness and unlovability.
- Typical and *short-circuited* are the outbursts of anger that may also result in clastic manifestations with subsequent restorative behaviours of compulsive caring for the other in a manner with often circular characteristics.
- These individuals tend to make an internal attribution of randomness in the events in which they find themselves, which generally relates to personal negativity, but which in some respects guarantees a possibility of more effective management in the situation in which they find themselves.
- The common and constant experience for these subjects is a condition whereby they feel themselves to be protagonists in a destiny of *election*, precisely because they are aware of a personal superiority in grasping things more than others, and at the same time victims of a destiny of *condemnation*, due to the fact that it *is not given to them*, because they feel they are destined *not to be true, to lose anyway*.

To better understand the intimate essence of Depressive functioning, Fernando Pessoa comes to our rescue: from *Bernardo Soares' Book of Disquiet* (1986, p. 23):

> ... a single thought fills my soul: the intimate desire to die, to end, to see no more light on any city, to think no more, to feel no more, to leave behind, like wrapping paper, the path of the sun and the days; to take off from me, like a heavy dress, by the big bed, the involuntary effort of being.

3 Operating Aspects of the Four PMOs

3.1 Awareness and Self-deception in a Recursive Circularity

Awareness fully represents one of the functions of the self-organisation of a complex system, the reflexive aspect of self-referentiality, which indicates how the system refers experiencing itself in order to maintain its internal coherence in its relations with the surrounding environment. The paradigm has changed: objectivity gives way to the subjective construction of the experiencer. In essence, *'when we perceive our environment, we ourselves invent it'* (von Foerster, 1987, p. 215). Each step of self-awareness is linked to an act aimed at maintaining systemic coherence; thus, when the individual explains an experience that has occurred, he or she does not do so *objectively*, but rather uses what he or she feels is most consistent with him or herself, evaluating discrepancies, eliminating contradictions. This happens within each act of rearranging immediate experience: it is the experiencing that is *subjectively* lived and explained. Each narrative has the purpose of putting the *pieces in place* regarding the experience, making them all assimilable in their own identity coherence.

Self-deception can make it feasible to maintain this systemic coherence so that it can continue to unfold, threatened as little as possible by disturbing discrepancies. *'To each level of knowledge corresponds its level of ignorance, the more the level of knowledge increases, the more the domain of ignorance increases'* (Guidano, 1998). Principles and values such as justice, moral freedom, ethics, etc. can actually be useful in self-deception processes in order to make the experiences we have consistent within our personal range of expectations, predictions and intentions in order to avoid discontinuities in the existential path. Basically, every self-organised system behaves in this way: when an emotional activation occurs, in order to keep it at an acceptable and stable level, the data are put out of focus. Subsequently, they can be progressively decoded.

Some examples within the four organisations of personal meaning guide us in understanding the functioning of *self-deception mechanisms*.

- PEDs, by their structure, do not grasp the continuous need to refer to the outside world in order to perceive themselves, they keep out of decoding many elements that otherwise cannot be integrated into their own narrative. These subjects have a consciousness that particularly lends itself to being permeated with chiaroscuro, vagueness and poor definition, which, on the other hand, allows them to keep many discrepant elements in the background without focusing on them too much. Let us imagine as an example a disappointment with an affectively significant person. This is handled in such a way that the emerging data, which would lead to a dramatic change in the other's image, is kept out of focus.
- PHOBICS experience continual constriction, a sense of unprotection, a loss of control and eventualities that these individuals must quickly resolve, on pain of decompensation, even symptomatic decompensation. To this end, these

individuals often use *illness* as an expedient to ensure the maintenance of a stable and acceptable conscious self-image in situations where there are failures or failures that threaten their feeling of *agency* in events and relationships. This allows them an attribution of external causality that enables them to maintain a good self-image.
- OBSESSIVES have to deal with the constant instability of the sense of unity of the self, implementing systematic doubt in the search for *certain certainty*. The capacity for self-deception comes to the rescue in the various cases in order to resolve initial discrepancies, moving mainly on the level of logical explanations that keep *dangerous* emotions in the background because they can hardly be controlled and rearranged in one's own narrative.
- DEPRESSIVES almost never recognise the perception of loss they are experiencing, they do not realise it, they only notice the most conspicuous ones. Functioning with a low level of perception of this feeling, they are able to perform *impossible feats*, making a considerable cognitive investment. Often the mechanism of *emotional disconnection* allows them to keep blurred and nebulous aspects of themselves or of reality that are difficult to decode, assimilate and integrate into their personal narrative, which otherwise brought into focus would underline their negativity and consequently unlovability.

3.2 Anxiety in the Four PMOs

Anxiety has to do with identity aspects of the person, it is unquestionably a trait. So much so that it can be declined in the systemic coherence of the four PMOs. It is therefore fundamental to look for *meaning* in *the* anxious state, reconstructing the system's decompensation dynamics. Anxiety is the signal of the discrepancy between the I and the Me and represents the gateway to start working in psychotherapy. It provides an opportunity to reconstruct the imbalance that has occurred. A *stirring* can manifest with an anxiety peak. As described, *emotional sp*ikes, a fundamental component of the emotional life of the human being, are a clear expression of the moment-to-moment occurrence, representing the immediacy that is expressed in discordant patterns of the flow of experience, producing a sense of discontinuity, albeit very brief. For the purposes of this intervention, let us recall how such *emotional episodes* present themselves with their specific characteristics, such as the very high intensity of the emotion that is activated, the character of sudden happening, of apparent explanatory inderivability, of lasting emotional redundancy.

In clinical practice, therefore, anxiety manifests itself differently in the four types of PMO.
- Performance or performance anxiety is predominantly observed in PMO PED, centred on a marked sensitivity to external judgement due to the indefiniteness

and vagueness of the self. The anxiety is underpinned by the fear of failure and disappointment.
- A form of loss of control anxiety is typical in PMO PHOBIC, which is particularly sensitive to issues of constraint and non-protection, where fear and experiences of noncontrol have the upper hand. The person suffers if they realise that they are unable to set their own conditions in situations, feeling threatened by their need to perceive themselves as always being in *agency* in events, ascribing the direction to themselves.
- In the OBSESSIVE PMO, based on the uncertainty of the unity of one's self perceived as dichotomous, worthy/despicable, one observes a form of doubt anxiety with respect to one's perceived negative/positive self. The same symptoms, rituals and intrusive ideations generate anxiety.
- An anxiety about the inevitability of one's destiny of loneliness, which reactivates and sustains the typical themes of loss, is present in DEPRESSIVE PMO, alternating with despairing experiences of the threat to one's self-sufficiency if one is convinced that one cannot cope alone.

Anxiety is dealt with in all its forms and expressions, but it can be said that when it disappears, that is when the real psychotherapy on the peculiar themes of that specific systemic coherence begins. As Guidano explains: *'the symptom is not that it leaves a void, if it leaves through elaboration, it becomes a way of perceiving the immediate experience... this means that the person by now had developed ways of reading the symptom on the various emotional planes. Thus what was previously an indicator of illness has become a sign of emotional activation'* (1999).

3.3 Substance Use in the Four PMOs

Abuse attitudes are transversal behaviours and must be considered within the internal coherence of the specific organisational system as a concrete way of elaborating one's own experience, as they relate to the specific topics dear to the different PMOs.

- In PMO PED, the abuse behaviour occurs in order to increase self-perception and is more frequent in situations where there is a perceived difficult confrontation and the need to feel conformed to the group. Substance and alcohol use in a social, episodic manner, often careful not to cross a certain line, is more typical. The substances used are usually cannabinoids, cocaine, heroin, activators and hallucinogens. The abuse of drugs or alcohol provides exposure to contexts in which one feels inadequate or unable.
- Individuals with an PMO FOB tend to use substances to increase their ability to manage relationships; psychotropic drugs and alcohol are taken to manage activations of fear and loss of control. The most frequently used substances are anxiolytic or hypno-inducing psychotropic drugs, alcohol, cocaine, cannabinoids, and activating substances.

- The PMO OSS may manifest abusive behaviour to manage particularly perturbing emotional oscillations that are perceived as uncontrollable. More frequent is the use of alcohol and psychotropic drugs to control activations of uncertainty, doubt, anger, self-doubt and sexuality. Often such use also serves to manage exhausting and endless rituals or disturbing intrusive ideations.
- In the subject of an PMO DEP the attitude of heavy drug and high alcohol abuse becomes continuous and repeated to the point of even leading the subject to anticonservative behaviour. All this is intended to soothe and contain the emergence of a pain without shelter. The despairing experience of loss, with experiences of loneliness, unworthiness, unlovability underlies the abuse.

3.4 Mourning in the Four PMOs

Events of loss, be it physical, a separation, or a dramatic change in the image of an affectively significant figure have a disturbing fallout typically represented in the four PMO. The emotional experience related to the bereavement event must be considered consistently with the personal meaning supporting the specific system.

- In an PMO PED in which the *field with which to define oneself is of* vital importance, with the loss of an affective reference figure, in whatever form this takes place, the defining context with which to perceive oneself is lacking, giving the subject experiences of emptiness, disorientation, and cancelled struggle. Sometimes one observes for some, an increase in exposure due to the perception of lack of judgement from the outside that *frees* the person in his or her own self-expression.
- In the case of an PMO FOB, if there is a physical loss of a loved one or the end of a romantic relationship, with the loss of the figure experienced as protective, the subject feels alone and exposed, at the mercy of events and in some cases catapulted to the *front line* to face the vicissitudes of life.
- In the aftermath of a significant loss, individuals with PMO OSS find themselves left in uncertainty about the essence of the relationship with the other; they experience oscillating and conflicting emotional experiences. Frequent are themes of injustice for having suffered the pain of loss, and sometimes themes of suspended responsibility for the bond.
- For the PMO DEP, the main theme of loss as an inescapable event that renews and confirms a pain without solution, and the inexorable experience of *condemnation of not having*, of the inevitability of losing, is reproposed inexorably. Despair that oscillates recursively with anger is accompanied by the perceptive pervasiveness of profound loneliness in the unbearable weight of existence.

3.5 Severe Psychopathology in the Four PMOs

> One must always be surprised by mental illness. The thing I would be most afraid of, if I went mad, would be that you would adopt a common-sense attitude, that you would take my delusions for granted. (Ludwig Wittgenstein 1967)

As mentioned, *narrative identity* develops and takes shape in the processuality of the self, caught in the dialectic between the '*I*' that experiences and the '*Me*' that evaluates the very experience of living, reorders it and relates it to itself. This process is located in a self-referential model, which aims to preserve systemic coherence throughout the individual's life cycle. Ricoeur (1995, 1986, 1987, 1988 (trad. It. 2016)) conceives of two foundational components of narrative identity:

- identity *idem, 'being the same'* (persistence over time)
- identity *ipse, 'to be oneself'* (self-designation of self)

The relationship between the two aspects is constituted by the narrative that the individual gradually constructs the explanatory part of his or her identity. The abnormal prevalence of one aspect over the other or the pathological disconnection of the two are posited as the constituent matrix of a *psychotic identity* (Ballerini, 2008). If we imagine the functioning of a paranoid system in which '*the phenomenon of chance is lost*' (Minkowski, 1966–1973), here beliefs and convictions are intimately connected to the context, to social action. In paranoid schizophrenia, it is the subject itself that goes into crisis, it no longer recognises itself. In this case it is an ontological insecurity: the story is no longer narratable, its continuity is interrupted, the *other* becomes *an 'obscure anonymous threat'*, the sense of both 'being the *same*' and '*being oneself*' is lost (Ballerini, 2008). Delirium, hallucinations and other specific symptoms represent self-referential cognitive modes when emotional emergencies that cannot be decoded because they are neither recognised nor referred to oneself are experienced as external experiences. This is also due in large part to the:

- poor capacity of the system to distinguish between inside and outside itself
- to a severe deficit in narrative articulation and emotional regulation
- to important disorders of integrated chronological, cause-effect, thematic sequencing

The dysfunctional aspects in psychotic functioning are:

- a very low capacity for time-integrated unit sequencing
- the obvious impairment of the ability to adequately distinguish the boundaries of the self from the non-self
- the occurrence of a severely restricted range of recognisable and decodable emotions
- the impairment of the ability to construct an emotional experience in its basic ingredients (imaginative, cognitive, affective, sense-perceptual)
- a marked reduction in the ability to maintain a unified and continuous sense of self
- the tendency to remain tied to the immediate perceptual context (concreteness)

- a deficit in the ability to distinguish between immediate experience and explanation of it
- the inadequacy and lack of flexibility in the possibility of rapidly changing the reading of the current experience (rigidity)
- the inability to generate new insights into one's experience of oneself or the world around one. The system shows no generative aptitude
- the conscious self-image is rigid and stereotyped

Considering these variables of functioning in the *psychotic system*, let us see how this is declined in the four PMOs.

- Within the same systemic coherence, in this case of the PED type, we find that a sense of inadequacy and personal incompetence can be elaborated in a relatively concrete way and then become an eating disorder, if the concreteness and rigidity of the system increase, the same experience can give rise to delusional or dispersive productivity on issues of judgement and definition from outside. Clinical pictures related to this functioning are paranoid schizophrenia, or bipolar disorder with manic excitement, or forms of catatonia (non-exposure block), hebephrenic schizophrenia, the simplex form, paraphrenia and erotomanic delirium (Merigliano, 2002).
- In an PMO of the FOB type, in the case of a particularly rigid and concrete meaning processing as in the psychotic type, hallucinatory delusional disorders with themes of persecution, harm and venom, danger and threat, jealousy, alterations in the state of consciousness as psychogenic fugues and severe hypochondriac syndromes with delusions of illness will be observed.
- The emblematic example of obsessive psychotic processing is paranoia, lucid and systematic delirium, but one can also find pictures of paranoid schizophrenia with mystical, ethical, injustice, responsibility and catatonic forms (doubt paralysis) (Merigliano, 2004).
- For the PMO DEP, an inflexible, concrete and non-generative processing of experience can produce psychotic pictures of the type: severe depressive syndromes, twilighting, persecutory delusions of unworthiness and exclusion, uncontrolled outbursts of anger to the point of pantoclasticity, or even sociopathic and delinquent attitudes.

3.6 Dreams in the Four PMOs

Within the constructivist framework, the dream is regarded as an expression of individual personal meaning and thus used to achieve a greater degree of awareness of the dynamics involved in the modulation of one's emotional and cognitive world. Guidano explains: '*Dreams are no different from other imaginative acts. They have the same transparency as other phenomena of the imagination, both open-eyed fantasies and imaginative scenarios*' (1998). Guidano again on the form of dreams: '*In the dream, the imaginative scenarios acquire a few more characteristics of an epic type; they do not have a logical, linear and sequential course, they have neither head nor tail, but apart from this the transparency is immediate as is the content of the imaginative scenarios that accompany the emotions... recurrent dreams have specific scenarios that deal with the individual's theme of coherence (at that moment most significant). They generally have two aspects:*

- *one of transparency that can be shared by an external observer (the therapist at work who is familiar with the patient's consistency theme and his or her current life theme in particular)*
- *one of immediate transparency for the patient who refers to his emotional baggage, understanding why that dream has taken on that specific configuration. The dream has a meaning above all for the individual who experiences it personally'* (1998).

Dream activity, like perception, imagination, gives form to *tacit knowledge*. This is difficult to formulate and concerns the ontological aspects of experience. In dreams, the *explicit element, which pertains* to verbal, logical, conceptual knowledge and everything that belongs to the level of explanation, expresses itself in referring the dream experience to itself, making it consistent in a coherent and personal narrative (Guidano, 1998; Merigliano, 2015, 2019a, b).

If we consider the dream experience as a *cognitive-emotional unit*, we can state that it is characterised by four distinctive qualities:

- consists of imaginative material
- is organised in narrative form
- is characterised by an intense emotional poignancy
- can end in a prolonged and pervasive emotional reverberation

Given these characteristics, dreams can be treated like any other material brought by the subject, be it imaginative or the recounting of a real event, in search, again, of the central core that characterises an identity: *personal meaning*.

Dreams present themselves both in content and form in a specific way in relation to the different Personal Meaning Organisations:

- PED subjects, who already in waking life often present a dreamy, *imaginative* attitude, have a very florid dream activity: it is common for them to produce very rich, highly articulated dreams, and to report *'dreaming in instalments'*. The themes concern feeling defined from the outside, inadequate and fear of the judgement of others.
- Individuals belonging to the PMO PHOBIC carry transparent dreams, very often violent, truculent, vivid in sensory aspects and very colourful. Emerging themes concern threat, danger, loss of control, fear, duress and feeling lost.
- The dreams that OBSESSIVE patients tell are as a rule very structured and rigorous. Their content often constitutes a source of cognitive curiosity for the patients themselves, who sometimes claim to solve problems that occurred in waking life by dreaming. The themes present relate mainly to logical, ethical, justice and mystical aspects.

- The subjects who show a surprising scarcity of dream material are the DEPRESSIVE. Their dreams often consist of single images, poor and sparse in detail, simple and dry in development. The cherished themes of loss, unlovability, strain and loneliness are the obvious expression of the typical systemic invariant that sustains them (Guidano, 1998; Merigliano, 2015, 2019a, b).

3.7   The Generativity of a PMO

The *orthogenetic progression* of a narrative identity appears as the clear evidence of an articulation that gradually becomes more structured over time, maturing in its own complexity. The result is a substantially generative expression of the specific theme in question as a clear sign of the attainment of greater self-awareness and self-functioning. Perceived personal identity is actively constructed by the knowing subject. The individual in their experiencing and expressing themselves, as a complex, historical system, proves to be *autonomous* insofar as in the course of its temporal becoming, they subordinate every possible change or transformation to the *maintenance of their identity that* has been able to construct for themselves. At this point it is evident that a self-referential system is *adapted* insofar as it has the capacity to transform the perturbations that emerge from interaction with the outside or from its own internal oscillations into meaningful information with respect to its own order or personal meaning. Thus, as we know, the only way for a system to maintain adaptation is to *preserve its own internal coherence* at the expense of the environment. More precisely, the system is adapted when in the identity circularity the coherence between the I that experiences and the Me that explains and evaluates the experience is guaranteed.

We return to complex systems to arrive at the concept of *orthogenetic progression* useful for understanding the evolutionary development of the patient's functioning and its generative capacities. It is characteristic of a complex, cognitive system that temporal evolution takes place as a process in continuous becoming, in a progressive and generative directionality, characterised by the discontinuous emergence of more structured and integrated levels of self-referential order throughout the life span (Prigogine, 1982). This temporal becoming is characterised not by a point of arrival, but rather by an *orthogenetic progression*, meaning that a system with time undergoes a progressive increase in its internal complexity as a consequence of the continuous assimilation of experience. This complexity manifests itself in the discontinuous emergence of more articulated and more integrated levels of self-knowledge and reality. Critical increases in internal complexity permit the maintenance of systemic coherence only if a more or less profound *reorganisation* of its experiential order can take place. Such a '*crisis*' development, typical of the adult period in an individual's existence, recalls the concepts of the principle of *punctuated equilibria* proposed by the approach known as *post-Darwinian evolutionary pluralism* (Gould, 1984). According to this perspective, translated to human existence, periods of apparent stability are followed by intense phases in which minimal environmental changes are matched by significant existential crises and profound reorganisations of personal experience. As we know, the system tends towards progressively more integrated and complex levels (Werner 1948–1957), thus manifesting the unfolding of an orthogenetic progression that we can also recognise in the material brought by the patient considered in its evolution.

Let us therefore see how these concepts are declined in the four PMOs.

- PED subjects, if harmonious, show great ability to read external signals as informative about the other. They quickly grasp the point of view, finally used to better understand the interlocutor, being able to identify with the other's reality. They manifest high levels of adaptability in contexts. They are particularly creative and imaginative. The work that is carried out in the treatment of these subjects to achieve progress towards a more generative articulation is that of *demarcation from the outside*.
- Aspects that emancipate in an orthogenetic progression for FOB individuals are expressed in the capacity for exploration and predictability of events, in attitudes of curiosity and organisational control over self and others in inter-subjective relationships. They have remarkable leadership skills in managing relationships. They are nurturing and protective. Work in therapy should aim to promote autonomy and the management of control issues in an articulate and functional manner.
- For an PMO OSS, the realistically attainable goal may be to be able to allow oneself to oscillate by allowing oneself to activate knowledge procedures through doubt. The attitude of doubtfulness becomes possibility. Still desirable is the acquisition of abstract capacities also on a purely emotional level, deepening the focus on the self and reading the inner states of the other.
- Individuals belonging to an PMO DEP, if harmonious, can come to articulate the theme of loss to the point of being able to perceive it as a category of human experience rather than as a personal destiny irreversibly marked by a sense of unlovability and loneliness. It is precisely the experience of loneliness that poses itself as a field for possible personal creativity and planning, accompanied by a theme of constant struggle to secure a sense of dignity and lovability that is otherwise difficult to achieve. The other is more and more deeply and accurately grasped, especially in the eventual suffering shown, to which such organised individuals are particularly sensitive. The theme of loss from being a constraining factor of experience becomes a generative ordering principle.

4 The Relationship, the Method, the Therapist, Tools and Eventualities

Guidano (1988) remind us how knowledge of self and the world is only possible through the organisation of relationships based on emotional reciprocity. We know how the natural aptitude to share emotions with our peers, grasping emotional activations in the other, can now be correlated with specific brain areas deputed to regulate the *mirror circuit* (Rizzolatti & Sinigaglia, 2006). This is why our neurobiology necessarily links us to others (Iacoboni, 2008).

The postrationalist model sets as its main goal to be pursued in therapy work, a better articulation of personal meaning on the part of patients (Guidano, 2008), thus achieving the possibility that they can feel protagonists of their own existence that has taken place and takes place according to those particular personal meanings that provide it with continuity, uniqueness and coherence. As stated then, the postrationalist perspective sets the goal of therapeutic intervention as making the person more aware of the mechanism through which immediate experience is attributed, which is then the essence of the articulation of personal meaning. Working on this process implies bringing tacit and immediate experience to an increasingly evolved level of self-awareness.

4.1 The Relationship

When we speak of psychotherapeutic intervention, the essential ingredient that the therapist needs as a primary tool in the welcoming and listening relationship with the patient is the ability to grasp the other's state of mind. The *mirror neuron* system allows the therapist to experience the emotional experience of his client in a natural and immediate way. The idea of *empathy as* conceived by Maturana and Varela (1985) is explained through the functioning of the mechanisms of autopoiesis and cognition. The two authors argue that in order to create fruitful relationships with others, it is not necessary to impose one's own point of view, as it is absolutely subjective. In fact, relating to others means *entering into emotional resonance*, into empathy with them (Luigi Onnis in Gembillo, 2016). In essence, the discovery of the mirror neuron system has made it possible to derive subjectivity from intersubjectivity mainly by exploiting the peculiarities of the brain-body dyad, the embodied simulation. This mechanism represents to all intents and purposes the biological basis of the ability to attune to the other (Gallese & Guerra, 2015). Supported by the perspective of complex thinking, we then find ourselves questioning the relationship between subjectivity and reciprocity possible between two individuals within a psychotherapy. This is how the quality of the therapist-patient relationship becomes a determining variable in achieving generalised and lasting changes. This relationship, which is established with our patient within therapy, is the *instrument* and *object of* the intervention we initiate with him (Liotti, 1993; Safran & Segal, 1990).

- It is an *instrument* because through the emotional relationship we create with the patient we produce the disruptions that are useful for change.
- It is *object* because the relationship itself can become material to be reorganised as a product of possible discrepancies.

Unlike in ordinary relationships with others, in therapy what happens in the relationship in emotional terms is used for purposes that are outside the relationship and not for the relationship itself. The goal to be achieved is a better articulation of personal meaning on the part of the patient (Guidano, 2008).

4.2 Sequencing

In psychotherapy, the reconstruction of the relationship between symptoms, meaning and personal history has as its aim the identification of the patient's functioning mechanisms and the maintenance of his or her identity coherence. In reconstructing a history, we work on the relationships between *episodic memory* and *semantic* memory.

- *Episodic* memory is the set of perceptual sensory impressions that accompany the recording of an event in neuro-psycho-biological terms.
- *Semantic* memory consists of the web of explanations and meanings that the recorded event gradually suggests.

While *episodic* memory is more stable, *semantic memory* can vary in relation to life events and the meaning we attribute to them in the continuous rewriting we perform on our experience over time. In order to reconstruct the contexts and unfolding of events, it is necessary to reconstruct all the episodic memories that correspond to those particular semantic memories (Tulving, 1972). To this end, the method of decoding and focusing on the patient's personal sequential portrayal, be it imaginative or experiential material, or even dream material, sees its greatest expression in the *moviola technique* (Guidano, 1992, 1999; Dodet, 1998; Merigliano & Dodet, 2001). This consists in a genuine process of scripting the way the immediate experience unfolds, accompanied by the individual's reading of that experience. It makes use of a type of conversation in a *non-ordinary* form. Guidano describes it as a psychotherapeutic strategy rather than a technique, indicating its basic principles of intervention, reconciled with the personal style of the therapist himself who becomes a '*strategically oriented disruptor*' in the work of reconstructing with the patient his experience of himself and the world around him (1988, 1992).

The first step that is tackled in psychotherapy work involves the reconstruction of an *oriented anamnesis* of the patient's life history, of its development with the different occurrences and variables, of possible critical moments. This is then followed by the reconstruction of the *decompensation dynamic* in which the '*how*' the discrepant event is perceived by the person, referred to oneself and reordered so as to become consistent with its own coherence of meaning. The aim is to make the patient increasingly expert in reconstructing the essential invariants according to which one's way of functioning is organised.

This can be done by inducing the person to *pass in moviola* sequences of significant scenes of the event perceived as critical, bringing into focus the different emotions that take place in the flow of the episode. The sequencing of the experience thus takes shape.

In its progress, the *moviola* represents a process of:

- *self-observation* of the experience taking place in the event brought by the patient,
- *sequencing* of the experience into distinct frames, to be analysed mainly in its emotional components,
- *contextualisation* of emotional events, reconstructing their *immediate* and *extended context*, initiating a reconstruction from the subjective and objective point of view of the experiencer (Merigliano, 2009).

4.3 Resistances

Resistance to change on the part of the patient can be expressed in various ways. They can be seen in attitudes of non-understanding of the indications provided, of the reformulations given; in the recurrence of disturbances that returned some time ago; in manipulations of the setting itself (delays in the sessions, missed appointments); in explicit requests by the patient to *slow down the work*; etc. Such occurrences often express the subject's difficulties in integrating new aspects into his or her narrative, which is evidently not yet ready to accept the new data. For this reason, *resistances* are to be considered in the same way as the symptoms themselves. As cognitive, self-reflective modalities, they reveal to us how the patient processes his or her own experience. Contrary to the psychodynamic approach that indicates to proceed *against* the resistances of the subject being followed, according to our perspective, we find ourselves working *with the* resistances, within its systemic coherence in order to understand them, to signify them.

4.4 The Therapist

As mentioned, new attention is currently being given to the *empathy* variable in relationships, following the Italian discovery of the likely biological basis of empathy in the circuitry of mirror neurons (Rizzolatti et al., 1996; Rizzolatti & Fadiga, 1999; Fogassi et al., 2005). Emotions thus represent the *'biological functions of the brain'* (Le Doux, 1998). The natural aptitude to share states of mind with our peers, grasping emotional activations in the other, can now be correlated with specific brain areas deputed to regulate the mirror circuit (Rizzolatti & Sinigaglia, 2006). This is why we reiterate how our neurobiology necessarily and constantly keeps us related to the expression of others (Iacoboni, 2008). Empathy, then, understood as the capacity of parts of the human brain to be activated to perceive the emotions of others, expressed with facial movements, gestures and sounds, supports the therapist in his work. (Rizzolatti & Sinigaglia, 2006).

The postrationalist model adds as a founding variable within the therapy process, the specific PMO and the therapist's personal meaning-making mode, which is expected to be flexible, generative and well-articulated. Hence the indispensable necessity of a personal pathway faced by the clinician, which enables him/her to focus on personal emotional emergencies and then to be able to recognise and manage them appropriately and strategically in the work with patients.

As we know, the purpose of a therapeutic act is to construct the conditions capable of triggering a reorganisation of personal meaning in order to achieve change (Guidano, 1992). This will be possible if the therapist is discrepant and if the degree of emotional involvement in the relationship is high. To do this, the practitioner proceeds to *perturb* the *patient system*. This disruption only becomes meaningful in an emotional relationship (Guidano, 2008).

To this end, it is essential to structure a therapeutic context in which the emotional involvement and reciprocity of the relationship allow the patient to rely on being able to consider the alternative point of view offered in the various reformulations as meaningful. It is essential to utilise the perturbing emotional emergencies that gradually arise in the progressive acquisition of self-awareness and understanding, prompted by the reformulations on the problem presented.

Let us then consider what tools a therapist must rely on. They must certainly move according to a *theoretical reference model* that allows them to acquire a general conception of man in its normal and pathological functioning. They must be able to deploy a *technique* that includes an intervention strategy and respects their own personal style. Furthermore, they must be able to *build a relationship* in which they're able to know, manage and strategically use their own themes and internal states together with the patient's emotional emergencies.

On the strength of these tools, applying the method consistent with the theoretical basis, when the work is complete, the *conclusion of the therapy* will lead to the achievement of:

- a *general objective* that must include the reduction of emotional peaks experienced as discrepant, which often take the form of symptoms.
- a *specific objective* for the different organisational types described, allowing for the articulation of the particular theme belonging to that given PMO.

An increase in self-awareness and functioning is pursued and expected with the patient. This is also done more specifically when the symptom is in remission.

5 A Clinical Case

A male patient, about 40 years old, an entrepreneur, married to a woman of the same age, with two children aged nine and seven, comes to visit.

He presented himself at first observation, saying that he had been '*anxious, sad and distressed for some time because of the constant feeling that he might commit an aggressive act against his children, especially the young one. He has suffered and still suffers from panic attacks*'.

- *Current symptoms*: Panic attack disorder, thymic inflection with feelings of guilt, despicable sense of self, inability to get things done, anxious activation reactive to episodes of intrusive ideation with images in which the defenestration of one of the children acts, somatisations, hypochondriac attitude. Constant perception of loss of control.
- *Symptoms in the past*: constrictive type panic attacks with chest oppression, tachycardia, air hunger, choking, trembling, fear of dying and a sense of constriction. Generalised anxiety and somatisation. Pathophobia. Depressed mood. Feelings of non-management and non-control of things.

Given the patient's past and current condition, the therapy work carried out included training in focusing on one's own experiences, focusing on the *reconstruction in moviola* of the emotional aspects in the reported critical episodes.

Here is an example:

'... I return in the evening tired from work... I enter the house and the children throw themselves at me asking me to play with them... (I *begin to feel a little closed... as if trapped... with a sense of suffocation* ...)... my wife, without even saying goodbye, shouts that their room is in a mess, that the exercise books for school are not ready yet and that I have to take care of it... (*the feeling of oppression grows and in addition I feel like I have no support from her... I feel closed and a bit lost... I have a sense of weight on my chest... my throat closes and I feel like I cannot breathe* ...). We go to the table for dinner and continuously the boys get up, eating around the room, arguing with each other, with my wife who keeps shouting... I can't even watch the news because the channel is constantly being changed... I feel like I'm in the middle of a market... with everybody making a mess... the little one is the most turbulent... you cannot keep him still for five minutes... he asks me things continuously ... he throws tantrums... (*the feeling of constriction is getting stronger and stronger... I am suffocating* ...) all of a sudden... he throws himself at me to take me to the computer... my wife does not help me... she cannot keep discipline... neither can she... (*I recognise the anger that rises... I feel that I am not in control of the situation that is overwhelming me*...) it is here that I had a salvo of bad thoughts with the image of me grabbing and throwing my son out the window... (*sense of total loss of control... not managing a situation that gives me a strong sense of anger, as it is highly constraining... I am terrified... I could really lose control... and commit a reckless act... I am desperate... what kind of father am I if I think of doing away with my children... if that were the case then I could really commit anything...*').

The progressive training in the focusing of the discrepant emotional states in the reconstruction in sequence of the scenes edited in moviola of the uncomfortable situations, entailed a progressive acquisition of the capacity to recognise the internal states with the relative re-reading of the events. This gradually enabled a substantial change in the patient's global functioning, who progressively became more self-aware and was able to integrate hitherto discrepant and therefore disturbing data into his personal narrative. What before the intervention was perceived as a somatic aspect, '*I suffocate*', and thus reordered, at the end of the treatment was recognised as an integrated emotional experience consistent with one's own feeling, '*I feel constricted*'. The intervention carried out had as its first objective the achievement of a more generative reorganisation of the patient's personal meaning and subsequently also produced an effective restructuring in the dynamics of reciprocity in the couple and in the relationship with the children. The patient has a likely prevailing theme of loss of control expressed in constrictive experiences in a phobic PMO with a visibly concrete elaboration of personal experience.

6 Conclusion

The postrationalist approach thus offers a study of human experience from the perspective of the individual who experiences and knows. This perspective is absolutely attentive to the *person in his or her* complexity precisely because its ultimate aim is the reconstruction and articulation of the specific personal meaning of the individual: of that point of view of the person who experiences, imparting a unique and unrepeatable order to the narrated tale that takes shape from a particular meaning and carries it with it, variously articulated, throughout its unfolding.

This perspective thus proves to be a model that can be applied to different types of human functioning, from the normal one, with its harmonious modalities in its existential themes, to the neurotic one with its short and episodic discontinuities up to the ragged and coarse fragmentariness of psychotic mechanisms. It can be used in both developmental and adult age; it can be spent in diverse settings, individual and couple. Recently it has also been successfully tested in groups and in professional and sports contexts. The application of the model can also be employed as a reading of artistic, literary and film creativity, and as an analysis of dream material (Merigliano et al., 2011; Merigliano, 2015, 2017, 2019a, b).

I want to conclude with the words of Vittorio Guidano: *'this is a very difficult job, because it is very hard to do ... you have to be very flexible, available, change your attitude... as patients come and go. It is a job that you do in solitude, because you work with the patient and you are responsible for the patient ... and you have intense personal emotions that cannot be communicated ... that have to be seen on your own ... because it is quite hard work, I believe that even from this point of view, a good knowledge of one's own way of functioning can help a therapist to better hold up who in himself is quite strong humanly and emotionally ...'* (1998).

References

Ballerini, A. (2008, May–August). *I Paradossi dell'Identità Personale* (Vol. IX, No. 2). L'Altro.
Bennett, L., Wolin, S., & Mc Avity, K. (1988). Family identity, ritual, and myth: A cultural perspective on life cycle transitions. In C. J. Falicov (Ed.), *Family transitions*. Guilford Press.
Bruner, J. S. (1988). *The multidimensional mind*. Laterza.

Bruner, J. S. (1991). The narrative construction of reality. In M. Ammaniti & D. N. Stern (Eds.), *Representations and narratives* (144 pp). Laterza.
Bruner, J. S. (1992). *The search for meaning*. Bollati Boringhieri.
Ceruti, M. (1989). *La danza che crea*. Feltrinelli.
Crittenden, P. M. (1994). *New perspectives on attachment*. Guerini.
Crittenden, P. M. (1997). *Danger, development and adaptation*. Masson.
Dodet, M. (1998). The moviola. In *Psychotherapy* (Vol. 4, No. 13, pp. 89–93). Moretti and Vitali.
Fogassi, L., et al. (2005). Parietal lobe: From action organisation to intention understanding. *Science, 308*, 662–667.
Gallese, V., & Guerra, M. (2015). *Lo schermo empatico. Cinema and neuroscience*. Raffaello Cortina.
Garger, S., & Guild, P. (1984). Learning styles: The crucial differentiations. *Curriculum Review, 23*, 9–12.
Gembillo, G. R. (2016). The empathy of Luigi Onnis with Maturana, Damasio and Rizzolatti. In *Psicobiettivo* (Vol. XXXVI, No. 3). FrancoAngeli.
Gould, S. J. (1983). *Hen's teeth and horse's toes*. W. W. Norton. Trad. It. *When horses had fingers. Mysteries and oddities of nature* (L. Sosio, Trans., p. 415). Feltrinelli, 1984.
Guidano, V. F. (1988). *La Complessità del Sé*. Bollati Boringhieri.
Guidano, V. F. (1991). Dalla rivoluzione cognitiva all'approccio sistemico in termini complessità: Riflessioni sulla nascita e sull'evoluzione della terapia cognitiva. In G. De Isabella, W. Festini Cucco, & G. Sala (Eds.), *Psicoterapeuti, teorie e tecniche: Un incontro possibile?* FrancoAngeli.
Guidano, V. F. (1992). *Il Sé nel suo Divenire*. Bollati Boringhieri.
Guidano, V. F. (1998). *APC training lectures Rome*.
Guidano, V. F. (1999). *APC training lectures Rome*.
Guidano, V. F. (2007). *Postrationalist cognitive psychotherapy* (notes and comments on the text by Quinones Bergeret A.T.). FrancoAngeli.
Guidano, V. F. (2008). *La psicoterapia tra arte e scienza*. FrancoAngeli.
Guidano, V. F. (2010). *Le dimensioni del Sé*. ARPES.
Guidano, V. F., & Liotti, G. (1983). *Cognitive processes and emotional disorders*. The Guildford Press.
Iacoboni, M. (2008). *I neuroni specchio: Come capiamo ciò che fanno gli altri*. Bollati Boringhieri.
Le Doux, J. (1998). *The emotional brain. At the origins of the emotions* (Tr. It.). Baldini & Castoldi, 1998.
Lewis, M. (1992). *The naked self. At the origins of shame* (Tr. It.). Giunti, 1995.
Lewis, M. (1994). Myself and me. In S. T. Parker, R. W. Mitchell, & M. L. Boccia (Eds.), *Self-awareness in animals and humans: Developmental perspectives* (pp. 20–34). Cambridge University Press.
Liotti, G. (1993). *Le discontinuità della coscienza – Etiologia, diagnosi e psicoterapia dei disturbi dissociativi*. FrancoAngeli.
Maturana, H. R. (1978). Biology of language: The epistemology of reality. In G. A. Miller & E. Lenneberg (Eds.), *Psychology and biology of language and thought*. Academic Press.
Maturana, H. R. (1993). *Self-awareness and reality*. Raffaello Cortina.
Maturana, H. R., & Varela, F. J. (1985). *Autopoiesis and cognition*. Marsilio.
Maturana, H. R., & Varela, F. J. (1987). *The tree of knowledge*. Garzanti.
Mead, H. G. (1934). *Mind, self, and society*. Chicago University Press.
Merigliano, D. (2002). Joan of Arc: Luc Besson's film. Post-rationalist constructivist reading of the decompensation and evolution of psychotic meaning-making. *Psychobjective, XXII*(1), 109–118.
Merigliano, D. (2004). Cinema and psychopathology: Ron Howard's A Beautifull Mind. Post-rationalist reading of a psychotic development. *Psychobjective, XXIV*(1), 129–139.

Merigliano, D. (2009). Ricordando una conversation hour con Vittorio F. Guidano. VI International congress on constructivism in psychotherapy, Siena 1998. *Quaderni di Psicoterapia Cognitiva, 14*(2), 24–42.

Merigliano, D. (2013). La creatività dei numeri: Lettura Postrazionalista dell'opera del regista Peter Greenaway. *Psicobiettivo, XXXIII*(1), 151–161.

Merigliano, D. (2015). Il sogno in psicoterapia. In A. Quinones Bergeret, P. Cimbolli, & A. De Pascale (Eds.), *La Psicoterapia dei Processi di Significato Personale dei Disturbi Psicopatologici. Theoretical-practical manual*. Alpes.

Merigliano, D. (2017). *In a world of images, personal meaning between cinema, photography and the web*. Bononia University Press.

Merigliano, D. (2019a). The Shape of Water, reflections on Guillermo del Taurus according to the postrationalist perspective. *Constructivisms, 6*, 93–103. Copyright © AIPPC ISSN: 2465-2083. https://doi.org/10.23826/2019.01.093.103

Merigliano, D. (2019b). *Postrationalist psychotherapy. Clinical cases, intervention methods and application aspects*. FrancoAngeli.

Merigliano, D., & Dodet, M. (2001). ad vocem "*La Moviola*" and "*Narrativity*". In S. Borgo, G. Della Giusta, & L. Sibilia (Eds.), *Dictionary of cognitive behavioural psychotherapy* (pp. 177–178, 181–182). Mc Graw-Hill.

Merigliano, D., Diamante, M., & Moriconi, F. (2011). *Dietro lo schermo. Il cinema come percorso di costruzione del significato personale*. FrancoAngeli.

Minkowski, E. (1966). *Trattato di Psicopatologia*. Feltrinelli.

Ortega y Gasset, J. (1994). *Il tema del nostro tempo* (C. Rocco & A. Lozano Maneiro, Trans.). Sugarco Edizioni.

Pessoa, F. (1998). *Il libro dell'inquietudine by Bernardo Soares*. Feltrinelli [1986]. Impronte 40. ISBN 978-88-07-05040-4.

Picardi, A., & Mannino, G. (2001). The organisations of personal meaning: Towards an empirical validation. *Journal of Psychiatry, 36*(4), 224–233.

Prigogine, Y. (1982). *Dissipative structures. Self-organisation of non-equilibrium thermodynamic systems*. Sansoni, 1982.

Reda, M. A. (1986). *Complex cognitive systems and psychotherapy*. NIS.

Ricoeur, P. (1986). *Time and tale* (Vol. 1, G. Grampa, Ed.). Jaca Book. TR2.

Ricoeur, P. (1987). *Tempo e racconto* (La configurazione nel racconto di fzione, Vol. 2, G. Grampa, Ed.). Jaca Book. TR3.

Ricoeur, P. (1988). *Il tempo raccontato. Tempo e racconto* (Vol. 3, G. Grampa, Ed. It. 2016). Jaca Book.

Ricoeur, P. (1995). *The philosophy of Paul Ricœur*. Open Court. *The just* (Trans.). University of Chicago Press, 2000 (1995). *Critique and conviction* (Trans.). Columbia University Press.

Ricoeur, P. (2016). *Self as another* (Tr. It.). Jaca Book. (Original work published 1990).

Rizzolatti, G., & Fadiga, L. (1999). Resonance behaviors and mirror neurons. *Italiennes de Biologie, 137*(2–3), 85–100. PMID 10349488.

Rizzolatti, G., & Sinigaglia, C. (2006). *So quel che fai, Il cervello che agisce e i neuroni specchio*. Raffaello Cortina.

Rizzolatti, G., Fadiga, L., Gallese, V., & Fogassi, L. (1996). Premotor cortex and the recognition of motor actions. *Cognitive Brain Research, 3*, 131–141.

Safran, J. D., & Segal, Z. V. (1990). *Interpersonal process in cognitive therapy*. Jason Aronson.

Tulving, E. (1972). Episodic and sematic memory. In E. Tulving, W. Donaldson, & H. White (Eds.), *Organisation of memory*. Academic Press.

von Foerster, H. (1987). *Systems that observe* (M. Ceruti & U. Telfner, Eds.). Astrolabio-Ubaldini.

Witkin, H. A. (1949–1963). Perception of body position and of the position of the visual field. *Psychological Monographs, 63*(Whole No. 302), 1–46.

Wittgenstein, L. (1967). *Ricerche Filosofiche*. Einaudi.

The Assessment of Attachment for Case Formulation

Patricia M. Crittenden, Giuliana Florit, Andrea Landini, and Susan J. Spieker

1 Why to Assess Attachment

Over the past half-century, significant changes have been introduced in the definition and treatment of mental illness, in the recognition of childhood maltreatment and establishment of child protection services, and in fight against crime. However, progress in these areas has not led to a reduction in the prevalence of these problems, suggesting that the services in place may be using outdated and incomplete models to address the problems they seek to resolve (Kim et al., 2017; Edwards, 2019).

Similarly, the introduction of psychiatric diagnosis concurred over the past half-century with the worldwide establishment of mental health services. Despite such progress, psychiatric diagnoses have shown significant gaps over time. For instance, they do not correspond to discrete entities of distress (Kendell & Jablensky, 2003), fail to address the conditions that lie between adjustment and diagnosable disorders, such as poverty-related conditions (Wakefield, 2015), while the promise of leading to effective treatments remained unfulfilled (Khoury et al., 2014).

Psychiatric diagnoses do not provide explanations for problematic behaviors; they merely describe them. Relying solely on the presenting problem or psychiatric diagnoses is not enough. Often, families themselves are unable to describe the

---

P. M. Crittenden
Family Relations Institute, Black Mountain, NC, USA

G. Florit
Family Court, Milan, Italy

A. Landini (✉)
Family Relations Institute, Reggio Emilia, Italy

S. J. Spieker
Department of Child, Family and Population Health Nursing, School of Nursing, University of Washington, Seattle, WA, USA

underlying issue (if they could, they might be spontaneously able to resolve it), and diagnoses are neither linked to etiology nor to treatment of the problem.

We believe that sharing a theory of adaptation and maladaptation, along with integrated services grounded in a solid theoretical foundation, can help prevent the increase of distress in the population and can provide effective support for the most fragile people. Understanding the developmental and psychological processes that underly problematic behaviors can increase hope for a future where the most vulnerable individuals and their families can finally be safe.

1.1 Limitations of Descriptive Nosology and the Need for a Functional Nosology

The introduction of psychiatric diagnosis has fostered dialogue among psychotherapists of different orientations, and the use of the term "mental illness" has restored humanity to individuals in distress, placing their treatment within the realm of medicine. However, the notion of discrete psychiatric illnesses with specific causes is not supported by adequate evidence and is insufficient for understanding and treating patients. These and other limitations of descriptive diagnoses make it necessary to rely on new paradigms guiding decision-making in a clinical setting.

Diagnoses Are Not Directly Linked to Etiology or Treatment of the Patient's Problem

Some data indicate that there are no pathogenic agents or processes that define mental illness or the majority of psychiatric diagnoses (Banner, 2013). The search for genes, neurological conditions, or toxins that might cause psychopathology has not yielded the expected conclusive data. Furthermore, patients with the same diagnosis often do not benefit equally from the same treatment. Within a given psychiatric diagnosis, there are heterogeneous groups of patients; as a result, the treatment may be helpful for some, harmful for others, or ineffective for another subgroup. In data analysis, this aspect of descriptive diagnosis can contribute to making the treatment appear ineffective for some patients.

Descriptive Diagnosis Does Not Always Give an Account About Maladaptive Behaviors Observed in a Patient

Mental illnesses are treated as medical conditions, such as infections or fractures, rather than dimensional problems. However, there is evidence that many pathological behaviors exist along a continuum, and individuals may exhibit some dysfunctions only occasionally, while others display them more frequently and intensely (Coghill & Sonuga-Barke, 2012; Haslam et al., 2006; Raballo et al., 2014).

People who engage in dysfunctional or even severely dangerous behaviors toward themselves and their offspring sometimes do not fit into any nosological category. For example, it is not uncommon in legal assessments for serious harmful behaviors to find no evidence of psychopathology in the perpetrator.

Descriptive Diagnosis Is Primarily Formulated Relying on What the Patient Knows About Themselves or Intends to Share

This limits the diagnostic procedure, not only in forensic settings (where information is provided to an authoritative interlocutor in a dangerous context) but also in clinical settings, when patients, for cognitive, metacognitive, or emotional reasons, omit important information. Neither the clinical interview nor questionnaires are effective in accessing implicit information (what the patient doesn't know or doesn't want to say) that can explain nonadaptive behaviors.

Therefore, it is necessary to turn to a nosology with solid theoretical foundations that addresses the full range of human behaviors as they arise in everyday life contexts, explains the conditions that promote maladaptive behavior, and is organized to indicate potentially beneficial treatments for specific patients.

The Dynamic-Maturational Model of Attachment and Adaptation (DMM, Crittenden, 1995, 2016) offers an alternative nosology to psychiatric diagnosis. It is based on a solid theoretical foundation and addresses the causes, manifestations, and functions of behaviors. Empirically tested and falsifiable, it is useful for psychotherapists and those allocating resources for mental health and child protection. It is intuitively meaningful for patients, and it is sufficiently complex to cover the variability of human behaviors.

1.2 Adaptation and Attachment: Strategies for Perceiving, Paying Attention, Assigning Meaning, and Acting in a Protective Manner

In DMM, the principle of protection from danger and reproduction as the main motivations for behavior and changes in phenotype and genotype is borrowed from evolutionary biology. At the population level, adaptive behavior is a behavior that promotes the survival of the species despite exposure to danger and reproduction despite interpersonal threats. At an individual level, it refers to the individual's adaptation to specific life conditions; these conditions vary from person to person and throughout life.

Without protective responses facing danger, survival is threatened. It elicits strategic behaviors such as self-protection, protection of a partner, and protection of offspring.

For children, the best strategy is to ensure that an adult protects them. The one who provides protection is the "attachment figure," typically fulfilled by the mother and father. It is certainly advantageous to have parents securely attached in a relationship that binds them, and a network of interconnected individuals, as is the case in an extended family. If a range of protective strategies and the resources provided by both family networks are available, children can survive and thrive. Their developmental pathway depends on the combination of their genetic inheritance with what they learn about safety in their cultural and subcultural contexts (Fig. 1).

Children develop protective strategies for themselves, find reproductive partners, and continue the life cycle with their own offspring grounding on genetic, physiological, psychological, relational, and contextual influences.

Throughout life, the mind has access to information. Information is used to organize a self-protective response in the presence of a threat. If the self-protective response is followed by a reduction in threat or an increase in comfort, it shall be probably re-enacted if similar threats occur. The repetition of this cause-and-effect relationship strengthens the neural network from stimulus to elicited behavior. In behavioral terms, it can be said that the individual acquires a self-protective (or, after puberty, reproductive) strategy. To organize protective and reproductive behaviors, the mind relies on three sources of information.

Somatic information, through sensations of discomfort/pain and well-being, signals the need or absence of need of a protective or sexual behavior. However, it does not clarify which action should be taken. *Cognitive* information connects events temporally, allowing for the learning of temporal contingencies. Each learned contingency functions as a prediction of the future, while past consequences suggest actions to be taken or avoided. *Affective* information connects contextual elements

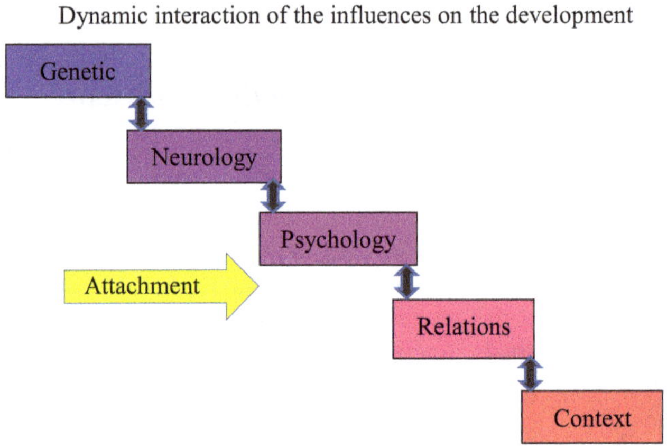

Fig. 1 The dynamic interaction of factors influencing adaptation. (Used by permission of Patricia M. Crittenden)

with psychological arousal. Innate responses to extreme variations in contextual stimulus intensity motivate or inhibit behavior and are subject to associative learning.

All behaviors are the result of activated neural networks, specifically somatic networks (information coming from the body), cognitive networks (information based on the temporal order of information coming to the brain), and affective networks (information coming from the external context). Therefore, mind represents "the self in connection with non-self" in different ways at the same time (Eagleman, 2011; Schacter & Tulving, 1994). Since activated neural networks dispose action (Crittenden, 1990; Damasio, 1996), we will refer to them as dispositional representations or DRs.

At any moment, multiple neural pathways are active, with some proceeding separately while others connecting together: the latter are more intense. Together, these networks result in multiple dispositional representations predisposing to action (Eagleman, 2011). There are two types of actions: (1) response and (2) inhibition of response (up to freezing and catatonia) (Baldwin, 2013). Representations and actions they give rise to are not necessarily identical or compatible with each other.

Concurrent with the increasing bottom-up information, there is a top-down attempt to fit existing models (Clark, 2016). This gives rise to different brain systems, each processing information differently, top-down and bottom-up, to find the best model of the "self in context." Moreover, the self is simultaneously a self-from-the-past and an actual self.

Since every context is somewhat new, the mind searches for discrepancies (Clark, 2016: 28–29); discrepancies are where information about new conditions can be found. By focusing on discrepancies, the mind maximizes the chances to discover the information that will be crucial for self-protection in the changing conditions of new contexts (cf. Bateson, 1972/2000).

Tulving and his colleagues clustered DRs as memory systems. With the introduction of new instrumental investigation techniques, the model has expanded to include five (Schacter & Tulving, 1994) or more (Schacter & Tulving, 1994; Devitt et al., 2017) memory systems.

Similarly, the DMM has evolved over time, progressively incorporating more memory systems, culminating in a 2016 model that describes eight memory systems (Fig. 2).

In humans, somatic, cognitive, and affective information exists in three forms: preconscious-implicit; verbal-conscious; integrated in episodes and reflections (Fig. 2). These levels of awareness have a sequential maturation (from infancy to adulthood) that is defined by our genome and needs to be activated by stimuli from the environment.

Individuals differ in perception and reliance on different types of information; these differences result from experience and influence behavior. Some people are more sensitive to somatic information, others to cognitive or affective information, while only a few individuals harmoniously utilize all sources of information.

Individuals also differ in whether they tend to act (1) quickly on preconscious DRs, (2) with moderate speed but greater clarity on conscious, verbal DRs based on

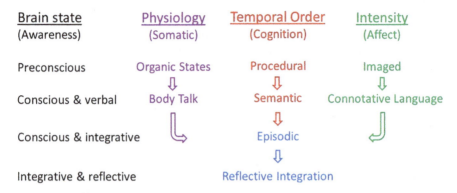

Fig. 2 Memory systems and levels of awareness. (Used by permission of Patricia M. Crittenden)

past integration, or (3) more slowly on DRs resulting from current conscious reflection.

Therefore, individual differences can be observed in preference for memory systems, in awareness, or in the tendency to engage in automatic responses. Another individual difference lies in the propensity to transform information more or less extremely.

Information can be considered truly predictive of future conditions, or instead irrelevant and thus "omitted" in subsequent processing. Other information, irrelevant to future dangers, may be privileged and mistakenly treated as important. Similarly, information can be distorted, falsified, denied, or created in a delusional manner by the mind itself. All of us transform information; some of us tend to transform information in a more extreme manner and with greater frequency.

This structure of genetic predisposition, neurological organization, multiple sources of information, and transformations disposes of behaviors that, when repeated frequently in similar circumstances, function strategically to protect the self.

In Fig. 3, the attachment strategies are represented in a bi-dimensional model based on the bias toward cognitive or affective information (the horizontal dimension) and on the amount of transformation of information (increasing from top to bottom of vertical dimension).

The DMM describes multiple strategic possibilities (Crittenden, 2016) in a two-dimensional model, with intelligence as a third dimension that affects the speed and complexity of processing. In the graph, the horizontal dimension indicates the extent to which cognitive or affective information is used by the strategies: in Type A strategies cognitive information prevails, in Type C strategies affective information prevails, while Type B strategies make a balanced use of cognitive and affective information. Intense or pervasive somatic activation, lacking organic dysfunction, usually corresponds to both cognitive and affective failure in resolving a threat.

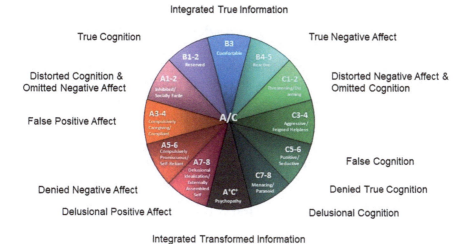

Fig. 3 Protective strategies and transformations of information in adulthood. (Used by permission of Patricia M. Crittenden)

The vertical dimension describes how affective or cognitive information gathered in the past is transformed to make predictions for the future: from top to bottom we observe the increasingly transformation of information (Crittenden, 2016). As previously emphasized, transformations range from truly predictive (untransformed) to omitted from processing, erroneously included, distorted, falsified, denied, and delusional. Several studies have confirmed that the use of extensively transformed information (typical of high-scoring strategies) is associated with psychiatric diagnoses (Hughes et al., 2000; Landini et al., 2016; Pace & Bufford, 2018).

Thus, many extreme strategies involve the use of erroneous information unsubmitted to proper scrutiny. Present behavior can be the result of DRs based on omitted, distorted, erroneous, falsified, denied, or delusional information. The DMM emphasizes how such behavioral responses can become maladaptive when used in contexts not fitting the past circumstances where these responses were learned as protective. Thus, the same strategy can be adaptive or maladaptive depending on the context in which it is used. Both pervasive maladaptation in psychiatric disorders and maladaptation due to psychological shortcuts resulting from exposure to danger result from a poor fit between strategy and context (Perry & Sullivan, 2014). For instance, a secure strategy based on open and clear communication (generally considered desirable) can turn out to be dangerous in the context of genocide, where an extreme strategy that foresees and employs distorted communication may instead result in being more protective.

This extreme example emphasizes the value of learning acquired as adaptation to danger (Ellis et al., 2020). Without such learning, a sudden threat can elicit psychological trauma; trauma can indeed be seen as the gap between what is known and what is necessary to know for safety in a given context.

1.3 Maladaptation and Attachment: Trauma—Maladaptive Strategies—Adaptive Strategies Are on a Continuum

Babies are born with a genetic predisposition to survive, provided that an adult takes care of them. Their brains expect stimuli (Sullivan, 2017) and develop in order to prepare them to benefit the best from information learned from relational experience with parents (Barrett, 2020). The parent has a mature brain already shaped by evolutionary environment and experiences of danger. The parent's brain responds to the needs expressed by the baby. Parents' response progressively shapes the synaptic connections of the neural networks activated in the baby's mind. When the adult's response overlaps what the child is already prepared to perceive and enact, that is, when it falls within the infant's zone of proximal development (ZPD; Vygotsky, 1978), development proceeds smoothly.

Conversely, in case of threats without any protection or comfort provided to the baby, the infant brain must whip up a neural chain to generate protective behavior. This network almost always includes some irrelevant information and excludes some relevant information. The elicited response is a "psychological shortcut." Of course, if the misrepresentations are corrected in adulthood, the shortcut can be revised. To do so, the adult must not feel threatened. In threatening conditions, the adult is not disposed to reflect about danger and is instead driven to enact automatic behavior. If this is the case, the individual shall carry on the shortcuts through further stages of development and subsequent contexts. In the new circumstances, shortcuts previously proved protective may prove unsuitable, thus generating maladaptation and distress.

The brain, as the organ that uses information to make predictions and trigger protective actions, is more vulnerable to errors when it is not yet mature. Thus, early experiences of unprotected and uncomforted dangers, generate more erroneous transformations of information compared to dangers experienced during adulthood (Opendak et al., 2017; Perry et al., 2017).

Furthermore, it should be emphasized that outdated and extremely transformed representations based on past exposure to dangers are at the core of mental disorders, child maltreatment, and criminal behaviors (Baetz & Widom, 2020; Crittenden, 1999; Wilkinson et al., 2019).

It is important to note that danger itself does not generate maladaptive behaviors or psychological trauma; instead, distorted information about danger leads to these risks. On the other hand, when we are prepared, we protect effectively ourselves and our offspring, and development proceeds without obstacles: we do not succumb, and our brains generate new and protective transformations (Ellis et al., 2020).

When the brain is immature, it processes information only in rudimentary ways; when dangers are too imminent, it is not advantageous to take time to process information; when certain aspects of danger are invisible, the necessary information is lacking. These three conditions limit the ability to effectively process information about danger.

Immaturity and the imminence and complexity of dangers can elicit behaviors based on insufficient processing. We referred to this type of incomplete processing as "psychological shortcut" (Crittenden, 2016).

Consistent with studies on adverse childhood experiences (ACE; American Psychological Association, 2021; Edwards et al., 2003; Felitti, 2009), we emphasize the risk associated with psychological shortcuts underlying maladaptive behaviors when they get organized before the child becomes aware of the problematic situation. In these cases, the strategy—and not the danger itself—causes maladaptation.

This perspective allows us to consider psychological problems, maltreatment, and deviant behaviors as arising from a single critical cause, operating in analogous ways despite different epiphenomena. It is a hypothesis that can be empirically tested and has the flexibility to match individual as well as the entire human species.

Current thinking differentiates typical behavior from traumatic behavior. We believe that such a distinction is inappropriate. The same principles apply to all neural networks, regardless of whether the resulting behavior is considered a traumatic response or not. The most important principle is that the mind develops to promote survival and reproduction (Sutherland & Mather, 2012). Consequently, any threat to survival or reproduction takes priority over other concurrent representations (Masson et al., 2020).

Behaviors are the result of a probabilistic game (Clark, 2016) regulated by three conditions that promote priming of neural networks: (1) events that threaten survival and reproduction, (2) repeated activation of specific neural circuits, (3) events that occur early in development. When these three conditions co-occur, the probability increases for rapid, preconscious behavioral responses, not always suitable for the current context, which are clinically referred to as "traumatic responses."

The neural networks underlying psychogenic trauma do not differ from other neural networks, but they have priority over non-traumatic, concurrently active networks. As a result, the neural networks that dispose protective behavior can be placed along a continuum: from the most urgent (both in terms of action and inhibition) to the less pressing—that allow for reflection. In between, we find usual behaviors—including strategic responses to danger—varying in terms of urgency.

This perspective suggests that urgent traumatic networks are nothing but protective responses not updated on current conditions (Crittenden, 1997; Feldman & Vengrober, 2011). Far from considering humans as vulnerable, these ideas highlight the human capacity to identify dangers and implement/enact protective responses even in early developmental stages (Ellis et al., 2020). This resource-based approach enables mental health professionals to understand maladaptive behavior and connect in a different way with those who enact harmful behaviors toward themselves, their partners, and their offspring.

1.4 Conclusions

Each strategy serves the purpose of preventing rejection or aggression in the short term and death in the long term. In evolutionary terms, young children must prevent rejection and abandonment to survive. Avoiding rejection is also necessary for reproduction, that is, for the survival of the species. When adults undertake a long-lasting relationship, they extend their self-protection strategies to the protection of their partner. When they have children, they adapt these strategies to protect their offspring. When the strategies for self-protection, partner protection, and offspring protection are incompatible or not suitable for the current context, imbalances, conflicts, and relationship-based dangers can arise (Dallos et al., 2019, 2020). Such circumstances underlie many of the challenges faced not only by therapists but also by professionals in child protection and social security services (Sloman & Sturman, 2012).

This perspective can therefore prove more effective than focusing on descriptive diagnosis and symptom reduction. Familiarity with strategies and an understanding of how individuals can act according to danger, as well as focus on conflicts between different ways of protecting oneself (or between self-protection, partner protection, and/or offspring protection), can be more effective and promising for diagnosis and intervention.

Current psychological treatments often focus on symptoms or changing personality structure. More recently, modifying attachment style has been introduced as a goal. According to the DMM, treatments should enable individuals to generate and apply protective strategies at the right time and in the right context. Psychological equilibrium refers to individual ability to use all information (both cognitive and affective, from every memory system) without biases favoring or excluding certain types of information in order to select in a reflective and conscious manner the most suitable strategy for the context.

The DMM emphasizes the utility of identifying the function of behaviors and words, viewing them from an interpersonal perspective, rather than focusing solely on the morphology of behaviors and explicit verbal content (as in descriptive diagnosis). DMM formulations can lead to innovative and sometimes counterintuitive hypotheses. They take into account the fact that the presenting problem is often not the "real" problem. Often, the designated patient offers a distorted version of the problem, which corresponds to what they know or want to reveal.

Users of non-B strategies are generally less aware of their preconscious actions. The deeper the unawareness, the more extreme the strategies, modified or influenced by unresolved traumas or losses. Thus, the clinical task is to unveil the "unspeakable" problem in ways as compassionate as to be acceptable to the patient's family (Dallos et al., 2019, 2020). For the DMM, the search for unspeakable problems is an essential task focused on investigation of current and past reproductive dangers and opportunities, pieced together through the patient's transformations of information. This complex task suggests the need for attachment assessment tools suitable for detecting such transformations.

2 How to Assess Attachment

Especially for those who work with at-risk families, attachment has become a crucial construct for decisions concerning child placement and preventive or treatment interventions for the family unit. However, practitioners still show uncertainties regarding the choice of assessment tools to employ, and only a few are aware of the implications of different methods of attachment assessment. Some practitioners refrain from formal assessments and instead propose interventions based on their own opinions, thereby increasing the risk of ineffective or iatrogenic interventions.

When information about self-protection strategies and about information processing mode is relevant for clinical application, it is necessary to rely on formal and replicable assessments, and experts must be able to choose suitable tools and use them correctly.

2.1 Tool Selection

Does the Tool Capture Implicit Information?

Some individuals rely predominantly on temporal cognitive contingencies (Type A), while others rely on their negative affective states (Type C). When both types of information are distorted and actions—motivated by preconscious information—are not recognized, the RDs become inaccurate: neither actions nor words mean what they seem to mean. In these cases, when asking the person how she is organized or why she behaved in a certain way, the person will say what she explicitly knows. This often does not correspond to her preferences in terms of information processing and to the underlying functional intention behind her manifest behaviors.

Clinical interviews and self-assessment tools, such as self-administered questionnaires, should therefore be complemented with assessment tools apt to capture preconscious information, using recordings of samples of behaviors motivated by implicit as well as explicit memory systems.

Preconscious memory systems correspond to procedural memory and imaged memory. These memory systems are available from birth and generate rapid protective behaviors (see Fig. 2). Procedures are sensorimotor patterns that operate based on contingencies and reinforcement. These patterns inhibit certain behaviors (e.g., crying or shouting) or produce repetitive sequences of behaviors (also known as compulsions) that the person often cannot rationally explain.

Sensory images associate aspects of the context (visual, auditory, olfactory, gustatory, tactile) with the expectation of what might happen in that context, eliciting bodily changes (somatic images) consistent with those expectations.

Semantic memory and connotative language are explicit forms of cognitive and affective representation—slower and more accessible to conscious revision. Semantic memory is verbal and consists of generalizations about how things have been in the past and, therefore, how they are expected to be in the future. Often, semantic information corresponds to how things should be. As a result, there can be a significant discrepancy between semantic representations (of which the person is aware) and their (preconscious) behaviors. Precisely this discrepancy requires the use of tools designed for going beyond the person's words (declarative semantic memory), and is apt to reveal what the person cannot say, especially if their strategies are extreme, modified, and suffer traumatic interference.

Is the Tool Able to Discern Complex Behavioral Organizations?

The mere distinction between B/non-B is useless to the clinician. Appropriate assessments must be chosen to reveal complex behavioral organizations. Identifying the pattern as non-B does not inform treatment, just like psychiatric diagnoses do not. The DMM also emphasizes how important it is not to equate non-B patterns in psychopathology, stating that patterns of pathological attachment do not exist; patterns can just be adaptive or maladaptive. All patterns may prove fitting in their developmental contexts while proving maladaptive and problematic in the current relational contexts; and the behavioral or psychological disorders may reflect the underlying maladaptation.

The assessment tool enables the clinician to evaluate whether the strategy fits the current context, or it is too inflexible and specific to the environment where it was learned, thus more likely to prove maladaptive in different settings, or it suffers disturbances due to unresolved traumas or losses. Such information enables the clinician to formulate hypotheses about the function of patients' symptoms or about potential risks, and guide treatment more effectively than descriptive diagnosis and clinician's opinions based on what the patient explicitly declares.

As a corollary to the above, we emphasize the importance of selecting theoretical models and assessment tools that encompass a wide range of classifications, it means, able to distinguish complex behavior organizations and to fit the evolutionary range of human behavior. DMM classificatory systems for different developmental stages reflect the greater strategic complexity permitted by maturation, including progressively more complex classifications. For example, while the classification system of the Preschool Assessment of Attachment (used for ages 2–6) includes patterns A1–4, C1–4, the combination of A/C patterns, and even a modifier (Dp), the Adult Attachment Interview (the tool for adulthood) encompasses a considerably expanded system with various modifiers and numerous potential traumatic response displays (see Fig. 3).

Precisely this aspect, crucial in assessment selection, turns out to be also an obstacle to the diffusion of more effective assessments. Analyzing increasing memory systems, identifying sub-patterns and modifiers, and screening traumatic response displays exposes the coder to a complexity that requires a time-consuming and costly training.

To overcome this obstacle, we propose drawing clinical practice nearer to the medical model, which involves greater compartmentalization and specialization of skills. As we will explain shortly, the skilled coder, able to browse through the many information that can be observed in the behavior sample or analyzed in the speech sample, can be seen as the professional who, in the medical field, analyzes tissues after acquiring magnetic resonance imaging on axial, coronal, or sagittal planes and provides information to guide the treatment they shall not personally organize or conduct.

We propose six kinds of specialization (Crittenden et al., 2021):

1. Screening for further assessment
2. Administering formal assessment
3. Coding of formal assessment
4. Formulating the problem based on attachment classifications, other tool results and case history
5. Planning treatments
6. Delivering treatment

Attempting to combine the above-mentioned skills into a single operator figure is ineffective and leads to frustration and dangerous shortcuts, such as avoiding evaluation altogether.

Does the Assessment Tool Provide a Standardized and Replicable Procedure for Gathering Information, and Specific Methods to Deduce the Results?

When assessing attachment is crucial, in order to reach valid conclusions, essential aspects have to be considered in selecting tools.

One obvious yet often overlooked aspect is threat: if we want to observe attachment strategy, both through behavior and speech, we need a procedure that activates a threat response in the observed person. Indeed, attachment is a bond between two individuals in which one person protects and comforts the other. Attachment behavior is the behavior used to elicit protection and comfort. The attachment pattern is the organization of attachment behavior used to elicit protection and comfort.

Without a threat that activates the protection strategy, we cannot observe how the person protects herself and how she seeks comfort.

However, in order to highlight individual differences, the procedure must be able to regulate the intensity of the threat since extreme threats tend to trigger stereotypical fight-flight-freeze behaviors. The threat must stay at moderate levels to elicit behaviors indicative of individual differences, thus enabling diagnostic judgments on protective strategies. In the Adult Attachment Interview, one of the interviewer's tasks is to regulate the interviewee's arousal through verbal and non-verbal behaviors. Similarly, in the Strange Situation, the director can anticipate the entry of the attachment figure into the room if the child's behavior indicates too high levels of stress.

The unpredictable absence of the mother in an unfamiliar room with or without the presence of a stranger in the Strange Situation, as the questions about dangers and losses in the Adult Attachment Interview, are examples of standardized threats included in the procedures.

In valid tools, rather than relying on the clinician's initiative, the progression and presence/absence of the threat are standardized.

The audio or video recording of the procedure (depending on the used tool) enables the coder to make an accurate subsequent examination based on review of the recording or on analysis of the transcript, in order to capture information that even the most experienced clinician may miss in a live observation. Recording also facilitates the comparison of expert coders' assessments on the same behavior sample making possible corrections and explanations of discrepancies between different coders' perspectives.

In the case of informal assessments, such as free play observation, the observed critical behaviors persist in the observer's mind connected with the deduced conclusions. The observer's ability to re-analyze this connection, and potentially correct it, is limited if the behavior cannot be reviewed. Without tangible evidence to scrutinize, every opinion is as valid as another.

Therefore, attachment assessment tools depend on (1) the surprise generated by introducing something unexpected, (2) the opportunity to regulate the threat, and (3) a careful, organized, and gradual collection of information. When some features of the procedure are omitted, used separately, or combined with other procedures or questions, the assessment is no longer valid. Extracted parts are unlikely to produce valid results since it is the overall structure that generates information (and activates strategies), not specific questions.

In the case of formal assessments that involve manuals and expert-led training courses, coders may and must undergo training, and their performance can be evaluated (compared to a standard) to determine their level of reliability. Thus, the reliability of the assessment depends not only on the choice of the tool, but also on the coder, who must adhere to a standard and demonstrate to maintain it over time.

Furthermore, the reliability of the result increases when the person doing the qualitative analysis of information is blind to all information about the case beyond the recorded behavior: this ensures that *the coder approaches the material to be evaluated with as little bias as possible.*

2.2 Assessment Tools

The assessment tools presented in this brief overview and presented in Table 1 are tailored to different developmental stages and focus on accurate observation of recorded behaviors that are understood in their function (vs morphology), in a relational context (the child with the adult and the interviewee with the interviewer).

The described assessment tools involve the introduction of a threat into the procedure (excluding the Infant CARE-Index) and the collection of information from different memory systems. They enable to identify complex behavior organizations:

The Assessment of Attachment for Case Formulation

Table 1 Assessment tools DMM

Tool	Age range	Method	Assessment of attachment strategy
Infant CARE-Index (ICI)	0–15 month	Adult-child play	Enacted
Toddler CARE-Index (TCI)	15–72 months	Adult-child play	Enacted
Strange Situation (SSP)	11–15 months	Separation and reunion	Enacted
Preschool Assessment of Attachment (PAA)	16–60 months	Separation and reunion	Enacted
School-aged Assessment of Attachment (SAA)	6–12 years	Story telling and child's autobiographical events	Represented
Transition to Adulthood Attachment Interview (TAAI)	16–25 years	Interview on attachment	Represented
Adult Attachment Interview (AAI)	Adulthood	Interview on attachment	Represented
Parents' Interview (PI)	Any	Interview on how to raise children	Enacted and represented

specific attachment sub-patterns for each developmental phase, modifiers, and unresolved traumas and losses (specifying how they are addressed in the mind).

Administering these tools is not difficult, although training is necessary to ensure the proper collection of material that might otherwise turn out to be uncodable.

The coder should be unaware of case information, rely on meticulous observation of verbal and non-verbal behaviors recorded in videos or transcribed (in the case of interviews), and *functionally* analyze behaviors based on in-depth knowledge of patterns, modifiers, and types of unresolved traumas, until a final classification is obtained.

Coding for every assessment requires extensive training before reaching the maximum level of reliability, which is desirable for forensic evaluations (90% agreement with the standard). Clinical assessments, as they can ideally be subjected to falsification and revisions at each session, might also be performed by coders with slightly lower levels of reliability.

The Infant CARE-Index (ICI)

Procedure The adult is asked to play with the child as they usually do, and the interaction is video-recorded for 3–5 minutes.

What it assesses It assesses the adult's ability to attune to the functional state of the child. Since it is used with very young children (before an attachment pattern has been formed) and since threats are not involved, it does not assess attachment directly. However, it can predict attachment patterns and inform on risk level for the child's future development. It can also be used with unfamiliar adults to assess their sensitivity to the child's signals of pleasure or distress. It can be administered multiple times without compromising its validity. It has been designed as a convenient screening tool and should always be considered taking other evidences into account.

Classification system The result includes a score of dyadic synchrony, and adults are evaluated in terms of sensitivity, control, and non-responsiveness, while children are assessed for cooperation, compulsivity, difficulty, and passivity.

Validity There are numerous publications supporting the validity of the ICI (Farnfield et al., 2010).

The Toddler CARE-Index (TCI)

Procedure It is the same as the ICI, but with the addition of a frustration and repair task administered to the child by the attachment figure after 3 minutes of free play.

What it assesses By eliciting the hierarchical structure of the relationship, which is a sensitive issue for the child's age, it provides an estimation of the child's attachment strategy toward the adult. It also assesses dyadic synchrony.

Classification system It recognizes patterns B, A1–4, and C1–4, as well as A/C and Dp.

Advantages and limitations It is a much simpler tool compared to the Strange Situation, making it useful as a screening tool. It suggests the most appropriate intervention on the base of dyadic synchrony score.

Validity There are two validation studies of the TCI (Crittenden, 1992; Künster et al., 2010), but many more on the ICI, which the TCI is based on.

The Strange Situation Procedure (SSP)

Procedure It consists of a sequence of eight 3-minute episodes. In the first episode, the child and the mother are together in the room. After 3 minutes, a stranger enters and, after chatting with the mother for about a minute, attempts to play with the child. At the sound of a knock, the mother leaves, and the stranger remains alone with the child for a maximum of 3 minutes. When the mother returns, the stranger exits. Mother and child have a minimum of 3 minutes to settle, then at the sound of a second knock, the mother leaves, leaving the child alone. After a maximum of 3 minutes, the stranger returns. The mother returns after a maximum of 3 minutes.

What it assesses SSP provides two types of information: (1) attachment strategy, and (2) in some cases, distortion of the basic strategy.

Classification system The DMM, in addition to the patterns proposed by Ainsworth (B1–4; A1–2, C1–2), allows for the identification of patterns B5, pre A3–4, pre C3–4, and A/C, as well as modifiers such as depression (Dp) and intrusion of forbidden negative affect states [ina].

Advantages and limitations It is the most validated tool but also requires more resources in terms of the setting (room with one-way mirror), equipment (closed-circuit camera), and personnel (video operator, stranger, and director). With the expansion provided in the DMM, it is particularly sensitive to nuances of attachment behavior in high-risk contexts.

Validity Numerous studies have been conducted from its implementation in the mid-1960s to its widespread acceptance in the mid-1980s. It is the most validated tool and is used as a benchmark in many studies on the validity of other attachment instruments.

The Preschool Assessment of Attachment (PAA)

Procedure The PAA utilizes the Strange Situation procedure, modified for children who are capable of walking, talking, and opening doors.

What it assesses It enables to identify child's self-protective strategy and possible prevailing distortion of the strategy, or evidence that the strategy is not functioning effectively for the child.

Classification system It is based on Ainsworth's three categories and identifies: patterns B1–5, patterns A1–2 and C1–2, and compulsive patterns A3–4 and obsessive patterns C3–4, as well as mixed patterns A/C and modifiers (Dp, [ina]).

Advantages and limitations Like SSP, it enables to distinguish low-risk anxious patterns from those requiring intervention. The limitations are the same as the SSP.

Validity PAA took over 5 years to be validated. It is currently the best attachment assessment tool for children aged 2–5. The other existing assessment method (Cassidy-Marvin) accounts for much less variance in results and predicts future development less well than the PAA (Crittenden, 2007a; Spieker & Crittenden, 2010).

The School-Age Assessment of Attachment (SAA)

Procedure The SAA (Crittenden, 2007b) is a semi-structured interview that is audio-recorded, then transcribed *verbatim*. The child is asked to tell a made-up story and then an autobiographical event on seven picture cards representing increasing levels of danger. The interviewer explores the child's understanding of their feelings and motivations, as well as their understanding of others' perspectives. Information is derived from discourse analysis, including what the child says, what they should have said but didn't, disfluencies, and how the child interacts with the interviewer.

What it assesses The SAA is particularly useful for identifying: (1) the child's primary problems (which experiences or relationships are currently a source of distress); (2) how the child obtains security and comfort and how they process information (their attachment strategies); (3) whether their self-protective strategies are functional.

Classification system DMM model up to school age (A1–4, B, C1–6, A/C), plus unresolved trauma/loss, Dp, and [ina].

Advantages and limitations The manifest behavior of children in this age group can be characterized by dissimulation or exaggeration of evidence regarding their problems, and therefore, true mental states can elude even the most trained "clinical eye." The SAA is a non-invasive tool that allows access to implicit information. It can be used in the child's home, at school, or in a clinical setting and requires approximately 1 hour for administration.

Among its limitations, it should be noted that many of the conditions that frighten or distress children are not fully understood by them, nor are they detailed in the seven stimulus figures. Additionally, the SAA does not provide information on parenting strategies and, therefore, should not be used *in isolation*.

Validity Several empirical studies have been published to date (e.g., Crittenden & Newman, 2010; Kwako et al., 2010; Nuccini et al., 2015; Carr-Hopkins et al., 2017).

The Transition to Adulthood Attachment Interview (TAAI)

Procedure It is a semi-structured interview lasting approximately 1 hour, audio-recorded, then transcribed *verbatim*. It uses a modified version of the Adult Attachment Interview (AAI). The modification takes into account the skills and salient issues of young adults during the transition to adulthood (~16–25 years). It includes questions about attachment relationships, friendships, romantic relationships, and autonomy from parents. Some questions "surprise" the interviewee, inducing moderate stress that activates their self-protective strategy. The TAAI is analyzed using the DMM method of discourse analysis (Crittenden & Landini, 2011), where the content of the interview (what happened) is less important than the form of the discourse.

What it assesses The attachment assessment through the TAAI identifies: (1) how the adolescent/young adult obtains security and comfort and they process information (their attachment strategies), (2) whether their self-protective strategies are functional and if there are unresolved traumas that could trigger extreme behaviors,

(3) what the main problems are. The TAAI probes the same information in multiple ways, enabling exploration of conflicting ideas that may motivate incompatible behaviors.

Classification system It identifies the same configurations and modifiers as the SAA, with the addition of strategies A5–6.

Advantages and limitations The same as we shall mention for the AAI.

Validity Validity studies are ongoing.

The Dynamic Maturational Model Version of the Adult Attachment Interview (DMM-AAI)

Procedure It is a semi-structured interview that takes between 60 and 90 minutes, focusing on childhood experiences and how they may influence current thoughts and behaviors, particularly as parents. The interview is audio or video-recorded, transcribed *verbatim*, and blind-coded using the DMM discourse analysis method (Crittenden & Landini, 2011). Like the TAAI, it elicits the same information through multiple representative modalities, and the topics are ordered from neutral to more dangerous.

What it assesses It provides a self-protective strategy, a list of unresolved dangerous events (losses or traumas that can be unresolved in different ways), and modifiers of the basic strategies (depressed, disoriented, reorganizing, intrusions of prohibited negative affective states, expression of somatic signs), as well as a subject-interpreted developmental history.

Classification system All DMM strategies, singularly or in combination, including traumas and modifiers.

Advantages and limitations It provides a comprehensive analysis of the information-processing mode, highlighting the functionality of the strategy, the degree of flexibility, and the impact of any traumatic experiences on behavior. It takes approximately 2 years to learn the coding system.

Validity It has been validated in studies that have used functional magnetic resonance imaging, the Strange Situation, and transgenerational configurations in normative population samples, as well as on a variety of clinical problems (for a review, see Farnfield et al., 2010).

The Parents' Interview (PI)

Procedure The Parents' Interview is a semi-structured audio and video-recorded interview that consists of a series of questions that require caregivers to consider (a) their own childhood, (b) their functioning as a couple and in raising their children. The children are present in the room, and parents are asked to manage any problems that may arise from the presence of their children. Managing multiple tasks and issues at the same time during the interview simulates the conditions that trigger parenting problems. The transcript is analyzed using the DMM discourse analysis method, and the video is also studied to gain a procedural view of family functioning.

What it assesses The information obtained includes: (1) an approximation of the attachment strategies of family members, (2) a brief developmental history of the parents, (3) the level of parental reasoning (LR), which is how the parent organizes decisions regarding child care. The LR provides insight into the parent's flexibility and sensitivity in interpreting their children's behaviors and responding to them, guiding recommendations for intervention in case of problems.

Classification system For basic protective strategies, the same system as the DMM-AAI is used; for parental reasoning, Levels of Parental Reasoning.

Advantages and limitations The Parents' Interview does not allow for a detailed analysis of strategies like in individual interviews, but it offers the advantage of capturing interactions in situations of moderate stress and observing how different strategic configurations function procedurally.

Validity The only published study that used the Parents' Interview indicated that it could differentiate four groups of parents: abusive, neglectful, marginally abusive, and adequate (Crittenden et al., 1991).

3 Applying Attachment Assessment to Case Formulation

3.1 Concept of Functional Family Formulation

Functional Family Formulations (FFF) provide an alternative to descriptive diagnosis by analyzing and explaining problems to indicate specific intervention strategies. They serve as a link between problems and their potential solutions (Flåm & Handegård, 2015; Johnstone & Dallos, 2013; Dallos et al., 2019). In FFF, problems are accurately described and related to the functioning of each individual, explaining the underlying need behind problematic behavior and identifying necessary interventions to modify problematic behavior. Instead of solely focusing on the needs of the designated patient, the needs of all family members are considered.

To explain many of the problems that arise within families, general functional formulations (GFF) are also employed, which synthesize common family experiences. For example, psychoses are considered responses to unresolved conflicts between behaviors and demands of the emerging context and incompatible demands from previous developmental environments. The psychotic crisis is the result of an inability to resolve such conflicts.

In FFF, Problem Description Is Functional

The focus of the DMM theory on protection and reproduction leads to a functional definition of behaviors. Observable behavior serves the purpose of promoting self, partner, and offspring safety and well-being, and it is considered "adaptive" to the extent that it achieves this goal.

Based on past experiences (especially those involving danger), we learn to transform information in a way that is advantageous for safety and comfort. The current response may be the result of transformed dispositional representations or interferences due to learning failures (trauma).

Understanding the nature of past and present dangers and the ways information is transformed from the perspective of each family member allows for the reconstruction of the function of problematic behaviors.

Different dangers may be addressed in a similar manner and lead to the same types of behavioral problems or symptoms (equifinality), while the same danger can be addressed with different behaviors (multifinality). Moreover, the function of a behavior or symptom at a given stage of development may change in subsequent developmental periods.

Functional meaning is primarily indicated by the form of the information, and this will be consistent with the content only in the presence of significant intra- and interpersonal coherence. Therefore, considerable attention must be given to the source and form of information, possible biases it may contain, and preconscious processes that influence behavior.

In FFF, Problem Description Connects Intrapsychic Functioning with Interpersonal and Family Functioning

Individual differences in response to danger coincide with patterns of interpersonal behaviors and intrapersonal modes of information processing. To understand behaviors, it becomes crucial to consider both dimensions instead of relying on just one.

DMM formulations integrate multiple sources of information gathered from assessment tools administered to each family member (in the case of PI with the family present).

Each strategy is related to those of other family members to explain problematic behaviors and hypothesize future risks. This holistic view not only allows for more accurate formulations but also guides changes in a way that does not threaten family dynamics, thus avoiding the activation of additional dysfunctional defensive modes.

Central elements of FFF are "critical dangers" and "critical causes of change." The former identifies factors around which family members' strategies have been organized (e.g., father's alcoholism, mother's fear of abandonment, parents' trauma from the death of a child, etc.). Critical causes of change, on the other hand, refer to the factors to intervene upon to generate intra- and interpersonal changes. A crucial critical cause of change often relates to attachment, i.e., the mode of information processing, opening up to awareness, more balanced ways of integrating information, reflection, and clear communication to enhance adaptation to the current context.

3.2 From Attachment Assessment to Case Formulation

After administering and coding attachment assessment tools and gathering historical information, the expert is ready for the process of reflective integration. In addition to attachment, it is necessary to assess organic adaptation (biochemical imbalances, sleep problems, chronic pain, etc.), developmental history (especially exposure to dangers), adaptation to the current context (employment, economic issues, social network, etc.), and the availability of appropriate services.

The formal coding of assessments highlights hidden or implicit problems, as well as the transformations of information used by each family member. The expert analyzes each person's self-protective strategies and, for parents, also identifies their strategies for protecting their partner and children.

This level of analysis helps identify needs that fall into the second and third levels of Maslow's hierarchy (Maslow, 1943; see Fig. 4), which should be addressed only after ensuring a response to the needs at the first level of the hierarchy.

The expert must keep in mind the complexity of perspectives, needs, and strategic modalities and avoid simplifications, maintaining an empathetic approach toward all family members. The result of this reflective process is a "functional family formulation" that places considerable importance on discrepancies between information, especially inexplicable ones that indicate obscure points for the expert, or those missing from the coding, unknown to the family, or deeply hidden ("the unspeakable").

3.3 From Formulation to Intervention

FFFs describe past and current functioning and indicate possible developmental pathways toward change, suggesting not only the necessary interventions but also the temporal sequence of these interventions based on what is urgent for the family and what its members can grasp.

In clinical practice, it is not always possible to derive a complete FFF, but it is necessary to proceed gradually through systemic reasoning, leaving open areas of

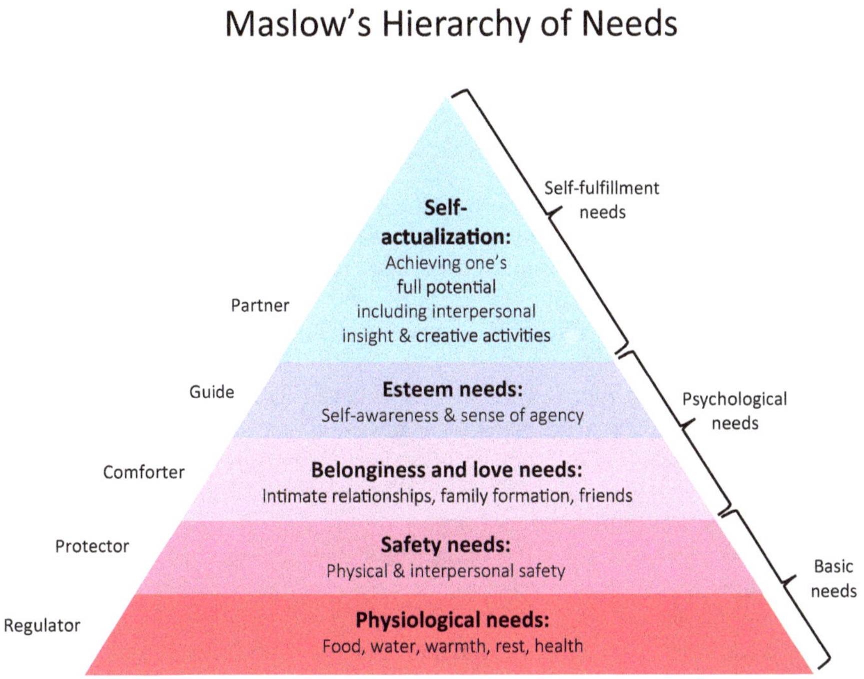

Maslow's Hierarchy of Needs

Pyramid levels (bottom to top):
- **Physiological needs:** Food, water, warmth, rest, health — Regulator
- **Safety needs:** Physical & interpersonal safety — Protector
- **Belongingness and love needs:** Intimate relationships, family formation, friends — Comforter
- **Esteem needs:** Self-awareness & sense of agency — Guide
- **Self-actualization:** Achieving one's full potential including interpersonal insight & creative activities — Partner

Right-side brackets: Basic needs (Physiological, Safety); Psychological needs (Belongingness, Esteem); Self-fulfillment needs (Self-actualization).

Fig. 4 Maslow's hierarchy of needs

unavailable information (ongoing dangers, family functioning level, Maslow's hierarchy of needs, parental reasoning, strategy exploration).

Formulation is a dynamic process that evolves and should be able to assimilate new information as it emerges in the clinical work process.

The most effective formulations are those that are not misled by transformations of family members, allowing the practitioner to gradually help the family discover implicit aspects of their experience, including those outside their awareness (Dallos, 2019).

DMM formulations are generated through a gradual and collaborative process of sense-making in relation to danger and comfort among the individuals involved and their perspectives.

3.4 A Case of Psychosis

As a child, Stefano had not raised major concerns with his parents. The mother recalls some reprimands from teachers for aggressive behavior toward classmates and a certain carelessness both in school and at home.

During adolescence, the first signs of distress emerged, particularly in the form of restrictive eating. He also used to spend a lot of time alone, mostly reading comics, and taking cannabis. During the summer after his exam failure, Stefano's emaciated body resembled that of his favorite superhero. Shortly thereafter, dressed as Captain America and wielding his legendary shield, he attempted to set fire to the house of an alleged pedophile.

After a brief stay in a psychiatric department, he was discharged with a diagnosis of schizoaffective disorder and prescribed medication.

About a year after the episode, Lucia, Stefano's mother, seeks a new clinical intervention with other practitioners when Stefano discontinues the treatment, not recognizing himself in the diagnosis, supported in his decision by his older sister, Valentina.

In the family, arguments over trivial matters have become unbearable for Lucia, who, widowed for a few years, must focus her efforts on saving the family assets, mortgaged because of her ex-husband's fraudulent behaviors and substance abuse. The eldest daughter, Valentina, who returned home after a failed attempt to become autonomous, is another concern for Lucia.

In the new clinical context, the Adult Attachment Interview (AAI) is administered to Lucia and Valentina, while Stefano receives the Transition to Adulthood Attachment Interview (TAAI).

The classification of the mother is rather complex: Dp Ul mother and father (v) maternal grandfather, (p) ex-husband, Utr (p) physical abuse by mother and father and between father and mother, (p) hospitalization of herself and ex-husband, (p) Stefano's breakdown, (p) substance addiction of the ex-husband A3(7)/C3(5)[ina]).

Explanation of the classification Despite evidence that her developmental history was indeed filled with threats, Lucia tends to exempt her attachment figures and excessively idealize them, sometimes even in a delusional manner (A7). She also employs another inhibitory strategy, that of compulsive caregiving (A3). Her solitude is seen as a resource, vulnerability is denied, except for occasional incipient intrusions of prohibited negative affective states ([ina]) and depressive markers (Dp).

Her strategic set also involves displaying anger through openly aggressive behaviors (C3), as well as more controlled and manipulative behaviors (C5), which allowed Lucia to protect herself from some threats from her family of origin. However, the strategy is not entirely functional in the current context as perceived by Lucia, as indicated by various markers during the interview (Dp). There are also numerous interferences with basic strategies caused by unresolved losses (parents, maternal grandfather, ex-husband) and traumas (physical abuse by parents, between parents, hospitalization of herself and the ex-husband, ex-husband's substance dependence, and Stefano's breakdown), most of which in a preoccupied form (p).

Valentina's strategy is also rigid, characterized by numerous transformations of information, and maladaptive: Dp Ul (p, dp, dlr) p, (v) paternal aunt, (dp) father, Utr (ds, v) parental separation, (ds, dn) physical abuse, (dpl) sexual abuse (A3(7) [ina]).

Explanation of the classification Valentina has developed a strategy of compulsive caregiving (A3). Like many children living in dangerous family contexts, in order to tolerate the proximity of dangers posed by attachment figures and match it with the need for protection and comfort, she has developed an extreme strategy of delusional idealization of attachment figures (A7). In her case as well, dysregulated behaviors may occur as a result of momentary inability to inhibit prohibited negative affective states [ina]. Valentina perceives the ineffectiveness of her protective strategies (Dp), which do not have a grip on her life context, presumably also because of unresolved losses (father and paternal aunt) and traumas (parental separation, abuse). Valentina's arousal is dysregulated, and her thought processes are highly distorted.

The delusional idealization does not seem ready to be accompanied by more functional strategies yet. Currently, it leads her toward delusional projects of "repairing the fate of the world," joining unruly people and thus expressing anger against movers and shakers. Traumas she has experienced (such as sexual abuse) are also exposed to this delusional transformation of information.

In the initial interview before her brother, Valentina appears to be more competent and compliant with the task of providing a presentation of herself and the problems from her point of view. Her opening statement: "We're here for him, who is schizophrenic." Stefano instead, pressed by his sister, indulges in rambling speeches not always coherent with the topic of the question, with torrential and obscure sentences about esoteric and idealistic topics, urged by his sister.

Surprisingly, these aspects related to the form of the discourse have not been observed in Stefano's TAAI interview, which is classified as: Utr (ds) parental separation and father's substance addiction R [C3,5,6△→B].

Explanation of the classification The most reassuring and unexpected information, if compared to the case history and the first interview, is the reorganization toward a more balanced strategy.

Like his sister and mother, Stefano has not learned enough from significant past events such as his parents' separation (during which he was also triangulated, △) and his father's substance dependence. Both events are treated in a distancing way (ds), meaning Stefano sets aside negative experiences and the impact of these events on himself. Over the years, he has developed a strategy focused on the manifestation of negative affective states, of both vulnerability and invulnerability (C3,5,6), but he is currently reorganizing (→B). He has already begun to include in his strategic mode previously excluded informations (e.g., his own vulnerability, the perspective of others), reflecting integration of different sources of information (without automatically prioritizing negative affective states, sensations, or images).

Functional Family Formulation Stefano's father died after a long agony, in a condition of destitution primarily linked to the consequences of his substance dependence. Around the events that led to the father's ruinous decline, all members of the family organized themselves in a dysfunctional way, starting with Lucia, each with their own strategic ways that, however, did not effectively function to ensure a satisfying balance against the repercussions of the events. Especially for Lucia, her husband is still unburied. The theme of the ruin he caused still worries her as if he could still squander the assets she has painstakingly preserved. The trauma thus originated affects her equilibrium and her relationships with her children. For example, when Stefano uses substances, Lucia acts reacting to traumatic memories (rather than tuning in to what is happening) and struggles to assume a normative containing role toward him. The mixed emotions she displays (fear, guilt, anger…) leave everyone confused.

Stefano had to face the unpredictability created by numerous family secrets (infidelities, serious illnesses, etc.) and maternal oscillations. Mother was certainly caring and focused on the boy's perspective and affective states (A3 component of the maternal strategy), but with an alternating preference for her own point of view and negative affective states that she displayed openly (C side of the strategy), and unregulatedly ([ina]). It was difficult for Lucia to tune in to Stefano when her mind was preoccupied with her traumas and/or when the boy displayed negative affective states. Over time, Stefano learned to control them (C5,6) without transforming them into words. Mother was present, but presumably not when he needed her most. She showed involvement, but often depending on the conflicts with her husband ($\triangle$). She was attentive to him and protected him from real dangers (better than she had done with his sister), but also from dangers her mind represented in distorted and anachronistic ways and that had to be kept hidden. Stefano lacked information about the dangers from which his mother wanted to protect him, and he lacked the ability to communicate clearly. By seeking help through his initially lethargic and resigned behaviors, and later with his emaciated body, he found a (distorted) way to communicate fear and suffering, but also anger toward his mother's inadequacy, and to gain more visibility and obtain predictability. At the cost of autonomy.

Mother's attempt to stop the progress of suffering generated new forms of distress that she herself found difficult to understand.

On the other hand, the older sister had learned to gain closer proximity by making her attachment figures feel good. She had been able to resolve the conflict between fear and the need for comfort by denying the former and delusionally representing the latter. For a long time and improperly, she had absolved her attachment figures by attributing excessive responsibility to herself when things went wrong. In the transition to adulthood, as often happens to individuals who use extreme Type A strategies, she had experienced anxiety about leaving the family. Without anger and fear, it was impossible for her to escape by granting herself a break without the burden of the past being too heavy, so as to prepare what was necessary for the future. She had attracted the wrong partner, as often happens to those who fail to orchestrate their own reorganization before important choices, and her excursion away from home had been brief and painful. She couldn't move forward, couldn't stay, couldn't blame others. Until Stefano's breakdown.

Stefano's breakdown brings the underlying family distress to the attention of extra-familial context. Similarly to when he was a child at school, albeit in a more extreme way, he expresses in relationships his fear of being too fragile with anger and resentment. The psychotic gesture of dressing as a superhero and seeking justice contrasts with the sense of futility and inhibition, offering an escape to the family.

Thus, the psychiatric diagnosis reveals the underlying family crisis while keeping the family problems obscure. The family focuses on cognitive problems and somatic symptoms, and the development of the children stagnates under the weight of the crisis. The rigidity of the family structure, the presence of unspeakable issues, particularly related to trauma, have prevented the necessary redefinition of family dynamics required for the transition to adulthood. The GFFG of psychosis helps to explain the temporal contingency of the breakdown. There may have been excessive fear regarding change (children leaving home) driven by irresolvable conflicts. For Lucia, who is so eager to rely on her own strength and autonomy, the self-sufficiency of those two apparently fragile children was both desired and feared. Perhaps, in witnessing the suffering and struggles of her children to achieve an independent life, she saw her own autonomy undermined while witnessing the reactivation of the theme of ruin.

For Valentina, taking care of her mother and seeking comfort outside in romantic relationships appeared as two irreconcilable desires. Stefano's breakdown represented both a threat to the stability of the mother and an opportunity to come back home to help her mother and make more acceptable the failure of her own autonomy project.

Stefano had not learned to trust his mind when it told him there were no dangers: his mother was too alarmed to make him feel truly safe, yet too secretive to focus his attention on defined dangers. With that distrust in his own mind, he felt safer within domestic boundaries where unspeakable problems were hidden, that could be brought to attention through his emaciated body. Mother's anxiety about financial collapse and need to regain autonomy had made impossible these solutions. He had to hurry, but how? He had never been efficient enough to feel capable of doing so. His exam failure had further hindered his timid progress. Vulnerability had to be fought against, and anger redirected.

Since the breakdown, Stefano and Valentina team up with each other and before his sister Stefano's dysfunctional patterns are reactivated, despite the availability of new, more functional patterns. Complex situations may seem made easier by symptoms and diagnoses; not unusually, after an initial resistance to the diagnosis, the family returns to the safety of the diagnostic label ("We're here because he is schizophrenic"), which keeps the unspeakable problems obscure.

Treatment Plan The change project should primarily address the issue that "obsesses" the mother (mortgages) and consequently concerns Valentina, who, on the other hand, disbelieves she can impact on the situation as she would like, so she shifts the struggle to extra-familial territories. Such translation has been more effective for Stefano, as he can rely on a Type C strategy that also engages his mother, activating her.

It is time for Lucia, Valentina, and Stefano to bury the hatchet and work together to protect common interests, to enhance the good remains amidst the ashes of their past, and to ensure the safeguarding of family assets: a necessary precondition for any other developmental project. There are first-level needs (see Fig. 4) the family must look after with the help of professional.

Once greater stability is achieved in concrete asset matters, they must be assisted in providing a "definitive burial" for the father and in giving up some past experiences. The work of processing traumas can be addressed in a therapeutic context where dialogue and reflection on complex family events are facilitated, and can subsequently be integrated with targeted and individual interventions (e.g., EMDR).

After clarifying the family history, reflection on future plans, particularly for the two children nearing adulthood, can be initiated. Valentina is the most challenged by this transition. She is excessively permeable to others' perspectives, while self-related information (especially fear) has a disintegrating effect on her. Although she has not received a diagnosed status, her functioning is significantly maladaptive. At this point, her vulnerabilities hinder the task of choosing a reproductive partner (she risks to attract complementary individuals) and of pursuing autonomous life plans. Certainly, she cannot proceed along those paths with her mind burdened by the history of her entire family.

Stefano's request for an update in therapy must be listened to. In the family's developmental pathway, he is the one situated at the most advanced point, the one who has signaled the distress within the family and is reorganizing his strategies. His positioning in the transitional phase to adulthood is an additional advantage. Having more opportunities than his sister, Stefano can be a resource for the family, and his autonomy can be an additional critical cause of change. The reorganization process needs to be consolidated and further promoted right away through specific individual support interventions.

3.5 When, Who, and How to Assess

When to assess Conducting a comprehensive assessment for the construction of a complete FFF (Functional Family Formulation) is time-consuming and costly. However, these burdens counterbalance the costs and impact of omitted or incorrect interventions. In cases where a screening of the family history shows few dangers and good availability of interpersonal resources, and when sufficiently high metacognitive capacities are observed, a complex evaluation may be unnecessary. In such cases, it may be sufficient to proceed directly with general services, such as psychoeducational interventions and stress reduction techniques.

Conversely, formal assessment should always be undertaken when:

1. Many important problems cannot be discussed explicitly from the beginning;
2. It is not possible to develop a meaningful formulation (because the data are too scarce to lead to explicit hypotheses about specific strategies used by family members, and about the critical danger that seems to organize family functioning).
3. Implemented interventions are not effective.

4. Before deciding to remove a child from her family.

As previously emphasized, some individuals are unable to put in words their most important problems and to account for their behaviors. This largely depends on their reflective skills and on their chances of reflecting on thinking the current context. Even people capable of reflection can have problems.

All families have periods in which the problems of their members affect the functioning of the entire family. It is important to differentiate between families able to manage properly their problems on their own—possibly requiring temporary assistance—and those in need of a comprehensive assessment of their needs.

Some individuals are able to recognize problems, attribute the appropriate importance to them, find for themselves a coherent meaning, take on the responsibility of solving them, and undertake proper actions (including seeking psychological help when the problem has a psychological side). Their level of information transformation does not compromise any step of information processing.

In these cases, the practitioner usually has a clear perception of the situation, agrees with the definition of the presenting problem, and can provide the required help, which often involves making available new information or different perspectives that the person (or parents, in the case of parent training) can integrate into their existing knowledge and effectively utilize.

Unfortunately, this is not the case in the majority of child protection cases, or with patients who tend to significantly transform information. In these cases, the practitioner feels confused, perceives many discrepancies or incongruences, and realizes she cannot rely on the terms in which the presenting problem is defined, nor she has the chance to develop a rough knowledge, i.e., a meaningful formulation (not even with the possibility of implementing it with the progress of treatment and the emergence of new information) or to identify who needs what.

Often, the attitude of these individuals is characterized by distrust in the possibilities of change and by suspicion towards the practitioner who, in turn, feels uncomfortable perceiving minimization, denial, displacement, or exaggeration of the problem from the patient's side.

Given their ways of processing and facing problems, usually these families have many problems gathered in their history. Several members of the family have long-standing, unresolved issues. Multiproblematic families, unlike resilient individuals, do not have any confidence in their ability to cope with problems. This lack of trust often stems from multiple failures of previous solution attempts, which are often generated by incorrect recommendations by professionals.

Different interventions or treatments require different skills and readiness on the part of their beneficiaries. If applied to patients or families who are not yet ready to receive them, interventions can be ineffective or even harmful. A gradient of change-focused interventions, ranging from educational interventions to psychotherapy, should be considered instead. Educational interventions, which are most commonly provided, require developed reflective abilities on the part of patients (or parents in the case of parent training). Whereas patients or parents who primarily act on an automatic and preconscious basis have limited chances of effectively using new information in their daily lives, especially when urged by personal or child-related dangers.

Furthermore, even when psychotherapy is necessary, if correct information about protective strategies and information processing is lacking, the approach can be incorrect, leading to consolidation of maladaptive transformations (such as inhibition or exaggeration of negative affective states), or proving to be futile (preventing the patient from learning the provisional and flexible quality of strategies).

Who to assess In DMM thinking, symptoms are seen beyond their negative and distressing appearances. Symptoms can serve as positive regulators, maintaining a sort of miraculous reciprocity in the significant relationships of the person, despite adverse or discrepant environmental conditions. Trauma symptoms are considered significant indications of an urgency to complete a learning process that was interrupted long ago.

The question is what the person is ready to learn. To make sound hypotheses in this regard, a thorough understanding of the person and her family is crucial. For individuals and for family, change can be necessary and threatening at the same time. Sometimes children protect the parents from the threat saying: "It's me, I'm the problem!" So, assessments and interventions are improperly focused on the problematic child. In such cases, if practitioners collude with this presentation, they get involved in the family's risk.

When a child is labeled as having a problem, such as autism, attention deficit and hyperactivity disorder (ADHD), conduct disorder, or an eating disorder, the focus might be diverted from the family processes that contribute to problematic behaviors. This occurs because discrepancies are often ignored rather than resolved. If a child employs an extreme strategy, it is because the dangers in her environment are extreme. Thus, attention must be directed to danger, with a comprehensive evaluation of *all* family members.

A DMM assessment addresses the contextual problems that a child tries to solve with symptoms, as well as the problems of adult patients seeking consultation. Among the collected information, the crucial focus is on the dangers experienced as well as the current problems and traumas.

How to assess The process from tool selection to feedback should be organized taking into account the Zone of Proximal Development of the individuals involved. The tools introduced above have the property of respecting the development of the person's acquired skills, and of assessing in a more structured way what the person is not yet able to grasp in terms of guidance and interventions. Information on the person obtained from these tools mainly concern experienced dangers, learned strategies to cope with these dangers, the strategy's adaptiveness, and possible interferences caused by traumas, provided that the tools are used correctly by experienced professionals.

In more complex cases, to create a treatment plan, a Functional Family Formulation (FFF) should be developed. FFFs focus on exposure to dangers, on the ability to transform the information gathered at the time of exposure to the significant events, and on subsequent reorganizations, as have been specified in the formal assessment. FFFs promote change suggesting an intervention plan consistent with the developmental level of each family member.

Change means that family members show a broader articulation of initial strategies; show strategies consistently adjusted with each member's developmental phase, functioning as a resource for interacting family members, and flexible to updating in order to suit new contexts. Often, individuals start since formulation to improve their skills to learn from the reviewed experience.

4 Conclusions

The main focus regarding change is on circumstances (current dangers, resources, etc.) and psychological processes (how individuals process information). Psychological processes change over the course of development creating new opportunities for strategic organization within families. Those who have not been protected from dangers and/or comforted have the opportunity to increase their sense of safety and comfort through new possible strategies. There is still hope.

In most extreme developmental contexts, the mind can either construct its own world in which it is never caught off guard by dangers, or create an illusory world. When strategies become progressively less adaptive, it is necessary to consider the distorted ways of perceiving and attributing meaning. Treatment should therefore focus on the shortcuts that generate maladaptation.

With disillusioned individuals who expect not to be understood, change occurs in relationships. Primarily with a therapist capable of assuming different perspectives and holding them in mind systemically, negotiating new trajectories as a good attachment figure should do.

It should not be underestimated that people who suffer often come from developmental contexts where they have experienced rejection and failures. The task of experts is to restore confidence in the possibility of change, reducing further experiences of failure and detachment. These individuals deserve the best opportunity for security and comfort: to do this, we must change the way we understand and help them.

Delivering useless or harmful interventions and overlooking necessary treatments has a significant impact on families and individuals. Experiences of failure are perceived in a way that assigns responsibility to the family rather than to the professionals who, with inadequate indications, contribute to the maintenance or exacerbation of maladaptation.

People who have not been helped to recognize, correct, and make their maladaptive strategies flexible are labeled as uncooperative, resistant to change, or oppositional. As failures accumulate, family resources become less accessible, and trust in change diminishes.

It has been repeatedly emphasized that a formal, comprehensive, and valid assessment focused on protective strategies and information processing allows for the identification of necessary and usable interventions for patients in pursuit of desired changes.

DMM is centered around hope. Even when individuals engage in behaviors that are dangerous for themselves or their children, there is hope. What individuals cannot do for themselves or their children can be done by figures who fulfill attachment functions and offer or facilitate safety and comfort to those who are suffering. The DMM approach suggests that individuals who engage in pathological behaviors resulting from mental illnesses, and those who endanger their children by violating ethical and legal standards, are not intrinsically different because: (1) they have experienced childhood dangers and have been in danger like their own children, (2) they suffer from the consequences of past dangers and problems they cannot resolve, (3) pathological and dangerous behaviors are generated, at least in part, by implicit processes.

An evaluation that captures these aspects and describes problematic behaviors from this perspective points the way toward change and increases the possibility of engaging even the most mistrustful individuals.

Recap Exercise

1. Which of the following statements are true and which are false?

   ___Attachment is a bond between two people in which one person protects and comforts the other.
   ___Attachment behavior is the behavior used to evoke protection and comfort.
   ___Attachment configuration is the organization of attachment behavior used to evoke protection and comfort.

2. How do you define maladaptation, and which theoretical model do you refer to, if any?

   _____
   _____
   _____
   _____

3. How is maladaptation defined in the DMM?

   _____
   _____
   _____
   _____

4. How do you define psychological trauma, and which theoretical model do you refer to, if any?

   _____
   _____
   _____
   _____

5. How is psychological trauma defined in the DMM?

   _____
   _____
   _____
   _____

6. Do you remember the four conditions that warrant a formal assessment?

   1. _____
   2. _____
   3. _____
   4. _____

7. What are the two central elements of Functional Family Formulations (FFF)?

   ☐ Critical dangers
   ☐ Functionality of strategies
   ☐ Critical causes of change
   ☐ Functioning of each family member

Recap Exercise Answers

Exercise 1. All three answers are true.

Exercise 3. Maladaptation, including pervasive psychiatric disorders, corresponds to the failure to adapt the strategy to the life context.

Exercise 5. Trauma coincides with failed learning, indicating a gap between basic strategies (what is known) and what is necessary to know for safety in a particular context.

Exercise 6. A formal assessment should be undertaken when many significant problems cannot be discussed verbally from the beginning, when it is not possible to develop a meaningful formulation, when implemented interventions are not effective, and before deciding to remove a minor from their family.

Exercise 7. The central elements of FFF are "critical dangers" (factors around which family members' strategies are organized) and "critical causes of change" (factors to intervene on to generate intra- and interpersonal changes).

References

American Psychological Association. (2021). Special issue: Adverse childhood experiences: Translating research to action. *American Psychologist, 76*, 2.

Baetz, C. L., & Widom, C. S. (2020). Does a close relationship with an adult reduce the risk of juvenile offending for youth with a history of maltreatment? *Child Maltreatment, 25*(3), 308–317.

Baldwin, D. V. (2013). Primitive mechanisms of trauma response: An evolutionary perspective on trauma-related disorders. *Neuroscience and Biobehavioral Reviews, 37*(8), 1549–1566.

Banner, N. F. (2013). Mental disorders are not brain disorders. *Journal of Evaluation in Clinical Practice, 19*, 509–513.

Barrett, L. F. (2020). *7 1/2 lessons about the brain*. Houghton Mifflin Harcourt.

Bateson, G. (2000). *Steps to an ecology of mind: Collected essays in anthropology, psychiatry, evolution and epistemology*. The University of Chicago Press. (Testo originale pubblicato 1972).

Carr-Hopkins, R., De Burca, C., & Aldridge, F. A. (2017). Assessing attachment in school-aged children: Do the SAA and Family Drawings work together as complementary tools? *Clinical Child Psychology and Psychiatry, 22*, 400–420.

Clark, A. (2016). *Surfing uncertainty: Prediction, action and the embodied mind*. Oxford University Press.

Coghill, D., & Sonuga-Barke, E. J. (2012). Annual research review: Categories versus dimensions in the classification and conceptualisation of child and adolescent mental disorders--Implications of recent empirical study. *Journal of Child Psychology and Psychiatry, 53*(5), 469–489.

Crittenden, P. M. (1990). Internal representational models of attachment relationships. *Infant Mental Health Journal, 11*(3), 259–277.

Crittenden, P. M. (1992). Quality of attachment in the preschool years. *Development and Psychopathology, 4*, 209–241.

Crittenden, P. M. (1995). Attachment and psychopathology. In S. Goldberg, R. Muir, & J. Kerr (Eds.), *John Bowlby's attachment theory: Historical, clinical, and social significance*. The Analytic Press.

Crittenden, P. M. (1997). Toward an integrative theory of trauma: A dynamic maturation approach. In D. Cicchetti & S. Toth (Eds.), *The Rochester symposium on developmental psychopathology*. University of Rochester Press.

Crittenden, P. M. (1999). "Atypical attachment in infancy and early childhood among children at developmental risk", VII. Danger and development: The organization of self-protective strategies. *Monographs of the Society for Research in Child Development, 64*(3), 145–220.

Crittenden, P. M. (2007a). CARE-Index: Infants coding manual [Unpublished manuscript]. Family Relations Institute, Miami, FL, USA.

Crittenden, P. M. (2007b). School-age assessment of attachment. Coding manual [Unpublished manuscript]. Family Relations Institute, Miami, FL, USA.

Crittenden, P. M. (2016). *Raising parents: Attachment, representation, and treatment* (2nd ed.). Routledge.

Crittenden, P. M., & Landini, A. (2011). *The adult attachment interview: Assessing psychological and interpersonal strategies*. Norton.

Crittenden, P. M., & Newman, L. (2010). Comparing models of borderline personality disorder: Mothers' experience, self-protective strategies, and dispositional representations. *Clinical Child Psychology and Psychiatry, 15*(3), 433–451.

Crittenden, P. M., Partridge, M. F., & Claussen, A. H. (1991). Family patterns of relationship in normative and dysfunctional families. *Development and Psychopathology, 3*, 491–512.

Crittenden, P. M., Spieker, S., & Farnfield, S. (2021). Turning points in the assessment and clinical applications of individual differences in attachment. In D. S. Dunn (Ed.), *Oxford bibliographies in psychology*. Oxford University Press.

Dallos, R. (2019). *Don't blame the parents: Intention and change in family therapy*. McGraw Hill.

Dallos, R., Crittenden, P. M., Landini, A., et al. (2019). Family functional formulations as guides to psychological treatment. *Contemporary Family Therapy, 42*, 190–201.

Dallos, R., Crittenden, P. M., Landini, A., et al. (2020). Correction to: Family functional formulations as guides to psychological treatment. *Contemporary Family Therapy, 42*, 190–201.

Damasio, A. R. (1996). The somatic marker hypothesis and the possible functions of the prefrontal cortex. *Philosophical Transactions of the Royal Society, 351*(1346), 1413–1420.

Devitt, A. L., Addis, D. R., & Schacter, D. L. (2017). Episodic and semantic content of memory and imagination: A multilevel analysis. *Memory & Cognition, 45*(7), 1078–1094.

Eagleman, D. M. (2011). *Incognito: The secret lives of the brain*. Canongate.

Edwards, F. (2019). Family surveillance: Police and the reporting of child abuse and neglect. *The Russell Sage Foundation Journal of the Social Sciences, 5*(1), 50–70.

Edwards, V. J., Holden, G. W., Felitti, V. J., et al. (2003). Relationship between multiple forms of childhood maltreatment and adult mental health in community respondents: Results from the adverse childhood experiences study. *American Journal of Psychiatry, 160*(8), 1453–1460.

Ellis, B. J., Abrams, L. S., Masten, A. S., et al. (2020). Hidden talents in harsh environments. *Development and Psychopathology, 16*, 1–19.

Farnfield, S., et al. (2010). DMM assessments of attachment and adaptation: Procedures, validity and utility. *Clinical Child Psychology and Psychiatry, 15*(3), 313–328.

Felitti, V. J. (2009). Adverse childhood experiences and adult health. *Academic Pediatrics*. https://doi.org/10.1016/j.acap.2009.03.001

Feldman, R., & Vengrober, A. (2011). Posttraumatic stress disorder in infants and young children exposed to war-related trauma. *Journal of the American Academy of Child and Adolescent Psychiatry, 50*(7), 645–658.

Flåm, A. M., & Handegård, B. H. (2015). Where is the child in family therapy service after family violence? A study from the Norwegian Family Protection Service. *Contemporary Family Therapy, 37*, 72–87.

Haslam, N., Williams, B., Prior, M., Haslam, R., Graetz, B., & Sawyer, M. (2006). The latent structure of attention-deficit/hyperactivity disorder: A taxometric analysis. *Australian and New Zealand Journal of Psychiatry, 40*, 639–647.

Hughes, J., Hardy, G., & Kendrick, D. (2000). Assessing adult attachment status with clinically-orientated interviews: A brief report. *British Journal of Medical Psychology, 73*(Pt 2), 279–283.

Johnstone, L., & Dallos, R. (2013). *Formulation in psychology and psychotherapy: Making sense of people's problems*. Routledge.

Kendell, R., & Jablensky, A. (2003). Distinguishing between the validity and utility of psychiatric diagnoses. *American Journal of Psychiatry, 160*(1), 4–12.

Khoury, B., Langer, E. J., & Pagnini, F. (2014). The DSM: Mindful science or mindless power? A critical review. *Frontiers in Psychology, 5*, 602.

Kim, H., Wildeman, C., Jonson-Reid, M., et al. (2017). Lifetime prevalence of investigating child maltreatment among US children. American *Journal of Public Health, 107*(2), 274–280. https://doi.org/10.2105/AJPH.2016.303545

Künster, A. K., Fegert, J. M., & Ziegenhain, U. (2010). Assessing parent–child interaction in the preschool years: A pilot study on the psychometric properties of the toddler CARE-Index. *Clinical Child Psychology and Psychiatry, 15*(3), 379–390.

Kwako, L. E., Noll, J. G., Putnam, F. W., & Trickett, P. K. (2010). Childhood sexual abuse and attachment: An intergenerational perspective. *Clinical Child Psychology and Psychiatry, 15*(3), 407–422.

Landini, A., Crittenden, P. M., & Landi, G. (2016). The parents of child psychiatric patients. *Annals of Psychiatry and Mental Health, 4*(7), 1087.

Maslow, A. H. (1943). A theory of human motivation. *Psychological Review, 50*(4), 370–396.

Masson, J. B., Laurent, F., Cardona, A., et al. (2020). Identifying neural substrates of competitive interactions and sequence transitions during mechanosensory responses in Drosophila. *PLoS Genetics, 16*, 2.

Nuccini, F., Paterlini, M., Gargano, G., & Landini, A. (2015). The attachment of prematurely born children at school age: A pilot study. *Clinical Child Psychology and Psychiatry, 20*, 381–394.

Opendak, M., Gould, E., & Sullivan, R. (2017). Early life adversity during the infant sensitive period for attachment: Programming of behavioral neurobiology of threat processing and social behavior. *Developmental Cognitive Neuroscience, 25*, 145–159.

Pace, A. L., & Bufford, R. K. (2018). Assessing adult attachment: Relation and validity of two dynamic maturational approaches. *Interpersona, 12*(3), 232–252.

Perry, R., & Sullivan, R. M. (2014). Neurobiology of attachment to an abusive caregiver: Short-term benefits and long-term costs. *Developmental Psychobiology, 56*(8), 1626–1634.

Perry, R. E., Blair, C., & Sullivan, R. M. (2017). Neurobiology of infant attachment: Attachment despite adversity and parental programming of emotionality. *Current Opinion in Psychology, 17*, 1–6.

Raballo, A., Meneghelli, A., Cocchi, A., Sisti, D., Rocchi, M. B., Alpi, A., & Hafner, H. (2014). Shades of vulnerability: Latent structures of clinical caseness in prodromal and early phases of schizophrenia. *European Archives of Psychiatry and Clinical Neuroscience, 264*, 155–169.

Schacter, D. L., & Tulving, E. (1994). *Memory systems*. The MIT Press.

Sloman, L., & Sturman, E. D. (2012). The impact of winning and losing on family interactions: A biological approach to family therapy. *The Canadian Journal of Psychiatry, 57*(10), 643–648.

Spieker, S. J., & Crittenden, P. M. (2010). Comparing the validity of two approaches to attachment theory: Disorganization versus danger-informed organization in the preschool years. *Clinical Child Psychology and Psychiatry, 15*, 97–120.

Sullivan, R. M. (2017). Attachment figure's regulation of infant brain and behavior. *Psychodynamic Psychiatry, 45*(4), 475–498.

Sutherland, M. R., & Mather, M. (2012). Negative arousal amplifies the effects of saliency in short-term memory. *Emotion, 12*(6), 1367–1372.

Vygotsky, L. S. (1978). *Mind and society: The development of higher psychological processes*. Harvard University Press.

Wakefield, J. C. (2015). Psychological justice: DSM-5, false positive diagnosis, and fair equality of opportunity. *Public Affairs Quarterly, 29*(1), 32–75.

Wilkinson, A., Lantos, H., McDaniel, T., et al. (2019). Disrupting the link between maltreatment and delinquency: How school, family, and community factors can be protective. *BMC Public Health, 19*(1), 588.

Part IV
Training in the Therapeutic Relationship

Alliance Ruptures and Repairs

Laura E. Captari and Catherine F. Eubanks

1 Introduction

A cisgender European-American man in his seventies, George presented to time-limited relational psychotherapy for depression and relationship problems at an alliance-focused training research program (Muran & Eubanks, 2020) in New York City. A cisgender European-American woman in my thirties, I [LEC] was in my final year of doctoral training. George explained that he was estranged from most of his family, and for the last decade, had been preoccupied with a woman he had grown to deeply care for, but felt paralyzed in expressing those feelings. In our sessions, I too felt rather paralyzed: sometimes lost in the details of George's meandering stories, often made sleepy by his monotone voice, frequently struggling to get a word in as he jumped in to fill the silence. It seemed that George's words obscured, rather than facilitated, meaningful connection. When I did successfully engage George in dialogue, his responses made it difficult to establish an alliance. Sometimes he questioned my ability to help, speaking down to me or hinting that I could not understand because of my younger age. In other moments, he turned the attack inward: "I'm so morose and boring—you'll get bored listening to me, just you wait. Nobody can stand me. That's why my relationships always fall apart." In

---

L. E. Captari (✉)
The Albert and Jessie Danielsen Institute, Boston University, Boston, MA, USA

Wheelock College of Education & Human Development, Boston University, Boston, MA, USA
e-mail: lcaptari@bu.edu

C. F. Eubanks
Gordon F. Derner School of Psychology, Adelphi University, Garden City, NY, USA

Brief Psychotherapy Research Program, Mount Sinai Beth Israel, New York, NY, USA

these moments, I often felt baffled and backed into a corner. But also, *he was on to me! I* was *bored sometimes!*

George shared, quite despondently, that he had worked with six therapists across his lifetime, including couples' therapists with both of his previous wives. When I expressed curiosity about what brought him back to treatment, George was upfront in admitting that he was not optimistic about our work. "This is just who I am... the way it's always been," he lamented. George described his childhood as "an emotional desert." He elaborated, "What I was feeling couldn't be shared at all, there was no one I knew who I could relate to, and anything remotely intense like sadness, desire, or attachment was forbidden." George found an escape in music "to cover the emotional emptiness... a kind of heavy deadness," and spent much of his career as a musician. When his first wife separated and took their young children, he did not protest, reasoning that "they are better off without my depressive influence." I felt that heavy deadness permeating our sessions but was unsure how to intervene. How could I spark some curiosity, some movement? If nothing else, how could I stay psychically alive and engaged?

In moments where we seemed to be getting closer to touching George's pain, he often shifted the conversation. With a deep sigh, he'd lament, "Whatever's in the past is in the past" or "I don't know... I'm not really sure what more to say. I've talked about all this stuff before," then move on quickly to another topic. Despite his ambivalence, George always came early, ensuring he brought payment and thanking me for my time. In our eighth session, George was once again trying to convince me that he was a hopeless case, and I found myself becoming paralyzed. Trying to regain my subjectivity, I said, "I'm getting the sense you feel *so* stuck and lonely, but when you describe these painful things, you discount your experience by saying 'that's just how it is,' and I'm sitting here feeling deeply sad." George began to cry. Pointing to his face, he said simply, "tears." We sat in silence, sharing this moment.

Just after this session, the COVID-19 pandemic hit New York City. I called to let George know that the clinic would be transitioning to telehealth, and we realized our only option would be to continue by phone, since George did not have Internet access. George pressed hard to come in person, emphasizing he did not think COVID was a big deal and, besides, therapy was very important to him. When I asserted that meeting in person unfortunately would not be an option, he snapped back, "I'm not interested. Meeting by phone would be an *impoverishment* of the process!" Caught off guard by the intensity of his affect, in supervision, I began to metabolize the many layers of George's emotional and relational impoverishment from which his anger emerged. I struck a deal with George—to meet for one session on the phone as an experiment and make a decision from there. We survived that phone session, and scheduled to meet again, but there was an echo of truth in his prediction. George spoke very quietly, and I often had to clarify or ask him to repeat himself. On one level, we were unwittingly sucked back in time, enacting the relational theme from his life of not feeling seen, heard, or understood.

During the pandemic, George spent a lot of time doing puzzles, and in our work, we aimed to put relational pieces together in the context of the therapeutic alliance. George reflected about how he tried to be easy-going and accommodating, but could not help being guarded and distant: "I feel like I can't ask for help. I can't say what I want... I'm always just so afraid of the hammer coming down." "The hammer?" I inquired. "With men, it's being punished, them being annoyed by me... with women, I'm always eventually left." In the next session, George elaborated about how "emotions and relationships are not so clear, it's like a language I never learned. .. I don't know the steps of the dance—who's leading, who's being asked to lead. I always just try to be there and be of service, but not request anything." As we continued to explore this area, George described a sense of "loosening... relief, regret. It's the beginning of a lot of things I missed. Things I miss even now." In moments of therapeutic traction, George was able to recognize, "When painful emotion comes out in me, I detach," and noted "a little bit of expectant curiosity inside, like something might be hidden there." Drawing on his expertise in foreign languages, we began to explore emotional communication as a language that can be learned. George noted little things he began to do more often: calling his kids, reaching out to old friends. Yet despite these signs of progress, George's despondency and profound aloneness spilled across the phone. At times, I found it difficult to bear this, and more than once broke down in supervision as I was hit with the deep sadness, regrets, and hopelessness that he carried. Given the context of the research program's 20-session limit, I would be yet another woman in his life who would leave. How could we best use the time we had?

In this chapter, we explore the vicissitudes of rupture and repair from the joint perspective of the clinician [LEC] and supervisor [CFE], drawing on key moments in treatment with George. While clinical training often emphasizes building the therapeutic alliance, considerably less attention is given to navigating alliance ruptures. This can lead to internalized pressure to be constantly "in sync" with patients, when in reality, mismatch and misunderstandings are a part of *all* human relationships. What happens *next* following a therapeutic rupture matters most.

2 What Are Alliance Ruptures?

The therapeutic alliance is a dynamic process that involves (a) developing and maintaining an emotional bond, (b) collaborating toward shared tasks and goals, and (c) intersubjective negotiation around differences (Bordin, 1979; Muran & Eubanks, 2020). Like other human relationships, the therapeutic dyad will inevitably experience tensions and disagreements, known as *alliance ruptures*. Ruptures can be understood as dyadic phenomena occurring on a continuum, ranging from small mismatches and misunderstandings (e.g., missing what a patient said) to significant conflicts and disagreements (e.g., divergent views about treatment focus) that result in a breakdown in collaboration.

For many beginning clinicians, the language of "ruptures" can stir up feelings of self-doubt and inadequacy—as if we have failed and the treatment is over. On the contrary, research suggests that ruptures are quite common across various theoretical orientations, occurring in 20–50% of sessions according to patients and 33–100%

of sessions based on observer-rated measures (Muran & Eubanks, 2020; Eubanks et al., 2018). Left unattended, ruptures can precipitate poor treatment response or premature termination; however, ruptures can be—and frequently are—successfully worked through in order to re-establish and potentially deepen trust, understanding, and collaboration. Rupture resolution occurs in 20–80% of cases according to patients and can catalyze positive outcomes (Eubanks et al., 2018). As one example, a study of cognitive behavioral and psychodynamic-interpersonal treatment for depression found that, across both groups, patients who reported repaired ruptures evidenced greater improvement compared with those who did not report ruptures at all (Stiles et al., 2004).

While ruptures that are not attended to can jeopardize the therapeutic process, when meaningfully addressed, repair and resolution processes can become a crucible for change and growth. This recognition frees us to become increasingly curious about how the alliance may be shifting in the moment-to-moment process—both verbal and non-verbal—of each session. A rupture is not evidence of being an incompetent therapist, but rather, a cue that something important is unfolding. Though it is uncomfortable to sit with and metabolize feelings of confusion, frustration, or anger—and difficult to do so while remaining attentive and connected to a patient—these moments are ripe with therapeutic potential. Across theoretical orientations and modalities, an alliance focus can provide rich understandings of patients' interpersonal difficulties and stuck points that brought them to treatment. Rather than *talking about* a problem, we begin to *live through it* together in real time. Working through discord and conflict in the context of an attuned, responsive other can be a corrective experience for patients who expect criticism and rejection. Maintaining a stance of humility, cultivating self-compassion, and becoming curious about what is happening in the here-and-now can free clinicians and supervisors to tap into a wealth of data.

3 Recognizing and Tracking Rupture Processes

Ruptures signal that the dyad is struggling to negotiate relational dialectics between motivations toward (a) personal agency and self-definition in tension with (b) communion and connectedness (Muran & Eubanks, 2020; Safran & Muran, 2000). Ruptures can be understood through the lenses of mentalization and intersubjectivity, as a breakdown in collaboration frequently involves difficulties recognizing and understanding the existence of others' mental states (e.g., thoughts, feelings, beliefs, desires) and life experiences as distinct from one's own. In contrast, a strong, flexible alliance facilitates mutual recognition, in which we can acknowledge—rather than trying to blot out—each person's subjective experience and cultural identities rather than collapsing "difference to sameness" (Benjamin, 1994, p. 234). With this theoretical framework in mind, let's get practical. What are the tell-tale signs of a rupture? We can focus on two indicators: interpersonal markers (e.g., patient and therapist behaviors) and intrapersonal markers (e.g., therapist emotions). The first can be seen, the second can be felt.

3.1 Interpersonal Rupture Markers

Ruptures involve relational movements that disrupt the dyad's ability to engage meaningfully and authentically. Like a dance gone wrong, these moves stem from difficulties negotiating and collaborating around issues of power, control, and intimacy. Each turn of speech and associated non-verbal behavior can move a person (a) *against* the other, oneself, or the work of therapy (confrontation ruptures) or (b) *away from* the other, oneself, or the work of therapy (withdrawal ruptures). In some cases, there may be a mix of both. These movements may be made by either member of a dyad—patient or therapist, supervisee or supervisor. Worksheet 1 outlines questions to help elucidate potential ruptures that may be in play.

Confrontation moves involve a dialectic compromise such that communion is sacrificed in pursuit of personal agency and autonomy. When a patient moves against the therapist or the therapeutic process, they may become defensive, reject an intervention (e.g., "this won't help me!"), complain about treatment tasks, progress or parameters, coerce the therapist by becoming seductive or overly friendly, or criticize the therapist as a person (e.g., question their competence, engage in microaggressions). Such moves are efforts to control or pressure the therapist and may range from passive aggressive behaviors to overt verbal attacks. Confrontation ruptures were interwoven in therapeutic work with George. Early on, he questioned my [LEC] ability to understand him and expressed skepticism that change was possible, especially via phone sessions. In other moments, he turned the attack inward to the tune of self-loathing.

When a therapist moves against the patient or the therapeutic process, they may unwittingly begin to pathologize, depersonalize, or talk down to the patient, rigidly enforce expectations (e.g., homework completion, session attendance) without collaborating to understand the patient's unique situation, or force-fit a theory by insisting on an interpretation or recommendation while neglecting the patient's perspective. In some moments with George, I [LEC] could get narrowly focused on linking his off-putting responses toward me with the relational challenges that brought him to treatment. It can be excruciating to sit with deep despair, and such interpretations offered me the tantalizing promise of regaining a sense of clinical efficacy, as if to communicate passive-aggressively, "It's not that you can't be helped—it's that you don't *want* to be helped." Yet, even if the content was accurate, this line of reasoning missed the intensity of George's mental anguish. Acknowledging the "inherently pejorative" pitfalls of such relational moves, Wachtel (2011) notes, "How we speak to patients is clearly not just a matter of technique but depends quite crucially on how we *think about* them" (p. 133).

In supervision, trainees may move against a supervisor (or, in group supervision, against fellow trainees) by rejecting their ideas, being overly defensive about the trainee's own ideas, criticizing the supervisor, challenging the supervisor's authority, blaming the supervisor or the supervision group for difficulties the trainee is experiencing in their clinical work, or putting excessive pressure on the supervisor or supervision group to rescue the trainee from a difficult case. Similar to therapists, supervisors can move against their trainees by criticizing them, condescending to them, or pushing the supervisor's view and agenda on the trainee without taking time to hear and validate the trainee's needs and experience. Supervisors need to work with a trainee's zone of proximal development (ZPD; Vygotsky, 1930/1980), the range between the trainee's current developmental level and the more advanced level that they can reach with scaffolding and support. Even a well-intentioned supervisor may inadvertently move against a trainee by failing to work within their ZPD. A supervisor who has unrealistically high expectations that exceed a trainee's ZPD may blame the trainee for failing to meet the supervisor's expectations, whereas a supervisor who underestimates a trainee's ZPD may be overly controlling and provide excessive structure or support that the trainee finds stifling or patronizing.

Withdrawal moves involve a dialectic compromise such that personal agency is sacrificed in order to maintain some semblance of communion. When a patient moves away from the therapist, the therapeutic process, or a difficult emotional state, they may give minimal responses (e.g., yes, no, mhm), become silent, shift the topic, engage in avoidant storytelling, or evidence a split between content and affect (e.g., laughing while speaking about something painful). In treatment with George, his long, meandering stories filled the space with words, but kept me [LEC] at a distance. When difficult affect surfaced, his minimizing responses of "whatever's in the past is in the past" or "this is just who I am" blocked meaningful exploration. Yet, over time, George began to develop the capacity to notice how "when painful emotion comes out in me, I detach" and became curious about learning the language of emotion. Paradoxically, patients may also withdraw from themselves and their own needs by becoming overly compliant, deferential and appeasing (e.g., passively agreeing to whatever the therapist says), or demeaning themselves, while idealizing the other. Echoes of this came through when George expressed the hope that I could offer life-changing insights that his six previous therapists had missed.

When a therapist moves away from the patient, the therapeutic process, or a difficult emotional state, they may begin to talk abstractly (e.g., intellectualizing, psychobabble), shift the conversation topic or session focus, or become overly accommodating and protective of the patient to avoid potential conflict. As my [LEC] work with George progressed, I became more aware of moments when I was talking too much, or in an abstract way, and how the more George withdrew from me, the more I felt pulled to fill the space with words, which only led to more withdrawal on his part.

Due to the evaluative nature of supervision, withdrawal ruptures are probably more common than confrontation ruptures in a supervisory context (Friedlander, 2015). Research on Alliance-Focused Training (AFT) has documented more frequent, impactful withdrawal ruptures in supervision compared with confrontation ruptures (Eubanks, Sergi, & Muran, 2021; Eubanks, Warren, & Muran, 2021). Trainees may move away from the supervisor, the supervisory process, and their own training needs by being overly deferential and passively complying with whatever the supervisor says. Trainees who are anxious about being criticized or appearing incompetent may be liable to present their clinical successes and avoid showing video or describing the moments of struggle, where they stand to benefit the most from supervision. I [LEC] definitely lapsed into this early on in group supervision; when my anxiety got the better of me, I tended to minimize just how lost and confused I felt. Over time, supervision supported a parallel process—I became more vulnerable with the group about my difficult countertransference feelings, and George became more forthcoming with me about the intensity of his sadness and regret. Trainees may also withdraw from supervision by taking up time and space with overly intellectualized theoretical discussions or unnecessary and tangential background information about their cases. Supervisors may withdraw via excessive focus on didactics or logistics and paperwork to avoid more challenging tasks such as providing difficult feedback about a trainee's limitations or clinical errors.

Moments of rupture can include elements of both confrontation and withdrawal, and these mixed ruptures are sometimes particularly confusing. Disentangling the elements of confrontation and withdrawal can be helpful for better understanding what is taking place. For example, a patient may suddenly harshly criticize the therapist, and the therapist may be bewildered by this criticism that seemed to come out of nowhere. The element of confrontation is obvious, but the therapist's confusion is a clue that there may be a more complex rupture process at work—the patient's confrontation may have also functioned as a withdrawal, as an effort to shift the topic away from a sensitive topic that was making the patient feel anxious or vulnerable. Mixed ruptures often emerged with George, which sometimes left me [LEC] feeling like I was herding cats—always trying to catch up and metabolize what was happening in our moment-to-moment process. With appreciation for what is realistically possible in any one session, supervision offered me an anchoring and reflective space to literally "replay the tape" and track one speech turn at a time. Yet, this sort of in-depth analysis in the presence of fellow trainees and my supervisor was only possible in the context of establishing a group alliance. Immersing ourselves together in a non-judgmental understanding of the unfolding process in George's treatment increasingly freed me from harsh and anxiety-provoking internal dialogue, which otherwise could have easily been projected onto others' remarks, questions, and feedback in supervision.

Therapists are generally interpersonally skilled at being supportive and validating, and as a result, may be particularly likely to engage in subtle, complex ruptures in an effort to smooth over conflicts or soften critical feedback. For example, a therapist may criticize a patient's lack of motivation, but enfold that criticism in an expression of empathy for the patient's difficult circumstances. There may be a particularly high likelihood of subtle ruptures in supervision (see Eubanks, Sergi, & Muran, 2021; Eubanks, Warren, & Muran, 2021). Supervisors and trainees may mask criticism or tension behind humor or intellectual discussions. From the supervisor's [CFE] perspective, this supervision group struggled at times with subtle ruptures. As has been observed, the group established a degree of trust and cohesion, but once that supportive space was created, trainees had difficulty expressing disagreements or grappling with the sense of competitiveness that they sometimes experienced. As the supervisor, I also wrestled with when and how to point out this process and invite exploration, and worried that if I launched an exploration prematurely, I would risk alienating or shaming a trainee. At times, the ruptures were so subtle that I was unsure about what was happening; for example, was the group bonding over a joke or smoothing over a conflict?

The risk with complex, mixed ruptures is that the strain in the alliance may be harder to recognize or understand, and this may obscure the need for an optimal path toward repair. A helpful line of exploration in supervision about George—as we reflected on both the therapeutic and the supervisory process—was *what is my agenda, hope, or fantasy behind this interpretation or intervention? Might there be an "edge" to that response, and if so, what's happening for me? What am I anxious about, frustrated by, or worried might happen? How might I be positioning or adapting myself, and in the service of what?*

3.2 Intrapersonal Rupture Markers

In the heat of a rupture, it can be difficult to keep a clear head and maintain a nondefensive stance of empathy, validation, and curiosity about what is unfolding. When we feel blindsided, we are much more likely to take up the maladaptive dance. The patient withdraws, we confront. They confront, we withdraw. Both of us withdraw, smoothing over potential conflict by intellectualizing or overaccommodating. Or both of us confront, engaging in power struggles to preserve our sense of self. Whatever the sequence of relational moves, emotions serve as the background music. After all, it's hard to dance without a tune! Our internal emotional states often signal the emergence of an alliance rupture. Yet, trainees may be initially uncomfortable discussing these experiences in supervision, presuming that these feelings substantiate their lack of skill and competence. On the contrary, these emotions arise as part of human experience and reveal important information about what is happening in the clinical situation. Worksheet 2 can serve as a starting point to explore relevant meanings.

A patient who is disengaged, gives minimal responses, or falls silent in a nonreflective manner often elicits feelings of frustration, anxiety, and powerlessness as the therapist grapples with how to best to engage them. This was certainly a clue for me [LEC] that some rupture process was unfolding with George, even if I could not immediately identify the specifics. Feeling bored or vaguely annoyed can indicate that avoidant storytelling or intellectualization is in play, moving the therapeutic process away from difficult or vulnerable emotion. When a patient unquestionably agrees with everything the therapist says, feelings of elation, discomfort, or confusion may arise. This could signal the patient's movement away from their internal experience (e.g., placating the therapist) in order to regulate the risks of authentic relational engagement. Finally, feeling pity rather than empathy may be a sign the patient is engaging in self-attack, which is also a form of withdrawal from relational collaboration. George's self-degrading remarks initially evoked a desire in me to prove him wrong. I idealistically tried to create a new relational experience (e.g., providing emotional attunement and responsiveness), but failed to recognize the kernel of truth in George's self-attack: while he complained of loneliness, another part of him was terrified of emotional vulnerability. Ironically, he "brought the hammer down" on himself before anyone else could.

Confrontation moves by the patient often feel controlling or off-putting. When a patient criticizes the therapist or questions their ability to help, the therapist may feel attacked or devalued. With George, this was captured in moments where I [LEC] felt talked down to or backed into a corner. Such dynamics may be intensified based on differences in cultural background and identities, as well as social location. George was an older white man whose dismissing comments communicated his skepticism that I could understand his experience. As an early career clinician who is a woman, this activated my own insecurities and sense of being an imposter. This patient's critique may have felt even more overwhelming and dysregulating for a therapist of color who lives within the sociocultural context of oppression. In supervision, I grappled with how to stay connected to my professional identity and a realistic awareness of my skills and training, rather than enacting patriarchal dynamics. I needed to learn to hold my ground, to intervene at times to slow George down, to challenge him and offer a different perspective. I needed to find a different way of approaching George than I would navigate talking with my grandpa. Trainees and supervisors should also attend to intrapersonal rupture markers when they emerge in the supervisory relationship. Anxiety is a common, and understandable, trainee emotion. When a trainee feels anxious, this may be due to remembering or anticipating an attack from their patient, or experiencing an attack from their own inner critic as they reflect on clinical mistakes and missed opportunities. However, trainee anxiety may also indicate that they are in a confrontation rupture process with their supervisor, who is perhaps subtly (or not so subtly) criticizing or pressuring them. Alternatively, anxiety could be an indication that the trainee feels alone and unsupported due to supervisor withdrawal.

From the supervisor's [CFE] perspective, I contributed to Laura feeling inadequately supported during the transition to telehealth at the beginning of the COVID-19 pandemic. As George pressured her to continue seeing him in person, she naturally turned to me for guidance on how to proceed and what the research program would allow. During this chaotic period, I was also trying to get clarification from the clinic administration, and for a time, I did not have an answer. Probably in part due to my own sense of being overwhelmed as the city began to shut down, I failed to appreciate how much pressure Laura was receiving from her patient. My withdrawal reaction can also be seen as part of a larger pattern that occurred throughout our work together. Laura was enthusiastic about AFT and bravely embraced every learning opportunity: she was always ready to show her videos, to participate in a role play, to engage actively in group discussions. Some fellow trainees were more wary about being vulnerable and taking risks, and at times I held myself back from inviting Laura to present in order to focus on coaxing other trainees to share with the group. When I would worry that I was going too far and neglecting Laura, I would reassure myself that Laura was doing well. Based on having been Laura's supervisor over the year, I had substantial evidence that she was a skilled and compassionate therapist. However, my confidence in her abilities likely contributed to a pattern of subtle withdrawals in which I provided insufficient support and failed to nurture my curiosity about our supervisory alliance. Laura probably also felt uncomfortable confronting me about this, and hence, we both kept the peace in group supervision with our withdrawals.

4 Pathways to Restoring the Alliance

The first step toward repairing a rupture is recognizing that a rupture is taking place. This idea is supported by research findings that therapist recognition of rupture is associated with improvements in alliance or outcome (Muran & Eubanks, 2020). Hence, the therapist who has recognized interpersonal or intrapersonal rupture markers has already begun the process of repair. In terms of next steps, therapists need to consider what approach will be most responsive to the patient's needs and the context of the therapeutic alliance in the moment (Stiles et al., 1998; see also Eubanks et al., 2021a). Because ruptures are complex and contextual, we cannot prescribe a specific repair strategy for each type of rupture. Instead, we offer a framework for approaching repair in terms of three pathways: (a) alliance-building strategies, (b) task-related repair strategies, and (c) exploratory strategies. Worksheet 3 provides some suggestions to help therapists in trying to decide which pathway to follow.

Each of these pathways can provide the patient with a corrective emotional experience that facilitates new learning (Alexander & French, 1946), as the patient who is accustomed to moving against or away from the other gains a new experience of what is possible in relationships when they collaborate with another to recognize their needs for agency and communion (Christian et al., 2012). To make this possible, we must remember that ruptures are co-constructed and be willing to acknowledge our contributions to rupture processes as the therapist. Clinicians also need to be prepared for the very real possibility that their initial attempts to address a rupture will not succeed and may contribute to new ruptures. Therapists should strive to flexibly move with the process so that they can respond to the rupture that is happening right now, and not become stuck trying to repair a rupture that has grown stale.

4.1 Alliance Building: Reattuning to Feelings and Intentions

When a therapist realizes that there is some misattunement in the alliance, one pathway to repair is to reattune to the patient's feelings and intentions by continuing to employ alliance-building behaviors that should be part of every therapist's repertoire: listening closely to the patient with compassion and curiosity, clarifying any misunderstandings, recognizing implicit feelings that lie behind the words, and validating the patient's experience. Sometimes these behaviors are sufficient for repair and can provide a corrective experience for a patient who is accustomed to being criticized or ignored.

It is particularly important for supervisors to attend to building a strong supervisory alliance, as the strength of the supervisory alliance impacts both the process and outcome of supervision (Watkins Jr., 2014). In order to help trainees explore ruptures in supervision—both alliance ruptures with their patients and supervisory ruptures—supervisors need to work within the trainee's ZPD, providing enough safety for the supervisee to be willing to be vulnerable, while also challenging the supervisee to tolerate some discomfort and take risks that will help them grow. Supervisors can use alliance-building strategies such as exploring and clarifying trainees' goals and building a supervisory bond by validating their trainee's concerns. Clinicians in training can contribute to a good supervisory alliance by checking the temptation to withdraw—recognizing when they are engaging in avoidant or abstract communication, presenting only their best work, or being overly deferential, and take the risk of sharing their real concerns and clinical struggles with their supervisor.

4.2 Task-Related Repair Strategies

Perhaps all ruptures to some extent involve movement against or away from a task of therapy. A patient might be uncomfortable with an exercise or homework assignment, or both patient and therapist might find that they are avoiding discussion of a sensitive issue. Another pathway to repair involves strategies for addressing these difficulties with therapy tasks. Therapists can clarify the obstacles, internal or external, to engaging with the task. If the patient is confused by the task or does not understand its aim, a therapist can acknowledge how they may have contributed to the confusion by not providing enough explanation, and they can then illustrate the task or provide the rationale for it. A therapist can also collaborate with the patient to renegotiate a therapy task by discussing and making changes to the task in response to the patient's needs and concerns. Therapists can also track when patients are avoiding a task, or withdrawing from a discussion of their concerns about a task, and gently redirect the patient back.

4.3 Exploring the Rupture Experience

Alliance-building reattunement and task-related repair strategies can be thought of as immediate strategies, as both focus on addressing a rupture and getting therapy "back on track." The third pathway involves expressive strategies in which the therapist aims to facilitate exploration of the rupture. A stage-process model of the repair process, refined based on empirical data (Safran & Muran, 1996), provides a framework for thinking about the stages of this exploration. In the first stage, the therapist recognizes and draws the patient's attention to the rupture. In the second stage, the patient and therapist collaboratively explore their negative feelings associated with the rupture. If this process becomes uncomfortable and either patient or therapist starts to withdraw from the exploration, the therapist can draw attention to and explore the avoidance maneuvers (stage 3). In the fourth stage, the therapist and patient focus on clarifying the patient's core relational need that underlies the initial rupture. In the case of confrontation ruptures, this usually involves moving from expressed anger to identifying feelings of disappointment and then making contact with underlying vulnerability and need to be nurtured: a movement toward communion. With withdrawal ruptures, this usually involves moving from exploring avoidance to helping the patient recognize and assert what they really need from the therapist: a movement toward agency. When ruptures involve mixtures of confrontation and withdrawal, we recommend starting with the withdrawal and helping the patient more directly assert the elements of confrontation.

Throughout the exploration process, the therapist can use metacommunication, or communication about the communication process, to invite the patient to collaborate on exploring what is taking place in the here and now (Muran & Eubanks, 2020; Safran & Muran, 2000). Therapists can metacommunicate by exploring the patient's experience (e.g., *What are you feeling right now?*), focusing on the interpersonal field between patient and therapist (e.g., *It seems like we're in some kind of power struggle*), or self-disclosing their experience (e.g., *I'm aware of feeling backed into a corner*). Metacommunication is a form of mindfulness in interaction—an effort to bring awareness to the interaction as it unfolds—and it is important that the therapist approach it with the same accepting, nonjudgmental stance that is encouraged in the mindfulness literature (Kabat-Zinn, 1991/2013). When considering self-disclosure of their experience, therapists should balance being authentic in the moment with making sure their feelings are not too raw, lest they become hostile toward patients. There may be notable individual differences in how patients are able to take in a therapist's subjectivity or not. Very intense feelings are often best processed in supervision before trying to employ self-disclosure with a patient.

As previously noted, therapists taking responsibility for their contribution to ruptures can be an important part of providing a corrective experience. At the same time, every repair strategy holds the potential to create a new rupture. Within the expressive pathway, therapist efforts to acknowledge their contribution by apologizing may function as a form of withdrawal: a hasty apology can foreclose additional exploration of negative feelings. Similarly, drawing links between a rupture and the patient's difficulties in other interpersonal relationships can be a helpful way to generalize their learning, but it can also function as a withdrawal from exploration of the here and now. As therapists engage in exploration of a rupture, it is important that they stay attuned to the interpersonal and intrapersonal rupture markers and the risk of new ruptures emerging—which is not really a question of if, but of when. Therapists can remind themselves that every new rupture is "grist for the mill" as it provides them more data about their alliance with their patient, and that their task is to keep moving with the process.

4.4 Repair Pathways in the Case of George

The three pathways to repair can all be illustrated with George's case. I [LEC] employed alliance-building strategies to attend closely to George's experience and to validate and foster curiosity about his feelings. In our eighth session, as George began to make more emotional contact with his internal experience and became tearful, I sought to validate and reinforce this through self-disclosure.

> Therapist : *You've expressed fear before that if anyone knew your pain, they'd run, but sitting here with you, I notice feeling more connected than we have been.*
> George : *[Nods head]. Huh. [Silence].*
> Therapist : *How does that land with you?*
> George : *It's different... different from what I thought.*

When the pandemic began and we had to transition to telehealth, I employed task-related repair strategies to address George's concerns about this change to the parameters of our work. I explained the rationale for switching to telehealth, explored obstacles to this switch, and brainstormed with him about adjustments we could make to ease the transition. An important part of our work was the third pathway of exploring the rupture experience. Over time, I began to note how both of us withdrew from each other in therapy sessions. The shared expression of "I think we're doing it again" injected playfulness and humor into our exchange, enabling us to pause and reorient the conversation toward what we might be avoiding.

> Therapist : *That relational pattern seems to show up whenever you begin to feel interested in a woman. It's a bit of a paradox. While one part of you really longs for closeness, you end up acting in ways that others experience as guarded or distant, and then she doesn't know where you stand.*
> George : *Ugh. I thought I was the abstract one.*
> Therapist : *You're right! I think we're doing it again... where were we?*
> George : *Me and women. Same old, same old...*
> Therapist : *And I started to get all intellectual on you.*
> George : *Yeah, that stuff doesn't help me much. I've talked about it with therapists before.*
> Therapist : *Yes, so what can we do differently here? I wonder what might be happening that we* both *could be moving away from?*
> George : *[Chuckles] How damn annoying it is to try to do this on the phone.*
> Therapist : *Yes, it sure is. Meeting over the phone sort of feels like we are flying blind. I'm throwing words and ideas at you and hoping that something sticks.*
> George : *Yeah, we're stumbling around in the dark.*

My hope is that exchanges like this provided George with a new relational experience that may have helped to shift, even a little, his beliefs about what is possible in interpersonal interactions. By exploring our shared experience of ruptures, I could, at least for a moment, join George, so that he was not alone in his hopelessness and despair. Reflecting together during termination, George noted how our work together had helped to increase his awareness of how he navigated relationships.

> George : *I'm beginning to accept the painful realities of life and realize that emotional awareness and sharing is what has been missing. But I'll probably go back to my usual routine of not reaching out to anyone. Part of me has this sense it's all a dead end. Maybe it's too late for me.*

Therapist	: *You sound defeated, like you feel like you're ending therapy in the same place you started.*
George	: *Well, I learned some things, and I appreciate you not giving up on me. But no therapy relationship is fully real, and I'm still so alone... At least, I hope you got what you needed for training.*
Therapist	: *Yes, I sense the loneliness you carry, and even more-so right now as things are so uncertain and scary. I remember back when we had to switch to the phone how you weren't sure about continuing. I'm glad you did. Maybe we've put a few puzzle pieces together, even if there are a lot left in the box...*

We continued by discussing George's perspective about therapy options moving forward, given the limitation of the context in which I was working. Our ending is a reminder that rupture repair truly is a process—it is not a one-time event in which a problem is solved in a neat and tidy way. Alliance ruptures, especially with patients with significant interpersonal difficulties, are complex, and every step forward in repair can contain the seeds of another rupture. The goal, especially in a time-limited treatment, is to increase the patient's—and the therapist's—awareness of how they navigate interpersonal interactions, and this includes awareness of our limitations. Particularly for trainees, who may feel pressure to prove their clinical worth, it is important to accept that ruptures and repairs are co-constructed and, hence, the therapist cannot save the day all on their own. But attending to ruptures does put us in the best possible position to facilitate collaboration and positive change by helping to keep patients engaged in therapy, as rupture repair is associated with reduced dropout (Muran et al., 2009; Safran et al., 2005).

4.5 *Repairing Supervisory Ruptures*

When ruptures in supervision emerge, supervisors can attend to them and use them as valuable opportunities to model skillful repair (Friedlander, 2015). Task-related repair strategies may feel more comfortable than exploring supervisory ruptures for supervisors and trainees, especially if the supervision is conducted in a group and there is concern about embarrassing or shaming a trainee. However, if a supervisor is willing to model humility and vulnerability by noting when supervisory ruptures occur and acknowledging their contribution to them, this can have a powerful impact on trainees and strengthen the supervisory alliance. As supervisors explore the supervisory rupture, they can use metacommunication to not only facilitate repair but also as a means of narrating some of their experience and decision-making in a way that is educational for trainees.

Exploring moments of rupture and attending closely to one's intrapersonal experience have the potential to bring up vulnerable feelings or painful memories for trainees, and supervisors and trainees need to be mindful of the teach/treat boundary and keep the focus on the trainee's struggles with their case. At the same time, just as therapists need to track the temptation to withdraw when exploring a rupture, trainees and supervisors need to attend to movements away from exploration of a supervisory rupture. For example, there may be a temptation to view a supervisory rupture as an instance of parallel process, where the trainee's difficulty with the supervisor is a reflection of the struggle the trainee is experiencing with their patient. This can be a useful observation, but it can also be an effort to move away from a strain in the supervisory alliance by shifting the focus to the therapy case and therefore may be a missed opportunity to gain a powerful firsthand experience of rupture repair.

5 Alliance-Focused Training and Supervision

Individual and group supervision can be powerful learning contexts for beginning to notice and track relational moves of withdrawal and/or confrontation. Supervisors can help contain trainees' anxieties about needing to get it "right" by modeling curiosity, humility, and empathic validation of the complexity—and fruitfulness—of attending to relational processes. Alliance-Focused Training (AFT; Eubanks et al., 2019; Muran & Eubanks, 2020) is a supervision approach that focuses on training therapists to recognize and repair alliance ruptures and has been demonstrated to contribute to improvements in interpersonal process for trainee therapists and their patients (Muran et al., 2018). AFT's three primary strategies are useful tools that can be incorporated into supervision and/or personal reflection to enhance rupture repair skills:

1. Mindfulness training, which usually takes the form of engaging in a mindfulness exercise at the beginning of supervision. This practice helps the trainee and supervisor orient themselves to noticing their interpersonal and intrapersonal experience in the present moment in a focused, yet nonjudgmental way. This awareness facilitates recognition of rupture markers.
2. Videotape analysis of rupture moments, where trainees are encouraged to bring their most difficult moments to supervision, ideally with videotape from the session. As supervisor and trainee watch the session clip, the trainee attends to their internal experience and tries to articulate it in words. This practice can help clinicians increase their awareness and understanding of their own emotions, as well as increase affect regulation capacities. Clearly, it is important that trainees develop sufficient safety in supervision in order to productively process most difficult moments.
3. Awareness-oriented exercises, which utilize techniques such as gestalt empty-chair and two-chair practice to support trainees in metacommunication. For example, a trainee may imagine their patient is in the empty chair and practice metacommunicating about their experience of a conflict that they and their patient are engaged in. Or, a trainee may move back and forth between the two chairs, alternately playing themselves and their patient, to explore how a metacommunication might be received and experienced by both members of the dyad.

These three strategies are opportunities for trainees to engage in a form of deliberate practice, that is, high concentration practice that leads to expert performance by stretching one's abilities and fostering the development of effective mental representations of important tasks (Ericsson et al., 1993).

In research studies (e.g., Muran et al., 2018; Urmanche et al., 2021), AFT is conducted as group supervision, and the group format is helpful in two ways. First, engaging in videotape analysis and awareness-oriented exercises in a group increases the pressure on the trainee similar to the pressure they may feel when navigating a rupture with a patient. The literature on athletic and academic performance highlights the importance of practicing under pressure to improve one's ability to perform in stressful situations (e.g., Beilock, 2010). Practicing under pressure also helps challenge the trainee to work in their ZPD, rather than staying where they feel most comfortable. The risk-taking involved in AFT contributes to a deeper supervision experience (Urmanche et al., 2021). Second, exploring ruptures in a group provides opportunities for validation and support as trainees bear witness to each other's difficulties and see firsthand that all therapists contend with challenging ruptures (Eubanks et al., 2019).

From the perspective of the supervisor [CFE], one way that AFT was helpful for Laura's work with George was through the use of role plays to help her cultivate a nonjudgmental awareness of and curiosity about her experience. Trainees are often uncomfortable when they experience a negative reaction to a patient, as it may violate their image of how an empathic therapist should be. When I saw that Laura was having difficulty understanding or accepting her reactions to George, I encouraged her to do a role play in which she would either play George while another trainee played the therapist, or she would play both George and herself, moving back and forth between the chairs. I encouraged her to metacommunicate about her experience in the therapist role, to not only explore her own negative reactions of boredom and frustration but also to risk sharing them with George. I reminded her that this was a role play—a space where she could experiment and "play" with being radically honest with herself and her patient without fear of going too far, as this was just an exercise. This process helped her take new risks, and in the process, become less stuck in the rupture and her own self-judgments. I knew we were making progress when we reached a point in the role play when Laura metacommunicated to her patient, moved to the other chair to respond as George, and then stopped. I asked her, "What do you think George would say now?" She said, with some surprise and confusion, "I don't know." I answered, "Good! We are onto something! This is new territory." This was a natural stopping point, as the goal of the role play was not to find all the answers or script out the next session, as therapists need to be ready and adaptable to meet the patient where they are at, but rather to help Laura move from feeling stuck and self-critical into a position of compassion and curiosity about what she and George were experiencing.

Clinicians in training who do not have the opportunity to engage in AFT group supervision can still draw on these strategies to enhance their rupture repair skills. For example, they can use mindfulness exercises (e.g., attending to their breath) to foster nonjudgmental awareness. Practicing mindfulness right before a therapy session has been linked to better session quality (Dunn et al., 2013; Stone et al., 2018). Trainees who are able to video record sessions can engage in their own videotape analysis of challenging moments in addition to bringing those moments to supervision. All trainees can also keep process notes, journaling about their emotional reactions to patients directly after each session. Emotion journals are a form of expressive writing, which has been shown to have positive impacts on psychological and physical well-being (Frattaroli, 2006). Trainees can also employ awareness-oriented exercises as part of individual deliberate practice. This could include playing out a difficult moment from a session, physically moving from one chair to another chair to role-play the patient and then themselves, practicing metacommunication out loud, and attending to their thoughts and emotions as they do so.

6 Multicultural and Systemic Considerations

Across clinical settings and theoretical orientations, a focus on rupture and repair can provide a shared language for trainees, supervisors, and treatment teams, helping everyone involved tune in with the "pulse" of the alliance in a flexible, transtheoretical manner (see Eubanks et al., 2022). We know from research that treatment responsiveness and collaboration matter more in real-world treatment settings than fidelity to any one particular model; as Norcross and Wampold (2018) describe, clinicians co-create "a new therapy for each patient" (p. 1889). Thus, the rupture markers and potential repair pathways described in this chapter are best understood as an orienting framework and guiding heuristic, rather than an exhaustive or prescriptive protocol. It is vital to recognize and be curious about the diverse ways the alliance may be negotiated based on (a) cultural values (e.g., individualistic vs. collectivistic), (b) communication styles (e.g., low vs. high context), (c) embedded norms for therapeutic relationships (e.g., the patients' expectation of a therapist being collaborative vs. prescriptive), (d) treatment setting (e.g., inpatient vs. outpatient vs. in-home or school-based), (e) similarities or differences in the therapeutic dyad (based on race, ethnicity, religion, class, gender, age, ability status, etc.), and (f) the patient's life history and transference dynamics. Core needs of agency and communion can be embodied in manifold ways and may be differentially salient based on individual and contextual factors (Asnaani & Hofmann, 2012).

As one example, in an individualistic, low-context culture, explicitly acknowledging a withdrawal rupture and exploring what is being avoided may be quite effective, because it is customary for information to be directly stated and individual experience is an important value. However, in more collectivistic, high-context cultures that prioritize maintaining harmony, such a directive approach by the therapist could evoke shame and exacerbate the rupture, as communication is typically more indirect, relying significantly on tone, non-verbal cues, and underlying meanings. In such treatment situations, rupture markers may be much more subtle and effective repair strategies are likely to be more nuanced and implicit. While a thorough examination of cultural responsiveness is beyond the scope of this chapter, we encourage trainees and supervisors to examine rupture and repair processes through the lens of cultural humility (Hook et al., 2017). This includes (a) maintaining an accurate view of oneself, including awareness of personal and professional limitations, as well as recognition of what one does not know, and (b) embracing an ongoing commitment to self-examination, inviting feedback from others, pursuing difficult conversations, and owning and working to alter implicit biases (Mosher et al., 2017). Therapists' cultural humility has been found to mediate the relationship between patients' difficult emotions due to a rupture and positive therapeutic outcomes (Davis et al., 2016).

While George's case exemplifies some considerations for individual treatment, a systemic perspective of rupture and repair can also be helpful for group work, which introduces multiple interrelated alliances. In group therapy, each patient develops an alliance with the therapist(s), the group as a whole, *and* other group members individually, any of which may become a context for mismatch, tension, or disagreement, as well as an opportunity for a new, generative experience. Research suggests that group alliance and patients' outcomes are dynamic and reciprocally related, such that strengthening the alliance is associated with individual symptom reduction, and concurrently, patients' clinical improvement predicts growth in their alliance to the group (Tasca & Lampard, 2012). Recognizing group as a social microcosm, recent empirical work has begun to explore how dynamics of privilege, power, and oppression may play out in microaggressions and other cultural ruptures (Miles et al., 2021). "Repairs of ruptures in group are quite complex," Coco et al. (2019) note, "because other group members have to process the rupture even if not directly involved" (p. 352). However, this is also one of group's unique interventional components: all members can gain awareness about how they navigate conflict by withdrawing or confronting and benefit indirectly from social modeling of potential repair strategies (Alldredge et al., 2021). For patients whose lives have been rife with ruptures that sever relationships, working through discord in a way that deepens bonds may be particularly impactful.

Couple and family work introduces unique complexities, including consideration of each member's (a) alliance with each other, (b) with the therapist, and (c) perception of the alliance between their spouse, child, or parent and the therapist. Here, clinicians are tasked with simultaneously developing multiple alliances in a system that has a history together, most often, a system fraught with conflict, tension, and misunderstanding. Each of these alliances interact "in covert as well as overt ways, particularly when family members are in conflict with one another or when one patient's alliance is notably stronger than that of another patient" (Friedlander et al., 2018, p. 356). Several unique dynamics have been noted in systemic therapies, including "split" alliances, which occur when family members develop disparate views about the therapist or the value of treatment, and problematic within-family alliances, which can precipitate therapeutic impasses. This calls for distinct systemically focused repair strategies (Friedlander et al., 2006; Carr, 2019). When withdrawal ruptures are noted, the therapist may support repair through facilitating family members' engagement with the therapeutic process, and in the face of confrontation ruptures, a focus on re-establishing safety within the therapeutic system may be a first step. To address within-family ruptures, therapists may focus on increasing within-family collaboration through developing a shared understanding of challenges and treatment goals. In the context of problematic alliances such as triangulation or scapegoating, therapists may prioritize strengthening boundaries between family subsystems in order to support differentiation. While this myriad of potential directions may feel overwhelming, an important takeaway is that "each person's alliance matters" (Friedlander et al., 2018, p. 368). Tracking and seeking to understand each member's perspective about treatment can serve as a ballast amid the inevitable challenges of engaging families in conflict.

7 Conclusion

In this chapter, we have explored therapeutic ruptures as both common in treatment and dynamically unfolding based on therapist and patient relational moves of withdrawal and/or confrontation. To help clinicians and supervisors track and apply these concepts practically, we encourage readers to reflect on and jot down interpersonal (Worksheet 1) and intrapersonal (Worksheet 2) rupture markers for a particular case and session. This exercise can be particularly helpful when reviewing video or process notes in order to increase awareness of what is happening in the alliance in a particular clinical moment (and across alliances for group, couple, or family therapy). Building on this, Worksheet 3 outlines decision points when identifying potential pathways to rupture repair, the nuances of which should be considered in the context of a patient's cultural background and communication style. Finally, Worksheet 4 can be used in conjunction with role plays to spark exploration and curiosity in the face of uncertainty by expanding clinicians' awareness of possible avenues toward a new relational experience.

As a supervisee who has benefited immensely from learning to track and scrutinize moment-to-moment clinical process, I [LEC] can also testify to the vulnerability of such moments and the need to consistently strengthen personal capacities for mindful awareness, humility, and self-compassion. This is not easy work, but it is *worth it* to develop the ability to hear the "music" of the alliance, notice our patients' dance steps and our own, and catalyze treatment by *working with* what is happening, rather than just smoothing things over. As a supervisor [CFE], I am grateful for the rupture repair framework as it helps us acknowledge how complicated and even messy human interactions can be, and it emboldens us to embrace that complexity rather than pushing against it or moving away from it. We can admit that we do not have all the answers and inevitably miss the mark. This attitude fosters our compassion for ourselves, our patients, and our colleagues, and also frees us to think flexibly, creatively, and responsively as we strive to be aware and present and move closer to recognizing each other's three-dimensional subjectivity. Every rupture is an opportunity to learn something new.

Worksheet 1. Identifying Interpersonal Rupture Markers

Is there a problem in the alliance?

- Are you and your patient collaborating on the work of therapy?
- Do you and your patient have a bond of mutual trust, acceptance, and respect?

If there is a problem, what does it look like?
Movement against: confrontation rupture markers
Are you and/or your patient:

- Complaining about or criticizing the other?
- Complaining about or criticizing therapy activities, parameters, or lack of progress?
- Pushing back against the other or the work of therapy by rejecting the other or defending oneself?
- Trying to control or pressure the other?

Movement away: withdrawal rupture markers
Are you and/or your patient:

- Shutting down or giving up on the work of therapy by going silent or being passive?
- Avoiding the work of therapy by shifting the topic or filling the space with avoidant stories or overly vague or abstract language?
- Masking one's real experience by displaying incongruent affect or being overly deferential and appeasing?

Worksheet 2. Identifying Intrapersonal Rupture Markers

If you feel…	Then ask yourself these questions and consider whether you and your patient might be in the midst of a rupture.
Angry	Do I feel under attack? *Possible confrontation rupture* Do I feel the need to defend myself against what is making me angry (and possibly also anxious or sad)? *Possible confrontation rupture*
Anxious	Do I feel under attack? *Possible confrontation rupture* Do I feel alone and unsupported? *Possible withdrawal rupture* Do I feel overwhelmed and want to control what is making me anxious (and possibly also angry or sad)? *Possible confrontation rupture* Do I feel overwhelmed and want to avoid what is making me anxious (and possibly also angry or sad)? *Possible withdrawal rupture*
Sad	Do I feel shut out or hopeless? Do I feel a sense of loss? *Possible withdrawal rupture*
Bored	Do I feel disengaged and distant from the other? *Possible withdrawal rupture*
Confused	Do I feel confused by irrelevant stories, shifting topics, vague language, or incongruent affect? *Possible withdrawal rupture* Do I feel confused because the other is moving against me and away from me at the same time? *Possible mixed confrontation and withdrawal rupture*
Guilty or self-doubting	Am I negatively evaluating my performance because I am being criticized by the other? *Possible confrontation rupture* Am I negatively evaluating my own performance to avoid criticizing the other? *Possible withdrawal rupture*

Ashamed, embarrassed	Am I afraid of being negatively evaluated by the other, who is attacking me? *Possible confrontation rupture* Do I want to hide? *Possible withdrawal rupture*
Proud	Am I positively evaluating my performance because the other is agreeing with me, deferring to me, idealizing me? *Possible withdrawal rupture*
Protective	Do I feel that the other is fragile and needs me to take control? *Possible confrontation rupture* Do I feel that the other is fragile and cannot tolerate any conflict or tension? *Possible withdrawal rupture*

Worksheet 3. Rupture Repair Choice Points

If...	Then consider...
It is early in the therapy and you think that the bond is too weak for exploring a difficult rupture.	Focus first on alliance building and/or task-related repair strategies. Also reflect with your supervisor on whether you are correctly gauging the bond or whether you are avoiding exploration due to anxiety.
You have tried alliance building and/or task-related repair strategies and they were unsuccessful.	Acknowledge your contribution to the rupture and the unsuccessful repair. Try exploring the rupture experience.
The rupture is closely related to the patient's presenting concerns or therapy goals.	Try exploring the rupture experience.
You have tried exploring the rupture and it was unsuccessful.	Acknowledge your contribution to the rupture and the unsuccessful repair. Consider shifting to alliance building and/or task-related repair strategies for a while, and then when another rupture emerges, try exploring again.
Your patient objects to a therapy task that you believe is essential for their progress.	Start with task-related repair strategies, and if those are unsuccessful, try exploring the rupture experience.
Your patient objects to a task and would benefit from a corrective experience in which the other hears them, takes them seriously, and respects their wishes.	Start with task-related repair strategies such as renegotiating the task, which demonstrate your willingness to be responsive to your patient.
Your patient objects to a task and would benefit from a corrective experience in which the other is assertive without being aggressive or avoidant.	Consider task-related repair strategies such as explaining the rationale, where you balance being responsive to your patient's concerns with appropriate self-assertion. Also consider exploring the rupture experience.
You feel stuck, frustrated, or hopeless and have not processed these feelings yet.	Focus on alliance building and/or task-related repair strategies in the session and bring these difficult feelings to supervision.
You feel stuck, frustrated, or hopeless, and you have started to process these feelings in supervision, an emotion journal, or mindfulness or experiential exercises.	Try exploring the rupture and metacommunicating about your experience.

Worksheet 4. Pathways to Repair
Briefly describe a rupture you recently experienced with a patient:
The three pathways to repair are listed below. For each pathway, write down at least one thing you could say to your patient to address the rupture following that pathway. Then write down how you think your patient would respond to each intervention.
Alliance-building: Reattuning to feelings and intentions
Task-related repair strategies
Exploring the rupture experience

Chapter Review Exercises

1. You ask your patient how they are feeling. They shrug and say nothing. What kind of rupture may be taking place?

   Answer: Withdrawal. The patient appears to be shutting down or giving up on the work of therapy.

2. You realize that you are talking a great deal in the session with your patient. You are using a lot of technical terms and giving long, detailed explanations of the theory that justifies your choice of intervention. What kind of rupture may be taking place?

   Answer: Mixed: withdrawal (avoiding the work of therapy by filling the space with vague or abstract language) and confrontation (pushing back against the other by defending oneself).

3. You feel very bored in a session. Explain what kind of rupture processes may be taking place.

   Answer: Withdrawal. You may be bored because you feel disconnected from what you and your patient are talking about. This may indicate that your patient is withdrawing from you (perhaps through vague, abstract speech or rambling stories that are unengaging and hard to follow), and/or that you are withdrawing from your patient, perhaps to avoid something that is making you uncomfortable.

4. You try to explore a rupture with a patient, and they keep changing the subject and avoiding the exploration. What should you do?

   A. Explore the avoidance—note how the patient is withdrawing and express curiosity about their internal experience.
   B. Shift to alliance-building or task-related repair strategies for a while and try exploring again later.
   C. In supervision, explore your reactions to this patient and practice metacommunicating how you feel when your patient avoids.
   D. Give up on exploration because it does not work with this patient.

   Answer: A, B, and C are all good options to try.

5. You realize that you have contributed to a rupture. Should you immediately apologize to your patient?

   Answer: It is important to acknowledge your contribution to ruptures. However, if you do this too quickly, you may miss an opportunity to further explore what is happening in the alliance. Think about what will be most responsive to this patient in this moment. Do you need to start with an apology in order to keep the patient engaged? Or can you start with some curiosity about the rupture and explore together first? If you are very unsure about how to proceed, another option is to metacommunicate about your uncertainty and invite the patient to collaborate with you on the repair. For example, "I feel very torn right now. Part of me wants to apologize to you and make everything OK again, but another part of me is worried that if we rush to fix things, we may miss an opportunity to learn more about what is happening between us right now. What do you think?"

References

Alexander, F., & French, T. M. (1946). *The corrective emotional experience*. The Ronald Press.
Alldredge, C. T., Burlingame, G. M., Yang, C., & Rosendahl, J. (2021). Alliance in group therapy: A meta-analysis. *Group Dynamics, 25*(1), 13–28.
Asnaani, A., & Hofmann, S. G. (2012). Collaboration in multicultural therapy: Establishing a strong therapeutic alliance across cultural lines. *Journal of Clinical Psychology, 68*(2), 187–197.
Beilock, S. L. (2010). *Choke: What the secrets of the brain reveal about getting it right when you have to*. Simon & Schuster.
Benjamin, J. (1994). The shadow of the other (subject): Intersubjectivity and feminist theory. *Constellations: An International Journal of Critical and Democratic Theory, 1*, 231–255.
Bordin, E. S. (1979). The generalizability of the psychoanalytic concept of the working alliance. *Psychotherapy, 16*, 252–260.
Carr, A. W. (2019). *Coding Rupture Indicators in Couple Therapy (CRICT): An observational coding scheme* (Master's thesis). Brigham Young University. https://scholarsarchive.byu.edu/etd/7533
Christian, C., Safran, J. D., & Muran, J. C. (2012). The corrective emotional experience: A relational perspective and critique. In L. G. Castonguay & C. E. Hill (Eds.), *Transformation in psychotherapy* (pp. 51–67). American Psychological Association.
Coco, G. L., Tasca, G. A., Hewitt, P. L., Mikail, S., & Kivlighan, D. (2019). Ruptures and repairs of group therapy alliance. *Research in Psychotherapy, 22*(1), 58–70.
Davis, D. E., DeBlaere, C., Brubaker, K., Owen, J., Jordan, T. A., Hook, J. N., & Van Tongeren, D. R. (2016). Microaggressions and perceptions of cultural humility in counseling. *Journal of Counseling & Development, 94*(4), 483–493.
Dunn, R., Callahan, J. L., Swift, J. K., & Ivanovic, M. (2013). Effects of pre-session centering for therapists on session presence and effectiveness. *Psychotherapy Research, 23*(1), 78–85.
Ericsson, K. A., Krampe, R. T., & Tesch-Römer, C. (1993). The role of deliberate practice in the acquisition of expert performance. *Psychological Review, 100*, 363–406.
Eubanks, C. F. (2019). Alliance-focused formulation: A work in process. In U. Kramer (Ed.), *Case formulation for personality disorders: Tailoring psychotherapy to the individual client* (pp. 337–354). Elsevier.
Eubanks, C. F., Muran, J. C., & Safran, J. D. (2018). Alliance rupture repair: A meta-analysis. *Psychotherapy, 55*, 508–519.

Eubanks, C. F., Muran, J. C., Dreher, D., Sergi, J., Silberstein, E., & Wasserman, M. (2019). Trainees' experiences in alliance-focused training: The risks and rewards of learning to negotiate ruptures. *Psychoanalytic Psychology, 36*(2), 122–131.

Eubanks, C. F., Sergi, J., & Muran, J. C. (2021). Responsiveness to ruptures and repairs in psychotherapy. In J. C. Watson & H. Wiseman (Eds.), *The responsive psychotherapist: Attuning to clients in the moment* (pp. 83–104). American Psychological Association.

Eubanks, C. F., Warren, J. T., & Muran, J. C. (2021). Identifying ruptures and repairs in alliance-focused training group supervision. *International Journal of Group Psychotherapy, 71*(2), 275–309.

Eubanks, C. F., Samstag, L. W., & Muran, J. C. (Eds.). (2022). *Rupture and repairs in psychotherapy: Multiple perspectives on common clinical challenges*. American Psychological Association.

Frattaroli, J. (2006). Experimental disclosure and its moderators: A meta-analysis. *Psychological Bulletin, 132*(6), 823–865.

Friedlander, M. L. (2015). Use of relational strategies to repair alliance ruptures: How responsive supervisors train responsive psychotherapists. *Psychotherapy, 52*(2), 174–179.

Friedlander, M. L., Escudero, V., & Heatherington, L. (2006). *Therapeutic alliances with couples and families: An empirically-informed guide to practice*. American Psychological Association.

Friedlander, M. L., Escudero, V., Welmers-van de Poll, M. J., & Heatherington, L. (2018). Meta-analysis of the alliance–outcome relation in couple and family therapy. *Psychotherapy, 55*(4), 356–371.

Hook, J. N., Davis, D., Owen, J., & DeBlaere, C. (2017). *Cultural humility: Engaging diverse identities in therapy*. American Psychological Association.

Kabat-Zinn, J. (1991/2013). *Full catastrophe living*. Bantam Books.

Miles, J. R., Anders, C., Kivlighan, D. M., III, & Belcher Platt, A. A. (2021). Cultural ruptures: Addressing microaggressions in group therapy. *Group Dynamics, 25*(1), 74–88.

Mosher, D. K., Hook, J. N., Captari, L. E., Davis, D. E., DeBlaere, C., & Owen, J. (2017). Cultural humility: A therapeutic framework for engaging diverse clients. *Practice Innovations, 2*, 221–233.

Muran, J. C., & Eubanks, C. F. (2020). *Performance under pressure: Negotiating emotion, difference, and rupture*. American Psychological Association.

Muran, J. C., Safran, J. D., Gorman, B. S., Samstag, L. W., Eubanks-Carter, C., & Winston, A. (2009). The relationship of early alliance ruptures and their resolution to process and outcome in three time-limited psychotherapies for personality disorders. *Psychotherapy, 46*, 233–248.

Muran, J. C., Safran, J. D., Eubanks, C. F., & Gorman, B. S. (2018). The effect of alliance-focused training on a cognitive-behavioral therapy for personality disorders. *Journal of Consulting and Clinical Psychology, 86*, 384–397.

Norcross, J. C., & Wampold, B. E. (2018). A new therapy for each patient: Evidence-based relationships and responsiveness. *Journal of Clinical Psychology, 74*(11), 1889–1906.

Safran, J. D., & Muran, J. C. (1996). The resolution of ruptures in the therapeutic alliance. *Journal of Consulting and Clinical Psychology, 64*, 447.

Safran, J. D., & Muran, J. C. (2000). *Negotiating the therapeutic alliance*. The Guilford Press.

Safran, J. D., Muran, J. C., Samstag, L. W., & Winston, A. (2005). Evaluating alliance-focused intervention for potential treatment failures: A feasibility study and descriptive analysis. *Psychotherapy, 42*, 512–531.

Stiles, W. B., Honos-Webb, L., & Surko, M. (1998). Responsiveness in psychotherapy. *Clinical Psychology: Science and Practice, 5*, 439–458.

Stiles, W. B., Glick, M. J., Osatuke, K., Hardy, G. E., Shapiro, D. A., Agnew-Davies, R., et al. (2004). Patterns of alliance development and the rupture-repair hypothesis: Are productive relationships U-shaped or V-shaped? *Journal of Counseling Psychology, 51*, 81–92.

Stone, M., Friedlander, M. L., & Moeyaert, M. (2018). Illustrating novel techniques for analyzing single-case experiments: Effects of pre-session mindfulness practice. *Journal of Counseling Psychology, 65*(6), 690–702.

Tasca, G. A., & Lampard, A. M. (2012). Reciprocal influence of alliance to the group and outcome in day treatment for eating disorders. *Journal of Counseling Psychology, 59*(4), 507–517.

Urmanche, A., Minges, M., Eubanks, C. F., Gorman, B. S., & Muran, J. C. (2021). Deepening the group training experience: Group cohesion and supervision impact in Alliance-Focused Training. *Group Dynamics, 25*(1), 59–73.

Vygotsky, L. S. (1930/1980). *Mind in society*. Harvard University Press.

Wachtel, P. L. (2011). *Therapeutic communication: Knowing what to say when*. Guilford Press.

Watkins, C. E., Jr. (2014). The supervisory alliance: A half century of theory, practice, and research in critical perspective. *American Journal of Psychotherapy, 68*(1), 19–55.

The Therapeutic Relationship as an Attachment Relationship: The Role of Epistemic Trust

Alessandro Talia

> *If there is one lesson that I have learned during my life as an analyst, it is the lesson that what my patients tell me is likely to be true—that many times when I believed that I was right and my patients were wrong, it turned out, though often only after a prolonged search, that my rightness was superficial whereas their rightness was profound.*
>
> —Heinz Kohut (1984)

1 Introduction

While not a self-sufficient clinical model, attachment theory provides a valuable theoretical framework for understanding psychopathology and its treatment from an integrated perspective. In this framework, psychological problems can be seen as reflecting difficulties patients have in trusting others and themselves (Talia & Holmes, 2021). Some patients have had inconsistent or unreliable caregivers, for example, because they disconfirmed the patient's perceptions and sense of self. Other patients report stories of threats or abuse. Still others have felt abandoned, due to prolonged separations or actual bereavement. Attachment theory views various psychological disorders as self-protective strategies employed by the individual to cope with these and other relational traumas, adaptive in their developmental

---

A. Talia (✉)
Institut de Psychologie, Faculté des Sciences Sociales et Politiques, Université de Lausanne, Switzerland

Université de Lausanne, Faculté des SSP, Lausanne, Switzerland

Department of Public Health and Primary Care, University of Cambridge, Cambridge, UK

Institute for Psychosocial Prevention, University of Heidelberg, Heidelberg, Germany
e-mail: alessandro.talia@unil.ch; https://www.researchgate.net/profile/Alessandro_Talia

© The Author(s), under exclusive license to Springer Nature Switzerland AG 2024
B. Poletti et al. (eds.), *Training in Integrated Relational Psychotherapy*,
https://doi.org/10.1007/978-3-031-71904-2_7

context, but now constraining people's affective lives and limiting their ability to learn from experience (Slade & Holmes, 2019). The task of psychotherapy in this perspective is to reactivate in patients the ability to trust, so that such self-protective strategies can be mitigated or abandoned altogether.

This chapter aims to illustrate how the therapeutic relationship can become an attachment relationship and, by that route, how it can contribute to strengthening patients' ability to trust. In particular, we will discuss in detail the functions that must be performed by the therapeutic relationship in order for it to be considered in all respects an "attachment relationship." Traditionally, attachment theory defines an attachment relationship as one whose main task is to offer protection, and by extension a sense of safety, whenever we feel vulnerable or helpless. More recently, some authors have pointed out that attachment relationships have other functions besides providing protection, such as providing a context in which it is possible to learn from others (Fonagy et al., 2017). In this chapter we will discuss both points of view and examine the clinical implications and technical recommendations related to each.

Less attention will be given here to how different early developmental circumstances give rise to individual relational differences, which are usually referred to as attachment styles, attachment classifications, or states of mind with respect to attachment. In recent years, the lion's share of attachment research has focused on individual variations and their measurement, at the expense of general applications of attachment theory (see Granqvist, 2021b). Going against this general trend, in this chapter we will address the clinical relevance of the normative, species-typical features of attachment theory, which are relevant to all patients, while setting aside the study of individual differences in attachment, which reflect somewhat more superficial variation (the reader is referred to Chapter 2 by Crittenden and colleagues for an in-depth discussion of these important differences and to Talia et al., 2019, for a description of them in the context of psychotherapy).

2 The Tasks of the Therapist According to Bowlby

In a perspective informed by attachment theory, the therapist's main task is to restore the patient's ability to seek proximity to his or her significant others. According to this meta-theoretical perspective, a patient with a mental disorder has developed an unconscious belief that he or she is not safe, in part as a result of early experiences in which he or she felt threatened and unprotected by his or her reference figures. As a consequence, the patient according to Bowlby continues in the present to experience anxiety or fear, inhibits his innate ability to resort to attachment behaviors (because he expects that they will lead to rejection by the other), and enacts interpersonal strategies that lead to calamitous outcomes: inhibition of exploration, chronic avoidance of proximity, or exaggerated search for protection from others (Bowlby, 1973).

Bowlby believed that in order to restore the patient's ability to approach others, it was necessary to provide insight (Bowlby, 1988). According to Bowlby, the patient and therapist were to examine the relational patterns that guide the patient's interpersonal behavior (called "internal working models"); that they were to trace the origin of these patterns to early experiences with parents; and that they were to assess the usefulness (or lack of usefulness) of these patterns in the present context, encouraging the patient to abandon them when pathogenic, and to adopt new ones. As Bowlby himself noted, this way of viewing psychotherapy is very similar to that of cognitivists such as Aaron T. Beck (Bowlby, 1980) or even more so Gianni Liotti (Bowlby, 1990).

The importance of insight as a predictor of the outcome of psychotherapies is now well known (Jennissen et al., 2018). Bowlby emphasized, however, that none of the therapeutic tasks listed above can be performed appropriately if the therapist does not first and foremost become a reference figure, capable of offering proximity—emotional if not physical—to the patient. From a perspective informed by attachment theory, in order to provide support for insight, the therapist must facilitate a sense of security in the patient, just as a good parent provides a secure base for the child to find the courage necessary to explore. From this perspective, the reflective activities that advance the therapeutic process are grounded in a more fundamental aspect of the therapeutic relationship: its being an "attachment" relationship. The following section will be devoted to examining and defining such a relationship.

3   A Traditional View of the Function of Attachment Relationships: Protection

What relationships can be called "attachment relationships"? This deceptively simple question is of fundamental importance to anyone interested in determining whether a specific relationship is in effect an "attachment" relationship, or, when the answer is negative, how it can become one. Inspired by earlier work by Ainsworth (1979), Hinde (1976), and of course Bowlby (1973), several authors in the field of psychotherapy research informed by attachment theory have compiled lists of characteristics that attachment relationships should possess. For example, Mikulincer and Shaver (2007) define an attachment bond as (a) an affective bond, meaning a bond in which the partners are individuals who consider themselves at least partly irreplaceable (although they may have more than one such bond); (b) a relationship that gives at least some measure of security to the individual when he or she experiences anxiety or fear, comforting and encouraging him or her; (c) a bond that elicits separation anxiety and grief whenever the attachment figure is not accessible; and (d) a relationship with a person perceived at least in some respect as wiser and stronger than oneself.

Although this list may seem exhaustive, many "attachment figures" sometimes do not possess some of the characteristics listed above, at least at certain times. In our case, research suggests that psychotherapeutic relationships with adult patients may occasionally exhibit all the essential elements of the attachment bonds listed above (see for example, Parish & Eagle, 2003), but that at any given time some of these elements may be missing (Mallinckrodt, 2010). For example, some therapists may sometimes fail to console the patient, or fail to appear as wiser and stronger, while setting themselves up as important reference figures for the patient. In other cases, the therapist might be seen as competent and capable of reassuring the patient, but the therapeutic relationship might be perceived as unimportant in itself, on a par with a merely professional relationship, the conclusion of which can be accepted without too much trouble (Fearon & Belsky, 2021).

According to an alternative strategy, to assess whether or not a therapeutic relationship is an attachment relationship, we might refer to the function performed by that relationship. One of Bowlby's (1969/1982) basic assumptions was that the behavioral system of attachment evolved because it served the adaptive function of protecting the child, through physical closeness, against dangers such as predation. This was, in Bowlby's assessment, the single adaptive function of the attachment system. And—at least in the context of relationships between the child and his or her caregivers—we can apply such a functional consideration to decide whether or not a particular relationship is an attachment relationship, depending on its ability to provide at least some degree of physical protection for the child through closeness.

Some difficulties arise, however, when we apply this same approach to attachment relationships after childhood. In childhood, our attachment figures are parents, grandparents, or sometimes a nanny. In adolescence, peers may assume this role. In adulthood, partners or friends become attachment figures, and in later life they are often professional caregivers, or one's own children. In many of these contexts, the physical protection provided by the closeness of the other is only one of many functions performed by the attachment figure, and certainly not the primary one. The question remains whether there is a function that all these different relationships have in common.

4 Another Function of Attachment Relationships: Fostering Information Transmission

Several attachment scholars have pointed out that attachment relationships not only protect children from immediate threats to their survival but also have the function of supporting cultural transmission (Csibra & Gergely, 2011; Fonagy et al., 2017; Fonagy & Campbell, 2015; Grossmann & Grossmann, 2005). For most contemporary evolutionary biologists and anthropologists, it is well established that the behaviors of organisms (humans included) not only make them adapted but also adaptive. In their evolutionary history, human infants have been vulnerable to a range of natural hazards in addition to predation: not only to starvation, thirst, sudden cold, infection, burns, bruises, suffocation, drowning, violence by conspecifics but also to a myriad of events whose occurrence is signaled by culturally learned clues—the list would be very long—such as cars, weapons, and local varieties of mushrooms. In all these cases and many others, cultural transmission should be considered a process almost as important to physical proximity to ensure survival and, in the long run, reproduction (Tomasello, 2014). It is through interpersonal communication that the child learns not only how in a given culture one protects oneself from what is dangerous but also how utensils are employed, what forms of interaction are acceptable, and what institutions organize communal life.

As is obvious, in order to learn from others, an individual—child or adult—must harbor at least an unconscious expectation that communication can enhance their knowledge about the world and their place in it (Fonagy et al., 2017). In other words, the child must have epistemic trust in the communicator. Epistemic trust is a type of trust that is tacitly directed toward interpersonal communication and guides our attention within it. Almost no explicit communication would occur in its absence. Note that epistemic trust involves not only the expectation that others will be sincere, but also that informants are competent, that the information they communicate is relevant to the interests of the recipients, and that it adds something new. In most cases, in early relationships with caregivers, the child gradually develops increasing confidence that all these expectations will be met.

Trusting others is vitally important, and it also exposes us to great risks. It allows us to depend on others—as people who teach us, who support us, who love us—but it carries the danger that others will give us the wrong information, fail to provide the information we need, or mislead us. Considering these dangers, Dan Sperber and his colleagues (Sperber et al., 2010) have proposed that in humans a set of cognitive epistemic vigilance mechanisms have evolved that automatically adjust their level of epistemic trust in others so that communication remains, on average, beneficial.

Based on these views, we might describe an attachment relationship (including one with a psychotherapist) as a relationship with a person toward whom we have epistemic trust. Such a person will be in a sense irreplaceable, because he or she will be the bearer of somewhat unique knowledge. He or she will be able to reassure and encourage us, because to feel reassured or encouraged we must have the conviction that the other is, at the very least, trustworthy and honest. This person will seem wiser and stronger to us, at least when he or she seems better informed about the topic being discussed than we are. And finally, when the attachment figure is not accessible, we will experience separation, anxiety, and depression, because these emotions—and their expression—function as communicative signals that manifest our need to maintain communication with others.

It is important to note that, according to this interpretation, no relationship always and consistently performs an "attachment" function. In fact, given that someone might be competent with respect to one topic but not another, or well-meaning at one time and dishonest at another, the mechanisms that establish epistemic trust—which is in part influenced by the individual's relational history—also necessarily draw on many other contextual cues: the perceived trustworthiness of the communicator, the strength of the evidence he or she provides, and the consistency between what is being communicated and what was previously known to the recipient (Mercier & Sperber, 2011).

The hypothesis that one function of attachment relationships is to bring out epistemic trust is particularly interesting in light of Fonagy et al.' (2017) hypothesis that a lack of epistemic trust is the common risk factor underlying all forms of psychopathology. Fonagy and colleagues' emphasis on epistemic trust is inspired by large longitudinal studies with psychiatric patients, which suggest that mental disorders in general are sequentially comorbid, recurrent, or chronic, and may be statistically represented by a single overarching factor of psychopathology called the "p-factor." Fonagy and his colleagues have argued that the "p-factor" cannot be equated with a deficit in a single cognitive or affective skill. According to these authors, this general factor common to psychiatric disorders can be better conceptualized as a product of the relationship between individual dispositions and the social environment, or, in short, as a lack of resilience within a given social system. Fonagy and his colleagues have tentatively linked such lack of resilience to an inability to learn from others and be receptive to their support, or low epistemic trust.

5 Epistemic Trust and the New Tasks of Attachment-Informed Therapy

The emphasis on supporting epistemic trust and communication as a central function of an attachment relationship allows us to reread and partly modify the tasks Bowlby assigned to the therapist. We can argue that if the therapist is to present himself as a secure base for the patient, crucial is the therapist's ability to present himself as a reliable and relevant source of information-in the broadest sense.

And yet "offering a secure base" cannot consist only in posing as trustworthy communicators, toward whose therapeutic interventions patients will be duly receptive. Epistemic trust is the result of a dyadic and reciprocal process. Children turn to their "wiser and stronger" attachment figures when they are in distress, but—to a greater or lesser extent–this is conditional on their caregivers trusting them: to be attuned to their emotions, validate their perceptions, and be appropriately responsive. In other words, the child who relies on his or her attachment figure not only expects to receive reliable information from the latter but also expects the caregiver to trust him or her. Under ideal conditions, these two forms of trust feed off each other, creating a virtuous circle (Talia & Holmes, 2021).

It is possible to conceptualize secure base formation in the therapeutic context in a very similar key. Already Bowlby wrote that while the prevailing posture of therapists in his days was, "I know and I will explain it to you," a therapeutic attitude more consistent with his attachment theory was rather akin to saying, "you know and you will explain it to me" (Bowlby, Bowlby, 1988). And so the preferred role of attachment-informed therapists is that of a trusted companion for patients' autonomous attempts to make meaning and affectively regulate their experiences, both negative and positive. But the therapist must not only subvert the implicit asymmetry of the therapeutic relationship and avoid assuming the role of the expert or that of the teacher. He must make the effort to develop his own epistemic trust in the patient in order to create the conditions through which the patient can feel understood and trust the therapist.

Establishing a secure foundation is the first step in attachment-informed therapy, and is probably a healing ingredient in itself. But as every therapist knows, this is not an easy task. First, because of their adverse developmental experiences, patients may not want to learn from others or be receptive to their communications (Fonagy & Allison, 2014). Second, therapists may find themselves driven to unconsciously distrust or reject patients. As with Collodi's Pinocchio, patients' problems in inspiring trust in others go hand in hand with their difficulties in trusting others. It is in these cases that it may be especially important for the therapist to make more conscious efforts to understand the patient's "profound rightness."

6 Understanding the Motivations of the Patient and the People in His or Her Life

Sometimes the therapist may come to feel that the patient is lying to himself, is afraid to admit an uncomfortable truth, or has simply misinterpreted a behavior of one of his reference figures. In such circumstances, the therapist need not show agreement with the manifest content of the patient's communication. If anything, the therapist's role in such cases is to identify an interpretation of what the patient is saying with which the therapist or therapist can agree.

One possible strategy the therapist can adopt when he or she does not understand or believe what the patient intends to communicate is to make conjectures about the patient's emotions and needs that arise in the conversation. For example, the patient might make a critical statement about a person in his or her life that the therapist does not agree with ("My husband is a good-for-nothing, he doesn't understand anything about me"). The therapist may then focus on the emotions communicated by the patient ("You seem very angry with him") or on her needs ("Maybe you need a different kind of support from him"). In this way, the therapist has the opportunity to make a statement expressing a belief that both he and the patient might consider true.

Drawing from a pioneering study by Dozier et al. (1994), in a recent study, Talia et al. (2020) found that the use of interventions similar to those described above is particularly typical of psychotherapists classified as "secure" on the Adult Attachment Interview (AAI, Main et al., 1985), the gold standard measure of attachment research in adults. In this study, insecure therapists were distinguished by one of two alternative characteristics. Some therapists attempted to make the patient's current beliefs explicit without relating them to their own views, for example, by asking many open-ended questions or by repeating and clarifying the patient's views. While striving to understand the patient, they thus neglected to show to the patient that they believed them.

Other therapists tended to focus consistently on real details of the patient's life, expressing assessments of the patient's interpersonal experience that were independent of the patient's own. Secure therapists, on the other hand, were characterized by an apparent ability to maintain balance and affective impartiality. They communicated what they believed the patient meant to say and partly sought agreement with him, but posed their perspective without undue detachment or omniscience.

This is also the essence of the mentalizing attitude, the ability to see the other subject as an autonomous individual with intentionality, seeing oneself from the outside and the other "from the inside" (Fonagy et al., 2017). By not limiting themselves to open-ended questions and trivial repetition, nor by informing the patient of "how things really are," secure therapists seem to accept that they do not know, but show confidence that it is possible to learn.

7 Negotiating the Therapeutic Alliance

However carefully a therapist acts, there will invariably be occasions when trust between patient and therapist breaks down momentarily and communication suffers. However, if patient and therapist are able to meta-communicate (i.e., communicate about their communication), these ruptures can also create therapeutic opportunities. Research suggests that successive cycles of rupture and repair lead to stronger therapeutic alliances than relationships that appear positive all the time (Eubanks et al., 2018). This is consistent with research showing that child-caregiver dyads subsequently judged "secure" in the Strange Situation are characterized not by perpetually synchronous interactions but by repeated cycles of rupture and repair (Beebe & Lachmann, 2003).

In this perspective, relational ruptures are defined as events that signal a decrease in trust in the therapy or therapeutic relationship, either in the patient or therapist. Ruptures in the therapeutic alliance can occur in one of two situations: withdrawal or confrontation (Safran & Muran, 2000). In withdrawal, the patient has low expectations of being believed by the therapist. Breakups of this type are manifested through decreased emotional closeness, an effort to limit one's communication, sometimes shifting the conversation from immediate experience or problematic affect to less personally relevant topics. In confrontational ruptures, the patient has low expectations of being listened to by the therapist, and here the patient will refute the therapist's perspectives or criticize him/her harshly. In both scenarios, not unlike the model proposed by Safran and Muran, the therapist informed by attachment theory and the epistemic trust perspective tries to focus on the patient's and on his or her own subjective experience of the rupture in open and non-blaming ways. Beyond that, the therapist does not simply note that a rupture seems to have occurred and question the patient about its meaning. He or she might feel that something is frustrating him or her in the relationship and decide to talk about it, actively proposing possible experiences that the patient might be experiencing (without showing absolute certainty), or sharing his or her own.

8 Adapting to the Patient

As mentioned briefly at the beginning of this chapter, a number of clinically relevant individual differences, called attachment patterns, have been identified by developmental research on attachment relationships. Attachment patterns reflect ways of entering into relationships with caregivers, which take shape in early life and can be assessed during childhood. The Adult Attachment Interview (AAI) identifies parallel categories in adults' autobiographical narrative styles: secure-autonomous, dismissing, preoccupied, and unresolved (Main et al., 1985). Recent research has studied these same patterns in the context of psychotherapy (Talia et al., 2017). Patients classified as secure in the AAI are able to be open and share their attitudes with candor and to support them with clear examples and convincing accounts of internal experiences. In doing so, they make their communication easy to understand and accept as true. Patients classified as dismissing in the AAI try to maximize the chances of being understood by being concise but undermine their communication by offering dry, emotionless narratives, empty of narrative detail. Preoccupied patients strive for therapist support, but express themselves in sometimes rambling or otherwise one-sided ways, which make it difficult for the listener to understand or empathize with their point of view.

Together with other colleagues, we have proposed that attachment patterns are stable communicative patterns that reflect fundamental—and not inherently pathological—ways of increasing the listener's trust in the speaker, which are independent of the topic discussed or the speaker. If this is true, therapists should aim to validate and work with, rather than summarily change, the patient's attachment patterns. Dismissing patients' responses can be thought of not as reflecting avoidance of the therapist, but as an attempt to be clear, and as an invitation to the therapist to add more. Prolonged or confusing repetition of past episodes by preoccupied patients may not be seen as an attempt to devalue or ignore the therapist's comments, but as reflecting the patient's efforts to provide as much information as possible to the therapist, and be believed (Talia et al., 2019). At this juncture, a two-step therapeutic approach may be suggested in which the therapist initially follows and mirrors the patient's communication style, and then gradually, through a combined use of empathic validation and meta-communication, moves toward a more secure and more coherent conversational mode.

Implicit in this approach is the view that, at least initially, the therapist will adapt to the patient's style in order to minimize the possibility of ruptures. And yet this is typically not sufficient in the long run. Insecure attachment patterns limit patients' ability to communicate openly and thus slow down therapeutic work. Such difficulties are particularly problematic during ruptures, the resolution of which relies on the assumption that therapist and patient are able to openly express their experiences of a relational problem. This perspective is confirmed by recent research suggesting that secure attachment is characterized by the ability to communicate openly with the therapist even or especially when problems arise. At these junctures, therapists must work hard to help insecure patients express themselves with the clarity and vivacity typical of secure attachment.

9 Conclusion: The Goal of Psychotherapy

In *A Secure Base*, Bowlby (1988) writes that "the human psyche, like our bones, is prone to self-healing. The job of the psychotherapist, like that of the orthopedic surgeon, is to provide the conditions under which self-healing can best take place." The perspective proposed in this chapter suggests a similar perspective, emphasizing in addition how self-healing can only take place through contact and communication with others. In this sense, just as Bowlby thought, it is not the psychotherapist who "cures" the patient, nor is it the patient who alone finds the key to get out of his or her problems. The role of the psychotherapist is to rebuild the patient's ability to trust others, but it is only through encounters with real others, whom one can truly trust, that the patient can consolidate his or her nascent ability to trust and put it to use to further his or her own psychic growth.

Chapter Review Exercises

1. Thinking about your last psychotherapy session, which of the five tasks listed by Bowlby do you feel were present? Can you give an example for each?
2. Are there any of these tasks that you feel you rarely accomplish in session, or that you feel are less important than the others? Try to argue your point of view.
3. (In pairs) Try to remember something in your recent work that one of your patients told you that you found hard to believe at the time. Try to write down what the patient said as faithfully as you can, and write down what you feel you answered him or her. Now read the patient's communication aloud to one of your classmates or colleagues, who will try to respond to the intervention as if they believed every word the patient said. Reflect on how this intervention makes you feel and compare it with your own.
4. Read the following excerpt from a psychotherapy session with a dismissing patient. How do you rate the therapist's work and why?

    P: [...] Okay, before we start, I just want you to know that uhm, just for the purpose of putting my personal problems in perspective, that in my daily life I have some positive interpersonal experiences, because they all seem to be, all bad, and I just want you to know that, just so that way you can put my problems in perspective.

T: Any experiences that come to mind, specifically? Or that you had in mind when you were saying that?

P: Well, I think the reason I said that is because most people, when they come to therapy, tend to focus on the negative, on their problems and issues, and they often leave out some of the positive experiences that they have. And I think it's important to notice that, just so that I can put things in perspective and have a more objective view of the person that I am.

T: It sounds like you want to prevent me from misperceiving you?

P: Well, I mean, that's not what I was thinking initially, it's just that this is just the way my mind works, maybe, I mean, if a person shares certain things with you, then your perception is based on what you share, so. Ah- ah that has nothing to do with you, it has to do with human nature, that's how I think human interactions work, so...

T: So you're thinking about how I'm perceiving you.

P: Yeah...(. . . 4 sec). Um.

T: And what are you thinking?

P: Well, I just—I just—I thought I wanted to bring this up so that when you evaluate me, my problems and issues, you can put everything in perspective and hopefully that will allow us to narrow down and focus on the key problems and issues in a bigger perspective.

5. What interventions could be substituted for those above in this session so as to show more epistemic trust in the patient?

References

Ainsworth, M. S. (1979). Infant-mother attachment. *American Psychologist, 34*(10), 932.
Beebe, B., & Lachmann, F. (2003). *Infant research and adult processing*. Raffaello Cortina.
Bowlby, J. (1969/1982). *Attachment and loss: Attachment*. Bollati Boringhieri.
Bowlby, J. (1973). *Attachment and loss: Separation, anxiety, and anger*. Bollati Boringhieri.
Bowlby, J. (1980). *Attachment and loss: Loss, sadness, and depression*. Bollati Boringhieri.
Bowlby, J. (1988). *A secure base*. Raffaello Cortina Editore.
Bowlby, J. (1990). Interview. *Clinical Neuropsychiatry, 2*, 159–171.
Csibra, G., & Gergely, G. (2011). Natural pedagogy as evolutionary adaptation. *Philosophical Transactions of the Royal Society, Biological Sciences, 366*(1567), 1149–1157.
Dozier, M., Cue, K. L., & Barnett, L. (1994). Clinicians as caregivers: Role of attachment organization in treatment. *Journal of Consulting and Clinical Psychology, 62*(4), 793.
Eubanks, C. F., Muran, J. C., & Safran, J. D. (2018). Alliance rupture repair: A meta-analysis. *Psychotherapy, 55*(4), 508.
Fearon, P., & Belsky, J. (2021). What is an attachment relationship? In R. Thompson, J. Simpson, & J. Berlin (Eds.), *Attachment: The fundamental questions*. Guilford Press.
Fonagy, P., & Allison, E. (2014). The role of mentalizing and epistemic trust in the therapeutic relationship. *Psychotherapy, 51*(3), 372.
Fonagy, P., & Campbell, C. (2015). Bad blood revisited: Attachment and psychoanalysis. *British Journal of Psychotherapy, 31*(2), 229–250.
Fonagy, P., Luyten, P., Allison, E., & Campbell, C. (2017). What we have changed our minds about: Part 2. Borderline personality disorder, epistemic trust and the developmental signifi-

cance of social communication. *Borderline Personality Disorder and Emotion Dysregulation, 4*(1), 1–12.

Granqvist, P. (2021a). Attachment, culture, and gene-culture co-evolution: Expanding the evolutionary toolbox of attachment theory. *Attachment & Human Development, 23*(1), 90–113.

Granqvist, P. (2021b). The god, the blood, and the fuzzy: Reflections on cornerstones and two target articles. *Attachment & Human Development, 23*, 1–10.

Grossmann, K. E., & Grossmann, K. (2005). Universality of human social attachment as an adaptive process. In C. S. Carter, L. Ahnert, K. E. Grossmann, S. B. Hrdy, M. E. Lamb, S. W. Porges, & N. Sachser (Eds.), *Attachment and bonding: A new synthesis* (Vol. Dahlem Workshop Report 92, pp. 199–229). The MIT Press.

Hinde, R. A. (1976). On describing relationships. *Journal of Child Psychology and Psychiatry, 17*(1), 1–19.

Jennissen, S., Huber, J., Ehrenthal, J. C., Schauenburg, H., & Dinger, U. (2018). Association between insight and outcome of psychotherapy: Systematic review and meta-analysis. *American Journal of Psychiatry, 175*(10), 961–969.

Main, M., Kaplan, N., & Cassidy, J. (1985). Security in infancy, childhood, and adulthood: A move to the level of representation. *Monographs of the Society for Research in Child Development, 50*, 66–104.

Mallinckrodt, B. (2010). The psychotherapy relationship as attachment: Evidence and implications. *Journal of Social and Personal Relationships, 27*(2), 262–270.

Mercier, H., & Sperber, D. (2011). Why do humans reason? Arguments for an argumentative theory. *Behavioral and Brain Sciences, 34*(2), 57–74.

Mikulincer, M., & Shaver, P. R. (2007). *Attachment in adulthood: Structure, dynamics, and change*. Guilford Press.

Parish, M., & Eagle, M. N. (2003). Attachment to the therapist. *Psychoanalytic Psychology, 20*(2), 271.

Safran, J. D., & Muran, J. C. (2000). *Negotiating the therapeutic alliance: A relational treatment guide*. Guilford Press.

Slade, A., & Holmes, J. (2019). Attachment and psychotherapy. *Current Opinion in Psychology, 25*, 152–156.

Sperber, D., Clément, F., Heintz, C., Mascaro, O., Mercier, H., Origgi, G., & Wilson, D. (2010). Epistemic vigilance. *Mind & Language, 25*(4), 359–393.

Talia, A., & Holmes, J. (2021). Therapeutic mechanisms in attachment-informed psychotherapy with adults. In R. Thompson, J. Simpson, & J. Berlin (Eds.), *Attachment: The fundamental questions*. Guilford Press.

Talia, A., Miller-Bottome, M., & Daniel, S. I. (2017). Assessing attachment in psychotherapy: Validation of the patient attachment coding system (PACS). *Clinical Psychology & Psychotherapy, 24*(1), 149–161.

Talia, A., Taubner, S., & Miller-Bottome, M. (2019). Advances in research on attachment-related psychotherapy processes: Seven teaching points for trainees and supervisors. *Research in Psychotherapy: Psychopathology, Process, and Outcome, 22*(3).

Talia, A., Muzi, L., Lingiardi, V., & Taubner, S. (2020). How to be a secure base: Therapists' attachment representations and their link to attunement in psychotherapy. *Attachment & Human Development, 22*(2), 189–206.

Tomasello, M. (2014). The ultra-social animal. *European Journal of Social Psychology, 44*(3), 187–194.

Mentalization in the Therapeutic Relationship

Paula Ravitz and Giorgio A. Tasca

1 Introduction

This chapter focuses on using mentalizing within an integrated model to improve the therapeutic alliance and patient mental health outcomes especially for individuals with a history of unresolved developmental trauma and insecure attachment. Mentalizing involves making inferences to understand what might be in our own and others' minds, including understanding that behaviors are the result of mental states (feelings, behaviors, intentions, needs, desires, and beliefs) (Bateman & Fonagy, 2019). This involves the process of "seeing others from the inside, and ourselves from the outside" (Holmes, 2015). The capacity for mentalizing emerges from attachment security in which children grow to experience others as sensitive and responsive to their psychological motivations or inner lives (Zeegers et al., 2017; Aival-Naveh et al., 2019; Luyten et al., 2020). One develops an ability to mentalize, be empathic, consider alternative perspectives and "to learn from social experience that enables people to respond effectively to adversity and challenge" when supportive others demonstrate and communicate care and understanding [p. 73 in: (Bateman & Fonagy, 2019)]. A key aspect of this social learning is the development of epistemic trust—that is, the coming to trust that what is in the mind of a caring other is reliable and a safe source of information about the social world. Mentalizing is important for interpersonal effectiveness, for perspective taking, empathy, resilience, and the forming and sustaining of relationships. It is also

---

P. Ravitz (✉)
Department of Psychiatry, Temerty Faculty of Medicine, University of Toronto, Toronto, ON, Canada
e-mail: Paula.Ravitz@sinaihealth.ca

G. A. Tasca
School of Psychology, University of Ottawa, Ottawa, ON, Canada

© The Author(s), under exclusive license to Springer Nature Switzerland AG 2024
B. Poletti et al. (eds.), *Training in Integrated Relational Psychotherapy*,
https://doi.org/10.1007/978-3-031-71904-2_8

important for survival and optimal functioning, to be able to understand and predict what might be in others' and one's own minds.

Mentalizing emphasizes balancing attention with exploration of both internal experiences such as feelings, thoughts, intentions or needs, and external actions, in oneself and others in relationships. In the therapeutic context, therapists can use meta-communication to bolster epistemic trust, model mentalizing, and encourage mentalizing in patients.

Metacommunication is therapist intervention that transparently explores intentions and impacts of interpersonal behaviors. According to Safran and Muran (2000), metacommunication involves therapists exploring the therapeutic interactions with skillful tentativeness, establishing a sense of "we-ness" or shared experience in the here and now of the relationship with the patient, accepting responsibility for one's own contribution to any misunderstandings or alliance ruptures, and recognizing alliance ruptures. Mentalizing provides a powerful model for therapists to understand and intervene in the context of alliance ruptures. We propose that mentalizing can be compatibly used with and can be fostered by metacommunication to help therapists recognize and work through therapeutic impasses, tensions, or ruptures in the alliance (Fonagy & Allison, 2014; Leszcz et al., 2015; Bateman & Fonagy, 2019; Fonagy et al., 2019; Law et al., 2022). Figure 1 shows the aspects of overlap between meta-communication as conceptualized by Safran and Muran and mentalizing interventions as conceptualized by Fonagy and Bateman.

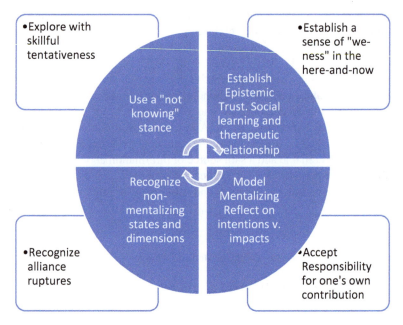

Fig. 1 Comparing aspects of metacommunication (squares outside of the circles) with mentalizing interventions (quadrants within the circle)

In a recent knowledge translation randomized controlled trial, we used an integrated model of mentalizing to formulate and repair alliance ruptures by emphasizing psychotherapy's common factors and relational theories. In our training model, therapists were taught to identify the effects of attachment insecurity, their own countertransference, the role of interpersonal style and interpersonal complementarity, and the impact of unresolved developmental trauma in patients. We used mentalizing theory as an overarching model to inform therapist interventions to recognize and repair alliance ruptures. That is, therapists were encouraged to use metacommunication to unpack the intentions of their own and patients' behaviors, to clarify and align therapeutic goals and tasks, and to model mentalizing as a means of increasing epistemic trust in the therapeutic relationship among patients. We found that compared to those with no training, community-based therapists with training in our model reported a steeper growth in the therapeutic alliance across sessions of therapy (unpublished data, Tasca et al. 2023).

Mentalizing, theory of mind and impairments of social cognition, has been explored in patients with autism and several personality disorders, including borderline personality disorder (BPD) and narcissistic personality disorder. Bateman and colleagues proposed BPD as a disorder of mentalizing and social cognition, with loss of resilience resulting from problems with epistemic trust and an inability to derive benefit from the social environment. For these reasons, Bateman and colleagues used principles of mentalizing to develop mentalizing-based treatment (MBT), an evidence-based therapy for BPD. Therapeutic process in MBT strives to foster generalizable experiences from being mentalized by a therapist and learning to mentalize. This is achieved in part from seeing and experiencing mentalization modeled in the therapist's behavior (Bateman et al., 2018). In a seminal study of MBT as compared to treatment as usual for patients with BPD, 8-year follow up demonstrated that MBT led to significantly greater decreases in self-harm, remission (i.e., patients no longer meeting diagnostic criterial for BPD) and improved vocational status (Bateman & Fonagy, 2008). Since this study, MBT has been rolled out in the United Kingdom through the Increasing Access to Psychological Therapies national program.

People with a history of early childhood adversity, abuse, neglect, or invalidation likely were not mentalized by an attachment figure. Thus, they may not develop a capacity to understand their own or others' minds, and they may be mistrustful, assuming that others are uncaring or maliciously intended. This can lead to social isolation and disconnection from others that further perpetuate a felt sense of exclusion and tendencies to mistrust (Fonagy & Allison, 2014). The result is a maladaptive cycle that further curtails opportunities for social learning, from and within relationships. One way of interrupting this self-perpetuating cycle is to both understand the patient and therapeutically intervene with mentalizing. Although the therapeutic principles and techniques of mentalizing were developed for individuals with BPD (Bateman & Fonagy, 2008), their operationalization is also conceptualized as "plain old therapy" and more broadly applied in various psychotherapeutic contexts to advance therapeutic processes.

Case Example

Joel is a 42-year-old man who works full time as a store manager and lives with one of his brothers for the past 6 months since separating from his wife of 5 years. Their 3-year-old daughter lives with his wife who allows Joel only supervised visits every other weekend since their separation. Joel came to psychotherapy reluctantly. He was urged by others to attend, but he doubts that psychotherapy will be helpful. The case of Joel and this integrated therapeutic approach was originally presented in a book and video on "Achieving Psychotherapy Effectiveness" (Leszcz et al., 2015) and is also presented in the chapter on Case Formulation in this volume (Tasca & Poletti, 2023).

Joel struggles with anger, irritability, sadness, insomnia, decreased appetite, difficulties with concentration, and a growing sense of anhedonia that have worsened over the past year in the context of heightened conflicts with his wife and at work. He endorses an increasing sense of feeling "out of control" and hopeless; however, he denies panic symptoms, suicidal ideation, or substance misuse.

The psychotherapist at the first session sought to establish a therapeutic alliance and to begin to get to know Joel, asking what brought him to treatment. Joel replied that he came to therapy because others have told him that he should. The therapist enquires, "why do you think they are concerned?," and Joel replies, "I don't know… you're probably going to tell me how messed up I am," conveying his expectation of harsh judgement by others including the therapist. The therapist attempted to disconfirm Joel's negative expectations of others in a non-shaming, non-blaming, and non-defensive manner. The therapist empathically communicated his sense of Joel's suffering and legitimate need for care, along with the therapist's intention to be helpful. The therapist also acknowledged his sense that Joel did not think that psychotherapy can help him to improve how he is feeling or his situation. Joel sarcastically replied, "Do your worst," once again demonstrating his expectation that others will hurt him and that they are not reliable, thus indicating problems with epistemic trust.

Joel's rejection of the therapist's attempts to empathize and show caring exemplifies a "confrontation rupture," defined as a patient moving against a therapist by complaining or be defending themselves against the therapist (Safran et al., 2011). This also alerted the therapist to Joel's irritability and provocative, distancing hostile interpersonal pulls that may be emblematic of how Joel can be off-putting to others. Others will likely respond in a complementary manner indicating disinterest or counter hostility, which would confirm Joel's internal working model and core interpersonal belief that others are uncaring, judgmental, or hurtful (Kiesler, 1983; Ravitz et al., 2008; Leszcz et al., 2015). The chapter on Case Formulation in this volume has a more detailed discussion of interpersonal complementarity (Tasca & Poletti, 2023).

The therapist communicated to Joel a hypothesis of Joel's dismissing avoidant or fearful attachment style, and a hostile dominant interpersonal stance that may evoke hostility or rejection from others, leaving him alone in his suffering (Bowlby, 1982; Hunter & Maunder, 2001). The therapist wondered if this may be rooted in a history of early childhood adversity with parents or primary caregivers who were invalidating, unavailable, abusive, frightening, or frightened. Thus, Joel might have learned early on in his life to mistrust what was in the minds of others and to protect himself from their intentions. However, what was true "then and there," in the past, is not necessarily true, "here and now." The therapist was offering Joel an opportunity for experiential learning both from and within the therapeutic alliance to modify Joel's internal working model of himself and relationships.

The therapist noticed and tried to control his own objective countertransference tendencies to retaliate, to defend himself, or to reject Joel and his accusations (Betan et al., 2005). The therapist made efforts to disconfirm Joel's negative beliefs about others within the therapeutic alliance. That is, the therapist tried to validate Joel's suffering and communicated his intentions that underlie his questions and that might help to align their goals for therapy in an attempt to repair the alliance tensions: "I get the sense you expect little from me or from psychotherapy, but my aim is to try to find a way to understand you and your situation in order to be helpful, and towards that end I'd like to get to know you and learn more of your current struggles." Joel softened a little and began to open up with a narrative that focused on others, including work colleagues and his wife. He described his wife as critical, "against him," and blind to his well-intended actions such as working hard at his job and buying gifts for his daughter. He was unable to appreciate how he negatively impacts others, and why people are upset with him when he raises his voice and loses his temper regarding things about which he feels justifiably angry.

2 Mentalizing and the Therapeutic Alliance

The therapeutic alliance as described in an earlier chapter is critically important to outcomes. The alliance refers to the collaborative agreement between patient and therapist on the tasks and goals of therapy, and their relational bond. In a meta-analysis of 295 independent studies with more than 30,000 psychotherapy patients (1978–2017), the authors found a robust positive relation between alliances and outcomes regardless of treatment approaches or patient characteristics (Fluckiger et al., 2018).

The detection and repair of therapeutic alliance ruptures or tensions can improve outcomes (Safran et al., 2011; Eubankset al, 2018b). Generally, an alliance rupture is a disagreement on the tasks or goals of therapy, or a breakdown in the relational bond. A meta-analysis examining the relation between rupture repair episodes and outcomes found a moderate effect size in 11 studies of 1314 patients ($r = 0.29$, $p < 0.003$). Eubanks and colleagues (2018b) also found in their meta-analysis that training in identifying and repairing alliance ruptures was associated with improved patient outcomes.

Alliance rupture repair strategies emphasize the importance of experiential, here-and-now, alliance-focused interventions that validate patients' experiences and explore ruptures during the session in which they occur (Eubanks et al., 2018a). One model of alliance repair involves therapeutic meta-communication as elaborated by

Safran and Muran (2000). Over the past two decades they have refined and tested their model of detecting and repairing therapeutic alliance ruptures (Safran et al., 2011; Eubanks et al., 2018b). Two types of recognizable alliance ruptures in psychotherapy are withdrawal and confrontation ruptures (Muran et al., 2021). Withdrawal ruptures are those in which the patient moves away from the therapist by going silent, giving minimal responses, engaging in avoidant storytelling, or being overly deferential to the therapist. Confrontation ruptures, like we saw in the case of Joel, include complaints about the therapy or therapist, defending oneself against the therapist, or pressuring and controlling the therapist. A more detailed discussion of alliance ruptures is presented in the chapter by Eubanks and colleagues in this volume.

3 Alliance Ruptures and Countertransference

Therapist emotional experiences and counter-transference are additional intrapersonal markers that may be useful to understanding an alliance rupture. Countertransference refers to therapist feelings, thoughts, or behaviors that are evoked by a patient's dynamics of maladaptive interpersonal patterns rooted in insecure attachment experiences. Countertransference can be considered objective if it stems from a reaction to the patient behaviors, thoughts, and feelings that would be evoked in any individual. For example, a patient who often ignores a therapist, is frequently late, or is abrasive might evoke complementary distancing feelings of annoyance or eventual disinterest in most individuals. Joel, in the case example above, may evoke objective counter transference in a therapist. On the other hand, subjective countertransference might occur if the patient's behaviors interact with unresolved inner conflict of the therapist (Gelso & Hayes, 2018). For example, had the therapist in the case example of Joel had an angry and abusive attachment figure, then his reactions to Joel might be complicated by this attachment history and its effects on his current functioning.

Countertransference, especially if objective in nature, can provide extremely useful information to the self-aware therapist about the patient's interpersonal style, expectations of others, and others' typical complementary responses. This understanding may also highlight pathways toward helping the therapist repair an alliance rupture. These resolution strategies might involve renegotiating therapy tasks or goals by exploring patient and therapist contributions or needs, "as critical change processes that can transform obstacles in treatment into opportunities" (Muran et al., 2021).

One method of doing this is for the therapist to use meta-communication as a means of making intentions more explicit. Many principles of meta-communication are like some of the principles of mentalizing. Meta-communication guides therapists to "explore with skillful tentativeness," similar to mentalizing's "not-knowing stance," by acknowledging that we make inferences about what might be in others' minds but cannot know with certainty. These therapeutic principles emphasize subjectivity to stir curiosity about internal experiences within interpersonal interactions.

4 Use of Mentalizing to Identify an Alliance Rupture

Countertransference as a Rupture Marker We encourage therapists to use their countertransference experience (boredom, confusion, distraction, anger, not feeling present) as indicators of non-mentalizing states of their patients. These may be signs of a withdrawal or confrontation rupture in the therapeutic alliance. At the same time, it can be helpful for therapists to appreciate how a patient's evocative or distancing interpersonal pulls may be emblematic of the patient's attachment patterns that contribute to interpersonal problems in the present. We find it helpful to remember that such attachment patterns may have developed as adaptive responses to untenable situations in the patient's early attachment relationships. Keeping this in mind can help therapists to remain empathic and resist distancing or hostile tendencies in response to rupture behaviors from a patient.

Recognize Non-mentalizing States Bateman and Fonagy (1996) identified three non-mentalizing states that can be detected in patients: *Teleological Mode, Psychic Equivalence,* and *Pretend Mode*. The Teleological Mode is characterized by selective attention to external actions and misattention to inner experiences such as intentions or feelings of oneself or others—where only actions have currency. For example, teleological mentalizing may be seen in a patient who believes that care is contingent on demonstrating it. That is, by a therapist taking the patient's calls in the middle of the night, or by a therapist extending the therapy session, or by any action that the therapist would not normally do. Such patients may also have a difficult time expressing intense feelings verbally, and so they express despair by self-harm behaviors and act out their anger. Psychic Equivalence refers to being overly certain of the rightness of one's appraisal, oblivious or dismissing to others' perspectives, and unable to consider alternative hypotheses about intentions or motivations behind actions. For example, a patient might feel that someone hates them or is out to undermine them with no evidence for this appraisal and no willingness to consider other viewpoints.

Teleological Mode and Psychic Equivalence non-mentalizing states can be evident in confrontation ruptures, such that patients may be angry if a therapist does not bend the therapeutic frame, or a patient might defend themselves against imagined thoughts, intentions, or feelings that the therapist does not hold. Finally, Pretend Mode describes when people are intellectualizing, engaged in avoidant story telling with little discussion of emotionally charged material, perhaps as a means of defending against their difficult emotions. These can be characteristic of withdrawal ruptures in the therapeutic alliance.

5 Restore Mentalizing to Repair an Alliance Rupture

Once a non-mentalizing state and alliance rupture are identified, the immediate goal is to restore mentalizing in part by returning the patient to a zone of optimal arousal. Ogden and colleagues (2006) described a window of tolerance in which an optimal zone of arousal was ideal for smooth everyday functioning. Mentalizing, for example, requires individuals to be able to both think and feel simultaneously which is only possible in this optimal zone. However, people may find themselves in a state of hyper-arousal (overly anxious, blind with rage, overwhelmed with grief) or hypo-arousal (frozen with fear or in a dissociative state), both of which make it difficult if not impossible to mentalize. If this is the case, a preliminary focus is to help patients to move to the zone of optimal arousal to restore their mentalizing capacity.

Helping a patient to restore their mentalizing can be done in several ways. First, a therapist can *model mentalizing*. That is, a therapist can verbalize their own intentions or feelings, they can accurately empathize with the patient's internal experiences, or they may reflect and wonder aloud on others' intentions. Second, a therapist can *take a not-knowing stance*. This involves a position of open non-defensive curiosity about the patient's feelings, thoughts, or intentions, by checking in with the patient in the here-and-now to validate and explore their experiences. In the context of an alliance rupture, a not-knowing stance can focus on inadvertent, unintended negative impacts the therapist or therapy may have had, accompanied by attempts to clarify and realign treatment goals and tasks.

A third and important mentalizing strategy is to deliberately explore unconsidered dimensions of mentalizing with "*contrary moves*." By dimensions of mentalizing, we mean the mental states that underlie the capacity to mentalize. A lack of balance along these dimensions are indicative of a non-mentalizing state. For example, *thoughts* versus *emotions* is a dimension of mentalizing. A patient in a non-mentalizing state like Pretend Mode might be overly focused on thoughts to the exclusion of emotions. In this case, a contrary move might be to ask patients to consider their emotions related to a particular situation or experience. However, another patient might overly focus on emotions without thoughts or appraisals, and so a contrary move might focus on thoughts. Another dimension of mentalizing includes *inner experiences* versus *external actions*. Some patients are overly focused on their own internal experiences without regard for actions or vice versa. For example, a patient in the Teleological Mode may overvalue and focus on external actions, unaware of others' potential inner experiences of feelings or intentions. A contrary move may focus on asking the patient to consider the internal motivations or intentions of others. On the other hand, someone engaged in Psychic Equivalence may overvalue and be overly focused on inner experiences, and so contrary a move intervention may direct attention to behaviors and expression of feelings. A final dimension of mentalizing is *self* versus *others*. For example, some patients tend to over-focus on their own thoughts and feelings to the exclusion of others, whereas other patients who engage in Psychic Equivalence might be overly focused with over certainty on what others think. Actively listening to patients' narrative allows the therapist may use contrary moves to identify "blind spots" related to aspects and perspectives of experience indicating a narrow attention or misattention on the self or on the other.

> **Therapist Worksheet**
> Identify when a patient is not mentalizing and how they are not mentalizing.
> 1. Notice non-mentalizing states of mind and withdrawal ruptures or tensions in the therapeutic alliance. Identify if the patient is using a Teleological Mode (only actions matter), Psychic Equivalence (I think therefore it is), or Pretend Mode (intellectualization or avoidant story telling) and reflect on whether there is a shared understanding or misunderstanding related to therapeutic goals.
> 2. Notice if there is an unbalance of key mentalizing dimensions when the patient over-focuses on one pole or the other in these dimensions: self versus others, thoughts versus emotions, and/or internal experience versus external actions. Use contrary moves to refocus and rebalance one or more of these dimensions.
> 3. Monitor the patient's affect during the session and seek to keep the patient in an optimal zone of arousal in order to maintain their mentalizing capacity. Help the patient to reduce their emotional arousal if hyper-aroused, or help the patient to increase their arousal if they are numb or dissociated.

6 Mentalizing-Based Interventions

Once non-mentalized dimensions are identified, the therapist can use "*contrary moves*" to help the patient rebalance the non-mentalizing dimension. First, the therapist must provide validation with a summative, empathic reflection to model mentalizing. This can provide the patient with an experience of safety within the alliance, in which the patient feels "held in mind" through the therapist's caring intention to understand and make sense of what the patient may be feeling or thinking. Following this, therapists can deliberately redirect the patient's attention with questions that stir reflection of unconsidered aspects of experience with respect to these dimensions, i.e., a contrary aspect of experience. For example, if a patient is overly focused on thoughts or abstract constructs, the therapist might empathically reflect and validate how this might help the patient to maintain equilibrium in the face of emotions. Then, in a contrary move, the therapist might ask the patient to speculate about their emotions. A similar approach can be taken for the dimensions of self versus other and for internal experiences versus external actions. Contrary moves are not done with the intention of discovering a secret or generating specific insights, e.g., into maladaptive interpersonal patterns, but with the intention to "switch on" reflective functioning with mentalizing of others and oneself, and a broadened awareness of thoughts, feelings, motivations, needs and their impacts.

Finally, a therapist might help the client who was previously mentalizing to return to mentalization by using the technique of "*stop, stand, and rewind.*" For example, a client who was in the optimal zone of arousal might experience a derailment of mentalizing caused by a memory, an emotional experience, or an association with another person or event in their past. In such instances, the therapist who recognizes that a patient is no longer in a mentalizing state might stop the patient's train of thought or content of the session and ask the patient to return to a point in the session during which the patient was mentalizing. For example, a therapist might say: "I lost track of what you were saying when you started talking about your brother's illness. Let's go back to before you started talking about him. What were you thinking then?" Or the therapist can *model mentalizing* and say, "I noticed that you got really angry a moment ago when I asked you about your father. I wonder if I said something that might have touched off your anger?"

To illustrate therapist interventions to recognize and respond to non-mentalizing states and dimensions of mentalizing, we discuss two possible patient personalities that might be challenging in terms of therapeutic alliance tensions. For example, patients with BPD tend to have a sense of psychic equivalence. That is, they are overly certain of their own perspective with little tolerance for others' perspectives. Such patients also tend to operate with a teleological mode by focusing on actions rather than inner experiences or intentions of others. With respect to dimensions of mentalizing, they might externalize blame onto others and selectively attend to emotions, assuming that the negative impacts they experience are caused by others' malicious intentions. Following a validating statement, the therapist might ask the patient questions using "contrary moves" to stir reflection of unconsidered parts of dimensions—from feelings to thoughts or appraisals, or from external actions to internal needs or intentions. On the other hand, patients with narcissistic personality also tend to psychic equivalence by being overly certain and convinced of their perspective and tend to focus on themselves and their own appraisals/thoughts with little consideration of what may be in the minds of others. In this case, following a validating statement, the "contrary moves" would involve asking the patient to reflect on what others may be feeling or needing, and asking them about their own and others' feelings.

> **Therapist Worksheet**
> Use the following therapeutic stances and techniques to restore mentalizing in your patient:
>
> 5. Use metacommunication to tentatively explore implicit intentions and to help the patient to understand interpersonal interactions and their impacts on self and others.
> 6. Use a not-knowing stance of caring curiosity to encourage mentalizing.
> 7. First validate what is valid, then use contrary moves to activate reflective functioning through a process of rebalancing of mentalizing dimensions.
> 8. Stop, stand, and rewind: politely interrupt and stop the process or train of thought and return to a point in the session when the patient was mentalizing.
> 9. Model mentalizing by judicious self-disclosure and wondering aloud about what might be in the mind of the patient.

Case Example Continued

Returning to Joel, when the therapist asked him about workplace stress, Joel stated, "sometimes I have to use the whip" to get workers that he supervises to do their jobs. Although this can be interpreted metaphorically, the therapist felt compelled to explore if there were safety concerns both in the workplace and at home, such as using corporal punishment with his daughter. The therapist asked Joel what he meant about using the "whip" at work and does it apply at home as well. Recall that Joel is very sensitive to expectation that others will criticize him, and so he angrily replied, "Nothing untoward is going on in my family home. I'm not a crazy creep. I'm not going to let you ask me that question." In this response, Joel demonstrated two aspects of a confrontation rupture: he defended himself from a therapist whom he believed was critical (thus also demonstrating psychic equivalence) and he may have been trying to control or coerce the therapist into "not asking that question." Joel went on to provide a clue to early childhood adversity, and stated to his therapist, that he (Joel) does not use "the whip" with Charlotte at home. He loves his daughter, wants to be close to her, and to provide a very different home environment for Charlotte from the house he grew up in. Joel also stated that he did not want to talk about his childhood and that he did not want to relive the past (likely because it was painful and traumatic). Joel likely did not feel much positive nurturing or positive regard from his parents. Likely in past, he felt criticized and invalidated with little sense of control or agency, and presently, he endorses feeling that his wife has "control" and power over him.

The therapist used principles of mentalizing in this moment of tension as a therapeutic opportunity. With respect to dimensions of mentalizing, the therapist noted that Joel was primarily focused on external actions, others, and negative opinions/appraisals. He regularly made assumptions and explanations in what appeared to be teleological and psychic equivalence non-mentalizing states. This was particularly true in relation to the custody arrangement and his perception of wife's attempt to control him (teleological mode), and the belief that his supervisees will not be productive at work unless he "uses the whip" (psychic equivalence). These non-mentalizing states and emblematic distancing interpersonal pulls come to life in the alliance rupture with the therapist when Joel experiences with psychic equivalence that the therapist's question was an attack and negative judgement. In response, the therapist modeled mentalizing by offering his understanding in a validating, non-defensive, and empathic manner that this may be what is in Joel's mind. The therapist tried to clarify possible misunderstandings from a not-knowing stance, and shared his therapeutic intent with Joel in a transparent manner. He also used contrary moves to switch from thoughts to marking Joel's feelings.

> Therapist: "Do you think that's what I am thinking. That you are some crazy creep? I can tell you what I am thinking. I'm thinking that you feel pretty angry, pretty threatened and you see me as part of the problem. I would like to see what else is going on so that I can be part of the solution."
>
> By validating and staying with a focus on the non-mentalized dimensions of affect and self, the therapist goes on to say:

"You said that people don't want to be with you. That generates some feelings for you right now that are pretty painful, I imagine. What we are talking about obviously generates a lot of feelings for you..."

Continuing to use mentalizing strategies, contrary moves, and a "not-knowing" stance of curiosity, the therapist invited the patient to "wonder or explore together." He asked Joel to look beyond the actions or rules around custody arrangements and to consider what his wife's internal experience, viewpoint, or perspective might be.

Therapist: "Do you think that when Sarah asks you, or even when I ask you how you are feeling that it might be coming from a place of interest or concern?"

Joel revealed that what he hears in those moments is a critical voice, and he imagines that others are thinking of him in a judgmental way, "what is wrong with you?". Again, the therapist continued to model mentalizing and to provide Joel with an experience of feeling "held in mind" and without judgment. The therapist validated how painful it must feel to be thinking that others are viewing him in a critical, rejecting way, and by acknowledging that Joel experienced this in his family of origin. Joel began to open up with subsequent therapeutic exploration, and the therapist continued to validate that what was true there-and-then in past relationships is not necessarily true in all present relationships. With time, Joel experienced a growing sense of epistemic trust with the therapist, and he was better able to approach the dispute with his wife in more interpersonally effective ways. Joel became less depressed, and more attuned to himself, his wife, and their daughter. With shared goals of wanting to provide a safe loving and secure experience for their daughter, he and his wife begin to reconcile.

In summary, we encourage therapists to use mentalizing principles to restore reflective functioning for social learning from and within the therapeutic alliance. Therapists must notice therapeutic alliance tensions, non-mentalizing states in their patients, and when the patient is not in an optimal state of arousal. Therapists can model mentalizing by using a "not-knowing stance," "stop, stand, and rewind" to a point in the session in which the patient was mentalizing, and contrary moves to rebalance mentalizing dimensions. For example, a therapist might ask about feelings when patients appear to be stuck on appraisals and vice versa or ask about intentions behind behaviors when patients selectively attend to emotional impacts. In here-and-now moments of the therapeutic relationship, mentalizing focuses therapists' attention on the inevitable lapses and blind-spots of both therapists and patients. When mentalizing goes offline or is absent, then the priority is for therapists to restore a mentalizing state in patients. "Common manifestations of restricted mentalizing, such as unwarranted certainty, unsubstantiated presumptions about feelings and beliefs, or insistence on actions, are most likely found in the gaps between the intentions and impacts of communication" [Law, Ravitz et al. under review]. Thus, we propose that therapeutic alliance tensions or ruptures can be repaired via the use of mentalizing strategies in the process of clarifying and finding agreement on the goals and tasks of therapy.

Chapter Review Exercises

1. Maria is a 42-year-old woman who lives with her elderly, recently widowed mother. Maria was referred to psychotherapy for worsening depression with tearfulness, terminal insomnia, difficulties concentrating, anergia, and an increased appetite with weight gain of 10 kg over the past six months since her father's death. She never previously sought treatment, though she has a history of depressive episodes in which her functioning decreased, but she never had to stop work due to depressive symptoms. She has long looked after her parents; and her late father was described as demanding and critical. Sometimes she witnessed him being violent with her mother. The father did not appreciate that Maria was devoted and supportive daughter. Maria's mother is described as always overwhelmed and as having parentified Maria as the eldest daughter. Maria's younger siblings are married with children. At her first therapy session, Maria was tearful and silent, she was highly self-critical and felt guilty for not doing enough for her parents, and she appeared to be in a disorganized and emotionally charged state. From this brief vignette, (1) discuss whether she is in an optimal zone of arousal, (2) what imbalance might you expect in terms of mentalizing dimensions, and (3) what might be ways to promote mentalizing?

   Answers: (1) Maria is in a state of hyper-arousal. (2) The self-criticism and guilt for not doing enough for her parents suggests an over focus on others and not herself, and perhaps on external actions and not internal experiences. (3) Help to calm her emotional state so that she can begin to mentalize. Once calmed, validate her experiences of loss and of feeling invalidated by her father and use contrary moves to help her focus on others and their actions.

2. After Maria and her therapist established a trusting bond within the alliance, and an agreement on some goals to help her to feel and do better, the therapy seems to stall and is at an impasse. Maria brings in baked goods at every therapy session. She tends to speak of the many helping activities she does for others both for her mother and in the workplace.

   Which *non-mentalizing states of mind* might likely be contributory to the impasse?

   A. Teleological Mode
   B. Psychic Equivalence
   C. Pretend Mode

   Answer: A. Teleological Mode

3. Based on the above case description of Maria, and to guide the use of contrary moves, which mentalizing dimensions of selection attention are prominent?

   A. Thoughts/appraisals
   B. Emotions
   C. External actions

D. Internal experiences
   E. Self
   F. Others
   Answers: C and F.

4. If you were to model mentalizing, what would you say?

   Answer (example): "I get the sense that you bring me these wonderful baked goods as a way of helping me see what a good person you are. What if I already know that about you without the baking?"

5. If you were to use contrary moves regarding Maria's imbalance in the self versus other dimension, what would you say?

   Answer (example): "I can see that you are concerned about your aging mother, I wonder if you can talk about what have you thought about when it comes to your own future?"

6. Maria starts session #7 tearfully telling you about Father's Day and visiting her father's gravesite with her mother. Then Maria describes a visit to her brother's home, and in some detail, she describes the delicious menu of food that her sister-in-law served. With mentalizing in mind, how might the therapist respond and why?

   Answer (example): The therapist might validate that it might be difficult for Maria to stay with her sadness and mixed feelings about her father. Then using *contrary moves* and *stop, stand, and rewind*, the therapist might bring Maria's attention back to her own feeling at the gravesite and away from the discourse about what her sister-in-law cooked.

References

Aival-Naveh, E., Rothschild-Yakar, L., & Kurman, J. (2019). Keeping culture in mind: A systematic review and initial conceptualization of mentalizing from a cross-cultural perspective. *Clinical Psychology: Science and Practice, 26*(4), 25.

Bateman, A., & Fonagy, P. (2008). 8-year follow-up of patients treated for borderline personality disorder: Mentalization-based treatment versus treatment as usual. *American Journal of Psychiatry, 165*(5), 631–638.

Bateman, A., & Fonagy, P. (2019). *Handbook of mentalizing in mental health practice*. American Psychiatric Association Press.

Bateman, A., Campbell, C., Luyten, P., & Fonagy, P. (2018). A mentalization-based approach to common factors in the treatment of borderline personality disorder. *Current Opinion in Psychology, 21*, 44–49.

Bateman, A., & Fonagy, P. (1999). The effectiveness of partial hospitalization in the treatment of borderline personality disorder - a randomised controlled trial. *Am J Psychiatry. 156*, 1563–1569.

Bateman, A., & Fonagy, P. (2001). Treatment of borderline personality disorder with psychoanalytically oriented partial hospitalisation: an 18-month followup. *Am J Psychiatry. 158*, 36–42.

Betan, E., Heim, A. K., Conklin, C. Z., & Westen, D. (2005). Countertransference phenomena and personality pathology in clinical practice: An empirical investigation. *American Journal of Psychiatry, 162*(5), 890–898.

Bowlby, J. (1982). Attachment and loss – Retrospect and prospect. *American Journal of Orthopsychiatry, 52*(4), 664–678.

Eubanks, C. F., Burckell, L. A., & Goldfried, M. R. (2018a). Clinical consensus strategies to repair ruptures in the therapeutic alliance. *Journal of Psychotherapy Integration, 28*(1), 60–76.

Eubanks, C. F., Muran, J. C., & Safran, J. D. (2018b). Alliance rupture repair: A meta-analysis. *Psychotherapy, 55*(4), 508–519.

Fluckiger, C., Del Re, A. C., Wampold, B. E., & Horvath, A. O. (2018). The alliance in adult psychotherapy: A meta-analytic synthesis. *Psychotherapy, 55*(4), 316–340.

Fonagy, P., & Allison, E. (2014). The role of mentalizing and epistemic trust in the therapeutic relationship. *Psychotherapy, 51*(3), 372–380.

Fonagy, P., Luyten, P., Allison, E., & Campbell, C. (2019). Mentalizing, epistemic trust and the phenomenology of psychotherapy. *Psychopathology, 52*(2), 94–103.

Hayes, J. A., Gelso, C. J., Goldberg, S., & Kivlighan, D. M. (2018). Countertransference management and effective psychotherapy: Meta-analytic findings. *Psychotherapy (Chic), 55*(4), 496–507. https://doi.org/10.1037/pst0000189. PMID: 30335461.

Holmes, J. (2015). Attachment theory in clinical practice: A personal account. *British Journal of Psychotherapy, 31*(2), 208–228.

Hunter, J. J., & Maunder, R. G. (2001). Using attachment theory to understand illness behavior. *General Hospital Psychiatry, 23*(4), 177–182.

Kiesler, D. J. (1983). The 1982 interpersonal circle – A taxonomy for complementarity in human transactions. *Psychological Review, 90*(3), 185–214.

Law, R., Ravitz, P., Pain, C., & Fonagy, P. (2022). Interpersonal Psychotherapy and Mentalizing — Synergies in clinical practice. *American Journal of Psychotherapy*. (Am J Psychother 2022 Jan 1;75(1):44–50. https://doi.org/10.1176/appi.psychotherapy.20210024. Epub 2022 Mar 2.

Leszcz, M., Pain, C., Hunter, J., Maunder, R., & Ravitz, P. (2015). *Psychotherapy essentials to go: Achieving psychotherapy effectiveness*. WW Norton.

Luyten, P., Campbell, C., Allison, E., & Fonagy, P. (2020). The mentalizing approach to psychopathology: State of the art and future directions. *Annual Review of Clinical Psychology, 16*, 297–325.

Muran, J. C., Eubanks, C. F., & Samstag, L. W. (2021). One more time with less jargon: An introduction to "rupture repair in practice". *Journal of Clinical Psychology, 77*(2), 361–368.

Ogden, P., Minton, K., & Pain, C. (2006). *Trauma and the body: A sensorimotor approach to psychotherapy (norton series on interpersonal neurobiology)*. WW Norton & Company.

Ravitz, P., Maunder, R., & McBride, C. (2008). Attachment, contemporary interpersonal theory and IPT: An integration of theoretical, clinical, and empirical perspectives. *Journal of Contemporary Psychotherapy, 38*(1), 11–21.

Safran, J. D., Muran, J. C., & Eubanks-Carter, C. (2011). Repairing alliance ruptures. *Psychotherapy, 48*(1), 80–87.

Safran, J. D., & Muran, J. C. (2000). *Negotiating the therapeutic alliance: A relational treatment guide*. Guilford Press.

Tasca, G. A., & Poletti, B. (2023). Formulazione del caso: Costruire una comprensione condivisa del mondo relazionale del paziente. In Poletti, B., Tasca, G.A., Pievani, L., & Compare, A (Eds.), Psicoterapia integrata: Il modello evidence based practice. Italy: FrancoAngeli.

Zeegers, M. A. J., Colonnesi, C., Stams, G., & Meins, E. (2017). Mind matters: A meta-analysis on parental mentalization and sensitivity as predictors of infant-parent attachment. *Psychological Bulletin, 143*(12), 1245–1272.

The Role of Trauma in the Therapeutic Relationship

Luca Pievani, Cristina Mapelli, and Isabel Fernandez

1 The Trauma

A potentially traumatic event is defined as a sudden and direct confrontation with death or its equivalents (such as serious harm, assault, or witnessing catastrophic events) (APA, 2013, 1980, 2000). The DSM also defines the possibility of indirect exposure, caused by communication from afar of the death or serious harm of relatives or close friends (APA, 2013, 1980, 2000; Guina et al., 2016). A traumatic event, as such, includes an immediate subjective feeling of traumatic or peritraumatic distress, characterised by negative emotions of fear, helplessness, revulsion, and/or horror (WHO, 2013; APA, 2013). We can therefore state that there are two aspects of trauma to be considered: one related to the type of event that causes a rupture in the internal dynamics of the organism and another related to the representation that the subject creates of that particular event and its consequences (Cyrulnik, 2000). The impact of psychological trauma is therefore subjective. Depending on personality characteristics, surroundings, emotional and cognitive structure, an event may have a more or less traumatic impact on a person's functioning.

The authors would like to thank Dr. Giovanni Tagliavini for his valuable contribution in revising the chapter.

L. Pievani (✉)
Scuola di Psicoterapia Integrata, Bergamo, Italy

C. Mapelli
ASST San Gerardo di Monza, Monza, Italy

I. Fernandez
Centro di Ricerca e Studi in Psicotraumatologia (CRSP), Milan, Italy

1.1 Post-traumatic Stress Disorder—Simple or Complex

Post-traumatic stress disorder, or PTSD, refers to a set of symptoms that may begin following exposure to a traumatising event. It was only included within the diagnostic categories of the DSM in the third edition, published in 1980 (APA, 1980). Initially introduced in the category of anxiety disorders, with the publication of the DSM V (APA, 2013), it was moved to the category 'traumatic and stressful event-related disorders'. Although the exact definition of PTSD and its categorisation have changed over the years, the four core symptom criteria have remained largely unchanged.

The basic criterion requires that the individual has been personally exposed to a *traumatic event* or has become aware of a seriously dangerous/deadly situation that happened to a close family member or friend. One of the pathognomonic signs of the disorder is re-experiencing (the person re-experiences the traumatic event) with the same distress, perceptions, emotions, and dissociative components that were originally experienced. The emotional component (fear, anxiety, distress) and related negative thoughts are also re-experienced. These episodes can occur during sleep (as traumatic nightmares) and during the waking period (in the form of flashbacks) (Auxéméry, 2018). Other manifestations are also possible: intrusive memories perceived as distinct from the original events; mental ruminations about the event; delusions of reliving the event by recognising elements of it in the environment; elementary motor phenomena that replicate the motor response from the time of the event; or repetitive behaviour (APA, 2013; Crocq, 1999). Another fundamental symptom cluster, which originates from the fear of new traumatic events, or from flashbacks during moments of decreased consciousness, concerns *symptoms of arousal dysregulation,* which most frequently fall into the category of hyperarousal symptoms (hypervigilance, irritability, startle response, restlessness), although some authors claim that there is a 'dissociative' subtype of PTSD characterised by the presence of hypoarousal symptoms including the collapse of cognitive functions (Lanius et al., 2010). Finally, the last cluster comprises cognitive and behavioural strategies of stimulus avoidance (places, activities, people, objects, internal perceptions) designed to avoid the resurfacing of traumatic memories (Auxéméry, 2018).

Prevalence data on PTSD in the general population vary significantly between studies. Some authors estimate that the percentage of people with PTSD in the US population may be as high as 6–9% (Kessler et al., 2005). Similar percentages are also provided by the American Psychological Association, which claims that the disorder affects about 5% of men and 10% of women (again taking the United States as the sample). As for the percentage of individuals who develop PTSD following exposure to a traumatic event, it ranges between 12% and 40% (Shalev et al., 2019; Sareen, 2014; Hidalgo & Davidson, 2000). There is general agreement within the different studies that the probability of developing PTSD depends on both risk factors and the type of traumatising event. The main risk factors include female gender, low education, poverty, the presence of mental health disorders, certain personality traits, and genetic factors (Atwoli et al., 2015). With regard to the type of trauma, it would appear that victims of physical assault or sexual violence are the groups most at risk of developing a post-traumatic clinical disorder. Finally, according to the literature, there are post-event conditions that may facilitate the emergence of PTSD. These include a lack of social support, financial difficulties, and the presence of disability or chronic pain (Sareen et al., 2007; Zalta et al., 2021). PTSD is therefore a frequent pathology in the clinical population.

The diagnostic category described so far fits well with those individuals who manifest the above-mentioned symptoms following a single traumatic event. In the 1990s, however, clinicians began to observe that the criteria for PTSD as they were described from DSM-III onwards failed to provide a comprehensive explanation of the complexity of symptoms manifested by individuals who had experienced cumulative traumatic experiences (Bryant, 2010; Chu, 2010). Judith Herman was the first to coin the term complex PTSD and, together with eminent colleagues, including Bessel van der Kolk, to propose its inclusion in the DSM IV under the acronym *DESNOS* (Disorder of Extreme Stress Not Otherwise Specified; Herman, 1992).

Complex PTSD typically manifests following repeated traumatic events of an interpersonal nature, particularly if these events occur in childhood (Ford & Courtois, 2009). In addition to the typical symptoms of uncomplicated PTSD, individuals presenting with this clinical picture show a constellation of additional symptoms such as severe difficulties with relationships and emotion regulation, impulsivity, self-injury, dissociative symptoms, identity alterations, and somatisation (Herman, 1992). According to Liotti and Farina, one of the main risk factors for the development of complex PTSD are experiences of maltreatment, abuse, or a history of severe neglect in childhood (Liotti & Farina, 2011). It was only in 2018 that this diagnostic category was included in the 11th edition of the International Classification of Diseases (ICD-11; WHO, 2019). The criteria provided by ICD-11 include the three main symptom clusters of simple PTSD (i.e. intrusive memories, avoidance symptoms, and hyperarousal), as well as three additional symptom clusters characteristic of patients with complex PTSD: emotional dysregulation, interpersonal difficulties, and negative self-view.

1.2 Dissociation

Optimal psychological functioning requires the ability to integrate a broad spectrum of cognitive functions, emotional processes, and somatic sensations. The integration of these factors helps the individual to 'treasure' the events of their past in order to live fully in the present and to make wise and conscious decisions for their future. van der Hart et al. (2006) speak of integration as realisation, understanding realisation as a complete acceptance of reality combined with an effective ability to adapt to events.

The term dissociation thus refers to the failure to achieve or the loss of coherence and integration of psychic activities (Janet, 1898). Within the DSM-5 (Diagnostic and Statistical Manual, 5th Ed.; APA, 2013), dissociation is defined as 'disconnection and/or discontinuity of the normal integration of consciousness, memory, identity, emotionality, perception, bodily representation, motor control, and behaviour'.

What is the relationship between trauma and dissociation? The association between the two variables appears to be strong and bidirectional. In favour of the hypothesis that dissociation is a consequence of trauma is the substantial body of literature that shows that among patients with dissociative disorder, there is a higher percentage of histories of emotional and physical abuse or neglect in childhood compared to other psychiatric disorders (Dutra et al., 2009; Sar et al., 2014; van Huijstee & Vermetten, 2018; Krüger & Fletcher, 2017). In these cases, dissociation would play a protective role, at least initially.

The individual, when faced with an overwhelming experience (trauma), would put in place a protective mechanism in order to avoid a complete disorganisation of the mind (dissociation), excluding traumatic experiences from conscious experience. Charcot, Freud, and especially Janet, already spoke of personality separation as a consequence of psychological trauma in the late 1800s (Dorahy & Van der Hart, 2007). However, if in the short term dissociation has a protective effect, over time this mechanism tends to become chronic, becoming the process through which the person organises experiences even when faced with situations in which the degree of danger is not high. Dissociative functioning would then lead the individual to implement maladaptive coping strategies, favouring the emergence of relational and work difficulties and, potentially, increasing the risk of re-traumatisation. Finally, the link between trauma and dissociation also appears well supported by neurobiological studies (Farina et al., 2014; Reinders et al., 2016; Lanius et al., 2018). According to reports in the literature, patients with post-traumatic disorders experience a reduction in brain grey matter in the hippocampus, anterior cingulate and medial prefrontal cortex, amygdala, and insular cortex, structures considered crucial for the proper functioning of autobiographical memory and attentional and metacognitive functions, which are essential in experiential integration processes (Bremner, 2006; Thome et al., 2020).

Categories of Dissociative Symptoms

Over the years, the term 'dissociation' has become an 'umbrella' category, within which numerous dissociative manifestations, some of them very different from each other, fit. Among the main ones are derealisation and depersonalisation, psychogenic amnesia, altered sense of identity, major emotional dysregulation, mental confusion and attentional difficulties, and even multiple personality disorders. In 2005, Holmes was the first to attempt to clarify and classify these phenomena into two main categories: dissociation as detachment and dissociation as compartmentalisation (Holmes et al., 2005; Brown, 2006). In the case of detachment, dissociation would manifest as a *symptom*, causing frequent discontinuities in the individual's experience. Dissociation as compartmentalisation, on the other hand, would represent the *process* through which the system creates fractures within the personality in which it encloses emotional parts that, if activated, would be incompatible with adaptation to the reality of everyday life. Let us see in more detail which clinical manifestations can be found within these two categories.

Liotti and Farina, in their book *Traumatic Developments* (Liotti & Farina, 2011), define detachment symptoms as that set of sensations that refer to the experience of feeling alienated from one's self, one's emotions, one's body, and the surrounding reality in response to threatening events. *Depersonalisation*, i.e. the persistent feeling of being detached from one's body and one's psychic processes, and even phenomena in which patients report being able to observe their bodies from the outside (autoscopy), fall into this category. *Emotional numbing is* also considered a form of depersonalisation. When the persistent sensation concerns feeling detached from external reality, one speaks instead of *derealisation*. In this case, in addition to the sense of unreality, patients may come to perceive objects as distorted, colours altered, or familiar places or people as unfamiliar.

Dissociative compartmentalisation symptoms occur most frequently following complex and repeated traumatisation over time, when it is impossible for the individual's mind to reach a level of integration that is functional for adaptation to reality. The sense of self, therefore, instead of being unitary, becomes fragmented. This fragmentation of the self may manifest as *dissociative amnesia* i.e. the inability to recall important autobiographical information, up to and including *dissociative fugue,* understood as a sudden departure from one's everyday life associated with confusion about one's identity (APA, 2000). The most severe picture of compartmentalisation certainly manifests itself with *dissociative identity disorder*, in which various dissociative parts of the personality develop autonomous and independent executive capacities in the course of the patient's everyday life (and not only within his or her inner world; van der Hart et al., 2006).

As mentioned at the beginning of the paragraph, according to van der Hart's (van der Hart et al., 2006) theory of Structural Dissociation, compartmentalisation constitutes the actual dissociative pathology, while the symptoms of detachment represent the expressive modalities of the process that generates it.

We emphasise how the DSM-5 (APA, 2013) includes within the category of dissociative disorders both syndromes referred to as detachment symptoms (depersonalisation/derealisation disorder) and others referred to as compartmentaliation symptoms (dissociative identity disorder, dissociative amnesia).

Finally, it is worth mentioning the concept of somatoform dissociation, first introduced by Nijenhuis in Nijenhuis, 2009, which refers to those dissociative disorders that involve the body and include both negative symptoms such as loss of sensory perception or motor control and positive symptoms such as tingling, trembling, or pain syndromes (e.g. psychogenic pain symptoms). Historically, conversion disorders also fall into this category.

2 Trauma in the Therapeutic Relationship

2.1 Trauma, Disorganised Attachment, and Metacognitive Functions

According to Bowlby, the child is born with a biological predisposition to develop an attachment to the caregiver. The attachment system would thus have the function of activating the caregiver to provide protection and security (Bowlby, Bowlby, 1983). On an evolutionary level, attachment is an innate system that fulfils a protective function exercised through the active search for closeness to a member of one's own species. Activating the attachment system, therefore, increases the individual's chances of survival. Again according to Bowlby, this system fosters both physiological and psychological development by facilitating the creation of a secure base from which the child explores the world and to which it returns for refuge when overwhelmed or threatened in some way (Pearlman & Courtois, 2005). Attachment is an interpersonal motivational system (IMS), an innate tendency of the individual that regulates our behaviour and emotions according to specific goals (Gilbert, 1989; Liotti, 1995). The basic IMSs are attachment (aimed at obtaining protection), caring (aimed at providing care), sexuality (aimed at maintaining the couple), agonistic or rank system (aimed at defining a hierarchy), the social game system and the cooperative system (aimed at achieving a common goal).

Depending on the quality of the relationship with the attachment figure, at around 18 months of age, the child will begin to create an image of himself, of others, and of their relationship with others (Internal Working Models or IWMs). What we are saying, then, is that a child who has the opportunity to have a responsive and caring caregiver will probably develop a secure attachment that will lead him or her to trust others and to have a positive and integrated self-image and sense of self. But what happens when a child grows up in sub-optimal care contexts to the point of violence or neglect?

The strange situation paradigm (Ainsworth et al., 1978) made it possible to identify two insecure attachment styles, in addition to the secure attachment style, on the basis of children's behavioural responses to separation and reunion with caregivers: an insecure-avoidant attachment style, characterised by an absence of protest and high emotional control, and an insecure-ambivalent or resistant style, characterised instead by a high index of expressiveness of emotions associated with inconsolability.

In later years, observation of children in the strange situation led to the hypothesis of the presence of a fourth attachment style, termed disorganised (Main & Solomon, 1986). The child with a disorganised attachment style, during moments of separation and reunion with the caregiver, manifests contradictory behaviour in rapid sequence (e.g. the child's arms and legs are projected towards the parent, but the head and gaze turn in the opposite direction). In more severe cases, dissociative symptoms may be observed at reunion or separation, in which the child may appear motionless, detached, absent, or blocked looking (Main & Morgan, 1996). Liotti has been one of the most important scholars of the relationship between developmental trauma, disorganised attachment, and Interpersonal Motivational Systems or IMS (Cortina & Liotti, 2014) and the first to build a bridge between ethological and neurophysiological studies and between cognitivism and psychoanalysis, delving into the relationship between disorganised attachment and pathological dissociation (Tagliavini & Boldrini, 2021). This is particularly the case in situations of severe and continuous abuse and neglect in which the caregiver is both the source of threat and the source of care. According to Liotti, the mechanism behind this may lie in the simultaneous activation of two motivational systems: the defence system and the attachment system. Under optimal developmental conditions, these two systems interact harmoniously: a frightened child runs away from danger and seeks comfort and protection from the attachment figure, thus defusing the defence system. In disorganised attachment, however, the attachment figure is both a source of danger and comfort, generating in the child unbridled terror and conflicting emotional reactions and leading him to develop an IWM characterised by incoherence and fragmentation. Liotti (2001) hypothesises that the activation of the disorganised IWM is accompanied by the experience of a painful mental state of annihilation and dissolution of the sense of self. As a defence against this unbearable feeling of instability and helplessness, attachment would be inhibited and in its place another motivational system would be activated. The child, in order to avoid the activation of the attachment system considered dangerous, will develop controlling strategies in the relationship with the caregiver, based on other motivational systems, such as the controlling-punitive strategy, based on the rank system, or the controlling-caring strategy, based on the caregiving system. In the controlling-punitive strategy, the child takes over by directing the parent and becoming overbearing (clinically some of these children become tyrannical and take control of the family). This is a co-option of the hierarchical dominance system we see in primates. The other form is a controlling-caring strategy in which the child becomes caring for the perceived frightened and weak parent. This strategy is an indication of the reversal of the normal direction of the attachment-care interaction between parent and child (Bureau et al., 2009). According to Lyons-Ruth, at around 6 years old, about 80 percent of children who are found to be disorganised in the strange situation paradigm manifest caring or punitive strategies to control parental behaviour (Lyons-Ruth et al., 2005).

Monticelli hypothesised the existence of sexualised controlling strategies that would serve to regulate the sense of and the relationship with the fearful attachment figure; in the course of development, these strategies could result in perverse behaviour potentially triggered by situations of vulnerability and loneliness, i.e. those situations that, under normal conditions, would activate the attachment system (Monticelli, 2005).

Controlling strategies, although they may be considered dysfunctional in the long term and for the development of the child's personality, are in the short term adaptive to the maintenance of an internal organisation of the child, avoiding the activation of a disorganised and dissociated Internal Working Model (IWM).

The collapse of controlling strategies may occur when the attachment system is activated more intensively (Hesse et al., 2003). This collapse would also lead to a sudden impairment of the individual's metacognitive abilities, functions that are highly sensitive to both the effect of emotional dysregulation and repeated traumatic experiences (Liotti & Prunetti, 2010). In essence, repeated traumas would have an impact on the mechanisms that allow us to quickly and implicitly understand our own mental states and those of others, favouring the appearance of maladaptive interpersonal patterns (e.g. perceiving others as threatening). Even alexithymia, i.e. the inability to perceive and identify emotions, can sometimes be a metacognitive outcome of a traumatic development.

2.2 Trauma Within the Therapeutic Relationship

To explore the ways in which trauma influences the therapeutic relationship, it is first necessary to give a definition of therapeutic alliance. The most widely accepted definition is that of Bordin, who defined the therapeutic alliance as an agreement on therapy goals and tasks, and an emotional bond between client and therapist (Bordin, 1979). As we mentioned earlier, however, in patients with histories of traumatic development, the traumas experienced are typically interpersonal in nature. The therapeutic relationship, as well as relationships in general, represents one of the greatest triggers for the traumatised patient since some of their deepest wounds were inflicted within a meaningful bond. Establishing a climate of trust and cooperation may be particularly challenging for the therapist, who will have to deal with frequent ruptures and repairs of the alliance and with particularly complex relational dynamics.

Hence, the importance of catching signs that may point towards the psychotraumatological field as early as possible, in order to implement from the very first interviews relational interventions that increase regulation and decrease the patient's internal conflicts.

Some patients come to psychotherapy practices complaining of symptoms typical of complex post-traumatic stress or recounting traumatic childhood episodes. These categories include those patients who already report stories of severe neglect, abandonment, or maltreatment in the first sessions, who complain of major dissociative symptoms, multiple personalities, or sometimes self-injurious acts. In many other cases, the clinical pictures that motivate the start of a therapeutic pathway may 'deceive' the clinician, concealing behind a non-specific symptom (e.g. a panic attack) a psychopathological functioning typical of the traumatic environment.

What, then, are the indirect but often pathognomonic clinical signs of complex PTSD? According to Liotti and Farina (2011), important information can be gleaned from autobiographical narratives, from the use of relational modalities typical of controlling strategies, from barely evident or latent clinical symptoms, and from the therapist's experiences.

The theme of the therapist's experiences as a 'marker' of possible dissociative functioning of the patient will be addressed in the next section, which focuses on the impact of hypo- and hyper-arousal states on therapy.

Regarding the issue of the patient's autobiographical narrative, it is important to pay attention both to what the patient is saying and how he/she says it. As already mentioned, special attention should be paid to the presence of episodes of severe neglect or mistreatment in the first years of life, accounts of significant bereavements involving a caregiver of reference in the pre- or peri-natal phase, conditions of extreme poverty, and attachment figures affected by major psychological pathologies. With regard to the qualitative aspects of the patient's narrative, an autobiographical account characterised by excessive confusion in placing events in a diachronic perspective or by frank amnesia for events that occurred in childhood may be considered a red flag. Another characteristic concerns the patient's inability to access episodic memory, instead exploiting semantic memories to answer the therapist's questions (e.g. 'my father was always angry').

Case 1

Lucia is a 42-year-old woman, married and the mother of two children, who comes to therapy following the onset of a panic attack disorder that began about six months earlier, after the premature death of a relative of her own age. During the first interview, she recounts that the most significant event in her early years was a hospital admission for prolonged hyperpyrexia at the age of 16 months. According to the patient, at that time parents could not spend the night in hospital with their children, so she was left alone and found by her mother in the morning tied to her bed. About five interviews later, Lucia returns to that event; this time, however, she remembers that she is a two and a half year old girl and when her mother arrives at the hospital in the morning she does not find her tied to the bed but in a state of trance while incessantly repeating 'quiet, mummy will be here soon'. When asked by the therapist to clarify whether it was a different episode from the one recounted in the first session, Lucia is astonished and confirms that it is the same episode she had already talked about. Throughout the sessions, it emerged that Lucia's mother had suffered from severe depression during those years, even going so far as to develop a suicidal ideation that she never materialised.

According to Liotti and Farina (2011), other possible signs of chronic traumatisation can be found in the relational modalities that patients use in their relationship with their therapist. As we mentioned in the previous section, individuals who suffer trauma in their relationship with attachment figures in the first years of life will frequently develop a disorganised type of attachment and will need to use controlling strategies to maintain the relationship with caregivers without activating the attachment system. Without intervention, these same strategies will also be used in adulthood. Catching indicators of the use of controlling strategies in therapy may therefore be an important clue to the presence of complex PTSD. The therapist may thus find themselves involved in therapeutic relationships characterised by strategies based on the rank system (in the dominant or submissive form), the nurturing system, or the sexuality system. A patient who uses control through the rank-submission motivational system is a compliant patient who tends to gratify the therapist through compliments or gifts. He may appear extremely compliant to the therapist's requests (e.g. homework), but in reality the therapist may perceive this as inauthentic. In the case of the controlling-punishing strategy, one may detect a critical, contemptuous and sometimes oppositional attitude from the patient towards the relational moves made by the therapist. The clinician will be made the object of attacks and therapy will be considered a useless investment of time and money. The controlling-accommodating strategy, on the other hand, manifests as excessive concern for the therapist and his or her health. Typically, these patients also manifest this attitude outside of therapy, as they are unable to establish boundaries in their requests for help from relatives and friends. Finally, patients with histories of sexual abuse may make use of seduction and sexuality in order to be accepted by the therapist. In terms of symptoms, this category of patients may come to therapy reporting symptoms from the realm of sexual disorders (e.g. perversion or paraphilias). Therapy with patients who seduce and eroticise the relationship, including patients with perversions, can be very difficult for the clinician to sustain. These difficulties can be traced back to the particular emotional reactions induced in the therapist, and the intensity and eroticisation of the relationship that could lead to a hostile and intrusive attitude that could make the therapist feel overwhelmed.

We reaffirm that in those cases the motivational systems of dominance and protection are strategies designed to avoid the upsetting dissociative feelings, the unbearable experience of fear without solution, and a relational chaos that creates feelings of helplessness. The interpersonal problems that emerge from attempting to regulate dissociative experiences and the controlling strategies associated with disorganised attachment histories create formidable challenges during the clinical exchange. During a therapeutic process that is proceeding well, it is not unusual to observe a sudden emergence of dominant-punitive behaviours and attitudes. These sudden ruptures are difficult to understand on the basis of previous interactions. The conflictual activation of attachment and defence systems, together with the activation of controlling strategies, is at the root of many traumatic transference and countertransference (Howell, 2011). These controlling patterns may also be accompanied by the fluctuation of affect regulation strategies that minimise or magnify attachment needs.

Sudden and dramatic changes between the roles of victim, persecutor, and rescuer could be another manifestation of complex and cumulative traumatic attachment experiences, in which a patient feels an urgent need to rescue a loved one using overprotective behaviours in the rescuer role, followed by a sudden switch to persecutor roles (Liotti, 2000).

Finally, according to Steele and van der Hart et al. (2013), there is one last strategy that the patient may employ to unconsciously activate the therapist's caretaking to achieve a greater sense of safety: the attachment cry. The attachment cry is usually elicited by feelings of loneliness and abandonment. For a patient with complex trauma, even a session drawing to conclusion may represent a trigger for the activation of overwhelming experiences, leading him or her to manifest the attachment cry with episodes of weeping and despair in the final phase of the interview, and difficulty in leaving the therapy room or the waiting room. Similarly, a patient employing the attachment cry may go so far as to attempt to contact the therapist outside of sessions, sometimes in an exaggerated and manipulative manner.

Case 2

Rossella is a 38-year-old single woman who comes to therapy following a diagnosis of an autoimmune disease that has led to a long hospitalisation. From the very first interview she made it explicit that she wanted to deepen her relational dynamics with the men she was seeing, which prompted her quickly move from the weaker role within the couple (victim) to a decidedly more aggressive, controlling, and provocative one (perpetrator), to the point of leading her to countless relationships breakups. During the interviews, Scarlett described her childhood as a 'place' in which she never felt safe. Her mother, in particular, was a woman with strong narcissistic traits and extremely manipulative and provocative attitudes towards her husband, who eventually gave in to repeated provocations and became physically violent with both his wife and children. On the Adverse Childhood Experiences questionnaire (Felitti, 1998), Scarlett scored a 5. Around the 20th interview, Scarlett cancelled four appointments in a row, skipping about a month of therapy. Once she resumed her work, she was able in the session to focus on a mechanism that has always governed her functioning: following a series of particularly positive sessions, she began to experience a feeling of imminent danger and sadness, which led her to withdraw from therapy. In this case too, the relational mechanism re-proposed within the therapy concerned the relationship with the mother, who 'destroyed' everything the daughter liked, conditioning her to create an association between positive emotions, feelings of danger and experiences of loss. Even later in the therapy, in the first session following a break for the summer holidays, Scarlett attacked the therapist, discrediting the therapy and the results obtained up to that moment, only to present herself at the next session with a gift for the therapist and showing a caring attitude towards the clinician.

Let us add one last factor: dissociative pathology is a pathology that tends to hide and take other forms; rarely will the patient be able to talk about it openly. Sometimes it may take the form of other psychopathological disorders. It is not unusual for the dissociative patient to come to therapy referring to the numerous diagnostic labels that have been attributed to him or her in previous courses of treatment or psychiatric visits (Liotti & Farina, 2011; Rezzonico & Furlani, 2019).

Once the possible signs of chronic traumatisation that the patient might bring to therapy are understood, what are other specific indications for a therapist working with a complex patient, in addition to the basic rules for creating a good therapeutic alliance?

Drawing from Winnicott's concept of the 'good enough mother', Cozolino (2004) proposes the term 'good enough therapist', i.e. a therapist who is able to provide consistency and security to the patient, but at the same time accepts they will go through frequent desynchronisations and ruptures within the therapeutic relationship that need to be mended. The characteristics that make a therapist able to establish an effective therapeutic relationship with a complex patient are a good awareness of one's own functioning and of the motivational systems that are activated in therapy in order to avoid as much as possible the activation of the patient's attachment system (Liotti & Farina, 2011; Schore, 2012), the habit of asking the patient for feedback on the work done and on the relationship (Norcross & Lambert, 2011), and the ability to 'hold together' the patient's numerous contradictions by seeing the system as a whole (Bromberg, 1993).

No less important, the therapist should be able to maintain clear and predictable setting and relationship boundaries that are ideally consistent with the therapist's personal boundaries. According to Steele et al. (2017), the more aware therapists are of their boundaries, the more they will be able to identify when the patient crosses them or when they themselves fail to respect them.

Finally, a good awareness of one's own functioning will enable the clinician working with trauma to identify in good time the unconsciously enacted relationship mechanisms (re-enactments) that arise within the therapist-patient dyad (Bromberg, 2006). In these situations, some non-integrated parts of the patient (e.g. controlling-punishing) may lead the therapist to implicitly assume the corresponding opposing role (e.g. fearful-conciliating therapist).

2.3 The Impact of Hypo- and Hyperarousal in the Therapeutic Process

Attachment insecurity and trauma have a profound and often severe impact on the neurophysiological development of the individual, leading to limited capacities and somatic and emotional dysregulation (Siegel, 1999). In order to address this section more effectively, it is necessary to provide some background information on two of the theories most psychotraumatologists refer to: Stephen Porges' Polyvagal Theory and Siegel's Tolerance Window.

The Polyvagal Theory provides therapists with a neurophysiological framework to consider the motivations behind the way people behave (Dana, 2019). It actually originated with the intention of studying how vagus nerve tone (the tenth cranial nerve) could be an indicator of resilience as well as a risk factor in infants. From there, Porges continued his research until he postulated his theory in 2014.

Until recently, the predominant description of the autonomic nervous system saw a contrast between the sympathetic autonomic system, responsible for activating arousal and pooling resources to cope with danger, and the parasympathetic autonomic system, responsible for restoring homeostasis and thus lowering arousal.

Through a series of studies, Porges was able to shed light on how the parasympathetic system (which functions primarily through the vagus nerve) is further subdivided into two circuits belonging to different periods of our phylogenetic history: the ventral vagal (more recent) circuit that drives facial muscles, voice, and breathing; and the dorsal vagal (older) circuit that maintains balance and control of basic visceral functions (stomach, small intestine, colon, bladder). According to Porges, the ventral vagal system has a calming effect by reducing the level of activation of the sympathetic system and promoting social engagement. When we are in this state, we communicate to the nervous system of others that it is safe to enter into relationships. The dorsal vagus, on the other hand, is the most primitive part of the autonomic nervous system, and thus used for survival in the face of extreme danger by collapsing and shutting down. According to Porges (2014), one of the outcomes of the dorsal vagal response is a reduction in the flow of oxygenation in the brain, which causes alterations in cognitive functioning and experiences of dissociation. When we feel confused, numb, or 'not present', it is possible that the dorsal vagal system is active.

Between these two levels of functioning, one active in safe conditions and one in extreme danger, lies the sympathetic system. With the emergence of the sympathetic system, the immobilisation response is no longer the only mode of defence available to us. Sympathetic activation protects us through movement, preparing us to act.

Speaking in terms of defence systems, we can attribute the attack (fight) and flight (flight) responses to the sympathetic system and the hypotonic immobility (faint) responses to the dorsal vagal parasympathetic system. The freezing response would instead appear to be caused by a simultaneous activation of the sympathetic and dorsal vagal parasympathetic systems.

At this point, in order to understand and work with patients with complex trauma, a descriptive model of autonomic functioning is indispensable: the 'window of tolerance' (FdT). With this model, the author, Daniel Siegel (1999), attempts to provide an explanation for the emotional dysregulation that is so frequent in this clinical population. The underlying concept is to assume that the arousal tone, or level of physiological activation, undergoes fluctuations over time, produced by both the environment and the person's internal state (triggers). In the absence of perturbations, these fluctuations should travel within an optimal window (ventral vagal system) in which we function with the best possible activation and regulation capacity. In the event of danger, the tone of our arousal leaves the optimal window to enter a state of hyperactivation (sympathetic system) and prepare us to activate the attack/escape defence systems. Faced with an even more extreme danger, the more primitive defences will be activated and our arousal will fall into a state of hypoactivation. According to Siegel, the greater the amplitude of the FdT, the greater the capacity for regulation even in the face of an event or thought that causes us frustration or discomfort.

Patients with a history of traumatic development have never had the opportunity to widen their window of tolerance and thus learn to regulate themselves even in the face of non-intense triggers. They therefore possess a reduced FdT: consequently, the slightest emotional activation may result in significant dysregulation upwards (hyperactivation states) or downwards (hypoactivation states). Marked dysregulations of arousal would therefore represent a specific sign of traumatisation (Tagliavini, 2011).

What are the effects within therapy? One of the risks in working with patients who easily dysregulate both upwards and downwards is that even the slightest stimulation is enough to send therapy and the therapeutic relationship 'out of the window', causing a feeling of insecurity in the patient or the activation of defence mechanisms. In the early stages of therapy, above all, the therapist must have a rhythm (*pacing*) appropriate to the patient, characterised by an alternation between the investigation of emotional experiences and actions of containment and grounding (Steele et al., 2017). An important rule to follow is to end the session with the patient within the window of tolerance.

A final observation: through a mirroring mechanism, highly dysregulated and dissociated patients can also induce alterations in arousal in the therapist, who may then experience fear, confusion, or sudden drowsiness (Liotti & Farina, 2011).

Detecting the presence of complex trauma in therapy:

Pays attention to the qualitative aspects of the patient's autobiographical narrative.

Assesses the possible presence of controlling strategies and/or dissociative phenomena.

Observes changes in the patient's arousal during the interview.

Pays attention to how you feel during the session, monitoring any occurrence of drowsiness, detachment, or "feeling different from usual". At the end of the interviewer try to review the session for possible re-enactments.

Evaluates the possibility of using psychodiagnostic instruments.

---

3 Clinical Intervention in the Trauma Patient

3.1 *The Therapeutic Alliance with the Complex Trauma Patient*

As one would expect, those with secure attachment internal working models (IWM) generally have higher levels of self-esteem and more integrated cognitive functioning: this leads to being generally more capable of expressing emotions and resolving conflicts (Pearlman & Courtois, 2005), and more likely to enjoy successful relationships, including therapeutic ones. Insecure-attachment patients tend to exhibit affect-based behaviour, without the capacity for cognitive organisation found in the secure client. They function on the basis of strong emotions such as anxiety, dependency, anger, and jealousy and often relate to others in extreme and opposite ways (i.e. alternating between idealisation and devaluation). Their interpersonal skills are generally not well developed: they may paradoxically cling to unhealthy relationships in a frantic attempt to avoid loneliness (Pearlman & Courtois, 2005). Treatment with this type of patient requires continuous attention and consistency and reliability of response on the part of the therapist in order to model and teach relational reliability that, if internalised, reduces anxiety, crucial in this attachment style, leading to greater interpersonal security. On the contrary, patients with insecure-avoidant attachment will present considerable difficulties in 'entering' the therapeutic relationship and will use predominantly cognitive strategies to regulate the emotional set-up and distance within the relationship. They will tend to normalise negative events that occurred during childhood. The therapeutic course, in this case, will aim to validate and legitimise the emotional experience and its expression, leading the patient to tolerate greater closeness within the relationship.

Adults with a history of childhood abuse present particular challenges in alliance formation due to interpersonal problems associated with an early breach of trust, safety, and protection from harm (Courtois & Ford, 2013). At the same time, a strong therapeutic alliance is crucial for the successful treatment of adults with histories of traumatic development (Cloitre et al., 2002, 2004). Two factors that have received little attention in the alliance literature are dissociation and retraumatisation (Cloitre et al., 2009).

Pearlman and Courtois (2005) noted that dissociative aspects are activated at times of intense negative emotions (such as fear, shame, rejection) associated with past interpersonal experiences of trauma: this disrupts the connection between therapist and patient and between the patient and their own internal experiences. Retraumatisation is exposure to multiple physical and/or mental traumatic events, such as multiple exposures to one type of traumatic event and/or multiple exposures to different types of traumatic events. Retraumatisation that begins in childhood is often associated with a pervasive distrust of others (Cloitre et al., 2009). Consequently, victims of childhood abuse report significant interpersonal problems in the social sphere (Cloitre & Koenen, 2001; Zlotnick et al., 1996). Patients' interpersonal problems also influence the therapeutic alliance. Paradoxically, it is precisely the therapist's attempts to establish a safe and trusting relationship that may activate defences (including dissociation) in the patient, associated with previous experiences of abuse in which intimacy was demanded: the therapist's own trustworthiness and consistency may in fact be threatening rather than comforting to these patients, who, in turn, put in place major defensive manoeuvres not knowing how to respond to the kind of consistent relationship proposed by their caregiver (Pearlman & Courtois, 2005).

Fortunately, over the last 30 years, scientific attention to the subject of trauma and dissociation has grown exponentially, enriching the scientific literature with efficacy studies, clinical cases, and diagnostic tools. The increasing amount of available literature has led to the creation of scientific societies specialising in the field of psychotraumatology (e.g. ISSTD, ESTD, EMDRIA). The merit of these societies has also been to propose treatment guidelines, with the aim of identifying what does not work, both clinically and relationally, and what does work to bring the patient towards greater emotional regulation and integration (Cloitre et al., 2011).

3.2 Treatment of Post-traumatic Stress Disorder

As described above, PTSD is a disorder that can begin following direct exposure to emotionally overwhelming experiences such as serious accidents, assaults, or natural disasters or if one learns of a traumatic event that occurred to a person with whom one has a close relationship. Symptomatically, it is characterised by re-experiencing (flashbacks) of the event, hyperarousal, and avoidance behaviour.

According to the guidelines published by the APA (American Psychological Association) in 2017, post-traumatic stress disorder should be treated and this should be done for several reasons (Courtois et al., 2017). Firstly, because of the distressing condition that the disorder itself causes. Secondly, it has been shown how being affected by PTSD creates a vulnerability to retraumatisation and revictimisation. Finally, it increases the risk of comorbidity with substance abuse, other axis I psychopathological disorders, in particular anxiety and depressive spectrum disorders, and violent behaviour.

The APA guidelines strongly recommend four types of psychotherapy for PTSD: cognitive behavioural therapy (CBT), cognitive *processing* therapy (CPT), cognitive therapy (CT), and prolonged exposure (PE). They also suggest the use of eye movement desensitisation and reprocessing (EMDR), *narrative exposure therapy* (NET), and short eclectic therapy (Courtois et al., 2017).

Let us look specifically at the most relevant features of the main approaches mentioned.

Prolonged Exposure (PE) Therapy

PE is a therapy that originated in the late 1980s but was only formalised as a treatment for PTSD in 2007 (Foa et al., 2007). It is based on a conceptual model called emotional processing theory (Foa & Kozak, 1986). According to this theory, we possess emotional structures, i.e. a cognitive network in which we store information about stimuli and their meaning. Within these structures, stimuli can make associations with each other and sometimes, based on life experiences, an association is made between neutral stimuli (neutral conditioned stimuli) and aversive stimuli (unconditioned stimuli), and this will lead to the activation of reactions, for example, fear (conditioned response). Conditioned emotional responses will contribute to keeping a danger signal active even in the face of neutral stimuli, maintaining avoidance symptoms. In order to dissolve this association, according to the authors, it is necessary to reactivate the emotional structure (fear) in order to incorporate new information that will reduce generalisations and avoidance behaviour and to trigger emotional processing of the aversive event. The exposure technique itself is based on both in vivo and imaginative exposure to which two further components of psycho-education and breathing re-education are added. The indicators of changes that are detected are therefore emotional activation of fear, habituation to fear within the same session, and habituation to fear between sessions.

EMDR Therapy (Eye Movement Desensitisation and Reprocessing)

The main objective of the EMDR approach is to focus on the unprocessed memory of a traumatic experience. The ultimate aim of the method is to work on the dysfunctionally stored memory together with the emotions, bodily sensations, and negative cognitions experienced at that time so that it, in the here and now, stops being perceived as disturbing and causing emotional suffering. EMDR therapy has as its basic conceptual assumption the theoretical model of *Adaptive Information Processing* (AIP, Shapiro, 2001, 2007, 2014). According to this model, the current problems reported by the patient are nothing more than the result of unprocessed life experiences that have been stored dysfunctionally within the memory system. Day after day, each individual goes through a series of daily experiences that are processed correctly and manage to integrate perfectly with the neural networks already present in the brain. When an individual experiences an extremely stressful and/or traumatic life event, the normal processing inherent in the brain is interrupted. In such cases, in fact, the memory remains crystallised within the memory system together with the characteristics associated with it, will not be able to integrate with the adaptive mnestic networks present in the brain, and will therefore continue to be perceived by the subject as disturbing even after a long time (Shapiro, 2001, 2014).

According to the AIP model, in the present, a subject may experience situations that are called 'triggers' because they reactivate the mnestic networks containing all the information related to the traumatic event and stored in a dysfunctional way. As a consequence, the subject will find themselves re-experiencing the strong emotional activation, physical sensations, and painful cognitions related to the unprocessed traumatic moment (Kaptan et al., 2021).

Pathology is therefore seen as the result of unprocessed experiences. Through the use of EMDR, it will be possible to access dysfunctionally stored information, reactivate the brain's natural processing, and allow the memory to integrate adaptively with the mnestic networks already present in the brain. With EMDR, the memory will stop being experienced as painful and will be stored adaptively (Solomon & Shapiro, 2008).

EMDR is an eclectic psychotherapy that contains elements that are compatible with most psychological approaches. As far as the psychodynamic approach is concerned, it places great importance on early childhood, and it is evident how life events that occurred in the early stages of development also play a fundamental role in the EMDR approach, which sees the failure to process traumatic memories of early childhood as the basis for the individual's psychopathological development. As far as the cognitive-behavioural approach is concerned, there are also similarities and overlaps. Both approaches, for example, place great emphasis on dysfunctional beliefs as fundamental ingredients related to the traumatic experience. Scientific research on the subject and World Health Organisation guidelines have emphasised that the trauma-focused cognitive behavioural approach and EMDR are both valid approaches for the resolution of PTSD. However, several comparative studies have pointed out that EMDR is able to achieve the same results, but faster (Schnyder et al., 2015). A further strength lies in the fact that EMDR therapy does not require the patient to describe in detail the traumatic episode experienced, as is the case with expositional techniques typical of the cognitive-behavioural approach; in this way, the patient can feel much more comfortable and complete the processing of the traumatic memory in a more favourable way. A further example could be the exercise of holding the image of the trauma in the mind, typical of the imaginal exposure techniques used in trauma-centred cognitive behavioural therapies and also central to the trauma processing phases of EMDR (Cusack & Spates, 1999). Finally, the EMDR approach does not involve the patient being given homework, making the therapeutic approach lighter (Ho & Lee, 2012).

A fundamental aspect that, however, differentiates the EMDR approach from CBT therapies lies in the fact that the latter tend to address the problems reported by the patient in the here and now, acting directly on the symptom; EMDR therapy, on the other hand, which is based on the AIP approach, considers negative beliefs and emotions not as the cause of the problem, but as their effect. Instead, the cause must be sought in unprocessed and dysfunctionally encoded early memories that influence current negative feelings, emotions, and perceptions.

EMDR was discovered by Francine Shapiro in 1987 during a walk in a forest; the author, in fact, realised that moving her eyes with saccadic movements while concentrating on disturbing memories allowed the disturbing component linked to these memories to diminish quickly and spontaneously (Shapiro, 1995). EMDR has been the subject of a great deal of scientific interest in recent years, with scientific research focusing on identifying and explaining the method's mechanisms of action, focusing on the role of eye movements. Some randomised studies, for example, have shown how the use of eye movements in the processing phase of traumatic memories led to a decrease in emotional arousal related to the memory and in the vividness of the traumatic image and to an increased attentional capacity and memory retrieval (Barrowcliff et al., 2004; Engelhard et al., 2011).

Over the years, there have been several hypotheses attempting to explain the mechanism of action concerning eye movements in particular. The first of these hypotheses is that concerning the orientation response; this mechanism manifests itself with an initial phase of an alerting response; however, if the stimulus that triggers this response is perceived as non-threatening, then a habituation response occurs that leads to a decrease in arousal levels. According to Armstrong and Vaughan (1996) and MacCulloch and Feldman (1996), the orientation responses triggered by eye movements allow the patient to focus attention on the traumatic material they are processing and, at the same time, allow access to adaptive information related to the trauma. Furthermore, this mechanism increases vigilance and facilitates exploration behaviour that makes cognitive processes more flexible and efficient (Lee & Cuijpers, 2013). The second hypothesis refers to working memory and its limited capacity. During EMDR therapy, when the patient is asked to focus simultaneously on the memory to be processed and on following the bilateral stimulation, an overload of the working memory is produced. This overload leads the patient to perceive the image used as a target as deteriorated, less vivid, and disturbing (Engelhard et al., 2010; Littel et al., 2016). This mechanism will allow the patient to take psychological distance from the event and allow the memory to be stored adaptively within the memory system. The last hypothesis that has been taken into greater consideration by studies on the subject concerns REM sleep. Specifically, researchers argue that the continuous orientation responses elicited by eye movements are capable of leading to a brain state similar to that found in REM sleep, in which memories can be processed and integrated within the memory system in a more adaptive form (Stickgold, 2002). In addition, it is important to mention that one of the fundamental hypotheses regarding eye movements is that EMDR is able to promote re-processing and integration of traumatic memories as it promotes communication between the two cerebral hemispheres through the use of eye movements (Propper et al., 2007). According to Shapiro (2001), therefore, when the clinician induces eye movements (or any other alternating bilateral stimulation) while the patient focuses and re-enacts the traumatic image, an integration of the information contained in the two hemispheres is achieved, thus leading to a resolution of the traumatic emotional conditioning.

The EMDR approach consists of a standardised eight-step protocol that aims to focus on the traumatic memories and, through bilateral stimulation, arrive at the re-elaboration of the traumatic material, which will then be stored in an adaptive and functional way within the memory system. The EMDR approach requires the clinician to focus, together with the patient, on the past, i.e. the clinical picture that the patient brings to therapy and that must necessarily be re-read starting from the unprocessed traumatic experiences that have contributed to the current psychopathology—on the present, i.e. the life events of the present that act as 'triggers' and cause suffering in the subject's life, and then on the future, i.e. all the situations that the patient would like to face, with desired skills, attitudes, and behaviour, free from the symptomatological picture that he/she brings to therapy today.

Phase 1 of the EMDR protocol corresponds with the patient's anamnesis and information gathering; the aim of this phase is to fully understand the patient's clinical picture, which is useful for outlining an adequate treatment plan and formulating shared therapeutic goals. It is essential, therefore, to investigate the patient's life history, his or her attachment dynamics, and the presence of any difficult and/or traumatic events; furthermore, it is fundamental, during this phase, to investigate the history of the disorder in depth, so as to understand the deeper meanings linked to the patient's history. During phase 2, or the preparation phase, the clinician has the important task of explaining to the patient what an EMDR treatment consists of, informing him/her about the dynamics and emotional activation he/she may undergo during processing, explaining what is meant by trauma, and making him/her understand, according to the AIP model, the impact that traumatic events have on an individual's developmental trajectories. The preparation phase is also useful because it is during this phase that the clinician understands and establishes together with the patient his or her degree of emotional tolerance and can provide him or her with a series of tools, such as the stop sign or the safe place setting, which the patient can refer to in moments of difficulty both during and between the EMDR session. In conclusion, phase 2 aims to increase the patient's level of emotional tolerance, so as to enable him/her to sustain and process traumatic targets adaptively (J. Dworkin,

2005). Phase 3 is where the patient is prepared for the subsequent processing of the traumatic event. In order to make this possible, the clinician asks the patient to focus on the most disturbing image of the traumatic event to be worked on; in this way it will be possible to access the mnestic network containing all the information related to the event that has remained 'crystallised' within the patient's memory system. Therefore, the negative cognition related to the image and the positive cognition (i.e. the verbalisation of the desired state belonging to the same thematic area as the negative cognition) will be identified; once the CP has been established, the patient is asked to measure it on a scale from 1 to 7, through the Validity of Cognition (VoC) scale. At this point, the patient is asked to verbalise the emotional reaction associated with the target and is then asked to measure, on the SUD scale, (Subjective Disturbance Unit, ranging from 0 to 10) the current degree of disturbance of his or her negative emotions, associated with the target. Finally, the patient will be asked in which part of his/her body he or she feels the disturbing sensation associated with the memory. The objective of phase 4, the desensitisation phase, is to help the patient and reduce the suffering and negative emotional load related the traumatic memory that has been chosen to work on. During the desensitisation phase, the therapist guides the patient through several sets of eye movements until the SUD is reduced to '0'; this means that the distress related to that specific target has been adequately processed and removed (Shapiro, 2000).

Once the patient has adequately processed the memory he or she is working on, one can proceed to the Installation of Positive Cognition phase. The aim of this phase of the EMDR protocol is to replace the original negative belief and to increase the patient's sense of self-esteem and self-efficacy (Shapiro, 2000). In the body-scanning phase, the patient is asked to focus on any residual body activations while thinking about the traumatic memory they have been working on. At the end of this phase, the patient should be able to recall the processed memory without it being accompanied by bodily tension or negative feelings. The closing phase aims to make sure that the patient leaves the therapy room in an optimal state of equilibrium. It will be the task of the therapist, in this phase, to explain to the patient that between sessions he/she may experience any other memories, emotions, and physical sensations related to the traumatic event he/she has been working on, and that it may be important to write down everything that emerges in order to give a detailed account of it in the next session. In the re-evaluation phase, the therapist makes sure that all the milestones reached in the previous session are stable and consolidated and listens to the account of what the patient experienced in the period between sessions.

Currently, EMDR has been the subject of numerous research studies and has been recognised as an efficient and effective treatment for PTSD in civilised populations by the American Psychological Association. The International Society for Traumatic Stress Studies (ISTSS) has also considered EMDR to be an effective procedure for the treatment of PTSD; numerous other bodies, such as the Clinical Resource Efficacy Team of the Northern Ireland Departement of Health, the Quality Institute Health Care CBO/Trimbos Institute, the French National Institute of Health and Medical Research, and the American Psychiatric Association, have considered

EMDR to be an elective treatment for PTSD along with CBT. Furthermore, EMDR is considered one of the three recommended methods for victims of terrorism (Bleich et al., 2006). Regarding the comparison of EMDR with other approaches for the treatment of PTSD, a study by Arnone et al. (2012) showed a greater decrease in PTSD symptoms following EMDR treatment than drug therapy.

Numerous studies have also compared the EMDR approach with trauma-focused CBT with regard to the resolution of PTSD; the studies considered have shown similar results with regard to the resolution of post-traumatic symptoms. However the EMDR approach, compared to CBT, seems to achieve the same results in less time and above all does not require the use of homework, which is a fundamental ingredient for the cognitive-behavioural approach (Ho & Lee, 2012).

3.3 Treatment of Complex Post-traumatic Stress Disorder

The diagnosis of complex PTSD, as reported earlier, has been much debated over the years. It all started with the observations of Herman in 1992, who argued that some patients with histories of repeated trauma, typically relational and frequently occurring in childhood, could not be treated simply as PTSD cases. They clearly needed specifically designed approaches, that took into account the severe emotional dysregulation and relational problems manifested by these patients. As previously reported, this diagnosis was only included in an official international classification in 2018, within the ICD-11. Finally, we recall that in order to make a diagnosis of complex PTSD, the patient must manifest the classic symptoms typical of PTSD in association with severe relational and emotion regulation difficulties, impulsivity and self-harm, frank dissociative symptoms, identity alterations, and somatisation.

All this makes the treatment of complex PTSD particularly challenging, starting with building a good therapeutic alliance. In addition to the relational difficulties to which the complex patient is immediately subjected, characterised mainly by conflicting experiences between the need to be helped by the therapist and an innate distrust of others, the initial phases of therapy are often also characterised by the presence of numerous dissociative symptoms and dysregulation of physiological arousal.

Although there are no official guidelines for the treatment of complex PTSD, the scientific societies specialised in trauma and dissociation agree that the most effective approach is the *phased treatment*, initially proposed by Pierre Janet at the beginning of the 20th century and taken up over the last 30 years by numerous contemporary authors (Herman, 1997; Van der Hart et al., 2006; Cloitre et al., 2011; Courtois & Ford, 2013). It is a three-phase treatment, which is linear in its basic proposal but often becomes recursive as these patients often show the need to return several times to previous phases in a 'spiral' pattern. The three phases are (1) stabilisation and reduction of symptoms; (2) treatment of traumatic memories; and (3) integration and rehabilitation of personality. The aim is to gradually build better integration skills.

Before describing the different treatment phases in more detail, it is necessary to make a premise: as we have said, the more severe, repeated, and early in childhood the trauma is, the more impossible it will be for the individual to integrate the different parts of the Self (which physiologically we all possess) into a more unified and cohesive personality. Consequently, as we have already mentioned in Sect. 1.2, the more overwhelming the traumatic events have been, the greater will be the patient's internal 'compartmentalisation'. In order to describe the mechanism by which trauma generates psychopathology, Van der Hart et al. (2006) proposed the theory of *Structural Dissociation of Personality*. According to this theory, the personality, understood as a system integrating cognitive, emotional, and somatosensory patterns, fractures into parts (dissociative parts of the personality) following traumatisation: one or more parts called apparently normal parts (ANP) dedicated to 'functioning' during daily activities and one or more emotional parts (EP) dedicated to defending the system. Since the performance of daily activities is incompatible with the activation of defence systems, different parts will be activated alternately and competitively. Among its various strengths, this model allows us to place the different post-traumatic clinical pictures along a continuum in which we find at one extreme simple PTSD (an ANP, or 'part that carries on daily life', and an EP, or 'part stuck in the time of the trauma'); in this case, we speak of primary structural dissociation. Increasing in severity, we find secondary structural dissociation pictures, usually clinically identifiable with NAS dissociative disorders and trauma-based personality developments (including borderline personality disorder with a post-traumatic component), in which we have one ANP and several EPs in contradicting each other. At the opposite end of the spectrum from simple PTSD, and at the highest degree of severity, is dissociative identity disorder or tertiary structural dissociation. In this case, in an attempt to remain functional, the patient's personality becomes increasingly divided: in addition to numerous EPs, there are also various ANPs.

Let us now look in more detail at the phases of the three-phase approach. The first phase of therapy with the complex patient is that of *stabilisation*: the aim is to reduce symptoms, in particular dissociative symptoms, develop resources, establish boundaries, develop skills for the self-regulation of arousal, and the creation of an initial internal sense of security, a completely new experience for these patients. The reduction of symptoms and the simultaneous development of skills will facilitate the creation of the therapeutic alliance during the interviews. Much attention will be given, in this first phase, to helping the patient develop a healthy model of self-care characterised by regularity and listening to one's primary needs and the development of physical, emotional, and relational boundaries (Chu et al., 2011).

In this first phase, there are many approaches and techniques that can be integrated to help the patient learn to stay within the window of tolerance. A basic psycho-education on what trauma is, what dissociation is, and how these two aspects affect personality functioning will help the patient begin to make sense of his or her internal experiences and to self-regulate following a top-down pathway. Boundary work can be done effectively using body techniques (Ogden & Fisher, 2016), while resources and internal regulation skills can be developed, e.g. through EMDR (e.g. resource work, safe place), mindfulness, or sensorimotor techniques.

The aim of the stabilisation phase is also to prepare the patient for phase 2, the *processing and integration of traumatic memories*. It should be pointed out that, before entering into work on specific traumatic events, internal phobias and resistance to working on traumatic memories must be resolved (Steele et al., 2017). Crucial in this second phase is to work with caution. One of the approaches that has proven to be effective is an adaptation of the EMDR protocol for the severe patient devised by Gonzalez and Mosquera (2016), called the 'progressive approach', which aims to approach the traumatic cores starting from the processing of small fragments of memories, while maintaining constant attention to the related dissociative dynamics.

Another modality of intervention, which can be integrated with the others already proposed, is that of working with the dissociative parts, with the aim of increasing internal communication, understanding the functioning of the whole parts system, and listening to the patient's primary emotional and relational needs. Operationally, in addition to the clinical interview, it could be useful to work with the patient through techniques that facilitate internal communication between the parts by promoting the recognition of the parts, cooperation between them, the distinction between past and present, and the creation of a shared awareness (Fraser, 2003; van der Hart et al., 2010; Gonzalez & Mosquera, 2016; Rezzonico & Furlani, 2019).

Case 3
Marco is a 50-year-old man who comes to therapy at a particularly delicate moment in his life: he has in fact decided to tell his family and acquaintances about his homosexuality, which he has kept hidden since he was a boy to the point of marrying a woman around the age of 35, from whom he will separate about 10 years later. Marco has a significant psychiatric history: from adolescence to 25, in order to detoxify from drug use (heroin), he attended several rehabilitation facilities, where he received a double diagnosis of borderline personality disorder associated with psychoactive substance use disorder. During the years of his marriage, he undertook a therapeutic course, motivated by the presence of impulsive behaviour that had led him to abuse substances and to overspend to the point of accumulating significant debts with credit companies. On that occasion he had been diagnosed with bipolar disorder. Finally, Marco reports an incident in his primary school days of which he has very hazy memories, but during which he may have been sexually assaulted in the school bathroom by an older boy. In the current therapy, Marco started to work on structural dissociation: the work on the parts led him to identify an 'adolescent' part responsible for enacting risky behaviour as an extreme attempt to regulate the intense emotion of shame and fear of abandonment felt by the 'child' part. Such experiences were triggered by a very critical part, which Marco initially called 'the Evil One'. Stabilising work and establishing internal communication between the parts enabled Marco to understand these internal dynamics and focus on the missing experiences from his childhood. Over the months, Marco learned to

listen and validate the emotional needs of the parties, achieving a degree of emotional and behavioural regulation he had never experienced before.

Finally, we come to the final phase of treatment, that of *Integration and Rehabilitation of Personality*. Although this is an advanced phase of treatment, it requires demanding work for both patient and therapist: the processing of grief related to past losses; the acceptance of healthy risks and change; and the adaptation to a daily life characterised by greater integration, fulfilment, closeness to others, and intimacy. Although the use of specific techniques may also be indicated during this phase (e.g. EMDR or sensorimotor techniques), the most commonly used approach is the one most typical of psychotherapy: the clinical interview. Being faced with a more integrated patient and with more developed metacognitive abilities will allow the therapist to also work on a deeper emotional level, but still be safe for the patient.

Over the past thirty years, numerous therapeutic approaches have developed that provide clinicians with valid and effective tools for working with complex trauma in all three phases, but particularly in the more delicate phase of processing traumatic memories. These approaches have one feature in common: they are developed as integrated models rooted in different methodologies. Below is an overview of some of the therapies that are most widely used in clinical practice today.

Sensomotor Psychotherapy

Sensorimotor psychotherapy (SP) represents one of the most effective approaches for processing traumatic experiences and attachment trauma (Tagliavini, 2011). Developed in the 1980s by Pat Odgen and his collaborators, it incorporates different methodologies, such as Ron Kurz's approach (Kurtz, 1990), mindfulness, the theories and techniques of cognitive-behavioural and psychodynamic psychotherapy, neuroscience and attachment theory (Ogden et al., 2006; Fisher & Ogden, 2009; Ogden & Fisher, 2016). The assumption on which SP is based is that traumatic memories remain inscribed in the body at a procedural, hence unconscious, level. SP provides clinicians with numerous tools for the creation of somatic and non-somatic resources, for the creation of relational boundaries, and for the somatic regulation of arousal, tools that are extremely effective in stabilising the patient's symptoms (phase one of treatment). During phase two, the patient is gradually exposed to the traumatic memory, in order to maintain arousal at the limit of the tolerance window and thus a good level of awareness; this modality will allow the patient to avoid abreactions, thus facilitating the integration of the somatic, emotional, and cognitive components of the memory. The aim of the treatment of the traumatic memory is to achieve the restoration of the mobilisation defences and the execution of those physical movements that could not be performed at the time of the trauma. The completed act thus promotes the patient's capacity for integration.

Schema Therapy

Schema therapy (ST) is an approach developed to work with patients with chronic disorders, such as complex PTSD, focusing on the patient's developmental history, the resulting early *maladaptive* patterns (or *EMS*), and their impact on trauma (Young et al., 2003). EMS originate from the individual's negative childhood experiences and unmet emotional needs and can lead to the development of dysfunctional responses such as flight, attachment, or freezing in front of a relational trigger. In this approach, work on disturbing memories is done through the use of experiential techniques, such as imagery rescripting (Arntz & Jacob, 2012). In the case of patients with complex PTSD, in order to avoid becoming emotionally overwhelmed, the focus of the rewriting of events will be on changing the meaning and needs related to the trauma, rather than direct exposure to the memory.

Interpersonal Metacognitive Therapy

Interpersonal metacognitive therapy (IMT; Dimaggio et al., 2013) is initially structured as a treatment of patients with personality disorders. Its primary goal is the improvement of the subjects' metacognitive abilities (monitoring, agency, and differentiation). It integrates different techniques, among which a large space is left to the use of experiential techniques such as guided imagination, body work, or mindfulness (Dimaggio et al., 2013; Centonze et al., 2020). Recently, Dimaggio and colleagues have also extended the application of IMT to complex trauma disorders (Dimaggio, 2021). The approach is based on the presence of maladaptive interpersonal schemes (MIS) in the patient's functioning, schemes that make him/her more vulnerable to traumatic events. According to the authors, the relationship between childhood trauma and MIS is bidirectional. Regarding the treatment in phases, IMT involves the use of grounding techniques, mindfulness, and power poses for stabilising and reducing symptoms, while for the processing of traumatic memories, it relies on experiential techniques, especially imaginative ones, with a particular focus on somatic experience.

To sum up, if the therapy of simple PTSD in many cases envisages the use of techniques and approaches involving direct exposure to traumatic memories, the therapy of the complex patient must necessarily envisage a long initial stabilisation phase that creates the basis for work on specific memories and an equally long subsequent phase of adaptation to a new, more integrated and cohesive functioning. Finally, it is important to emphasise how integration, besides being the goal of the step-by-step approach, also represents the underlying process of therapy, a process that the therapist must always have in mind in order to help the patient reduce the emotional and experiential chaos with which he/she arrives at the session.

> **Setting up treatment with a patient with complex trauma and dissociative disorders:**
> Formulate a conceptualisation of the case and a treatment plan.
> In the early stages, keep the patient within the tolerance window.
> Work on creating a patient's internal sense of security, reducing symptoms, creating healthy boundaries, and containing flashbacks.
> Once the patient is stabilised, access the work of processing traumatic memories and resolving disorganised/insecure attachment bonds.
> Assess the possibility of using techniques that facilitate the processing and integration of memories.
> In the last phase of treatment, he/she works on adaptability to the new everyday life and the grieving of past losses.

4   The Cost to the Therapist in Working with Trauma

Working with patients with complex traumatisation is definitely tiring and sometimes frustrating. First of all, the emotional load to which the therapist is subjected session after session has a negative effect on him/her both physically and emotionally. One of the highest risks for those working in this field is that of 'vicarious trauma', which can be seen as a psychotrauma-specific version of *burnout* (McCann & Pearlman, 1990). The main characteristics of this syndrome are signs of emotional exhaustion, a progressive detachment from the patient's clinical situations (but also an increased level of social withdrawal in private life) and a perception of low effectiveness or inadequacy in the work environment (Imperatori et al., 2014). On a symptomological level, clinicians may develop irritability, anxious-depressive symptoms, and even substance abuse. The mechanism underlying vicarious trauma could reside in *'mirroring'*, i.e. the neurophysiological mechanism of empathic understanding of pain (*emotional empathy*), which would be achieved through the activation of the same brain areas (in this case, the areas of emotional pain perception) that are active in the patient at that time.

Another aspect that makes working with the complex patient particularly challenging concerns what Wilson and Thomas (2004) have called *physiological empathy*. When there is a deep connection in the therapeutic dyad, the therapist's body will mirror the patient's hyper- and hypo-activations, leading him/her to experience even sudden feelings of fear or anger or, on the contrary, a sudden lowering of activation (drowsiness, boredom, mental confusion; Liotti & Farina, 2011).

What tools are available to us in these cases? Steele, Boon, and Van der Hart (Steele et al., 2017), in their handbook entirely dedicated to therapists working with dissociative patients, argue that there are two protective modalities available to clinicians. First, the ability to care for oneself (self-care): it is indeed not uncommon for therapists to work with patients to develop a healthy and functional lifestyle, without being able to adopt it for themselves. Caring for our bodies, health and relationships protects us from vicarious traumatisation. The second protective aspect is the therapist's awareness: the more we learn to listen to ourselves and to notice the effects of the therapeutic relationship on our body in the here and now of the session, the more we will be able to distinguish whether that specific activation we are experiencing is due to the reactivation of a personal functioning or to a mirroring of the patient's experiences. Awareness, therefore, helps to manage and regulate sudden activations, thus lowering perceived fatigue.

5 Post-traumatic Psychopathology

5.1 Beyond Post-traumatic Stress Disorder

Although PTSD is the most widely used post-traumatic diagnosis, it is not the only possible post-traumatic psychiatric disorder diagnosis (Dworkin et al., 2017). Many other post-traumatic symptoms are related to re-experiencing the traumatic event, among which the following should be considered: mood disorders, pathological bereavement, anxiety disorders, obsessive-compulsive disorders, psychotic disorders, psychoactive substance abuse (especially alcohol and drugs), somatoform expressions, psychosomatic and somatic symptoms, disorders in instinctual behaviour, conduct disorders, personality changes, and difficulties adapting in professional and personal life (Auxéméry, 2018). Traumatic events experienced during development, i.e. Early Life Stress (ELS), which include emotional abuse, physical aggression with risk of injury in general, sexual abuse, emotional and physical neglect (Bernstein et al., 2003), can cause damage to certain neurobiological and neuroendocrine aspects, which persist for the rest of the individual's life, as Carr et al. (2013) have shown by confirming the association between ELS subtypes and the development, persistence, and severity of psychopathology in adults.

The psychopathologies with the highest correlations with traumatic events are listed below.

Mood Disorders

There is a growing awareness that trauma is a relevant risk factor for the development of depressive disorders in adults (Mandelli et al., 2015). Childhood trauma is one of the most robust and significant risk factors for depressive disorders (Kuzminskaite et al., 2021). Among people who have been sexually assaulted, depressive disorder and PTSD seem to be particularly common; in fact, more than one-third of people show depressive disorders that tend to become chronic (39%) (Dworkin, 2020), conditioning an increased risk of self-harm and increased levels of impulsivity (Brodsky et al., 2001; Wiersma et al., 2009; Dworkin et al., 2017). In addition, Mandelli et al. (2015) demonstrated that childhood neglect is the strongest risk factor for the development of depression, especially in females, followed by emotional abuse (Bifulco et al., 1998).

Bipolar Disorder

Interacting with pre-existing genetic vulnerabilities, childhood traumatic events are a risk factor for the development of bipolar disorder, which would lead to a more severe clinical presentation over time, such as an earlier age of onset, rapid cyclicity, high levels of psychiatric comorbidity, higher likelihood of delusional beliefs in patients, and increased suicide attempts (Etain et al., 2013, 2016). Etain et al. (2017) therefore suggested that patients with a more severe and unstable form of bipolar disorder should be systematically screened for childhood trauma. It has also been shown that a traumatic event such as sexual assault appears to be associated with a substantially increased risk of developing bipolar conditions (Dworkin et al., 2017).

Anxiety Disorders

Childhood trauma is one of the most robust and significant risk factors for anxiety disorders, particularly for the development of generalised anxiety disorder, social phobia, panic attack disorder, and agoraphobia (Kuzminskaite et al., 2021). A study by Schimmenti and Bifulco (2015) also shows how experiences associated with parental emotional neglect can lead to the development of an anxiety disorder. Furthermore, it has been shown that exposure to sexual violence is associated with an increased risk of onset of all anxiety disorders (except for specific phobias and lifelong agoraphobia) and this could indicate that specific phobia is relatively less related to trauma (Dworkin, 2020).

Obsessive-Compulsive Disorders

It has been shown that PTSD and OCD are highly comorbid (Brown et al., 2001) and that the two disorders share similar symptomatologies (e.g. intrusive thoughts, stimulus avoidance, and elevated psychological arousal; APA, 2013). In a meta-analysis of the effect of trauma on the severity of obsessive-compulsive spectrum symptoms by Miller and Brock (2017), a significant association between trauma exposure and the severity of obsessive-compulsive symptoms was found for women in particular. Finally, it has been shown that sexual violence appears to be associated with a substantially increased risk of developing obsessive-compulsive conditions (Dworkin et al., 2017).

Eating Disorders

Among the many factors that may contribute to the pathogenesis of eating disorders, childhood trauma appears to be a predictor of symptom severity (Jacobi et al., 2004; Molendijk et al., 2017). In a study by Monteleone et al. (2019), it was found that patients with anorexia nervosa (AN) and bulimia with elimination behaviours (BP) showed a more severe reported experience of trauma with some differences with respect to trauma type (Monteleone et al. 2019). In particular, emotional abuse showed a direct connection with DCA symptoms, whereas sexual and physical abuse were associated with DCA psychopathology through the mediation of one or more psychiatric comorbidities.

Borderline Personality Disorder

Some authors have shown that the relationship between childhood trauma and borderline personality disorder (BPD) is consistent, especially in a multifactorial aetiological model (Scalabrini et al., 2016). In the study, it appears that levels of dissociation in BPD are higher than in psychiatric disorders in general. Therefore, the authors postulated that dissociation is a trauma-related phenomenon that is particularly present in BPD. Debated, however, is the issue of overlap between complex post-traumatic disorder (Herman, 1992; Reed et al., 2016), PTSD, and BPD (Giourou et al., 2018). BPD is characterised by oscillation between emotional inhibition and emotional lability, often associated with prolonged childhood trauma, such as abuse and neglect, present in between 30% and 90% of BPD patients (Battle et al., 2004; Yen et al., 2002; Zanarini et al., 2006; van Dijke et al., 2010). The latter, in addition to high comorbidity with PTSD (McLean & Gallop, 2003), also shares some of the main symptoms described in complex PTSD (affective dysregulation, dysfunctional relationships and interpersonal problems, unstable sense of identity, dissociative symptoms, impulsive or reckless behaviour, irritability, and self-destructive behaviour) (Herman, 1992; Reed et al., 2016; van Dijke et al., 2010). This symptomatological overlap has led to a number of arguments as to whether BPD represents a comorbidity of a trauma-related disorder or in fact duplicates complex PTSD (Giourou et al., 2018). Ultimately, whereas BPD has as its core symptom an unstable sense of self that oscillates between a very high and very negative self-evaluation and a relational attachment style between idealisation and denigration of others' perceptions, complex PTSD involves exposure to traumatic stress as a diagnostic criterion (not included in the definition of BPD despite its importance especially in the early stages of life) and is defined by a deeply negative sense self of and avoidant attachment style that is stable and is consequential to complex trauma (Giourou et al., 2018).

Substance and Behavioural Addictions

In addition to the aforementioned systematic review by Carr et al. (2013) that highlighted how early stressful life events are related to substance abuse, being a victim of sexual assault also places the individual at risk for all substance use disorders (Dworkin et al., 2017; Dworkin, 2020). In a study by Schimmenti et al. (2017) that aimed to explore the relationship between traumatic experiences, alexithymia, and Internet addiction symptoms in a sample of adolescents in their final year of high school, it was found that trauma was predictive of Internet addiction symptoms among males while alexithymia among females. In this sense, whereas males might abuse the Internet to gain greater self-direction and a sense of mastery after being exposed to significant trauma, females who develop problems identifying and describing their feelings might find the Internet to be helpful in building relationships with other people (Schimmenti et al., 2017).

Chapter Review Exercises

1. What are the typical controlling strategies of attachment D and how do they arise? Provide an explanation by mentioning the attachment system, internal operating models, and interpersonal motivational systems.
2. Alan is an 18-year-old boy, adopted by an Italian family, who lived until he was 4 years old in an orphanage in South America with his 1-year-old brother. Once in Italy, the brothers were adopted by different families who, over the years, increasingly decreased contact between them. During psychotherapy sessions, every time Alan mentions his brother, he begins to feel drowsy, eventually falling asleep in his chair. How would you rate Alan's level of activation, based on the Tolerance Window model? What interventions could be useful to bring arousal back to a more functional level?
3. List five situations in which you felt you were able to maintain a healthy boundary in your relationship with a patient, exploring the following areas: contact outside the session, giving personal information, whether and when to schedule extra sessions, aggressive patient behaviour, accepting gifts from the patient, and rules regarding the collection of professional fees or any credits.
4. What relational challenges and personal difficulties might a therapist working with complex trauma patients face?
5. Stefano is a young man in his thirties who came to therapy about five weeks after suffering a physical assault for the purpose of robbery while walking down the street in the evening. From that moment on, he started to manifest a symptomatology characterised by hyperarousal with numerous somatisations (nausea, vomiting, trembling), feeling 'immobilised', and intrusive thoughts concerning the assault. Following the assault, Stefano was no longer able to return to work or leave home alone to go shopping. In the past, Stefano had never had any significant relationship, work, or family difficulties, with the exception of his parents' separation when he was in primary school. What is the diagnosis for this patient? According to the APA guidelines, what interventions would be most recommended in this situation?

Bibliographic References

Ainsworth, M. D. S., Blehar, M. C., Waters, E., & Wall, S. (1978). *Patterns of attachment: A psychological study of the strange situation.* Erlbaum.
American Psychiatric Association (APA). (1980). *DSM III. Manuale diagnostico e statistico dei disturbi mentali.* Masson. (trad. it.: 1983).
American Psychiatric Association (APA). (2000). *DSM IV-TR. Manuale diagnostico e statistico dei disturbi mentali.* Masson. (trad. it.: 2001).
American Psychiatric Association (APA). (2013). *DSM-5. Manuale diagnostico e statistico dei disturbi mentali.* Raffaello Cortina. (trad. it.: 2014).
Armstrong, M. S., & Vaughan, K. (1996). An orienting response model of eye movement desensitization. *Journal of Behavior Therapy and Experimental Psychiatry, 27*(1), 21–32.
Arnone, R., Orrico, A., D'aquino, G., & Di Munzio, W. (2012). EMDR e terapia psicofarmacologica nel trattamento del disturbo da stress post-traumatico. *Rivista di Psichiatria, 47*(2 Suppl), 8–11.
Arntz, A., & Jacob, G. (2012). *Schema therapy in practice: An introductory guide to the schema mode approach. An introductory guide to the schema mode approach.* Wiley-Blackwell.
Atwoli, L., Stein, D. J., Koenen, K. C., & McLaughlin, K. A. (2015). Epidemiology of posttraumatic stress disorder: Prevalence, correlates and consequences. *Current Opinion in Psychiatry, 28*(4), 307–311.
Auxéméry, Y. (2018). Post-traumatic psychiatric disorders: PTSD is not the only diagnosis. *Presse Médicale, 47*, 423–430.
Barrowcliff, A. L., Gray, N. S., Freeman, T. C. A., & MacCulloch, M. J. (2004). Eye-movements reduce the vividness, emotional valence and electrodermal arousal associated with negative autobiographical memories. *Journal of Forensic Psychiatry & Psychology, 15*(2), 325–345.
Battle, C. L., Shea, M. T., Johnson, D. M., Yen, S., Zlotnick, C., Zanarini, M. C., et al. (2004). Childhood maltreatment associated with adult personality disorders: Findings from the Collaborative Longitudinal Personality Disorders Study. *Journal of Personality Disorders, 18*, 193–211.
Bernstein, D. P., Stein, J. A., Newcomb, M. D., Walker, E., Pogge, D., Ahluvalia, T., et al. (2003). Development and validation of a brief screening version of the Childhood Trauma Questionnaire. *Child Abuse & Neglect, 27*, 169–190.
Bifulco, A., Brown, G. W., & Moran, P. (1998). Predicting depression in women: The role of past and present vulnerability. *Psychological Medicine, 28*, 39–50.
Bleich, A., Gelkopf, M., Melamed, Y., & Solomon, Z. (2006). Mental health and resiliency following 44 months of terrorism: A survey of an Israeli national representative sample. *BMC Medicine, 27*, 4–21.
Bordin, E. S. (1979). The generalizability of the psychoanalytic concept of the working alliance. *Psychotherapy: Theory, Research & Practice, 16*(3), 252–260.
Bowlby, J. (1983). *Attachment: Attachment and loss, Volume One.* Basic Books.
Bremner, J. D. (2006). Traumatic stress: Effects on the brain. *Dialogues in Clinical Neuroscience, 8*(4), 445–461.
Brodsky, B. S., Oquendo, M., Ellis, S. P., Haas, G. L., Malone, K. M., & Mann, J. J. (2001). The relationship of childhood abuse to impulsivity and suicidal behavior in adults with major depression. *The American Journal of Psychiatry, 158*, 1871–1877.
Bromberg, P. M. (1993). Shadow and substance: A relational perspective on clinical process. *Psychoanalytic Psychology, 10*(2), 147–168.
Bromberg, P. M. (2006). *Clinica del trauma e della dissociazione. Standing in the spaces.* Raffaello Cortina Editore.
Brown, R. J. (2006). Different types of "dissociation" have different psychological mechanisms. *Journal of Trauma & Dissociation, 7*(4), 7–28.

Brown, T. A., Campbell, L. A., Lehman, C. L., Grisham, J. R., & Mancill, R. B. (2001). Current and lifetime comorbidity of the DSM-IV anxiety and mood disorders in a large clinical sample. *Journal of Abnormal Psychology, 110*(4), 585–599.

Bryant, R. A. (2010). The complexity of complex PTSD. *The American Journal of Psychiatry, 167*(8), 879–881.

Bureau, J. F., Easlerbrooks, M. A., & Lyons-Ruth, K. (2009). Attachment disorganization and controlling behavior in middle childhood: Maternal and child precursors and correlates. *Attachment & Human Development, 11*(3), 265–284.

Carr, C. P., Martins, C. M. S., Stingel, A. M., Lemgruber, V. B., & Jurena, N. F. (2013). The role of early life stress in adult psychiatric disorders. A systematic review according to childhood trauma subtypes. *The Journal of Nervous and Mental Disease, 201, 12*, 1007–1020.

Centonze, A., Inchausti, F., MacBeth, A., & Dimaggio, G. (2020). Changing embodied dialogical patterns in metacognitive interpersonal therapy. *Journal of Constructivist Psychology, 34*(2), 123–137.

Chu, J. A. (2010). Posttraumatic stress disorder: Beyond DSM-IV. *The American Journal of Psychiatry, 167*(6), 615–617.

Chu, J. A., Dell, P. F., Van der Hart, O., Cardeña, E., Barach, P. M., Somer, E., et al. (2011). Guidelines for treating dissociative identity disorder in adults, third revision. *Journal of Trauma & Dissociation, 12*(2), 115–187. Routledge.

Cloitre, M., & Koenen, K. C. (2001). The impact of borderline personality disorder on process group outcome among women with posttraumatic stress disorder related to childhood abuse. *International Journal of Group Psychotherapy, 51*(3), 379–398.

Cloitre, M., Koenen, K. C., Cohen, L. R., & Han, H. (2002). Skills training in affective and interpersonal regulation followed by exposure: A phase-based treatment for PTSD related to childhood abuse. *Journal of Consulting and Clinical Psychology, 70*(5), 1067–1074.

Cloitre, M., Chase, S.-M. C. K., Miranda, R., & Chemtob, C. M. (2004). Therapeutic alliance, negative mood regulation, and treatment outcome in child abuse-related posttraumatic stress disorder. *Journal of Consulting and Clinical Psychology, 72*(3), 411–416.

Cloitre, M., Stolbach, B. C., Herman, J. L., van der Kolk, B., Pynoos, R., Wang, J., & Petkova, E. (2009). A developmental approach to complex PTSD: Childhood and adult cumulative trauma as predictors of symptom complexity. *Journal of Traumatic Stress, 22*(5), 399–408.

Cloitre, M., Courtois, C.A., Charuvastra, A., Carapezza, R., Stolbach, B.C., & Green, B.L. (2011). Treatment of complex PTSD: results of the ISTSS expert clinician survey on best practices. *Journal of Traumatic Stress, 24*(6), 615–27.

Cortina, M., & Liotti, G. (2014). An evolutionary outlook on motivation: Implications for the clinical dialogue. *Psychoanalytic Inquiry, 34*(8), 864–899.

Courtois, C. A., & Ford, J. D. (2013). *Treatment of complex trauma: A sequenced, relationship-based approach*. Guilford Press.

Courtois, C., Sonis, J., Brown, L. S., Cook, J., Fairbank, J. A., Friedman, M., Gone, J. P., Jones, R., & La Greca, A. (2017). *Clinical practice guideline for the treatment of posttraumatic stress disorder (PTSD) in adults*. American Pyschological Association. Testo disponibile al sito (visitato il 13/01/2022).

Cozolino, L. (2004). *The making of a therapist: A practical guide for the inner journey*. W W Norton & Co..

Crocq, L. (1999). *Les traumatismes psychiques de guerre*. Odile Jacob.

Cusack, K., & Spates, C. R. (1999). The cognitive dismantling of Eye Movement Desensitization and Reprocessing (EMDR) treatment of posttraumatic stress disorder (PTSD). *Journal of Anxiety Disorders, 13*(1-2), 87–99.

Cyrulnik, B. (2000). *Il dolore meraviglioso*. Frassinelli.

Dana, D. (2019). *La teoria polivagale nella terapia. Prendere parte al ritmo della regolazione*. Giovanni Fioriti Editore.

Dimaggio, G. (2021). *Affrontare il trauma. Verso una psicoterapia integrata*. ApertaMenteWeb.

Dimaggio, G., Montano, A., Popolo, R., & Salvatore, G. (2013). *Terapia metacognitiva interpersonale*. Raffello Cortina.

Dorahy, M. J., & van der Hart, O. (2007). *Relationship between trauma and dissociation: A historical analysis*. In E. Vermetten, M. Dorahy, & D. Spiegel (Eds.), *Traumatic dissociation: Neurobiology and treatment* (pp. 3–30). American Psychiatric Publishing, Inc.

Dutra, L., Bureau, J. F., Holmes, B., Lyubchik, A., & Lyons-Ruth, K. (2009). Quality of early care and childhood trauma: A prospective study of developmental pathways to dissociation. *The Journal of Nervous and Mental Disease, 197*(6), 383–390.

Dworkin, M. (2005). *EMDR and the relational imperative: The therapeutic relationship in EMDR treatment*. Routledge.

Dworkin, E. R. (2020). Risk for mental disorders associated with sexual assault: A meta-analysis. *Trauma, Violence & Abuse, 21*(5), 1011–1028.

Dworkin, E. R., Menon, S. V., Brystrynski, J., & Allen, N. E. (2017). Sexual assault victimization and psychopathology: A review and meta-analysis. *Clinical Psychology Review, 56*, 65–81.

Engelhard, I. M., van den Hout, M. A., Janssen, W. C., & van der Beek, J. (2010). Eye movements reduce vividness and emotionality of 'flashforwards'. *Behaviour Research and Therapy, 48*(5), 442–447.

Engelhard, I. M., van den Hout, M. A., Dek, E. C. P., Giele, C. L., van der Wielen, J.-W., Reijnen, M. J., & van Roij, B. (2011). Reducing vividness and emotional intensity of recurrent 'flashforwards' by taxing working memory: An analogue study. *Journal of Anxiety Disorders, 25*(4), 599–603.

Etain, B., Aas, M., Andreassen, O. A., Lorentzen, S., Dieset, I., Gard, S., et al. (2013). Childhood trauma is associated with severe clinical characteristics of bipolar disorders. *The Journal of Clinical Psychiatry, 74*(10), 991–998.

Etain, B., Lajnef, M., Bellivier, F., Henry, C., M'bailara, K., Kahn, J. P., et al. (2016). Revisiting the association between childhood trauma and psychosis in bipolar disorder: A quasi-dimensional path-analysis. *Journal of Psychiatric Research, 84*, 73–79.

Etain, B., Lajnef, M., Henry, C., Aubin, V., Azorin, J. M., et al. (2017). Childhood trauma, dimensions of psychopathology and the clinical expression of bipolar disorders: A pathway analysis. *Journal of Psychiatric Research, 95*, 37–45.

Farina B., Speranza A.M., Dittoni, S., Gnoni V., Trentini C., Maggiora Vergano C., ..., and Della Marca G. (2014), Memories of attachment hamper EEG cortical connectivity in dissociative patients. *European Archives of Psychiatry and Clinical Neuroscience, 264*: 449–458.

Felitti, V. J., Anda, R. F., Nordenberg, D., Williamson, D. F., Spitz, A. M., Edwards, V., Koss, M. P., & Marks, J. S. (1998). Adverse Childhood Experiences Study Questionnaire [Database record]. APA PsycTests.

Fisher, J., & Ogden, P. (2009). *Sensorimotor Psychotherapy*. In C. A. Courtois & K. D. Ford (Eds.), *Treating complex traumatic stress disorders: An evidence-based guide* (pp. 312–328). The Guildfor Press.

Foa, E., & Kozak, M. J. (1986). Emotional processing of fear: Exposure to corrective information. *Psychological Bulletin, 99*(1), 20–35.

Foa, E., Hembree, E. A., & Rothbaum, B. O. (2007). *Prolonged exposure therapy for PTSD: Emotional processing of traumatic experiences*. Oxford University Press.

Ford, J. D., & Courtois, C. A. (2009). Defining and understanding complex trauma and complex traumatic stress disorders. In C. A. Courtois & J. D. Ford (Eds.), *Treating complex traumatic stress disorders: An evidence-based guide* (pp. 13–30). The Guilford Press.

Fraser, G. A. (2003). Fraser's "dissociative table technique" revisited, revised: A strategy for working with ego states in dissociative disorders and ego-state therapy. *Journal of Trauma & Dissociation, 4*(4), 5–28.

Gilbert, D. T. (1989). *Thinking lightly about others: Automatic components of the social inference process*. In J. S. Uleman & J. A. Bargh (Eds.), *Unintended thought* (pp. 189–211). The Guilford Press.

Giourou, E., Skokou, M., Andrew, S. P., Alexopoulou, K., Gourzis, P., & Jelastopulu, E. (2018). Complex posttraumatic stress disorder: The need to consolidate a distinct clinical syndrome or to reevaluate features of psychiatric disorders following interpersonal trauma? *World Journal of Psychiatry, 8*(1), 12–19.

Gonzalez, A., & Mosquera, D. (2016). *EMDR e Dissociazione: l'approccio progressivo*. Giovanni Fioriti editore.

Guina, J., Welton, R. S., Broderick, P. J., Correl, T. L., & Peirson, R. P. (2016). DSM-5 criteria and its implications for diagnosing PTSD in military service members and veterans. *Current Psychiatry Reports, 18*(5), 43.

Herman, J. L. (1992). Complex PTSD: A syndrome in survivors of prolonged and repeated trauma. *Journal of Traumatic Stress, 5*(3), 377–391.

Herman, J. L. (1997). *Trauma and recovery: The aftermath of violence – Ffrom domestic abuse to political terror*. Basic Books.

Hesse, E., Main, M., Abrams, K., & Rifkin, A. (2003). Unresolved states regarding loss or abuse can have "second-generation" effects. In M. F. Solomon & D. J. Siegel (Eds.), *Healing trauma: Attachment, mind, body, and brain* (pp. 57–106). Norton.

Hidalgo, R. B., & Davidson, J. R. (2000). Posttraumatic stress disorder: Epidemiology and health-related considerations. *The Journal of Clinical Psychiatry, 61*(7), 5–13.

Ho, M. S. K., & Lee, C. W. (2012). Cognitive behaviour therapy versus eye movement desensitization and reprocessing for post-traumatic disorder—Is it all in the homework then? *European Review of Applied Psychology, 62*(4), 253–260.

Holmes, E. A., Brown, R. J., Mansell, W., Fearon, R. P., Hunter, E. C., Frasquilho, F., & Oakley, D. A. (2005). Are there two qualitatively distinct forms of dissociation? A review and some clinical implications. *Clinical Psychology Review, 25*(1), 1–23.

Howell, E. F. (2011). *Understanding and treating dissociative identity disorder: A relational approach*. Routledge/Taylor & Francis Group.

Imperatori, C., Farina, B., & Bossa, C. (2014). Il dolore degli altri: il trauma vicario. In E. Faretta (Ed.), *Trauma e Malattia. L'EMDR in psiconcologia*. Mimesis.

Jacobi, C., Hayward, C., de Zwaan, M., Kraemer, H. C., & Agras, W. S. (2004). Coming to terms with risk factors for eating disorders: Application of risk terminology and suggestions for a general taxonomy. *Psychological Bulletin, 130*(1), 19.

Janet, P. (1898). *Névroses et idées fixes, Vol. 1*. Félix Alcan.

Kaptan, S. K., Dursun, B. O., Knowles, M., Husain, N., & Varese, F. (2021). Group eye movement desensitization and reprocessing interventions in adults and children: A systematic review of randomized and nonrandomized trials. *Clinical Psychology & Psychotherapy, 28*(4), 784–806.

Kessler, R. C., Berglund, P., Demler, O., Jin, R., Merikangas, K. R., & Walters, E. E. (2005). Lifetime prevalence and age-of-onset distributions of DSM-IV disorders in the National Comorbidity Survey Replication. *Archives of General Psychiatry, 62*(6), 593–602.

Krüger, C., & Fletcher, L. (2017) Predicting a dissociative disorder from type of childhood maltreatment and abuserabused relational tie. *Journal of Trauma & Dissociation, 18*(3), 356–372

Kurtz, R. (1990). *Body-centered psychotherapy: The Hakomi method*. LifeRithm.

Kuzminskaite, E., Pennix, B. W. J. H., van Harmelen, A., Elzinga, B. M., Hovens, J. G. F. M., & Vinkers, C. H. (2021). Childhood trauma in adult depressive and anxiety disorders: An integrated review on psychological and biological mechanisms in the NESDA cohort. *Journal of Affective Disorders, 283*, 179–191.

Lanius, R. A., Vermetten, E., Loewenstein, R. J., Brand, B., Schmahl, C., Bremner, J. D., & Spiegel, D. (2010). Emotion modulation in PTSD: Clinical and neurobiological evidence for a dissociative subtype. *The American Journal of Psychiatry, 167*(6), 640–647.

Lanius, R. A., Boyd, J. E., McKinnon, M. C., Nicholson, A. A., Frewen, P., Vermetten, E., Jetly, R., & Spiegel, D. (2018). A review of the neurobiological basis of trauma-related dissociation and its relation to cannabinoid- and opioid-mediated stress response: A transdiagnostic, translational approach. *Current Psychiatry Reports, 20*(12), 118.

Lee, C. W., & Cuijpers, P. A. (2013). Meta-analysis of the contribution of eye movements in processing emotional memories. *Journal of Behavior Therapy and Experimental Psychiatry, 44*(2), 231–239.

Liotti, G. (1995). *Disorganized/disoriented attachment in the psychotherapy of the dissociative disorders*. In S. Goldberg, R. Muir, & J. Kerr (Eds.), *Attachment theory: Social, developmental, and clinical perspectives* (pp. 343–363). Analytic Press Inc.

Liotti, G. (2000). Disorganized attachment, models of borderline states and evolutionary psychotherapy. In Gilbert, P., & Bailey, K.G. (Eds.). *Genes on the couch: Explorations in evolutionary psychotherapy*. Brunner-Routledge.

Liotti, G. (2001). *Le opere della coscienza. Psicopatologia e psicoterapia nella prospettiva cognitivo-evoluzionista*. Raffaello Cortina.

Liotti, G., & Farina, B. (2011). *Sviluppi Traumatici. Eziopatogenesi, clinica e terapia della dimensione dissociativa*. Cortina Editore.

Liotti, G., & Prunetti, E. (2010). *Metacognitive deficits in trauma-related disorders: Contingent on interpersonal motivational contexts?* In G. Dimaggio & P. H. Lysaker (Eds.), *Metacognition and severe adult mental disorders: From research to treatment* (pp. 196–214). Routledge.

Littel, M., van den Hout, M. A., & Engelhard, I. M. (2016). Desensitizing addiction: Using eye movements to reduce the intensity of substance-related mental imagery and craving. *Frontiers in Psychiatry, 7*, 14.

Lyons-Ruth, K., Yellin, C., Melnick, S., & Atwood, G. (2005). Expanding the concept of unresolved mental states: Hostile/helpless states of mind on the Adult Attachment Interview are associated with disrupted mother-infant communication and infant disorganization. *Development and Psychopathology, 17*(1), 1–23.

MacCulloch, M. J., & Feldman, P. (1996). Eye movement desensitisation treatment utilises the positive visceral element of the investigatory reflex to inhibit the memories of post-traumatic stress disorder: A theoretical analysis. *The British Journal of Psychiatry, 169*(5), 571–579.

Main, M., & Morgan, H. (1996). *Disorganization and disorientation in infant strange situation behavior: Phenotypic resemblance to dissociative states*. In L. K. Michelson & W. J. Ray (Eds.), *Handbook of dissociation: Theoretical, empirical, and clinical perspectives* (pp. 107–138). Springer.

Main, M., & Solomon, J. (1986). *Discovery of an insecure-disorganized/disoriented attachment pattern*. In T. B. Brazelton & M. W. Yogman (Eds.), *Affective development in infancy* (pp. 95–124). Ablex Publishing.

Mandelli, L., Petrelli, C., & Serretti, A. (2015). The role of specific early trauma in adult depression: A meta-analysis of published literature. Childhood trauma and adult depression. *European Psychiatry, 30, 6*, 665–680.

McCann, I. L., & Pearlman, L. A. (1990). Vicarious traumatization: A framework for understanding the psychological effects of working with victims. *Journal of Traumatic Stress, 3*(1), 131–149.

McLean, L. M., & Gallop, R. (2003). Implications of childhood sexual abuse for adult borderline personality disorder and complex posttraumatic stress disorder. *The American Journal of Psychiatry, 160*, 369–371.

Miller, M. L., & Brock, R. L. (2017). The effect of trauma on the severity of obsessive-compulsive spectrum symptoms: A meta-analysis. *Journal of Anxiety Disorders, 47*, 29–44.

Molendijk, M. L., Hoek, H. W., Brewerton, T. D., & Elzinga, B. M. (2017). Childhood maltreatment and eating disorder pathology: A systematic review and dose-response meta-analysis. *Psychological Medicine, 47*, 1402–1416.

Monteleone, A. M., Ruzzi, V., Patriciello, G., Pellegrino, F., Cascino, G., Castellini, G., et al. (2019). Parental bonding, childhood maltreatment and eating disorder psychopathology: An investigation of their interactions. *Eating and Weight Disorders - Studies on Anorexia, Bulimia and Obesity, 25*(3), 577–589.

Monticelli, F. (2005). Le perversioni sessuali nella prospettiva cognitivo-evoluzionista. In *Psicobiettivo: Rivista quadrimestrale di psicoterapie a confronto, 1*. Franco Angeli.

Nijenhuis, E. R. S. (2009). *Somatoform dissociation and somatoform dissociative disorders*. In P. F. Dell & J. A. O'Neil (Eds.), *Dissociation and the dissociative disorders: DSM-V and beyond* (pp. 259–275). Routledge/Taylor & Francis Group.

Norcross, J. C., & Lambert, M. J. (2011). Evidence-based therapy relationships. In J. C. Norcross (Ed.), *Psychotherapy relationships that work: Evidence-based responsiveness* (pp. 3–21). Oxford University Press.

Ogden P. and Fisher J. (2016), *Psicoterapia sensomotoria. Interventi per il trauma e l'attaccamento.* .

Ogden, P., Minton, K., & Pain, C. (2006). *Trauma and the body. A sensorimotor approach to psychotherapy*. Norton.

Pearlman, L. A., & Courtois, C. A. (2005). Clinical applications of the attachment framework: Relational treatment of complex trauma. *Journal of Traumatic Stress, 18*(5), 449–459.

Porges, S. W. (2014). *Teoria polivagale fondamenti neurofisiologici delle emozioni, dell'attaccamento, della comunicazione e dell'autoregolazione*. Hoepli.

Propper, R. E., Pierce, J., Geisler, M. W., Christman, S. D., & Bellorado, N. B. S. (2007). Effect of bilateral eye movements on frontal interhemispheric gamma EEG coherence. *The Journal of Nervous and Mental Disease, 195*(9), 785–788.

Reed, G. M., First, M. B., Elena, M.-M. M., Gureje, O., Pike, K. M., & Saxena, S. (2016). Draft diagnostic guidelines for ICD-11 mental and behavioural disorders available for review and comment. *World Psychiatry, 15*, 112–113.

Reinders, A. A. T. S., Willemsen, A. T., Vissia, E. M., Vos, H. P. J., den Boer, J. A., & Nijenhuis, E. R. S. (2016). The psychobiology of authentic and simulated dissociative personality states: The full monty. *Journal of Nervous and Mental Disease, 204*(6), 445–457.

Rezzonico, G., & Furlani, F. A. P. (2019). *La dissociazione nella costruzione della realtà. Prospettive cliniche*. Franco Angeli.

Sar, V., Alioğlu, F., & Akyüz, G. (2014). Experiences of possession and paranormal phenomena among women in the general population: Are they related to traumatic stress and dissociation? *Journal of Trauma & Dissociation, 15*(3), 303–318.

Sareen, J. (2014). Posttraumatic stress disorder in adults: Impact, comorbidity, risk factors, and treatment. *Canadian Journal of Psychiatry. Revue Canadienne de Psychiatrie, 59, 9*, 460–467.

Sareen, J., Cox, B.J., Stein, M.B., Afifi, T.O., Fleet, C., & Asmundson, G.J. (2007). Physical and mental comorbidity, disability, and suicidal behavior associated with posttraumatic stress disorder in a large community sample. *Psychosomatic Medicine, 69*(3), 242–248.

Scalabrini, A., Cavicchioli, M., Fossati, A., & Maffei, C. (2016). The extent of dissociation in borderline personality disorder: A meta-analytic review. *Journal of Trauma & Dissociation*.

Schimmenti, A., & Bifulco, A. (2015). Linking lack of care in childhood to anxiety disorders in emerging adulthood: The role of attachment styles. *Child and Adolescent Mental Health, 20*(1), 41–48.

Schimmenti, A., Passanini, V., Caretti, V., La Marca, L., Granieri, A., Iacolino, C., Gervasi, A. M., Maganuco, N. R., & Billieux, J. (2017). Traumatic experiences, alexithymia, and Internet addiction symptoms among late adolescents: A moderated mediation analysis. *Addictive Behaviours, 64*, 314–320.

Schnyder, U., Ehlers, A., Elbert, T., Foa, E. B., Gersons, B. P., Resick, P. A., Shapiro, F., & Cloitre, M. (2015). Psychotherapies for PTSD: What do they have in common? *European Journal of Psychotraumatology, 14*(6), 281–286.

Schore, A. N. (2012). *The science of the art of psychotherapy*. W. W. Norton & Company.

Shalev, A. Y., Gevonden, M., Ratanatharathorn, A., Laska, E., van der Mei, W. F., Qi, W., et al. (2019). Estimating the risk of PTSD in recent trauma survivors: Results of the International Consortium to Predict PTSD (ICPP). *World Psychiatry, 18*(1), 77–87.

Shapiro, F. (1995). *Eye movement desensitization and reprocessing: Basic principles, protocols, and procedures*. Guilford Press.

Shapiro, F. (2000). *EMDR. Desensibilizzazione e rielaborazione attraverso movimenti oculari*. McGraw-Hill.

Shapiro, F. (2001). *Eye movement desensitization and reprocessing: Basic principles, protocols, and procedures*. Guilford Press.

Shapiro, F. (2007). EMDR and case conceptualization from an adaptive information processing perspective. In F. Shapiro, F. Kaslow, & L. Maxfield (Eds.), *Handbook of EMDR and family therapy processes* (pp. 3–36). Wiley.

Shapiro, F. (2014). The role of eye movement desensitization and reprocessing (EMDR) therapy in medicine: Addressing the psychological and physical symptoms stemming from adverse life experiences. *The Permanente Journal, 18*(1), 71–77.

Siegel, D. J. (1999). *The developing mind: Toward a neurobiology of interpersonal experience*. Guilford Press.

Solomon, R. M., & Shapiro, F. (2008). EMDR and the adaptive information processing model: Potential mechanisms of change. *Journal of EMDR Practice and Research, 2*(4), 315–325.

Steele, K., Boon, S., & van der Hart, O. (2017). *La cura della dissociazione traumatica. Un approccio pratico e integrative*. Mimesis.

Stickgold, R. (2002). EMDR: A putative neurobiological mechanism of action. *Journal of Clinical Psychology, 58*(1), 61–75.

Tagliavini, G. (2011). Modulazione dell'arousal, memoria procedurale ed elaborazione del trauma. Il contributo clinico del modello polivagale e della terapia sensomotoria. *Cognitivismo Clinico, 8*(1), 60–72.

Tagliavini G., Boldrini P. (2021), La ricerca sull'attaccamento disorganizzato e la terapia della traumatizzazione complessa. In Rezzonico G., Ruberti S. (Eds.), Attualità e prospettive dell'attaccamento. Dalla teoria alla pratica clinica. Franco Angeli, .

Thome, J., Terpou, B. A., McKinnon, M. C., & Lanius, R. A. (2020). The neural correlates of trauma-related autobiographical memory in posttraumatic stress disorder: A meta-analysis. *Depression and Anxiety, 37*(4), 321–345.

van der Hart, O., Nijenhuis, E. R. S., & Steele, K. (2006). *The haunted self: Structural dissociation and the treatment of chronic traumatization*. W.W. Norton & Co.

van der Hart, O., Nijenhuis, E. R. S., & Steele, K. (2010). *Fantasmi nel sé. Trauma e trattamento della dissociazione strutturale*. Raffaello Cortina.

van der Hart, O., Steele, K., & Boon, S. (2013). *La Dissociazione Traumatica: Comprenderla e Affrontarla*. Mimesis.

van Dijke, A., Ford, J. D., van der Hart, O., van Son, M., van der Heijden, P., & Bühring, M. (2010). Affect dysregulation in borderline personality disorder and somatoform disorder: Differentiating under- and over-regulation. *Journal of Personality Disorders, 24*, 296–311.

van Huijstee, J., & Vermetten, E. (2018). The dissociative subtype of post-traumatic stress disorder: Research update on clinical and neurobiological features. *Current Topics in Behavioral Neurosciences, 38*, 229–248.

Wiersma, J. E., Hovens, J. G., van Oppen, P., Giltay, E. J., van Schaik, D. J., Beekman, A. T., & Penninx, B. W. J. H. (2009). The importance of childhood trauma and childhood life events for chronicity of depression in adults. *The Journal of Clinical Psychiatry, 70*, 983–989.

Wilson, J. P., & Thomas, R. B. (2004). *Empathy in the treatment of trauma and PTSD*. Brunner-Routledge.

World Health Organization. (2013). *Guidelines for the management of conditions specifically related to stress*. WHO.

World Health Organization. (2019). *International Statistical Classification of Diseases and Related Health Problems (11th ed.)*. WHO.

Yen, S., Shea, M. T., Battle, C. L., Johnson, D. M., Zlotnick, C., Dolan-Sewell, R., et al. (2002). Traumatic exposure and posttraumatic stress disorder in borderline, schizotypal, avoidant, and obsessive-compulsive personality disorders: Findings from the collaborative longitudinal personality disorders study. *The Journal of Nervous and Mental Disease, 190*, 510–518.

Young, J. E., Klosko, J. S., & Weishaar, M. E. (2003). *Schema therapy: A practitioner's guide*. Guilford Press.

Zalta, A.K., Tirone, V., Orlowska, D., Blais, R.K., Lofgreen, A., Klassen, B., Held, P., Stevens, N.R., Adkins, E., & Dent, A.L. (2021) Examining moderators of the relationship between social support and self-reported PTSD symptoms: A meta-analysis. *Psychological Bulletin. 147*(1), 33–54.

Zanarini, M. C., Frankenburg, F. R., Hennen, J., Reich, D. B., & Silk, K. R. (2006). Prediction of the 10-year course of borderline personality disorder. *The American Journal of Psychiatry, 163*, 827–832.

Zlotnick, C., Shea, M. T., Pearlstein, T., Simpson, E., Costello, E., & Begin, A. (1996). The relationship between dissociative symptoms, alexithymia, impulsivity, sexual abuse, and self-mutilation. *Comprehensive Psychiatry, 37*(1), 12–16.

Training Therapists in Common Interpersonal Skills

Tao Lin and Timothy Anderson

1 Introduction

Training therapists to master interpersonal skills is a cornerstone of effective psychotherapy. Yet, any approach to empirically supported training of therapist interpersonal relational skills is inherently complicated. The complexity arises from multiple training goals, such as mastering different therapy modalities and treating various disorders, each requiring distinct training methods. Traditional training methods, such as supervised individual sessions and small group discussions, have been somewhat effective in addressing the complexity (Barnard & Goodyear, 2018) but often fail to emphasize the importance of relational skills adequately. Unfortunately, many training programs have focused on specific procedures in implementing these protocols without maintaining at least an equal focus on the interpersonal messaging needed to bring these specific techniques alive within the lives of clients. Optimal training should balance the implementation of defined treatments with the cultivation of interpersonal skills that enhance therapeutic engagement.

Interpersonal skills, mostly viewed as a common factor that permeates the expression of most, if not all, psychological treatments, are essential not only for implementing specific therapeutic techniques but also for engaging with the unique interpersonal traits and expressiveness of each client. In addition to customizing interpersonal expressions for different techniques and treatments, therapists also

T. Lin (✉)
Department of Psychology, Ohio University, Athens, OH, USA

Department of Psychiatry, University of Pennsylvania, Philadelphia, PA, USA
e-mail: tl860218@ohio.edu

T. Anderson
Department of Psychology, Ohio University, Athens, OH, USA

customize their interpersonal abilities to the unique interpersonal traits and expressiveness of the client. That is, therapists simply don't implement techniques or interpersonal skills onto a passive client, but clients also bring their own interpersonal skills into the treatment (Anderson & Perlman, 2022). Clients' interpersonal skills match and complement the therapist in ways that activate common factors of treatment (e.g., persuasion of treatment rationale, an alliance bond that drives treatment involvement, sparking positive expectations for treatment success). These relational processes are potent in and of themselves (Wampold & Owen, 2021) and are catalyzed as the necessary ingredient of a specific psychotherapy treatment to which both client and patient can ally.

However, common interpersonal relationship skills often use some constructs that seem broad at first flush (e.g., "warmth") and are not as precisely defined as some trainees may desire. Even more, learning to relationally engage with real clients in practice requires, broadly speaking, a capacity to use the therapist's genuine self in a *real relationship* with clients (Farber et al., 2022), many of whom have limited abilities to reciprocate.

Recent research on professional training of a wide range of professions has identified multiple innovative training methods (e.g., Ericsson, 2018) that could be adapted for psychotherapy (Rousmaniere et al., 2016), such as deliberate practice and high-risk simulations. Our approach aims to address therapists' interpersonal skills by integrating multiple methods, including brief exposures (e.g., workshops), longer-term practices (deliberate practice, longer-term relational practice of skills with others, didactic training), personal and professional development (e.g., scaffolding to individualized stages of career development), and professional practice in implementing interpersonal skills with real clients.

2 Why Are Interpersonal Skills So Important in Psychotherapy?

The core of these therapist interpersonal skills was identified in the early years of psychotherapy research, many of which have historical links to foundational figures such as Rogers (1957 empathy, warmth, and genuineness), Freud (1913; the alliance bond, resistance/rupture), and persuasiveness (Frank & Frank, 1993). A strong body of research has since evolved, empirically supporting that these elements, between therapists and clients, are strongly associated with improved client outcomes (Norcross & Lambert, 2019).

Recently, therapists' interpersonal skills have been defined using performance-based metrics, focusing on skill-based characteristics of these interpersonal constructs. Isolating these foundational skills into performance-based expressions is designed to enhance the focus of these interpersonal skills in a variety of client characteristics and contexts. These interpersonal skills have gathered momentum in significantly predicting client outcomes (Anderson et al., 2009). For example,

Schöttke et al. (2017) used a performance-based measure of therapist interpersonal skills and found that more positively rated therapist interpersonal dispositions were significantly predictive of client outcomes. Furthermore, the effect of therapist interpersonal skills was independent of treatment techniques and occurred for a long-term period (i.e., across a 5-year period) after the interpersonal assessment of the therapists. Through an observation-based measurement, Heinonen et al. (2014) were successful in isolating therapist skills as independent of client reactions, and thus an independent influence on clients.

A focus on therapists' interpersonal skills in clinical training is empirically supported for several reasons, foremost being the strong effect sizes (about 0.7 to 0.8) for interpersonal skills (e.g., empathy) as predictors of treatment outcome (Wampold & Imel, 2015). While arguments for the relative strength of interpersonal skills relative to specific treatments have been made, and are convincing (see Wampold & Imel, 2015), the point is not to compare which is stronger. Instead, therapist interpersonal skills are important *regardless* of whatever specific treatment is chosen. By focusing on building therapists' interpersonal skills, therapists are engaging in skills that have the strongest effects on client outcomes.

3 How to Assess and Train Interpersonal Skills?

A challenge for training therapists is how to define and measure therapists' interpersonal skills within the real-world practice when therapy relationships are complex, interactive, and constantly changing. Stiles (2021) referred to this problem as one of responsiveness in human relating, and that the individual reactions within the relationship are in constant flux within and always developing with an emergent context. A therapist may often ask themselves: "What interventions should I use?" "Which skill should I present with?" "What target should I respond to?" Depending on what a patient presents, the answers may vary a lot. Even the most manualized and "standardized" therapist would probably adjust the treatment according to client needs and characteristics as this emergent context unfolds. As a result, the therapist's performance may vary across different patients, different sessions, and even within the same session (Kring et al., 2022).

Although therapy occurs within a defined context with the overarching benevolent goal of promoting positive client change, there are additional difficulties in defining therapist skills that extend beyond the observed client-therapist interactions. The needs of the client may not always be stated, or observable, but are also influencing the therapeutic processes. For example, a therapist may need to demonstrate strong alliance bond capacity when working with a client with trust issues, but relatively little bond is needed for clients with secure attachments. In contrast, persuasiveness might be needed more when working with a client who is hesitant to reduce alcohol use in a mandated treatment, but less prevalent for a client who returns to treatment and is facing similar issues after experiencing new life stressors. In addition, the expression of interpersonal skills should be adjusted to the setting and environment. For example, researchers have suggested that therapists should exaggerate voices and facial expressions in teletherapy to compensate for the loss of nonverbal cues in remote communication (Lin & Anderson, 2024).

Thus, therapists will need to adjust their skills according to the setting, the emerging context, and the client's goals. How can we assess a construct that varies from moment to moment? In the following sections, we consider how traditional methods were used in the assessment and training of therapist interpersonal skills.

Therapists' Self-Evaluation Therapists' self-evaluation is perhaps the easiest option. However, to which extent can we really trust self-evaluations? Numerous studies have documented the ubiquity of self-assessment bias in clinical skills among therapists and trainees (Anderson et al., 2020; Loades & Myles, 2016; Longley et al., 2023; Parker & Waller, 2015). A striking illustration of this bias was described by Walfish et al. (2012). In their sample of 129 mental health professionals, all self-rated their skills above average, and over 90% self-rated their skills at the 75th percentile or above. Researchers have also identified therapists' tendency to underestimate their skills compared to their supervisors (Loades & Myles, 2016; McManus et al., 2012). The self-assessment bias may hinder therapists from identifying areas of growth and continuing to develop their skills.

Supervisor Observation Supervisor observation of trainees performing clinical skills with actual patients is an important assessment tool for performance-based clinical skills in healthcare professions. Although this method can reduce self-report bias, the use of direct observation is very infrequent due to a lack of supervisory resources (Amerikaner & Rose, 2012; Holmboe, 2004). How many sessions or videotapes can a supervisor observe each week?

Even assuming the supervisor has the resources and availability for direct observation, their evaluations are not always accurate and unbiased. As mentioned above, trainees' performances vary from moment to moment. The trainee may be skillful in one scenario but seems clumsy in another. Apparently, it is not feasible for the supervisor to observe each session of each client. How can supervisors possibly know which session/client can best represent the trainee's skill? The trainee's skills might be overestimated if an easy client/session is selected for observation, but underrated if a difficult session was observed.

Previous research has also suggested significant deficiencies in faculty direct observation evaluation skills (Holmboe, 2004). Some may expect that supervisors should have a more nuanced understanding of the client's needs or stronger skills than the trainee. However, this may not always be correct, especially when observing a new case. The supervisor may even have a different or even less accurate understanding of the therapeutic context and expect the trainee to respond in a different way. The ambiguity in performance criteria could lead to biased evaluation. Additionally, supervisors who employ varying therapeutic approaches might have distinct definitions and place different levels of importance on interpersonal skills in supervision, resulting in inconsistent training.

Client Report Some may argue that, since the treatment goal is to facilitate positive changes and symptom relief, why don't we just use client report to assess therapists' skills? A good therapist is supposed to achieve a higher patient recovery rate than a less good therapist (Saxon & Barkham, 2012). Yet, treatment outcome is determined by a variety of factors, and therapist effect only accounts for 5–10% of the treatment outcome. In other words, client outcomes are largely dependent on other factors such as client traits, diagnosis, and clinical setting. Is it fair to compare a therapist working with psychotic patients in a psychiatric hospital versus another therapist working with high-functioning clients at a university counseling center by simply evaluating their patients' treatment outcome? Likewise, it is much easier to establish a strong working alliance with a friendly patient compared to a hostile client. How can we compare the grades from different exams?

To summarize, traditional training methods may fail to accurately capture therapists' variable skills in complex practice as these skills fluctuate in response to the context. How can we control for the client- and context-related variability? Our approach involves two key strategies: (1) conceptualizing common interpersonal skills as conceptually unique from any specific treatment, or "pan-theoretical," and (2) employing well-defined, artificial scenarios as performance-based exercises to initially train therapists to apply broadly defined interpersonal skills within the complex environment of real-world practice.

Specifically, we have used standardized videos to stimulate difficult therapy scenarios (Anderson et al., 2019). Anderson and colleagues (2019) developed the Facilitative Interpersonal Skills (FIS) task, during which participants are presented with a set of video clips that depict challenging interpersonal situations performed by actors. These video clips were developed based on actual, difficult therapy sessions. Once the video is paused, the participants are asked to respond to the stimulated client immediately as if they were the therapist in the session. Their responses will then be recorded and rated by trained raters on the eight FIS items (verbal fluency, emotional expressiveness, persuasiveness, warmth and acceptance, empathy, hope, alliance bond capacity, and alliance rupture repair responsiveness) using a 5-point Likert-type scale from 1 (skill deficit) to 5 (optimal presence of skill). The raters are instructed to set their initial rating at 3, which is considered the ordinary level of skills, and adjust the ratings based on the participants' performance.

The FIS task has several key advantages in skill assessment. First, these stimulus clips provide a controlled, standardized environment, thereby accounting for client characteristics and environmental factors. By responding to the same set of clients/scenarios, each therapist and trainee is assessed under the same condition. Therefore, their responses can be evaluated and compared with others on the same scale. As the stimulus clips are meticulously pre-designed to present specific challenges, evaluators are fully aware of the key issues that need to be addressed and the appropriate responses expected in each scenario. Consequently, this design can minimize ambiguity in performance criteria and allow for a targeted assessment of the trainee's ability to manage the predefined challenges. With proper training, graduate students and even undergraduate coders can achieve good reliability of FIS rating (e.g., Hill et al., 2016). This can greatly alleviate the workload of supervisors.

Second, the FIS stimulus clips were based on actual clinical interactions the FIS clips were selected to include a wide range of interpersonal experiences in therapy, such as expressing disappointment about treatment progress, feelings of being judged, and idealizing the therapist, and to represent a variety of clients, including a confrontational angry client, a passive withdrawn client, a confused and yielding client, and a controlling and blaming client (Anderson et al., 2009). These clips represent different styles of communication regarding the interpersonal circumplex and various interpersonal needs (Anderson et al., 2016a). Therefore, the FIS task can comprehensively evaluate trainee's performance across scenarios.

Moreover, the simulated clients were designed to be "difficult." The fact that the video simulations are challenging is part of their appeal that makes them useful as a training tool. Most therapists and trainees perform fine with an "easy," compliant client. What really differentiates good versus bad therapists is how they perform with a challenging client/scenario. Previous research has demonstrated that the FIS ratings generated based on therapists' responses to FIS clips consistently and robustly predict treatment outcome (Anderson et al., 2009, 2016a, b). The task is limited in that the clips are brief, and the context of the video-simulated clients is fixed and not created by the therapist being assessed or trained. Therapists responding to the clips sometimes complain that *their clients* would never be as dissatisfied with them in their real practice (even though all FIS simulations are from transcripts of actual therapies, they are from different therapists). As individuals tend to overestimate their competence and effectiveness, (Walfish et al., 2012), using the challenging FIS clips in training may aid some therapists, especially those with extensive clinical experience to reconsider the limits of their skill and help them engage in continuing education Relatedly, the FIS task does not provide the opportunity for therapists to practice genuinely interactive responding that essential to genuine interpersonal relatedness where each client and therapist create a unique narrative and therapists respond immediately to their client's response to something the therapist actually said.

Notwithstanding these challenges, the standardized stimulus clips have great potential in facilitating skill training. For nearly a decade our research has focused on how to use these standard stimuli from the FIS task to training. The standardization of training materials ensures that all trainees are exposed to the same scenarios under a controlled setting, which promotes uniformity in training experiences and outcomes. In real clinical training, the training quality is not always under the supervisor's control. Some trainees may get all the easy, compliant cases and feel unchallenged whereas others may get all the hard, defensive cases and feel defeated. Video simulations can depict a wide range of situations and clients, including rare or difficult cases that trainees might not frequently encounter in real-life practice.

Additionally, we can control the learning curve by adjusting the stimulus clips depending on the trainees' strengths and weaknesses. That is, trainees can benefit from responding to simulated clients that are moderately challenging or at certain levels of difficulty. Trainees can watch these videos multiple times to observe and learn different approaches to handle the same situation. This repetition can be crucial for mastering clinical skills and understanding subtle nuances in patient interactions. The brief, repeatable exposure is ideal for deliberate practice of micro-skills.

Moreover, using video simulations allows trainees to learn and make mistakes in a risk-free environment, without the potential for harming actual patients. For example, the trainee can practice addressing trusting issues with a simulated client before encountering a real one. This can significantly reduce the pressure and anxiety associated with clinical training. Simulation has been widely used in skill acquisition in various fields (Fraser et al., 2009; Rourke, 2020).

Furthermore, FIS is rated on the eight domains. This standardization allows instructors to provide specific, objective feedback based on clearly defined criteria. Trainees can benefit from this structure by seeing exactly where they need improvement, which can be directly tied to actions and responses shown in the videos. Finally, the video simulation can be accessed easily, making it possible to train a large number of students. The evaluation of a trainee's performance does not necessarily require supervisors but can be reliably achieved by students. This scalability helps in reducing training costs and resources.

After three outcome studies demonstrating that therapist responses on the simulated FIS clips predicted the therapists' outcomes with their real clients (Anderson et al., 2009, 2016a, b), work began on developing trainings that would help therapists build those abilities. A workshop-style training was developed that included eight modules that were parallel to the FIS items, referred to as Facilitative Interpersonal Relationship Skills Training (FIRST). Because the FIS items mostly were grounded on many of the strongest process variables throughout the history of psychotherapy research, the training topics were nothing new, and thus very familiar, within foundational training of therapy training programs. There is a paradox here: a brief performance rating of these skills from a brief client simulation predicted outcomes and yet, after years of long-term training and practice, there were no appreciable gains in therapists' outcomes (e.g., Goldberg et al., 2016), and again that therapists were not especially perceptive of their own abilities (Walfish et al., 2012). Given this paradox, we thought there might be some room for developing innovative training that might build these skills, both in early training and established therapists.

Initially, FIRST was created as an integration with Alliance Focused Training (AFT; Eubanks et al., 2015), specifically on the Alliance Rupture Repair ratings, responsiveness (Stiles, 2021), and building the therapists' abilities to form an alliance bond. There are several defining characteristics to the FIRST:

1. The approach to these training modules differs in several ways, including the fact that our conceptualization was a direct outgrowth of the foundational contributions of seminal contributions of Hans Strupp (Strupp & Binder, 1984), Lorna Benjamin (Critchfield & Benjamin, 2024; Frank & Frank, 1993).
2. An innovation to our approach is the use of standardized client videos, which not only has an advantage of standardization in assessing performance clips but also creates a sharper focus for examples within training. Using some of the same

simulations that are used in the FIS assessment allows for a direct link to the materials that has proven capacity for predicting outcomes and the elements with the training.
3. The FIS simulus clips are administered as the initial phase of training. This approach provides all trainees with a common experience and allows for shorthand and even stereotypic interpersonal patient characteristics as realistic examples for the training.
4. The fact that the FIS clips were drawn from actual psychotherapy cases allows for these stereotypic problems to be anchored in real clinical practice and, to some extent, allows for trainers to contextualize the examples during the training.
5. From the beginning, an emphasis was given to the use of Internet technologies. Perlman et al. (2020, 2022) began collecting FIS responses remotely with the aim of providing therapists more privacy in giving their responses and increasing efficiency in collecting sample responses.
6. FIRST also was committed to integrating innovative training and educational methods, such as deliberate practice. As the modules develops, the focus increases on exploring aspects of deliberate practice that might boost training. For example, Anderson et al. (2019) showed that simple modeling, or "Modeled Practice" of demonstrated "good" and "poor" FIS processes on a video, significantly increased therapists' abilities after a few repetitions of practice (i.e., without a supervisor).

FIRST has also been expanded to a variety of meaningful training situations and settings. Notably, Lin et al. (2024a, b) developed and examined a 2-h synchronous training that was specifically focused on the interpersonal challenges of conducting tele-therapy, tele-FIRST. An advantage of Lin's work is that it was founded on several studies that identified unique interpersonal challenges within tele-therapy (Lin et al., 2021, 2024a, b). The features of these interpersonal challenges within the tele-therapy context (Békés, et al., 2021) formed a structure for developing new tele-FIS situations from a two-site research team (Antebi-Lerman et al., 2024). Lin et al. (2024a, b) led this two-site team with a cumulative project that comprehensively evaluated the effectiveness of the tele-FIRST training in a randomized controlled trial (RCT). The RCT of tele-FIRST found that those who underwent the training had relatively higher ratings in tele-FIS responses. Lin et al. (2024a, b) also found that there were relative increases in self-ratings of FIS, tele-therapy skills, and competencies, as well as increased self-efficacy in helping skill interventions.

The development of these materials has expanded further into other practice situations, also offering opportunities for unique training based on the FIRST model. For example, the FIS clips have expanded to Child Clients (Bate & Tsakas, 2022), Client Risk (Duffy, 2022); Text Application (Zech et al., 2023); hospital-based social work context (Maserow, 2023), and nine different languages using the same core interpersonal situations. These developments have allowed for vastly expanded practice within an international community of practitioners and trainers to be organized around a common set of interpersonal situations.

However, several issues have arisen as the FIS and training have expanded. First, consisting of eight domains that are highly correlated, FIS is broadly defined. The broad definition lacks the precision needed to accurately measure and differentiate between various skills or behaviors, making it challenging to identify and target specific areas for improvement. It can result in some overlaps between FIRST and previous skill training. Second, despite the trainable nature of FIS (e.g., Lin et al., 2024a, b), some have argued that certain elements of FIS are more trait-like and may be less amenable to change.

Third, the coding of FIS responses is labor-intensive. Coders need to fully understand the concepts, interpersonal needs in the simulated therapeutic scenarios portrayed in the FIS stimulus clips, and rating criteria, which typically takes months of training. Providing timely feedback on therapists' performance, which is often a key component of clinical training, is challenging due to the time-consuming nature of FIS coding. Recently, researchers have been working to develop a machine learning algorithm that aims to automatically and rapidly code FIS responses, potentially reducing the burden on human coders and facilitating more timely feedback (Aafjes-van Doorn et al., under review).

4 Conclusion

Training therapists to master interpersonal skills is fundamental to effective psychotherapy, yet presents significant challenges due to the complexity of clinical practice. The FIS task, with its performance-based approach, offers a promising solution by providing standardized, controlled environments for skill assessment and training. The brief and standardized FIS clips can simulate various challenging scenarios in psychotherapy. These stimulus clips allow therapists and trainees to repeatedly and deliberately practice a micro skill, with the benefits of observer-rated feedback. FIRST, a training integrating FIS and deliberate practice, was found to effectively and significantly increase the interpersonal skills of both therapists and trainees (Perlman et al., 2020, 2022). Moreover, FIRST can be easily adapted to various settings and situations. By integrating FIS training into clinical training, we can enhance the development of therapists' interpersonal skills, ultimately improving client outcomes and advancing the field of psychotherapy.

References

Amerikaner, M., & Rose, T. (2012). Direct observation of psychology supervisees' clinical work: A snapshot of current practice. *The Clinical Supervisor, 31*(1), 61–80.

Anderson, T., & Perlman, M. R. (2022). Therapists and clients facilitative interpersonal skills in psychotherapy. In J. N. Fuertes (Ed.), *The other side of psychotherapy: Understanding clients' experiences and contributions in treatment*. American Psychological Association. https://doi.org/10.1037/0000303-000

Anderson, T., Ogles, B. M., Patterson, C. L., Lambert, M. J., & Vermeersch, D. A. (2009). Therapist effects: Facilitative interpersonal skills as a predictor of therapist success. *Journal of Clinical Psychology, 65*, 755–768.

Anderson, T., Crowley, M. J., Himawan, L., Holmberg, J., & Uhlin, B. (2016a). Therapist facilitative interpersonal skills and training status: A randomized clinical trial on alliance and outcome. *Psychotherapy Research, 26*, 511–529. https://doi.org/10.1080/10503307.2015.1049671

Anderson, T., McClintock, A. S., Himawan, L., Song, X., & Patterson, C. L. (2016b). A prospective study of therapist facilitative interpersonal skills as a predictor of treatment outcome. *Journal of Consulting and Clinical Psychology, 84*, 57–66. https://doi.org/10.1037/ccp0000060

Anderson, T., Patterson, C., McClintock, A. S., McCarrick, S. M., Song, X., & The Psychotherapy and Interpersonal Lab Team. (2019). *Facilitative interpersonal skills task and rating manual*. Ohio University.

Anderson, T., Perlman, M. R., McCarrick, S. M., & McClintock, A. S. (2020). Modeling therapist responses with structured practice enhances facilitative interpersonal skills. *Journal of Clinical Psychology, 76*(4), 659–675.

Antebi-Lerman, E., Anderson, T., Lin, T., & Aafjes-van Doorn, K. (2024). Tele-therapy training's impact on therapist's perspectives and self-efficacy: The role of emotion. In [Conference paper] *The 55th annual conference for the international society for psychotherapy research*. Ottawa, CA.

Barnard & Goodyear. (2018). *Fundamentals of clinical supervision*. Merrill Counseling.

Bate, J., & Tsakas, A. (2022). Facilitative interpersonal skills are relevant in child therapy too, so why don't we measure them? *Research in Psychotherapy: Psychopathology, Process, and Outcome, 25*(1), 595.

Békés, V., Aafjes-van Doorn, K., Luo, X., Prout, T. A., & Hoffman, L. (2021). Psychotherapists' challenges with online therapy during COVID-19: Concerns about connectedness predict therapists' negative view of online therapy and its perceived efficacy over time. *Frontiers in Psychology, 12*, 705599. https://doi.org/10.3389/fpsyg.2021.705599

Critchfield, K. L., & Benjamin, L. S. (2024). *Structural Analysis of Social Behavior (SASB): A Primer for Clinical Use*. American Psychological Association.

Duffy, M. (2022). *Facilitative interpersonal skills (FIS) and high-risk scenarios: An adaptation of the FIS task for working with suicidal clients*. Doctoral dissertation, The New School for Social Research.

Ericsson, K. A. (2018). The differential influence of experience, practice, and deliberate practice on the development of superior individual performance of experts. In K. A. Ericsson, R. R. Hoffman, A. Kozbelt, & A. M. Williams (Eds.), *Cambridge handbook of expertise and expert performance* (2nd ed., pp. 745–769). Cambridge University Press. https://doi.org/10.1017/9781316480748.038

Eubanks-Carter, C., Muran, J. C., & Safran, J. D. (2015). Alliance-focused training. *Psychotherapy, 2015*(52), 169–173. https://doi.org/10.1037/a0037596

Farber, B. A., Suzuki, J. Y., & Ort, D. (2022). *Understanding and enhancing positive regard in psychotherapy: Carl Rogers and beyond*. American Psychological Association.

Frank, J. D., & Frank, J. B. (1993). *Persuasion and healing: A comparative study of psychotherapy* (3rd ed.). The Johns Hopkins University Press.

Fraser, K., Peets, A., Walker, I., Tworek, J., Paget, M., Wright, B., & McLaughlin, K. (2009). The effect of simulator training on clinical skills acquisition, retention and transfer. *Medical Education, 43*(8), 784–789.

Freud, S. (1913). On the beginning of treatment: Further recommendations on the techniques of psychoanalysis. In J. Strachey (Ed.), *The standard edition of the complete psychological works of Sigmund Freud* (Vol. 12, pp. 122–144). Hogarth.

Goldberg, S. B., Rousmaniere, T., Miller, S. D., Whipple, J., Nielsen, S. L., Hoyt, W. T., & Wampold, B. E. (2016). Do psychotherapists improve with time and experience? A longitudinal analysis of outcomes in a clinical setting. *Journal of Counseling Psychology, 63*(1), 1–11. https://doi.org/10.1037/cou0000131

Heinonen, E., Lindfors, O., Härkänen, T., Virtala, E., Jääskeläinen, T., & Knekt, P. (2014). Therapists' professional and personal characteristics as predictors of working alliance in short-term and long-term psychotherapies. *Clinical Psychology & Psychotherapy, 6*, 475–494. https://doi.org/10.1002/cpp.1852

Hill, C. E., Anderson, T., Kline, K., McClintock, A., Cranston, S., McCarrick, S., et al. (2016). Helping skills training for undergraduate students: Who should we select and train? *The Counseling Psychologist, 44*(1), 50–77. https://doi.org/10.1177/0011000015613

Holmboe, E. S. (2004). Faculty and the observation of trainees' clinical skills: Problems and opportunities. *Academic Medicine, 79*(1), 16–22.

Kring, M., Cozart, J. K., Sinnard, M. T., Oby, A., Hamm, E. H., Frost, N. D., & Hoyt, W. T. (2022). Evaluating psychotherapist competence: Testing the generalizability of clinical competence assessments of graduate trainees. *Journal of Counseling Psychology, 69*(2), 222–234. https://doi.org/10.1037/cou0000576

Lin, T., & Anderson, T. (2024). Reduced therapeutic skill in teletherapy versus in-person therapy: The role of non-verbal communication. *Counselling and Psychotherapy Research, 24*(1), 317–327.

Lin, T., Stone, S. J., Heckman, T. G., & Anderson, T. (2021). Zoom-in to zone-out: Therapists report less therapeutic skill in telepsychology versus face-to-face therapy during the COVID-19 pandemic. *Psychotherapy, 58*(4), 449–459.

Lin, T., Aafjes-van Doorn, K., Antebi-Lerman, E., & Anderson T. (2024a). *Efficacy of telefacilitative interpersonal and relational skills training on teletherapy skills: A randomized controlled trial.*

Lin, T., Stone, S. J., & Anderson, T. (2024b). A head start in the long race: Therapists are learning to adapt their therapeutic skills within teletherapy. *Professional Psychology: Research and Practice.* Advance online publication. https://doi.org/10.1037/pro0000572

Loades, M. E., & Myles, P. J. (2016). Does a therapist's reflective ability predict the accuracy of their self-evaluation of competence in cognitive behavioural therapy? *The Cognitive Behaviour Therapist, 9*, e6.

Longley, M., Kästner, D., Daubmann, A., Hirschmeier, C., Strauß, B., & Gumz, A. (2023). Prospective psychotherapists' bias and accuracy in assessing their own facilitative interpersonal skills. *Psychotherapy, 60*(4), 525–535. https://doi.org/10.1037/pst0000506

Maserow, J. (2023). *FIRST for medical social workers: Evaluating the impact of facilitative interpersonal and relational skills training (FIRST) on medical social workers' interpersonal skillfulness.* Doctoral dissertation, The New School for Social Research.

McManus, F., Rakovshik, S., Kennerley, H., Fennell, M., & Westbrook, D. (2012). An investigation of the accuracy of therapists' self-assessment of cognitive-behaviour therapy skills. *British Journal of Clinical Psychology, 51*(3), 292–306.

Norcross, J. C., & Lambert, M. J. (2019). *Psychotherapy relationships that work: Volume 1: Evidence-based therapist contributions.* Oxford University Press.

Parker, Z. J., & Waller, G. (2015). Factors related to psychotherapists' self-assessment when treating anxiety and other disorders. *Behaviour Research and Therapy, 66*, 1–7.

Perlman, M. R., Anderson, T., Foley, V. K., Mimnaugh, S., & Safran, J. D. (2020). The impact of alliance-focused and facilitative interpersonal relationship training on therapist skills: An RCT of brief training. *Psychotherapy Research, 30*(7), 871–884. https://doi.org/10.1080/10503307.2020.1722862

Perlman, M. R., Anderson, T., Finkelstein, J. D., Foley, V. K., Mimnaugh, S., Gooch, C. V., David, K. C., Martin, S. J., & Safran, J. D. (2022). Facilitative interpersonal relationship training enhances novices' therapeutic skills. *Counselling Psychology Quarterly, 1–16.* https://doi.org/10.1080/09515070.2022.2049703

Rogers, C. (1957). The necessary and sufficient conditions of therapeutic personality change. *Journal of Consulting Psychology, 21*, 95–103.

Rourke, S. (2020). How does virtual reality simulation compare to simulated practice in the acquisition of clinical psychomotor skills for pre-registration student nurses? A systematic review. *International Journal of Nursing Studies, 102*, 103466.

Rousmaniere, T. G., Swift, J. K., Babins-Wagner, R., Whipple, J. L., & Berzins, S. (2016). Supervisor variance in psychotherapy outcome in routine practice. *Psychotherapy Research, 26*(2), 196–205. https://doi.org/10.1080/10503307.2014.963730

Saxon, D., & Barkham, M. (2012). Patterns of therapist variability: Therapist effects and the contribution of patient severity and risk. *Journal of Consulting and Clinical Psychology, 80*(4), 535–546. https://doi.org/10.1037/a0028898

Schöttke, H., Flückiger, C., Goldberg, S. B., Eversmann, J., & Lange, J. (2017). Predicting psychotherapy outcome based on therapist interpersonal skills: A five-year longitudinal study of a therapist assessment protocol. *Psychotherapy Research, 27*, 642–652. https://doi.org/10.1080/10503307.2015.1125546

Stiles, W. B. (2021). Responsiveness in psychotherapy research: Problems and ways forward. In J. C. Watson & H. Wiseman (Eds.), *The responsive psychotherapist: Attuning to clients in the moment* (pp. 15–35). APA Books. https://doi.org/10.1037/0000240-002

Strupp, H. H., & Binder, J. L. (1984). *Psychotherapy in a new Key: A guide to time-limited dynamic psychotherapy*. New York Basic Books.

Walfish, S., McAlister, B., O'Donnell, P., & Lambert, M. J. (2012). An investigation of self-assessment bias in mental health providers. *Psychological Reports, 110*(2), 639–644.

Wampold, B. E., & Imel, Z. E. (2015). *The great psychotherapy debate: The evidence for what makes psychotherapy work* ((2nd ed.). ed.). Routledge/Taylor & Francis Group.

Wampold, B. E., & Owen, J. (2021). Therapist effects: History, methods, magnitude, and characteristics of effective therapists. In M. Barkham, W. Lutz, & L. Castonguay (Eds.), *Bergin & Garfield's handbook of psychotherapy and behavior change* (pp. 297–326). Wiley.

Zech, J., Foley, V. K., Hull, T. D., & Anderson, T. (2023). Assessing the quality of digital patient-therapist communication: The development and validation of a text-based facilitative interpersonal skills task. *Psychotherapy Research, 33*(6), 743–756.

iCAST: Possible Steps Toward the Integration of Nonverbal Signals into Psychotherapeutic Practice

Fabian T. Ramseyer

1 Introduction

In psychotherapy, there are a few factors that are considered central to the success of therapy across all schools of therapy: These can be summarized as general factors (common factors; Pfammatter & Tschacher, 2012). In this chapter, I propose to place the factor "nonverbal behavior" in an equally prominent position. In many schools of therapy, nonverbal behavior is explicitly emphasized and highlighted, which can also be seen in numerous publications on this topic (e.g., Geissler, 2005; Hermer & Klinzing, 2004; Philippot et al., 2003; Westland, 2015). Many practitioners would undoubtedly agree with the relevance of nonverbal behavior at the interpersonal level. This chapter uses a simple model to attempt to integrate "nonverbal behavior" into psychotherapeutic practice at a higher level. The concrete presentation of how and when nonverbal behavior can be used and changed seems to me to be insufficiently developed, above all in the field of cognitive-behavioral approaches (with positive exceptions, e.g., Roediger, 2016), but especially in the introductory literature, general calls to pay attention to nonverbal behavior (without further indications of how this should be done) are so abstract that prospective therapists can probably draw little practical benefit from them. When an introductory work states that "for example, the ability to consciously use a wider range of nonverbal

This chapter is a translation of an article by FT Ramseyer, which appeared in "Die Psychotherapie". Ramseyer, F.T. iCAST: Ein praktisches Modell für die Integration nonverbaler Signale in die Psychotherapie. *Psychotherapie* 68, 36–43 (2023). https://doi.org/10.1007/s00278-022-00618-6. A number of updates and extensions have been added to the original text.

F. T. Ramseyer (✉)
Department of Clinical Psychology and Psychotherapy, Institute of Psychology,
University of Bern, Bern, Switzerland
e-mail: fabian.ramseyer@unibe.ch

behavior …" (Caspar, 2021, p. 46) is an advantage, then this makes perfect sense but still offers little in the way of concrete implementation in therapy. How can prospective psychotherapists integrate nonverbal behavior into their practical work? The model presented here attempts to point out a possible—initially simplified—direction. A specific emphasis will be put on phenomena that are emerging at the level of dyads or bigger groups—a focus that has gained more traction in recent years (Wheatley et al., 2023).

2 Nonverbal Behavior

Current reviews on nonverbal behavior (Hall et al., 2019) illustrate well the broad area of influence of this phenomenon, which is also expressed in the following statement: "There is hardly an area in the study of human behavior where nonverbal behavior is not involved" (Harrigan et al., 2005, p. 2). This is also true in psychotherapy; human behavior occurs in a defined form on a regular basis between two or more people. In this setting, nonverbal expression is always present and influences the quality and course of therapy. However, the significance that nonverbal behavior has taken on in psychotherapy research in recent decades is to be found elsewhere, as a review of various introductory books on the topic of "psychotherapy" speaks a different language: "Nonverbal" is rarely dealt with in a separate section in such works (Rief et al., 2021).

2.1 Nonverbal Behavior and Psychotherapy

Various meta-analyses on nonverbal behavior in the field of psychotherapy (Hall et al., 1995) or on communication in doctor–patient contact (Schmid Mast, 2007) are available and illustrate the general relevance of the topic. In the field of body psychotherapy (Geißler & Heisterkamp, 2013; Geuter, 2024), there are also various detailed treatises on nonverbal behavior and concrete tips for implementation. The findings reported in the meta-analyses also regularly appear in concrete instructions on "favorable" behavior by therapists. Here I will focus on a single, frequently mentioned aspect as an example and try to briefly place it in its empirical context. This is the sitting configuration of therapists: An upright posture and a slight inclination of the upper body toward the patient is recommended. This can be found in a book on the therapeutic relationship and conversation (Lammers, 2017, p. 93), in an introductory book on psychological therapy (Rief et al., 2021), and also in Grawe's explicit therapist suggestions in his book *Psychological Therapy,* where he stated that therapists should incline their upper body towards patients (Grawe, 1998, p. 435). This specific constellation of the body is intended to signal interest and commitment and it has been associated by patients with more empathy, commitment, and competence (Trout & Rosenfeld, 1980). However, such a recommendation is actually based on a limited number of studies that have operated with 30-s, posed video clips (e.g. Harrigan & Rosenthal, 1983). The only empirical test in "comparably normal" counseling sessions (with an acting patient) even found the opposite of the expected correlation: In minutes with low rapport, the forward-leaning position was more often observable than in minutes with high rapport (Sharpley et al., 2001). The authors also conclude that it is not the display of a forward tilt "per se" but its flexible and varying use that makes sense. However, I will not attempt to argue on this specific level in the following but rather advocate an "open" basic attitude with regard to the use of nonverbal behavior in therapy sessions. Further concrete suggestions can be found in books from the field of body or Gestalt psychotherapy (e.g. Geuter, 2024; Joyce & Sills, 2018)—for the time being, I am trying to describe the phenomenon of "nonverbal behavior and psychotherapy" on a general level and with a primarily cognitive-behavioral background.

3 Model

3.1 Acronym iCAST

The acronym iCAST introduced here is primarily intended as a mnestic anchoring of the various central elements for dealing with nonverbal behavior in psychotherapy. The exact order and weighting are secondary, and both individual as well as multiple aspects of the aspects mentioned below can be implemented in a session. The English word *cast* has a wide range of meanings, which I will discuss repeatedly at the end of each aspect. "*Cast*" can be used both as a noun and as a verb (*to cast*). As a noun, "*cast*" is suitable in the sense of actors in a play, film, or another production; and also the members of a band (music): Each element of iCAST contributes in its own sense to the success and character of a therapist's working with nonverbal signals in psychotherapy sessions.

I—Information

The model begins with the conscious awareness and the registration of visible information or information that can be accessed through interaction. This information forms the basis for further steps in dealing with nonverbal signals, because in order to be able to work with nonverbal behavior on a conscious level, it must also be registered. This first step has often been mentioned in previous instructions on dealing with nonverbal signals and can be "retained": The habitual noticing and processing of nonverbal signals could make every therapist part of a basal "encounter stance," because this source of information offers essential clues about the process (in the session) and also about the patient's general behavior/interaction. The way in which a patient acts nonverbally in the session is also part of their acquired way of "facing the world" (Rosa, 2016) and thus potentially relevant for therapy. In addition to such receptivity to nonverbal signals, I would also add here the current knowledge of nonverbal abnormalities of the various disorders: Only if prospective therapists are equipped with this constantly growing knowledge can they use the nonverbal signals specifically for the session or for further therapy planning. Comparable to knowledge on a disorder-specific level, knowledge of the nonverbal characteristics of various psychological phenomena could thus be enriched. As an example, I refer here to a study on the nonverbal behavior of patients with a disorder from the depressive spectrum (Altmann et al., 2021). The *i* for information thus stands for the linking of knowledge about disorder-relevant nonverbal specificities (Hall et al., 1995), and also for the conscious perception of such signals. With the *i* of iCAST, "to cast" can be seen in the sense of *molding* (casting, making an impression): The perceived information leaves an imprint on the therapist, it gives *form* to the unfolding therapeutic process; that is, "cast" in the area of information can be seen as a form/imprint that arises and leaves its mark from the interaction between patient and therapist.

C—Comment/Confront

If something relevant is perceived in the nonverbal area, it can be communicated in many cases. Relevant can mean many things, whether in the sense of "not having occurred before" (e.g. a clenched fist in the case of previously suppressed anger), or in the sense of "more/less pronounced" (e.g., more emotional expression on the face in the case of previously flat affect), in the sense of "disagreement with verbal content" (e.g. a smile when recounting an argument with a caregiver), and in many other situations that the therapist deems important. The verbal response to such an observation can also assume a broad spectrum, ranging from a neutral description of the observation to explicit confrontation. Such an active therapist intervention takes place either on the linguistic level (e.g. "I notice that …"; "Can you make that sigh again …", "I wonder if your foot movement has a meaning …"), or also on the nonlinguistic level, for example, a "not laughing along" as has been described in the area of the exchange of facial expressions (Bänninger-Huber, 1992). The main aspect of this step is thus that the patient is made aware of nonverbal aspects of the current situation through verbal or behavioral actions of the therapist. Patients are invited to reflect on the phenomenon with this (benevolent) response. In a subsequent step, this information can be followed up in several ways, either by means of clarification-oriented deepening or by means of coping-oriented methods. A number of therapeutic methods have always explicitly included this or a comparable step in their therapeutic approach. Gestalt therapy and its phenomenological focus on the here and now is an example of such a direction (Perls et al., 2006); intensive psychodynamic brief therapy (ISTDP) and body psychotherapy (Geißler & Heisterkamp, 2013; Geuter, 2024) could also be mentioned here. In current third-wave therapy methods, suitable elements can be found in the Cognitive Behavioral Analysis System of Psychotherapy (CBASP), Emotion-Focused Therapy (EFT), and also in some other therapeutic orientations. Historically, this part of iCAST can be explicitly assigned to Beier and Young's (1998) writings, because in their analysis of therapist behavior, they speak in many places of "nonsocial" behavior—behavior that has the potential to surprise/confront patients to such an extent that a breaking of previous reaction and processing habits is made possible in the first place (Beier & Young, 1998). In the C of iCAST, the meaning aspect of *movement* (eye movements, the movement used when fishing, or to cast a dice) can be mentioned as examples of this aspect. In other words, raising a patient's awareness (verbally or scenically) on aspects outside of the verbal domain, a transformation process can be initiated. By picking up on nonverbal aspects, the therapists aims to capture a potentially important aspect of their patient.

A—Attune/Acknowledge

In all stages/steps of the model, it is worthwhile for therapists to be aware of the effect or mutual influence of the other person and, in particular, to open up to this process: The resonance occurring between interaction partners creates a dyadic phenomenon, which has attracted a marked increase of empirical research in the past decade. A specific example for this kind of resonance has been investigated under the term of nonverbal synchrony: the phenomenon of coordinated body movement between patient and therapist. Nonverbal (movement) synchrony was already described in the 1960s (Condon & Ogston, 1966); a current empirical method for recording synchrony is Motion Energy Analysis (MEA; Ramseyer, 2020). The first randomized study on nonverbal synchrony in outpatient psychotherapy showed that more nonverbal synchrony was associated with higher relationship quality (from the patient's perspective) and better therapy success (Ramseyer & Tschacher, 2011). A positive correlation between synchrony and therapy outcome was also reported in youth psychotherapy, but an association between alliance and synchrony was not confirmed (Zimmermann et al., 2021). Subsequent comparable studies to the first randomized study were able to reproduce the correlation between synchrony and alliance (Altmann et al., 2020; Cohen et al., 2021), whereas other studies—with sometimes significantly different parameters used—have also led to contradictory findings (Paulick et al., 2018; Schoenherr et al., 2019a). Part of the inconsistency can be seen in the high variablity of parameters used to quantify nonverbal synchrony (Schoenherr et al., 2019b), another factor could also lie in the multiple determinacy of the phenomenon: synchrony is not only influenced by affect or relationship, but also, for example, by cognitive load (Van der Zee et al., 2020), the nature of the task (Tschacher et al., 2014), the socio-cultural composition of the dyad (Hamel et al., 2022), or medical conditions such as hearing impairment (Völter et al., 2024). Overall, however, attunement and instances of synchrony appear to be promising phenomena in the area of mutual influence between therapist and patient (Wiltshire et al., 2020), which will hopefully be further differentiated in future studies. The A of iCAST thus focuses on the aspect of *triggering/delivering* (casting a shadow, casting a vote, casting a spell in magic): Patients bring about changes in their therapists at the level of experience and behavior (nonverbally), and these influences continue to have their effects in both directions (in the sense of an evolving process at the level of the dyad).

S—Shape/Soothe/Stimulate

Many clients come to psychotherapy because their experiences in everyday life are not shaped in such a way that further growth and/or processing of the problem would be possible. In this sense, therapists always have the function of enabling clients to have different and new experiences that have a corrective or healing effect on their social sphere: In addition to the (linguistic) content platform that a therapeutic interaction creates, the nonverbal experience can analogously also be described as a (new) field of experience. When therapists are present (Geller & Greenberg, 2002) and fully attentive to their patients, this relational experience in itself holds enormous potential for change, which Carl Rogers also emphasized in a late interview (Baldwin, 2000). With an appropriate way of relating nonverbally, corrective experiences can thus be further promoted on an interpersonal level. Therapists can influence their clients in the appropriate direction (e.g., calming in the case of over-activation; stimulating in the case of under-activation) if they are aware of this and shape their nonverbal behavior appropriately. The *S* of iCAST, therefore, focuses on influencing or assisting in the sense of *providing support/ structure* (as seen in a casting mold, or in a plaster bandage). By consciously shaping the relationship situation and the nonverbal signals sent out by the therapist, a new or more helpful experience or state can be embedded on an interpersonal level.

T—Train/Test/Transfer

"Talk is silver, real experience is gold" (Grawe, 1995, p. 136; translation by the author): This very clearly also applies to the area of nonverbal behavior: only when the relevant physical elements are activated in a processual way can this experience be *embodied,* and in a second step, a transfer from the therapy situation to everyday life may later take place. The concept of corrective experience (Castonguay & Hill, 2012) fits well with this step: A corrective (new) experience can be made possible for the patient in the session or by means of guided implementation between sessions. While this can be mostly implicit in the shape/soothe/stimulate described above, the usual mode in train/test/transfer is to explicitly create or instruct situations. Behavioral therapy has always upheld the value of enactments (or role plays) and also offers specific instructions for their implementation (Hautzinger, 2022). Various third-wave approaches have long since incorporated this activating part into their approach (whether on an emotional or interactional level), and many eclectic therapists incorporate such elements into their work. In addition to these widely known possibilities in the field of scenic activation, there are now also a number of computer-based methods that enable experiencing/practicing in the therapy room

(Schmid Mast et al., 2018). The *T* of iCAST, thus, concerns the upheaval, the change, which is appropriately captured with *losing/discarding* (casting off horns: animal kingdom; cast off leaves: plants). A new state can only be achieved through such a process, an overcoming of previously established structure. Therapists can shape this implementation by means of suitable staging inside the therapy room and also outside of sessions.

4 TRAIN: Also for Therapists?

What do the steps just described mean for psychotherapeutic practice? "The systematic consideration of therapists' nonverbal communication behavior and its targeted modification should therefore be an explicit component of psychotherapeutic training and especially of supervision." (Grawe, 1998, p. 311; translation by the author). This statement by Klaus Grawe can be fully endorsed in the light of what has been said so far. If it is possible to make prospective therapists aware of the relevance and possible fascination of nonverbal behavior, then this will create an additional opportunity for change.

4.1 Therapy Phase

In my experience, the iCAST model can be applied more or less explicitly in all phases of therapy. For therapists, directing attention to nonverbal behavior (in general) from the first seconds of interaction is a good idea. Nonverbal cues can be used by "perceptually open" therapists from the first moment of the encounter and provide relevant possibilities for the design of a session per se, and of course for the further design of the relationship.

4.2 Conditions for Use

The elements of iCAST described above should not be "worked through" in a prescriptive way, as situational and patient-specific elements should guide the respective choice. The sequence presented here is also partly due to the formation of acronyms: While "information" and also "attunement" may always play a role, other elements are easier to separate from the others: "training and testing" things can be done both in the therapy session itself, but one can also easily plan and commission these elements as projects ("therapy tasks") for the time between sessions. What is important for the use in sessions is not the sequence, but the appropriate use at the right moment.

5 Empirical Example

The previous explanations of the iCAST model will be illustrated very briefly here with a simple empirical example. I refer to a publicly accessible data set in the OpenScienceFramework (OSF; https://osf.io/gkzs3/), which was created with an automated program for video-based, objective quantification of body movement (MEA; Ramseyer, 2020), and for which suitable statistical evaluation methods are available (Kleinbub & Ramseyer, 2021). The data consists of $N = 103$ initial interviews of one therapist with 103 different patients. This specific configuration has the advantage that intraindividual peculiarities that may depend on e.g. demographic or diagnostic characteristics of the different patients can be explored in this data set.

5.1 Results

MEA captures body movement, which may also be differentiated into pre-defined regions. For the example used here, the extent of the therapist's head movement will be examined: Fig. 1 shows the distribution of movement activities separately for affective disorders ($n = 31$; pink color) and anxiety disorders ($n = 19$; turquoise color). The time course within the sessions is shown from the beginning (bottom, "window") of the interview up to minute 55 (top, "window_50"). One can see a difference in the extent of head movement depending on the diagnosis: In patients with affective disorders, the therapist moved his head more frequently ($T(430.3) = 3.34$; $p < 0.001$; $d = 0.30$). The patients also show a difference in the same direction—patients with affective disorders move their heads more than those with an anxiety disorder—but with a much lower effect size ($p = 0.036$; $d = 0.20$). These diagnosis-specific differences in movement suggest a mutual influence, that is, patients and therapists seem to influence each other in the extent of their head movement. This conclusion may be drawn if we assume that the therapist did not consciously alter his movement according to the diagnosis of his patients.

This effect of bidirectional influence can be further explored on the basis of the extent of synchronous movement: the so-called nonverbal synchrony (Ramseyer & Tschacher, 2011)—the coordination of body movement between patient and therapist in this dataset does not differ between the two diagnostic groups ($d = 0.06$), but it is significantly above the random value of pseudosynchrony with a high effect size ($d = 0.94$; $p < 0.001$). Synchrony of body movement, on the other hand, is of interest in this data set in connection with another parameter: The further course of therapy after the initial consultation was surveyed in each case: After the

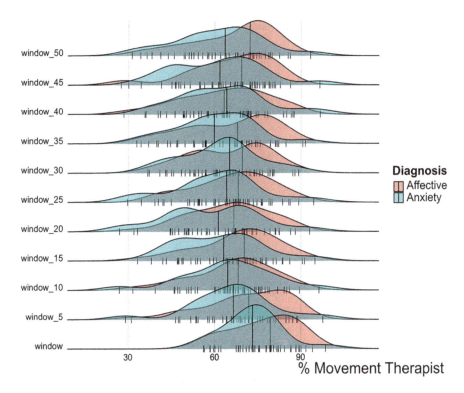

Fig. 1 Course of the therapist's head movement, separated by diagnosis. (Window time segment of the analysis (5 min segments), movement therapist percentage head movement therapist)

consultation, patients either switched to a therapist in training at a University clinic (norm; $n = 76$) or they decided against therapy (dropout; $n = 14$). Another subgroup ended treatment with the new therapist prematurely (term; $n = 13$). Differences are visible across all three groups and over the entire time shift (±10 s) (see Fig. 2), although these are not significant due to the small group sizes. However, there is a trend for differences in the extent of the therapist's imitation ($F(2) = 2.89; p = 0.060$). The two sub-groups "dropout/out" and "premature termination/term" differ in how strongly they were imitated by the therapist in the initial interview: Patients who only attended the initial interview were imitated less by the therapist than those who terminated their treatment prematurely ($T(21.3) = -2.61; p = 0.016; d = 1.03$), and patients with regular therapy completion were between these two groups. No significant differences were found in the area of imitation of the therapist by the patients. The respective differences in the extent of synchrony can be seen graphically in Fig. 2.

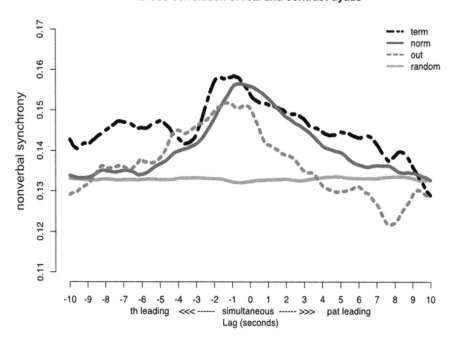

Fig. 2 Extent of synchrony across different time shifts (= lag); nonverbal synchrony absolute cross-correlation, Fisher's Z-standardized. Term (black-dashed) therapy discontinuation, norm (dark-grey) regular course of therapy, out (gray-dashed) dropout after initial interview, random (light-grey) pseudosynchrony (comparison with chance)

6 Discussion of the Findings

A detailed interpretation of these findings is beyond the scope of this article, and the data are presented primarily for illustrative purposes. Nevertheless, it can be concluded that the variable "head movement," which is generally under little conscious control, exists as an expression of movement-based alignment processes (= nonverbal synchrony) and that the movement similarities found between patients and therapists have something to do with the respective psychopathology presented at intake. The differential imitation pattern in patients who responded differently to the therapy offer or not indicates that differences in the extent of synchrony may emerge very quickly (at the initial interview) and that these differences may be prognostically relevant. Future studies could make use of these correlations for prognostic purposes. I hope that these two examples make it clear how richly very simple nonverbal parameters such as body movement (and synchrony) can be recorded and evaluated, and how much potential there can be in such quantifications.

According to Grawe, one can imagine that "actors would also make good psychotherapists" (Grawe, 2002, personal communication in a seminar). After all, they are experts in *embodying* different roles, which means that the majority of them have a high degree of flexibility in their nonverbal expression. The parallel regarding flexibility can also be drawn with psychotherapists, because in this profession, it is also an advantage to be able to embody different (nonverbal) functional modes with different patients. When I use the term "embodiment" here, it deliberately refers to the research field of *embodiment* (Tschacher & Pfammatter, 2016): Processes at the cognitive level are not decoupled or independent of processes in the body; there is a bidirectional influence. The iCAST model outlined here could therefore create a simple basis that enables the rich area of nonverbal behavior to be perceived on a conscious level in psychotherapy and, above all, to actively influence the therapy process. Such influence not only serves to shape the therapeutic relationship, it also helps to recognize and address difficulties. How and when observations and personal (nonverbal) experiences are addressed should be decided by the therapist on a case-by-case basis during the process. Looking inward also helps with this decision: The therapist's most important instrument is herself—her reactions to the client and her own perception in the here and now (Joyce & Sills, 2018, p. 39).

7 Conclusion for Practice

Nonverbal behavior is an important factor for many therapeutic approaches, but the specific work with nonverbal signals has so far been little systematized. In cognitive-behavioral therapy-based approaches, in particular, there is a lack of concrete guidance. The iCAST model represents a cross-school approach that can make it easier for therapists to perceive and work with nonverbal signals. The proposed basic approach conceptualizes therapists as sensitive measuring instruments who allow themselves to be influenced in the process of interacting with patients, perceive this influence and, by explicitly picking up on these events, invite the other person to reflect in a clarification-oriented manner and to experience and work on them in a coping or experience-oriented manner. They use their own nonverbal behavior to lead patients to an increase in their degree of freedom (expansion of possibilities). The concept of *embodiment* can be seen as the theoretical basis for these processes.

References

Altmann, U., Knitter, L. A., Meier, J., Brümmel, M., & Strauss, B. (2021). Nonverbal correlates of depressive disorders. *Zeitschrift für Klinische Psychologie und Psychotherapie, 49*(4), 231–240.

Altmann, U., Schoenherr, D., Paulick, J., Deisenhofer, A. K., Schwartz, B., Rubel, J. A., Stangier, U., Lutz, W., & Strauss, B. (2020). Associations between movement synchrony and outcome in patients with social anxiety disorder: Evidence for treatment specific effects. *Psychotherapy Research, 30*(5), 574–590.

Baldwin, M. (2000). Interview with Carl Rogers on the use of the self in therapy. In M. Baldwin (Ed.), *The use of self in therapy* (pp. 29–38). Haworth Press.

Bänninger-Huber, E. (1992). Prototypical affective microsequences in psychotherapeutic interaction. *Psychotherapy Research, 2*(4), 291–306.

Beier, E. G., & Young, D. M. (1998). *The silent language of psychotherapy*. Aldine De Gruyter.

Caspar, F. (2021). Flexible design of interaction situations. In W. Rief, E. Schramm, & B. Strauss (Eds.), *Psychotherapy* (pp. 45–47). Elsevier.

Castonguay, L. G., & Hill, C. E. (2012). Corrective experiences in psychotherapy: An introduction. In L. G. Castonguay & C. E. Hill (Eds.), *Transformation in psychotherapy: Corrective experiences across cognitive behavioral, humanistic, and psychodynamic approaches* (pp. 3–9). American Psychological Association. https://doi.org/10.1037/13747-001

Cohen, K., Ramseyer, F. T., Shachaf, T., & Zilcha-Mano, S. (2021). Nonverbal synchrony and the Alliance in psychotherapy for major depression: Disentangling state-like and trait-like effects. *Clinical Psychological Science: A Journal of the Association for Psychological Science, 9*(4), 634–648.

Condon, W. S., & Ogston, W. D. (1966). Sound film analysis of normal and pathological behavior patterns. *The Journal of Nervous and Mental Disease, 143*(4), 338–347. https://doi.org/10.1097/00005053-196610000-00005

Geissler, P. (2005). *Nonverbal interaction in psychotherapy: Research and relevance in the therapeutic process*. Psychosozial-Verlag.

Geißler, P., & Heisterkamp, G. (2013). *Introduction to analytical body psychotherapy*. Psychosozial-Verlag.

Geuter, U. (2024). *Body psychotherapy: A theoretical foundation for clinical practice.*. Taylor & Francis.

Geller, S. M., & Greenberg, L. S. (2002). Therapeutic presence: Therapists' experience of presence in the psychotherapy encounter. *Person-Centered & Experiential Psychotherapies, 1*(1–2), 71–86.

Grawe, K. (1998). *Psychologische Therapie*. Hogrefe.

Grawe, K. (1995). Grundriss einer Allgemeinen Psychotherapie. *Psychotherapeut, 40*(3), 130–145.

Hall, J. A., Harrigan, J. A., & Rosenthal, R. (1995). Nonverbal behavior in clinician-patient interaction. *Applied and Preventive Psychology, 4*(1), 21–37.

Hall, J. A., Horgan, T. G., & Murphy, N. A. (2019). Nonverbal communication. *Annual Review of Psychology, 70*, 271–294.

Hamel, L. M., Moulder, R., Ramseyer, F. T., Penner, L., Albrecht, T. L., Boker, S., & Eggly, S. (2022). Nonverbal synchrony: An indicator of clinical communication quality in racially-concordant and racially-discordant oncology interactions. *Cancer Control*. https://doi.org/10.1177/10732748221113905

Harrigan, J. A., & Rosenthal, R. (1983). Physicians' head and body positions as determinants of perceived rapport. *Journal of Applied Social Psychology, 13*(6), 496–509.

Harrigan, J. A., Rosenthal, R., & Scherer, K. R. (Eds.). (2005). *The new handbook of methods in nonverbal behavior research*. Oxford University Press.

Hautzinger, M. (2022). Verhaltensübungen–Rollenspiele. In M. Linden, & M. Hautzinger (Eds.), *Verhaltenstherapiemanual–Erwachsene* (pp. 285–288). Springer.

Hermer, M., & Klinzing, H. G. (2004). *Nonverbal processes in psychotherapy*. dgvt-Verlag.

Joyce, P., & Sills, C. (2018). *Skills in gestalt counseling & psychotherapy*. SAGE.

Kleinbub, J. R., & Ramseyer, F. T. (2021). Rmea: An R package to assess nonverbal synchronization in motion energy analysis time-series. *Psychotherapy Research, 31*(6), 817–830.

Lammers, C.-H. (2017). *Therapeutic relationship and conversation: Techniques of behavioral therapy*. Beltz.

Paulick, J., Deisenhofer, A.-K., Ramseyer, F., Tschacher, W., Boyle, K., Rubel, J., & Lutz, W. (2018). Nonverbal synchrony: A new approach to better understand psychotherapeutic processes and drop-out. *Journal of Psychotherapy Integration, 28*(3), 367–384.

Perls, F. S., Hefferline, R. F., & Goodman, P. (2006). *Gestalt therapy*. Klett-Cotta.

Philippot, P., Feldman, R. S., & Coats, E. J. (2003). The role of nonverbal behavior in clinical settings. In P. Philippot, R. S. Feldman, & E. J. Coats (Eds.), *Nonverbal behavior in clinical settings*. Oxford University Press.

Pfammatter, M., & Tschacher, W. (2012). Effective factors of psychotherapy-an overview and assessment. *Z Psychiatr Psych Ps, 60*(1), 67–76.

Ramseyer, F., & Tschacher, W. (2011). Nonverbal synchrony in psychotherapy: Coordinated body-movement reflects relationship quality and outcome. *Journal of Consulting and Clinical Psychology, 79*(3), 284–295.

Ramseyer, F. T. (2020). Motion energy analysis (MEA). A primer on the assessment of motion from video. *Journal of Counseling Psychology, 67*(4), 536–549.

Rief, W., Schramm, E., & Strauß, B. (2021). *Psychotherapy*. Elsevier Health Sciences.

Roediger, E. (2016). Resource activation through a change of perspective. Just stand up once! A plea for more movement (En) in behavior therapy. *Behavior Therapy, 26*(2), 117–123.

Rosa, H. (2016). *Resonanz*. Suhrkamp Verlag.

Schmid Mast, M. (2007). On the importance of nonverbal communication in the physician-patient interaction. *Patient Education and Counseling, 67*(3), 315–318.

Schmid Mast, M., Kleinlogel, E. P., Tur, B., & Bachmann, M. (2018). The future of interpersonal skills development: Immersive virtual reality training with virtual humans. *Human Resource Development Quarterly, 29*(2), 125–141.

Schoenherr, D., Paulick, J., Strauss, B. M., Deisenhofer, A. K., Schwartz, B., Rubel, J. A., Lutz, W., Stangier, U., & Altmann, U. (2019a). Nonverbal synchrony predicts premature termination of psychotherapy for social anxiety disorder. *Psychother (Chic), 56*(4), 503–513.

Schoenherr, D., Paulick, J., Worrack, S., Strauss, B. M., Rubel, J. A., Schwartz, B., et al. (2019b). Quantification of nonverbal synchrony using linear time series analysis methods: Lack of convergent validity and evidence for facets of synchrony. *Behavior Research Methods, 51*(1), 361–383. https://doi.org/10.3758/s13428-018-1139-z

Sharpley, C. F., Halat, J., Rabinowicz, T., Weiland, B., & Stafford, J. (2001). Standard posture, postural mirroring and client-perceived rapport. *Counselling Psychology Quarterly, 14*(4), 267–280.

Trout, D. L., & Rosenfeld, H. M. (1980). The effect of postural lean and body congruence on the judgment of psychotherapeutic rapport. *Journal of Nonverbal Behavior, 4*(3), 176–190.

Tschacher, W., & Pfammatter, M. (2016). Embodiment in psychotherapy-a necessary complement to the canon of common factors. *European Psychiatry, 13*, 9–25.

Tschacher, W., Rees, G. M., & Ramseyer, F. (2014). Nonverbal synchrony and affect in dyadic interactions. *Frontiers in Psychology, 5*, 1323. https://doi.org/10.3389/fpsyg.2014.01323

Van der Zee, S., Taylor, P., Wong, R., Dixon, J., & Menacere, T. (2020). A liar and a copycat: Nonverbal coordination increases with lie difficulty. *Royal Society Open Science*. https://doi.org/10.1098/rsos.200839

Völter, C., Oberländer, K., Brüne, M., & Ramseyer, F. T. (2024). Impact of hearing loss and auditory rehabilitation on dyads: A microsocial perspective. *Journal of Nonverbal Behavior*. Advance online publication. https://doi.org/10.1007/s10919-024-00468-7

Westland, G. (2015). *Verbal and non-verbal communication in psychotherapy*. W. W. Norton & Company.

Wheatley, T., Thornton, M. A., Stolk, A., & Chang, L. J. (2023). The emerging science of interacting minds. *Perspectives on Psychological Science*. Advance online publication. https://doi.org/10.1177/17456916231200177

Wiltshire, T. J., Philipsen, J. S., Trasmundi, S. B., Jensen, T. W., & Steffensen, S. V. (2020). Interpersonal coordination dynamics in psychotherapy: A systematic review. *Cognitive Therapy and Research, 44*, 752–773.

Zimmermann, R., Fürer, L. E., Kleinbub, J. R., Ramseyer, F. T., Hütten, R., Steppan, M., & Schmeck, K. (2021) Movement synchrony in the psychotherapy of adolescents with borderline personality pathology –a dyadic trait marker or resilience? *Frontiers in Psychology, 12*. https://doi.org/10.3389/fpsyg.2021.660516

Part V
The Therapist's Experiential Training and Self-Awareness Development

Personal Experiential Training Within the Integrated Psychotherapy Pathway

Monica Bononi, Silvia Busti Ceccarelli, Emilia Martino, and Martina Manzoni

> *Every time we learn something new, we ourselves become something new.*
>
> Leo Buscaglia

1 Experiential Training from an Integrated Perspective

Why train the therapist? Jay Haley (1997), in defining the therapist, argues:

> If psychotherapy were only a question of skill, it would be possible to teach it as a series of techniques; however, the therapists are themselves the instrument through which the therapeutic techniques are expressed, and sometimes this instrument presents problems, because of the intensity of the emotions that, in session, he/she may feel (Haley, 1997 in Onnis 2010, p. 80).

Reflecting on what is reported, *personal training is* of undoubted importance. Addressing this aspect means reflecting on a series of issues related to the attention paid to the person-therapist, to the Self in its complexity, to the emotional world, and related reactions characterizing its functioning. It reflects on the centrality of the student, who will become an indispensable container of the therapeutic relationship and an expert who uses, strategically, knowledge, techniques, and tools, integrating them in his or her person and declining them in an inter-subjective dimension with the other.

The therapist, seen in his or her complexity (Guidano, 1991), is indeed placed within a *field* of *observation* as part of the therapeutic process and the outcomes of the process itself.

In an interesting metaphor, Guidano (1991) defines the therapist as a *strategically oriented disruptor*; as such he/she is *able to* facilitate the process of change without knowing a priori the outcome of the disruption (Cionini & Ranfagni, 2009a,

---

M. Bononi (✉) · S. Busti Ceccarelli · E. Martino · M. Manzoni
Scuola di Psicoterapia Integrata, Centro Clinico Integrato, Bergamo, Italy

b), calibrating at the same time the intervention on the patient's personological characteristics in an integrated perspective (Poletti et al., 2023). In this perspective, knowledge seen on the one hand as the set of theories, methods, and techniques, and on the other hand as the construction of a self that *facilitates change,* is a complex and global learning "tailored" on the patient (Cionini & Ranfagni, 2009a, b), but that does not go beyond the work on the Self of the therapist.

In this complex two-way dynamic called *psychotherapy,* then the need for *training* that pays attention not only to the model and constructs but, at the same time, to the person-therapist and his or her subjective dimension, inexorably implicated in the psychotherapeutic process, is unquestionable. In this sense, the two trainers, whose functions will be specified later on, are positioned as *solicitors* aimed at facilitating the exploration of the relational dynamics, life plot, and trainees' inner world, proceeding toward a deeper level of knowledge. The exploration of one's own dynamics, as well as the tracing of personal experiences, makes it possible to identify and redesign, under a magnifying glass, one's own *meanings* that resonate in the construction of the professional role and in the work dimension itself. The ultimate aim of the training is to allow one to acquire self-observation skills, exploring aspects of the Self, reactions, emotions, and life themes, touching a more hidden and deeper level of learning, in order to arrive at defining oneself as an indispensable tool and resource for the therapy itself. Specialized training in psychotherapy aims to create the conditions for building one's own professional role, which is not only consistent with the epistemological constructs of the school's therapeutic model but which adheres to and reflects the peculiarities of one's own being as a person. Consequently, actively constructing and defining one's own professional identity implies learning by experiencing oneself within an interactive process where a therapist's core competencies can be acquired by means of a purposive *experiential training* (Cionini & Ranfagni, 2009a, b). For this reason, training in an integrated perspective follows defined times and spaces. Organization and methodologies are structured and defined in line with the principles outlined above.

1.1 The Role of Trainers as Guides in the Learning Process

Trainers are an important guiding element within the 4-year course. The acquisition of an active role on their part as trained and competent specialists is aimed at guiding a process of self-observation that seeks to enhance awareness of the learner's subjective mechanisms, through circular and reflexive questions that follow a profound process, enriched by strategically oriented interventions and ad hoc reformulations. The trainer's intervention encourages the exploration of the individual's complexity, without providing solutions or answers: He/she positions himself/herself as an *active agent* and a *beneficiary of* a constant process of epistemological change. This change is governed by an individual and collective time (Onnis, 2010, p. 808).

The importance of a double lens on the group, following its change, makes clear the indispensability of having two trainers for the same class; they become an operational reference model and a *secure base* during the 4-year course.

With this in mind, the trainers divide up the work on the basis of specializations and competencies in order to provide the group with two different but complementary outlooks: On the one hand, they work on their own *memoires, experiences, and emotional memories*, while on the other hand, they experience with the *body* a world that is often not treated and seen, thus allowing future therapists to have concrete emotional experiences, which will be added to their own baggage of competence. The languages used are also multiple: Word and image are placed side by side, allowing each other to become a useful channel for self-exploration and a present and future tool for working with the patient. Particularly relevant is the use of the *metaphor* as an immediate key to personal experience and a meeting point between patient and therapist, without the interference of the word with the personal meanings that it carries (Faccio & Salvini, 2007). The metaphor identified by each pupil accompanies them over the course of the 4 years just as it accompanies the patient during the sessions.

The careful guidance of the trainer will enable the trainee to bring his or her own personal story into the group in a safe context, testing experiences with people and points of view sometimes very different from his/her own, and thus trying out concrete experiences that will later be reused in therapy with patients.

The path followed by the trainers is consistent with the school's theoretical proposal and follows the evolution of the group in both its construction and change phases.

The training topics proposed are *distributed by year*: During the first year, the themes of *trust* and group building are central. The first trainer proposes experiences of telling one's own story related to the proposed theme and the second trainer proposes bodily exercises useful to permit the first-hand experience of what the patient feels when he/she entrusts himself/herself to a stranger. This is where the first form of relationship/alliance arises, which in therapy will correspond to the basis of everything and in the group will make it possible to experience a safe context in which to let oneself go. One begins to speak, theoretically, of the first interview and construction of the therapeutic alliance.

The second year is the one of *exploration*: The group and the individual begin to allow themselves to explore, experiment, and look also at hidden or little-treated aspects of everyday life, with the help of a guide and the group that is now able to provide support for them, just as a secure base would do. In this year, from a perspective informed by the attachment theory, the future therapist experiences the possibility of exploration and inhibition of dysfunctional fears and beliefs, in light of an increasing openness to the other and to the world, experiencing the possibility of being welcomed and supported by the group considered as a secure base (Poletti et al., 2023). All the exercises proposed, both of emotional nature and of bodily exploration, are aimed at the sharing and practical experimentation of what is expressed by the theory of reference ("The five tasks of the therapist according to Bowlby"; Bowlby, 1988 in Poletti et al., 2023).

The third year has the task of exploring the themes of *conflict* and *cooperation*: The now-formed group is able to confront in both cooperative and critical terms, with a constructive view to enriching skills. Emotional themes related to anger and conflict are proposed by the trainers, so that everyone can feel free to express and tell parts of themselves, while in body exercises, in body exercises, games are provided to encourage cooperation and also put on the field a part of healthy competition towards others. This is the year in which one experiences the differentiation from the other and the ability to move, with absolute respect, according to characteristics that appear to be different and that can lead to the creation of subgroups. After an initial falling in love and growth of the group, one works (consistently with what happens in preadolescence and adolescence) on individual differences from a cooperative point of view. The possibility of disagreement with the other begins to be expressed, which, if known and recognized also in the therapeutic context, becomes a valuable weapon with which growth can be experienced.

As we approach the fourth year, it is time to prepare the group for the end of the training course and it is the task of the trainers to propose topics related to *closure, mourning, and saying goodbye*. One experiences what it means to let someone go and which emotions are linked to this theme, both on a bodily and emotional level, as in therapy; particular emphasis is placed on body-centered techniques (e.g., mindfulness, progressive muscle relaxation).

The two trainers propose, in absolute harmony, two major aspects of work: one more *theoretical/emotional* and another of *bodily experimentation*. Over the course of the years, they aim to make people experience exactly what happens in a *therapeutic cycle* and in the relationship between patient and therapist:

- Start of therapy with confidence building
- Exploration and consolidation of bonds
- Conflict and cooperation, that is, fielding the patient's dysfunctional cycles
- Greeting and closing of the therapy

This linearity in the training proposal makes it possible to experience a true therapeutic journey, mirroring what the patient and future therapist will then experience together.

1.2 Supervision

Supervision finds its place in the training process as a *tool guide* in learning the correct intervention modalities, through a focused attention on emotions, resonances, prejudices, and meanings found in the therapeutic relationship, in a constant process of co-construction of specific competencies. It starts from the sharing and formulation of the clinical case, then moves on to the problems encountered by the trainee in the setting. The co-trainer (reference figure of the group) or the supervisor uses the supervision space to act as a *conductor* in the clinical reasoning and as a facilitator of the pupil's self-observation starting from the specific difficulties reported.

Supervision does not, therefore, aim at mere theoretical-technical transmission, but it is a shared experiential moment that encourages deep reflection, which touches the student's professional identity in its entirety.

The *question* posed may concern a problem of a theoretical nature to be investigated in depth (nosographic and functional analysis), presuppose the sharing of a targeted reasoning with which to re-read the life plot of the case presented (verifying the most appropriate approach and techniques), or require the trainee's introspection on what has emerged and on the difficulties encountered in his/her psychotherapeutic work. The co-trainer or supervisor, in this sense, positions himself/herself as an expert able to make himself/herself available as a strategic tool (Haley, 1988).

As mentioned above, supervisions in an integrated perspective start concretely from the *formulation of the case,* which is based on a multi-level investigation, deepened through the articulation of specific questions that guide the trainee in clinical reasoning, allowing him/her to progressively acquire clinical reading and analysis skills.

The first level to probe is the *nosographic framework*. The symptom is placed within a more "epidermic" reading of the complexity of the patient's functioning. The nosographic analysis allows to move forward/advance progressively to a deeper level, arriving at an understanding of the evolutionary meaning and logic underlying the reported symptomatology, with the possibility of proceeding towards a targeted analysis on the use of methods and diagnostic instruments calibrated to the patient's specificity. The use of evidence-based techniques and a theoretical framework integrated and calibrated to the complexity of the individual (Poletti et al., 2023) leads, in a climate of co-construction of the comparison, to an analysis of the *functionality of* the symptom, thus passing to a further and deeper level of reading related to the personological and structural setup. At the same time, possible tools for managing the symptomatology are discussed and shared, maintaining a focused attention on the relational process in which the student-therapist is involved. From the nosographic analysis, the structured and interactive exploration, acted out within a cooperative framework, is directed toward the deepening of a psychopathological perspective of great explanatory value, in which the symptom is read in its functional, evolutionary, and "identitary" meaning. It is necessary for the student to acquire profound reading skills of the *symptom's meaning*, guided by a specific theoretical framework that sees in Attachment Theory the matrix from which to start (Bowlby, 1988). At this point, the lens with which to jointly read the disorders passes to the postrationalist theorization through the construct of Personal Meaning Organisation (Guidano & Liotti, 1983) and to the cognitive-evolutionist strand (Liotti, 1994; Liotti & Monticelli, 2008, 2014) that follows an ethological and evolutionary approach centered on the analysis of Interpersonal Motivational Systems.

From the above, there is no doubt that supervision thus becomes fertile ground for the acquisition of an *inferential process* that moves from the most superficial to the deepest level, articulating specific and "strategically" oriented questions. The ultimate goal is not only the understanding of the case and a structured formulation of the treatment plan but a clear definition of three pillars that presuppose a precise diagnosis (Pievani & Poletti, 2024):

Nosographic diagnosis: What symptoms? What disorders? What kind of question does the patient ask?
Functioning diagnosis: How does the patient function "psychologically" and "relationally"? What is the patient's attachment? What are the patient's Personal Meaning Organizations? What are the patient's Motivational Systems? What are the relational bonds in which the patient is embedded (couple, family, friends), and how are they characterized?
Explanatory diagnosis: What was the "relational history" that led the patient to function "psychologically" and "relationally" in that way? What are the critical and traumatic events that characterize the patient's relational history? What are the relational dynamics that characterized the family of origin and in which the patient grew up?

From these three pillars, the co-trainer or supervisor guides toward an in-depth understanding of the therapist's experiences, both in relation to the patient and in resonance with his/her personological setup. Supervision (whether carried out in a group by the co-trainer or in an individual context by the supervisor) then becomes not only a tool for learning possible modes of psychotherapeutic intervention or in-depth theoretical investigation but also a fertile space for knowledge and sharing of the professional self, focusing on difficulties in case management or highlighting a problematic trait of the therapist himself/herself.

Supervision in this perspective stands in the middle between the technical part relating to skills and the personal part of the therapist and can be carried out individually or in the teaching group. The aim is to achieve not only greater self-knowledge and "tools" that can be used in clinical work but also to foster awareness of who one is and how one operates in the therapeutic context (Butera & Zaratti, 2003).

1.3 Educational Therapy

In scientifically oriented training schools, didactic psychotherapy constitutes a focal point of the student's evolutionary and training process. It makes it possible to trace aspects of the future therapist's personal and family history, becoming a parameter of his/her personal and professional evolution (Onnis, 2010, p. 548), through a work on oneself that involves the retrieval of emotional memories, recurring life themes, significant experiences, and thus reorganizing one's perception of oneself, one's relational modality, and functioning structure.

In a continuous evolutionary process, didactic therapy allows one to recognize and highlight one's own aspects that act in the therapeutic relationship, in a constant emotional learning aimed at reorganizing one's personal constructs, with the purpose of configuring oneself as the main therapeutic instrument. The therapist, an active agent in the relationship, can feel specific emotions within the work with the patient and, during the psychotherapeutic process, perceive the amplification of one's own history and functioning: The dominion over one's own experiences then becomes the ultimate goal. According to Liotti (2001), assuming the duality of human consciousness, the psychotherapist's work cannot avoid the effects that move within the psychotherapeutic framework where the interpersonal components of patient and clinician intertwine. Indeed, the school of integrated psychotherapy places emphasis on the therapeutic relationship (Poletti et al., 2023), which takes priority over psychopathological symptoms.

This element undoubtedly illustrates the importance of didactic therapy, through which one can learn to recognize one's own blind spots (Bara & Sconci, 2019, p. 23), understood as the *mental processes that* cannot be identified and observed with mere self-referentiality. The didactic therapy becomes the means for the future therapist to manage what is elicited by the patients in the clinical setting, not only in terms of self-awareness and self-awareness in relation to the other but also in terms of managing the therapeutic relationship and the intervening processes. Being aware of the dominant intersubjective patterns in the relationship in the dyadic relationship, whether in the clinical setting or in everyday life (Bara, 2007), thus assumes centrality in psychotherapeutic work.

Given the evolutionary and formative value, it is unquestionable that the choice of the didactic therapist respects an epistemological coherence and adheres to the psychotherapeutic model of the chosen training pathway. Indeed, didactic therapy also moves from the possibility of *assimilation of* an intervention model given by the encounter between two professionals, one an expert and the other in training, which leads to the acquisition, albeit tacitly, of a *trace* in the future therapist's clinical consciousness. The evolutionary advantage in this sense is not only a work on oneself, but a gradual and meaningful exposure to a psychotherapeutic approach that allows one to experience the *effects of* psychotherapy firsthand: Not infrequently, "the internalization of one's trainer" leads the trainee to intimately experience him/her as an example, model, and implicit comparison in the most difficult situations. We, therefore, speak of a dual value of didactic therapy, that is, *"a double track of engagement: it must move effectively in a therapeutic mode and at the same time its acts have an important and lasting formative value"* (Bara & Sconci, 2019, p. 27); this makes it clear that it is an obligatory passage for a 4-year training that is complete.

1.4 The Formative Function of the Group

The group represents the context in which to guarantee a continuous and circular flow of thoughts, emotions, and bodily activation, becoming itself a "training tool."

The group dimension fosters the capacity for self-observation and reflection, allowing one to become an autonomous knower of oneself over time. Bateson (1976) had highlighted with the term "collective mind" the potential of the group.

Here we would like to take this as a starting point to emphasize its peculiarities not only as an "amplifier of the formative potentialities" (Onnis, 2010, p. 140) but also as a container of mirroring and differentiation between its members. In it, the different representations of the self, images, and meanings are brought together, in a constant process of circular sharing. Each movement within the group is "orchestrated" by the *trainer* who, like an orchestra conductor, rearranges the melody, making the composition musical, which, in this case, is the emerging sharing. Everyone will move their own notes, reflecting colors and nuances in each personal intervention, following their own speed and, at the same time, respecting others' dimensions. Self-knowledge is fostered by reciprocal resonances and the echo of one's own words, by the experience of oneself in relation to others, and by one's own structural and historical arrangement, thus facilitating individual and collective growth.

Group work consists of exposing and dealing with relevant personal issues and aspects in order to analyze one's relational patterns from a training perspective and acquire greater knowledge and skills on one's own functioning. In the group, the trainers use specific bodily and experiential techniques that make it possible to experience, within a controlled and protected context, situations that one normally avoids, often for fear of exposing fragile or hidden parts. Sharing stages of one's own developmental history and main themes of interpersonal functioning allows one to confront different relational styles and ways of attributing meaning (Bara, 2005). Over time, the group becomes a small world in which to immerse oneself, with different inhabitants and reactions, in an atmosphere of exploration and sharing without judgment.

Despite its undoubted experiential and formative value, the group context often conceals issues that involve the world outside the classroom: The group, by its very nature, evolves and gives rise not only to new ideas and resources but also to critical issues.

During the 4-year period, the group, as we will see more clearly in the next chapter, following the course of a real path of psychotherapy, changes itself and its members, always following a similar pattern.

In the first year, positive and purposeful aspects emerge in an overall dimension, but, at the same time, specific traits of each participant begin to emerge. The pleasure of discovery, being together, and experimenting, gradually takes shape in a process of differentiation and reconstruction, within a context made up of new rules and the possibility of a greater openness of its components.

During the second year, focused on exploration, the first differentiations emerge: The individual member begins to feel similar but, at the same time, different from the others. The other appears different and the bearer of a relational style that is not always understandable and manageable. The group mates, as happens with patients, begin to solicit critical elements in each other, with the possibility of individual confrontation in cases of particular fatigue. The role of the trainers, as we have seen, is a fundamental part of the process of differentiation and reconstruction: They maintain a focused and attentive gaze on the evolution of the group in its constituent elements.

The third year is usually the year of conflicts, bad feelings, the creation of subgroups, and discussions among members, even among the tightest ones; it is the year in which the group experiences ruptures which, as happens in therapy, must then be repaired, so that they themselves become a meaningful and formative experience.

Finally, the fourth year is the year of the acceptance of differences and preparation for separation; it is the year in which, in view of the final goodbye, disagreements are often settled or faced with the mature awareness of the 'goodbye' of the educational journey.

In all the steps just described, the figure of the co-trainer acts as a facilitator of the learning process, taking a look at the individual student and at the whole, ensuring individual growth in the relationship with oneself and with the group.

2 Simulations: Definition and Phases

The importance of self-monitoring as therapists-in-training (but not only) is widely acknowledged in the literature (Prasko et al., 2023; Bara & Sconci, 2019; Weck et al., 2017; Chigwedere et al., 2021; Hahn et al., 2023) and finds its place not only in the supervising and didactic therapy spaces, but also in the classroom simulation moments. In fact, the "in vivo" experience carried out in the classroom allows the student-therapist to begin the process of self-monitoring, which is essential in order to be able to immediately grasp any difficulties encountered and/or useful strategies for his or her clinical work. As theorized by Bruno Bara (2005), knowledge of one's own issues and difficulties is essential and unavoidable in order to approach the patient without prejudices or personal emotions interfering with the treatment process.

The process of awareness, which finds its way into personal analysis, group work, and supervision, is experienced here in an experiential manner with the use of a well-defined structure, which is useful to support the knowledge and deepening of the future therapists' inner world, also through guided and controlled experimentation.

The classroom simulation experience implies an exercise involving a student-therapist and a student-patient, with the supervision of the trainer and the active participation, as observers, of the rest of the group. It also involves the use of video recordings that can be subsequently reviewed by both students involved in the simulation, as described in the next section.

On a practical level, the setup involves the use of a room equipped with cameras that frame the patient and therapist and play the video in the room where the rest of the group is present. During the simulated interview, the trainer can provide the class with some considerations regarding specific indicators worthy of attention. The trainee-therapist is instructed to interrupt the interview after approximately 15/20 min, to leave the room and go to the classroom for an initial debriefing moment in which to confront with the trainer, the co-trainer, and the rest of the class. The purpose of this space is to promote the therapist's self-awareness of what they are feeling and to be able to reorient themselves toward a less impulsive and more therapeutic direction, focusing on "how I am, what I am doing, and why I am doing it." The therapist's training process must be aimed at increasing their knowledge through theoretical and experiential preparation (Cionini, 1991; Bara, 2005): It is, therefore, fundamental to explore "knowing how to do," having theoretical and knowledge competencies, and "knowing how to be," understood as the process according to which the therapist acquires and arrives at a good knowledge of himself, of his cognitive and emotional processes, and is able to use them to the best within the therapy room.

Returning to the simulation setting, by the time the therapist reaches the rest of the group, the patient remains in the therapy room; for him too, this break of about 10 min often proves to be a useful and productive moment, stimulating reflexivity and awareness, in which to allow feelings, emotions, and thoughts to settle before the therapist returns and the interview can be resumed. After another 20 min or so, the interview is closed and both the students return to the classroom for a final discussion with the group and the trainers, in which the therapist's and patient's experience is explored, and feedback, questions, and reflections are shared in a participative and non-judgmental atmosphere.

In this phase, it is possible to retrace the focal points of the interview in the best possible way, either by reviewing the video or by leaving room for the storytelling of those involved, with the active participation of the group. At the end of the simulation, the product video can be further used as useful material for the therapist-pupil to revisit and rethink the focal points of the interview, as will be seen in more detail in the video-feedback analysis. It can also be taken up in the therapeutic context to focus, in more detail, on aspects of personal functioning that emerge in the relational context of therapy. Indeed, the relationship is the main and privileged instrument for modifying personal functioning, through interpersonal patterns and self-image modification processes (Safran & Segal, 1993; Bara, 2005).

Patient and therapist communicate with each other within the room and, at the same time, more or less consciously for a third person (in this case the group) who observes; the simulation structured in this way can be traced back to the systemic tradition in which there is a triad of actors in the field. The observers maintain an eye on the patient-therapist dyad, while the dyad works in a setting that also contemplates a "third eye" that goes beyond the dyad itself and moves in the direction of a systemic hermeneutic.

3 Video-Feedback in Clinical and Educational Practice: Theoretical Principles and Practical Developments

Video-feedback is a well-known technique with consolidated clinical efficacy in the field of developmental psychology for research and intervention to promote mentalization in parents (Lionetti et al., 2015; Downing, 2015). It is also proposed as a pivotal tool for the analysis of the therapeutic alliance, one of the variables that best predicts the effectiveness of the psychotherapeutic treatment (Norcross & Lambert, 2011; Fluckiger et al., 2018), and it is defined as the ability of the psychotherapist and the patient to: (a) agree on treatment goals; (b) collaborate during therapeutic tasks; (c) maintain an affective bond (Bordin, 1979). The crucial aspect for which the use of video-feedback is essential, especially in training, is for the therapist to be aware of what is happening between himself/herself and the patient. If the therapist finds himself/herself under pressure during a clinical situation, he/she risks to adhere so closely to the protocol that he/she is no longer useful to the patient (Muran & Eubanks, 2021). Therefore, it is extremely important that in training, one does not exclusively anchor oneself to protocols in a rigid manner but it is essential that the therapist is taught to know how to be with the patient (Poletti et al., 2023). Knowing how to "be with patients" means to catch moments of tension and stress in the therapeutic relationship, understood as ruptures: disagreements between patients and therapists on treatment goals, failure of collaboration on therapy tasks, and/or stress in the emotional bond. Research tells us that ruptures are much more prevalent than we think: from 33% to 100% of sessions (Eubanks et al., 2018). Breakups can be about withdrawal (movement away from the other person as isolation, attempts to deny an aspect of the self, stifling a desire to indulge the other person) or confrontation (movements against another person, aggressive or controlling urges). Through video and audio analysis of a session, the coding procedures described by the Therapeutic Alliance Rupture Resolution Rating System (3RS, Eubanks-Carter et al., 2015; Eubanks et al., 2019) can be applied. The authors recommend coding segments of 5 min at a time within which to identify any markers of withdrawal or confrontation, or both. It is crucial to use video as non-verbal data is diriment to some of the breakdowns, which can be very small and difficult to identify with just the transcript or audio of the session.

In the classroom training context, video-feedback is proposed as a tool that provides a space for the therapist's self-monitoring during simulation that is useful for both the supervisor and the therapist-in-training (Abbass, 2004; Alpert, 1996; Goldberg, 1983; Huhra et al., 2008). For the supervisor, it is a tool that favors greater objectivity, as it is possible to work directly on what is observed in the therapist and in the patient (also grasping nonverbal aspects), rather than on what is solely reported. There are benefits well documented in the literature for the therapist too; these include the possibility of enhancing skills of self-observation, self-reflexivity, and self-awareness, but it is also possible that it brings in the therapist experiences of anxiety, fear of judgment, and therefore less willingness to show parts of their work (Topor et al., 2017).

In order to limit the risk of these aspects affecting the therapist's involvement and willingness to work, it is essential to take care of a few aspects right from the start: to manage exposures gradually, starting with brief simulations focused on a few elements at a time; to cultivate a climate of nonjudgment within the class group; and finally, to emphasize right from the start how this tool is a fundamental and valuable learning opportunity. If these conditions are present, the use of video-feedback allows the clinician-in-training to maintain a look on the *therapist-self that is* curious and open to confrontation, without being frightened by it. Each trainee has an SD card on which he/she can record simulations in which he/she plays the role of therapist (with the written consent of the colleague playing the role of patient).

The simulations recorded in this way serve the student to:

- Observe oneself at a later time through the guidance (feedback) of the lecturer/co-trainer in order to increase one's awareness, to learn and improve in clinical practice, and to observe oneself independently.
- Observe the evolution of one's learning in terms of clinical practice skills over the 4 years of training by viewing simulations in chronology.

Having the opportunity to re-observe oneself at the end of the session under the guidance of the trainer allows the trainee to reflect primarily on how one's own emotional state acts on the non-verbal aspects and the quality of the relationship, rather than focusing before on words or techniques used, in line with the importance of "knowing how stay" in that setting before "knowing how to be" and therefore with an experiential training (Cionini & Ranfagni, 2009a, b). This technique allows an in-depth and focused attention on the therapist's experiences, interpersonal motivational systems (Monticelli, 2019), and active interpersonal cycles (Salvatore et al., 2019). Only afterward observation of the techniques used proceeds, stimulating in the student an awareness of the clinical process that guided him/her.

During a lesson dedicated to video-feedback, a simulation is usually carried out in the first part of the day and one in the second part: Once the simulation is over, the video-recorded interview is reviewed in the group with the guidance of the trainer who focuses on the most significant verbal and nonverbal aspects. Thus, for example, a trainee-therapist who is very focused on the questions to be asked is invited to observe how much this attracts his/her attention while something very interesting is happening in the patient from a nonverbal point of view, or a trainee-therapist who is very emotionally attuned may be so involved and activated on the level of care that he/she does not notice the fast pace with which he/she intervenes at the expense of times of silence. Often, especially in the first 2 years, the student-therapist reports the difficulty of keeping together the more "didactic/performance" plan (of knowing how to be) with the more "emotional/relational" plan (of knowing how to stay): Video-feedback helps them to acquire more and more awareness of how these two parts move, sometimes disharmonically, other times in a much more harmonious way towards ever greater integration. Video-feedback thus becomes one of the many training opportunities of proven efficacy, together with simulations, didactic therapy, and supervision that the *self-therapist* can draw on during his or her personal and professional growth.

4 The Experience of the School of Integrated Psychotherapy: "Where We Are" Project

In the year 2023, the Bergamo and Milan School of Integrated Psychotherapy (SPI) developed the "Where We Are" project, which aims, through validated instruments, to monitor the acquisition of theoretical knowledge and the development of students' metacognitive skills over the 4 years.

Respecting the canons of evidence-based practice, the project wishes to make the awareness of one's own functioning and theoretical and experiential learning more concrete and as far as possible objectifiable (Poletti et al., 2023).

In fact, this practice, wisely used by students and co-trainers, could become the training compass for the 4 years of specialization and help to personalize the pathway of the individual and the group by focusing on those little-known areas, weaknesses, and strengths, in order to be able to return the dynamic evolution of these aspects.

In practical and concrete terms, the School of Integrated Psychotherapy has begun to structure a well-organized and planned system of "call to action" that envisages students and co-trainers filling in some questionnaires at the end of each training year. At the end of the compilation, the student will only be able to see his or her personal page and only the results of the current academic year in order to favor as much as possible the absence of judgment and the focus on the mere numerical result of the questionnaire. The co-trainer, on the other hand, will be able to compare the results of the individual's and the group's performance over the 4 years. This latter, indeed, will be able to use the outputs in the end-of-year interviews so as to return with greater accuracy, the points of improvement and the resources of the individual and, at the same time, to have an idea of how the student, with respect to the co-trainer's assessment and self-assessment, is positioned within his or her class group.

The instruments used are two validated questionnaires: QACP (Questionnaire for the Self-Assessment of Psychotherapist Competencies, Settanni et al., 2022) and MMQ (Multidimensional Mentalizing Questionnaire, Gori et al., 2021) and a questionnaire regarding the number of supervisions and interviews the student can take advantage of during the year:

- The QACP questionnaire (Questionnaire for the Self-Assessment of Psychotherapist Competences): Monitors the competencies and the acquisition of skills across different theoretical models. It consists of 63 items with 5 macro areas: assessment and case formulation, therapeutic relationship, implementation of the intervention, monitoring and conclusion of therapy, and ethics and cultural sensitivity, divided into 15 sub-scales.
- The MMQ (Multidimensional Mentalizing Questionnaire): Monitors the ability to be aware of oneself, one's own functioning, and how one relates to other people. It is a 33-item self-report instrument that investigates the construct of mentalization from different aspects: cognitive-affective, self-other, external-internal,

and explicit-implicit. It has six subscales, three positive and three negative; the response format is on a five-point Likert scale.
- SUPERVISIONS AND INTERVIEWS: The proposed questionnaire monitors how much and how students engage in the supervisions or interviews organized each year. In this sense, the comparison with what emerges from the monitoring concerning the skills acquired as a future therapist is very useful: For example, if the perceived result concerning the skills acquired is low but at the same time no supervisions are requested, these data can be discussed with the co-trainer and can mean an underestimation of one's own skills or a difficulty in exposing oneself in training contexts.

Outputs are discussed with individual students in periodic discussions with co-trainers in order to have a basis for the joint work on the future psychotherapists' objective and personal learning skills. At the end of each year, indeed, qualitative dimensions (thanks to the interviews that the student carries out at the end with their co-trainer) and quantitative dimensions (thanks to the output of the questionnaires) are discussed and analyzed in order to monitor the evolution of learning and personal perception related to the work done.

The "Where We Are" project, introduced for the first time in the academic year 2022/2023, has made it possible to start looking at learning as a constantly evolving process, within a flow of continuous and constant improvement, also impacting the quality of the training plan offered. Together with the other tools we talked about earlier, it provides the possibility for future therapists to monitor themselves more and more both in terms of competencies and skills acquired also in relation to the other, as it happens within the therapeutic pathway. Constant self-monitoring as a working tool (Cionini, 2014) is in fact essential for a good awareness of the therapist's functioning, which, as we have seen, enriches the relational context and supports the promotion of alliance in the therapeutic context.

5 Conclusions

The chapter aimed to show an overview of what happens within an integrated orientation training course, which originates from the fusion of different therapeutic styles, which take their cue from evidence-based cognitive and systemic therapeutic programs. Quoting Bara (2005), *"If the primary goal of specialization schools is to enable a change in individual professional skills, coherence will be shown by fostering change in ways that are in line with the relevant theories."*

In this regard, the entire training course is orchestrated down to the smallest detail in order to allow the future therapist, and the group, to experience what happens in therapy with the patient, also and above all with a focus on the person as a working tool. This focus allows for a perfect integration of theory and practice, techniques, and personal experimentation through the body, emotions, and thoughts in a constant and continuous learning process.

The figures of trainers, supervisors, and co-trainers are fundamental tools for learning and growth, but also for coping with any difficulties that may arise within such an articulated and complex pathway. It is indeed true that students, facing a path that is also personal, may experience crises and doubts, both in their own person and in their profession and future (Bara, 2005): This is where the support network created around the group comes into play. The aim is always to foster learning and growth and, as we know from our experience with patients, this also involves sudden storms that appear on the path to awareness. As with patients, gaining awareness of one's own functioning and mechanisms is often the only way to bring about change and that is why the main focus is on making the future therapist more and more aware.

From an integrated perspective, the therapist's feelings and emotions become a working tool and are essential to fostering change within a functional relationship (Poletti et al., 2023). They are often the starting point for understanding the other and they provide a useful direction for orienting future therapeutic choices, in a process of reciprocal regulation of the relationship, also made up of ruptures and repairs of the alliance (Cionini, 2014).

In the light of all these considerations, an increasing focus on personal training in accordance with precise patterns, in harmony with the theoretical and technical training process, provides essential tools for the training of future therapists who will skilfully use themselves and their relationship with the patient to broaden their awareness of the patient's experiences and functioning, with the ultimate aim of promoting real and perceived change.

References

Abbass, A. (2004). Small-group videotape training for psychotherapy skills development. *Academic Psychiatry, 28*(2), 151–155.

Alpert, M. C. (1996). Videotaping psychotherapy. *The Journal of Psychotherapy Practice and Research 1996, 5*(2), 93–105.

Bara, B. G. (2007). *Dinamica del cambiamento e del non-cambiamento*. Bollati Boringhieri.

Bara, B. G. (a cura di). (2005). *Nuovo manuale di psicoterapia congitiva-volume primo*. Bollati Boringhieri.

Bara, B., & Sconci, M. (2019). La psicoterapia didattica nella formazione dei terapeuti cognitivi. *Cognitivismo clinico, 16*(1), 19–32.

Bateson, G. (1976). *Verso un'ecologia della mente*. Adelphi.

Bordin, E. S. (1979). The generalizability of the psychoanalytic concept of the working alliance. *Psychotherapy: Theory, Research & Practice, 16*(3), 252.

Bowlby, J. (1988). *A secure base*. Routledge. Trad. it. (1989). *Una base sicura: Applicazioni cliniche della teoria dell'attaccamento*. Raffaello Cortina.

Butera, N., & Zaratti, R. (2003). La supervisione in psicoterapia cognitiva: un modello sistemico-processuale. *Quaderni di Psicoterapia Cognitiva, 6*, 2.

Chigwedere, C., Bennett-Levy, J., Fitzmaurice, B., & Donohoe, G. (2021). Personal practice in counselling and CBT trainees: the self-perceived impact of personal therapy and self-practice/self-reflection on personal and professional development. *Cognitive Behaviour Therapy, 50*(5), 422–438.

Cionini, L. (1991). *Psicoterapia cognitiva: teoria e metodo dell'intervento terapeutico*. Carocci.
Cionini, L. (2014). La persona del terapeuta come strumento del cambiamento: implicazioni per il processo formativo. *Costruttivismi, 1*, 29–33.
Cionini, L., & Ranfagni, C. (2009a). Dire, fare, imparare: un modello di formazione alla psicoterapia in ottica cognitivo-costruttivista. *Rivista di Psicologia Clinica, 2*, 42–62.
Cionini, L., & Ranfagni, C. (2009b). Dal setting descrittivo al setting funzionale: Regole d'improvvisazione nel gioco della terapia. In C. Loriedo & F. Acri (Eds.), *Il setting in psicoterapia: lo scenario dell'incontro terapeutico nei differenti modelli clinici di intervento*. FrancoAngeli.
Downing, G. (2015). Promuovere la mentalizzazione tramite la Video Intervention Therapy. In *La genitorialità. Strumenti di valutazione e interventi di sostegno*. Carocci.
Eubanks, C. F., Muran, J. C., & Safran, J. D. (2018). Alliance rupture repair: A meta-analysis. *Psychotherapy, 55*(4), 508.
Eubanks, C. F., Lubitz, J., Muran, J. C., & Safran, J. D. (2019). Rupture resolution rating system (3RS): Development and validation. *Psychotherapy Research, 29*(3), 306–319.
Eubanks-Carter, C., Muran, J. C., & Safran, J. D. (2015). Alliance-focused training. *Psychotherapy, 52*(2), 169.
Faccio, E., & Salvini, A. (2007). Le "metaforizzazioni" nelle pratiche discorsive della psicologia clinica. In *Psicologia clinica: dialoghi e confronti*. Springer.
Flückiger, C., Del Re, A. C., Wampold, B. E., & Horvath, A. O. (2018). The alliance in adult psychotherapy: A meta-analytic synthesis. *Psychotherapy, 55*(4), 316.
Goldberg, D. A. (1983). Resistance to the use of video in individual psychotherapy training. *The American Journal of Psychiatry, 140*(9), 1172–1176.
Gori, A., Arcioni, A., Topino, E., Craparo, G., & Lauro Grotto, R. (2021). Development of a new measure for assessing mentalizing: The multidimensional mentalizing questionnaire (MMQ). *Journal of Personalized Medicine, 11*(4), 305.
Guidano, V. F. (1991). *The self in process: Toward a post-rational cognitive therapy*. Guilford. Trad. it. (1992). *Il Sé nel suo divenire: Verso una terapia cognitiva post-razionalista*. Bollati Boringhieri.
Guidano, V. F., & Liotti, G. (1983). *Cognitive processes and emotional disorders* Guilford. New York.
Hahn, D., Weck, F., Witthöft, M., & Kühne, F. (2023). What characterizes helpful personal practice in psychotherapy training? Results of an online survey. *Behavioural and Cognitive Psychotherapy, 51*(1), 74–86.
Haley, J. (1988). Reflections on supervision. In H. A. Liddle, D. C. Breunlin, & R. C. Schwartz (Eds.), *Handbook of family therapy training and supervision* (pp. 3358–3357). The Guilford Press.
Haley J. (1997). *Formazione e supervisione in terapia*, Erickson, Trento.
Huhra, R. L., Yamokoski-Maynhart, C. A., & Prieto, L. R. (2008). Reviewing videotape in supervision: a developmental approach. *Journal of Counseling and Development, 86*(4), 412–418.
Lionetti, F., Barone, L., Juffer, F., Bakermans-Kranenburg, M. J., & van IJzendoorn, M. H. (2015). Il protocollo VIPP-SD: tra sensibilità e disciplina sensibile. In *La genitorialità. Strumenti di valutazione e interventi di sostegno*. Carocci.
Liotti G. (1994). *La Dimensione Interpersonale della Coscienza*, Carocci, Roma.
Liotti G. (2001). *Le Opere della Coscienza*. Raffaello Cortina, Milano.
Liotti, G., & Monticelli, F. (2008). *I sistemi motivazionali nel dialogo clinico*. Cortina Editore.
Liotti, G., & Monticelli, F. (2014). *Teoria e clinica dell'alleanza terapeutica*. Cortina Editore.
Monticelli, F. (2019). Editoriale: i vantaggi del monitoraggio dei sistemi motivazionali in seduta per facilitare l'uso appropriato della relazione terapeutica. *Quaderni di Psicoterapia Cognitiva, 45*(2), 5–10.
Muran, J. C., & Eubanks, C. F. (2021). *Il terapeuta sotto pressione: riparare le rotture dell'alleanza terapeutica*. Raffaello Cortina.

Norcross, J. C., & Lambert, M. J. (2011). *Psychotherapy relationships that work II* (Vol. 48, No. 1, p. 4). Educational Publishing Foundation.

Onnis, L. (Ed.). (2010). Lo specchio interno. La formazione personale del terapeuta sistemico in una prospettiva europea: La formazione personale del terapeuta sistemico in una prospettiva europea. FrancoAngeli.

Pievani, L., & Poletti, B. (a cura di). (2024). *La terapia familiare basata sull'attaccamento per la depressione in adolescenza*. Fioriti editore.

Prasko, J., Ociskova, M., Abeltina, M., Krone, I., Kantor, K., Vanek, J., et al. (2023). The importance of selfexperience and self-reflection in training of cognitive behavioral therapy. *Neuroendocrinology Letters, 44*(3), 152–163.

Poletti, B., Tasca, G., Pievani, L., & Compare, A. (a cura di). (2023). *Psicoterapia integrata. Il modello Evidence-Based Practice (EBP)*. Franco Angeli.

Safran, J. D., & Segal, Z. V. (1993). *Il processo interpersonale nella terapia cognitiva*. Feltrinelli.

Salvatore, G., Dimaggio, G., Popolo, R., & Ottavi, P. (2019). La relazione terapeutica nella terapia metacognitiva interpersonale. *Quaderni di Psicoterapia Cognitiva, 45*(2), 119–139.

Settanni, M., Bronzini, M., Carzedda, G., Godino, G., Manca, M. L., Martini, L., et al. (2022). Introducing the QACP: Development and preliminary validation of an instrument to measure psychotherapist's core competencies. *Research in Psychotherapy: Psychopathology, Process, and Outcome, 25*(2), 599.

Topor, D. R., AhnAllen, C. G., Mulligan, E. A., & Dickey, C. C. (2017). Using video recordings of psychotherapy sessions in supervision: Strategies to reduce learner anxiety. *Academic Psychiatry, 41*, 40–44.

Weck, F., Kaufmann, Y. M., & Höfling, V. (2017). Competence feedback improves CBT competence in trainee therapists: A randomized controlled pilot study. *Psychotherapy Research, 27*(4), 501–509.

The Path of Self-Awareness Development and the Role of the Co-trainer

Laura Carelli, Cristina Morrone, and Mara Zanni

> ... When I help my students expand their horizons, I do not emphasise the transmission of specific techniques or skills, but the maturation of mature attitudes, including: emotional honesty, respect for patients, curiosity and open-mindedness, genuine empathy... an ability to mentalise even patients who do not attract the therapist's sympathy, an integration of their clinical knowledge into their most authentic personality style, an enhancement of skills through exposure to theoretical aspects outside their own training, humility, ethical sensitivity, openness to recognising their mistakes, and knowing where to turn for help.
> These changes do not occur through the transmission of skills, but take place in the context of a relationship that proceeds naturally towards the establishment of a more intimate and secure attachment bond ...
>
> Nancy McWilliams, Supervision. Psychoanalytic Theory and Practice

1 The Figure of the Co-trainer as an Experiential and Didactic Mediator Between Motivational Systems and Attachment Theory

The co-trainer is a didactic, clinical and training figure who can represent an added value within the psychotherapy training pathway.

In a training project in which the person of the therapist appears to be central –in terms of not only technical competence acquired but also, and above all, personal

L. Carelli (✉) · C. Morrone
Scuola di Psicoterapia Integrata, Centro Clinico Integrato, Bergamo, Italy

M. Zanni
Scuola di Psicoterapia Integrata, Centro Clinico Integrato, Alzano Lombardo, Bergamo, Italy

maturation work—it is indeed important to accompany the student during the 4-year learning process on both a professional/methodological and personal level.

Co-training, therefore, poses challenges to those who decide to take on the role.

First and foremost, it represents a complex function. On the one hand, it involves mediating among the various actors of the training school (students, teachers, directors, secretariat) and supporting the student in the assimilation and integration of the various contents proposed. On the other hand, the co-trainer acts as a facilitator in the path of both personal and professional growth of each student; all this by holding an active and emotionally involved position within the group. The co-trainer is hence called upon to create a stimulating training environment and embodies in his or her figure the concepts of cooperation and sharing (Bara, 2018) in a context characterised by multiple intersubjectivities and in which different motivational systems can be activated (Liotti & Monticelli, 2008). The co-trainer represents, in fact, a vicarious agent of cooperative learning among several plans: the individual, the group, and the group with the training institution. The co-trainer constitutes a 'third observational pole' on the interactions among the learners and between the learner and the teacher or trainer.

He/she is, therefore, sometimes a discreet promoter of the creation of a relationship both with each pupil and with the entire group; keeping the relationship alive, monitoring it and repairing, when necessary, any relational ruptures (Bara, 2018). Such ruptures become a way of analysing together the difficulties that are created. For the learner, this is a useful confrontation to experience him/herself in relational modes that differ from his/her own habitual ones, and for the co-trainer to have a reminder of how he/she is perceived—both in terms of role and, sometimes, in personal terms—within a specific interaction or context. What happens in the ruptures and their analysis, in fact, makes both the actors involved more aware, since they have the opportunity to reflect on the relational drives that have come into play and that, ultimately, have to do with their own peculiar way of interpreting what is happening, themselves, and the others (Bara, 2018).

This appears particularly relevant in a school of training in integrated psychotherapy, characterised by a greater training complexity in terms of content and notions and which that envisages, within it, a variegated articulation of approaches—cognitivist, behavioural, systemic, psychodynamic—and specific techniques. On the basis of this approach, we can find attachment theory and the therapeutic relationship as common denominators.

The role of the co-trainer that is proposed has different functions, which can be performed on several dimensions potentially interconnected with each other:

– *Interpersonal/group*: Stimulation of the relational climate and management of critical phases within the group's training and development and of any difficulties in relations between pupils and the school or certain teachers.
– *Personal*: Point of reference and support for personal struggles that occur during training, timing in undertaking didactic therapy and support in choosing a didactic therapist, monitoring interviews about the training course, and conducting supervision.

- *Professional*: Support at the beginning of the psychotherapeutic profession and conducting group and/or individual supervision.
- *Didactics*: Facilitation of the integration of the different components of the therapeutic model, verification of learning, review of the thesis work, bibliographic suggestions, and assessment of the suitability for specialisation.

The following will illustrate the modalities and the underlying theoretical constructs, through which the co-trainer promotes group training.

1.1 The Co-trainer in the Group: Promoting Identity and Self-Awareness

As illustrated above, the co-trainer represents a model to work on an interpersonal relationship in which he/she is actively involved. As Bruno Bara (2018) suggests, a parallelism can be found with what happens in the 'canonical' therapeutic relationship: The patient (in this case the pupil) and the therapist (in this case the co-trainer) work on structuring a relationship, not without difficulties, relational ruptures, and their repair. Similarly to the therapist's role, the co-trainer is called upon to support the individual pupil in the development of self-awareness, which, in the specific sphere of psychotherapy training, also translates into the construction of one's own personal identity based on processes of both belonging to and differentiation from the reference group.

Moreover, as with most group settings, there is a greater complexity regarding the need to tune in to different subjective and emotional perceptions and interpretative styles (Bara, 2018; Liotti, 2001, 2005; Liotti & Intreccialagli, 2003; Liotti & Farina, 2011; Liotti & Monticelli, 2008).

Self-awareness can be characterised by impartial and nonjudgmental attention to oneself (Prasko et al., 2023), which is associated with self-reflexivity (self-consciousness), the latter being understood as both an intellectual and affective activity that can be used to better understand what is happening during an interaction (Boud et al., 1985). The role of metacognition, which is also linked to the recognition and self-monitoring of one's own emotions, thoughts, and somatic activations (cf. section on 'co-trainer and metacognitive functions'), is central in this regard.

Concerning the purpose of the training, the role of the co-trainer cannot therefore disregard the intersubjectivity that characterises it. Indeed, it appears to be a supramodular dimension (Fodor, 1983) and entails by definition the sharing of explicit and implicit information about the ongoing social experience. The relationship between intersubjectivity and higher-order consciousness (Edelman, 1989; Liotti, 1994/2005)—which the concept of intersubjective consciousness is based on (Stern, 2004)—implies that the co-trainer also has a hierarchical predisposition to communicate with others, like the other group members. Understanding their point of view, cooperating, and developing a sense of identity and belonging is the implicit effect of an immediate affective attunement of the co-trainer with the members of his own group, for the same belonging to a so-called hypersocial species (Tomasello, 1999). In the light of the evolutionary perspective, in the absence of other motivations the co-trainer and the group members find themselves predisposed to cooperation without necessarily being aware of it.

However, the actual sharing of experiences between the members of a group requires not only commonality but also differentiation, that is the recognition of others as individuals separate from oneself. Thus, sharing no longer means only identity but also implies distinction in terms of neural circuits and cognitive representations. An example of this is a student who raises his hand to ask a question: Another sufficiently attentive person in the group will spontaneously follow the interaction and will be able to reflect on the question that he/she had not asked.

Therefore, in his/her presence and desired awareness, the co-trainer offers the group members a triadic interaction that allows them to develop an I/Other distinction (Becchio et al., 2006), which consists of a transition from the WE as an undifferentiated group to the "WE as I think of it," therefore subjective and no longer absolute (Bara, 2018). This shift is built in managing, modelling, mirroring, and forming alliances for educational purposes, investing in the skills associated with belonging to a group while nurturing the possibility of exploring a clearer perspective of the individual position that can be differentiated from it.

For these reasons, by providing his/her group with both symmetrical and complementary sharing, the co-trainer will have to promote organisational autonomy within it. Picking up on a metaphor by Vittorio Guidano (1991), he/she can sometimes take on the role of a strategically oriented disruptor, without, however, ever being able to know exactly what the effect of the disruption on the system will be. In his/her group, he/she constitutes a territory in which the group can find the tools to arrive at its peculiar responses: tools understood as ways of approaching listening and self-knowledge, to arrive at understanding and explaining 'himself by himself' according to the situations experienced from time to time.

In short, he/she appears as a linking figure between the needs of belonging and of intra- and intergroup differentiation that represent the motivational drive to create relationships, orienting our behaviour, our emotions, and our thoughts (Liotti & Farina, 2011).

1.2 The Co-trainer in the Relationship: Motivational Systems and Attachment Theory

Interpersonal motivational systems (IMSs) are human phasic dispositions that take shape only in social interaction: Intersubjectivity, rather than the subjectivity of the isolated individual, is the locus of their existence (Liotti, 1994/2005). IMSs organise and finalise both interpersonal conduct and the emotional experience and discursive thought that accompany it, without their activity necessarily being the object of

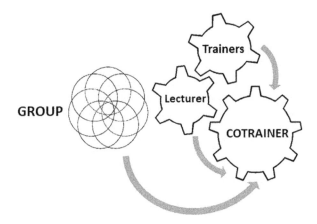

Fig. 1 The co-trainer's point of view

attention and reflexive consciousness (Liotti & Monticelli, 2008). We can imagine how the co-trainer, during the 4-year training course, observes many of the relational motivations that organise social and interpersonal behaviour, as well as emotional experience and the representation of 'self-with-others'. One only has to think of the innumerable relational plans with which one simultaneously relates: the observation of the relationship between students (in dyadic and group form), between students and the teacher (in dyadic and group form), and between students and themselves (in dyadic or group form). Trying to depict the concept from the co-trainer's point of view (omitting for obvious necessity the complexity of everyone's points of view), a rather interconnected figure appears (Fig. 1).

As is well known, not all human relationships can be considered attachment relationships, not even when significant. However, we can argue that the co-trainer, for the group, is one of these attachment figures. Weiss in 1982 argued that at least three basic conditions had to be present for this description: (a) the search for closeness between the person who requires care and the person who provides it; (b) the presence of protest reactions in the face of separation, such as protests or accusations; (c) the development of a 'secure base', that is, a particular condition of security and trust that is established between the figure who requires protection and comfort and the figure who offers care in a complementary manner. Bowlby's (1988) metaphor of the secure base is therefore applicable to the co-trainer's relationship with the group: In fact, it can be full-fledged considered a potential, important, and formative attachment figure. As we know, the *attachment system* concerns the request for care or protective closeness (Bowlby, 1969) that is activated when a person is in difficulty (due to tiredness, fear, pain, or vulnerability). The system predisposes the person in question to approach a known member of their social group who appears stronger or wiser. According to Bowlby's attachment and motivational systems theory, every individual needs to feel safe, supported and understood in order to be able to explore new experiences and grow in a healthy way. In a group of psychotherapy trainees, the co-trainer can play the role of a safe and reliable attachment figure, offering support, guidance, and constructive feedback to foster the students' learning and professional development. The co-trainer can act as a model of a 'safe and competent adult' who promotes a climate of trust and openness in the group. At times, analysing the processes that occur in the relationship with him/her, or through his/her point of view towards the involvement of a different relational nature (e.g. in simulation exercises), offers unique opportunities to re-read together with the student the characteristics of his/her motivational systems at the very moment they are put into action.

It is human to describe how groups of psychotherapy trainees are not exempt from being confronted with the *sexual system* too: The rules of this system (Fisher, 1992) call for the search for a partner of the opposite sex who is willing to mate. The interpersonal sexual motivational system is aimed at the formation and maintenance of the sexual couple with the biological value of reproduction and the sustenance of offspring and is triggered by physiological signals within the organism (hormonal changes) and by courtship behavioural signals emitted by another individual, usually of the opposite sex. The gender ratio in this context tends to be very unbalanced, with future female therapists in a clear majority. Undoubtedly, hormonal variations can condition the sensitivity of female students and amplify, at specific moments, the emotional reactions triggered by the lesson. Furthermore, the formation of important affective relationships between two members of a group is not improbable: In this situation, the co-trainer is called upon to monitor the impact of a couple on the group so that this spontaneously arisen relationship does not collude with avoidance or with relational asymmetries that are dysfunctional for experiential and training purposes. Other examples of the activation of the sexual interpersonal motivational system may be the controlling modes that some students may activate towards a teacher, or the co-trainer himself/herself, with particularly seductive attitudes: This is a way of controlling the relationship with one's interlocutor, regulating one's emotions, and giving cohesion to the self. There may be an activation of the sexual system in case of emotions of fear when faced with the establishment of intimate relations in the group in individuals who may have experienced trauma from sexual abuse, or modesty exacerbated by experiential lessons in sexuology or clinical cases in which the future therapist is confronted with issues related to the sphere of sexuality. Last but not least, physiological sexual activations may arise during experiential body lessons as a result of physical proximity or body contact between students. In all these situations, the co-trainer (where he/she can see) is called upon to monitor the student's activation that concerns what is happening in the context, supporting a subjective awareness or intervening by reflecting back to the students some activation that occurs over time without them being fully aware of it.

The activation of the *agonistic (or competition system for social rank)* is frequent: According to Gilbert (1989), the rules of the system assert that when faced with competition with a member of one's own group for any good or resource, the individual must show his/her strength. If in the contest the individual risks to be harmed because his/her opponent proves to be stronger, he/she must acknowledge the opponent's superiority by signalling submission; conversely, if it is the opponent who signals submission, he/she ceases to attack him, allowing him/her to remain close so that group cohesion is allowed after the dispute. Once, a student exposed herself in front of the class in a role-playing where she portrayed a patient pressing the therapist for reassurance. Commenting on how she felt, after the simulation was over, the student emphasised how she was not at all sensitive to control issues and a choral response from the group invoked a rather discordant *no*. The student, feeling misunderstood in her fictitious intentions to that simulation, acted towards the group in a reactive response and asked for an explanation of what they all had noticed to support it. The teacher accepted the group's message and offered the student a disruptive experience, which the student later integrated with her co-trainer. Other illustrative activations of the rank system can be the failed exposure of learners prone to emotions of shame: this represents a psychological component of self-perception as belonging to a low social rank (Troop et al., 2008) and is activated when individuals judge themselves negatively, fostering low self-esteem and a sense of inferiority and powerlessness (Doran & Lewins, 2011). Thus, the purpose of shame is to protect the self-image one would like to show others (Carni et al., 2013). In these cases, too, the co-trainer, after some recursiveness, invites the student to become aware of how he/she 'chooses' to participate in his/her own learning by withdrawing from the experience. This allows the student to share personal meanings attached and find a dialogical openness on this susceptible issue.

On the contrary, it frequently happens that learners are emphasised that the efficacy of help does not consist in 'rescuing' the patient or replacing the other, but rather in accompanying the patient along the path of self-exploration and towards the construction of possible alternatives, thanks to the offer of a relational point of view, according to one's own constructive potential for reorganisation in a moment of distress. When the *caretaking system* is activated, normally, there is a relational offer of care. Its rules (George & Solomon, 1999) correspond to the formula: 'if a known member of your group asks you for help, offer it – and offer it with particular solicitude if it is one of your genetic descendants'. It may seem counterintuitive that, in providing a care service, one does not 'materially' offer care to the patient. This is not to say that it is indispensable when needed, but the student is taught not to dwell on the distorted idea that the patient does not need someone to take charge of his or her life, but rather to realise this need and implement behaviours aimed at satisfying this need in his/her affections. It is frequent to meet students who, empathising with the suffering of their colleague manifested in front of the class in a role-playing, come out of those emotions with intentionally deactivating questions. Often, the explicit explanation concerns an acknowledged caring motion to protect the colleague. In many cases, it is a caring motion towards oneself, in the fatigue of 'being' with one's own negative affective states that the suffering of the colleague has exacerbated. This is an example of how, from an experiential training perspective, the motivational system of caretaking precludes the activation of a cooperative system, which is much more constructive at that moment for everyone. In these cases, the didactic intent of the co-trainer is therefore to accompany the student in building up a critical awareness that 'doing therapy' is not 'doing by giving to the other' but rather 'doing by doing with the other'. Thus, the student can experience what it means to take care of the suffering encountered or, rather, to work with the suffering encountered, and this shift is possible thanks to the activation of an *equal cooperation system*.

The rules of this system induce one to consider a member of the group, who is interested in achieving a given goal more easily through a joint effort, as an equal and not only on the basis of the dominance rank possibly defined through previous agonistic competitions. DeWaal (1989) has extensively explored the emergence of particular social behaviours suggestive of empathy and reciprocity that are required by peer cooperation, which stem from an innate human disposition. Furthermore, taking a preventive perspective, a cooperative setup is what most guarantees the therapist's relational comfort over time. Bruno Bara wrote: 'It is better not to delude oneself that one can do it alone: I can try to support someone but only if I am aware that it must be him/her who bears the direct effort, without illusory substitutions. The instrument of care is the shared awareness and the patient's own commitment is as indispensable as the co-empathic presence of a therapist'. Co-participation in dyadic symmetrical work within the therapy could be, with regard to burnout, one of the therapist's indispensable elements to monitor that feeling of frustration and discomfort in not feeling 'used at best' (Maslach & Pines, 1977). A safeguard not only for the therapist, if that can at least be consoling: A number of clinical observations have shown that the cooperative interpersonal motivational system is the one most conducive to the exercise of metacognition (Di Maggio & Semerari, 2003).

1.3 Co-trainer and Metacognitive Functions

Much research has investigated the correlation between metacognition and attachment. Teasdale (1999), Carcione (1997), and Semerari (2006) have described metacognition as 'an individual's ability to perform heuristic cognitive operations on one's own and others' psychological conduct, as well as the ability to use such knowledge for strategic purposes in solving tasks and mastering specific mental states, which are the source of subjective suffering'. With these theoretical premises, it is important to position the co-trainer as the promoter of a group climate that is sufficiently safe for training and exposition purposes. It is now recognised that the metacognitive components have a fundamental role as variables capable of conditioning how an individual learns is now scientifically recognised (Cornoldi, 2006). The role of metacognition in learning is crucial as it enables individuals to become active in and responsible for their own learning, through self-assessment, self-control, and self-reflection skills. Through empathic and respectful communication, the co-trainer can help participants explore their own emotions, thoughts, and behaviour, facilitating reflection and awareness of themselves and their learning process. Where it appears to be lacking, it can sometimes come to reflect the observed relational dynamics from one's own perspective, becoming the object of an explicit or implicit metacommunication. This is because if a dyad is limited by the need for both individuals to be involved in direct communication, when a triad is constructed, the opportunity is created for one person to observe and be observed by the two people engaged in direct communication. This 'meta' point of view allows the observer to make constructive comments on the interaction within the dyad (Andolfi & Haber, 1995) and can help students acquire a sensitivity to otherness: Understanding the other and being open to the novelty of his/her narrative, quoting Gadamer (1960), 'presupposes neither an objective neutrality nor an oblivion of oneself, but implies a precise awareness of one's own pre-assumptions and prejudices'. One can, therefore, summarise the role of the co-trainer as an experiential and didactic mediator, acting on a multiplicity of levels, which can be integrated with each other. In the next section, we will take a closer look at the versatility of this role, characterising it within the dynamic and evolutionary processuality of the class group.

2 The Role of the Co-trainer in the Group's Evolutionary Transitions: Birth, Growth, Maturity, and Separation

The interpersonal/group dimension is an indispensable part of specialised psychotherapy training (Bennett-Levy & Finlay-Jones, 2018). Some research has shown that group training in psychotherapy leads students to recognise positive effects regarding their self-awareness, communication style, interpersonal behaviour, acceptance of self and others, empathy, theory of mind, personal sensitivity, clinical insights, professional growth, and, finally, greater connection between theoretical and practical aspects (Ieva et al., 2009; Kline et al., 1997; Schneider & Rees, 2012; Chigwedere et al., 2020). It is well known that a member's individual sense of belonging and commitment to the group helps to build mutual trust, support, and collective commitment to learning within the group (Burlingame et al., 2001). Therefore, the co-trainer is the guarantor of a positive relational climate within the group, which is essential to foster effective communication, cooperation, and cohesion among individual group members, as well as the group as a whole. Cohesion would increase empathy among colleagues and mutual acceptance of feedback as a form of interesting dissonance to one's own self-perception, which would foster greater understanding and motivation for change. Therefore, the co-trainer, by sustaining these forms of both relational and didactic mutual support, cultivates and enhances the 'human' resources of the group itself, with a focus on the particular (the individual student) and a simultaneous general overview (the group).

The stages of group development are presented below, over the 4 years of training, examining, more specifically, the roles of the co-trainer listed above. The phases can, in fact, trace the stages of individual development and envisage a pathway that, through separation-individuation mechanisms (Mahler et al., 1975), accompanies the training of future psychotherapists both in the acquisition of precise methodologies and techniques and in the direct exposure to the emotional exchange with the other.

2.1 The Formation of the Group: The Birth

A critical phase in the life of a group is the training phase, when individuals meet: in a residential setting of 4 days and three nights, the group's first contact with its co-trainer takes place. This residency is often a highly disruptive condition, experienced with considerable emotional intensity by all participants, including the trainers. On the first sharing concerning significant parts of one's own life story, the co-trainer contains and regulates the emotional activation of some students whose suffering cannot be sustained in front of the group. Moreover, in the residency, the first formal and informal exchanges begin through social contact situations such as, for example sharing lunches, dinners, and recreational moments of group fun.

At this stage, since secure attachment is a prerequisite for the individual to explore his or her experiences with confidence, the task of the co-trainer is to engage in the construction of welcoming, supportive, and validating reciprocal interactions. The hypothesis, echoing Bowlby's (1988) attachment theory, is that the secure attachment pattern, insofar as it is flexible, allows for the establishment of a good didactic and interpersonal relationship, based on trust and exploration (Slade, 2008). As the group of students is heterogeneous in terms of attachment style, the co-trainer will notice individual interpersonal peculiarities from the very first interactions: for example distancing students who show more discomfort at the level of affective closeness in the relationship and preoccupied students who tend to be very demanding in relational engagement. Reflection, from the outset, is, therefore, on the particular ways in which one's interpersonal experiences can be revealed and communicated within a cooperative relationship (Miller-Bottome et al., 2017).

Already at this stage, group members begin to establish relationships with each other. This is a phase of mutual acquaintance and the creation of a sense of belonging to the group: in keeping with the motto 'the first impression is the one that counts', it is not at all uncommon for certain affinities, which arose in the immediacy of a residential meeting, to become relationships cultivated over the years, after the training course has ended, on a personal and/or professional level.

2.2 The Early Years: Growth

During the first year, students are confronted with a theoretical preparation across multiple approaches. Integrated training is inescapably grounded in evidence from the literature and the School guides students in the use of evidence-based practices (EBP). During this period, students are exposed to different theories and models of psychotherapy, with an emphasis on the integration of different perspectives. The focus on the relationship and the use of the attachment framework allow students to develop knowledge of psychotherapeutic relational processes, learning how to prevent and manage possible ruptures in the therapeutic alliance. Students begin to measure themselves with different types of settings (individual, couple, family, and group) and approaches. In this first year of indispensable and preparatory training work, the co-trainer supports students mostly for needs of a purely concrete and practical nature: Students contact him/her for information related to didactics, doubts concerning the modalities of their annual placement, bibliographic references, and theoretical clarifications. A frequently reported feeling in the end-of-year interviews with one's co-trainer is a feeling of bewilderment and confusion on the part of the student, who, depending on his/her style, reacts differently to the frustration of 'wanting to do' but, in a certain sense, 'having to learn'. This year also provides the first opportunities to practise the so-called first interviews and refine one's clinical skills through the presentation of clinical cases that the lecturers share in their lectures. During this year, the co-trainer has only one lesson in supervising clinical cases, demonstrating that, at this point in the course, the co-trainer's energies are being directed towards other needs. From the second year, the didactic focus shifts to the developmental age and more experiential learning is intensified: Students are encouraged to explore their own identity and style of entering into a relationship with the patient, to probe their personal beliefs, values, and prejudices regarding clinical work.

In these first 2 years, from an individual point of view, the co-trainer interfaces with what, according to a parallelism of individual development, represents the first steps of the child who interacts with the socio-cultural conditions of the environment that surrounds him or her, starting from his/her own biological predisposition and endowment. Certainly, these needs cannot be generalised; they can manifest themselves at different times and only in certain students. By way of example, to mention a few, we refer to: disorientation towards theoretical models, overload of stimulation and enthusiasm with correlated anxiety, attitudes of expressive and affective deficiency, difficulty in processing frustrations, feelings of omnipotence, pretension to immediate satisfaction of every desire, lack of autonomy, little sense of responsibility for one's own actions, lack of respect for rules, lack of delicacy in comments to colleagues, and, finally, intellectual investment to the detriment of emotional experiential investment.

In general, the figure of the co-trainer welcomes and responds to requests for didactic and/or emotional support, monitoring students who manifest the first recurring fatigue concerning transient crises or particular life events/stories and, in some cases, guiding the student to undertake his/her own personal didactic therapy. The co-trainer can manage 'outside the classroom' some dysregulations that the student is unable or unwilling to share with the group. He observes the students' interactions by reflecting on their learning needs and perceived satisfaction, especially in students who are not very interactive at an explicit level. Moreover, by working side by side with the two trainers in charge of the experiential lessons with the students, the co-trainer becomes a point of continuity and comparison between the different therapeutic styles, which, although tend to be homogeneous, will nevertheless be differentiated in relation to the personal differences of the trainers themselves that cannot be eliminated. Working alongside the trainer, he/she provides a different perspective and additional guidance during discussions and practical exercises. This supportive role is crucial in helping students explore their own emotional reactions and better understand the teaching material. Overall, the first two formative years of an integrated approach psychotherapy school provide students with a solid theoretical and practical foundation to begin to develop their clinical skills and prepare them to enter into the psychotherapy profession.

A final task of the co-trainer pertains to the monitoring of annual progress, with the collection of both individual and group indicators, conducted through an interview dedicated to each student (relational feedback) and an examination (didactic feedback). At the end of the first year, a written examination is conducted with open questions centred on the integration of the various theoretical contributions acquired. From the end of the second year, on the other hand, a video-recorded session of a first interview (at the end of the second year) or a session at a late stage of therapy or a follow-up session (from the end of the third year) is presented, with the aim of engaging the student in the application of the theoretical concepts of the integrated approach and in the formulation of the case in terms of diagnostic hypotheses and the consequent planning of the therapeutic work.

2.3 *Between Protest and Autonomy: Maturity*

Most groups go through critical phases at some point: in the physiological relational asymmetries that, in the middle of the journey, begin to become more consistent, there are those who already want to go, those who would never want to finish, those who already feel ready, those who think they never will, those who want to have their say, those who have never said it, those who need to join, those who want to assert themselves. The maturity of the group is reached by passing through a delicate phase, which in general could be represented by the third year. This is a time for the group to consolidate and experiment with the skills acquired and to potentially redefine the boundaries between possible subgroups and/or of each pupil within their own class. On a didactic level, during this period, students can deepen their understanding of the theory and practice of integrated psychotherapy through their own clinical experience, certainly internship experience, and for many also professional experience. The co-trainer starts having to manage time well in order to deal with the numerous 'clinical' or supervisory questions. Indeed, the literature shows how the percentage of students in supervision increases significantly towards the end of the training and decreases 1 year after the end (Ying Zhang et al., 2022). For these reasons, in line with the group's needs, formally, the co-trainer's didactic supervision classes with the group are increased to 3 days. From a training point of view, the students are provided with tools and techniques belonging to the different approaches studied, integrating them into the relational framework of the therapeutic dyad, and addressing the whole spectrum of psychopathology (from the neurotic to the psychotic area, with particular reference to personality disorders) in the different phases of life, including adulthood and senescence. Once this material has been received, students engage in the practice of the acquired techniques and frequently the co-trainer has the task of promoting in the students an awareness of how the conceptualisation of the case goes hand in hand with the selection of which specific intervention or technique is most suitable for that particular moment in the therapy with that patient, thus encouraging a tailor-made approach to therapeutic work (Norcross, 2002).

In this phase of the training, the co-trainer supports students who have not yet started their personal therapy in evaluating the most suitable trainer. Many studies have sustained the positive association between personal therapy and professional learning: Through a greater understanding of one's own personal suffering and internal conflicts, the student will be better prepared to understand others (Orlinsky & Rønnestad, 2005; Orlinsky et al., 2011). Other empirical research also suggests positive effects on personal and professional development during training, through an increase in interpersonal skills, self-awareness, mentalisation processes, and functioning patterns (Edwards, 2018; Gale & Schröder, 2014; Moe & Thimm, 2021; McMahon & Rodillas, 2020; Scott et al., 2021; Strauß & Taeger, 2021). At this stage, group members have clarified their responsibilities and roles within the group, which works more autonomously. Some students become active in support of others by proposing intervision exchanges. With regard to the critical phases at the relational level, there are difficulties for individual students with other colleagues, with the group, or with part of it, for example intra-group divisions or a siding of a more or less numerous groups of students against figures belonging to the school (teachers, trainers, and co-trainers). In spite of the delicacy of this phase and, probably, precisely because of the fragility that characterises this moment of relationship breakdown, the students concerned and the group as a whole have the opportunity to analyse their own needs and to express them to each other; this can lead to a potential generativity in terms of redefining and making explicit their own needs, negotiating with the 'counterpart's' demands and creating new interpersonal balances. In order to be effective, this process requires metacognitive and self-awareness work, with the co-trainer at the forefront. His/her aim is to help in the creation of a shared meaning capable of giving coherence and continuity to the experience of each of the actors involved, in an intersubjective dimension and emotional reciprocity (Guidano, 2008; Nardi & Capecci, 2005, 2006). The co-trainer is not exempt from engaging in conflicts that involve a rupture from withdrawal or confrontation (Safran & Muran, 2019): it is desirable to suggest to readers that it is highly inconvenient for this to happen, yet it is human to admit its plausibility. Whatever the type of the rupture, the purpose of these interventions is to "make the interlocutor more aware of how to manage other personal relationships" (Muran & Eubanks, 2021, p. 55) and turn the therapeutic rupture into a cooperative opportunity, identifying one's own contribution in maintaining the dysfunctional interpersonal cycle and using tools to safeguard work and relationship goals in the group. Resuming the therapist-patient and co-trainer–pupil parallelism proposed above, the therapist/co-trainer, as an act of self-reflection, re-examines what happened in therapy also in the light of his/her own thoughts, moods, and behaviour, considering them as the indispensable object of analysis for improving the therapeutic process itself. The process of self-reflection enables the therapist to differentiate his/her own needs from those of the patient, to analyse the quality of the therapeutic relationship, to make therapy more effective, and, ultimately, to increase the therapist's and patient's sense of competence and trust in the therapeutic relationship itself (Prasko et al., 2023). The positive management of these critical phases is central in the promotion of a subsequent greater cohesion and autonomy of the group itself, also starting from the redefinition of relational and identity boundaries, in fact favouring the passage to the next phase of the group's life: detachment.

2.4 Closure: The Separation

And then comes the separation phase, the phase in which the group prepares to say goodbye. Both the students and the co-trainer may feel sad or nostalgic and/or may feel relief and well-being in preparing for future projects or meetings. The students can also project themselves more concretely onto the professional life that awaits them and, before that, onto the writing of their thesis. It is a time in which they can reflect further on themselves in the therapist role, with their own peculiarities, resources, and personal struggles. Throughout the course of the final year, the themes suggest a didactic accompaniment to concrete leave-taking: ageing, closure, and death. The co-trainer, in this last period, will be a figure increasingly peripheral to the group, which by now must anchor itself on its own constructed securities, preparing for the detachment from what is an educational institution made up of teachers, fellow travellers, and co-trainers. It is essential to approach this transition by celebrating the successes achieved over the years and to face the separation consciously, giving oneself time to wait for it, prepare for it, and experience it. For this reason, the co-trainer and trainers spend a final residential experience with the group where the protagonists become tears, sighs of relief, melancholy, pride, disbelief, fear, joy, and affection.

This moment is an emotionally moving experience and requires personal, as well as professional, closure for the co-trainer too. He therefore conducts the last individual interviews with his/her students, who cease to be students and instantly become fellow therapists. On this occasion, he does not hold an end-of-year exam but rather begins to correct the elaboration of the two clinical cases of the students who are gradually preparing for specialisation. It is at that appointment that he/she formally concludes his/her commitment to each student: an institutional moment that becomes a meaningful closing experience for both.

The end of the training course in psychotherapy is a moment charged with meaning and has a strong symbolic value. It is time for the group to act as its own supervisor, to test a change in relationships, first personal and then professional. It is time to share a general point of view as a set of individual contributions, with respect to the integration of the contents that have emerged over the years, with the specific and exclusive process modalities of the group. The students can say goodbye to each other by virtue of the training objectives achieved. The last step to be tackled together is the meaning and importance of the final separation (for that specific modality) as a true recognition of autonomy, not as anguish and fear of loss as it often was for some life stories. With each new knowledge, new problems and new sources of non-knowledge open up: awareness is not a panacea, it cannot be pursued in itself, because each awareness one arrives at corresponds to an increase in the sense of ambiguity. However stressful, these must be experienced as personal emotions from which one can take information about oneself, in the continuation of a life in which to observe the uniqueness of one's self in its becoming (Guidano, 2008). In conclusion, it is important to emphasise the originality of each group's developmental path: The developmental stages may vary according to its composition, the set goals, the internal dynamics, the influence of the co-trainer, and of life events, be they of the trainees, the co-trainer, or the trainers.

3 The Integrated Approach: Specificities and Implications for the Role of the Co-trainer

The panorama of psychotherapy schools in Italy is vast and constantly growing. It is common knowledge that in some Schools of Specialisation in psychotherapy the figure of the co-trainer/co-didactor is foreseen, in relation to the training programmes and to the cardinal constructs of that specific therapeutic approach, which, when present, can be declined in very different ways. Some Schools envisage a figure who performs some additional functions to the main didactic ones: (a) supervisor; (b) tutor with traineeship orientation functions; (c) in a specific case, some tutor figures dedicated to a group training part that change every year following specific modules. In other Schools, we can find greater emphasis on the didactic skills of the co-trainer as teacher, providing an ad hoc training pathway and the development of practical training modules, in an autonomous way or alongside the main trainer. In yet others, instead, a more relational, continuous, and polyvalent function of the co-trainer is envisaged. In fact, one figure (in some cases two) is envisaged who accompanies the class for the 4 years is envisaged, carrying out functions regarding the interpersonal/group, personal, didactic, and professional dimensions described at the beginning of this chapter.

A recent article reports that similarly in different approaches (cognitive-behavioural, psychodynamic, constructivist, and systemic), the *relational characteristics of trainers* are considered the most important aspects in the training pathway by students in training and already specialised professionals (Rocco et al., 2019). These aspects are considered superior even compared to supervision and the transmission of technical skills, for two possible reasons hypothesised by the authors. First, such characteristics convey to students the perception of themselves as suitable for the profession of therapists, providing reassurance and support necessary to face the challenges of the profession. Second, through this relational modelling, students learn a possible way of being within an (effective) therapeutic relationship. We can consider that these considerations on the relevance of relational aspects also apply to the figure of the co-trainer in the integrated approach.

Moreover, group experiential training, which is a pivotal element in the personal and professional growth of the trainee therapist, is also onerous and emotionally destabilising and requires the availability of adequate emotional support in order to be effective and generative (Hahn et al., 2023). In addition to this relational function, in the integrated approach, the co-trainer plays the role of facilitator of the integration process. This facilitation takes place along multiple and partly sequential dimensions: (a) first, the orientation within the different conceptual products that are added in the training arena; (b) then the progressive development of a deep and mature integration, that is the ability to think in a fluid and creative way; (c) together with the personalisation, in the person of the therapist-in-training, of the learnings with the identification of his/her own style and preferences on a technical and conceptual level (Norcross & Popple Leah, 2017).

3.1 Special Personal and Professional Challenges of the Integrated Co-trainer

The main aspects that characterise the integrated approach—not exclusively but certainly to a greater extent than single-model therapies—include a focus on research and EBP practice, the use of constant feedback, collaboration and agreement on goals, monitoring of the therapeutic relationship, and personalisation of treatment (Norcross & Popple, 2017; Norcross & Wampold, 2018). These dimensions characterise not only the therapeutic process but also the training pathway to become an integrated psychotherapist (Norcross & Wampold, 2018). This focus on process aspects, together with the plurality of theoretical models and techniques proposed during training, make the figure of the co-trainer essential, with the challenges and specificities described below.

Having a Didactic Mediation Role in a Context Based on Experiential Learning and the Use of Feedback

The request for feedback, obtained from patients in more formal and structured or informal and colloquial ways, is a primary aspect in the integrated approach and also permeates the training to become a psychotherapist (Muran & Eubanks, 2021). This aspect is essential to ensure an empathic and collaborative relationship, and to promote awareness and change. In order to train for such constant monitoring of the therapeutic process and relationship, the training environment must encourage students to expose their own insecurities and potential errors in clinical practice. The figure of the co-trainer represents a didactic and experiential mediating figure also from this point of view: By placing him/herself on a more accessible level than the lecturers, he/she can show the human and therefore fallible dimension of the therapist through self-disclosure and the revealing of therapy experiences, reducing shame and modulating the tendency to avoid exposure in the group. This can help develop a 'compassionate internal supervisor' in the student to cope with self-criticism and reduce the sense of threat in therapy (Bell et al., 2017).

Being a Supervisor Who Adopts Different Techniques and Approaches According to Increasing Needs

The co-trainer also acts as a supervisor for the class on a regular basis and individually according to the needs of the students and the availability of the co-trainer. From the point of view of the integrated approach, the supervision provided to students must also progress through a series of evolutionary stages reflecting increasing needs, techniques, and complexity: from a more structured and directive initial stage, more oriented towards the promotion and consolidation of diagnostic and technical skills in the student, to a more collaborative and dynamic stage, capable of integrating the different approaches and techniques in a flexible manner according to the patient's needs (Norcross & Popple, 2017). In the beginning, supervisions can be more centred on the framing of the case and, as the training progresses, they can also be enriched with those dimensions of intersubjectivity that characterise, in fact, the therapeutic relationship, thanks also to the student's acquisition of a greater awareness of himself/herself and of his/her own therapeutic tools.

A characteristic of experienced therapists, as opposed to those in training, is indeed 'responsivity', understood as the ability to flexibly tune into what is happening in the relationship with the patient, using both bodily and cognitive-affective indicators (Spagnuolo Lobb et al., 2022; Norcross & Wampold, 2018). For this to happen, self-knowledge as a person (including the dimensions concerning personal meaning organisations, motivational systems, and attachment patterns) and self-knowledge as a therapist are required in order to distinguish what is mine, what is the patient's, and what is of the therapeutic relationship in place. Accompanying students in such a dynamic and evolutionary supervision also implies a challenge for the co-trainer, as it requires adequate self-knowledge as a person, as a therapist, and as a supervisor, in a necessarily less mature way at the beginning, but gradually becoming more and more structured over time (Nancy McWilliams, 2022).

Managing Complexity

The complexity to which the students are exposed is composed of several aspects, including: a mind, and a motivational setup, no longer so predisposed to continuous and systematic study, together with work and family burdens that make the time to devote to one's own learning burdensome; the illusion of having arrived at an exhaustive self-awareness that clashes with new, and sometimes disorienting, personal learning, especially when exposed to theoretical models different from those that had become familiar during one's training or personal therapy; an integration built in a personal way during the years after specialisation, an integration that does not necessarily overlap with the models presented in school and therefore requires an additional integrative load. To sum up, these aspects require the following skills: (a) tolerance of the permanent and potentially frustrating state of being a student, considering that 'even the simple experience of learning something one did not know before can produce a small narcissistic wound' (Nancy McWilliams, 2022); (b) a sufficiently broad motivation; (c) the availability of emotional and personal resources to cope with the destabilising effect of the new self-awareness that is gradually emerging.

Compared to those who choose single theoretical models, among students who choose an integrated approach we find to a greater extent traits of perfectionism (Norcross & Popple, 2017; Castonguay, 2006). These perfectionistic traits can be characterised by: (a) tension to implement the best therapeutic approaches in order to identify the optimal treatment for each patient, in the positive components; (b) in the negative dimensions, cumbersome performative aspects with excessive fear of therapeutic failure, impatience with progress in therapy and chronic anxiety of not doing 'well enough' with excessive fear of exposing one's vulnerabilities (shirking opportunities for practice and learning). In these cases, the cognitive complexity and multiplicity of approaches that students are exposed to often lead to an increase in such anxious and performative aspects, with possible defensive attitudes of various kinds (e.g. anger and criticism of the model, accentuation of perfectionism, experiential avoidance), especially in the initial phases (first and second year). What are the possible collusive movements of the co-trainer? The co-trainer could be inclined to (a) favour integration by seeking connections between concepts that need to be understood and assimilated before they can be integrated with each other; (b) provide additional materials and bibliographical indications in order to meet the students' need for control, with the risk of further overloading learning and making it even more cognitively mediated (collusion on the rank motivational system); (c) act with a protective attitude towards students' anxiety (collusion on the motivational system of nurturing), perhaps developing an overly critical attitude towards the integrated model itself, similar to how apprehensive and overprotective parents do with teachers who cause 'pain' to their children. The path to pursue remains an open stance of listening to and welcoming the students' travails, within an adjusted position that is attentive to one's own motivational systems in action, when different from the cooperative one, in order to place oneself as a truly secure base, which promotes a sense of trust in order to foster the process of exploring past and present relationships (Bowlby, 1989).

4 The Person of the Co-trainer: Life Stages, Illnesses, Personal Difficulties, and Changes Over Time

After outlining the functions of the co-trainer within the training course, it becomes evident how the specific characteristics of the co-trainer as an individual can influence the course of each student within the class, as well as the class group as a whole.

The various functions of the co-trainer serve to support the professional and personal growth of the student when performed within an alliance that is certainly didactic, which hopefully also takes on the form of a therapeutic alliance, at certain times more than others. As it happens in psychotherapy, but more generally in all meaningful relationships, it appears inevitable that the co-trainer's attachment model and the associated relational and communicative style interact with those of the students, involving different levels and types of reciprocal attunement (Talia et al., 2019).

Certainly, both for the co-trainer and the students, being aware of one's own attachment style can help to understand, foresee, and repair ruptures in the didactic and therapeutic alliance that may occur in the relationship with the students. Such flexions and ruptures in the alliance become known, and therefore repairable, thanks to the continuous cooperative exchanges on the progress of this relationship, within the group and in the cadenced individual interviews.

However, numerous changes occur throughout the 4-year period, whether small or more significant, progressive or sudden, such that they disrupt the co-trainer's emotional balance and activate to a greater extent or in a less effective way the cognitive and behavioural strategies associated with his/her attachment style and the lenses he/she has constructed and uses to view him/herself and the world. An interesting recent article shows that there is a significant relationship between the therapist's quality of life (and personal/interpersonal stress) and the quality of the therapeutic alliance with patients (Nissen-Lie et al., 2013). This influence appears to be recognised differently by the two members of the relationship. In particular, the therapist appears to minimise this impact, whereas the patients seem to show increased sensitivity to the therapist's negative reactions: Every single signal of disinterest, rejection, aggression, or defensive behaviour resulting from an increased burden in the therapist's life can deteriorate the therapeutic alliance. This sensitivity is evident to each co-trainer who finds in the feedback received from the students a mirror of their own states of mind and changes in their own relational set-up over the 4 years, partly deformed by their own personal plots of meaning.

Some significant events have a greater impact on quality of life and personal stress levels, such as the onset of illnesses (one's own or those of close ones), significant bereavements, separations, and major job changes, but also positive events such as pregnancy. Among such events, more space has been devoted in the literature to the condition of pregnancy and motherhood with regard to the figure of the psychotherapist (Way et al., 2019). Such experience would seem to entail some main consequences: (a) changes in the level of identity of the therapist, with the need to harmoniously reconcile the new maternal role with the professional one, both partly concerning care and nurturing; (b) the need to communicate personal aspects to patients, which in some therapeutic approaches represents an important change in the setting; (c) therapeutic challenges related to new emerging contents; (d) experiences of guilt towards patients due to the fear of feelings of abandonment or of exposing positive aspects of one's own life in front of the suffering Other. To some extent, all these aspects can also concern the person of the pregnant co-trainer, but there are some differences to be taken into consideration: (a) the element of unveiling aspects of oneself appears significantly less critical, as the co-trainer figure is more accessible and informal compared to the therapist's one; (b) the presence in the training course of a plurality of attachment figures (personal therapy, trainers, class group) make the students' possible fear of abandonment more tolerable and the co-trainer's feelings of guilt more contained. However, since pregnancy represents a delicate moment in life for the co-trainer too, its implications should be worked out within the context of intervision, individual supervision, or personal therapy. In particular, it will be necessary to understand how the activation of the motivational system of caring intrinsic to the motherhood condition is experienced by the co-trainer and how it is reflected in the relationship with the students and the class group, in more or less harmonious ways, with more or less distancing or amplifying strategies.

Other changes with negative valence, such as illness or significant relational losses due to separation or bereavement, lead to significant stress and activate the attachment system with its associated strategies. Where avoidant attachment prevails, the co-trainer may continue to carry on with their work activities without modification or accentuate their investment in their work assignments; in the presence of ambivalent attachment, the reaction may be one of emotional amplification, with momentary declared or perceived inability to cope with their tasks. Both strategies entail criticality and an impact on the relationship with the students and the class group, since the co-trainer is a relational and professional role model as well as an attachment figure. Likewise, such unfavourable events may alter the way students perceive the co-trainer figure in terms of strength and reliability as a secure base. Cooperative arrangements may result, but also the accentuation of self-sufficient dynamics or, on the contrary, the students' ambivalent, and potentially angry, search for closeness.

Other changes concerning the professional and career sphere may be impacted by the increased stress level, but also by the activation of motivational systems such as the rank system, both in the co-trainer and in the students. For some students, where the rank motivational system is particularly active, the co-trainer may be perceived as a figure to be appreciated by, or a role model to compete against in order to feel sufficiently adequate. In such situations, changes in the perceived status of the co-trainer, whether in an improving or worsening direction, may lead to slippage in the rank system, and a possible further distancing from a cooperative system. Such a distancing in fact represents a risk because this motivational system is the only one that creates the conditions for exercising metacognition and mentalisation (Liotti & Monticelli, 2008).

5 After Specialisation

The first moment of closure of the educational pathway is the conclusion of the teaching activities of the fourth year, followed by further moments of closure, some of which are for all intents and purposes institutional, such as the preparation and delivery of the specialisation thesis, and others more qualitative and informal. The way in which these occasions are approached provides information on how each student approaches the closure of his/her training. There may be theses that are difficult to complete, hand in, or finalise; didactic therapies that have never been completed, or begun again; the continuation of professional roles not inherent to psychotherapy; the search for new training opportunities without a break; the relationship with the co-trainer that is maintained without changing over time. Therefore, the co-trainer's role may not end with the correction of the theses, and even this more didactic-evaluative phase may become a further moment of confrontation not only on the content level but also on the process level, representing a further occasion of relational exchange between the co-trainer and the student.

As far as the person of the co-trainer is concerned, too, the conclusion of the training course may be accompanied by very different emotions, that sustain in more or less harmonious or difficult ways the necessary accommodations in one's role required by such a transition. There may be dimensions of sadness and nostalgia associated with the loss, fear of not being taken into account once one's formal assignment is over, disorientation due to the loss of a now familiar relational and identity setup, as well as aspects of solicitous curiosity towards one's students' paths and interest in maintaining a form of continuity by nourishing relationships and transforming them.

Inevitably, for such a multifaceted, polyvalent, and relational role as the one played for 4 years by the co-trainer, the 'moment' of closure cannot but decline according to blurred, subjective, and dynamic space-time coordinates. Regardless of the specific ways in which this passage is managed, even after specialisation the co-trainer remains in fact a person one can refer to in order to tackle the subsequent steps in the construction of one's professional identity, outside the more guided context of the specialisation school.

A typical way of continuing the relationship with the student is as a supervisor.

After specialisation, having an affective bond and personal acquaintance with one's supervisor, a former co-trainer, makes it easier to handle the feelings of shame that arise when presenting one's professional difficulties, which may increase once training has ended, providing a form of legitimation for one's mistakes (Bilodeau et al., 2012).

In the supervisor-psychotherapist relationship, as well as in the therapeutic context, shame is an emotion that—if made explicit and elaborated in its occurrence in the various *enactments* (Bromberg, 2012) in the here and now—can promote a real attunement and access to the real nuclei of suffering, of the patient as well as of the therapist in supervision (Salvatore, 2023). From this perspective, having a supervisor to whom one is relationally attached allows one to deal with shame, experiencing it in one's window of tolerance, rather than avoiding it through a safe context or perfectionistic coping.

The transition from the co-trainer-student relationship to the colleague (senior)-colleague (junior) relationship opens up more mature and equal spaces for sharing and collaboration. In this context, possibilities are opened up for sharing work projects and extra-work dimensions more guided by spontaneity and personal and professional affinities, also experienced during the 4-year course, but always subordinate to the primacy of the training mandate towards all students. Similarly, some co-trainer–student relationships that during the 4-year course have been sustained primarily by the training role, in the absence of a free and sincere bond may lead to an interruption of the relationship or to a purely concrete and methodological-professional reference to the figure of the co-trainer.

A virtuous aspect of the continuation of the relationship with students after specialisation consists in the opportunity to remain up-to-date, through their subsequent professional experiences, on the advances in approaches and techniques in psychotherapy from an evidence-based and continuous education perspective. In this way, a generative circularity is built, in which the former co-trainer becomes a beneficiary of what the young specialists bring to the table in terms of energy and planning, and the process of knowledge and change is nurtured in a dynamic way. Likewise, former students can participate in, or carry out themselves, research paths on the efficacy of the integrated model and integrated training, promoting a continuous and dynamic exchange and interconnection between clinical practice, research, and training (Castonguay, 2011).

6 Conclusions

This chapter has outlined the ways in which the co-trainer's functions of *affective, interpersonal, didactic,* and *experiential* mediator *are* carried out within the dynamic and evolutionary training process that unfolds over the 4 years of the specialisation school. It has been described how certain pivotal constructs that inform the therapeutic process, such as attachment theory, personal meaning organisations, metacognition, and interpersonal motivational systems also support and guide the co-trainer's relational and practical actions, serving as guides and detectors of alliance changes, as well as repairers of relational ruptures. This anchorage to theoretical constructs and 'meta' reflections is even more so essential when looking at the 'person' of the co-trainer, exposed to the unpredictable and perturbing (not always strategically) events of personal and working life that happen throughout such a significant period of time, such as that required by the completion of the school of psychotherapy.

The tools provided by the integrated approach, in particular the constant monitoring of ongoing processes, the experiential mode of awareness acquisition, and the fostering of the integration of different therapeutic approaches in an all-encompassing framework, represent challenges for the co-trainer, but at the same time opportunities for self-awareness, reflective integration of changes in the here and now of their manifestation, and enrichment also in professional terms.

Albeit modulated and progressive, the constant exposure of oneself, of one's own nuclei of suffering, and of one's own professional actions that characterise the integrated approach as outlined here, allows a familiarisation with one's own experiences of shame and their harmonious integration with the other parts of oneself.

Only in this way will it be possible to realise with oneself and with one's patients an authentic and therapeutic intersubjective attunement, rather than a purely performative attitude that risks being painful and not very productive.

Once it comes to an end, the exciting and enriching journey of the psychotherapy school will therefore find not only the students but also the trainers and the co-trainer profoundly, and consciously, changed.

References

Andolfi, M., & Haber, R. (1995). *La consulenza in terapia familiare: una prospettiva sistemica*. Raffaello Cortina.
Bara, B. (2018). *Il terapeuta relazionale. Tecnica dell'atto terapeutico*. Bollati Boringhieri.
Becchio, C., Adenzato, M., & Bara, B. (2006). How the brain understands intention: Different neural circuits identify the componential features of motor and prior intentions. *Consciousness and Cognition, 15*(1), 64–74.
Bell, T., Dixon, A., & Kolts, R. (2017). Developing a compassionate internal supervisor: Compassion-focused therapy for trainee therapists. *Clinical Psychology & Psychotherapy, 24*(3), 632–648. https://doi.org/10.1002/cpp.2031. Epub 2016 Jul 25. PMID: 27456393.
Bennett-Levy, J., & Finlay-Jones, A. (2018). The role of personal practice in therapist skill development: A model to guide therapists, educators, supervisors and researchers. *Cognitive Behaviour Therapy, 47*, 185–205. https://doi.org/10.1080/16506073.2018.1434678
Bilodeau, C., Savard, R., & Lecomte, C. (2012). Trainee shame-proneness and the supervisory process. *Journal of Counselor Preparation and Supervision*. https://doi.org/10.7729/41.0020
Boud, D., Keogh, R., & Walker, D. (1985). *Reflection: Turning reflection into learning*. Routledge.
Bowlby, J. (1988). *Una base sicura. Applicazioni cliniche della teoria dell'attaccamento*. Tr.it. Raffaello Cortina, Milano 1989.
Bowlby, J. (1969). *Attachment and loss* (Vol. I). Hogarth Press.
Bowlby, J. (1989). *Una base sicura. Applicazioni cliniche della teoria dell'attaccamento*. Raffaello Cortina. ISBN: 9788870780888.
Bromberg, P. M. (2012). *L'ombra dello tsunami. La crescita della mente relazionale*. Raffaello Cortina.
Burlingame, G. M., Fuhriman, A., & Johnson, J. E. (2001). Cohesion in group psychotherapy. *Psychotherapy: Theory, Research, Practice, Training, 38*, 373–379.
Carcione, A., Falcone, M., Magnolfi, G., & Manaresi, F. (1997). La funzione metacognitiva in psicoterapia: Scala di Valutazione della Metacognizione (S.Va.M.). *Psicoterapia, 9*, 91–97.
Carni, S., Petrocchi, N., Del Miglio, C., Mancini, F., & Couyoumdjian, A. (2013). Intrapsychic an interpersonal guilt: A critical review of the recent literature. *Cognitive Processing, 14*, 333–346.
Castonguay, L. G. (2006). Personal pathways in psychotherapy integration. *Journal of Psychotherapy Integration, 16*(1), 36–58.
Castonguay, L. G. (2011). Psychotherapy, psychopathology, research and practice: Pathways of connections and integration. *Psychotherapy Research, 21*(2), 125–140. https://doi.org/10.1080/10503307.2011.563250
Chigwedere, C., Bennett-Levy, J., Fitzmaurice, B., & Donohoe, G. (2020). Personal practice in counselling and CBT trainees: The self-perceived impact of personal therapy and self-practice/self-reflection on personal and professional development. *Cognitive Behaviour Therapy*, 1–17.
Cornoldi, C. (2006). *Metacognizione e apprendimento*. il Mulino.
DeWaal, F. (1989). *Peacemaking among primates*. Harward University Press.
Di Maggio, G., & Semerari, A. (2003). *I Disturbi di Personalità: Modelli e trattamento. Stati mentali, metarappresentazioni, cicli interpersonali*. Roma-Bari.

Doran, J., & Lewins, C. A. (2011). Components of shame and eatig disturbante among clinica lan non clinical populations. *European Eating Disorder Review, 20*, 265–270.

Edelman, G. M. (1989). *The remembered present: A biological theory of consciousness*. Basic Books.

Edwards, J. (2018). Counseling and psychology student experiences of personal therapy: A critical interpretive synthesis. *Frontiers in Psychology, 9*, 1732.

Fisher, H. E. (1992). *Anatomy of love*. Norton.

Fodor, J. (1983). *La mente modulare*. Il Mulino.

Gadamer, H. G. (1960). *Wahreit und methode: Grundzuge einer philosophischen hermeneutik*. Tubingen: J.C.B.Mohr. Trad.it. (1983). Verità e metodo. Bompiani.

Gale, C., & Schröder, T. (2014). Experiences of self-practice/self-reflection in cognitive behavioural therapy: A meta-synthesis of qualitative studies. *Psychology and Psychotherapy, 87*, 373–392.

George, C., & Solomon, J. (1999). Attachment and caregiving: The caregiving behavioral system. In J. Cassidy & P. R. Shaver (Eds.), *Handbook of attachment: Theory, research, and clinical applications* (pp. 649–670). The Guilford Press.

Gilbert, P. (1989). *Human nature and suffering*. Erlbaum.

Guidano, V. (1991). *The self in process: Towards a post rationalist cognitive therapy*. Guilford.

Guidano, V. (2008) *La Psicoterapia tra arte e scienza*. A cura di Giovanni Cutolo, Angeli, Milano.

Hahn, D., Weck, F., Witthöft, M., & Kühne, F. (2023). What characterizes helpful personal practice in psychotherapy training? Results of an online survey. *Behavioural and Cognitive Psychotherapy, 51*(1), 74–86. https://doi.org/10.1017/S1352465822000406. Epub 2022 Oct 25. PMID: 36281883.

Ieva, K. P., Ohrt, J. H., Swank, J. M., & Young, T. (2009). The impact of experiential groups on master students' counselor and personal development: A qualitative investigation. *The Journal for Specialists in Group Work, 34*, 351–368. https://doi.org/10.1080/01933920903219078

Kline, W. B., Falbaum, D. F., Pope, V. T., Hargraves, G. A., & Hundley, S. F. (1997). The significance of the group experience for students in counselor education: A preliminary naturalistic inquiry. *Journal for Specialists in Group Work, 22*, 157–166.

Liotti, G. (1994/2005). *La dimensione interpersonale della coscienza*. Carocci editore.

Liotti, G. (2001). *Le opere della coscienza. Psicopatologia e psicoterapia nella prospettiva cognitivo-evoluzionista*. Raffaello Cortina, Milano.

Liotti, G. (2005). *La dimensione interpersonale della coscienza*. Carocci.

Liotti, G., & Farina, B. (2011). *Sviluppi Traumatici. Eziopatogenesi, clinica e terapia della dimensione dissociativa*. Raffaello Cortina Editore.

Liotti, G., & Intreccialagli, B. (2003). Disorganized attachment, motivational systems and metacognitive monitoring in the treatment of a patient with Borderline Syndrome. In M. Cortina & M. Marrone (Eds.), *Attachment theory and the psychoanalytic process*. Whurr.

Liotti, G., & Monticelli, F. (2008). *I sistemi motivazionali nel dialogo clinico*. Raffaello Cortina.

Mahler, M., Pine, F., & Bergman, A. (1975). *The psychological birth of the human infant*. Basic Books.

Maslach, C., & Pines, A. (1977). The burnout syndrome in the daycare setting. *Child Care Quarterly, 62*, 100–113.

McMahon, A., & Rodillas, R. R. (2020). Personal development groups during psychotherapy training: Irish students' expectations and experiences of vulnerability, safety and growth. *Counselling Psychology Quarterly, 33*, 163–186.

Miller-Bottome, M., Talia, A., Safran, J. D., & Muran, J. C. (2017). Resolving alliance ruptures from an attachment-informed perspective. *Psychoanalytic Psychology, 35*, 175–183. https://doi.org/10.1037/pap0000152

Moe, F. D., & Thimm, J. (2021). Personal therapy and the personal therapist. *Nordic Psychology, 73*, 3–28.

Muran, J. C., & Eubanks, C. F. (2021). *Il terapeuta sotto pressione. Riparare le rotture dell'alleanza terapeutica*. Raffaello Cortina.

Nardi, B., & Capecci, I. (2005). Organizzazioni di significato personale: adattamento e fisiopatologia. In *Approccio all'Adolescente Difficile* (pp. 103–116). Quaderni Asur Marche.

Nardi, B., Capecci., & I. (2006). I processi di organizzazione degli stili di personalità e le basi dell'unicità individuale. *Quaderni di Psicoterapia Cognitiva, 18*, 48–83.

Nancy McWilliams. (2022). *La supervisione. Teoria e pratiche psicoanalitiche*. Raffaello Cortina Editore. ISBN: 9788832854343.

Nissen-Lie, H. A., Havik, O. E., Høglend, P. A., Monsen, J. T., & Rønnestad, M. H. (2013). The contribution of the quality of therapists' personal lives to the development of the working alliance. *Journal of Counseling Psychology, 60*(4), 483–495. https://doi.org/10.1037/a0033643. Epub 2013 Aug 19.

Norcross, J. C. (Ed.). (2002). *Psychotherapy relationships that work: Therapist contributions and responsiveness to patients*. Oxford University Press.

Norcross, J. C., & Popple Leah, M. (2017). *Supervisione in Psicoterapia Integrata: Elementi essenziali* (Italian Edition). Leal M. Norcross John C.; Popple Leah M. Published by Sovera Edizioni. ISBN 10: 8866520187 ISBN 13: 9788866520184.

Norcross, J. C., & Wampold, B. E. (2018). A new therapy for each patient: Evidence-based relationships and responsiveness. *Journal of Clinical Psychology*. https://doi.org/10.1002/jclp.22678

Orlinsky, D. E., & Rønnestad, M. H. (2005). *How psychotherapists develop: A study of therapeutic work and professional development*. American Psychological Association.

Orlinsky, D. E., Schofield, M. J., Schroder, T., & Kazantzis, N. (2011). Utilization of personal therapy by psychotherapists: A practice-friendly review and a new study. *Journal of Clinical Psychology, 67*(8), 828–842. https://doi.org/10.1002/jclp.20821

Prasko, J., Ociskova, M., Abeltina, M., Krone, I., Kantor, K., Vanek, J., Slepecky, M., Minarikova, K., Mozny, P., Piliarova, M., & Bite, I. (2023). The importance of self-experience and self-reflection in training of cognitive behavioral therapy. *Neuroendocrinology Letters, 44*(3), 152–163.

Rocco, D., Gennaro, A., Filugelli, L., Squarcina, P., & Antonelli, E. (2019). Key factors in psychotherapy training: An analysis of trainers', trainees' and psychotherapists' points of view. *Research in Psychotherapy, 22*(3), 415. https://doi.org/10.4081/ripppo.2019.415. PMID: 32913816; PMCID: PMC7451323.

Safran, J. D. & Muran, J. C. (2019). Teoria e pratica dell'alleanza terapeutica.

Salvatore, G. (2023). *La Vergogna del terapeuta. Da nucleo di sofferenza a fattore di cura*. Raffaello Cortina Editore.

Schneider, K., & Rees, C. (2012). Evaluation of a combined cognitive behavioural therapy and interpersonal process group in the psychotherapy training of clinical psychologists: Evaluation of psychotherapy training. *Australian Psychologist, 47*, 137–146.

Scott, J., Yap, K., Bunch, K., Haarhoff, B., Perry, H., & Bennett-Levy, J. (2021). Should personal practice be part of cognitive behaviour therapy training? Results from two self-practice/self-reflection cohort control pilot studies. *Clinical Psychology & Psychotherapy, 28*, 150–158.

Semerari, A. (2006). *Storia, teorie e tecniche della psicoterapia cognitiva*. Laterza.

Slade, A. (2008). The implications of attachment theory and research for adult psychotherapy: Research and clinical perspectives. In J. Cassidy & P. R. Shaver (Eds.), *Handbook of attachment: Theory, research, and clinical applications* (pp. 762–783). Guilford Press.

Spagnuolo Lobb, M., Sciacca, F., Iacono Isidoro, S., & Di Nuovo, S. (2022). The Therapist's intuition and responsiveness: What makes the difference between expert and in training gestalt psychotherapists. *European Journal of Investigation in Health, Psychology and Education, 12*(12), 1842–1851. https://doi.org/10.3390/ejihpe12120129. PMID: 36547030; PMCID: PMC9777848.

Stern, D. N. (2004). *The present moment: In psychotherapy and everyday life*. W W Norton & Co.

Strauß, B., & Taeger, D. (2021). *Untersuchungen zur „Wirkung" von Selbsterfahrung in der Psychotherapieausbildung – Ein systematisches Review* [Effects of personal therapy during psychotherapy training – a Systematic Review]. Psychotherapie, Psychosomatik, medizinische Psychologie. Advance online publication.

Talia, A., Taubner, S., & Miller-Bottome, M. (2019). Advances in research on attachment-related psychotherapy processes: Seven teaching points for trainees and supervisors. *Research in Psychotherapy,* 22(3), 405. https://doi.org/10.4081/ripppo.2019.405. PMID: 32913812; PMCID: PMC7451314.

Teasdale, J. D. (1999). Multi-level theories of cognition–emotion relations. In T. Dalgleish & M. J. Power (Eds.), *Handbook of cognition and emotion* (pp. 665–681).

Tomasello, M. (1999). *The cultural origins of human cognition.* Harvard University Press.

Troop, N. A., Allan, S., Serpell, L., & Treasure, J. L. (2008). Shame in women with a history of eating disorders. *European Eating Disorder Review,* 16, 480–488.

Way, C., Lamers, C., & Rickard, R. (2019). An unavoidable bump: A meta-synthesis of psychotherapists' experiences of navigating therapy while pregnant. *Research in Psychotherapy,* 22(3), 386. https://doi.org/10.4081/ripppo.2019.386. PMID: 32913808; PMCID: PMC7453161.

Weiss, R. (1982) Attachment in adult life. In C. M. Parkes, & J. Stevenson Hinde (a cura di) (Eds.), *The place of attachment in human behavior.* Tavistock.

Ying Zhang, Lili Shi, Jing Wei, Armin Hartmann, Rainer Leonhart, Markus Bassler, & Kurt Fritzsche. (2022). Perceived professional development of Chinese psychotherapy trainees: A pilot study. *Research in Psychotherapy,* 25, 229–238.

Part VI
Evidence-Based Techniques

Interweaving Techniques and Therapeutic Relationship for the Treatment of Personality Disorders

Antonella Centonze, Tiziana Passarella, Raffaele Popolo, Paolo Ottavi, and Giancarlo Dimaggio

1 Introduction

Despite the proven efficacy of psychotherapy (Lambert, 2013; Muran et al., 2021), there is much room for improvement: Many patients, in fact, do not benefit (30–40%) and many drop out (20%, see Lambert, 2010; Swift & Greenberg, 2015). One way to improve efficacy and reduce dropout is to pay attention to adjusting the alliance between patient and therapist (Muran et al., 2021). In efficacy studies, the alliance has been described as an "integrative variable par excellence" and a "common factor" (Wampold & Imel, 2015). A "second generation" of alliance research now aims to study the repair of ruptures (Flückiger et al., 2018, 2020; Horvath et al., 2011; Horvath & Symonds, 1991; Martin et al., 2000). Breakups have been broadly defined as any disagreement about how the patient and therapist work together (e.g., on cognitive and emotional exploration tasks in session, exercises during sessions, and experiments between sessions) and to what end (Safran & Muran, 1998, 2000, 2006).

Alliance ruptures can be signaled in session by the presence of markers: Muran et al. (2021) distinguish them into markers of withdrawal and confrontation: the former include movements away, avoidance, and movements toward isolation, such as keeping quiet or changing the subject, trying not to do an in-session exercise, or homework. Withdrawal markers can also include actions that are distant from one's own desires and aimed at pleasing others, thus defining withdrawals as efforts to preserve a bond with someone, to keep the peace, or to gain their approval. As for confrontational markers, they are defined as movements against the other, movements that involve aggression or control, such as criticism or manipulation.

In addition to interpersonal markers, ruptures can also be defined in terms of intrapersonal markers: These countertransferential experiences, that is, therapist's

A. Centonze (✉) · T. Passarella · R. Popolo · P. Ottavi · G. Dimaggio
Centro di Terapia Metacognitiva Interpersonale, Rome, Italy

reactions to the patient—such as anxiety, anger, despair, guilt, shame, competitiveness, boredom, and seduction—are emotional experiences that, like a compass, can indicate where the therapist is in relation to his or her patient at a certain time (Muran et al., 2021).

Working on the therapeutic relationship, however, is not easy: Several studies have shown how patients may be reluctant to disclose negative feelings about the therapist or therapy and how therapists may have difficulty acknowledging patients' negative feelings (Eubanks et al., 2021; Hill, 2010), as well as their own, making it difficult to metacommunicate about the relationship when necessary. The overall results of these works indicate an association between good relationship functioning and good treatment outcome (Horvath et al., 2011; Lambert & Ogles, 2004; Muran et al., 2018) although it seems more effective when the sample includes fewer patients with personality disorders (Eubanks et al., 2018). Therefore, although the therapeutic relationship is a crucial factor in treatment, it is necessary to address other aspects to increase its effectiveness, particularly in patients with personality disorders (PD) to whom this chapter is devoted. Indeed, in recent years, experiential techniques are being used effectively as a central working modality with these patients, although these have a strong impact on the therapeutic relationship.

Among the empirically supported treatments for patients with PD or complex trauma, some approaches make heavy use of experiential techniques, among them, Emotion Focused Therapy (Greenberg, 2002), Compassion Focused Therapy (Gilbert, 2010), Schema-Therapy (Arntz & Jacob, 2013), EMDR (Shapiro & Forrest, 2001), Dialectical Behavior Therapy for complex trauma (Bohus et al., 2020), and Metacognitive Interpersonal Therapy (TMI; Dimaggio et al., 2013, 2019b). All of these approaches use techniques such as: role-playing, guided imagination and rewriting, two-chairing, and bodywork. Consistent with what developmental psychology, neuroscience, and experimental psychopathology have shown, most maladaptive cognitive-affective processes also unfold at a level that can be called: implicit, tacit, procedural, unconscious (Bargh, 2017), and embodied. This, therefore, requires modes of intervention that go beyond simple cognitive attributions: working experientially becomes an important factor for change. Our hypothesis is that experiential work is effective in modifying the automatic, unconscious, and implicit part of maladaptive interpersonal patterns. However, it is necessary, in order to make it fruitful in patients with PD, to monitor its impact on the therapeutic relationship. Proposing to the patient the use of a technique or performing it after agreeing to it can in the first instance generate relational micro-fractures that then need to be monitored and repaired; in parallel it can generate positive changes in the relationship, making it more intimate, deep and solid. Attention to relational work is crucial because if the therapist does not pay attention to and carefully monitor the relationship with these patients, the inevitable fractures will not be repaired and this would make it difficult to apply techniques. The consequence would be that therapy could not benefit from the effect of the techniques, and therapeutic change would be slowed or hindered.

Therefore, in order to make the work on the therapeutic relationship and experiential work with PD patients synergistic, it is necessary to take into account a number of specific factors that characterize the psychopathology of these patients.

2 The Impact of Personality Pathology on the Therapeutic Relationship

PDs are common in most clinical settings, and it is well known how their presence can slow down the treatment process or facilitate dropout. Suffering in this type of disorder is the result of problematic expectations about interpersonal relationships, where patients predict that others will frustrate some of their basic desires. The impact of these predictions influences the treatment process and affects the outcome.

TMI is a recently manualized (Dimaggio et al., 2007) model of therapy for treating patients with PD (Dimaggio et al., 2013, 2019a). To better understand the complexity of working with these patients, it is necessary to briefly describe the aspects that generate and maintain psychopathology.

The first level of difficulty concerns impaired metacognition (Carcione et al., 2016; Dimaggio & Lysaker, 2015; Semerari et al., 2003, 2014), Metacognition includes skills by which people: (a) recognize mental states and attribute them to themselves or others; (b) think, reflect, and reason about their own mental states (self-reflexivity) and others' states (understanding others' minds); (c) use this knowledge and reflect to make decisions, solve psychological and interpersonal problems, and master subjective suffering (mastery, Carcione et al., 2011). Conversely, the better the metacognition, the stronger the therapeutic alliance, which, in turn, by facilitating experiential work, affects the outcome of therapy. This, therefore, makes metacognition a therapeutic goal in therapy with these patients (Dimaggio et al., 2019a). Individuals diagnosed with PD report significant difficulties in recognizing and naming the emotions they feel. They have difficulty describing their thoughts and cognitive antecedents that elicit affective states or social behaviors. For example, they may report avoiding meeting with friends but are unable to tell the therapist that they have done so because, for example, they may be ashamed and unconsciously be inclined to avoid exposing themselves and recounting their internal states or performing any experiential exercise.

Self-reflexivity includes monitoring, that is, the ability to distinguish and name a range of thoughts and affects and describe them with different nuances, for example, "I am sad because I feel abandoned" instead of "I am tense." A patient with poor monitoring, for example, might feel "fatigued" in session and not understand the deeper meaning such as, "I am ashamed of my frailties in front of the therapist whom I experience as judgmental." Without this understanding, he might come to feel that therapy is too tiring for him and decide to leave.

Self-reflexivity also includes differentiation, that is, the ability to view one's ideas as hypotheses and not objective descriptions of external reality, particularly in the relational domain. It includes the realization that we sometimes make sense of relationships on the basis of our own learned tendencies. If we apply it to the relationship with the clinician in practice it means, for example, going from "I think the therapist will belittle me and that's a given" to "I think he will belittle me but I'm not sure. I realize that throughout my history I have learned that if I do something my way, I will be harshly criticized." This is a differentiation in which the patient moves from "My belief is true" versus "My belief is learned." Another type of differentiation is possible through access to healthy aspects of schemas (Dimaggio et al., 2013). The patient goes from "It is always true" to "In some cases, I see myself and others in a more benevolent way." In a state of nondifferentiation, the patient keeps repeating to himself, "I'm a mess. I have always been a failure." When, on the other hand, the patient can notice that in session or during homework he has experienced different, valued images of himself in front of the perceived supportive therapist, differentiation is increased. The possibility of also noticing during an exercise that different images of Self and Other coexist in the patient, some more benevolent than others, brings an increase in agency: "I can see myself and others more benevolently, I have power and agency over my mental state."

A second order of problems in working with these patients concerns the application of the relational patterns of patients with PD to the relationship with the therapist: The maladaptive interpersonal pattern applies to the clinical relationship (Dimaggio et al., 2019b), and if the therapist somehow confirms that he or she is consistent with negative expectations (by appearing directive, critical, neglectful, obstructive, etc.) the relationship may go into an impasse.

Interpersonal schemata (Dimaggio et al., 2013, 2019b; Crits-Christoph et al., 1990) are used to give meaning to interpersonal exchanges and to predict whether others will fulfil some basic desires, for example, to be approved, cared for, loved, helped to explore, included, etc. Schemas are formed mainly during developmental history, and through them, humans have quick tools to decode communicative signals, which function as maps for their social action (Dimaggio et al., 2013, 2019b). Interpersonal schemas are built around an evolutionarily selected set of motivations (Gilbert, 1989; Lichtenberg, 1989; Liotti & Gilbert, 2011; Panksepp, 1998), namely: (a) attachment, that is, the need to be protected, cared for, and to feel safe and nurtured (Bowlby, 1969); (b) social rank, which defines hierarchies of access to limited resources within a group; (c) autonomy-independence and exploration, that is, the drive to act according to one's preferences and interests (Panksepp & Biven, 2012) and to explore the environment, both physically and intellectually, in order to find resources and new solutions to problems; (d) nurturing, which is providing assistance to those who are suffering or in distress; (e) group inclusion, which is the need to belong (Baumeister & Leary, 1995; Lichtenberg, 1989); (f) sexuality, which is mating aims combined also with the need to form long-term relationships; and (g) cooperation, aimed at achieving shared goals once each individual's role and tasks are defined (Tomasello et al., 2005).

The main elements of schemas are:

(a) nuclear self-images underlie each specific desire/motivation. For example, when social rank is active, the person may be dominated by a self-idea of unworthiness, alongside which coexists a self-idea of self as worthy, which, however, appears difficult to access consciousness in this type of patient; (b) the other's response, which has more than one facet. The dominant representation in personality disorders is negative, for example, in the social rank domain, the other is described and perceived as strongly critical, or dominate. An alternative representation is also present here, in which the other is seen as benevolent and valued in the social rank domain. However, even if these benevolent representations are present, the person is less likely to notice them and interpret the communicative behaviors of the other as manifestations of their existence and take them as true; (c) the response of self to the response of the other. This aspect includes cognitions, affects, and somatic reactions and usually rises to confirm the negative self-image.

For example, a patient driven by social rank hopes to be appreciated but expects the other to criticize or ignore her if she shows her qualities in certain situations. Painful memories may appear in her mind where her father criticized her harshly, making her feel incapable. The memories trigger suffering that is sustained in the mind by a fundamental idea of herself as unworthy and unable to respond. When preyed upon by these ideas about herself and others, the patient enters a mental state of sadness, loneliness, shame, low self-esteem, and so on. At the same time, she will feel deprived of energy and decrease the tendency to engage in pleasant or creative activities. Since she anticipates that she has only marginal hopes that the other person will appreciate her, she will withdraw by being lonely, emotionally and socially. This coupling of negative images of self and other, for example, I feel inadequate while expecting that the other will judge me negatively, is itself a path to suffering.

The clinical relationship will not be exempt from this pattern: the patient herself may easily fall prey to the negative self-image in relation to the therapist. She may hope, while recounting a personal story or while performing an exercise in session, to be appreciated by the therapist, but with ease, she will read the therapist's interventions through the lens of the pattern. The therapist will seem critical or not validating enough or worse dismissive, regardless of the actual exchange. The selective focus is on the signs that confirm the maladaptive schema, within which the patient as usual will feel incapable and inadequate in the presence of others who consider her not up to par, etc.

Another aspect of DP psychopathology (Dimaggio et al., 2019b) is maladaptive coping. When these patients are about to experience emotions that they are unable to regulate, such as shame, guilt, anxiety, or sadness, they adopt a variety of strategies aimed at minimizing discomfort. A frequent mechanism is avoidance at any level: behavioral, cognitive, and affective. To self-protect themselves, they do not ask a partner for a date, they do not meet with peers, they do not try to do the things they would like to do, that is, they do not perform an exercise in session. When they are about to experience negative emotions, they distract themselves, such as by playing video games, surfing the Internet, or dealing with other topics, to the point that they become confused about what they were experiencing. Or, when they realize that some interactions are distressing, their thoughts move elsewhere and they are easily distracted and unable to concentrate, even in session. Avoidance is not the only maladaptive strategy: patients with personality disorders may resort to perfectionism, hoping that others will not notice their mistakes, or they may submit and tend to please the other, or they may become paralyzed, avoiding asserting their own point of view.

Other strategies are built in the cognitive domain and include various forms of repetitive thinking, for example, worrying and rumination, aimed at trying to figure out the causes of suffering and possibly solve them, which, however, results in endless thinking effort that does not solve the problem and further worsens mood and reduces self-esteem, cognitive efficiency, and the ability to feel pleasure and motivation (McLaughlin et al., 2007; Nolen-Hoeksema et al., 2008). The person becomes trapped in a sequence of thoughts, such as "Is it better to stay home and risk boredom, to go out with friends and risk humiliation? But if I go out, what should I wear? Will I be able to tell any jokes? But my jokes are poor, so they will notice that I am stupid and then refuse to include me again."

For example, a patient moved by a maladaptive schema within the autonomy system sees himself as stuck and the other as constricting and overbearing. If the clinician proposes a behavioral exercise to him between sessions, even though it has been agreed upon within the therapeutic contract, he will easily tend to read this task and the therapeutic relationship as constrictive, with respect to which he will adopt his usual coping, such as angry protest or avoid performing the exercise out of rebellion. These oppositional behaviors, if read as coping activated by the patient's maladaptive pattern, will be able to help the clinician easily and quickly highlight the activation of the dysfunctional pattern at that precise moment. At that point, the focus of work will shift from experiential exercise to reflection on the therapeutic relationship, as we will show in the clinical case. Usually, these operations increase metacognition, consolidate the working alliance, and facilitate the emergence of autobiographical memories more easily.

Another aspect concerns the clinician's own fear of using the techniques with these patients, as he fears damaging them, invading them, invalidating them, etc., thus risking compromising the working alliance that is already so difficult to consolidate.

3 The Experiential Techniques in TMI

In Metacognitive Interpersonal Therapy, we use experiential techniques from the earliest moments of therapy (Centonze et al., 2020; Dimaggio et al., 2019b) with a specific purpose: to allow better access to the patient's internal states and to arrive more effectively at case formulation: we call this dynamic assessment (Dimaggio et al., 2019b). In TMI we make use of different types of techniques that we use singly or in combination, such as guided imagination (Hackmann et al., 2011), role-playing and two-chair play (Moreno & Moreno, 1975/2012; Greenberg, 2002; Perls 1951), bodily and sensorimotor exercises (Lowen, 1971; Ogden & Fisher, 2015), and behavioral experiments (Dimaggio et al., 2013).

Experiential techniques serve several functions, which, schematized, are:

1. Enhancing metacognitive monitoring (Semerari et al., 2003) to increase awareness of affective experiences and helping patients to recognize and name them.
2. Enhancing agency over mental states and guiding patients to discover that they have power and control (agency) over what they think and feel.
3. Promoting differentiation, that is, awareness that one's idea of oneself and others is subjective, related to one's perspective, and can therefore be modifiable.
4. Facilitating access to healthy self-images. This refers to gaining awareness of having experienced positive experiences within which one has created benevolent self-images, such as "lovable," "worthy," "strong," and so on. Usually, the more severe the patients' difficulties, the poorer the awareness of the existence of such images, and the lower the ability to call them to consciousness and use them to deal with problematic tasks or interactions and ground a firm and benevolent sense of self.
5. Rewriting some episodic memories that exemplify the interpersonal pattern, both remote and recent, ranging from negative childhood experiences with a caregiver to episodes of social exclusion in school age to recent problems with important people such as partners, colleagues, and friends. The rewriting intervention serves a central function in TMI (Centonze et al., 2020; Dimaggio et al., 2019b). When we ask people to write different endings to scenes re-experienced in imagination or to adopt different body postures when facing problematic relational interactions, we are helping the person to perform a rewriting of maladaptive interpersonal patterns, particularly in their procedural/embodied component.

At this stage, we also ask the patient to act in coherence with the wish that is active at that moment (Dimaggio et al., 2019b). For example, we ask patients to persist in pursuing wishes related to autonomy, playfulness, and exploration. Or in a situation where they need help, we invite them to actively ask for it without letting the schema-related prediction that the Other will not be available stop them. Or even when they are driven by social rank, we invite them to persist in their efforts, staying in touch with their worthy self-image instead of giving up because they position the Other in the critical and invalidating role. At this stage, we also ask the patient to curb maladaptive coping behaviors. Patients will then try to refrain from perfectionism, social avoidance, complacency, and so on. Based on these interventions, new and more specific emotions and thoughts usually appear, gradually increasing patients' awareness of their inner world.

Although they are a valuable modality for exploring the patient's inner world, the techniques may, however, contribute to generating alliance ruptures where their proposal to the patient may activate the patient's schemata precisely within the context of the relationship with the clinician; reading and repairing these difficulties constitutes an important therapeutic opportunity to intervene directly and "live" on patients' schemata (Centonze et al., 2021a). If the clinician succeeds in repairing the rupture, the patient may realize that he or she sees the relationship with the clinician through the lens of the schema and the possibility opens up to read the relationship through different lenses in which the nuclear self-image is more positive and the other is seen as benevolent.

4 The Intersection of Techniques and the Therapeutic Relationship

The main objective of this chapter is to highlight how the proposal of an exercise in session may lead the patient, consistent with his maladaptive schema, to see exercises as situations in which negative self-images are reactivated in the face of another, the therapist, perceived as cold or critical or overbearing, etc. Often overlooked, however, is the opposite effect of the techniques: Through their use, the patient can experience positive, adaptive, functional relational modes in the relationship with the therapist. This is an aspect that is often overlooked in the clinic, since there is a prevailing concern about the risk that the use of techniques may undermine the relationship, whereas it is also important to emphasize that techniques can consolidate it or create new positive states.

In summary, the proposed use of experiential techniques can have an impact on the therapeutic relationship of three types: (a) it generates a temporary rupture that once repaired allows the patient to feel the relationship consolidated and with new and beneficial aspects as a result of the use of the technique; (b) it improves the therapeutic relationship and enhances the clinical work; and (c) it generates a prolonged rupture that requires commitment to be repaired.

(a) *The technique generates a temporary rupture that once repaired allows the patient to feel the relationship consolidated and with new and beneficial aspects.*

The patient with a maladaptive pattern driven by social rank will experience, for example, the proposal of an in-session experiential exercise or a behavioral experiment between sessions as a performance, will enter an agonistic setup experiencing the clinician's proposal as a performance in which to strive to do the best, or will tend to give up, as he is assailed by the fear of not being capable. Images of other patients who will do the task better than him may surface in his mind, and above all he will represent the therapist as a critical and demanding figure ready to misjudge him. The patient may avoid the exercise or may perform it in a forced manner, suppressing the real affections that the task arouses in him.

When the patient is moved by the idea that if he needs care, he will find no one to take him in, clinical work and experiential techniques may activate in him a sense of helplessness against which the technique appears to be a futile attempt to get better. To this the patient may react in various ways and adopt various copings: He may become sad and shut down, resigning himself to the inescapable fate that the technique will not work; he may avoid the work or become angry about it. He may perceive the therapist as absent or unreliable with respect to whom he will therefore feel distrust, distancing himself.

Proposing an exercise to a patient driven by a maladaptive schema within the autonomy system may activate a sense of compulsion in him, and the patient may refuse or become angry at the clinician's proposal. This patient sees himself as "hindered," always blocked by others experienced as bullies, for example, and applies this to the therapeutic relationship as well.

There will be instances when patients will adopt coping that is more usual to them even in session: For example, a patient who is used to pleasing others by not showing his true feelings may please the therapist in order to avoid negative judgment, for example, and thus feel inadequate. He will perform the required exercise wishing not to do it but instead imposing on himself the opposite. Relational markers will be able to signal the presence of a complacent attitude and help the clinician who catches them to easily and quickly highlight the activation of the dysfunctional pattern at that precise moment. Exploration of what is happening in the here and now of the therapeutic relationship will allow these patients to recognize their emotional reactions, explore their internal states, or begin to differentiate by reconnecting their response to their pattern, reactivating autobiographical memories in which they experienced the same reaction, the same feeling of self in front of another experienced as constricting or cold or judgmental.

The therapist attentive to relational markers will then be able to explore what is happening, and such a process of metacommunication will aim to increase the patient's awareness of the internal world and, by preventing fractures in the relationship, will help the therapist to pass the relational test and consolidate the working alliance.

At that point, the working focus will shift from experiential exercise to reflection on the therapeutic relationship, as we will show in the clinical case. Usually, these operations increase metacognition, consolidate the working alliance, and facilitate the emergence of autobiographical memories more easily.

(b) *The technique fosters therapeutic relationship and clinical work.*

Within a maladaptive attachment-based schema, the patient is driven by a desire to feel helped, cared for, driven by the self-image of being fragile, weak, or alone in the face of another seen as absent, neglectful, or too weak to care. Instead, the patient hopes to find someone ready to care for him, although he thinks this is unlikely. If the patient comes to the session agitated and the therapist helps him, for example, to regain calmness through regulating exercises such as slow breathing and grounding (Lowen, 1971), the therapist becomes the other who provides care when the patient needs it. The patient understands experientially, in the here and now of the session, that the therapist considers him worthy of care and lovable, unlike his schema, the patient explores this perception and the image of himself as worthy of care finds consolidation here. The same patient in performing an imaginative exercise might relive intense pain related to the episode he is reenacting.

If the therapist, unlike the patient's predictions, is calm with respect to his pain, if he shows himself to be strong and solid in not giving up the task, in not giving up the technique for fear of hurting the patient, it will help him to experience something different, such as: If I am scared, anxious and sad, the other person does not get scared in turn, but remains calm with respect to my emotions, shows himself to be solid, and that he does not give up. This makes me feel worthy of care and safe. At that point, the patient may discover that there are positive, benevolent images of himself and the other that are often obscured by negative ones in which he sees himself as worthy of care and the other as capable of helping him. Thus, more than the use of the technique, it will be the relationship between patient and therapist that is activated around the technique that will be central. If the therapist became frightened of the excess of pain, giving up the technique would, for example, lead to the reactivation of the patient's maladaptive pattern: If I am in pain, the other is frightened of my pain, does not help me, and I feel lonely, unhelpful, and sad.

Within a maladaptive pattern activated by social rank, the patient may view the other (the therapist) as critical, dominant, and devaluing, being guided by an image of himself as inept and inadequate while hoping to be appreciated and valued. There is, however, an "image of adequacy" within him but it is not accessible, and the hope of seeing it confirmed is active, but the patient does not think it likely: Experimenting with a rehearsal between sessions (e.g., a behavioral reactivation exercise based on playing sports) and finding the therapist in session ready to welcome the experience carried out with an attitude of appreciation, regardless of the result, not performance-oriented but curious, will allow the consolidation of the positive self-image. The patient will get to explore the feeling of confronting a validating other, and it will be possible, if the therapist is shrewd, to explore what this activates in him. The patient will likely see himself as adequate, amused, and strong if the therapist leads him to dwell not on the miles traveled but on how worthwhile it was to try and the pleasure of doing so. It is useful in such cases to help the patient also feel in the body the "embodied" feeling of being valid, acknowledging it and inviting him to "photograph" it so that he can recall it whenever he feels he is reactivating the maladaptive pattern, thus enhancing the differentiation process (Centonze et al., 2021b). The therapist will have to continuously transition so that the patient can become aware of these aspects. The working alliance at that point is strengthened, metacognition improves, and the therapeutic work benefits. It becomes easier for autobiographical memories to emerge and easier for experiential techniques to be adopted in session, welcomed with less and less resistance.

When the patient is moved by a maladaptive schema activated by the desire for autonomy/exploration, he may represent the other as hindering, feeling blocked or turned off, describing himself as powerless, constricted, and not entitled to be autonomous. If the therapist, through in-session or between-session exercises, helps the patient to accommodate the need and, for example, to go on a trip, to plan a change of job (through guided imagination, for example), he will position himself as supportive toward the need for autonomy: for autonomy and support its image as "free and in right" will help the patient to feel not constricted, stuck but free. The patient will then move from "every time I want to do something I feel a block and understand that the other is never supportive" to "I feel that my therapist is supportive and I understand that I can feel free and in law."

(c) *The technique generates a prolonged rupture that the therapist must spend time repairing.*

It sometimes happens that the proposal of the technique leads the patient to refuse to carry it out since it is read, as mentioned above, through the lens of maladaptive schemas. The patient may say he is against it, is uncomfortable, say he does not like certain things, and that he prefers "just talking." He may express this rejection with shame, but also with aggression. The therapist may in turn feel guilty or inadequate.

The patient also may become frightened at the suggestion of the technique and arouse protective feelings in the therapist, who with the idea that he does not want to make him feel bad may act an avoidance, giving up his work purpose. The therapist fears a rupture but in fact fuels a rupture since avoidance may lead to:

- Not proceeding in the direction of the agreed therapeutic goals
- Feeding the maladaptive pattern through an unconscious disabling attitude
- Missing the opportunity to explore in the here and now of the session the patient's emotions and patterns in action

These situations are often at the root of clinical experiences characterized by impasses in therapeutic work, with both parties feeling that they are "going around in circles" even for sessions, risking a dropout. It sometimes happens that the therapist may experience negative feelings before meeting with the patient, feel anxious, or feel a desire to not meet that person. These are markers indicative of a prolonged rupture that deserve attention.

In this context, the therapist should refrain from using techniques until the rupture is repaired. It is necessary to explore what is happening in the patient's internal world as well as pay attention to the patterns that are activated in the therapist. How the patient is constructing the therapist and how he or she sees himself or herself become the central purpose of the exploration, trying to make the patient understand that different things are happening in the "real" therapeutic relationship than what the patient feels through the lens of the schema. The therapist will have to help the patient understand that what he or she hears is an expression of his or her internal world, since it is similar to what has already transpired in relationships in his or her life before. This is far from easy and requires a shift in the focus of the work and also a redefinition of the therapeutic contract, which might shift, for example, from working on symptoms to working on relational patterns.

We will show through a clinical case how the use of experiential techniques creates beneficial effects in clinical work and on other occasions may have generated ruptures that the therapist readily repaired with beneficial effects on the process of change.

Gloria is 30 years old and comes to therapy for Panic Attack Disorder, asking to be helped to decrease the fear she feels on all fronts and be safer. Gloria asks the therapist that she wants to feel pride, strength, and a sense of dignity and face the male world that terrifies her. In the course of therapy, it will become clear that Gloria not only suffers from panic attacks but on the personality level she suffers from a Dependent Personality Disorder and has borderline and narcissistic traits.

Gloria is a painter, and at the moment, when she begins to be known through fine work, she is hired by a famous French ceramist to participate, with themed paintings, in one of her pottery exhibitions. She moves to France for a time, where she sees the possibility of fulfilment of her desire to succeed in a competitive professional world. She rejects other proposals and puts all her energy into the success of this project. She soon discovers that the client does not respect her creativity but imposes on her a style that does not match her own. At first, she tries to comply by going along with the demands, but it is not enough. The ceramist begins to dislike her work, first criticizing and yelling at her in private, then beginning to insult and humiliate her in public. Gloria feels sadness, fear, and shame wants to disappear and reacts by paralyzing herself and increasing her efforts to please the patron in vain. As a result, Gloria sees herself as incapable and a failure and experiences intense anxiety, depression, and shame. During the exhibition, she notices that her works are met with subtly derisive looks of contempt. Two art critics attack her in two separate articles published in French national newspapers. Gloria comes out of this with a feeling of defeat and psychic shattering.

After this failure, she does not know where to start to think about the future: She has no romantic relationship; with her family of origin prevails a sense of relational distance that Gloria has cultivated over the years and that her father, mother, and brother do not seem interested in bridging; she does not know whether to return to Italy or stay in France; she does not understand what to start investing in again, and she no longer knows if painting is what she wants. From there shortly panic attacks begin, leading her to seek psychotherapy.

In her life story is a melancholy, idealistic father who pursues his social and political ideals in a passive, recriminatory manner and from whom she feels, in her words, "unseen … he is so caught up in himself that I disappear." She describes her father as critical and dismissive of her and the world, distant and closed in his ivory tower. In front of her father, she perceives herself as invisible, unimportant, and inadequate and feels a strong sense of loneliness and deep sadness. She describes her mother as passive and weak, unable to stand up to her father when he despises or belittles her, with a tendency to express her grievances covertly and with moral blackmail, and extremely interested in her social image. Gloria reports that her mother never respected her for who she really was and never supported her autonomy.

As a result, it is clear from her words how both parents contributed to building in her mind a nuclear image of herself as lonely, invisible, and wrong. In her adolescent memoirs, she reports feeling rejected and mocked by men, never living up to their expectations. She had her first romantic relationship at age 25 with an abusive man from whom she suffered verbal assault, contempt, and severe bullying during sexual intercourse. Her accounts show that he humiliated and belittled her, even insulting her, and that during intercourse, for example, he would block her by pressing her knees to her chest while penetrating her with objects with which he caused her pain.

5 Case Formulation

Through the analysis of multiple narrative episodes reported by Gloria in session and through a joint work of reflection on the episodes themselves, Gloria and the therapist observe how family experiences first, and sentimental ones later, have generated and crystallized her interpersonal patterns: The desire that seems to orient Gloria is that of autonomy, and from these, other motivational systems are activated.

More specifically, Gloria has learned that if she follows her own path, if she expresses herself, if she manifests what she feels and thinks:

- The other ignores her, does not support her, rejects her, and leaves and the self-image that is elicited has to do with perceiving herself as alone, invisible, and transparent and is accompanied by sadness, pain, emptiness, shutdown, paralysis, anaesthesia in the belly area, and a sense of death.
- The other attacks her, blocks her, is violent, and activates a vulnerable, fragile, "prey" self-image, accompanied by an emotional and somatic experience of terror, alarm, crushing, constriction, helplessness, and paralysis. In this case, from the system of exploration, Gloria transitions into that of seeking safety.
- Facing the violent other and feeling in danger, vulnerable, and fragile, she perceives herself inept in coping with that situation and in need of help. However, perceiving the other as dangerous or distracted or incapable of giving care, she further perceives herself in danger and helpless, with no way out, and reacts by stiffening her body in an attempt not to let her suffering show and choosing not to ask for help but to always fend for herself. In this case, Gloria moves from the safety-seeking system to the attachment system;
- The other criticizes and despises her and elicits an inadequate, substandard, incapable, and failed self-image. This self-image is accompanied by emotions of anxiety, sadness, and shame. In this case, from the autonomy-related system, the patient transitions into the rank motivational system.

In order to get out of the lonely and transparent self-image and put an end to the emotions of sadness, emptiness, shutdown, and paralysis Gloria enacts behaviors aimed at making herself invisible in turn, renounces showing herself, activates processes of depressive rumination through which she constantly self-condemns herself, and further closes in on herself feeling wrong and unworthy.

In order to cope with the vulnerable, prey, inept, and unhelpful self-image; the emotions of terror and helplessness; and the feelings of alarm, crushing, and paralysis, not only does Gloria give up expressing what she feels but she also becomes compliant: In order to appease the other, she submits, lets the other decide what is best for her, and at the same time gives up asking for help.

To cope with the inadequate and incapable self-image, she hyper-invests on performance and succeeding, she broods, stiffens, closes herself off, and shies away from situations that challenge her in order to feel safe: "I put on armor and block action because it is reassuring."

Painting is a vehicle for expressing all the suffering Gloria feels invested in, but it is not a real means by which she is able to process it.

Within this reconstruction, it is also clarified how panic attacks are the symptom that emerges when, as a result of the activation of the fragile self-image, Gloria experiences anxiety and is frightened of the sensations related to this emotion.

6 Promotion of Change

At the beginning of therapy, Gloria feels welcomed but is very frightened by the figure of the therapist by whom she fears being harmed, judged, and rejected. In fact, when the therapist asks the patient to recount narrative episodes in which she experienced sadness or fear and panic to explore them together, Gloria is frightened by the request and asks not to talk about it. The therapist invites the patient to verbalize how she feels, and Gloria states that she is afraid to open up, that she is hurt, harmed by the therapist, and thus in danger, vulnerable, and powerless; Gloria also states that she fears being judged and deemed unworthy as well as unfit for psychotherapy. The therapist at first explores these issues in relation to the retrieval of associated more recent and older memories present in the patient's life history. This allows Gloria to become aware of how fear of being harmed and judged, as well as the tendency to run away from the situation, are central themes in her own life. In light of this, when the therapist proposes to explore the physiological and bodily correlates that characterize the themes of vulnerability and unworthiness, the patient accepts although still very frightened. Through a mindfulness practice, the therapist asks the patient to explore the sensations and emotions present in the body at that moment in relation to fear, and at that moment Gloria's mental state changes: "I feel stronger...the firm and warm voice and the fact that for the first time someone descends with me into my pain without using it but in a gentle and strong way, holding me and not judging me...makes me feel stronger."

At this point, Gloria and the therapist observe with even greater clarity how Gloria's fear was: on the one hand feeling prey and vulnerable in the hands of a "ruthless tormentor" who could hurt her voluntarily or an "incapable being" who was unable to approach her pain as he was too self-absorbed and unable to help her; on the other hand, feeling judged for whatever she felt and thus feeling wrong and inept. The therapist, by her standing firm on the proposition of getting in touch with the pain in the body, and by her constant validation of what Gloria was feeling, is experienced as a strong, helpful, and welcoming figure allowing the patient to have a first experience of a part of herself in which she, in turn, feels centered, strong, and right. The experiential technique fostered the emergence of a healthy relational experience that patient and therapist could talk about.

From this initial experience of accessing a positive self-image, all subsequent therapy work is focused, in addition to working on panic attacks from a cognitive-behavioral perspective, on identifying interpersonal patterns in different narrative episodes, rewriting painful scenes, exploring new and more functional parts of herself, and achieving autonomy goals. Gloria learns to recognize the activation of her own interpersonal patterns, to look at them as patterns and not as reality, and to regulate brooding as a factor in maintaining suffering.

Through the bodywork of activating and regulating procedural memories and by rescripting the images related to the memories underlying the interpersonal pattern, carried out through EMDR, sensorimotor, mindfulness, and gestalt techniques, the patient begins to perceive the body, to value her sensations and emotions, to affirm what she feels and thinks, and to act in line with her needs and desires.

Gloria begins to become autonomous in her work, carrying out projects in which she enjoys and expresses her creativity, selecting collaborators on the basis of mutual pleasure and support in working together, adjusting the drive to have to be perfect and please everyone, and distancing herself from the inner drive to get it done in the shortest possible time. She gets involved in romantic relationships, recognizes when men are emotionally unavailable, turns away from them, and begins to perceive herself as respectable and feel that there is a real possibility of experiencing an equal and exchangeable relationship with each other. A desire arises in her to understand what she really likes and follow her own aptitudes, and she begins to experiment with a range of activities, discovering a love of nature and a deep passion for scuba diving, which becomes her main hobby.

Gloria begins to perceive, albeit still on and off, the body as present, calm, and solid and accesses a strong, worthy, and lovable self-image.

At this time in therapy, interpersonal patterns, and thus procedural memories, still activate but do so with less intensity and are less pervasive. Hanging out with men who are more emotionally present and who respect her, she meets a man a little older than her, Giulio, who like her has a passion for painting and diving. During the more stable dating that ensues, in some episodes, the old patterns become active again.

An example of this is a particular episode reported by Gloria in session. The episode is interesting because in it, as a result of the use of body techniques, a rupture in the alliance is generated that, once repaired, will help Gloria first to increase awareness of her own patterns and then to rework them toward new access to healthy parts.

Gloria, 2 days before the session, receives confirmation that she can exhibit paintings in France. Upon hearing the news, she feels joy, elation, a sense of accomplishment, hope, and strength. She feels that she is about to go and do what she desires, and in her body, she feels a tendency to move to arrange for her departure. When that evening she informs Julius that she would be leaving 2 weeks from then, she is assailed by the fear that he will leave her; she feels lost and perceives herself to be alone, transparent, and wrong; she feels sadness, emptiness, and fear and begins to brood about the advisability of leaving. Moved by the desire to put an end to the emotions and feelings generated by the image of herself as lonely, transparent, and wrong, she begins to look for arguments aimed at convincing herself that not leaving is the best thing to do and tells herself that "after all, for the other person it is also right to make sacrifices." The consequence is that she struggles to trace within herself the desire to leave, which was originally crystal clear, and begins to feel a sense of shutdown.

She recognizes, however, that this is nothing more than her pattern and brings it to the session with a request to be helped to figure out what to do.

The therapist proposes that Gloria come to an understanding of what to do by exploring together, in a guided imagery practice, the emotions, bodily reactions, and interpersonal patterns that are activated by reentering the episode in which she communicates to Julius about the departure. Gloria agrees and, with her eyes closed, describes the scene in detail. Gloria is in the living room, sitting on the sofa, and Giulio is sitting next to her. It is dark outside and the light in the house is dim. As Gloria informs Giulio that the project has been accepted and she is about to leave, he caresses her and smiles at her. The patient feels the feelings of fear, sadness, and emptiness resurface; the therapist asks not to try to make them go away but to feel them and describe their physiological correlates. Gloria suddenly becomes rigid, refuses any intervention by the therapist, and expresses mild anger nonverbally. At this point, the therapist asks Gloria what she is feeling. Gloria pays attention to her own emotions for a few seconds and explains that she is angry because, she says, "she wants to treat me too fast…she's in too much of a hurry and I can't do it." Faced with the therapist's questions as she begins to explore and asks at what point the patient felt this hurry, Gloria responds that she perceived the therapist to be spaced out and irritated as she said she was exploring the physical sensations and not doing anything to try to make them go away. This episode with the therapist becomes a new scene to explore. Continuing to remain with her eyes closed, Gloria is asked to retrieve and describe the exact moment when she had the perception of hurry and irritation in the therapist and by what signs she had sensed these reactions. At first, Gloria describes the scene and talks about the therapist's tone of voice, then stops and explains, "No… actually she didn't do it… it's just that I don't want to let go of this part where I suffer because it makes me feel strong." The therapist does not understand, communicates this to Gloria, and asks her to describe in more detail what she is feeling. Gloria explains that she perceived the therapist as "harmful because if I feel my emotions I will end up healing and if I heal I will no longer have the armor that makes me feel strong." The therapist explores the feelings again and a memory emerges: Gloria stands in the center of the pottery and painting exhibition, now 2 years earlier, as she is mocked, criticized, and humiliated. As she observes the participants and hears their words, she perceives how in that moment she activated "an armor that makes me feel strong… if I remain silent and resist in the face of humiliation, it means I am strong and I feel strong."

Out of the guided imagination exercise, patient and therapist reconstruct all the interpersonal patterns that were activated during the practice. In the first one, which concerns the episode that happened at home 2 days before the session, while observing how Julius remains close and welcoming, Gloria imagining that she is leaving and thus realizing her desire for autonomy, predicts that Julius will reject this choice of hers by ending the relationship, she perceives herself as lonely and inconsistent and feels fear, sadness, and emptiness. To put an end to these painful emotions at that moment, she only wishes to give up what she desires and puts on the "armor" and stiffens, she stiffens and enters a state of momentary strength given by the forced renunciation of what she likes. When the therapist, on the other hand, invites her to let her emotions be present without doing anything to make them pass, she perceives the therapist as harmful in that she is paradoxically healing her, since this prevents her from adopting the coping (the armor) that she feels at that moment is her only way to perceive the mental state of strength by causing her to fall into the image of herself as vulnerable again, which she wants to avoid instead.

In the memory, Gloria recovers when she is humiliated during the exhibition, this aspect appears very clear: in front of the other, who mocks and humiliates her, Gloria feels inadequate and unworthy, feels emotions of sadness and shame, and manages to transit into a temporary state of strength through a dysfunctional mode of coping: She tries to "resist" and puts on the "armor," and in this way, she manages to access a strong self-image. However weak, transient, and a source of collateral problems, the state of strength that Gloria accesses through the armor is the state that allowed her to achieve goals in the past, never give up to the end what she wanted, and even to seek help in therapy.

Patient and therapist more precisely articulate the formulation of the therapeutic contract: the goal of therapy is to seek an internal state of stability, strength and consistency that will enable Gloria to achieve her goals and, thus, to realize the desire for autonomy that moves her. To get to this Gloria must give up the armor as a means of perceiving strength and stability and be willing to contact the negative emotions internal to the patterns in order to deal with them in new and more functional ways.

At this point, bodywork is resumed using a gestalt technique in which the therapist asks the patient to move the armor by placing it on the chair in front of her. Gloria agrees and feels that "the body has the consistency of a shellfish ... as if in the armor are my bones ... without it I have no consistency."

Using sensorimotor therapy techniques (Ogden & Fisher, 2015), the patient is guided in maintaining a mental posture of observation with respect to the physical sensations present and in holding these sensations together with her perception of the rhythm of her breath and, when Gloria expresses a desire to move, the rhythm of her own steps.

Asking Gloria what she is feeling at that moment she notices that the body has changed consistency and "now has a consistency like bread" and therefore feels full and light.

The therapist asks Gloria if she can close her eyes and imagine getting up and leaving for France feeling this texture in her body. In doing so, Gloria feels joy, energy, and lightness.

In summary, then, beginning with the use of experiential and bodily techniques designed to increase monitoring of interpersonal patterns in order to understand what action to enact, an alliance rupture is generated and explored through the clinical interview and experiential techniques. Once the interpersonal patterns that generated the relational difficulty have been detected, the therapeutic alliance has been restored, and the therapeutic contract clarified, patient and therapist proceed toward changing the interpersonal patterns through bodily practices aimed at getting rid of old coping patterns, in order to make room for healthy parts of the Self perceived in the body as fullness, lightness, and energy.

After this session, Gloria's therapy proceeds by continuing with work aimed at modifying interpersonal patterns and fostering the fortification of solid, strong, worthy, and capable self-image accompanied by body sensations such as, warm, soft and yet solid.

One of the illustrative images from this period of therapy has to do with a dream in which when confronted with the ceramist who accuses her she stands firm and does not feel the need to justify herself because "I don't need to sanitize my image in her eyes", feels strong and "feels legs I never felt and breathes in my belly."

The story with Julius ends, and Gloria experiences it with a sadness that she does not, however, read in light of the pattern in which she sees herself as alone, vulnerable, inept, or wrong. Instead, she feels worthy and solid. From here begins a period in which she travels, continues to paint in different countries, studies new approaches and techniques for her work, and experiments with how she is with the new people she meets, in different contexts and activities.

7 Results

Gloria, therefore, began psychotherapy by presenting interpersonal patterns, underlying Dependent Personality Disorder, and borderline and narcissistic traits, characterized by a lonely, vulnerable, inept, and mistaken self-image. These patterns did not allow her to realize her desire for autonomy, a desire that had been consistently frustrated in her life history. At the conclusion of therapy, Gloria presents a self-image in which she perceives herself as solid, strong, worthy, and capable, and her life is set on autonomous experimentation with different relational contexts and situations. The patient no longer meets the criteria for Panic Attack Disorder or Dependent Personality Disorder. The same is true for the other personality traits. This evolution was possible by means of the work on the therapeutic relationship, also thanks to the relational facilitations or ruptures brought about by the use of experiential techniques, as well as the specific work on panic attacks, the identification of interpersonal patterns, bodywork and rescripting in imagination, and the promotion of change through the identification and fortification of healthy parts.

8 Conclusions

In this chapter, we have described how the use of experiential techniques together with the work on the therapeutic relationship were central to the work with a patient with Dependent Personality Disorder. Patients with personality disorders exhibit maladaptive interpersonal patterns, dysfunctional coping, and impaired metacognition underlying their suffering. With this type of patient, the therapeutic relationship becomes the place where aspects of psychopathology manifest themselves, as well as in relational life outside the session. We have shown how techniques can play a role as an accelerator of healthy or dysfunctional relational patterns with the therapist, the explication and discussion of which in session facilitated the emergence of emotions and autobiographical memories, then increasing metacognitive monitoring, facilitating cooperative arrangement, and accelerating the healing process.

Our case description aims, therefore, to encourage clinicians to adopt experiential work from the very beginning of psychotherapy, not allowing themselves to be held back by the resistances that patients manifest, operating instead with curiosity toward them and with constant monitoring of the therapeutic relationship, giving great space for metacommunication work on it.

We acknowledge that we have illustrated this approach through a single successful case, with no formally evaluated results. Future studies could focus on replication of results and evaluation of therapeutic outcomes.

References

Arntz, A., & Jacob, G. (2013). *Schema therapy in practice: An introductory guide to the schema mode approach*. Wiley-Blackwell.

Bargh, J. (2017). *Before you know it: The unconscious reasons we do what we do*. Simon and Schuster.

Baumeister, R. F., & Leary, M. R. (1995). The need to belong: Desire for interpersonal attachments as a fundamental human motivation. *Psychological Bulletin, 117*(3), 497–529. https://doi.org/10.1037/0033-2909.117.3.497

Bohus, M., Kleindienst, N., Hahn, C., Müller-Engelmann, M., Ludäscher, P., Steil, R., et al. (2020). Dialectical behavior therapy for posttraumatic stress disorder (DBT-PTSD) compared with cognitive processing therapy (CPT) in complex presentations of PTSD in women survivors of childhood abuse: A randomized clinical trial. *JAMA Psychiatry, 77*(12), 1235–1245. https://doi.org/10.1001/jamapsychiatry.2020.2148

Bowlby, J. (1969). *Attachment and loss (Attachment)* (Vol. 1). Basic Books.

Carcione, A., Nicolò, G., Pedone, R., Popolo, R., Conti, L., Fiore, D., et al. (2011). Metacognitive mastery dysfunctions in personality disorder psychotherapy. *Psychiatry Research, 190*(1), 60–71. https://doi.org/10.1016/j.psychres.2010.12.032

Carcione, A., Semerari, A., & Nicolò, G. (2016). *Curare i casi complessi: la terapia metacognitiva interpersonale dei disturbi di personalità*. Gius. Laterza & Figli Spa.

Centonze, A., Inchausti, F., MacBeth, A., & Dimaggio, G. (2020). Changing embodied dialogical patterns in metacognitive interpersonal therapy. *Journal of Constructivist Psychology*, 1–15. https://doi.org/10.1080/10720537.2020.1717117

Centonze, A., Popolo, R., MacBeth, A., & Dimaggio, G. (2021a). Building the alliance and using experiential techniques in the early phases of psychotherapy for avoidant personality disorder. *Journal of Clinical Psychology, 77*(5), 1219–1232. https://doi.org/10.1002/jclp.23143

Centonze, A., Ottavi, P., MacBeth, A., Popolo, R., & Dimaggio, G. (2021b). Modular treatment for complex depression according to metacognitive interpersonal therapy. In *Depression and personality dysfunction* (pp. 245–276). Springer. https://doi.org/10.1007/978-3-030-70699-9_10

Crits-Christoph, P., Luborsky, L., & Barber, J. (1990). Overview of psychodynamic treatment. Handbook of Outpatient Treatment of Adults: Nonpsychotic Mental Disorders, 51–70.

Dimaggio, G., & Lysaker, P. H. (2015). Metacognition and mentalizing in the psychotherapy of patients with psychosis and personality disorders. *Journal of Clinical Psychology, 71*(2), 117–124. https://doi.org/10.1002/jclp.22147

Dimaggio, G., Semerari, A., Carcione, A., Nicolò, G., & Procacci, M. (2007). *Psychotherapy of personality disorders: Metacognition, states of mind and interpersonal cycles*. Routledge.

Dimaggio, G., Montano, A., Popolo, R., & Salvatore, G. (2013). *Terapia metacognitiva interpersonale: dei disturbi di personalità*. Cortina.

Dimaggio, G., Maillard, P., MacBeth, A., & Kramer, U. (2019a). Effects of therapeutic alliance and metacognition on outcome in a brief psychological treatment for borderline personality disorder. *Psychiatry, 82*(2), 143–157. https://doi.org/10.1080/00332747.2019.1610295

Dimaggio, G., Ottavi, P., Popolo, R., & Salvatore, G. (2019b). *Corpo, immaginazione e cambiamento*. Raffaello Cortina.

Eubanks, C. F., Muran, J. C., & Safran, J. D. (2018). Alliance rupture repair: A meta-analysis. *Psychotherapy, 55*(4), 508–519. https://doi.org/10.1037/pst0000185

Eubanks, C. F., Sergi, J., Samstag, L. W., & Muran, J. C. (2021). Commentary: Rupture repair as a transtheoretical corrective experience. *Journal of Clinical Psychology, 77*(2), 457–466. https://doi.org/10.1002/jclp.23117

Flückiger, C., Del Re, A. C., Wampold, B. E., & Horvath, A. O. (2018). The alliance in adult psychotherapy: A meta-analytic synthesis. *Psychotherapy, 55*(4), 316. https://doi.org/10.1037/pst0000172

Flückiger, C., Del Re, A. C., Wlodasch, D., Horvath, A. O., Solomonov, N., & Wampold, B. E. (2020). Assessing the alliance–outcome association adjusted for patient characteristics and treatment processes: A meta-analytic summary of direct comparisons. *Journal of Counseling Psychology, 67*, 706. https://doi.org/10.1037/cou0000424

Gilbert, P. (1989). *Human nature and suffering*. Psychology Press.

Gilbert, P. (2010). An introduction to compassion focused therapy in cognitive behavior therapy. *International Journal of Cognitive Therapy, 3*(2), 97–112. https://doi.org/10.1521/ijct.2010.3.2.97

Greenberg, L. S. (2002). *Emotion-focused therapy: Coaching clients to work with their feelings*. American Psychological Association.

Hackmann, A., Bennett-Levy, J., & Holmes, E. A. (2011). *Oxford guide to imagery in cognitive therapy*. Oxford University Press.

Hill, C. E. (2010). Qualitative studies of negative experiences in psychotherapy. In J. C. Muran & J. P. Barber (Eds.), *The therapeutic alliance: An evidence-based guide to practice* (pp. 63–73). The Guilford Press.

Horvath, A. O., & Symonds, B. D. (1991). Relation between working alliance and outcome in psychotherapy: A meta-analysis. *Journal of Counseling Psychology, 38*(2), 139.

Horvath, A. O., Re, A. C. D., Flückiger, C., & Symonds, D. (2011). Alliance in individual psychotherapy. In J. C. Norcross (Ed.), *Psychotherapy relationships that work: Evidence-based responsiveness* (pp. 25–69). Oxford University Press. https://doi.org/10.1093/acprof:oso/9780199737208.003.0002

Lambert, M. J. (2010). *Prevention of treatment failure: The use of measuring, monitoring, and feedback in clinical practice*. American Psychological Association. https://doi.org/10.1037/12141-000

Lambert, M. J. (2013). Outcome in psychotherapy: The past and important advances. *Psychotherapy, 50*(1), 42–51. https://doi.org/10.1037/a0030682

Lambert, M. J., & Ogles, B. M. (2004). The effcacy and effectiveness of psychotherapy. In M. J. Lambert's (Ed.), *Bergin and Garfeld's handbook of psychotherapy and behavior change* (pp. 139–193). Wiley.

Lichtenberg, J. D. (1989). *Psychoanalysis and motivation*. The Analytic Press Inc.

Liotti, G., & Gilbert, P. (2011). Mentalizing, motivation, and social mentalities: Theoretical considerations and implications for psychotherapy. *Psychology and Psychotherapy: Theory Research and Practice, 84*(1), 9–25. https://doi.org/10.1348/147608310X520094

Lowen, A. (1971). *The language of the body*. Macmillan.

Martin, D. J., Garske, J. P., & Davis, M. K. (2000). Relation of the therapeutic alliance with outcome and other variables: A meta-analytic review. *Journal of Consulting and Clinical Psychology, 68*(3), 438. https://doi.org/10.1037/0022-006X.68.3.438

McLaughlin, K. A., Borkovec, T. D., & Sibrava, N. J. (2007). The effects of worry and rumination on affect states and cognitive activity. *Behavior Therapy, 38*, 23–38. https://doi.org/10.1016/j.beth.2006.03.003

Moreno, J. L., & Moreno, Z. T. (1975/2012). *Psychodrama, Vol. 3rd, action therapy and principles of practice*. The North-West Psychodrama Association.

Muran, J. C., Safran, J. D., Eubanks, C. F., & Gorman, B. S. (2018). The effect of alliance-focused training on a cognitive-behavioral therapy for personality disorders. *Journal of Consulting and Clinical Psychology, 86*(4), 384–397. https://doi.org/10.1037/ccp0000284

Muran, J. C., Eubanks, C. F., & Samstag, L. W. (2021). One more time with less jargon: An introduction to "Rupture Repair in Practice". *Journal of Clinical Psychology: In Session, 77*, 361–368. https://doi.org/10.1002/jclp.23105

Nolen-Hoeksema, S., Wisco, B. E., & Lyubomirsky, S. (2008). Rethinking rumination. *Perspectives on Psychological Science, 3*(5), 400–424. https://doi.org/10.1111/2Fj.1745-6924.2008.00088

Ogden, P., & Fisher, J. (2015). *Sensorimotor psychotherapy: Inter-ventions for trauma and attachment*. WW Norton & Company.

Panksepp, J. (1998). The periconscious substrates of consciousness: Affective states and the evolutionary origins of the self. *Journal of consciousness studies, 5*(5–6), 566–582.

Panksepp, J., & Biven, L. (2012). A meditation on the affective neuroscientific view of human and animalian MindBrains. From the couch to the lab: trends in psychodynamic neuroscience, 145–175.

Perls, F. (1951). Gestalt therapy. Excitement and Growth in Human Personality/Delta.

Safran, J. D., & Muran, J. C. (1998). *The therapeutic alliance in brief psychotherapy: General principles*. American Psychological Association.

Safran, J. D., & Muran, J. C. (2000). Resolving therapeutic alliance ruptures: Diversity and integration. *Journal of Clinical Psychology, 56*(2), 233–243. https://doi.org/10.1002/(SICI)1097-4679(200002)56:2%3C233::AIJCLP9%3E3.0.CO;2-3

Safran, J. D., & Muran, J. C. (2006). Has the concept of the therapeutic alliance outlived its usefulness? *Psychotherapy: Theory, Research, Practice, Training, 43*(3), 286. https://doi.org/10.1037/0033-3204.43.3.286

Semerari, A., Carcione, A., Dimaggio, G., Falcone, M., Nicolo, G., Procacci, M., & Alleva, G. (2003). How to evaluate metacognitive functioning in psychotherapy? The metacognition assessment scale and its applications. *Clinical Psychology & Psychotherapy, 10*(4), 238–261. https://doi.org/10.1002/cpp.362

Semerari, A., Colle, L., Pellecchia, G., Buccione, I., Carcione, A., Dimaggio, G., et al. (2014). Metacognitive dysfunctions in personality disorders: Correlations with disorder severity and personality styles. *Journal of Personality Disorders, 28*(6), 751–766. https://doi.org/10.1521/pedi_2014_28_137

Shapiro, F., & Forrest, M. S. (2001). *EMDR: Eye movement desensitization and reprocessing*. Guilford.

Swift, J. K., & Greenberg, R. P. (2015). *Premature termination in psychotherapy: Strategies for engaging clients and improving outcomes*. American Psychological Association. https://doi.org/10.1037/14469-000

Tomasello, M., Carpenter, M., Call, J., Behne, T., & Moll, H. (2005). Understanding and sharing intentions: The origins of cultural cognition. *Behavioral and Brain Sciences, 28*(5), 675–691. https://doi.org/10.1017/S0140525X05220125

Wampold, B. E., & Imel, Z. E. (2015). *The great psychotherapy debate: The evidence for what makes psychotherapy work*. Routledge. https://doi.org/10.4324/9780203582015

Attachment-Based Family Therapy: Theory, Clinical Model, and Training

Guy Diamond, Suzanne Levy, and Brianna Brennan

1 Introduction

How do we create change in therapy? How do we organize and move forward on the many possible themes or directions that emerge when having a therapeutic conversation? We can focus on cognitions, emotions, behaviors, histories, current stressors, internal representations, and social expectations. In family therapy, all these dimensions are present with multiple people simultaneously. Each person brings their own internal world, psychological landscape, and history of internalized experiences to therapy. However, there is an added dimension in family therapy: interactions among people that have shaped their internal landscape, their sense of self, and their view of others. These interactions reinforce their expectations of themselves and others. Interactions shape internal experiences, and internal experiences shape how we interact with others. In family therapy, all of these are possible topics of exploration or conversation. They become targets of interventions, either as small steps or as main process goals.

Then, how do therapists choose what to focus on? How do we organize these multiple opportunities when working with a family? When do we focus on internal processing? On interactions? On behavior? On emotions? How do we focus on these dimensions? What strategies do we use for each domain and what is the goal? Therapists may not realize it, but every speech-turn and every statement we make is a decision about what to focus on, how to focus on it, and what we aim to accomplish.

G. Diamond (✉)
University of Pennsylvania School of Medicine, Philadelphia, PA, USA

ABFT International Training Institute, LLC, Newtown, PA, USA

S. Levy · B. Brennan
ABFT International Training Institute, LLC, Newtown, PA, USA

Some therapy models have a more circumscribed parameter; the range of choices is prescribed by the theoretical framework. In general, cognitive behavioral therapy (CBT) focuses on cognitions. Dialectical behavior therapy (DBT) focuses on regulating emotions. Psychodynamic therapy focuses on internal conflicts. Traditional family therapy focuses on family interactions. However, some therapy models are more integrative (Norcross & Goldfried, 2005). In a recent survey of 1000 psychotherapists, 15% indicated using only one theoretical model (Tasca et al., 2015). The challenge of working with a more integrative model is knowing when and how to use each theory and technique. Here, the dilemma has been referred to as "integration" vs. "eclectic." Whereas the former has a framework to help make selections, the latter consists of a more random use of techniques (Zarbo et al., 2016). In our work, we promote an integrationist perspective where principles and theory guide the mixing and matching of patients with clinical targets and techniques.

Attachment-based family therapy (ABFT) offers a road map to help organize these infinite therapeutic possibilities (Diamond et al., 2014, 2021). It begins with theory but moves into practice. Unlike many family therapy models, it has a clear direction as well. The proposed mechanism of change is cumulative, building from one process to another. The order of the processes is not prescribed, but rather a recommended sequences of tasks which offer an elegant scaffold for delivering this complex multiperson therapy. At its core, the model is integrative, helping the therapist focus on a wide range of psychological (within) and interactive (between) functions.

2 Theoretical Framework

ABFT is rooted in Bowlby's (1969) attachment theory. Bowlby, breaking with his intrapsychic-oriented psychiatry community, believed that the quality of the interactions between a parent and infant shaped the latter's internal psychological landscape. Attachment theory is organized around the innate, biologically wired, attachment instincts of a child. This attachment need is activated when a child senses danger or experiences distress. As an instinctual response, the child turns to their parents, usually the mother, for protection and comfort. If the caregiver is available, sensitive, and responsive, the child feels protected. Over time, after repeatedly experiencing this responsiveness, the child begins to feel that the world is a safe place and that they are worthy of being loved and protected (Bosmans et al., 2022). Thus, Bowlby observed and theorized that a parent's responses play a significant role in shaping how a child views themselves and others. Further, these representations become internalized as working models or expectations of future relationships. As the child grows older, these early experiences provide the template for the kinds of relationships a person will seek as an adolescent or an adult. If one is treated well as a child, one will more likely look for relationships where one feels treated well as an adult (Kobak & Bosmans, 2019).

This secure attachment experience also helps children internalize skills related to emotion regulation. Consider a child who falls off their bike and runs to their mother with a scraped knee. The attentive parent comforts the child and helps them regulate their fear and pain. Over time, and with repeated experience of their parent's attention, the child begins to internalize self-soothing skills. Eventually, the child no longer needs their mother to help them downregulate their emotions because they have done it so many times, they know how to do it themselves (Brumariu, 2015).

When parents are not available and not responsive, children feel less taken care of. They begin to see the world as unsafe and themselves as unworthy of love and protection. They guard against these feelings and further disappointment by developing relational strategies to protect themselves (Mikulincer et al., 2009). Some children become disengaged and deny their need of protection (avoidant). Some children constantly try to win love and protection knowing their mother is incapable of providing this, so they end up pushing people away (ambivalent). Some children do not have an organized way to reach out or protect themselves so they become dysregulated or dissociated during times of need (disorganized). Such children have often experienced trauma at their parents' hands, which has deeply disturbed their psychological understanding of love and safety. These insecure attachment styles or orientations become relational strategies for protecting oneself from further hurt.

When adult patients come for psychotherapy, they bring these relational strategies with them (Slade & Holmes, 2019). Many patients continue to struggle with what their parents did or did not do for them. Of course, this is not the only dynamic with which patients struggle. Biology, temperament, life stress, and trauma experienced as an adult contribute to the psychological dilemma a patient brings to therapy. Nevertheless, their early relationships with their parents lay the foundation for their psychological makeup. These early relationships sometimes tie up the patient's emotional energy in a psychological knot that many psychotherapies aim to untie. Many contemporary theorists believe psychotherapy is the re-experiencing of a trustworthy parent who is available in times of distress (Steele & Steele, 2017).

In ABFT, therapists access a child's memories and recollections: a history that has contributed to the child's internal psychological development. Therapists can validate and empathize with a history of attachment ruptures. However, having the parent listen to and validate the child's experiences can deepen the psychological penetration of that acknowledgment. Additionally, when the parent soothes the child's internal landscape in the present, we change the interactional patterns between them: patients are expressing their vulnerable feelings, and their parents are available, sensitive, and attuned to those feelings. Therefore, ABFT aims to use family therapy to challenge both internal functioning and interactional functioning.

How does the ABFT framework guide our decision-making in therapy? ABFT is tenaciously focused on trying to untie the knots of insecure attachment. This means putting the topic of attachment security at the center of the therapeutic conversation. From the first session, ABFT proposes that family members discuss what has come in the way of trust in the family. What things have happened (e.g., divorce) or what processes continue to happen (e.g., high criticism) that damage the relational fabric? These questions become the focus of the very first session. Then, similar themes are developed in individual sessions alone with the adolescent and with the parents. Next, we incorporate these themes into a conjoint discussion during family sessions. If we keep attachment rupture and repair at the center of the therapy, it provides a framework to guide our decisions about what intervention to use and when, what topics to focus on and when, what emotions to amplify and reduce, which processes to promote and block, and which topics to keep front and center. The attachment lens helps the therapist navigate the complex possibilities of a multi-person therapeutic conversation.

3 Clinical Framework

Along with a theoretical framework, ABFT offers a clinical framework or scaffold to support the implementation of attachment-focused therapy. ABFT is organized around five tasks. Tasks are not sessions, but a set of operations to address a specific therapeutic objective. ABFT has five main tasks made up of several subtasks or topics. The five tasks are reframing, alliance building with the youth, alliance building with the parents, attachment repair, and promoting autonomy. Whereas the reframing task often requires one session, the other tasks might be two-to-four sessions per task. ABFT is designed as a short therapy course (12–16 weeks). If the therapist remains focused, the tasks can be delivered within this time frame.

3.1 Task I: Reframing

The Relational Reframe Task sets the essential foundation for ABFT. It has three parts. It begins like any therapy: with joining. Usually, we spend the first 10-to-15 min just talking with the clients about, for example, a recent sports event or the weather. However, we can also talk about their lives. For example, where do they live? Who lives in their home? Where are they from? What kind of work do their parents do? How is everyone's health at home? What are the young family members' hobbies or interests, skills, and competencies? Although one can carry out general small talk, it is also important to understand the context of patients' lives so that the therapist is not taken by surprise later about critical life stressors (e.g., health).

Part two focuses on the problems that brought the family to therapy. This is a standard intake assessment that anyone would conduct in a new case. We ask about presenting problems, recent crises, past treatments, current medications, and school and peer functioning. We also ask about parental teamwork, or parenting more generally, because this is a cornerstone of family life. We aim for the essential details, but do not let this become an elongated story-telling session. We balance information gathering and alliance formation, closely monitoring the conversation to ensure parents are not feeling blamed for the child's problems. This also goes beyond just information gathering. The therapist establishes that the youth is in distress. The therapist begins to uncover some of the psychological challenges that might be driving negative behavior. This begins to establish for the parents a broader understanding of why the adolescent is in pain. The therapist also attempts to identify the parent's distress and worry that might fuel their frustration and concerns.

The third part begins the relational reframing process. About 40 min into the session, the therapist shifts the conversation to relational ruptures. The defining question is, "When you are feeling suicidal, why don't you go to your parents for help?" This pivotal question puts the quality of the relationship and its ruptures squarely at the center of the therapy conversation. Navigating this phase of the conversation can be complicated. To keep things productive, therapists try not to go too far into any rupture story, just far enough to discuss how the events or processes have gotten in the way of the family feeling more connected. Therapists explore the impact of the youth not reaching out for support and help on both the youth and the parents. This topic allows the therapist to promote a softer emotional state. We move the topic from anger and behavior problems to love and longing. When we get enough of this softened mood in the room, we suggest that the therapy initially focus on repairing the relationship rather than fixing the behavioral problems. We give the rationale that if the relationship were stronger, it would be easier to solve such problems.

3.2 Task II: Alliance Building with the Adolescent

Therapeutic alliance builds on three principles: bonds, goals, and tasks (Horvath, 2018). Clients have to like the therapist and feel that the therapist likes them. However, clients also need to feel therapists share a mutual goal for therapy. If the therapist wants the client to stop smoking marijuana and the young person wants more freedom at home, then therapy conversations will be stiff and frustrating. We also need to agree on a task. In ABFT, we want patients to agree to talk with his or her parents about attachment ruptures, which often initially seem unappealing. Thus, the alliance session with adolescents aims to build agreement on bonds, goals, and tasks.

The session often begins with the therapist trying to better understand the patient's world. This can include friends, hobbies, romance, goals, and dreams. Sometimes therapists talk about sexuality and drugs as a means to show our nonjudgmental interest in patients' lives. At other times, therapists start conversations about sexual and gender identity or about race and racism. The aim is to try and connect with what feels authentic and pertinent to the youth.

Eventually, the conversations turn to the mental health narrative. Here the therapist reviews the patients' view of the mental health challenges they are facing. Therapists want to hear the young person's version of the story. We also help them take their problems seriously. For example, we can say, "I know you say things are OK, but I cannot imagine you're very happy with your life given some of the things that got you here." We want adolescents to feel like they are in this therapy for themselves. We want them to acknowledge that they are not happy with how their life is going and they want to be in therapy to change it.

With this commitment to therapy, therapists turn their attention to the attachment narrative. The therapist tries to make the client's understanding of the circumstances that have contributed to the formation of an insecure attachment more coherent (Waters et al., 2021). The therapist helps the patient sort through family processes or events that have damaged their trust in the relationship. The therapist uses this opportunity to help patients identify the underlying vulnerable meanings (e.g., attachment themes) that result from these problems but have been avoided. For example, a child may be angry at and feel abandoned by their father because he left them after the divorce. A child may feel worried about their anxious or sick mother while also feeling unprotected by her. These primary, and often avoided or ignored, emotions sometimes drive self-destructive behavior (Greenberg & Goldman, 2019). Linking these more "authentic" feelings with traumatic events or deleterious processes can help the patient develop a more cohesive narrative about themselves and others. In ABFT, we also use attachment themes to help bring a new layer of meaning to such narratives. Anger covers abandonment; fear covers neglect (Greenberg & Goldman, 2019).

Once the mental health and attachment narratives are more fleshed out, the therapist begins the linking process. First, the therapist begins to link the attachment narrative to the depression narrative. For some youth, the caregivers contribute to their distress. "I know it is complex, but I worry that some of your anger at your parents fuels your depression and desire to kill yourself." Some youth have stressors outside the home (e.g., bullying) but feel they cannot go to their parents for support. "This leaves you vulnerable and unsupported." If these kinds of assumptions are eventually embraced, then the therapist can also link the attachment narrative to Task IV: "Talking to your parents about these problems might be your only way out of them." Attachment ruptures fuel depression, which the young person does not want to feel anymore. However, "the only way out of this pickle is to look your parents in the face and tell them how you feel." Even with all this preparation, many young people may say no. ABFT offers many strategies to help patients work through this resistance.

3.3 Task III: Alliance Formation with the Parents

Parent sessions focus on preparing parents for the conversation in Task IV. However, as therapists know, joining with and guiding parents toward therapeutic progress can be difficult. We employ several strategies to join with parents. We usually start by understanding their current stressors. We ask for permission to briefly talk with them about themselves, separate from problems with the young person. Therapists explore work, health, finances, racism, mental health, and other stressors that might distress parents. This is meant to be a way of achieving an empathic understanding of circumstances in their lives that might impinge on their parenting: "No wonder you are having a tough time with Jonny. Anyone going through what you are would feel distracted." When working with two caregiver families, therapists always spend a session on parental teamwork (e.g., mother/father, parent/grandparent). These conversations aim to identify where and how caregivers agree or disagree on parenting strategies and how to bring them more into alignment.

Another strategy of collaborating with parents focuses on their experience of being parented when they were a child. The therapist aims to identify who the parents went to for emotional support when they were a child and how that experience went. Unfortunately, when working with troubled young people who have mental health distress, therapists find that they often come from homes with conflict or stress and that the parents may have their own history of attachment ruptures. The aim here, as it also is with young people's attachment narratives, is to motivate parents to remember how they felt as a child when their emotional needs were not met. In this moment of self-reflection, we help parents consider their child's psychological experience of not having their needs met. This moment of reflective functioning or mentalization (Fonagy & Bateman, 2016) activates caregiving instincts of love and protection in parents. In this softened state, we offer parents emotion coaching and attachment promoting skills that might help Task IV go well.

3.4 Task IV: Attachment Task

In many ways, the attachment task serves as the centerpiece of the therapy. Tasks I, II, and III are therapeutic in and of themselves, but they also serve as preparation for Task IV. Like in shuttle diplomacy, therapists have met alone with the young person and with the parents to develop themes and skills and seek agreement to engage in Task IV. In Task IV, it is time for the actual conversation. No more preparation, no more teaching, and no more winning people over—just practicing having actual conversations. These sessions are in vivo, experiential moments where family members talk directly to each other, and the therapist coaches them to keep the conversation on track and helpful.

The attachment task works at many levels. First, we help families discuss core relational ruptures that have undermined family trust and cooperation. These might be events like divorce or a death in the family that have never been discussed, even though all members have thought about them individually. They might also be instances of chronic parental negativity and criticism that leaves the child feeling unloved and uncared for. We identify these content themes in Task II and III, and we bring them forward in Task IV. At another level, because the conversations are conducted in real time, family members can practice the communication skills they learned in the previous tasks. Here, the emphasis is on the family talking to each other and the therapist coaching and challenging them to remain regulated, honest, and present.

At a third level, this conversation creates a reattachment experience. The young person is talking about emotional experiences that were painful for them and their parents are listening while being sensitive and available. This replicates what secure attachment should be. The "experience" of parent availability challenges the internal working model the young person holds about their parent. This helps the young person revise the model to see their parents as more reliable. It also creates the possibility that this kind of interaction will be repeated in the future: "My mother can be there for me when I need her ... Maybe I will give her a try again." Simultaneously, the parent has experienced the young person in a new way. They think to themselves, "I have never seen her talk so honestly without being angry or withdrawn. It was painful to hear, but a relief to know what she was actually thinking. Maybe she has more legitimate complaints than I gave her credit for."

3.5 Task V: Promoting Autonomy

The initial three tasks serve as preparation for Task IV. Similarly, Task IV serves as preparation for Task V. For many families that come to therapy, bad experiences, bad processes, and life problems can leave them waging a constant battle. Behavioral problems become the battleground of unspoken emotional problems. We find, however, that Task IV does not have to resolve all the emotional problems facing each family. Instead, when the family has a few productive, emotion-focused conversations, family members begin to feel more competent and start trusting that they can have these kinds of conversations in the future. Task IV bursts through that relational expectation of insecure attachment and opens up family members to the possibilities of more loving and effective interactions. Task V then becomes the testing ground where family members have to prove they are capable of maintaining a secure attachment even in the face of day-to-day stress.

Conversations in Task V can focus on a range of topics. Sometimes the young person needs help with day-to-day operations: going back to school, looking for a job, or rejoining the basketball team. Oftentimes, the young person will not trust the parent to help with these goals. In Task V, they can communicate slightly better, and parents can provide more support. Sometimes, the young person needs help navigating their mental health needs. This might include medication management, treatment visits, or suicide risk management. Sometimes young people just need to vent and be heard. Therapists hope the young person will more willingly allow their parents to help with these challenges, and that parents will provide that help in a way that the young person needs and wants. Conversations in Task V can focus on values and identity development. Relevant topics might include love, sex, drugs, sexual identity, racism, and future plans. As parents become more trustworthy, young people might rely on them to help navigate life's challenges.

4 Integrative Thinking

How does the map outlined above assist with ABFT's integrative nature? As we progress through each task, we have outlined different topics, different kinds of therapeutic actions, and different kinds of directions and goals. In Task II, for example, the therapy uses psychodynamic reflection to recall early memories of attachment ruptures. Emotion-focused strategies from EFT can help the therapist deepen their encounters with these memories (Greenberg & Goldman, 2019). However, by the end of the task, the therapist is asking for behavioral change: that is, for conversations among family members. If they agree to have these conversations, therapists turn to psycho-education strategies to help prepare family members learn new skills to make these conversations successful. In Task IV, we turn to in vivo experiential sequences of family members "doing" what we had talked about in earlier tasks. This complex task involves emotional processes as family members go deeper and deeper into their stories. This task also has elements of exposure therapy, where we continue with this process of going deeper even if the family members feel uncomfortable or scared. We want them to have this conversation long enough to know that they are capable of it. Thus, the tasks themselves have different moments and elements that require different skills and strategies. A good ABFT therapist has to wear many hats and be comfortable with many different therapeutic strategies. The ABFT model itself helps guide the therapist about when each strategy might be more relevant. However, the therapist has to remain on their toes and responsive to the ebb and flow of therapeutic progress. We must be ready at any minute to change our direction and try a different strategy if the current one is failing.

5 Training and Supervision

Because we are clinical trial researchers, we have imported training standards from clinical trials research into practice. This strategy rests on the assumption that training therapists up to fidelity in a treatment protocol requires more intensive training than just a weekend workshop. It includes reading a manual, attending an introductory workshop, treating two or three pilot cases with weekly supervision, rating the degree of adherence of those sessions using adherence checklist measures, and providing final training to consolidate all this learning. In clinical trial research, the therapist needs to reach a high enough score on the adherence/fidelity measures to be a provider in a study. We, like others, have come to find that fidelity in non-research, real-world clinical settings may require more flexibility. For many, this may not be achievable (Kendall & Frank, 2018). This has led us to adjust our training expectations and our certification standards. We have observed however, that in the United States, advanced clinical training seems to take place in empirically supported treatment training courses. In Europe, training programs/externships continue to provide advanced training to therapists. Workshops can be held in person or online.

5.1 The Training Process

The ABFT International Training Institute has a well-defined process for training and certifying therapists. There are three levels to ABFT training, each building upon the other. The certification process takes a minimum of 1 year (most complete the process in 18 months) and consists of 3-day workshops, 22 biweekly group supervision sessions, a 3-day advanced workshop, and intensive tape reviews. Therapists in training may say they are conducting ABFT-informed work. Therapists who have been certified may refer to themselves as ABFT-certified therapists. Therapists in the United States need to have at least a Master's degree in social work, mental health counseling, clinical or counseling psychology, or couple and family therapy. If therapists are not licensed, they need to be employed somewhere where they are receiving supervision. International therapists need to have local certification or licensure allowing them to practice therapy. Further, therapists must ensure they have sufficient clinical time to treat ABFT clients (at least two to three clients at a time).

The target audience for ABFT training is counselors, couple and family therapists, mental health professionals, psychiatrists, psychologists, psychotherapists, and social workers. However, day one of our 3-day introductory workshop is appropriate for case workers, emergency room physicians, health-care administrators, frontline mental health staff, primary care physicians, and school-based therapists. When working with health-care programs, like residential care, having line staff be exposed to ABFT can improve treatment coherence across the organization.

(A) Level I: Introductory Workshop or Webinar

Therapists must attend a 3-day introductory in-person or online workshop. Day one provides an overview of the model using lectures, slides, and recorded examples. This provides a good overview of the model, including its theoretical foundation and clinical strategies. Faculty reviews how attachment theory, emotional regulation, and trauma resolution inform the delivery of ABFT. We also review the goals and structure of the five treatment tasks that provide a road map for delivering this interpersonally focused psychotherapy effectively and rapidly. Because day one is in a lecture format, the audience can be large. Agencies often invite their nonfamily therapy staff to orient other staff members to the framework.

Days two and three of the introductory workshop provide a more in-depth look at the procedures and processes involved in facilitating ABFT. Case discussions, tape reviews, and role-play deepen participants' understanding of the approach. These 2 days provide a more in-depth exposure to the scaffold of each task. We review extended clips of therapy sessions, talk about challenges, and then role-play the core elements of each task. This gives therapists a more practical sense of how to apply the model with moderately cooperative families. The goal is to learn to apply the basic structure, not to modify the model to more difficult, or different kinds of, families—that comes in supervision and advanced training. In addition, therapists are taught how to use the self-report ABFT adherence checklists. Because these 2 days are more hands-on, enrollment is usually limited to 30 participants per trainer.

(B) Level II: Supervision

After the initial workshop, therapists begin a series of 22 fortnightly, 60-min individual or group case consultation meetings with an ABFT-certified consultant. These groups are conducted on a HIPAA-compliant Zoom program. Trainees are expected to discuss their current cases in which they are applying ABFT. Therapists send a short case write-up using the ABFT Case Write-up Outline when presenting a case. Additionally, they present 5–10-min recordings of their therapy sessions each time they present.

Supervision sessions help therapists implement ABFT more effectively with clients. During supervision, therapists learn how to conceptualize from an ABFT framework so that they can utilize ABFT with a variety of different clients, presenting problems, and difficult situations. Video reviews of sessions allow supervisors to offer detailed feedback on the moment-by-moment decisions that occur in the therapy room. Supervisors also help therapists identify and work through person-of-the-therapist issues that arise when doing this interpersonal, emotionally deep work.

5.2 Advanced Workshop

The final step in Level II certification training involves attending an advanced 3-day workshop (in person or online). Therapists attend the advanced workshop typically after participating in supervision for approximately 6 months. This workshop helps advance and solidify therapist's ABFT skills. Therapists engage in POTT exercises to further understand their own attachment histories and how their own attachment history creates barriers or can help facilitate their delivery of therapy. They learn how to utilize their own personal experiences in life to build empathy and understanding of their clients' experiences. Therapists also learn a variety of emotion-deepening skills in the context of ABFT. Challenges faced when implementing the model for each task are discussed along with how to adapt or modify ABFT with more challenging clients. Therapists are then provided time to practice how to manage their POTT and task-related challenges and utilize the emotional deepening skills during role-play activities. Through practice in role-plays and receiving feedback, participants refine new skills and concepts.

To reach Level II Therapist status, therapists must attend the majority of supervision sessions in a year, and present at least four times with the ABFT case write-up and at least twice with video. Therapists must also attend the advanced workshop. When all criteria are met, therapists are eligible to take the Level II therapist exam. If these criteria are met, therapists become a level II certified ABFT therapist.

6 Certification

Level III therapist training is our full therapist certification where therapists demonstrate fidelity to the model. Certification has become a standard clinical training procedure throughout the world of empirically supported treatments. After attending the advanced workshop and participating in supervision (supervision does not need to be finished), trainees begin submitting video recordings of complete (i.e., 1 h) ABFT sessions for review. When submitting tapes, therapists must provide a case write-up (template provided) and self-feedback on their tapes with suggestions for how to improve portions of their sessions that are not consistent with ABFT or could be improved in general. Therapists also rate their own tapes with the ABFT adherence measure. ABFT-certified supervisors review the tapes and provide in-depth written feedback and adherence ratings and offer a 20-min phone consultation (as needed) regarding the tape. Therapists completing Level III Certification can feel confident that they are implementing the model the way it is intended. We are also confident that certified ABFT therapists can represent the work as it is intended.

Trainees submit a minimum of 10 tapes at a rate of one to two videotapes a month. Tapes should be of recent sessions so that therapists can demonstrate their use of feedback from the group supervision and advanced workshop. When submitting tapes, we ask trainees to use the ABFT case write-up format to explain the progression of the case. We also ask that they review the recording and provide their own commentary on what they have observed. What do they see in the therapy session that was good or could have gone differently? What opportunities were missed or could have gone deeper or lasted longer? We also ask them to observe themselves: "What did I do well, what might I have changed, and what seemed difficult for me?" This self-review is very important. We do not expect that therapists will submit perfect sessions. However, we do expect that they understand the model well enough to know what they did well and where they could improve. Therapists also rate their own tapes with the ABFT adherence measure.

An ABFT-certified supervisor then reviews the submitted tape. We provide nearly a line-by-line analysis of the therapy process. At a meta level, we look for how well the therapist keeps attachment at the center of the therapy conversation and how well they manage emotions and activate more vulnerable primary emotions. We also look at the use of the task structure. We do not overly prescribe adherence, and we expect much complexity in the cases. We do want to see the therapist leaning in when they are going deep and linking as they are moving toward Task IV activity. Finally, we look for micro skills in the room. Is the therapist addressing resistance appropriately? Is the therapist moving too fast or not fast enough? Is the therapist facilitating conversation between family members or doing too much of the talking themselves? These kind of skills have been a major part of the conversation in supervision groups. When the review is done, we offer a 20-min phone review with the trainee to go over the feedback.

7 Conclusion

ABFT is an empirically supported and transdiagnostic therapy model that can be used with children, adolescents, young adults, and even adults with their parents. The model provides a road map for delivering core intervention strategies of an emotion focused, attachment informed, family psychotherapy model. In addition, it offers thinking strategies for how and when to integrate different clinical strategies to guild a sort of theoretical eclecticism (Castonguay et al., 2015). The model has been well validated (Diamond et al., 2021) and teaching methods are well developed. Readers interested in learning more about the work can visit our website at ABFT International.com

References

Bosmans, G., Van Vlierberghe, L., Bakermans-Kranenburg, M. J., Kobak, R., Hermans, D., & van IJzendoorn, M. H. (2022). A learning theory approach to attachment theory: Exploring clinical applications. *Clinical Child and Family Psychology Review, 25*(3), 591–612. https://doi.org/10.1007/s10567-021-00377-x

Bowlby, J. (1969). *Attachment and loss: Attachment* (2nd ed.). Basic Books.

Brumariu, L. E. (2015). Parent–child attachment and emotion regulation. *New Directions for Child and Adolescent Development, 2015*(148), 31–45.

Castonguay, L. G., Eubanks, C. F., Goldfried, M. R., Muran, J. C., & Lutz, W. (2015). Research on psychotherapy integration: Building on the past, looking to the future. *Psychotherapy Research, 25*, 365–382. https://doi.org/10.1080/10503307.2015.1014010

Diamond, G. S., Diamond, G. M., & Levy, S. A. (2014). *Attachment-based family therapy for depressed adolescents.* American Psychological Association Press.

Diamond, G. S., Diamond, G. M., & Levy, S. A. (2021). Attachment-based family therapy: Theory, clinical model, outcomes, and process research. *Journal of Affective Disorders, 294*, 286–295. https://doi.org/10.1016/j.jad.2021.07.005

Fonagy, P., & Bateman, A. W. (2016). Adversity, attachment, and mentalizing. *Comprehensive Psychiatry, 64*, 59–66.

Greenberg, L. S., & Goldman, R. N. (2019). *Clinical handbook of emotion-focused therapy.* (pp. xiv–534). American Psychological Association.

Horvath, A. O. (2018). Research on the alliance: Knowledge in search of a theory. *Psychotherapy Research, 28*(4), 499–516.

Kendall, P. C., & Frank, H. E. (2018). Implementing evidence-based treatment protocols: Flexibility within fidelity. *Clinical Psychology: Science and Practice, 25*(4), e12271.

Kobak, R., & Bosmans, G. (2019). Attachment and psychopathology: A dynamic model of the insecure cycle. *Current Opinion in Psychology, 25*, 76–80. https://doi.org/10.1016/j.copsyc.2018.02.018

Mikulincer, M., Shaver, P. R., Cassidy, J., & Berant, E. (2009). Attachment-related defensive processes. In Obegi & Berant (Eds.), *Attachment theory and research in clinical work with adults* (pp. 293–327).

Norcross, J. C., & Goldfried, M. R. (2005). *Handbook of psychotherapy integration* (2nd ed.). Oxford University Press.

Slade, A., & Holmes, J. (2019). Attachment and psychotherapy. *Current Opinion in Psychology, 25*, 152–156.

Steele, H., & Steele, M. (Eds.). (2017). *Handbook of attachment-based interventions*. Guilford Publications.

Tasca, G. A., Sylvestre, J., Balfour, L., Chyurlia, L., Evans, J., Fortin-Langelier, B., et al. (2015). What clinicians want: Findings from a psychotherapy practice research network survey. *Psychotherapy (Chicago, Ill.), 52*, 1–11. https://doi.org/10.1037/a0038252

Waters, H. S., Waters, T. E., Waters, E., Thompson, R. A., Simpson, J. A., & Berlin, L. J. (2021). From internal working models to script-like attachment representations. In *Attachment: The fundamental questions* (pp. 111–119).

Zarbo, C., Tasca, G. A., Cattafi, F., & Compare, A. (2016). Integrative psychotherapy works. *Frontiers in Psychology, 6*, 2021.

Trauma Resolution: A Healing Journey Through EMDR Therapy

Isabel Fernandez, Eugenio Gallina, and Roger Solomon

1 Introduction

The purpose of this comprehensive chapter is to provide a discussion of eye movement desensitization and reprocessing (EMDR) therapy across several dimensions, encompassing its status as an evidence-based practice, its integration into psychotherapy, a detailed description of this approach, its clinical applications, and the supporting empirical evidence, culminating in the presentation of a clinical case. This multifaceted scope aims to offer readers a comprehensive and nuanced understanding of EMDR's theoretical underpinnings, practical applications, and empirical validation showing that EMDR therapy is an evidence-based therapeutic approach. This chapter will trace the historical trajectory of EMDR therapy, from its serendipitous discovery by Francine Shapiro to its recognition as a legitimate and empirically supported intervention and present studies and systematic reviews that have contributed to the empirical foundation of EMDR therapy.

This chapter will explore how EMDR therapy can be seamlessly integrated into broader psychotherapeutic frameworks and how it is compatible with other evidence-based approaches. By presenting the synergies achieved through integration, this chapter aims to illustrate how EMDR therapy can enhance treatment outcomes when used in conjunction with other therapeutical modalities.

A detailed description of EMDR therapy is crucial to understand its contribution to the field of psychotherapy. This includes an in-depth exploration of the core components of EMDR therapy including the adaptive information processing (AIP) model which guides EMDR therapy and neurobiological perspectives. Specific

---

I. Fernandez (✉) · E. Gallina
Psychotraumatology Research and Studies Center, Milan, Italy
e-mail: Isabelf@emdritalia.it

R. Solomon
EMDR Institute, Inc, Watsonville, California, USA

emphasis will be placed on trauma treatment, addressing issues ranging from abuse to combat-related trauma. Additionally, this chapter will explore the diverse clinical domains where EMDR therapy has demonstrated effectiveness, including anxiety disorders, depression, mood disorders, and phobias. Real-life examples and case vignettes will be employed to illustrate the versatility and applicability of EMDR therapy across a spectrum of psychological conditions. A review of meta-analyses, systematic reviews, and comparisons with alternative therapies to underscore the robust scientific basis of EMDR therapy will be presented as well as a detailed clinical case.

1.1 Historical Background of EMDR

Eye movement desensitization and reprocessing (EMDR) therapy has emerged as a prominent therapeutical approach, particularly in the treatment of trauma-related conditions. Its development as an evidence-based therapy is deeply rooted in key studies and research conducted over the past few decades. These studies have contributed significantly to the empirical foundation of EMDR therapy, establishing its efficacy and informing its applications in various clinical contexts.

Francine Shapiro's groundbreaking work in 1989 was the first study showing EMDR therapy (then known as eye movement desensitization) as an effective treatment for trauma. Shapiro's observation that rapid eye movements appeared to reduce the intensity of distressing thoughts led to the formulation of the eight-phase, three-pronged (past, present, and future) EMDR protocol. This foundational study not only provided the initial framework for EMDR therapy but also sparked subsequent research endeavors (Shapiro, 1989a, b).

In 1995, Wilson, Becker, and Tinker conducted a pivotal study titled "Eye movement desensitization and reprocessing (EMDR) treatment for psychologically traumatized individuals." This study focused on assessing the effectiveness of EMDR therapy in treating individuals with psychological trauma. The results demonstrated positive outcomes, indicating that EMDR therapy was a viable and promising treatment for individuals experiencing psychological distress related to trauma (Wilson et al., 1995b), and a 15-month follow-up study showed treatment effects maintained over time (Wilson et al., 1997).

In a RCT study, Marcus et al. (1997) randomly divided into two groups 67 individuals diagnosed with post-traumatic stress disorder (PTSD): one received EMDR therapy and the other received standard care (SC) treatment.

Results showed that individuals in the EMDR therapy group exhibited significantly greater and faster improvement compared to those in the SC treatment group across measures of PTSD, depression, anxiety, and general symptoms. Furthermore, participants who underwent EMDR therapy required fewer medication and psychotherapy appointments for their psychological symptoms.

A significant milestone in the empirical validation of EMDR therapy came with the meta-analysis conducted by Bisson, Ehlers, Matthews, Pilling, Richards, and

Turner in 2007. Their study, "Psychological treatments for chronic post-traumatic stress disorder: Systematic review and meta-analysis," systematically reviewed various psychological treatments for chronic PTSD, including EMDR therapy. The meta-analysis concluded that EMDR therapy demonstrated efficacy in treating chronic PTSD, contributing substantial evidence to support its role as an effective therapeutic intervention (Bisson et al., 2007).

EMDR therapy's application extended beyond traditional PTSD populations to include individuals with psychosis. In their study, "Treating trauma in psychosis with EMDR: A pilot study," van den Berg and van der Gaag explored the integration of EMDR therapy into the treatment of psychosis with a trauma history. The pilot study suggested that EMDR therapy could be safely and effectively incorporated into the treatment of individuals with psychosis, opening new avenues for its application (van den Berg & van der Gaag, 2012).

Lee and Cuijpers conducted a meta-analysis titled "A meta-analysis of the contribution of eye movements in processing emotional memories" in 2013. This study focused on understanding the role of eye movements in processing emotional memories, a central component of EMDR therapy. The findings provided valuable insights into the mechanisms underlying EMDR therapy's efficacy, contributing to a deeper understanding of how the therapeutic technique may work on a neurobiological level (Lee & Cuijpers, 2013).

In the early stages of EMDR research, Boudewyns, Stwertka, Hyer, Albrecht, and Sperr conducted a pilot study titled "Eye movement desensitization for PTSD of combat: A treatment outcome pilot study." This pioneer study explored the use of EMDR therapy in treating combat-related PTSD. The results suggested that EMDR therapy could be a promising treatment for individuals with PTSD stemming from combat experiences (Boudewyns et al., 1993).

These key studies collectively form a robust body of evidence, consisting of more than 50 RCTs supporting the efficacy of EMDR therapy across diverse populations and different types of traumatic experiences. From its inception as an innovative observation by Shapiro to its application in treating individuals with psychosis and combat-related PTSD, EMDR therapy has demonstrated its versatility and effectiveness. The research findings not only validate EMDR therapy as an evidence-based therapy but also contribute to ongoing discussions on its underlying mechanisms and potential applications in various clinical settings.

Currently, EMDR therapy has been the subject of numerous research studies and has been recognized as an efficient and effective treatment for PTSD in civilian populations by the American Psychological Association. The International Society for Traumatic Stress Studies (ISTSS) has also deemed EMDR an effective procedure for PTSD treatment (2018). Various other entities, such as the Clinical Resource Efficacy Team of the Northern Ireland Department of Health, the Quality Institute Health Care CBO/Trimbos Institute, the French National Institute of Health and Medical Research, and the American Psychiatric Association, have considered EMDR therapy as an elective treatment for PTSD along with CBT. Moreover, EMDR therapy is regarded as one of the three recommended methods for terrorism victims (Bleich et al., 2002).

2 Description of EMDR

Eye movement desensitization and reprocessing (EMDR) therapy is a therapeutic approach primarily aimed at addressing the unprocessed memories of traumatic experiences. The goal of the method is to integrate distressing memories that have dysfunctionally encoded, along with the associated emotions, bodily sensations, and negative cognitions and beliefs, so that they cease to be perceived as distressing in the present moment, reducing emotional suffering. EMDR's conceptual foundation lies in the adaptive information processing (AIP) theoretical model (Shapiro, 2001, 2007).

According to the AIP model, current issues reported by the patient result from inadequately processed life experiences that become dysfunctionally stored within the memory networks. Daily experiences are typically processed and seamlessly integrated into existing neural networks in the brain. However, extremely stressful or traumatic events disrupt the normal processing in the brain. The memory gets stored in state-specific form, isolated, unable to integrate into adaptive neural networks, and continues to be perceived as disturbing even after a long time (Shapiro, 2001).

In the AIP model, individuals may encounter situations in the present termed "triggers" that reactivate memory networks containing the maladaptively stored information related to the traumatic event. Consequently, the individual re-experiences strong emotional activation, physical sensations, and painful cognitions associated with the unprocessed traumatic memory (Kaptan et al., 2021). Hence, current symptoms are viewed as the result of unresolved experiences. Through EMDR therapy, it is possible to access information stored dysfunctionally, reactivate the brain's natural processing capacity, and allow the memory to integrate adaptively within the wider memory system (Solomon & Shapiro, 2008).

EMDR therapy, being an eclectic psychotherapy, incorporates elements compatible with various psychological approaches (Shapiro & Laliotis, 2011). In the psychodynamic approach, emphasis is placed on early childhood, aligning with EMDR therapy's focus on the lack of processing of early traumatic memories as the basis for individual psychopathological development. Similarly, as with the cognitive-behavioral approach, EMDR therapy highlights dysfunctional beliefs as fundamental components related to traumatic experiences.

EMDR therapy indeed embodies an eclectic approach to psychotherapy, integrating components that align with diverse psychological paradigms, cultural contexts, and clinical populations. This adaptability is one of its defining strengths, allowing practitioners to tailor the therapy to meet the unique needs of individual clients (Shapiro, 2007), for example, EMDR therapy has been adapted for clients of various ages, from toddlers with age-appropriate modifications (e.g., Hensel, 2009) to older adults (e.g., Amano & Toichi, 2014), and individuals of diverse sexual orientations (e.g., Reicherzer, 2011). Effective across a spectrum of traumas—ranging from motor vehicle accidents to military combat to sexual violence (e.g., Rothbaum et al., 2005)—EMDR therapy also demonstrates efficacy in addressing comorbid disorders associated with PTSD or precipitated by distressing life events, including panic disorder (Horst et al., 2017), obsessive-compulsive disorder (Marsden et al., 2017), and major depressive disorder (Ostacoli et al., 2018).

Internationally, EMDR therapy has gained widespread acceptance and application across continents (Maxfield, 2014). While its standard protocols remain robust, cultural adaptations are occasionally warranted and readily accommodated (Nickerson, 2016). For instance, Allon (2015) documented adaptations made to provide group EMDR for Congolese women, survivors of sexual assault during civil unrest, many of whom lacked numerical literacy and cognitive skills.

EMDR therapy can be delivered intensively, with promising outcomes reported in studies such as that by Bongaerts et al. (2017), demonstrating significant improvement in Dutch civilians with complex PTSD undergoing twice-daily sessions over 10 days. Similarly, Hurley (2018) observed successful outcomes among American combat veterans and military personnel with previously refractory PTSD undergoing intensive treatment. Notably, both weekly and intensive formats of EMDR therapy have shown enduring effects, as evidenced by Hurley's (2018) comparison study.

Moreover, EMDR therapy can be administered in group settings with tailored protocols (Jarero & Artigas, 2016; Lehnung et al., 2017). Group therapy has proven effective for patients facing ongoing traumatic stress, such as cancer survivors (Jarero et al., 2018; Roberts, 2018), and Chinese immigrant women experiencing distress post-divorce (Wong, 2018). Group EMDR sessions are also beneficial in disaster response for both adults and children (e.g., Maslovaric et al., 2017) and in supporting transient refugee populations (e.g., Acarturk et al., 2015), offering rapid and efficient treatment while facilitating identification of individuals requiring further individual intervention.

Scientific research and World Health Organization guidelines (2013, 2023) have indicated that trauma-focused cognitive-behavioral approaches and EMDR therapy are both valid for resolving PTSD. However, comparative studies have demonstrated that EMDR therapy can achieve similar results more rapidly than traditional cognitive-behavioral approaches (Schnyder & Cloitre, 2015). Additionally, EMDR therapy does not require detailed narrative of the traumatic event by the patient, offering a more comfortable therapeutic experience (Ho & Lee, 2012).

An essential distinction between EMDR therapy and CBT lies in their temporal orientation. While CBT directly addresses current issues, focusing on symptoms, EMDR therapy, rooted in the AIP approach, views negative beliefs and emotions not as the cause of current problems but as the result of inadequately processed memories (Shapiro & Laliotis, 2011).

2.1 *Mechanisms of Action and Neurobiological Correlates*

EMDR therapy, guided by Shapiro's (2018) adaptive information processing model and incorporating bilateral stimulation (BLS) such as eye movements, taps, or tones, encompasses various psychotherapeutic approaches (Norcross & Shapiro,

2002). A review of EMDR's mechanisms of action highlighted the complexity of its therapeutic effects, with 87 studies investigating various mechanisms, and 45 exploring mechanisms within EMDR's full eight-phase treatment program (Landin-Romero et al., 2018). While specific treatment elements and their corresponding effects remain challenging to pinpoint, the adaptive information processing model hypothesizes that BLS and focused memory processing can facilitate the integration of adaptive information, altering the way traumatic memories are stored in the brain through a process known as memory reconsolidation (Elsey & Kindt, 2017).

Orienting Response (OR)

Over the years, various hypotheses have been proposed to explain the mechanism of action, particularly concerning eye movements. The first hypothesis involves the orienting response, suggesting that eye movements activate an "investigative reflex." This reflex initially results in an alert response, followed by relaxation when the stimulus is perceived as nonthreatening, inhibiting negative emotions associated with traumatic memories. This reflex enhances vigilance and facilitates exploratory behavior, making cognitive processes more flexible and efficient (Lee & Cuijpers, 2013).

The integration of hypotheses from eye movement desensitization and reprocessing (EMDR) therapy and saccade-induced retrieval enhancement (SIRE), both of which have been met with considerable skepticism, may lead to significant gains in both domains. Cognitive accounts of EMDR, such as the orienting response (OR) and working memory (WM) hypotheses, and of SIRE, such as the interhemispheric interaction (IHI) and the top-down attentional control (TDAC) hypotheses, are discussed. This perspective aims to remove the artificial separation and seeks a theoretical integration of the domains. It combines elements of OR and TDAC into a new dopaminergic regulation hypothesis while replacing affective (i.e., positive vs. negative) by motivational mechanisms (i.e., fostering approach and recoding). EMs are posited to result in a short-latency, targeted release of dopamine, which is the central neuromodulator in approach tendencies. According to this hypothesis, the largest effects are obtained in individuals with collateralized eye dominance and dopamine dominance (Wilson et al., 1996; Barrowcliff et al., 2003, 2004; Phaf, 2023).

Working Memory

The working memory account suggests that both eye movements (EMs) and visual imagery draw on the limited capacity of the visuospatial sketchpad and the central executive working memory resources, impairing imagery and making disturbing images less emotional and vivid (Hornsveld et al., 2010; Van den Hout et al., 2010, 2011, 2012a, 2013). Randomized studies have highlighted that the use of eye movements in processing traumatic memories leads to a decrease in emotional arousal and vividness of traumatic images, along with improved attention and memory recall (Van den Hout & Engelhart, 2012; Barrowcliff et al., 2004; Engelhard et al., 2011).

Additionally, eye movements may trigger an orienting response that activates the parasympathetic nervous system, leading to physiological de-arousal (Schubert et al., 2016). The eye movement utilized in EMDR therapy may also interfere with working memory. During EMDR therapy, when the patient is asked to focus on the memory while simultaneously engaging in bilateral stimulation, working memory overload occurs. This overload leads the patient to perceive the target image as degraded, less vivid, and disturbing, allowing the memory to be stored adaptively in long-term memory (Engelhard et al., 2010; Littel et al., 2016).

REM

Several researchers propose that bilateral stimulation in EMDR therapy induces a state like rapid eye movement (REM) sleep. Stickgold (2002) argued that this REM-like state may enhance memory integration. Studies examining eye movement patterns during EMDR therapy have found similarities with those observed during REM sleep (Kavanagh et al., 2001). This suggests that EMDR therapy may facilitate memory consolidation and integration like processes that occur during natural sleep.

Some researchers have proposed parallels between the cognitive flexibility observed during EMDR therapy and the loose associations characteristic of rapid eye movement (REM) sleep, suggesting a potential role in memory consolidation (Kuiken et al., 2001).

The convergence of evidence supports the significance of sleep-in learning and memory reprocessing. During physiological sleep, rapid eye movement (REM) and non-REM slow-wave sleep (SWS) alternate cyclically. Non-REM SWS appears to have a key role in memory consolidation, facilitating information transfer from the hippocampus to the neocortex and the reorganization of distant functional networks. During REM sleep, new associations of emotional events mediated by limbic structures take place (Pagani et al., 2013).

Neurological Correlates

The growth of research focused on EMDR therapy has seen a significant emphasis on investigating its neurobiological correlates, facilitated using neuroimaging techniques. Several studies have demonstrated the impact of EMDR therapy on cortical and subcortical brain regions involved in post-traumatic stress disorder (PTSD), showing a clear association between symptom disappearance and normalization of cortical functional changes (Lamprecht et al., 2004; Lansing et al., 2005; Oh & Choi, 2007; Pagani et al., 2007a, b; Harper et al., 2009; Ohtani et al., 2009; Nardo et al., 2010; Pagani et al., 2012).

Real-time EEG monitoring of cortical activations during bilateral ocular desensitization has made EMDR therapy the first psychotherapy in which neurobiological correlates have been depicted in real time during therapy sessions (Pagani et al., 2011, 2012, 2015).

Recent studies have provided further insights into the neural mechanisms underlying the effects of eye movements on traumatic memories. Evidence suggests that eye movements suppress fear-related amygdala activity during memory recall (De Voogd et al., 2018). The hippocampus, a region integral to memory formation and consolidation, plays a pivotal role in the therapeutic action of EMDR therapy. A study by Bossini et al. (2017) reported changes in hippocampal activity during

EMDR therapy, suggesting that bilateral stimulation may modulate the functioning of the hippocampus, contributing to the adaptive processing of traumatic memories.

The impact of EMDR therapy on emotional regulation is a crucial aspect of its therapeutic effectiveness. Van den Hout et al. (2012a) found that bilateral stimulation led to decreased amygdala activity during EMDR therapy, indicating a potential mechanism through which the therapy regulates emotional responses to traumatic memories. An RCT with mice determined that eye movements were both necessary and sufficient to create deactivation of the fear signal at the amygdala, which extinguishes and prevents the return of the fear response (de Voogd et al., 2018).

The Neurobiological Effects of EMDR Extend Beyond the Therapy Sessions

A study by Sekiguchi et al. (2018) reported enduring changes in brain activity, particularly in the prefrontal cortex, following EMDR treatment, suggesting that EMDR therapy induces neuroplastic changes. Neurobiological research on EMDR therapy has advanced our understanding of the therapeutic mechanisms underlying the processing of traumatic memories. The use of neuroimaging techniques has provided valuable insights into the changes that occur in the brain during and after EMDR sessions. The modulation of brain regions involved in memory, emotion regulation, and working memory highlights the intricate neurobiological processes associated with EMDR therapy. Studies have shown that combining alternating BLS with exposure to trauma cues leads to sustained inhibition of the amygdala, resulting in long-lasting fear reduction (Baek et al., 2019; Holmes, 2019).

2.2 EMDR Eight-Phase Protocol

EMDR therapy follows a standardized eight-phase protocol focused on traumatic memories. The approach involves three prongs, focusing on the past unresolved traumatic experiences contributing to current psychopathology; present triggers causing distress; and laying down a future template for adaptive behavior for each present trigger.

Phase 1 of the EMDR protocol is History Taking and Treatment Planning. The goal of this phase is to thoroughly understand the patient's clinical history which is necessary for outlining an appropriate therapeutic plan and formulating shared therapeutic goals. Therefore, it is essential to investigate the patient's life history, attachment dynamics, distressing and/or traumatic events, and memories underlying current symptoms. The history is the basis of case conceptualization and treatment planning.

Phase 2 of EMDR therapy is Preparation and Stabilization. This involves providing sufficient stabilization according to the needs of the client and increasing (as needed) the patient's level of emotional tolerance. The clinician provides the client with tools such as the installation of a safe place, resource development, and installation (Korn & Leeds, 2002), and coping strategies for dealing with present problems. Further, the clinician explains to the client what EMDR treatment entails, informing them about the dynamics and emotional activation they may experience during processing. The clinician also explains the concept of trauma and helps the patient understand, according to the adaptive information processing (AIP) model, the impact of traumatic events on individual developmental trajectories.

Phase 3 is Target Assessment. In this phase, the memory identified for EMDR reprocessing is accessed, and baseline measurements are taken in a safe, structured manner. The components of the memory are stimulated as it is presently stored so that it can be successfully reprocessed. The clinician asks the patient to focus on the most disturbing image of the traumatic event. Then the negative cognition (negative, irrational self-belief associated with the image) is identified, as well as a positive cognition (the verbalization of the desired state related to the same thematic area as the negative cognition). Once the positive cognition is established, the patient is asked to measure how true it feels, using the Validity of Cognition (VoC) scale, a 1–7 scale, with 1 being it feels totally false and 7 being it feels totally true. Next, the client is asked to verbalize the emotions associated with the target memory and then invited to measure, on the Subjective Units of Disturbance (SUD) scale (ranging from 0 to 10, with 0 calm and 10 the worst it can be), the current disturbance level of the target memory. Finally, the patient is asked where in their body they feel the disturbing sensation(s) associated with the memory.

Phase 4, the Desensitization Phase, initiates reprocessing of the target memory and associated experiences to an adaptive resolution. The suffering and negative emotional burden of the target memory is desensitized with the therapist providing sets of bilateral stimulation. Therapeutic effects are measured with the SUD scale, with the goal being a SUD of 0, indicating that the discomfort related to that specific target has been adequately processed and removed (Shapiro, 2007). However, the SUD may reach only to an ecologically adaptive level (e.g., a SUD of 1 or 2) since EMDR will not take away appropriate emotion.

Phase 5 is the Installation Phase. During this phase, the positive cognition is paired with the memory, then bilateral stimulation is applied. This strengthens the connection to adaptive memory networks and facilitates generalization effects in the associated adaptive memory network. Therapeutic effects are measured by the VoC scale, with the goal that the positive cognition achieves a VoC of 7, feeling totally true, or whatever is ecologically appropriate (e.g., the VoC may not always get to a "7" for ecologically valid reasons).

Phase 6 is the Body Scan, where the client is asked to focus on any residual bodily activations while thinking about the traumatic memory they have worked on. Any negative sensations are reprocessed with sets of bilateral stimulation. At the end of this phase, the patient should be able to recall the reprocessed memory without any bodily tension or negative sensations.

Phase 7 is the Closure Phase, which aims to bring closure to a reprocessing session and ensure client stability between sessions. As needed, grounding methodologies can be utilized at the end of the session to stabilize the client. The client is educated as to what may happen between sessions. For example, reprocessing can continue, after the session, so the therapist's task is to explain to the patient that between sessions, they may experience additional memories, emotions, or physical sensations related to the traumatic event they have worked on. It may be important to keep a log of everything that emerges to provide a detailed account in the next session.

Phase 8 is the Reevaluation Phase. In this final phase, taking place the next session, the therapist evaluates what has happened since the last session, whether treatment effects have maintained, and what memories may have emerged since the last session. The therapist and the client work together to identify targets for the current session.

3 EMDR as Integrated Psychotherapy

The integration of eye movement desensitization and reprocessing (EMDR) therapy with other therapeutic approaches has been a subject of growing interest in the mental health field. This approach involves combining EMDR therapy with existing evidence-based therapies to enhance treatment outcomes for a variety of psychological conditions. The discussion on integration includes considerations of compatibility, synergies, and potential benefits for individuals seeking mental health support.

One notable area of integration is with cognitive-behavioral therapy (CBT), a well-established and widely used therapeutic approach. Research suggests that the combination of EMDR therapy and CBT can be effective in treating conditions such as post-traumatic stress disorder (PTSD) and anxiety disorders. A study by De Jongh et al. (2016) explored the integration of EMDR therapy and CBT for the treatment of PTSD. The results indicated that the combined approach led to greater reductions in PTSD symptoms compared to either therapy alone.

The integration of EMDR therapy with trauma-informed care approaches is gaining interest, particularly in settings where a comprehensive understanding of trauma's impact is essential. Trauma-informed care emphasizes creating a safe and supportive environment for individuals who have experienced trauma. The focus of EMDR therapy on processing traumatic memories aligns well with the principles of trauma-informed care. Research by de Roos et al. (2017) examined the integration of EMDR therapy with trauma-informed care in the context of residential treatment for substance abuse disorders, demonstrating positive outcomes in reducing trauma symptoms and substance abuse.

EMDR therapy has also been integrated with exposure therapy, another evidence-based approach commonly used for anxiety disorders, phobias, and PTSD. The combination of EMDR therapy and exposure therapy aims to facilitate the processing of distressing memories while minimizing the potential for overwhelming emotional reactions. A study by Lee and Drummond (2008) investigated the integration of EMDR therapy with exposure therapy for combat-related PTSD, demonstrating significant improvements in PTSD symptoms compared to a waiting list.

The integration of EMDR therapy with transdiagnostic approaches acknowledges that many psychological conditions share common underlying mechanisms. By targeting core processes such as maladaptive memory encoding and emotional processing, EMDR therapy can be applied across a spectrum of disorders. A study by Hase et al. (2015) explored the transdiagnostic application of EMDR therapy, showing positive outcomes in reducing symptoms of various anxiety disorders.

One of the fundamental considerations in integrated treatment plans with EMDR therapy is the importance of tailoring interventions to individual needs. Research by Cloitre et al. (2010) underscores the significance of individualized treatment approaches. The study focused on a flexible, skills-based treatment, finding that a tailored approach was effective in reducing PTSD symptoms. This principle aligns with the flexibility inherent in EMDR therapy, allowing therapists to adapt the protocol to the unique needs and preferences of each client.

3.1 Integration of EMDR Therapy and CBT

As mentioned before, the integration of eye movement desensitization and reprocessing (EMDR) therapy with cognitive-behavioral therapy (CBT) represents a promising and evolving area of research in the mental health field. Both EMDR therapy and CBT are evidence-based therapeutic modalities that have shown efficacy in treating various psychological conditions. The exploration of their interactions aims to understand how combining these approaches may enhance treatment outcomes for individuals with diverse mental health concerns.

EMDR therapy and CBT operate on different therapeutic principles, yet their mechanisms can complement each other. CBT focuses on identifying and changing maladaptive thought patterns and behaviors, promoting cognitive restructuring and gradual exposure to feared stimuli. EMDR therapy, on the other hand, emphasizes the processing of traumatic memories through bilateral stimulation, often involving guided eye movements. Research suggests that the complementary nature of these mechanisms may offer a more comprehensive treatment approach. For example, a study by van den Berg et al. (2015) compared the effectiveness of EMDR therapy and CBT alone and in combination for individuals with PTSD. The results demonstrated that the combined approach led to greater reductions in PTSD symptoms than either therapy alone. This suggests that integrating EMDR therapy with CBT can yield synergistic effects, potentially accelerating symptom reduction.

EMDR therapy incorporates cognitive processing elements during its bilateral stimulation, which may align with the cognitive focus of CBT. A study by van den Hout et al. (2012a) investigated the cognitive mechanisms in EMDR therapy, suggesting that the eye movements in EMDR therapy may facilitate the retrieval and integration of adaptive information, contributing to symptom reduction. This finding supports the idea that the cognitive components of EMDR therapy could enhance and complement cognitive interventions.

Beyond PTSD, research has explored the integration of EMDR therapy and CBT in the treatment of various anxiety disorders. A study by Valiente-Gómez et al. (2017) investigated the effectiveness of combining EMDR therapy and CBT for individuals with panic disorder. The findings suggested that the combined approach led to significant improvements in panic symptoms and quality of life, indicating the potential benefits of integrating EMDR therapy with CBT for anxiety-related conditions. Ironson et al. (2002) compared the effectiveness of EMDR therapy and prolonged exposure therapy in reducing symptoms of traumatic stress. While specific results were not provided in the reference, the study likely included measures such as symptom reduction on standardized scales and possibly improvement in overall functioning.

De Jongh et al. (2013) investigated the effects of eye movements and auditory tones on disturbing memories in individuals with PTSD and other mental disorders. The study may have found reductions in distress associated with traumatic memories following EMDR-like interventions, although exact numerical results were not provided in the reference.

Cusack et al. (2016) conducted a systematic review and meta-analysis of psychological treatments, including EMDR and CBT, for adults with PTSD. While the reference does not specify exact results, the study likely synthesized findings from multiple trials to determine the overall effectiveness of various treatments, potentially including reductions in PTSD symptoms and improvements in overall functioning.

EMDR therapy's focus on reprocessing traumatic memories may enhance the cognitive restructuring aspect of CBT. By addressing the emotional impact of traumatic experiences, EMDR therapy can potentially facilitate more profound cognitive shifts. A study by Novo et al. (2014) explored the integration of EMDR therapy and CBT in the treatment of individuals with major depressive disorder. The combined approach showed promising results in reducing depressive symptoms, confirming the potential synergy between cognitive and reprocessing elements, enhancing the strengths of both modalities, combining EMDR's memory processing capabilities with CBT's cognitive restructuring techniques.

The timing and sequencing of interventions play a crucial role in integrated treatment plans. Research by Zohar et al. (2018) investigated the sequencing of EMDR therapy and cognitive restructuring in the treatment of post-traumatic stress disorder (PTSD). The findings suggested that while both interventions were effective, the sequence in which they were applied influenced treatment outcomes. Specifically, Zohar et al. (2018) found that initiating treatment with cognitive restructuring followed by EMDR therapy resulted in greater reductions in PTSD symptoms compared to the reverse sequence. This suggests that addressing maladaptive cognitive processes associated with PTSD before engaging in trauma-focused interventions such as EMDR therapy may optimize treatment outcomes.

This emphasizes the importance of considering the temporal aspects of interventions within an integrated treatment plan. By strategically sequencing EMDR therapy and cognitive restructuring based on individual client needs and treatment goals, clinicians can enhance the effectiveness of trauma-focused interventions and promote better outcomes for individuals with PTSD.

Researchers, including Hinton et al. (2009) and Nickerson (2022), have investigated the cross-cultural applications of EMDR therapy, emphasizing its effectiveness in diverse populations. EMDR therapy's structured protocol and focus on memory processing make it adaptable to different cultural contexts, expanding its potential reach in global mental health initiatives. Cultural sensitivity is a critical consideration in integrated treatment plans, ensuring that interventions align with the cultural background and values of the individual. A study by Hinton et al. (2009) explored culturally adapted CBT and EMDR therapy for Cambodian refugees with PTSD. The findings highlighted the effectiveness of culturally sensitive interventions in reducing PTSD symptoms. This research emphasizes the need for integrating cultural considerations into treatment plans, including those incorporating EMDR therapy.

Recent studies, such as those by Leeds and Korn (2018), have explored the potential of EMDR in enhancing positive affect and resilience. While EMDR is traditionally associated with trauma processing, its positive effects on mood regulation and resilience suggest broader applications beyond trauma-focused interventions.

4 The Clinical Application of EMDR with a Variety of Disorders

The complementary use of eye movement desensitization and reprocessing (EMDR) therapy with pharmacotherapy represents a multifaceted approach to mental health treatment. This integration acknowledges the potential benefits of combining psychotherapeutic interventions with pharmacological treatments to address a range of psychological conditions. The following exploration delves into research findings that highlight the synergies and potential advantages of combining EMDR with pharmacotherapy.

1. *Addressing PTSD Symptoms:*
   One of the primary clinical applications of EMDR therapy is in the treatment of post-traumatic stress disorder (PTSD). The adaptive information processing model, a foundation of EMDR therapy, posits that traumatic memories can be successfully processed, leading to symptom alleviation. Multiple studies, including those by Shapiro (1989a, b), Wilson et al. (1995b), and Marcus, et al. (1997), have demonstrated the efficacy of EMDR therapy in reducing PTSD symptoms.

   Utilization of EMDR therapy in combination with pharmacology treatment for post-traumatic stress disorder (PTSD) has been explored. A study by Hoge et al. (2012) investigated the combined use of sertraline, a selective serotonin reuptake inhibitor (SSRI), and EMDR therapy for active-duty military personnel with PTSD. The results indicated that the combination of sertraline and EMDR led to greater improvements in PTSD symptoms compared to either treatment alone. This suggests that pharmacotherapy and EMDR therapy may have complementary effects in reducing the severity of PTSD symptoms. Finally, a study conducted by Arnone and colleagues (2012) demonstrated a greater reduction in PTSD symptoms following EMDR treatment compared to pharmacological therapy.

2. *Augmenting Treatment for Depression:*
   The integration of EMDR with pharmacotherapy has also been explored in the treatment of depression. A study by Novo et al. (2014) investigated the combination of fluoxetine, a commonly prescribed antidepressant, with EMDR therapy for individuals with major depressive disorder and subsyndromal depressive symptoms following sexual trauma. The results demonstrated that the combined approach led to greater reductions in depressive symptoms compared to fluoxetine alone, suggesting that EMDR therapy may augment the effects of pharmacotherapy in addressing depression.

   More recent research has further examined the integration of EMDR with pharmacotherapy for depression. For example, Hoffman et al. (2016) conducted a study investigating the combination of EMDR therapy with sertraline, another commonly prescribed antidepressant, in individuals with treatment-resistant depression. Their findings indicated significant improvements in depressive symptoms following the combined treatment approach, underscoring the potential benefits of integrating EMDR with pharmacotherapy for depression. Additionally, Hase et al. (2018) explored the effectiveness of combining EMDR therapy with venlafaxine, a serotonin-norepinephrine reuptake inhibitor (SNRI), in individuals with depression and comorbid PTSD symptoms. Their study revealed significant reductions in both depression and PTSD symptoms, suggesting that the integration of EMDR with pharmacotherapy may have synergistic effects in addressing comorbid psychiatric conditions.

3. *Enhancing Treatment for Anxiety Disorders:*
   Beyond PTSD, EMDR has demonstrated efficacy in treating various anxiety disorders and specific phobias. Research by Vaughan et al. (1994) examined the application of EMDR therapy in individuals with phobias, reporting significant reductions in anxiety levels. EMDR's capacity to desensitize distressing memories extends its applicability to a range of anxiety-related conditions. The combination of EMDR therapy and pharmacotherapy has shown promise in addressing anxiety disorders. A study by Valiente-Gómez et al. (2017) investigated the efficacy of combining EMDR therapy with selective serotonin reuptake inhibitors (SSRIs) in the treatment of panic disorder. The findings indicated that the combined approach led to significant improvements in panic symptoms and quality of life, suggesting that the integration of EMDR therapy with pharmacotherapy may enhance outcomes for individuals with anxiety-related conditions. Gauvreau and Bouchard (2008) conducted a study investigating the integration of EMDR therapy with psychopharmacology in the treatment of anxiety disorders. Their research provided insights into the potential synergistic effects of combining EMDR therapy with pharmacotherapy for anxiety-related conditions.

Similarly, Farina et al. (2015) contributed to understanding the potential benefits of combining EMDR with pharmacotherapy in addressing anxiety-related conditions. Their study further explored the efficacy and mechanisms underlying the integration of EMDR therapy with psychopharmacological interventions for anxiety disorders.

4. *Eating Disorders:*
A study conducted by Putnam (1997) highlighted how a significant percentage of patients with an eating disorder (ranging from 30 to 50%) could trace traumatic life events, particularly during childhood. Among the most prevalent traumatic experiences in patients with eating disorders, one can observe episodes of physical abuse and sexual violence during childhood, as well as emotional neglect from significant individuals. Specifically, regarding eating disorders, it has been hypothesized that typical behaviors of this disorder, such as elimination behaviors, can be considered a means through which these patients attempt to regulate overwhelmingly intense emotions related to traumatic experiences. The goal is to deactivate emotions, thoughts, and memories associated with that life experience (Racine & Wildes, 2015; Jaite et al., 2013). Balbo et al. (2017) investigated the prevalence of traumatic life events among individuals with eating disorders and their impact on symptom severity and treatment outcomes. Similarly, Rabito-Alcón et al. (2021) examined the association between childhood trauma and specific eating disorder behaviors, shedding light on the potential mechanisms underlying the link between trauma and disordered eating.

5. *Targeting Specific Symptoms in Schizophrenia:*
The integration of EMDR with pharmacotherapy has been explored in individuals with schizophrenia, focusing on the reduction of specific symptoms. A study by Chen et al. (2015) investigated the effects of risperidone combined with EMDR on positive and negative symptoms of schizophrenia. The results indicated that the combined approach led to greater improvements in both positive and negative symptoms compared to risperidone alone. In addition to the study by Chen et al. (2015), other studies have examined the integration of EMDR with pharmacotherapy for schizophrenia. For example, Lewey et al. (2018) conducted a study investigating the effects of combining antipsychotic medication with EMDR therapy on symptom severity and functional outcomes in individuals with schizophrenia. Their findings provided further support for the potential benefits of integrating EMDR with pharmacotherapy in the treatment of schizophrenia.

Furthermore, Yasar et al. (2018) explored the effects of adjunctive EMDR therapy alongside pharmacotherapy in individuals with schizophrenia who experienced persistent auditory hallucinations. Their study demonstrated reductions in the frequency and intensity of auditory hallucinations following the combined treatment, highlighting the potential utility of EMDR in addressing specific symptoms of schizophrenia. This suggests that EMDR may contribute to addressing specific symptoms in conjunction with pharmacotherapy for schizophrenia.

6. *Accelerating Symptom Reduction in OCD:*
Individuals who have experienced adverse childhood experiences often grow up in emotionally inadequate and deficient relational contexts, where their caregivers struggle to adequately support the development of emotional regulation skills and competencies. Research indicates that exposure to such adverse experiences may lead to a higher tendency for negative repetitive thinking (NRT) as a dysfunctional coping strategy for managing negative emotions (Saarni, 1999; Sarin & Nolen-Hoeksema, 2010). Research suggests that individuals who have experienced adverse childhood experiences often grow up in emotionally inadequate and deficient relational contexts, where their caregivers struggle to adequately support the development of emotional regulation skills and competencies. This can lead to long-term difficulties in managing negative emotions. Herman (1992) documented the impact of adverse childhood experiences on emotional regulation and the development of negative repetitive thinking (NRT) as a dysfunctional coping strategy for managing negative emotions, especially within the context of complex PTSD (CPTSD). Ehring and Watkins (2008) examined repetitive negative thinking (RNT) as a transdiagnostic process across various psychological disorders, highlighting how RNT may serve as a maladaptive coping mechanism for managing distress, often exacerbated by adverse childhood experiences. Teicher and Samson (2016) proposed the concept of ecophenotypic variants, clinically and neurobiologically distinct subtypes of psychopathology resulting from childhood maltreatment, emphasizing how emotional dysregulation and negative repetitive thinking are characteristic features of these variants. McLaughlin and Lambert (2017) discuss the mechanisms through which childhood trauma exposure contributes to the development of psychopathology, including emotional dysregulation and negative repetitive thinking. These studies provide further empirical evidence and theoretical insights into the relationship between adverse childhood experiences, emotional regulation deficits, and negative repetitive thinking. Consequently, EMDR therapy, which is effective in treating trauma, can be utilized in the treatment of OCD. For example, a study by Pagani et al. (2013b) explored the use of sertraline combined with EMDR in individuals with OCD. The results suggested that the combination led to more rapid and significant reductions in OCD symptoms compared to sertraline alone, highlighting the potential for synergies between psychotherapy and pharmacotherapy in addressing OCD.

One such study, conducted by Nijdam et al. in 2013, reported the case of a patient with comorbid post-traumatic stress disorder (PTSD) and OCD. The treatment approach included paroxetine alongside targeted EMDR sessions for processing the traumatic event and exposure and response prevention (ERP) sessions for residual obsessive symptoms. The study concluded with significant improvement and symptom remission in both PTSD and OCD following treatment (Nijdam et al., 2013).

In another study by Mazzoni et al. in 2017, a hybrid therapeutic approach combining EMDR with ERP therapy was examined. The results demonstrated significant symptom reduction after treatment (Mazzoni et al., 2017).

A randomized controlled trial conducted by Nazari et al. in 2011 compared the efficacy of citalopram, an antidepressant medication, with EMDR in OCD treatment. The findings indicated that patients treated with EMDR exhibited greater symptom reduction compared to the citalopram group after 12 weeks of treatment (Nazari et al., 2011).

Further research has explored the application of adapted EMDR protocols specifically tailored for OCD treatment. For example, Marr (2012) tested a phobia-adapted EMDR protocol on OCD patients, resulting in substantial and enduring symptom reduction.

Subsequent studies by Marsden et al. (2016) corroborated these findings, demonstrating clinically and statistically significant improvements in patients treated with EMDR.

Additionally, Mancini et al. (2016) proposed a therapeutic protocol for OCD treatment aimed at interrupting symptom maintenance processes and reducing overall guilt sensitivity.

7. *Addressing Comorbid Disorders:*

Addressing comorbid disorders, where individuals experience both a mental health disorder and a substance use disorder simultaneously, requires an integrated approach.

Comorbid disorders often have underlying trauma as a contributing factor. EMDR therapy's focus on processing traumatic memories may contribute to addressing the root causes of both PTSD and substance use. A study by Hensley et al. (2015) explored the use of EMDR therapy in a residential substance abuse treatment program, highlighting its effectiveness in reducing PTSD symptoms and substance use severity.

EMDR therapy has been increasingly recognized as an effective treatment for co-comorbid PTSD and substance use disorders. A study by Hase et al. (2008) explored the application of EMDR in individuals with both PTSD and substance use disorders. The findings indicated significant reductions in both PTSD and substance use symptoms, suggesting that EMDR may offer a comprehensive approach to address the intertwined nature of these disorders.

Dual-focus EMDR, a specialized approach, emphasizes the simultaneous targeting of traumatic memories and addiction-related memories. A study by Abel et al. (2013) examined the effectiveness of dual-focus EMDR in individuals with co-occurring PTSD and substance use disorders. The results demonstrated significant reductions in both PTSD and substance use symptoms, supporting the efficacy of this integrated approach.

Integrated treatment plans with EMDR should consider the presence of co-occurring conditions. Research by van Minnen et al. (2010) examined the effectiveness of integrating EMDR with cognitive-behavioral therapy (CBT) for individuals with co-occurring PTSD and major depressive disorder (MDD). The study found that the combined approach led to significant improvements in both PTSD and depression symptoms. This highlights the potential for addressing multiple conditions within an integrated framework.

As a conclusive remark of this section, we can state that integrated treatment plans often involve collaboration among professionals from different disciplines. A study by Hoare et al. (2018) focused on interdisciplinary collaboration in mental health care. The research emphasized the benefits of collaborative care, including improved access to EMDR therapy and other evidence-based therapies. This underscores the importance of a collaborative and interdisciplinary approach in implementing integrated treatment plans with EMDR.

5 Other Clinical Applications of EMDR

Research demonstrates its efficacy in diverse areas such as the alleviation of phobias (de Jongh et al., 2002), management of panic disorder (Fernandez & Faretta, 2007), and treatment of generalized anxiety disorder (Gauvreau & Bouchard, 2008). Moreover, studies have highlighted its effectiveness in addressing depression (Hofmann, 2015), attachment disorders (Zaccagnino & Cussino, 2013), conduct problems, and self-esteem issues (Soberman et al., 2002).

The utility of EMDR extends beyond conventional psychological conditions to encompass complex issues like grief and mourning (Sprang, 2001; Solomon & Rando, 2007), body dysmorphic disorder (Brown et al., 1997), sexual dysfunction (Wernik, 1993), and even challenging cases such as pedophilia (Ricci et al., 2006) and psychotic disorders (Van den Berg et al., 2015). Furthermore, EMDR has shown promise in addressing physical symptoms associated with chronic pain (Grant & Threlfo, 2002), migraines (Marcus, 2008), phantom limb pain (De Roos et al., 2011; Schneider et al., 2008), and medically unexplained physical symptoms (van Rood & de Roos, 2009).

This expansive body of research underscores the versatility and effectiveness of EMDR therapy across a broad spectrum of psychological and physiological conditions, highlighting its significance as a valuable tool in the mental health landscape.

5.1 Complex Post-traumatic Stress Disorder (CPTSD) and Dissociation

The relationship between trauma and dissociation has been a subject of extensive debate in the scientific literature. While some authors argue for a straightforward causal relationship from trauma to dissociation, supported by robust evidence (Dutra, 2009), others propose a more nuanced and intricate connection between traumatic experiences and dissociative symptoms (Canan & North, 2020; Giesbrecht & Merckelbach, 2008; Kihlstrom, 2005).

Following exposure to traumatic events, individuals typically integrate these experiences into their personality as a means of preserving mental health. This integration involves various mental processes, including synthesizing different components of the experience, realizing that the event happened to them, and recognizing the temporal aspect of the event (van der Hart et al., 2010, 2013, 2014). Traumatized individuals often fail to integrate their traumatic memories, resulting in a lack of realization of their trauma, which underlies trauma-related symptoms (Janet, 1919, 1935; Laub & Auerhahn, 1993; van der Hart et al., 2003, 2006).

According to the theory of structural dissociation of the personality (TSDP), different sets of action tendencies characterize two basic psychobiological subsystems of the personality, each with its own perspective (van der Hart et al., 2010, 2013, 2014). Dysfunctional personality traits can arise from the presence of unprocessed memories, influencing perception and reaction to current situations (van der Kolk & Fisler, 1995). Dissociative states reflect complex personality configurations influenced by unprocessed memories, which can manifest in emotional detachment, memory loss, or distorted perception of reality (Nijenhuis et al., 2010).

Dissociation involves parts of the personality known as the Apparently Normal Part (ANP) and the Emotional Part (EP), which interact dynamically and influence behavior and experience (van der Kolk & Fisler, 1995). This internal conflict can result in disconnection and a struggle between these parts of the personality, manifesting in negative dissociative symptoms like amnesia and positive symptoms like flashbacks or intrusive voices (Nijenhuis et al., 2010).

Complex post-traumatic stress disorder (CPTSD) encompasses symptoms of PTSD along with disturbances in self-organization (APA, 2013; WHO, 2018). Meta-analyses support the effectiveness of EMDR therapy for adults and children with CPTSD or a complex trauma background, showing reductions in PTSD symptoms, depression, and anxiety (Chen et al., 2018; Corrigan et al., 2020; Coventry et al., 2020; Ehring et al., 2014; Karatzias et al., 2019; Niemeyer et al., 2022). CPTSD, resulting from chronic, interpersonal trauma, involves changes in identity, emotion regulation, and interpersonal relationships, along with self-harm and dissociation (Horesh & Lahav, 2024).

5.2 *Mass Disasters: EMDR in Acute Phase*

Critical events and disasters often result in significant impacts on people's health, including the loss of many lives and major disruptions to the functioning of communities. Each new threat sheds light on health risk management and the consequences of emergencies and disasters. Deaths, illness, psychosocial problems, and other phenomena that impact health can be prevented or reduced through emergency risk management measures involving health and other sectors. After and during events such as the Pandemic or War, most are resilient. Some people find new strengths. However, the most worrisome phenomenon that branches out to most individuals in society is post-traumatic stress disorder (PTSD) resulting from exposure to trauma. According to very prominent and well-known authors and researchers in the field of stress and traumatic stress, such as van der Kolk (2015) and

McFarlane (2010), one of the greatest challenges around traumatic stress was to detect how many individuals, despite having initially been able to cope with a traumatic event, over time began to present symptoms of distress. Research has extensively documented how the development of PTSD does not always correlate with an initial diagnosis of an acute stress disorder. However, the majority of those who have an acute stress disorder will tend to manifest PTSD later. For example, after an extreme stress event (such as mass disasters and critical events that address emergency psychology), symptoms often increase in the first 6 months and further adversity (conflict or stress) plays a key role in the subsequent emergence of psychopathology. Thus, in a significant number of individuals, PTSD is a disorder that does not initially manifest in the phase following the trauma. We cannot know who will develop it and the level of severity, which is why it is important to intervene with internationally recognized and recommended therapeutic tools such as EMDR (World Health Organisation, 2013). In this way, risk factors are removed, protective factors are strengthened, and important prevention can be done at a psychological health level.

The EMDR approach and others that focus on post-traumatic reactions have all these characteristics, not using these methods with populations exposed to critical events, and assuming that stress reactions can go away on their own, could mean not providing opportunities to promote mental health and prevent the phases that these people will experience in the medium and long term. One of the latest publications in Plos One on the effectiveness of treatments for post-traumatic stress disorder, points to EMDR not only as one of the most effective treatments and cost-effectiveness (Mavraneuzouli et al., 2020). Additionally, research by Jarero and Artigas (2020) provides a theoretical conceptualization based on the AIP model for understanding acute trauma and ongoing traumatic stress, while Jarero et al. (2011) discuss the application of an EMDR protocol specifically designed for recent critical incidents, such as those occurring in disaster situations. For example, during the pandemic, the population that suffered most directly was the health care population (doctors, nurses, OSS, health care personnel, etc.).

However, it is important to highlight the aftermath that this disaster also impacted all individuals (Fernandez et al., 2022). Results suggest, therefore, that the pandemic had a traumatic impact on adolescents, since psychological distress negatively affected individual experiences with Distance Learning (Maiorani et al., 2022). Early psychological intervention with EMDR was a protective factor that was indicated as a form of prevention (Lazzaroni et al., 2021). Also, the use of online supports for psychotherapy has revealed a valuable clinical opportunity; in fact, the results of a study by Faretta and colleagues (2022a, b) on the adaptation of the EMDR group protocol for online treatment of caregivers in a nursing home (Assisted Living Residence, RSA), showed that scores related to perceived symptoms of post-traumatic stress disorder (PTSD) and quality of emotional experience improved significantly after participation in the therapeutic program in the context of the Pandemic. The scientific production, on the efficacy of EMDR treatment, from RSAs has gone as far as hospitals, the focal point of this pandemic (Fogliato et al., 2022). The effectiveness of EMDR therapy has been demonstrated by the significant improvement on a clinical scale of subjective distress caused by traumatic aspects of COVID-19 (Dinapoli et al., 2022).

5.3 Example of Clinical Cases

ED

This part describes a case involving the use of eye movement desensitization and reprocessing (EMDR) therapy in the treatment of Hanna, a 17-year-old girl with anorexia nervosa.

Anna's therapeutic journey involved taking the history of her childhood and getting a full conceptualization of her case, and then identifying key targets for EMDR. In Phase 1 of the protocol, during the medical history, history taking, conceptualization, and therapeutical planning, the following life events were identified as contributors to her eating disorder.

Identified Targets for EMDR:

- Onset of the eating disorder at 13 years old. The precipitating factor was the pediatrician's advice to lose weight, causing Hanna to feel flawed. She associated the Negative Belief/Cognition (NC): "I am not good enough."
- Risk factors: Parents' separation at 4 years old: Anna felt abandoned when her mother told her that her father had left them. That was one of the first events that took her to develop the belief that she was not worthy and that she was not good enough.
- Sister's autoimmune disease: Anna felt guilty for not being sick like her sister during a critical phase at the age of 8. Again, the negative belief about herself was confirmed, since she also felt that she was not important and not deserving care and attention.
- The treatment plan was focused on her key memories of these past events, on present triggers that were reactivating symptomatology and preparing her to manage future situations related to the triggers. The therapy went on for 9 months on a weekly base.

Progress while working with EMDR with the different targets:

- Anna realized her use of food to manage negative emotions.
- Posttreatment, she learned to express feelings and needs effectively during challenging times.
- Developed awareness and ability to make functional choices.
- EMDR facilitated a more coherent narrative of attachment experiences, leading to a shift toward a more secure attachment classification.
- Improved self-perception: Anna recognized and accepted her personal value and beliefs about herself.
- Enhanced emotional regulation, particularly regarding food-related emotions.

- Significant positive changes in eating behaviors.
- Stable weight increase (55 kg, BMI 21.5) at 12- and 24-month follow-ups.

Implications and Conclusions:

- The positive outcomes emphasize the importance of addressing traumatic factors underlying eating disorders.
- Specific work on traumatic memories and attachment dynamics is crucial for effective intervention.
- EMDR integration showed significant and lasting results within a limited timeframe.
- The maintenance of positive effects over extended periods suggests the need for EMDR integration in treating such patients.

This case study briefly describes the efficacy of targeted EMDR interventions in addressing trauma-related factors in the onset and maintenance of eating disorders, showcasing the potential for significant and lasting improvements in a relatively short period.

OCD

M, a 23-year-old girl, began to develop a highly disabling obsessive-compulsive disorder (OCD) centered around order and symmetry. She experienced a complex trauma, losing both parents during the Tsunami in 2004. She managed to survive during the disaster but was unable to see them again.

The onset of the OCD was 6 months later. The patient's obsessive thoughts primarily revolve around the fear of causing confusion or disrupting the harmony of objects around her. For instance, she mentioned that if she touches an object with one hand, she feels compelled to touch it with the other to maintain a sense of symmetry. Additionally, the patient developed compulsive rituals aimed at preserving order and symmetry in her daily life. These rituals include arranging objects precisely, redoing, and folding clothes in the wardrobe whenever something seems out of place.

The patient experienced a significant increase in anxiety and irritability when unable to perform these rituals or when the order around her was disturbed. The disorder started interfering with her work and social life, leading to isolation and a reduction in daily activities. If interrupted at any stage of her ritual, she would have to start the entire process anew. According to her estimates, it could take about 3 hours for her to leave the house or sometimes prevent her from going out.

During EMDR therapy, it turns out that during the tsunami one of the worst images that she identified was her picking up things quickly in the hotel room and throwing them inside the suitcase. After realizing that her parents were dead during the wave, she had to leave the hotel to go to the airport where the rescue teams took her to go back home. So, she had to gather and put all the personal belongings of her parents quickly in the suitcases and leave the hotel room. She associated the disorder with the pain and traumatization of the death of her parents and the images of the Tsunami disaster.

In her vicious cycle, maintaining order serves to prevent something bad from happening again, as magic thinking.

Negative cognitions revolved around feelings of responsibility, guilt, and safety.

The current symptoms and disturbances were a manifestation of the unprocessed images and feelings associated with the traumatic moments she went through in the context of the Tsunami. The processing of these events with the EMDR therapy protocol helped her manage better the OCD symptomatology, also thanks to the transformation of beliefs about herself related to the event, from negative to positive. The protocol was applied also to reprocess the memories of the rituals, to desensitize them to prevent the repetition. The future template then was used to prepare her to manage moments of anxiety that could lead her to the rituals and to compulsive behaviors.

6 Future Directions

As we look toward the future of EMDR therapy, several exciting directions and possibilities emerge.

For example, the integration of technology in mental health interventions (Jauch et al., 2023) should open new avenues for EMDR therapy. Virtual reality (VR) applications and online platforms may enhance the accessibility and effectiveness of EMDR therapy, particularly for individuals who face geographical or logistical challenges in accessing traditional therapy (Van Meggellen et al., 2022).

Research and clinical exploration could delve into the application of EMDR therapy for conditions beyond traditional trauma. For instance, consider a scenario where an individual, let us call her Sarah, experienced subtle yet emotionally impactful events during her childhood. Sarah recalls moments where her mother's expression of anger or disappointment left a lasting impression, instilling feelings of inadequacy and fear of abandonment. Additionally, there were instances where Sarah felt alone and neglected, further exacerbating her sense of vulnerability and insecurity. While these experiences may not fit the conventional definition of "trauma," they nevertheless shape Sarah's perceptions of herself, others, and the world around her. They influence her ability to form healthy attachments, regulate emotions, and navigate interpersonal relationships. Left unaddressed, these attachment-based memories continue to exert a profound impact on Sarah's psychological well-being, manifesting in symptoms of anxiety, depression, and low self-esteem (Bowlby, 1988; Sroufe, 2005; Main et al., 1985; Ainsworth et al., 1978; Brenning et al., 2012; Rutter et al., 2007).

For this reason, investigating its efficacy in different areas or for specific populations, such as children and adolescents' survivors of trauma and abuse (Gint et al., 2022; Van der Asdonk et al., 2022), refugees (Cowling & Anderson, 2023; van Es et al., 2023), and individuals in low- and middle-income countries (Venturo-Conerly et al., 2023) can be an important avenue for future research. Understanding the nuances of applying EMDR in diverse cultural contexts is crucial for ensuring its effectiveness across varied demographics.

EMDR therapy can be further explored in combination with other therapeutic modalities. Integrating it into a holistic treatment approach that includes CBT, psychopharmacology, or other evidence-based therapies may provide synergistic effects and improve overall treatment outcomes.

EMDR therapy's journey from a groundbreaking innovation to an established therapeutic modality underscores its flexibility and efficacy in the mental health field. The comprehensive body of research supports its role as a first-line treatment for trauma-related conditions, and ongoing investigations continue to enrich our understanding of its mechanisms and applications.

The future trajectory of EMDR therapy involves embracing technological advancements, tailoring interventions for specific populations. As EMDR evolves, maintaining a commitment to cultural sensitivity and inclusivity will be crucial to its global relevance.

7 Conclusion

Finally, eye movement desensitization and reprocessing (EMDR) has emerged as a highly effective and widely recognized therapeutic approach for individuals grappling with the debilitating effects of trauma, particularly post-traumatic stress disorder (PTSD) (Yunitri et al., 2023). Over the years, extensive research and clinical applications have established EMDR as a valuable intervention with a solid evidence base and the long-term impact and sustainability of EMDR therapy interventions (Bisson et al., 2013; Chen et al., 2014; Lee & Cuijpers, 2013).

Meta-analyses and systematic reviews have consistently demonstrated the efficacy of EMDR in comparison to various therapeutic modalities. The approach exhibits notable success in reducing PTSD symptoms and addressing associated comorbidities. Moreover, its applicability extends beyond traditional trauma treatment, encompassing diverse clinical domains such as anxiety disorders, mood disorders, and specific phobias. Further, EMDR therapy has been effective with suicidal individuals (Burback et al., 2023), people with intellectual disabilities (Tapp et al., 2023), dementia (Ruish et al., 2023), personality disorder (de Jong & Hafkemeijer, 2023), and cancer (Anderson & Jones, 2023).

Comparative studies with cognitive-behavioral therapy (CBT), another well-established therapeutic approach, have indicated comparable outcomes in terms of symptom reduction. However, EMDR often shows advantages in terms of the cost-effectiveness, with shorter treatment durations and the absence of homework assignments, making it an attractive option for certain populations.

Clinical applications of EMDR have expanded to include cases of abuse, assault, and various types of trauma, keeping in mind that trauma is a transdiagnostic event of pathologies in today's diagnostic manuals. For these reasons, the versatility of

EMDR makes it applicable to a wide range of clinical scenarios (Högberg, et al., 2007), demonstrating its efficacy across different populations (Hoppen et al., 2023a, b, c; Hoppen & Morina, 2023; Kip et al., 2023) and settings (Silver et al., 1995).

In conclusion, EMDR not only addresses the immediate symptoms of trauma but also is a transdiagnostic approach that contributes to the broader landscape of mental health and well-being. Its continued growth and integration into diverse clinical settings reaffirm its status as a transformative force in psychotherapy. As we look to the future, EMDR's journey promises ongoing innovation, empowering therapists and bringing healing to individuals around the world.

References

Abel, N. J., O'Brien, J. M., & Peek, C. W. (2013). Dual-focus EMDR and the Twelve Steps in the treatment of chemical dependency and abuse. *Journal of EMDR Practice and Research, 7*(1), 22–29.

Acarturk, C., Konuk, E., Cetinkaya, M., Senay, I., Sijbrandij, M., Cuijpers, P., & Aker, T. (2015). The efficacy of eye movement desensitization and reprocessing for post-traumatic stress disorder and depression among Syrian refugees: Results of a randomized controlled trial. *Psychological Medicine, 45*(13), 2665–2678.

Ainsworth, M. D., Blehar, M. C., Waters, E., & Wall, S. (1978). *Patterns of attachment: A psychological study of the strange situation*. Psychology Press.

Allon, M. (2015). Providing group EMDR to women in The Congo. *Traumatology, 21*(2), 118–126.

Anderson, D., & Jones, V. (2023). Psychological interventions for cancer-related post-traumatic stress disorder: Narrative review. *BJPsych Bulletin, 1–10*, 100. https://doi.org/10.1192/bjb.2023.42

Amano, T., & Toichi, M. (2014). Effectiveness of the on-the-spot-EMDR method for the treatment of behavioral symptoms in patients with severe dementia. *Journal of EMDR Practice & Research, 8*(2), 50–65.

American Psychiatric Association. (2013). *Diagnostic and statistical manual of mental disorders* (5th ed.). Author.

Arnone, R., Orrico, A., D'aquino, G., & Di Munzio, W. (2012). EMDR and psychopharmacological therapy in the treatment of the post-traumatic stress disorder. *Rivista di Psichiatria, 47*(2 Suppl), 8–11.

Baek, J., Lee, S. H., Cho, T., Kim, S. H., & Lee, Y. (2019). Alternating bilateral stimulation induces high-frequency oscillations in the rat amygdala. *Neuroscience Letters, 706*, 107–112.

Balbo, M., Zaccagnino, M., Cussino, M., & Civilotti, C. (2017). Eye movement desensitization and reprocessing (EMDR) and eating disorders: A systematic review. *Clinical Neuropsychiatry, 14*(5), 321–329.

Barrowcliff, A. L., Gray, N. S., MacCulloch, S., Freeman, T. C. A., & MacCulloch, M. J. (2003). Horizontal rhythmical eye-movements consistently diminish the arousal provoked by auditory stimuli. *British Journal of Clinical Psychology, 42*, 289–302.

Barrowcliff, A. L., Gray, N. S., Freeman, T. C. A., & MacCulloch, M. J. (2004). Eye-movements reduce the vividness, emotional valence and electrodermal arousal associated with negative autobiographical memories. *Journal of Forensic Psychiatry and Psychology, 15*, 325–345.

Bisson, J. I., Ehlers, A., Matthews, R., Pilling, S., Richards, D., & Turner, S. (2007). Psychological treatments for chronic post-traumatic stress disorder: Systematic review and meta-analysis. *The British Journal of Psychiatry, 190*(2), 97–104.

Bisson, J. I., Roberts, N. P., Andrew, M., Cooper, R., & Lewis, C. (2013). Psychological therapies for chronic post-traumatic stress disorder (PTSD) in adults. *Cochrane Database of Systematic Reviews, 2015*, CD003388.

Bleich, A., Kotler, M., Kutz, I., & Shalev, A. (2002). *A position paper of the (Israeli) National Council for mental health: Guidelines for the assessment and professional intervention with terror victims in the hospital and in the community*. Jerusalem, Israel.

Bongaerts, H., van Minnen, A., de Jongh, A., & Dijkstra, T. (2017). Intensive EMDR to treat patients with complex PTSD: A case series. *Journal of EMDR Practice and Research, 11*(2), 68–81.

Bossini, L., Tavanti, M., Calossi, S., Polizzotto, N. R., Galli, R., Vatti, G., et al. (2017). Remote traumatic memories: A diffusion tensor imaging and neuropsychological study in war veterans. *NeuroImage: Clinical, 16*, 524–531.

Boudewyns, P. A., Stwertka, S. A., Hyer, L. A., Albrecht, J. W., & Sperr, E. V. (1993). Eye movement desensitization for PTSD of combat: A treatment outcome pilot study. *Behavior Therapy, 24*(4), 585–605.

Bowlby, J. (1988). *A secure base: Parent-child attachment and healthy human development*. Basic Books.

Brenning, K., Soenens, B., Braet, C., & Bosmans, G. (2012). Attachment and depressive symptoms in middle childhood and early adolescence: Testing the validity of the emotion regulation model of attachment. *Attachment & Human Development, 14*(3), 231–248.

Brown, T. A., Antony, M. M., & Barlow, D. H. (1997). Psychometric properties of the Penn State Worry Questionnaire in a clinical anxiety disorders sample. *Behaviour Research and Therapy, 35*(1), 33–42.

Burback, L., Brémault-Phillips, S., Nijdam, M. J., McFarlane, A., & Vermetten, E. (2023). Treatment of posttraumatic stress disorder: A state-of-the-art review. *Current Neuropharmacology, 21*, 557. https://doi.org/10.2174/1570159X21666230428091433

Canan, F., & North, C. S. (2020). The association between general and pathological dissociation and disasterrelated psychopathology in directly exposed survivors. *Psychiatry, 83*(3), 292–305.

Chen, Y. R., Hung, K. W., Tsai, J. C., Chu, H., Chung, M. H., Chen, S. R., & Chou, K. R. (2014). Efficacy of eye-movement desensitization and reprocessing for patients with posttraumatic-stress disorder: A meta-analysis of randomized controlled trials. *PLoS One, 9*(8), e103676. https://doi.org/10.1371/journal.pone.0103676

Chen, C. H., Lu, M. L., Chen, K. Y., Wang, T. Y., Cheng, J. J., & Yang, Y. K. (2015). Risperidone and eye movement desensitization and reprocessing therapy in the treatment of post-traumatic stress disorder in schizophrenia. *Psychiatry Investigation, 12*(1), 111–112.

Chen, R., Gillespie, A., Zhao, Y., Xi, Y., Ren, Y., & McLean, L. (2018). The efficacy of eye movement desensitization and reprocessing in children and adults who have experienced complex childhood trauma: A systematic review of randomized controlled trials. *Frontiers in Psychology, 9*, 534.

Cloitre, M., Petkova, E., Wang, J., & Lu Lassell, F. (2010). An examination of the influence of a sequential treatment on the course and impact of dissociation among women with PTSD related to childhood abuse. *Depression and Anxiety, 27*(10), 1051–1059.

Corrigan, J. P., Fitzpatrick, M., Hanna, D., & Dyer, K. F. (2020). Evaluating the effectiveness of phase-oriented treatment models for PTSD—A meta-analysis. *Traumatology, 26*(4), 447.

Coventry, P. A., Meader, N., Melton, H., Temple, M., Dale, H., Wright, K., et al. (2020). Psychological and pharmacological interventions for posttraumatic stress disorder and comorbid mental health problems following complex traumatic events: Systematic review and component network meta-analysis. *PLoS Medicine, 17*(8), e1003262.

Cowling, M. M., & Anderson, J. R. (2023). The effectiveness of therapeutic interventions on psychological distress in refugee children: A systematic review. *Journal of Clinical Psychology, 79*(8), 1857–1874. https://doi.org/10.1002/jclp.23479

Cusack, K., Jonas, D. E., Forneris, C. A., Wines, C., Sonis, J., Middleton, J. C., Feltner, C., Brownley, K. A., Olmsted, K. R., Greenblatt, A., & Weil, A. (2016). Psychological treatments for adults with posttraumatic stress disorder: A systematic review and meta-analysis. *Clinical Psychology Review, 43*, 128–141.

De Jongh, A., & Hafkemeijer, L. C. S. (2023). Trauma-focused treatment of a client with Complex PTSD and comorbid pathology using EMDR therapy. *Journal of Clinical Psychology, jclp.23521*, 824. https://doi.org/10.1002/jclp.23521

De Jongh, A., Ten Broeke, E., & Renssen, M. R. (2002). Treatment of specific phobias with Eye Movement Desensitization and Reprocessing (EMDR): Protocol, empirical status, and conceptual issues. *Journal of Anxiety Disorders, 16*(3), 235–246.

de Jongh, A., Ernst, R., Marques, L., Hornsveld, H., & Verdam, M. (2013). The impact of eye movements and tones on disturbing memories involving PTSD and other mental disorders. *Journal of Behavior Therapy and Experimental Psychiatry, 44*(4), 447–453.

De Jongh, A., Resick, P. A., Zoellner, L. A., van Minnen, A., Lee, C. W., Monson, C. M., et al. (2016). Critical analysis of the current treatment guidelines for complex PTSD in adults. *Depression and Anxiety, 33*(5), 359–369.

de Roos, C., Veenstra, A. C., de Jongh, A., den Hollander-Gijsman, M., van der Wee, N. J., Zitman, F. G., & van Minnen, A. (2017). Treatment of chronic phantom limb pain using a trauma-focused psychological approach. *Pain Research & Management, 15*, 65.

de Roos, C., Greenwald, R., den Hollander-Gijsman, M., Noorthoorn, E., van Buuren, S., & De Jongh, A. (2011). A randomised comparison of cognitive behavioural therapy (CBT) and eye movement desensitisation and reprocessing (EMDR) in disaster-exposed children. *European Journal of Psychotraumatology, 2*(1), 5694.

De Voogd, L. D., Kanen, J. W., Neville, D. A., Roelofs, K., & Fernández, G. (2018). Reduced emotional and physiological reactivity to negative events in the eye movement desensitization and reprocessing procedure. *Journal of Anxiety Disorders, 55*, 1–7.

de Voogd, L. D., Kanen, J. W., Neville, D. A., Roelofs, K., Fernández, G., & Hermans, E. J. (2018). Eye-movement intervention enhances extinction via amygdala deactivation. *The Journal of Neuroscience: The Official Journal of the Society for Neuroscience, 38*(40), 8694–8706. https://doi.org/10.1523/JNEUROSCI.0703-18.2018

Dinapoli, L., Ferrarese, D., Belella, D., Carnevale, S., Camardese, G., Sani, G., & Chieffo, D. P. R. (2022). Psychological treatment of traumatic memories in COVID-19 survivors. *Clinical Psychology & Psychotherapy, cpp.2771*, 225. https://doi.org/10.1002/cpp.2771

Dutra, L., Bureau, J. F., Holmes, B., Lyubchik, A., & Lyons-Ruth, K. (2009). Quality of early care and childhood trauma: a prospective study of developmental pathways to dissociation. *The Journal of nervous and mental disease, 197*(6), 383–390. https://doi.org/10.1097/NMD.0b013e3181a653b7

Ehring, T., & Watkins, E. R. (2008). Repetitive negative thinking as a transdiagnostic process. *International Journal of Cognitive Therapy, 1*(3), 192–205.

Ehring, T., Welboren, R., Morina, N., Wicherts, J. M., Freitag, J., & Emmelkamp, P. M. (2014). Meta-analysis of psychological treatments for posttraumatic stress disorder in adult survivors of childhood abuse. *Clinical Psychology Review, 34*(8), 645–657.

Elsey, J., & Kindt, M. (2017). Breaking boundaries: Optimizing reconsolidation-based interventions for strong and old memories. *Learning & Memory, 24*(10), 472–479.

Engelhard, I. M., van Uijen, S., & van den Hout, M. A. (2010). The impact of taxing working memory on negative and positive memories. *European Journal of Psychotraumatology*, 5623. https://doi.org/10.3402/ejpt.v1i0.5623

Engelhard, I. M., et al. (2011). Reducing vividness and emotional intensity of recurrent "flashforwards" by taxing working memory: An analogue study. *Journal of Anxiety Disorders, 25*, 599–603.

Faretta, E., Garau, M. I., Gallina, E., Pagani, M., & Fernandez, I. (2022a). Supporting healthcare workers in times of COVID-19 with eye movement desensitization and reprocessing online: A pilot study. *Frontiers in Psychology, 13*, 964407. https://doi.org/10.3389/fpsyg.2022.964407

Faretta, E., Maslovaric, G., Garau, M. I., Marmondi, G., Piras, L., Rezzola, S., Incerti, A., Nardoni, A., Pagani, M., & Gallina, E. (2022b). The psychological impact of the COVID emergency on Italian nursing homes staff and the effectiveness of eye movement desensitization and reprocessing. *Frontiers in Psychology, 13*, 969028. https://doi.org/10.3389/fpsyg.2022.969028

Farina, B., Imperatori, C., Quintiliani, M. I., Castelli Gattinara, P., Onofri, A., Lepore, M., et al. (2015). Neurophysiological correlates of eye movement desensitization and reprocessing sessions: Preliminary evidence for traumatic memories integration. *Clinical Physiology and Functional Imaging, 35*(6), 460–468.

Fernandez, I., & Faretta, E. (2007). EMDR in panic disorder with agoraphobia: Preliminary results of a controlled study. *Journal of EMDR Practice and Research, 1*(1), 2–11.

Fernandez, I., Pagani, M., & Gallina, E. (2022). Post-traumatic stress disorder among healthcare workers during the COVID-19 pandemic in Italy: Effectiveness of an eye movement desensitization and reprocessing intervention protocol. *Frontiers in Psychology, 13*, 964334. https://doi.org/10.3389/fpsyg.2022.964334

Fogliato, E., Invernizzi, R., Maslovaric, G., Fernandez, I., Rigamonti, V., Lora, A., Frisone, E., & Pagani, M. (2022). Promoting mental health in healthcare workers in hospitals through psychological group support with eye movement desensitization and reprocessing during COVID-19 pandemic: An observational study. *Frontiers in Psychology, 12*, 794178. https://doi.org/10.3389/fpsyg.2021.794178

Gauvreau, P., & Bouchard, S. (2008). Preliminary evidence for the efficacy of EMDR in treating generalized anxiety disorder. *Journal of EMDR Practice and Research, 2*(1), 26–40.

Giesbrecht, T., Lynn, S. J., Lilienfeld, S. O., & Merckelbach, H. (2008). Cognitive processes in dissociation: An analysis of core theoretical assumptions. *Psychological Bulletin, 134*(5), 617–647. https://doi.org/10.1037/0033-2909.134.5.617

Gindt, M., Fernandez, A., Zeghari, R., Ménard, M.-L., Nachon, O., Richez, A., Auby, P., Battista, M., & Askenazy, F. (2022). A 3-year retrospective study of 866 children and adolescent outpatients followed in the Nice Pediatric Psychotrauma Center created after the 2016 mass terror attack. *Frontiers in Psychiatry, 13*, 1010957. https://doi.org/10.3389/fpsyt.2022.1010957

Grant, M., & Threlfo, C. (2002). EMDR in the treatment of chronic pain. *Journal of Clinical Psychology, 58*(12), 1505–1520.

Harper, M. L., Rasolkhani-Kalhorn, T., & Drozd, J. F. (2009). Effects of eye movement desensitization on memory fragmentation: A comparison study. *Traumatology, 15*(4), 16–22.

Hase, M., Schallmayer, S., & Sack, M. (2008). EMDR reprocessing of the addiction memory: Pretreatment, posttreatment, and 1-month follow-up. *Journal of EMDR Practice and Research, 2*(3), 170–179.

Hase, M., Plagge, J., Hase, A., Braas, R., Ostacoli, L., Hofmann, A., & Huchzermeier, C. (2018). Eye movement desensitization and reprocessing versus treatment as usual in the treatment of depression: A randomized controlled trial. *Frontiers in Psychology, 9*, 1384.

Hase, M., Balmaceda, U. M., Hase, A., Lehnung, M., Tumani, V., & Huchzermeier, C. (2015). Eye movement desensitization and reprocessing (EMDR) therapy in the treatment of depression: A matched pairs study in an inpatient setting. *Brain and Behavior, 5*(5), e00342.

Hensel, W. (2009). The use of EMDR with infants and toddlers. *Journal of EMDR Practice and Research, 3*(2), 101–111.

Hensley, B. J., Jordan, M., & Gobin, R. L. (2015). The use of eye movement desensitization and reprocessing (EMDR) in the treatment of traumatized substance abusers: A controlled outcome study. *Journal of Chemical Dependency Treatment, 15*(1), 1–12.

Herman, J. L. (1992). Complex PTSD: A syndrome in survivors of prolonged and repeated trauma. *Journal of Traumatic Stress, 5*(3), 377–391.

Hinton, D. E., Rivera, E. I., Hofmann, S. G., Barlow, D. H., & Otto, M. W. (2009). Adapting CBT for traumatized refugees and ethnic minority patients: Examples from culturally adapted CBT (CA-CBT). *Transcultural Psychiatry, 46*(2), 409–442.

Ho, M. S. K., & Lee, C. W. (2012). Cognitive behaviour therapy versus eye movement desensitization and reprocessing for post-traumatic disorders it all in the homework then? *European Review of Applied Psychology, 62*, 253–260.

Hoare, P., Harris, M., Jackson, Y., & Barnett, B. (2018). Mental health interdisciplinary care in Australia: Implications for primary care settings. *Australian Journal of Primary Health, 24*(4), 312–317.

Hofmann, A. (2015). The efficacy of cognitive behavioral therapy: A review of meta-analyses. *Cognitive Therapy and Research, 39*(1), 1–14.

Högberg, G., Pagani, M., Sundin, Ö., Soares, J., Åberg-Wistedt, A., Tärnell, B., & Hällström, T. (2007). On treatment with eye movement desensitization and reprocessing of chronic post-traumatic stress disorder in public transportation workers—A randomized controlled trial. *Nordic Journal of Psychiatry, 61*, 54.

Hoge, C. W., Iverson, K. M., Gaylord, K. M., & Adler, A. B. (2012). The effect of mild traumatic brain injury on symptomatology in combat-deployed Iraq and Afghanistan veterans. *Psychological Services, 9*(1), 53–59.

Holmes, E. A. (2019). Connecting sleep with emotion: The practical use of REM sleep and its neurobiological basis in procedural emotional memory processing. *Biological Psychology, 146*, 107709.

Hoppen, T. H., & Morina, N. (2023). Psychological interventions for adult post-traumatic stress disorder are effective irrespective of concurrent psychotropic medication intake: A meta-analysis of randomized controlled trials. *Psychotherapy and Psychosomatics, 92*(1), 27–37. https://doi.org/10.1159/000527850

Hoppen, T. H., Jehn, M., Holling, H., Mutz, J., Kip, A., & Morina, N. (2023a). The efficacy and acceptability of psychological interventions for adult PTSD: A network and pairwise meta-analysis of randomized controlled trials. *Journal of Consulting and Clinical Psychology, 91*(8), 445–461. https://doi.org/10.1037/ccp0000809

Hoppen, T. H., Kip, A., & Morina, N. (2023b). Are psychological interventions for adult PTSD more efficacious and acceptable when treatment is delivered in higher frequency? A meta-analysis of randomized controlled trials. *Journal of Anxiety Disorders, 95*, 102684. https://doi.org/10.1016/j.janxdis.2023.102684

Hoppen, T. H., Meiser-Stedman, R., Jensen, T. K., Birkeland, M. S., & Morina, N. (2023c). Efficacy of psychological interventions for post-traumatic stress disorder in children and adolescents exposed to single versus multiple traumas: Meta-analysis of randomised controlled trials. *The British Journal of Psychiatry, 222*(5), 196–203. https://doi.org/10.1192/bjp.2023.24

Horesh, D., & Lahav, Y. (2024). When one tool is not enough: An integrative psychotherapeutic approach to treating complex PTSD. *Journal of Clinical Psychology., 80*(7), 1689–1697.

Hornsveld, H. K., Landwehr, F., Stein, W., Stomp, M. P. H., Smeets, M. A. M., & van den Hout, M. A. (2010). EMDR versus CBT: Effectiveness and suitability compared in PTSD treatment. *Clinical Neuropsychiatry, 7*(2), 74–82.

Horst, F., Den Oudsten, B. L., Zijlstra, W. P., de Jongh, A., Lobbestael, J., & De Vries, J. (2017). Eye movement desensitization and reprocessing (EMDR) therapy in the treatment of depression: A matched pairs study in an inpatient setting. *Journal of EMDR Practice and Research, 11*(3), 129–140.

Hurley, E. C. (2018). Comparing the outcomes of weekly versus daily EMDR in veterans with PTSD: A preliminary study. *Journal of EMDR Practice and Research, 12*(1), 25–37.

Ironson, G. I., Freund, B., Strauss, J. L., & Williams, J. (2002). Comparison of two treatments for traumatic stress: A community-based study of EMDR and prolonged exposure. *Journal of Clinical Psychology, 58*(1), 113–128.

Janet, P. (1919). Les fatigues sociales et l'antipathie. *Revue Philosophique de la France et de l'Étranger, 87*, 1–71.

Janet, P. (1935). Les débuts de l'intelligence. *Revue Philosophique de la France Et de l, 119*(5), 418–419.

Jaite, C., Pfeiffer, E., Lehmkuhl, U., & Salbach-Andrae, H. (2013). Childhood abuse in adolescents with anorexia nervosa compared to a psychiatric and healthy control group. *Zeitschrift fur Kinder-und Jugendpsychiatrie und Psychotherapie, 41*(2), 99–107.

Jarero, I., & Artigas, L. (2016). EMDR protocol for recent critical incidents: A randomized controlled trial in a technological disaster context. *Journal of EMDR Practice and Research, 10*(4), 186–194.

Jarero, I., Givaudan, M., & Osorio, A. (2018). Randomized controlled trial on the provision of the EMDR integrative group treatment protocol adapted for ongoing traumatic stress to female patients with cancer-related posttraumatic stress disorder symptoms. *Journal of EMDR Practice and Research, 12*(3), 94–104.

Jarero, I., & Artigas, L. (2020). AIP model-based acute trauma and ongoing traumatic stress theoretical conceptualization (third edition). *Iberoamerican Journal of Psychotraumatology and Dissociation, 10*(1), 1–10.

Jarero, I., Artigas, L., & Luber, M. (2011). The EMDR protocol for recent critical incidents: Application in a disaster mental health continuum of care context. *Journal of EMDR Practice and Research, 5*(3), 82–94. https://doi.org/10.1891/1933-3196.5.3.82

Jauch, I., Kamm, J., Benn, L., Rettig, L., Friederich, H.-C., Tesarz, J., Kuner, T., & Wieland, S. (2023). 2MDR, a microcomputer-controlled visual stimulation device for psychotherapy-like treatments of mice. *Eneuro, 10*(6), ENEURO.0394-22.2023. https://doi.org/10.1523/ENEURO.0394-22.2023

Karatzias, T., & Cloitre, M. (2019). Treating adults with complex posttraumatic stress disorder using a modular approach to treatment: Rationale, evidence, and directions for future research. *Journal of Traumatic Stress, 32*(6), 870–876.

Kaptan, S. K., Dursun, B. O., Knowles, M., Husain, N., & Varese, F. (2021). Group eye movement desensitization and reprocessing interventions in adults and children: A systematic review of randomized and nonrandomized trials. *Clinical Psychology & Psychotherapy, 28*(4), 784–806.

Kavanagh, D. J., Freese, S., Andrade, J., & May, J. (2001). Effects of visuospatial tasks on desensitization to emotive memories. *British Journal of Clinical Psychology, 40*(3), 267–280.

Kihlstrom J. F. (2005). Dissociative disorders. *Annual review of clinical psychology, 1*, 227–253. https://doi.org/10.1146/annurev.clinpsy.1.102803.143925

Kip, A., Iseke, L. N., Papola, D., Gastaldon, C., Barbui, C., & Morina, N. (2023). Efficacy of psychological interventions for PTSD in distinct populations—An evidence map of meta-analyses using the umbrella review methodology. *Clinical Psychology Review, 100*, 102239. https://doi.org/10.1016/j.cpr.2022.102239

Korn, D. L., & Leeds, A. M. (2002). Preliminary evidence of efficacy for EMDR resource development and installation in the stabilization phase of treatment of complex posttraumatic stress disorder. *Journal of Clinical Psychology, 58*(12), 1465–1487.

Kuiken, D., Bears, M., Miall, D., & Smith, L. (2001). Eye movement desensitization reprocessing facilitates attentional orienting. *Imagination, Cognition and Personality, 21*(1), 3–20.

Lamprecht, F., Köhnke, C., Lempa, W., Sack, M., Matzke, M., Köhnke, A. M., & van der Velden, W. (2004). Event-related potentials and EMDR treatment of post-traumatic stress disorder. *Neuroscience Research, 49*(3), 267–272.

Landin-Romero, R., Moreno-Alcázar, A., Pagani, M., & Amann, B. L. (2018). How does eye movement desensitization and reprocessing therapy work? A systematic review on suggested mechanisms of action. *Frontiers in Psychology, 9*, 1395.

Lansing, K., Amen, D. G., Hanks, C., & Rudy, L. (2005). High-resolution brain SPECT imaging and eye movement desensitization and reprocessing in police officers with PTSD. *The Journal of Neuropsychiatry and Clinical Neurosciences, 17*(4), 526–532.

Laub, D., & Auerhahn, N. C. (1993). Knowing and not knowing massive psychic trauma: Forms of traumatic memory. *The International Journal of Psycho-Analysis, 74*(Pt 2), 287.

Lazzaroni, E., Invernizzi, R., Fogliato, E., Pagani, M., & Maslovaric, G. (2021). Coronavirus disease 2019 emergency and remote eye movement desensitization and reprocessing group therapy with adolescents and young adults: Overcoming lockdown with the butterfly hug. *Frontiers in Psychology, 12*, 701381. https://doi.org/10.3389/fpsyg.2021.701381

Lee, C. W., & Cuijpers, P. (2013). A meta-analysis of the contribution of eye movements in processing emotional memories. *Journal of Behavior Therapy and Experimental Psychiatry., 44*, 231.

Lee, C. W., & Drummond, P. D. (2008). Effect of eye movement versus therapist instructions on the processing of distressing memories. *Journal of Anxiety Disorders, 22*(5), 801–808.

Leeds, A. M., & Korn, D. L. (2018). Preliminary evidence that positive emotion in memories of traumatic events can contribute to posttraumatic growth. *Journal of Positive Psychology, 13*(3), 250–261.

Lehnung, M., Shapiro, E., Schreiber, M., & Hofmann, A. (2017). EMDR group protocol with refugees: A group treatment program for traumatised refugees. *Intervention, 15*(2), 147–156.

Lewey, J. H., Smith, C. L., Burcham, B., Saunders, N. L., Elfallal, D., & O'Toole, S. K. (2018). Comparing the effectiveness of EMDR and TF-CBT for children and adolescents: A meta-analysis. *Journal of Child & Adolescent Trauma, 11*, 457–472.

Littel, M., van den Hout, M. A., & Engelhard, I. M. (2016). Desensitizing addiction: Using eye movements to reduce the intensity of substance-related mental imagery and craving. *Frontiers in Psychiatry, 7*, 14.

Main, M., Kaplan, N., & Cassidy, J. (1985). Security in infancy, childhood, and adulthood: A move to the level of representation. *Monographs of the Society for Research in Child Development, 50*(1–2), 66–104.

Maiorani, C., Fernandez, I., Tummino, V., Verdi, D., Gallina, E., & Pagani, M. (2022). Adolescence and COVID-19: Traumatic stress and social distancing in the Italian epicenter of pandemic. *Journal of Integrative Neuroscience, 21*(5), 143. 10.31083/j.jin2105143.

Mancini, F., Gangemi, A., & Melli, G. (2016). A cognitive-behavioral conceptualization of obsessive-compulsive disorder and a treatment protocol. *Journal of Clinical Psychology, 72*(7), 706–717.

Marcus, S. V. (2008). EMDR for migraine headaches: A pilot study. *Journal of EMDR Practice and Research, 2*(3), 228–238.

Marcus, S. V., Marquis, P., & Sakai, C. (1997). Controlled study of treatment of PTSD using EMDR in an HMO setting. *Psychotherapy: Theory, Research, Practice, Training, 34*(3), 307–315. https://doi.org/10.1037/h0087791

Marr, M. J. (2012). Eye movement desensitization and reprocessing (EMDR) for obsessive-compulsive disorder: A pilot study. *Journal of Anxiety Disorders, 26*(6), 590–593.

Marsden, Z., Lovell, K., & Blore, D. (2016). EMDR for obsessive-compulsive disorder: A pilot study. *Journal of EMDR Practice and Research, 10*(2), 66–77.

Marsden, Z., Lovell, K., Blore, D., Ali, S., & Delgadillo, J. (2017). Can group-based cognitive-behavioural therapy and brief guided self-help improve the well-being of distressed patients in primary care? A systematic review and network meta-analysis. *Health Technology Assessment, 21*(27), 1–172.

Maslovaric, G., Bandalovic, A., Valentic, B., & Filakovic, P. (2017). Eye movement desensitization and reprocessing in the treatment of post-traumatic stress disorder in children following the 2014 Southeast Europe floods. *Journal of EMDR Practice and Research, 11*(3), 109–118.

Mavranezouli, I., Megnin-Viggars, O., Grey, N., Bhutani, G., Leach, J., Daly, C., Dias, S., Welton, N. J., Katona, C., El-Leithy, S., Greenberg, N., Stockton, S., & Greenberg, N. (2020). Cost-effectiveness of psychological treatments for post-traumatic stress disorder in adults. *PLoS One, 15*(4), Article e0232245. https://doi.org/10.1371/journal.pone.0232245

Maxfield, L. (2014). Eye movement desensitization and reprocessing in North America: An introduction to the special issue. *Journal of EMDR Practice and Research, 8*(4), 157–160.

Mazzoni, G. P., Gugliotta, M., & Costa, A. (2017). Eye movement desensitization and reprocessing (EMDR) therapy in the treatment of obsessive-compulsive disorder (OCD): A case series. *Journal of EMDR Practice and Research, 11*(1), 31–41.

McLaughlin, K. A., & Lambert, H. K. (2017). Child trauma exposure and psychopathology: Mechanisms of risk and resilience. *Current Opinion in Psychology, 14*, 29–34.

McFarlane A. C. (2010). The long-term costs of traumatic stress: intertwined physical and psychological consequences. World psychiatry : official journal of the World Psychiatric Association (WPA), 9(1), 3–10. https://doi.org/10.1002/j.2051-5545.2010.tb00254.x

Nardo, D., et al. (2010). Gray matter density in limbic and paralimbic cortices is associated with trauma load and EMDR outcome in PTSD patients. *Journal of Psychiatric Research, 44*, 477–485.

Nazari, H., Momeni, N., & Jariani, M. (2011). A randomized controlled trial of the efficacy of eye movement desensitization and reprocessing (EMDR), fluoxetine, and pill placebo in the treatment of obsessive-compulsive disorder (OCD). *Psychological Trauma: Theory, Research, Practice, and Policy, 3*(3), 310–319.

Nickerson, L. I. (Ed.). (2022). *Cultural competence and healing culturally based trauma with EMDR therapy: Innovative strategies and protocols.* Springer.

Niemeyer, H., Lorbeer, N., Mohr, J., Baer, E., & Knaevelsrud, C. (2022). Evidence-based individual psychotherapy for complex posttraumatic stress disorder and at-risk groups for complex traumatization: A meta-review. *Journal of Affective Disorders, 299*, 610–619.

Nijdam, M. J., Baas, M. A., Olff, M., Gersons, B. P., & Heir, T. (2013). Eye movement desensitization and reprocessing treatment for posttraumatic stress disorder with comorbid anxiety disorder. *European Journal of Psychotraumatology, 4*(1), 21594.

Nijenhuis, E. R., Van der Hart, O., & Steele, K. (2010). Trauma-related structural dissociation of the personality. *Acta Psychiatrica Scandinavica, 121*(1), 75–85.

Norcross, J. C., & Shapiro, F. (2002). Eight critical issues in psychotherapy case formulation. *Psychotherapy: Theory, Research, Practice, Training, 39*(4), 216–220.

Novo, P., Landin-Romero, R., Radua, J., Vicens, V., Fernandez, I., Garcia, F., et al. (2014). Eye movement desensitization and reprocessing therapy in subsyndromal depressive symptoms after sexual trauma: A randomized controlled trial. *Frontiers in Psychology, 5*, 1036.

Oh, D. H., & Choi, J. A. (2007). A study on the effectiveness of eye movement desensitization and reprocessing (EMDR) on anxiety disorder patients. *Korean Journal of Clinical Psychology, 26*(2), 359–369.

Ohtani, T., Ito, Y., Yamashita, K., & Takahashi, T. (2009). Improvement of intrusive thoughts and a decrease in autonomic responses after a single session of eye movement desensitization and reprocessing: A case report. *Japanese Journal of Behavior Therapy, 35*(1), 17–25.

Ostacoli, L., Carletto, S., Cavallo, M., Baldomir-Gago, P., Di Lorenzo, G., Fernandez, I., et al. (2018). Comparison of eye movement desensitization reprocessing and cognitive-behavioral therapy as adjunctive treatments for recurrent depression: The European Depression EMDR Network (EDEN) randomized controlled trial. *Frontiers in Psychology, 9*, 1–13.

Pagani, M., Di Lorenzo, G., Monaco, L., Daverio, A., Giannoudas, I., La Porta, P., et al. (2007a). Neurobiological correlates of EMDR monitoring–an EEG study. *PLoS One, 2*(8), e701.

Pagani, M., Högberg, G., Salmaso, D., Nardo, D., Sundin, O., Jonsson, C., et al. (2007b). Effects of EMDR psychotherapy on 99mTc-HMPAO distribution in occupation-related post-traumatic stress disorder. *Nuclear Medicine Communications, 28*(10), 757–765.

Pagani, M., Högberg, G., Fernandez, I., & Siracusano, A. (2013a). Correlates of EMDR therapy in functional and structural neuroimaging: A critical summary of recent findings. *Journal of EMDR Practice and Research, 7*(1), 29–38.

Pagani, M., Högberg, G., Salmaso, D., Nardo, D., Larsson, S. A., & Törebjörk, E. (2013b). Effects of EMDR psychotherapy on 99mTc-HMPAO distribution in occupation-related post-traumatic stress disorder. *Nuclear Medicine Communications, 34*(5), 419–425.

Pagani, M., Högberg, G., Fernandez, I., & Siracusano, A. (2013). Correlates of EMDR therapy in functional and structural neuroimaging: A critical summary of recent findings. *Journal of EMDR Practice and Research, 7*(1), 29.

Pagani, M., Di Lorenzo, G., Monaco, L., Niolu, C., Siracusano, A., Verardo, A. R., et al. (2011). Pretreatment, intratreatment, and posttreatment EEG imaging of EMDR: Methodology and preliminary results from a single case. *Journal of EMDR Practice & Research, 5*(2), 42–56.

Pagani, M., Di Lorenzo, G., Verardo, A. R., Nicolais, G., Monaco, L., Lauretti, G., et al. (2012). Neurobiological correlates of EMDR monitoring–an EEG study. *PLoS One, 7*(9), e45753.

Pagani, M., Di Lorenzo, G., Monaco, L., Daverio, A., Giannoudas, I., La Porta, P., et al. (2015). Neurobiological response to EMDR therapy in clients with different psychological traumas. *Frontiers in Psychology, 6*, 1614.

Phaf, R. H. (2023). Merging and modifying hypotheses on the emotional and cognitive effects of eye movements: The dopaminergic regulation hypothesis. *New Ideas in Psychology, 70*, 101026.

Putnam, F. W. (1997). Dissociation in children and adolescents: A developmental perspective.

Rabito-Alcón, M. F., Baile, J. I., & Vanderlinden, J. (2021). Mediating factors between childhood traumatic experiences and eating disorders development: A systematic review. *Children (Basel, Switzerland), 8*(2), 114. https://doi.org/10.3390/children8020114

Racine, S. E., & Wildes, J. E. (2015). Emotion dysregulation and anorexia nervosa: An exploration of the role of childhood abuse. *International Journal of Eating Disorders, 48*(1), 55–58.

Reicherzer, S. (2011). Utilizing EMDR with lesbian, gay, bisexual, and transgender individuals: A case study. *Journal of EMDR Practice and Research, 5*(3), 101–106.

Ricci, R. J., Clayton, C. A., & Shapiro, F. (2006). Some effects of EMDR on pedophilic identity and sexual arousal in a case of multiple paraphilias. *Journal of Forensic Psychiatry & Psychology, 17*(3), 453–476.

Roberts, E. M. (2018). Group therapy for cancer-related post-traumatic stress disorder: Feasibility and effectiveness. *International Journal of Group Psychotherapy, 68*(4), 534–548.

Rothbaum, B. O., Astin, M. C., & Marsteller, F. (2005). Prolonged exposure versus eye movement desensitization and reprocessing (EMDR) for PTSD rape victims. *Journal of Traumatic Stress., 18*, 607.

Ruisch, J. E., Nederstigt, A. H. M., Van Der Vorst, A., Boersma, S. N., Vink, M. T., Hoeboer, C. M., Olff, M., & Sobczak, S. (2023). Treatment of post-traumatic stress disorder in people with dementia: A structured literature review. *Psychogeriatrics, 23*(3), 523–534. https://doi.org/10.1111/psyg.12951

Rutter, M., Kreppner, J., & Sonuga-Barke, E. (2007). Emanuel Miller lecture: Attachment insecurity, disinhibited attachment, and attachment disorders: Where do research findings leave the concepts? *Journal of Child Psychology and Psychiatry, 48*(6), 529–554.

Saarni, C. (1999). *The development of emotional competence*. Guilford Press.

Sarin, S., & Nolen-Hoeksema, S. (2010). The dangers of dwelling: An examination of the relationship between rumination and consumptive coping in survivors of childhood sexual abuse. *Cognition and Emotion, 24*(1), 71–85.

Schneider, J., Hofmann, A., Rost, C., & Shapiro, F. (2008). EMDR in the treatment of chronic phantom limb pain. *Pain Medicine, 9*(1), 76–82.

Schubert, S. J., Lee, C. W., & Drummond, P. D. (2016). The efficacy and psychophysiological correlates of dual-attention tasks in eye movement desensitization and reprocessing (EMDR). *Journal of Anxiety Disorders, 43*, 1–11.

Schnyder, U., & Cloitre, M. (2015). *Evidence based treatments for trauma-related psychological disorders*. Springer International Publishing.

Sekiguchi, A., Sugiura, L., Taki, Y., Kotozaki, Y., Nouchi, R., Takeuchi, H., et al. (2018). Brain structural changes as vulnerability factors and acquired signs of post-earthquake stress. *Molecular Psychiatry, 23*(3), 543–549.

Shapiro, F. (1989a). Efficacy of the eye movement desensitization procedure in the treatment of traumatic memories. *Journal of Traumatic Stress, 2*(2), 199–223.

Shapiro, F. (1989b). Eye movement desensitization: A new treatment for post-traumatic stress disorder. *Journal of Behavior Therapy and Experimental Psychiatry, 20*(3), 211–217.

Shapiro, F. (2001). *Eye Movement Desensitization and Reprocessing (EMDR): Basic principles, protocols, and procedures*. Guilford Press.

Shapiro, F. (2007). EMDR, adaptive information processing, and case conceptualization. *Journal of EMDR Practice & Research, 1*(2), 68–87.

Shapiro, F., & Laliotis, D. (2011). EMDR and the adaptive information processing model: Integrative treatment and case conceptualization. *Clinical Social Work Journal, 39*(2), 191–200.

Shapiro, F. (2014). The role of eye movement desensitization and reprocessing (EMDR) therapy in medicine: Addressing the psychological and physical symptoms stemming from adverse life experiences. *The Permanente Journal, 18*(1), 71.

Shapiro, F. (2018). *Eye movement desensitization and reprocessing (EMDR) therapy: Basic principles, protocols, and procedures* (3rd ed.). Guilford Press.

Silver, S. M., Brooks, A., & Obenchain, J. (1995). Treatment of Vietnam War veterans with PTSD: A comparison of eye movement desensitization and reprocessing, biofeedback, and relaxation training. *Journal of Traumatic Stress., 8*, 337.

Soberman, G. B., Greenwald, R., & Rule, D. L. (2002). A controlled study of eye movement desensitization and reprocessing (EMDR) for boys with conduct problems. *Journal of Aggression, Maltreatment & Trauma, 6*(1), 217–236.

Solomon, R. M., & Rando, T. A. (2007). The utilization of EMDR in the treatment of grief and mourning. *Journal of EMDR Practice and Research, 1*(1), 37–45.

Solomon, R. M., & Shapiro, F. (2008). EMDR and the adaptive information processing model: Potential mechanisms of change. *Journal of EMDR Practice and Research, 2*, 315–325.

Sprang, G. (2001). The use of Eye Movement Desensitization and Reprocessing (EMDR) in the treatment of traumatic stress and complicated mourning: Psychological and behavioral outcomes. *Research on Social Work Practice, 11*(3), 300–320.

Sroufe, L. A. (2005). Attachment and development: A prospective, longitudinal study from birth to adulthood. *Attachment & Human Development, 7*(4), 349–367.

Stickgold, R. (2002). EMDR: A putative neurobiological mechanism of action. *Journal of Clinical Psychology, 58*(1), 61–75.

Tapp, K., Vereenooghe, L., Hewitt, O., Scripps, E., Gray, K. M., & Langdon, P. E. (2023). Psychological therapies for people with intellectual disabilities: An updated systematic review and meta-analysis. *Comprehensive Psychiatry, 122*, 152372. https://doi.org/10.1016/j.comppsych.2023.152372

Teicher, M. H., & Samson, J. A. (2016). Childhood maltreatment and psychopathology: A case for ecophenotypic variants as clinically and neurobiologically distinct subtypes. *American Journal of Psychiatry, 173*(10), 971–982.

Valiente-Gómez, A., Moreno-Alcázar, A., Radua, J., Ruiz, V., Soriano-Mas, C., & Fullana, M. A. (2017). Efficacy of eye movement desensitization and reprocessing in children and adolescent with post-traumatic stress disorder: A meta-analysis of randomized controlled trials. *Frontiers in Psychology, 8*, 1750.

van den Berg, D. P., & van der Gaag, M. (2012). Treating trauma in psychosis with EMDR: A pilot study. *Journal of Behavior Therapy and Experimental Psychiatry, 43*(1), 664–671.

van den Berg, D. P., de Bont, P. A., van der Vleugel, B. M., de Roos, C., de Jongh, A., Van Minnen, A., et al. (2015). Prolonged exposure vs. eye movement desensitization and reprocessing vs. waiting list for posttraumatic stress disorder in patients with a psychotic disorder: A randomized clinical trial. JAMA. *Psychiatry, 72*(3), 259–267.

Van den Hout, M. A., Engelhard, I. M., Smeets, M. A. M., & Hornsveld, H. K. (2010). Neurobiological considerations of EMDR: Eye movements during retrieval reduce subjective vividness and objective memory accessibility. *Journal of Behavior Therapy and Experimental Psychiatry, 41*(4), 371–378.

Van den Hout, M. A., Engelhard, I. M., Rijkeboer, M. M., Koekebakker, J., Hornsveld, H., Leer, A., et al. (2011). EMDR: Eye movements superior to beeps in taxing working memory and reducing vividness of recollections. *Behaviour Research and Therapy, 49*(2), 92–98.

van den Hout, M. A., Engelhard, I. M., Rijkeboer, M. M., Koekebakker, J., Hornsveld, H., Leer, A., et al. (2012a). EMDR: Eye movements superior to beeps in taxing working memory and reducing vividness of recollections. *Behavior Research and Therapy, 50*(6), 422–427.

Van den Hout, M. A., Rijkeboer, M. M., Engelhard, I. M., Klugkist, I., Hornsveld, H., & Toffolo, M. B. (2012b). Tones inferior to eye movements in the EMDR treatment of PTSD. *Behaviour Research and Therapy, 50*(5), 275–279.

Van Der Asdonk, S., Kesarlal, A. R., Schuengel, C., Draaisma, N., De Roos, C., Zuidgeest, K., Rippe, R. C. A., & Alink, L. R. A. (2022). Testing an attachment- and trauma-informed intervention approach for parents and young children after interparental violence: Protocol for a randomized controlled trial. *Trials, 23*(1), 973. https://doi.org/10.1186/s13063-022-06902-9

Van der Hart, O., Steele, K., Boon, S., & Brown, P. (2003). The treatment of traumatic memories: Synthesis, realization, and integration. *Dissociation: Progress in the Dissociative Disorders, 6*(2–3), 162.

van der Hart, O., Nijenhuis, E. R. S., & Steele, K. (2006). *The haunted self: Structural dissociation and the treatment of chronic traumatization.* Norton.

Van der Hart, O., Nijenhuis, E. R. S., & Solomon, R. (2010). Dissociation of the personality in complex trauma-related disorders and EMDR: Theoretical considerations. *Journal of EMDR Practice and Research, 4*, 76–92.

Van der Hart, O., Groenendijk, M., Gonzalez, A., Mosquera, D., & Solomon, R. (2013). Dissociation of the personality and EMDR therapy in complex trauma-related disorders: Applications in phase 1 treatment. *Journal of EMDR Practice and Research, 7*, 81–94.

Van der Hart, O., Groenendijk, M., Gonzalez, A., Mosquera, D., & Solomon, R. (2014). Dissociation of the personality and EMDR therapy in complex trauma-related disorders: Applications in phase 2 and 3 treatment. *Journal of EMDR Practice and Research, 8*, 33–38.

van der Kolk, B. A., & Fisler, R. (1995). Dissociation and the fragmentary nature of traumatic memories: Overview and exploratory study. *Journal of Traumatic Stress, 8*(4), 505–525.

Van der Kolk, B. (2015). *El cuerpo lleva la cuenta. Cerebro, mente y cuerpo en la superación del trauma*. Elefhteria.

Van Es, C. M., Velu, M. E., Sleijpen, M., Van Der Aa, N., Boelen, P. A., & Mooren, T. (2023). Trauma-focused treatment for traumatic stress symptoms in unaccompanied refugee minors: A multiple baseline case series. *Frontiers in Psychology, 14*, 1125740. https://doi.org/10.3389/fpsyg.2023.1125740

Van Meggelen, M., Morina, N., Van Der Heiden, C., Brinkman, W.-P., Yocarini, I. E., Tielman, M. L., Rodenburg, J., Van Ee, E., Van Schie, K., Broekman, M. E., & Franken, I. H. A. (2022). A randomized controlled trial to pilot the efficacy of a computer-based intervention with elements of virtual reality and limited therapist assistance for the treatment of post-traumatic stress disorder. *Frontiers in Digital Health, 4*, 974668. https://doi.org/10.3389/fdgth.2022.974668

van Minnen, A., Hendriks, L., & Olff, M. (2010). When do trauma experts choose exposure therapy for PTSD patients? A controlled study of therapist and patient factors. *Behaviour Research and Therapy, 48*(4), 312–320.

van Rood, Y. R., & de Roos, C. (2009). Treatment of medically unexplained symptoms in primary care: A systematic review. *Psychosomatics, 50*(3), 269–280.

Vaughan, K., Armstrong, M. S., Gold, R., O'Connor, N., & Jenneke, W. (1994). A trial of eye movement desensitization compared to image habituation training and applied muscle relaxation in post-traumatic stress disorder. *Journal of Behavior Therapy and Experimental Psychiatry, 25*(4), 283–291.

Venturo-Conerly, K. E., Eisenman, D., Wasil, A. R., Singla, D. R., & Weisz, J. R. (2023). Meta-analysis: The effectiveness of youth psychotherapy interventions in low- and middle-income countries. *Journal of the American Academy of Child & Adolescent Psychiatry, 62*(8), 859–873. https://doi.org/10.1016/j.jaac.2022.12.005

Wernik, U. (1993). Treatment of sexual dysfunction. In *Handbook of EMDR and family therapy processes* (pp. 303–321). Wiley.

Wilson, S. A., Becker, L. A., & Tinker, R. H. (1995a). Eye movement desensitization and reprocessing (EMDR) treatment for psychologically traumatized individuals. *Journal of Consulting and Clinical Psychology, 63*(6), 928–937.

Wilson, S. A., Becker, L. A., & Tinker, R. H. (1995b). Fifteen-month follow-up of eye movement desensitization and reprocessing (EMDR) treatment for posttraumatic stress disorder and psychological trauma. *Journal of Consulting and Clinical Psychology, 63*(6), 1012–1018.

Wilson, D. L., Silver, S. M., Covi, W. G., & Foster, S. (1996). Eye movement desensitization and reprocessing: Effectiveness and autonomic correlates. *Journal of Behavior Therapy and Experimental Psychiatry, 27*(3), 219–229.

Wilson, S. A., Becker, L. A., & Tinker, R. H. (1997). Fifteen-month follow-up of eye movement desensitization and reprocessing (EMDR) treatment for posttraumatic stress disorder and psychological trauma. *Journal of Consulting and Clinical Psychology, 65*(6), 1047.

Wong, S. L. (2018). EMDR-based divorce recovery group: A case study. *Journal of EMDR Practice & Research, 12*(2), 58–70.

World Health Organization. (2013). *Guidelines for the management of conditions that are specifically related to stress*. World Health Organization.

Yaşar, A. B., Kiraz, S., Usta, D., Abamor, A. E., Zengin Eroğlu, M., & Kavakcı, Ö. (2018). Şizofreni Olgusunda Göz Hareketleri ile Duyarsızlaştırma ve Yeniden İşleme (EMDR) Uygulaması ve Kliniğe Etkileri: Olgu Sunumu [Eye Movement Desensitization and Reprocessing (EMDR)

Therapy on a Patient with Schizophrenia and Clinical Effects: A Case Study]. *Turk psikiyatri dergisi = Turkish journal of psychiatry, 29*(2), 138–142.

Yunitri, N., Chu, H., Kang, X. L., Wiratama, B. S., Lee, T.-Y., Chang, L.-F., et al. (2023). Comparative effectiveness of psychotherapies in adults with posttraumatic stress disorder: A network meta-analysis of randomised controlled trials. *Psychological Medicine, 53*(13), 6376–6388. https://doi.org/10.1017/S0033291722003737

Zaccagnino, M., & Cussino, M. (2013). EMDR and parenting: A clinical case. *Journal of EMDR Practice and Research, 7*(3), 154–166.

Zohar, J., Fostick, L., Juven-Wetzler, A., & Kaplan, Z. (2018). The impact of order of treatment on outcome of combined treatment with prolonged exposure and eye movement desensitization and reprocessing (EMDR) for post-traumatic stress disorder. *Journal of Psychiatric Research, 99*, 60–66.

Dialectical Behavior Therapy (DBT)

Cesare Maffei

1   The Fundamentals of Dialectical Behavior Therapy (DBT)

Dialectical behavior therapy (DBT) (Linehan, 1993) is based on a dialectical philosophical conception of reality, according to which reality is a system whose parts have no intrinsic essence but are related to each other. It follows that reality is not static, but is constantly changing due to the interaction between the parts. Change is mainly generated by the tension between opposites: day is the opposite of night, cardiac systole is the opposite of diastole, an affirmation is the opposite of its negation. Opposites are complementary: in fact, one does not exist without the other, and one transforms into the other. Reality thus consists of sequences of processes of change, that is, of transactions between opposites: day turns into night, systole into diastole, an affirmation into its negation. To sum up: reality is a totality, a system composed of parts, whose opposition generates transactional processes from which continuous change results.

The centrality of dialectics was discovered by Marsha M. Linehan when, in the 1980s, verifying that subjects at high chronic suicidal risk were unable to change their behavior, but also unable to accept their suffering, she understood that it was necessary to find a balance between two opposites, between change and acceptance. Dialectics represented the conceptual framework that allowed the balance between two opposite strategies.

Change and acceptance relate to the other two foundations of DBT: Behavioral Science and Zen. Marsha Linehan began her clinical practice as a behaviorist and has remained faithful to the principles and methodology of Behaviorism. The idea

---

C. Maffei (✉)
Department of Psychology, University "Vita-Salute San Raffaele", Milan, Italy

Sigmund Freud University, Milan, Italy
e-mail: maffei.cesare@hsr.it

that adaptive and maladaptive behavior obeys the same laws, with a central role attributed to learning, the observation of phenomena, the formulation of hypotheses, and the collection of data belong to the behavioral tradition. On the other hand, the idea that reality, as it is made up of events that follow one another according to a cause and effect relationship, and that therefore everything that exists has a reason for existing because something caused it, is "perfect" is a basic concept in Zen. This leads to the *radical* acceptance of reality, and therefore of the fact that suffering is inevitable, and that the more we try to escape it, the more it increases. The practice of mindfulness is the operational consequence of the application of the principles of Zen to treatment: DBT was the first treatment to introduce mindfulness among its therapeutic tools. The dialectical balance between opposites leads to a synthesis: acceptance is the foundation of change. If you don't accept that you have a problem, you won't be able to do anything to solve it, that is, to change. In synthesis: DBT is an integrative treatment based on dialectics, behavioral science, and Zen/mindfulness.

2 Biosocial Theory

The first patients to whom Marsha Linehan tried to apply behavioral treatment strategies, with negative results as has already been mentioned, were women at high suicide risk. The application for a grant to fund the research needed to identify a disorder. The choice fell on borderline personality disorder (BPD) because of the frequency of suicidal and self-injurious behaviors. However, it was first necessary to understand the mechanisms that generated the dysfunctional behaviors of BPD and then to develop a treatment that could modify the mechanisms, in harmony with the theoretical assumptions, and capable of generating research data. The solution was the biosocial theory, which was able to explain both the pathogenesis and stability of BPD. In summary, according to biosocial theory, the main problem is the pervasiveness and stability of emotional dysregulation. This is the cause of dysfunctional behaviors, which can be viewed as attempts to reduce emotional distress, as well as dysregulation of identity and interpersonal relationships.

Biosocial theory explains the pathogenesis of BPD as a result of transactions between the subject's biological vulnerability (high sensitivity, high reactivity, and slow return to baseline) and the pervasiveness of invalidation by the environment (Crowell et al., 2009, 2016). Biological sensitivity has been validated by extensive empirical research (Bortolla et al., 2020).

Research has recently shown that individuals with BPD are particularly sensitive to rejection by others, even when the behavior of others does not really have a rejecting intention, or is minimally rejecting. This shows how even interpersonal events that are not particularly significant can generate intense and unwarranted emotional reactions, with the risk of activating dysfunctional behaviors (Cavicchioli & Maffei, 2020).

Biosocial theory, therefore, shows how the pathogenesis of BPD represents a failure of the developmental dialectical process: transactions between the individual and the environment, and vice versa, lock the individual within insoluble dialectical dilemmas. The main dialectical dilemma is represented by the oscillation between emotional vulnerability and self-invalidation. Self-invalidation represents an attempt to adapt to a disabling environment: subjects assume a negative, judgmental attitude toward him/herself. They believe that they are the cause of problems and experience emotions of shame and guilt, from which avoidance behavior results. Avoidance increases emotional vulnerability because emotions of shame and guilt are often augmented by the tendency to ruminate, which can generate sadness, anger toward self, and envy toward others. When emotions become intolerable, the other side of the dialectical dilemma appears, emotional vulnerability, which is often accompanied by dysfunctional behaviors whose purpose is to reduce emotional suffering. Suicide attempts, self-injurious behavior, substance or alcohol use, binge eating, hetero-aggressive behavior, toward things or people, are the most frequent examples. Of course, all of these are likely to increase invalidation by the environment, exacerbating the systemic vicious cycle that sustains the disorder. Interestingly, the oscillation between emotional vulnerability and avoidance is in line with Gross's (2014) Modal Model of Emotion Regulation, which places emotion-driven behaviors and avoidance at the two ends of a continuum.

In conclusion, biosocial theory shows that BPD is not only about the individual, but is an expression of the dysfunctionality of the individual-environment system, in a dialectical, or rather anti-dialectical, developmental process. This has consequences for the structure of treatment, which is aimed at the individual, but also at the environment.

3 Comprehensive DBT: The Structure of Treatment

The treatment described in this section is the comprehensive treatment for subjects with BPD. DBT structures treatment by relating modes and functions. The modes are:

1. Individual psychotherapy
2. Skills training
3. Telephone consultation
4. Intervention in the environment/ancillary treatments
5. Consultation team

Each mode will now be discussed, along with its function.

3.1 Consultation Team

It is the treatment organizer, so it will be presented first.

Treating severe BPD patients can produce burnout both in therapists and in patients (Linehan et al., 2000). The usefulness of introducing a team was understood by Marsha Linehan during the progressive structuring of DBT in light of the difficulties of successfully conducting treatment with severe BPD sufferers by individual therapists. In fact, these are severely suffering individuals who tend to engage their therapists emotionally from the very beginning of the therapeutic relationship. The risk for therapists is thus to engage personally as well as professionally, losing the boundary between these two types of relationships. Especially when the therapist does not have a precise treatment model, specific and effective for the issues in question, the consequences of which are the poor treatment effect, patients become even more needy and demanding, or distrustful and uncooperative. The consequences of this are, for the therapist, negative emotional activation, a reduction in motivation, and a possible tendency to expel the patient from treatment, perhaps blaming him or her for the failure. From what has been described, it is clear that the risk for the therapist is to fall into a dialectical dilemma whose poles are overactivity and rejection.

The functions of the therapeutic team are aimed at avoiding the occurrence of these kinds of problems, as well as at resolving them when they appear. The team, therefore, increases the therapists' motivation, ensures their psychological balance, and helps implement treatment adherently and effectively.

A summary of the functions of the team can be expressed as follows: the team is to the therapist what the therapist is to the patient. Just as patients do not always have the skills to solve problems in their lives but need help, so therapists may not have the skills to solve their patients' problems. So, therapists also need help.

These statements introduce the relational climate of the team, which is a peer consultation team, who must have an accepting (mindful) and nonjudgmental attitude toward each other. Operationally, the team meets once a week with an agenda and certain roles. The meeting leader manages the agenda, the observer rings the Tibetan bell whenever he/she observes behaviors that are not in accordance with DBT principles (judgmental comments, unwarranted conclusions, digressions), the note-taker verbalizes the meeting. This begins with the reading of notes from the previous meeting, continues with a request for help from therapists in need, followed by the presentation of problems that have arisen in individual therapies or skills training groups. If there is time, which is not always possible in the two hours, or two and a half hours available, some theoretical or research topic is discussed in depth. The team consists of up to six to eight professionals, who may be psychotherapists, but also rehabilitation technicians, educators, nurses, and social workers, who have the skills to conduct skills training, which is the psycho-educational component of treatment. The roles described above are rotational, while the only stable role for a long time is that of the team leader. The latter has an administrative and organizational role, also being the intermediary between the team and the institution in which they work. As will be seen in the section on implementation, it is indeed important for the team to operate safely with respect to its stability, and to be able to apply DBT integrally.

3.2 Individual Psychotherapy

The function of individual psychotherapy is to increase and sustain motivation, helping subjects to reduce suffering and solve problems. The individual psychotherapist is responsible for the treatment and oversees its progress. Strategies of individual psychotherapy, as everything in DBT, need a dialectical balance between acceptance and change strategies: acceptance is expressed in validation, while change is about problem-solving.

Individual psychotherapy is administered weekly and begins with a pretreatment phase that typically lasts about four sessions. Frequently, referral to pretreatment is made after a diagnostic assessment has been conducted, the methods and tools of which may vary from situation to situation, both in terms of formulating a categorical and dimensional diagnosis. In addition, certain psychopathological features, such as emotional dysregulation, can be explored in depth through special instruments, such as DERS (Gratz & Roemer, 2004).

Pretreatment is the stage in which all the information necessary for case formulation is gathered, from which treatment decisions are derived. It is also the stage at which a collaborative relationship begins and at which it is necessary for the subject to be informed in detail of the nature of his or her problems, the characteristics of the treatment, and the reasons why the treatment is deemed appropriate. This allows for informed adherence to the treatment itself.

Case formulation involves a number of steps, which will now be summarily described:

1. Demographic information, including diagnosis, previous treatments, and reasons for referral to DBT.
2. Biosocial Theory. It is important to understand whether the subject's history is characterized by the presence of emotional vulnerability and environmental invalidation. As has been previously stated, biosocial theory is the tool for understanding the mechanisms that generate and maintain BPD.
3. Stage of treatment. DBT provides four stages of treatment depending on the nature of the problems. The standard treatment for individuals with BPD concerns Stage 1, where the level of the disorder is higher. The latter is defined according to the following criteria:

    - Imminent threat (What are the current threats to life?)
    - Disability (How and in what areas is adaptation impaired?)
    - Severity (What is the client's subjective experience of suffering?)
    - Pervasiveness (In what and how many contexts are the problems present?)

- Complexity (What and how many distinct problems does the client have? Are there other disorders?)

Individuals for whom Stage 1 is indicated suffer from a severe disorder in which assessment of biosocial theory has shown a major difficulty in emotion regulation, which often results in the occurrence of dysfunctional behaviors, of which life- or safety-threatening behaviors represent a very frequent percentage. In addition, there is intense subjective suffering, the dysfunctionality is pervasive and disabling, and there is often the presence of other psychopathological problems (e.g., bipolar disorder, major depression, panic attacks, and others) and socio-environmental difficulties.

Incidentally, formalization of DBT has been done only for Stage 1, while variable treatments may be implemented for the others. Stage 2 concerns the presence of still intense emotional suffering, but without any more dysfunctional behavior being enacted; Stage 3 concerns the presence of problems in the conduct of daily life; and Stage 4 concerns the need for help in spiritual realization.

4. Treatment goals. The ultimate goal of DBT is to achieve "a life worth living." In concrete terms, this means a life in which one is able to pursue and achieve goals derived from personal values. It is very important that the definition of values and goals be concrete and realistic, although it is not possible to define a priori whether it will, or will not, be possible to achieve a given goal. The desire to "feel better," to "lead a more satisfying life," or the like are not defined goals. It follows that such statements need to be translated into concrete terms, such as being able to have stable emotional relationships, that is, being able to find and keep a job. If the person is unable to define treatment goals, help with respect to this is a part of treatment from the very beginning.

Carefully assessing and concretely defining the goals in initial sessions will help clients engage in treatment, develop a strong commitment, and gain motivation to engage in the hard work needed to change their behavior. Without careful assessment, the therapist may inadvertently impose his or her own goals on the client, taking the client in a direction that perhaps does not fit his or her wishes. Ongoing assessment will also be essential, as the client's goals may evolve as treatment progresses, and treatment will be less effective if therapy is tied to an outdated goal.

The importance of defining treatment goals is that it makes it possible to identify which problems are interfering, and which are the primary targets of treatment.

5. Primary targets. Primary targets are anything that primarily prevents the achievement of treatment goals. In Stage 1 DBT, primary targets are divided into three categories:

- Behaviors that endanger life or safety: suicide attempts, nonsuicidal self-injury (NSSI), severe aggressive behaviors toward others, risk-taking behaviors. They can also be classified as thoughts, impulses, and actions.
- Behaviors that interfere with treatment: these are all behaviors that make treatment difficult, affect the motivation of even the therapist, and prevent change. Skipping sessions, arriving late, and arriving under the influence of alcohol or substances are examples of such kinds of behaviors.

- Behaviors that interfere with quality of life: alcohol use, substance use, eating binges, purging, gambling, spending money, not going to work or school, and staying in bed during the day are frequent problem behaviors. Symptoms and behaviors resulting from other psychiatric disorders can also affect quality of life.

All of these behaviors will be addressed during sessions, going on to identify what causes them, and what skills can be put in place to avoid their occurrence, instead pursuing what is helpful in achieving treatment goals. It is very important not to confuse these with targets, which relate to the means of achieving the goals. In fact, stopping cutting oneself, or drinking, instead enacting adaptive behaviors, are means to the achievement of goals. The therapist must always have the achievement of goals in mind and must work on targets in every session.

Validation and Problem-Solving

Validation
Change needs acceptation: if a problem is not accepted, it cannot be solved.

The relational climate in which the session takes place is validating, and this is conducive to building and maintaining collaborative work. Validating means communicating that someone else's thoughts, emotions, and behaviors are understandable in light of what the other person looks like, from emotional sensitivity, history, and current living conditions. Validating does not mean approving: a behavior may be understandable, in light of the above, but it is not necessarily agreeable.

DBT describes six levels of validation:

1. Staying awake: the therapist shows that he or she is actively present and participating, especially through nonverbal or paraverbal communication. Eye contact, tone of voice, and posture are essential components.
2. Reflecting: the therapist is responsive to what is expressed by the client, commenting and rephrasing, especially at times when content is particularly significant.
3. Mind reading: the therapist communicates, hypothetically, that he or she has perceived something that the client has not expressed, such as an emotion.
4. Validation in terms of past learning or emotional vulnerability: the therapist draws on biosocial theory to communicate understanding of something happening in the present, but which is understandable in light of the past.
5. Validation in terms of present context: it is similar to the previous one, but understandability is based on the present life situation.
6. Radical Genuineness: the therapist relates to the patient person-to-person, and can also talk about himself (self-disclosure), both in terms of the session and with respect to facts from his professional or personal life. Radical genuineness is the most complete expression of the fact that DBT is a treatment based on a real relationship between peers.

Problem-Solving

The key strategy for identifying behavioral problems, that is, targets, is behavior analysis, which draws information from the diary card that patients must fill out during the week prior to the session and bring to the session. The diary card contains a section on target behaviors and a section on core emotions. Behavior analysis involves identifying links that connect the target behavior with a prompting event, which occurred within minutes or hours prior, and with vulnerability factors, which may relate to the proceeding day(s). The prompting event, which may be external or internal, can be defined as an event without which the target behavior would not have occurred. Vulnerability factors are what favor the event being prompted. For example, a rejection may be the event that triggers self-injurious behavior (cutting) on the basis of intense shame activation. However, if the person did not sleep the night before the event, the event is likely to have a more intense effect on emotional activation. Vulnerability factors are mostly to be sought in biology (sleep, food, physical illness), but also in alcohol or substance use, or in relationship difficulties. Another link in the chain concerns the consequences of the problem behavior, both in the subject and in the environment, which may have a reinforcing or inhibiting effect on the likelihood that the behavior will be repeated. Finally, the links that connect the triggering event and the behavior are thoughts, emotions, and actions, which become the object of the analysis of possible solutions, starting with the question, "what could you have done differently and at what time?" or "what skill could you have used?" The identification of adaptive behaviors refers to skills training, the psychoeducational component of treatment, the purpose of which is skill learning in various areas.

Secondary targets are the problems that generate and sustain the primary targets and are usually identified during the course of treatment. They are the dialectical dilemmas referred to in the section on biosocial theory. Next to the oscillation between emotional vulnerability and self-invalidation, which has already been discussed, there are two dialectical dilemmas. The oscillation between apparent competence and active passivity appears when the client is only apparently capable of enacting adaptive behaviors, then delegating problem-solving to the therapist. Often apparent competence is supported by avoidance, which allows the client not to enact maladaptive behaviors. The last dialectical dilemma concerns the oscillation between avoidance of suffering and ongoing crisis. Often the presence of abandonment, loss, generates intolerable suffering that generates dissociative symptoms, freezing, as disconnection from emotions. These extreme forms of avoidance, however, in turn, generate intense and repeated emotional blizzards, which result in the appearance of dysfunctional behaviors.

3.3 Skills Training

Skills training is the psychoeducational component of treatment, which takes the form of a teaching-learning group led by a leader and co-leader. It consists of four modules: mindfulness, suffering tolerance and crisis management, emotion regulation, and interpersonal effectiveness. Weekly sessions last around 2–2.5 hours.

In standard DBT, each cycle lasts 6 months and the commitment required is at least 1 year, depending on the need to complete at least two modules. Each module begins with mindfulness, which is also the foundation of all treatment, starting with acceptance of reality as such. It is advisable for the group to be open-ended, so each participant completes his or her own cycle, because the co-presence of more experienced individuals and newcomers allows the former to be of use to the latter through their experience of learning and using skills.

Mindfulness skills are derived from the meditative tradition, with particular reference to Zen. They are divided into two areas: "What," which includes observing, describing, and participating, and "How," which includes doing one thing at a time, in a nonjudgmental way, being effective. Suffering tolerance skills include crisis survival and acceptance of reality. Crisis survival means implementing strategies to overcome moments when the risk of activating dysfunctional behaviors is highest. The skills included in this group relate to differentiated situations: for example, the STOP skill allows one to stop before acting out, especially anger, while Pros and Cons is to be used to evaluate the usefulness or otherwise of following the impulse of the moment. The TIP skill, which is to be used when nothing has worked, allows for physiological lowering of brain arousal. Acceptance, especially in the formulation of radical acceptance, refers back to the principles and practice of Mindfulness and Zen. Radical Acceptance develops the ability to accept especially that which generates suffering and cannot be changed.

The skills of Emotional Regulation contain a number of strategies ranging from understanding the functions of emotions to recognizing and naming them, to the ability to distinguish whether an emotion is generated by facts or interpretations of facts, to reducing emotional vulnerability, to the ability to increase positive emotions. The usefulness of these skills concerns the ability to keep the level of emotional activation contained, finding effective solutions in situations where suffering is not too pronounced.

Interpersonal Efficacy skills concern situations where you want to get something from someone, or want to say no, where you want to improve interpersonal relationships, or where you want to defend your self-respect.

3.4 Telephone Consultation

The function of telephone consultation is to help patients implement skills in everyday life situations between sessions. The consultation is the responsibility of the individual therapist but may involve the Skills Training presenters. Hourly availability is agreed on a case-by-case basis.

Three situations are provided: the patient should call when they are at serious risk of enacting dysfunctional behaviors, starting with suicide, having no other resources available. The phone call, therefore, is a crisis management strategy. The other two situations involve difficulties in the enactment of skills, that is, tensions with the therapist that are deemed best resolved before the next session. Phone calls should be brief and not become phone psychotherapy sessions.

3.5 Interventions in the Environment

They both concern issues with the environment, which can be social, family, and therapeutic, including managing relationships with other professionals treating the patient, for example, the psychiatrist administering medication. Client consultation is the key strategy, as it helps to be effective in problematic relational situations by involving the patient personally. Intervention by the therapist instead of the patient would be disabling and make the patient more fragile. When it is verified that consultation with the client is not feasible, it is the therapist who interacts directly with the environment. Often, especially with adolescent patients, the environment is too powerful, so it is necessary for the therapist to intervene, but always without excluding the patient.

3.6 Ancillary Treatments

DBT does not exclude pharmacological interventions, involvement of family members in support groups whose rationale is similar to that of skills training, or hospitalizations. Especially with respect to the latter, DBT urges careful weighing of the pros and cons, particularly in situations where it is believed, rightly or wrongly, that there is a suicidal risk.

4 Research Evidence

Since the early 1990s, the number of peer-reviewed scientific publications on various aspects of DBT has grown at an accelerating rate. Between 1993 and 2000, 10 publications appeared per year, between 2000 and 2010 the number was 64 per year, and as of 2010 about 94 per year. The review of Randomized Controlled Trials (RCTs) done by Miga et al. in 2018 showed the presence of 31 studies on comprehensive DBT and DBT skills only, culminating in about 38 publications derived from them.

Marsha Linehan conducted four RCTs on comprehensive DBT with BPD subjects. Two studies concerned women with BPD and chronic suicide (Linehan et al., 1991, 2006), and two on women with BPD and substance dependence (Linehan et al., 1999, 2002). DBT was compared to Tratment-As-Usual (TAU) and active treatments, showing more efficacy in nonsuicidal self-injury (NSSI), hospitalizations, substance dependence, experiential avoidance, and anger. Social and global adjustment were consistently improved 1 year after the end of the treatment.

Linehan et al. (2015) performed a component analysis by comparing females with BPD and suicidal behavior, randomized across comprehensive DBT, DBT

Skills training only (DBT- S), and DBT individual therapy only (DBT- I). Reduction in suicide attempts and ideation, as well as use of crisis services, were similar in all the treatments, while the presence of skills training was more effective in reducing NSSI. Comprehensive DBT reduced dropouts and hospitalizations.

Assuming that RCT studies are the "gold standard" for scientifically evaluating the effectiveness of a treatment, however, it is necessary to verify the quality of research. The review by Miga et al. (2018) addressed this issue by focusing mainly on the assessment of treatment adherence by therapists. In fact, measuring adherence allows for verification of treatment fidelity. Based on this, studies, both with adherence assessment and without, were identified in the following areas:

- Comprehensive DBT for BPD
- Comprehensive DBT for personality disorder traits and self-injurious behavior
- Comprehensive DBT for personality disorder traits with and without self-injurious behavior
- Comprehensive DBT for mood disorders
- DBT skills only for BPD
- DBT skills only for emotional dysregulation
- DBT skills only for mood disorders
- DBT skills only for eating disorders
- DBT skills only for ADHD
- DBT skills plus phone coaching for depression

Comparison of studies with and without assessment of treatment adherence does not allow conclusions to be drawn and needs further investigation. Regarding the overall results of the RCTs, the conclusions of Miga et al. (2018) are as follows: "Comprehensive DBT has well- established evidence for efficacy with suicidal and self- injurious behaviors, comorbid BPD, and substance use problems, as well as for high treatment retention. Following the same criteria, the DBT skills only treatment model has well-established empirical evidence for efficacy with treatment-resistant depression, binge eating, and bulimia disorders" (pp.446–447). Valentine et al. (2020) reviewed 31 studies of DBT skills only and concluded that their efficacy, as compared to comprehensive DBT, still remains unclear.

The results reported here are about efficacy in research context. Effectiveness studies in the clinical setting have shown that DBT is effective on suicidal and non-suicidal self-injury (NSSI), hospitalizations, depression, and overall psychiatric symptoms (Carter et al., 2010; McMain et al., 2009, 2012).

Mechanisms of change seem to be related to the components of the dialectical stance. Indeed, the balance between acceptance, that is validation, and change, that is problem-solving, helps the patients to be more open to their inner experience, to communicate it, to learn new skills, and to explore reality (Bedics et al., 2015; Barnicot et al., 2016; Lynch et al., 2006; Neacsiu et al., 2010). Recent research focused on neural changes (Iskric & Barkley-Levenson, 2021).

5 Adaptations of DBT

Since the comprehensive DBT for BPD patients, adaptations have appeared that have considered different psychopathological conditions. The rationale for the development of each adaptation implies that what is deemed useful in addressing clinical problems is included, while maintaining the core of fidelity to DBT. According to the evidence-based practice, an adaptation must be verified and validated through empirical research. The main adaptations will now be briefly listed, referring to the authors for further discussion.

5.1 DBT for Adolescence (DBT-A) (Rathus & Miller, 2015)

It is targeted at adolescents with multiple problems, at risk or not of suicide and/or NSSI. The modes are similar to comprehensive DBT; however, skills training is a multi-family group format, where adolescents are included together with their parents. Parental support is offered, through family or parenting sessions and parent telephone coaching. The first RCT was published in 2014 (Mehlum et al., 2014). Rathus and Miller (2015) published the manual of DBT-A.

5.2 DBT for Preadolescent Children (DBT-C)

It maintains the structure of comprehensive DBT, with a change in target hierarchy, where the parental capacity to respond to the child's emotions and behavior is emphasized (Perepletchikova et al., 2017)

5.3 DBT for Eating Disorders

It is recommended for nonresponders to other evidence-based treatments. They should show emotional dysregulation and complex clinical presentations. Rozaku-Soumalia et al. (2021) published a literature revision and a metanalysis that showed good results in patients with binge eating disorder and bulimia. However, the studies are few and with a small number of subjects.

5.4 DBT for Substance Use Disorder (SUD)

The presence of SUD together with BPD makes treatment more challenging and needs integration of strategies derived from both clinical conditions. Comprehensive DBT can be integrated with pharmacological interventions, toxicological controls, and a 12-step program. The risk of dropout needs attachment strategies and interventions on the environment (Dimeff & Linehan, 2008). A metanalysis of six studies by Haktanir and Callender (2020) showed that DBT is an effective approach in the treatment of substance-related issues, as evidenced by post-treatment assessment and follow-up assessment.

5.5 DBT PE

Adaptation of DBT for individuals with PTSD and BPD (DBT PE) (Harned, 2022) makes it possible to deal with complex clinical situations that until now have been a difficult problem to solve. In fact, the presence of severe emotional and behavioral dysregulation along with PTSD invites caution with respect to dealing with issues of trauma. DBT PE complements Comprehensive DBT with a modified version of Foa et al. (2007) Prolonged Exposure Therapy and allows treatment of such individuals in Stage 1 DBT after achieving (on average after 20 sessions) a reduction in dysfunctional behaviors, especially self-injury and suicide.

5.6 DBT-PTSD

DBT-PTSD (Bohus et al., 2020) is a multimodal treatment for individuals who were abused in childhood and have emotional and behavioral dysregulation due to the presence of Complex PTSD or BPD. The treatment is divided into phases and includes components from other 'third wave' therapies.

DBT is now used in forensic settings (Moulden et al., 2020), in intellectual disabilities (Brown et al., 2013), and in schools (Dexter-Mazza et al., 2020).

6 Implementation and Training

The implementation of DBT in different geographic, cultural, and clinical settings implies the need to have in mind, from the outset, two fundamental aspects: project sustainability and treatment fidelity. Sustainability refers to whether a project, once initiated, has a good chance of lasting over time. Fidelity concerns the ability to implement the treatment in a manner adherent to how it has been used in the research setting. In fact, the evaluation of effectiveness in a clinical setting starts with the need to be able to control for treatment-related variables in the first place. Barriers to implementation are numerous and an exhaustive list can be found in Proctor et al. (2011). In 2018, an International Committee started to work aiming at developing DBT in the world in a coherent, shared, way. Three areas are considered: training, research, and treatment development. The World DBT Association (WDBTA) is going to be established. Continental Chapters, where National DBT Societies are included, will structure it.

The implementation of an evidence-based treatment in different settings, as stated above, has necessitated the development of a standardized training model. Over the course of several years of work, the Behavioral Research & Therapy Clinics at the University of Washington and Behavioral Tech, LLC and its International Affiliates developed the Dialectical Behavior Therapy Intensive Training™. This model, based on teams' programs, is widely diffused and could be considered as a part of the success of DBT in dissemination and implementation in different countries. Before the training begins, participants are required to read the core texts of DBT, discuss them in teams, and attend a 16-hour introductory workshop. Other training initiatives are also possible, however, so that participants do not arrive at the training without adequate preparation.

The description of the Intensive Training™ here refers to the in-depth description by DuBose et al. (2018). The training comprises two parts of 5 days each, interspersed with a period of about 9 months that allows the teams to implement the program, face barriers, and start to treat patients, supported by mentors. The first part concerns the following subjects, taught with various methodologies, such as explaining, demonstrating, and modeling.

First day: Foundations of DBT (Behavioral Science and Acceptance), Dialectical Principles, DBT Case Formulation, Structure of the Treatment, DBT Consultation Team

Second day: Functions of Comprehensive Treatment, Levels of Disorder and Stages of Treatment, Targets of Treatment, Orientation and Commitment

Third day: Problem-Solving, Behavioral Analysis, CBT Procedures, Validation, Dialectical Strategies

Fourth day: Suicide Risk Assessment and Management, Crisis Strategies, Treatment of Suicidal Individuals

Fifth day: Stylistic Strategies, Case Management Protocols, Special Treatment Strategies

In the second part, trainers consult teams on their programs and help them to solve implementation problems. Case consultation is also offered by trainers.

References

Barnicot, K., Gonzalez, R., McCabe, R., & Priebe, S. (2016). Skills use and common treatment processes in dialectical behaviour therapy for borderline personality disorder. *Journal of Behavior Therapy and Experimental Psychiatry, 52*, 147–156.

Bedics, J. D., Atkins, D. C., Harned, M. S., & Linehan, M. M. (2015). The therapeutic alliance as a predictor of outcome in dialectical behavior therapy versus non- behavioral psychotherapy experts for borderline personality disorder. *Psychotherapy, 52*, 67–77.

Bohus, M., Kleindienst, N., Hahn, C., Müller-Engelmann, M., Ludäscher, P., Steil, R., et al. (2020). Dialectical behavior therapy for posttraumatic stress disorder (DBT-PTSD) compared with cognitive processing therapy (CPT) in complex presentations of PTSD in women survivors of childhood abuse: A randomized clinical trial. *JAMA Psychiatry, 77*(12), 1235–1245.

Bortolla, R., Cavicchioli, M., Fossati, A., & Maffei, C. (2020). Emotional reactivity in borderline personality disorder: Theoretical considerations based on a meta-analytic review of laboratory studies. *Journal of Personality Disorders, 34*(1), 64–87.

Brown, J. F., Brown, M. Z., & Dibiasio, P. (2013). Treating individuals with intellectual disabilities and challenging behaviors with adapted dialectical behavior therapy. *Journal of Mental Health Research in Intellectual Disabilities, 6*(4), 280–303.

Carter, G. L., Willcox, C. H., Lewin, T. J., Conrad, A. M., & Bendit, N. (2010). Hunter DBT project: Randomized controlled trial of dialectical behaviour therapy in women with borderline personality disorder. *Australian & New Zealand Journal of Psychiatry, 44*(2), 162–173.

Cavicchioli, M., & Maffei, C. (2020). Rejection sensitivity in borderline personality disorder and the cognitive–affective personality system: A meta-analytic review. *Personality Disorders: Theory, Research, and Treatment, 11*(1), 1.

Crowell, S. E., Beauchaine, T. P., & Linehan, M. M. (2009). A biosocial developmental model of borderline personality: Elaborating and extending Linehan's theory. *Psychological Bulletin, 135*, 495–510.

Crowell, S. E., Yaptangco, M., & Turner, S. L. (2016). Coercion, invalidation, and risk for self-injury and borderline personality traits. In T. J. Dishion & J. J. Snyder (Eds.), *The Oxford handbook of coercive relationship dynamics* (pp. 182–193). Oxford University Press.

Dexter-Mazza, E. T., Mazza, J. J., Miller, A. L., Graling, K., Courtrtney-Seidler, E., & Catucci, D. (2020). Application of DBT in a school-based setting. In *Dialectical behavior therapy in a clinical practice: Applications across disorders and settings* (pp. 121–137).

Dimeff, L. A., & Linehan, M. M. (2008). Dialectical behavior therapy for substance abusers. *Addiction Science & Clinical Practice, 4*(2), 39.

DuBose, A. P., Botanov, Y., Navarro-Haro, M. V., & Linehan, M. M. (2018). *The Oxford handbook of dialectical behaviour therapy* (pp. 965–979).

Foa, E. B., Hembree, E., & Rothbaum, B. O. (2007). *Prolonged exposure therapy for PTSD: Emotional processing of traumatic experiences.* Oxford University Press.

Gratz, K. L., & Roemer, L. (2004). Multidimensional assessment of emotion regulation and dysregulation: Development, factor structure, and initial validation of the Difficulties in Emotion Regulation Scale. *Journal of Psychopathology and Behavioral Assessment, 26*(1), 41–54.

Gross, J. J. (2014). Emotion regulation: Conceptual and empirical foundations. *Handbook of emotion regulation, 2*, 3–20.

Haktanir, A., & Callender, K. A. (2020). Meta-analysis of dialectical behavior therapy (DBT) for treating substance use. *Research on Education and Psychology, 4*(Special Issue), 74–87.

Harned, M. S. (2022). *Treating trauma in dialectical behavior therapy: The DBT prolonged exposure protocol (DBT PE).* Guilford Publications.

Iskric, A., & Barkley-Levenson, E. (2021). Neural changes in borderline personality disorder after dialectical behavior therapy–a review. *Frontiers in Psychiatry, 12*, 772081.

Linehan, M. M. (1993). *Cognitive- behavioral treatment of borderline personality disorder.* Guilford Press.

Linehan, M. M., Armstrong, H. E., Suarez, A., Allmon, D., & Heard, H. L. (1991). Cognitive-behavioral treatment of chronically parasuicidal borderline patients. *Archives of General Psychiatry, 48*, 1060–1064.

Linehan, M. M., Schmidt, H., III, Dimeff, L. A., Craft, J. C., Kanter, J., & Comtois, K. A. (1999). Dialectical behavior therapy for patients with borderline personality disorder and drug dependence. *American Journal of Addictions, 8*, 279–292.

Linehan, M. M., Cochran, B. N., Mar, C. M., Levensky, E. R., & Comtois, K. A. (2000). Therapeutic burnout among borderline personality disordered clients and their therapists: Development and evaluation of two adaptations of the Maslach Burnout Inventory. *Cognitive and Behavioral Practice, 7*(3), 329–337.

Linehan, M. M., Dimeff, L. A., Reynolds, S. K., Comtois, K. A., Welch, S. S., Heagerty, P., & Kivlahan, D. R. (2002). Dialectical behavior therapy versus comprehensive validation therapy plus 12- step for the treatment of opioid dependent women meeting criteria for borderline personality disorder. *Drug and Alcohol Dependence, 67*(1), 13–26.

Linehan, M. M., Comtois, K. A., Murray, A. M., Brown, M. Z., Gallop, R. J., Heard, H. L., & Lindenboim, N. (2006). Two-year randomized controlled trial and follow-up of dialectical behavior therapy vs therapy by experts for suicidal behaviors and borderline personality disorder. *Archives of General Psychiatry, 63*, 757–766.

Linehan, M. M., Korslund, K. E., Harned, M. S., Gallop, R. J., Lungu, A., Neacsiu, A. D., et al. (2015). Dialectical behavior therapy for high suicide risk in individuals with borderline personality disorder: A randomized clinical trial and component analysis. *JAMA Psychiatry, 72*(5), 475–482.

Lynch, T. R., Chapman, A. L., Rosenthal, M. Z., Kuo, J. R., & Linehan, M. M. (2006). Mechanisms of change in dialectical behavior therapy: Theoretical and empirical observations. *Journal of Clinical Psychology, 62*, 459–480.

McMain, S. F., Links, P. S., Gnam, W. H., Guimond, T., Cardish, R. J., Korman, L., & Streiner, D. L. (2009). A randomized trial of dialectical behavior therapy versus general psychiatric management for borderline personality disorder. *The American Journal of Psychiatry, 166*(12), 1365–1374.

McMain, S. F., Guimond, T., Streiner, D. L., Cardish, R. J., & Links, P. S. (2012). Dialectical behavior therapy compared with general psychiatric management for borderline personality disorder: Clinical outcomes and functioning over a 2- year follow- up. *The American Journal of Psychiatry, 169*(6), 650–661.

Mehlum, L., Tormoen, A., Ramberg, M., Haga, E., Diep, L. M., Laberg, S., et al. (2014). Dialectical behavior therapy for adolescents with recent and repeated self- harming behavior—First randomized controlled trial. *Journal of the American Academy of Child and Adolescent Psychiatry, 53*, 1082–1091.

Miga, M. M., Neacsiu, A. D., Lungu, A., Heard, H. L., & Dimeff, L. A. (2018). Dialectical behaviour therapy from 1991–2015. In *The Oxford handbook of dialectical behaviour therapy* (pp. 415–465).

Moulden, H. M., Mamak, M., & Chaimowitz, G. (2020). A preliminary evaluation of the effectiveness of dialectical behaviour therapy in a forensic psychiatric setting. *Criminal Behaviour and Mental Health, 30*(2–3), 141–150.

Neacsiu, A. D., Rizvi, S. L., & Linehan, M. M. (2010). Dialectical behavior therapy skills use as a mediator and outcome of treatment for borderline personality disorder. *Behaviour Research and Therapy, 48*, 832–839.

Perepletchikova, F., Nathanson, D., Axelrod, S. R., Merrill, C., Walker, A., Grossman, M., et al. (2017). Randomized clinical trial of dialectical behavior therapy for preadolescent children with disruptive mood dysregulation disorder: Feasibility and outcomes. *Journal of the American Academy of Child & Adolescent Psychiatry, 56*(10), 832–840.

Proctor, E., Silmere, H., Raghavan, R., Hovmand, P., Aarons, G., Bunger, A., et al. (2011). Outcomes for implementation research: Conceptual distinctions, measurement challenges, and research agenda. *Administration and Policy in Mental Health and Mental Health Services Research, 38*, 65–76.

Rathus, J. H., & Miller, A. L. (2015). *DBT skills manual for adolescents*. Guilford Press.

Rozakou-Soumalia, N., Dârvariu, Ş., & Sjögren, J. M. (2021). Dialectical behaviour therapy improves emotion dysregulation mainly in binge eating disorder and bulimia nervosa: A systematic review and meta-analysis. *Journal of Personalized Medicine, 11*(9), 931.

Valentine, S. E., Smith, A. M., & Stewart, K. (2020). A review of the empirical evidence for DBT skills training as a stand-alone intervention. In *The handbook of dialectical behavior therapy* (pp. 325–358).

CBT-E: Addressing Eating Disorder Psychopathology with Cognitive Behavioral Strategies and Procedures

Riccardo Dalle Grave, Simona Calugi, and Selvaggia Sermattei

Abbreviations

BMI	Body mass index
CBT	Cognitive behavior therapy
CBT-E	Enhanced cognitive behavior therapy
CBT-ED	Cognitive behavior therapy for eating disorders
DSM	Diagnostic and Statistical Manual of Mental Disorders
FBT	Family-based treatment
SSCM	Specialist supportive clinical management
MANTRA	Maudsley Model Anorexia Nervosa Treatment for Adults

1 Introduction

The treatment options offered to patients with eating disorders in real-world settings largely depend on the judgment and training of their assisting clinicians (von Ranson et al., 2013) and local constraints on which treatments can be offered. Unfortunately, few of these treatments are based on scientific evidence, and even fewer have been evaluated in clinical trials (Tobin et al., 2007; Waller et al., 2013; Turner et al., 2014).

There is a consensus that the mainstay of the treatment of eating disorders is the outpatient setting (National Guideline Alliance, 2017). It is less expensive and disruptive than day-hospital and inpatient treatments and can be effective in many patients (Byrne et al., 2017). However, some patients do not respond to the best

R. Dalle Grave (✉) · S. Calugi
Department of Eating and Weight Disorders, Villa Garda Hospital, Garda, Italy

S. Sermattei
Associazione Disturbi Alimentari e del Peso (AIDAP Empoli), Empoli, Italy

available outpatient treatments. The most common option in these cases is to provide them with a more intensive form of care (National Guideline Alliance, 2017) to improve their chances of recovery. However, it is common for patients being transferred from a less intensive (e.g., outpatient) to a more intensive form of care (e.g., day hospital or inpatient) and vice versa to be treated with different strategies and procedures regarding both theory and content. This type of transition produces discontinuities in the process of care and may confuse patients about the procedures and strategies that they should use to address their eating disorders. These problems indicate the need to promote the improvement of the implementation of evidence-based treatments in standard clinical settings and the process of patient transfer from outpatient to intensive settings, and vice versa.

The NICE guideline recommends cognitive behavior therapy for eating disorders (CBT-ED) as an evidence-based treatment for all eating disorders (National Guideline Alliance, 2017). CBT-E (E = "enhanced") is one major example of the specialist treatments covered by the umbrella term "CBT-ED." CBT-E was developed initially to address eating disorder psychopathology (rather than the DSM diagnosis) of adult outpatients (Fairburn et al., 2003a), but it was also adapted for adolescents (Dalle Grave & Calugi, 2020; Dalle Grave & Cooper, 2016) and intensive levels of care (Dalle Grave et al., 2008a; Dalle Grave, 2012).

CBT-E, having to be designed to treat all diagnostic categories of clinical eating disorders both in adults and adolescents in different settings of care (from outpatient to inpatient), offers the concrete possibility, for the first time in the field of evidence-based psychotherapy for eating disorders, to implement a stepped-care approach in real-world clinical settings overcoming some of the difficulties encountered in more conventional, fragmented clinical services. Indeed, the most distinctive feature of this approach, also termed multistep CBT-E (Dalle Grave, 2013), is that the same theory and procedures are applied at each level of care, as the main difference between the various steps is the intensiveness of treatment.

This chapter begins by providing an overview of transdiagnostic cognitive behavior theory. Then, it gives an overview of CBT-E, describing its goals, general treatment strategy, forms, adaptations for clinical groups and settings, and current status. Finally, it concludes by discussing the challenges that need to be addressed.

2 The Transdiagnostic Cognitive Behavior Theory of Eating Disorders

Several specific psychological theories have been proposed to explain the development and maintenance of eating disorders. Among these, cognitive behavioral theory has most influenced the evidence-based treatment for eating disorders. The theory was initially developed in the early 1980s to understand and treat bulimia nervosa (Fairburn, 1981). This theory was primarily concerned with the processes that maintain bulimia nervosa rather than those responsible for its initial development, although the two may overlap. Subsequently, the theory for bulimia nervosa was improved and expanded in two main aspects (Fairburn et al., 2003a): (i) it was extended to all disorders of clinical severity, and for this reason, it was defined as "transdiagnostic" and (ii) it included four additional maintaining processes that, in subgroup patients, interact with the eating disorder maintaining processes and constitute obstacles to change.

According to the transdiagnostic cognitive behavioral theory, the overvaluation of shape, weight, and eating and their control is of central importance in maintaining eating disorders (Fairburn et al., 2003a; Dalle Grave & Calugi, 2018). Indeed, the other clinical features seen in these disorders can be understood as stemming directly from this "core psychopathology," including extreme weight-control behaviors (e.g., dietary restraint, dietary restriction, self-induced vomiting, laxative and diuretic misuse, and excessive exercising), various forms of body weight and shape checking and avoidance, and preoccupation with thoughts about eating, weight, and shape.

The undereating and other extreme weight-control behaviors create a persistent caloric deficit, and this results in significantly low body weight, typical of most initial cases of eating disorders, and the development of secondary physiological and psychological consequences (called "starvation symptoms") that themselves perpetuate undereating and the overvaluation of shape and weight (Dalle Grave et al., 2007, 2011). For example, the sense of fullness even after eating modest amounts of food, as a result of delayed gastric emptying, may be interpreted as having eaten "too much" and intensifies dietary restriction; the secondary social withdrawal that often occurs has the effect of encouraging self-absorption while also isolating patients from external influences that might diminish their overvaluation of eating, shape, and weight and their control; the food preoccupations secondary to undereating and underweight may accentuate the adoption of strict and extreme dietary rules.

One prominent feature that is not an apparent direct expression of the core psychopathology is binge eating, which occurs in many patients with eating disorders, whatever their DSM-5 diagnosis. However, the transdiagnostic cognitive behavioral theory proposes that binge eating is maintained mainly by attempts to adhere to extreme and rigid dietary rules (Cooper & Dalle Grave, 2017). People with eating disorders tend to react in an adverse and extreme (often dichotomous) way to the almost inevitable breaking of these rules, and even a small dietary transgression is interpreted as evidence of poor self-control and personal weakness. The response to this perceived lack of self-control is a temporary abandonment of efforts to restrict eating, and, as a result, patients succumb to the urge to eat that arises from the restraint (and any accompanying dietary restriction). The result is a short-lived period of uncontrolled eating (i.e., an episode of subjective or objective binge eating). This binge eating maintains the core psychopathology by intensifying patients' concerns about their ability to control their eating, shape, and weight. It also encourages further dietary restraint, thereby increasing the risk of further binge eating.

Two additional processes also contribute to and maintain binge eating. First, adverse day-to-day events and associated mood changes increase patients' likelihood of breaking dietary rules. In part, this is because it is challenging to maintain dietary restraint under such circumstances, and in part, binge eating can become a way of coping with these difficulties. After all, it temporarily ameliorates such mood states and distracts patients from thinking about their problems. Second, if binge eating is followed by compensatory purging, this also maintains binge eating. This is because the commonly held mistaken belief in the effectiveness of such "purging" in preventing energy absorption removes a major deterrent to binge eating, i.e., fear of weight gain. Patients do not realize that vomiting only retrieves part of what has been eaten (Kaye et al., 1993), and laxatives have little or no effect. This explains why, when recurrent episodes of objective binge eating occur, patients tend to regain weight and, in many cases, lose their underweight status (satisfying the diagnostic criteria of bulimia nervosa or subthreshold bulimia nervosa) although they continue to maintain a severe dietary restraint outside the episodes of binge eating. For those patients who maintain a DSM-5 diagnosis of anorexia nervosa, binge eating may be mainly subjective or not present at all.

The transdiagnostic cognitive behavior theory proposes that in certain patients, one or more of four additional ("external") processes interact with the core eating disorder maintaining mechanisms (Fairburn, 2008). When this occurs, they constitute further obstacles to change. These external maintaining mechanisms are extreme perfectionism ("clinical perfectionism"), unconditional and pervasive low self-esteem ("core low self-esteem"), marked interpersonal problems ("interpersonal difficulties"), and mood intolerance.

Figure 1 shows the core processes involved in the maintenance of eating disorders according to the transdiagnostic cognitive behavioral theory. In our experience, this theory provides a good account of the processes that maintain any eating disorder, whatever its exact form or diagnosis. In some patients, only a limited number of these processes are active (e.g., in binge-eating disorder), whereas in others, many more are operating (e.g., anorexia nervosa with binge eating and purging). The

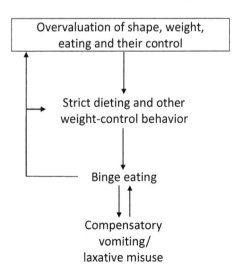

Fig. 1 The main maintenance processes of eating disorders according to transdiagnostic cognitive behavioural theory

transdiagnostic cognitive behavioral theory highlights the processes that need to be tackled in treatment and provides a guide (the road map) to its individualization.

3 Evidence Supporting the Transdiagnostic Theory

Several data support the cognitive perspective on the maintenance of eating disorders, including descriptive, comparative, and experimental investigations of the clinical characteristics of individuals with these disorders (Grilo, 2013; Shafran et al., 2007a; Shafran et al., 2007b; Watson et al., 2011).

In individuals with bulimia nervosa, studies have confirmed a relationship between the overvaluation of shape and weight and changes in dietary restraint and binge eating over time (Fairburn et al., 2003b). Additionally, binge eating has been correlated with self-reported calorie restriction (Zunker et al., 2011) and between intensification of weight concerns and increased restraint and vomiting frequency (Spangler et al., 2004). Furthermore, research has confirmed that a decrease in dietary restraint during treatment mediates a subsequent reduction in binge eating (Wilson et al., 2002). In a broader transdiagnostic sample involving patients with both bulimia nervosa and anorexia nervosa, reciprocal relationships have been established between the overvaluation of shape and weight and the adoption of moderate to extreme dietary restraint and excessive exercising (Tabri et al., 2015).

Cross-sectional assessments of the transdiagnostic model have been conducted using structural equation modeling, encompassing treatment-seeking patient samples and community samples. A comparison was made between the original cognitive behavioral theory and the enhanced version, which included additional maintaining mechanisms (e.g., clinical perfectionism, core low self-esteem, marked interpersonal difficulties, and mood intolerance), specifically in patients diagnosed with bulimia nervosa and atypical forms of the disorder. The results supported both models, with the enhanced model explaining a greater portion of the variance (Lampard et al., 2011). However, the hypothesized relationship between dietary restraint and binge eating did not receive support. Further evaluations in transdiagnostic samples were carried out, one involving referrals for intensive treatment to a tertiary center (Lampard et al., 2011; Tasca et al., 2011) and another comparing the original and enhanced models in referrals to various specialist eating disorder centers within one country (Dakanalis et al., 2015). In both samples, there was support for the theory, although variations were observed between diagnostic groups regarding the level of support for certain relationships tested by the models. Notably, restraint was found to be only indirectly associated with binge eating. Support for the theory has also been observed in community studies involving male students and women (Dakanalis et al., 2014; Hoiles et al., 2012).

Despite the large amount of direct support for both the original cognitive behavioral theory and the enhanced version, there has been an ongoing controversy about the relationship between dietary restraint and binge eating (Lowe et al., 2013). While this relationship is often observed to be operating in clinical situations, issues of measurement have complicated its investigation in a research context. Further discussion of this issue is beyond the scope of this chapter.

4 Overview of CBT-E

CBT-E is a specialized psychological treatment for eating disorders based on the transdiagnostic cognitive behavioral theory described above. The treatment has four general goals (Dalle Grave, 2022):

1. To actively engage the patient in deciding to change and treatment.
2. To help the patient eliminate their eating-disorder features (e.g., dietary restraint and restriction, low weight, self-induced vomiting, laxative misuse, excessive exercising, and preoccupation with shape, weight, and eating).
3. To correct the mechanisms maintaining the eating-disorder features.
4. To ensure lasting change and prevent relapse.

CBT-E treats the patient's psychopathology, not the eating disorder DSM-5 diagnosis. It does so by addressing the emotional, behavioral and cognitive maintaining mechanisms and the eating-disorder features operating in the patient in a flexible and personalized way. It is a comprehensive treatment and should not be associated with other forms of therapy. It is designed to help the patients feel in control, involving them actively from the decision to start to the choice of which problems to address and how.

During the assessment and preparation session, patients are educated on two main models that try to explain why a person persists in adopting unhealthy weight control behaviors and pursuing low weight despite the actual and or future physical and psychosocial impairment (i.e., the "disease model" and the "psychological model" adopted by CBT-E), and their clinical implications (Dalle Grave, 2023) (see Table 1).

The psychological model adopted by CBT-E requires not using "prescriptive" or "coercive" procedures. In other words, the CBT-E therapist never asks patients to do things they disagree with, which may increase their resistance to change. For example, the initial goal of the treatment in underweight patients is not weight regain but instead to help them understand the nature of their eating problem according to the CBT-E model and make an active decision to change. This "informed decision-making" approach is also used to address other egosyntonic features of eating-disorder psychopathology, like dietary restraint and/or excessive exercising. The therapist collaboratively creates with the patient the personal formulation of the main processes maintaining the eating psychopathology according to the cognitive behavioral transdiagnostic theory. Once they reach a shared understanding of the nature of the eating problem, some sessions are dedicated to discussing the implications of change, including addressing weight regain if indicated. If the patient does not conclude that they have a problem to address, the treatment cannot be started or postponed for some time, but this is not common.

Table 1 The disease model and the CBT-E psychological model of eating disorders

Disease model
The disease model postulates that the features of eating disorders (e.g., dietary restraint, dietary restriction, other extreme weight control behaviors, binge-eating and purging, fear of gaining weight, and preoccupation with shape and weight) are the symptoms of a specific "disease," namely anorexia nervosa, bulimia nervosa, binge-eating disorder, or other eating disorders. As in other medical models of mental disorders (Radden, 2018), it considers eating disorders in much the same way as physical diseases.
The disease model has important clinical implications. Indeed, if the eating disorder is a disease, the clinicians have the role to treat it by adopting an active and prescriptive approach. The patients are considered not to be in control of their thoughts and behaviors, as are symptoms of their disease and are encouraged/obliged to play a passive role in the treatment. Specifically, they are often asked not to trust their thoughts about shape, weight, and eating, as they are generated by the "ill" part of their brain. To get well, they must follow passively the prescriptions of their therapists. At the same time, their parents or significant others, as is recommended, for example, by family-based treatment (Lock & Le Grange, 2013), are actively involved as "controllers," overseeing the patient's meals and eating.
Psychological CBT-E model
The CBT-E model is based on a psychological explanation of the patient's eating disorder. According to this model, the person has difficulties seeing strict dieting, other extreme weight control behaviors, and low weight as a problem because they judge themselves predominantly or even exclusively in terms of shape, weight, and eating control (i.e., the overvaluation of shape, weight, and eating control) (Fairburn et al., 2003a). This core cognitive psychopathology explains why when they adhere to extreme and rigid dietary rules and achieve low weight, they usually perceive a sense of triumph and realization despite the physical and psychosocial negative consequences. However, despite these perceived positive consequences, the persons can be gradually helped to understand that their self-evaluation system is dysfunctional, and deciding to address the psychological and behavioral mechanisms maintaining their eating disorder mindset.
The psychological model has important clinical implications. Indeed, with this model, the patient plays an active role in understanding the psychological and behavior mechanisms maintaining their eating disorder, deciding to change. The therapists are "collaborators" of the patients in helping them to reach a shared understanding of the mechanisms maintaining the eating disorders, evaluating the pros and cons of change, and identifying the strategies and procedures to address the eating disorder features and their maintenance mechanisms (Dalle Grave, 2023). At the same time, the parents and significant others are involved as "helpers" of the patients in creating an optimum family environment and implementing some treatment procedures with the previous patient's consent (Dalle Grave & el Khazen, 2022).

Once the patient is engaged in the process of change, their eating-disorder psychopathology is addressed via a flexible set of cognitive, behavioral, and interpersonal strategies and procedures integrated with ongoing education. Two guiding principles underpin CBT-E: first, simpler procedures are preferred over more complex ones, and second, it is better to do a few things well rather than many things badly (the principle of parsimony) (Fairburn, 2008).

Patients are encouraged to observe how the processes illustrated in their formulation operate in real life and to monitor their eating and the associated events, thoughts, and feelings in real time. Then, they are asked to make gradual personalized behavioral changes and analyze the effects and implications of each change on their way of thinking. The disruption of the main eating-disorder maintenance mechanisms gradually reduces the patient's preoccupation with shape, weight, eating, and their control. In the later stages of treatment, when the patient reports periods free from such concerns, CBT-E focuses on helping them to recognize the early warning signs of eating-disorder mindset reactivation and to decenter from it to avoid relapse.

The parents of adolescents are actively involved in creating an optimal home environment favoring the patient's change and, with the young person's consent, providing support in implementing some procedures of the treatment (e.g., planning and preparing the meals, assisting the patient during the consumption of the meals). A detailed description of the parent's role can be found in the CBT parent's guide (Dalle Grave & el Khazen, 2022). A similar strategy is used with adult patients if both the therapist and the patient agree that involving their significant other(s) might aid their recovery.

5 Forms of CBT-E

CBT-E can be administered in two forms (Fairburn, 2008):

1. *Focused form.* It targets, in a flexible and personalized way, the patient's eating-disorder psychopathology.
2. *Broad form.* It addresses both the patient's eating-disorder psychopathology and one or more of their external maintenance mechanisms (i.e., clinical perfectionism, core low self-esteem, mood intolerance, or marked interpersonal difficulties).

The focused form is indicated for most patients. In contrast, the broad module(s) are introduced if the external psychopathology is pronounced, appears to maintain the eating disorder, and interferes with the treatment (Dalle Grave et al., 2021). The decision to use the broad form is made in a review session held after four weeks in non-underweight patients or in one of the review sessions later on in underweight patients.

6 Adaptations for Clinical Groups and Settings

6.1 Outpatient CBT-E

Adolescent Version

A detailed treatment description can be found in the official CBT-E manual for adolescents (Dalle Grave & Calugi, 2020). There are also manuals for the patients (aged 15–24) (Dalle Grave & Calugi, 2024) and the parents (Dalle Grave & el

Khazen, 2022), which explain clearly what eating disorders are, what CBT-E entails, and how to make the best use of CBT-E strategies and procedures.

CBT-E for underweight adolescent patients (i.e., those with a BMI-for-age percentile corresponding to a BMI <18.5 in adults (Cole et al., 2007)) is delivered in 30–40 fifty-minute sessions. This variability in the treatment duration depends on the patient's underweight degree and difficulties in addressing weight regain (Calugi et al., 2015). In non-underweight patients, the treatment usually lasts 20 weeks. Parents are asked to participate alone in an interview lasting approximately 50 minutes during the first week. Subsequently, the patient and parents are periodically seen together for 15–20 minutes immediately after the individual sessions four to six times (in non-underweight patients) or eight to ten times (in underweight patients).

The treatment involves two assessment/preparation sessions, and in underweight patients—the most common group of treatment-seeking adolescent patients with an eating disorder (Dalle Grave et al., 2022a)—it is delivered in three main "Steps" to achieve weight restoration. Every 4 weeks, there is a review session. There are further review sessions 4, 12, and 24 weeks after the end of treatment. Table 2 describes the principal procedures of the adolescents' version of CBT-E for underweight patients. CBT-E for non-underweight adolescents has a similar structure but is delivered for 20 weeks.

Since the physical organs of adolescents are not mature and medical complications associated with eating disorders, e.g., osteopenia and osteoporosis, may be severe in this age range and have lifelong repercussions, regular medical assessment, and a lower threshold for hospital admission in case of medical instability are integral parts of CBT-E for adolescents.

Outpatient CBT-E for Adults

The outpatient version of CBT-E is recommended for most adult patients with an eating disorder, and its detailed description can be found elsewhere (Fairburn, 2008). A manual for non-underweight patients that can be used as self-help, guided self-help, or guided reading during the treatment is also available (Fairburn, 2013).

The treatment lasts 20 weeks in non-underweight patients and 40 weeks in underweight patients, and it is delivered in 20 and 40 individual sessions, respectively. The adult version of CBT-E was initially divided into four "Stages." However, we prefer to use "Steps" rather than "Stages" also in the adult version of CBT-E because most treatment-seeking individuals with an eating disorder are underweight or have highly suppressed weight (maximum weight—actual weight) and need to regain weight (Dalle Grave et al., 2022a). Hence, three Steps are used to help them: (i) decide to address weight regain, (ii) regain a healthy weight, and (iii) maintain weight and prevent relapse. In our clinical experience, underweight adult patients appreciate this approach, finding the three steps easy to understand and implement. In particular, as they tend not to see being underweight as a problem, they

Table 2 The three steps, the review sessions, and the principal procedures of the CBT-E version for non-underweight adolescent patients

Step one—starting well and deciding to change
The aims are to engage the patient in treatment and change, including addressing weight regain. The appointments are twice weekly for 4 weeks and involve the following:
Jointly creating a formulation of the processes maintaining the eating disorder
Establishing real-time self-monitoring
Personalized education on eating disorder
Introducing and establishing weekly collaboratively in-session weighing
Introducing and adhering to a pattern of regular eating
Thinking about addressing weight regain
Involving parents to facilitate treatment
Review sessions
These are held 1 week after Step One and then every 4 weeks for:
Collaboratively reviewing treatment compliance and progress
Identifying barriers to change
Adjusting the initial formulation considering progress and/or emerging issues
Deciding to continue with the focused form of CBT-E rather than the broad form
Step two—addressing the change
The aim is to address weight regain and the key mechanisms that are maintaining the patient's eating-disorder psychopathology. The appointments are twice a week until the rate of weight regain stabilizes, at which time they are held once a week. This step involves the following CBT-E modules:
Underweight and undereating
Overvaluation of shape and weight
Dietary restraint
Events and mood-related changes in eating
Setbacks and mindsets
External modules (clinical perfectionism, core low self-esteem, mood intolerance, interpersonal difficulties)
Step 3—ending well
The aims are to ensure that progress made during treatment is maintained and the risk of relapse minimizes. There are three appointments, 2 weeks apart, covering the following:
Addressing concerns about ending treatment
Devising a short-term plan for continuing to implement changes made during treatment until the post-treatment review sessions
Phasing out treatment procedures
Devising a long-term plan for maintaining body weight and averting and coping with setbacks
Post-treatment review session
Reviewing the long-term maintenance plan around 4, 12, and 20 weeks after treatment has finished.

appreciate that in Step One, the goal is not weight regain but instead to collaboratively evaluate the implications of change.

Moreover, also with the non-underweight patients, in our clinical experience, it is helpful to discuss during Step One of the treatment the pros and cons to address some egosyntonic features of their eating disorder, such as dietary restraint and other extreme weight control behaviors before addressing them in Step Two of CBT-E. Finally, the periodical Reviews Sessions are implemented both at the end of Step One and every four weeks during Step Two (in underweight patients), and in the latter case, we think it is not precise to label these sessions as Stage Two (as a Stage Two cannot occur after the Stage Three). However, for readers familiar with the description of the adult version of CBT-E in four Stages, it may be helpful to remember that Stage One corresponds to Step One, Stage Two to the Review Sessions, Stage Three to Step Two, and Stage Four to Step Three of the adolescents' version.

6.2 Intensive CBT-E

The decision to expand the application of CBT-E to intensive settings was based on three primary considerations (Dalle Grave & Pike, 2023). First, some individuals do not improve with a well-delivered outpatient CBT-E, or they present with an eating disorder of such clinical severity that they cannot be safely managed in an outpatient setting. Second, existing evidence on changing the type of outpatient treatment for individuals unresponsive to CBT-E is inconclusive and has primarily been evaluated on bulimia nervosa. In such instances, especially in patients with anorexia nervosa, the alternative to outpatient care often involves hospitalization in specialized eating disorder units. These units typically embrace an eclectic approach rooted in the disease model rather than being guided by a singular empirically supported theory. Third, the inefficacy of outpatient CBT-E in certain patients may be attributed to insufficient intensive care rather than inherent limitations in the treatment methodology.

A detailed description of the different intensive versions of CBT-E can be found elsewhere (Dalle Grave et al., 2008a; Dalle Grave, 2012, 2013).

Intensive Outpatient and Day-Hospital CBT-E

These versions of CBT-E are designed for patients who may need more professional input than outpatient CBT-E can provide but whose conditions are not sufficiently severe to warrant hospitalization. This adaptation of CBT-E incorporates all of the strategies and procedures of outpatient CBT-E but includes several additional features developed specifically for this new approach (Dalle Grave et al., 2008a, b; Dalle Grave, 2012). Intensive outpatient CBT-E is usually delivered in an outpatient office, while day-hospital is organized inside a hospital and, therefore, can benefit from a specialist medical assessment and management.

These versions of intensive CBT-E can be flexibly adapted to both the clinical needs of the patient and the logistical characteristics of the clinical service that delivers it. However, they should include the following procedures on weekdays: (i) supervised daily meals; (ii) individual CBT-E sessions; (iii) sessions with a CBT-E-trained dietician to plan and review weekend meals; and (iv) regular reviews with a CBT-E-trained physician.

While the effectiveness of CBT-E has been evaluated in patients treated with a 12-week day-hospital treatment (Dalle Grave et al., 2022b), the length of the treatment may be personalized and reduced if patients successfully progress in the areas in which they were struggling in outpatient CBT-E (e.g., lack of weight progress regain, reducing binge eating, and/or eating regular meals). Toward the end of intensive treatment, patients who have responded well are gradually encouraged to eat meals outside the unit, thereby allowing the treatment to evolve into standard outpatient CBT-E.

Inpatient or Residential CBT-E

Inpatient CBT-E is indicated as a first-line option for patients requiring close medical supervision or those not responding well to the less intensive versions. The treatment is delivered in specialized rehabilitation hospital settings but can also be delivered in a residential environment in patients with medical stability.

Inpatient CBT-E maintains all the main strategies and procedures of outpatient CBT-E, which are delivered in a group format and individual sessions but has three main features that set it apart (Dalle Grave et al., 2008a, 2013a; Dalle Grave, 2012). First, the treatment is delivered by a non-eclectic multidisciplinary team rather than a sole therapist. This will comprise physicians, psychologists, dieticians, and nurses who have all been fully trained in CBT-E. Second, assistance with eating is provided in the early weeks of treatment. This approach is to help patients overcome their difficulties in real time. Third, adolescent patients can continue their studies during hospitalization with the aid of on-site educators.

Inpatient CBT-E, as organized at the Department of Villa Garda Hospital, also includes the following additional elements designed to reduce the high rate of relapse typically seen after discharge from the hospital (Dalle Grave et al., 2008a):

- The inpatient rehabilitative unit is open, with patients being free to go outside. This is so they are not sheltered from the environmental stimuli that tend to trigger their eating-disorder mindset and behaviors but can rely on professional support.
- The 13 weeks of inpatient treatment are followed by 7 weeks of day-hospital, during which the treatment intensity is gradually reduced to evolve toward a standard CBT-E. During this period, patients are helped to identify and address potential environmental triggers triggering relapse.
- Toward the end of treatment, parents are helped to create a positive, stress-free home environment in readiness for the patient's return.
- The intensive treatment is generally followed with 20 sessions of outpatient treatment over 20 weeks (twice weekly in the first month after discharge, and after that less frequently) to help patients consolidate the changes they have

achieved during their residential treatment, to provide them with strategies for dealing with the difficulties that occur once they return home, and to identify and address any residual eating disorder feature and maintenance mechanisms.

7 Multistep CBT-E

CBT-E, being designed to address a broad spectrum of eating disorders across various care settings, presents a tangible opportunity to overcome challenges encountered in more traditional, fragmented services. The distinctive feature of this approach, also referred to as "multistep CBT-E" (Dalle Grave, 2013), lies in the consistent application of the same theory and procedures at each level of care. The main difference among the levels of care lies in the intensity of treatment, where less severely affected patients receive outpatient CBT-E procedures. At the same time, those with more acute conditions are directed to inpatient CBT-E. This model facilitates a seamless transition for non-responders to outpatient treatment to a more intensive form of treatment within the CBT-E framework. Thus, patients can be moved seamlessly from outpatient care to different intensity levels of care with no change in the nature of the treatment itself.

This approach offers two key advantages. First, patients receive a singular, well-delivered, evidence-based treatment, as opposed to the evidence-free eclectic approaches often implemented in intensive eating disorder clinical services. Second, it mitigates challenges associated with transitions from adolescent to adult services (Poulsen et al., 2014) and outpatient to intensive treatment. It provides a more seamless continuum of care by avoiding confusing and counterproductive changes in therapeutic approaches commonly associated with such transitions. However, it is important to note that alternative forms of treatment must be considered for patients who do not respond to CBT-E.

8 The CBT-E Team

CBT-E in the intensive level of care and with severely underweight patients is delivered by a "non-eclectic" multidisciplinary team in which all members (i.e., psychologists, dietitians, physicians) receive extensive training on CBT-E and are aware of the entire clinical picture of patients (Dalle Grave, 2012, 2013). In this non-eclectic multidisciplinary team, the dietitians address undereating and dietary restraint, the physicians assess and manage medical complications and coexisting mental and general medical disorders (e.g., clinical depression, diabetes), and the psychologists deliver the core elements of CBT-E.

9 The Status of CBT-E

CBT-E has been tested in all diagnostic categories of eating disorders in several countries. In general, the research findings can be summarized as follows:

- CBT-E in bulimia nervosa and non-underweight patients was superior to all the psychological treatments it was compared with, including psychoanalytic psychotherapy (Poulsen et al., 2014) and interpersonal therapy (IPT) (Fairburn et al., 2015). In general, about 80% complete CBT-E, and about two-thirds achieve a full remission that appears well maintained over time.
- CBT-E is equally effective as other therapies (e.g., SSCM, MANTRA) in the treatment of adults with anorexia nervosa, with about 50% of patients achieving a healthy weight (Byrne et al., 2017).
- CBT-E has been to shown to be effective in patients with severe and extreme anorexia nervosa (66% completed the treatment, and among completers, about 50% have a full response at 60 weeks of follow-up) (Calugi et al., 2021).
- CBT-E has shown promising results for the treatment of adolescent patients with anorexia nervosa (about 72% complete the treatment, and among completers, about 62% have a full response at follow-up) (Dalle Grave et al., 2013b), with a similar outcome to family-based treatment (FBT) at 6- and 12-month follow-up (Le Grange et al., 2020). Similar promising results have been achieved when the treatment has been delivered in real-world clinical settings (Dalle Grave et al., 2019a) and among patients aged 14–25 (Dalle Grave et al., 2023). Therefore, it could be adopted by adolescents and across the transitional age to ensure continuity of care.
- Day-hospital CBT-E has similar promising outcomes in underweight and not underweight adults with eating disorders. About 86.0% complete the treatment; among these, about 54% of underweight and 65% of non-underweight patients achieve a full response at 20-week follow-up (Dalle Grave et al., 2022b).
- CBT-E can be used with promising results, both in adolescents and adults, in inpatient settings (85% complete the treatment, and among completers, about 50% have a full response at 60 weeks of follow-up) (Dalle Grave et al., 2013a; 2014, 2020).
- The inpatient CBT-E appears to be effective for patients with severe and enduring anorexia nervosa (85% complete the treatment, and among completers, 33% have a full response at 12-month follow-up) (Calugi et al., 2017).

10 Challenges and Future Directions

Several research and clinical challenges must be addressed in the future to enhance the effectiveness, efficacy, and accessibility of CBT-E.

Future investigations should aim to elucidate the relative efficacy of CBT-E and FBT in the treatment of adolescent patients with anorexia nervosa through randomized controlled trials. It is of theoretical interest and clinical significance to explore potential moderators of treatment response, allowing for the tailored matching of patients to CBT-E or FBT. The substantial differences in their conceptualization of eating disorders, strategies, procedures, and postulated modes of action suggest the potential existence of such moderators (Dalle Grave et al., 2019b). For instance, the nature of FBT (Lock & Le Grange, 2013) may be better suited for younger patients. At the same time, CBT-E, designed to address maintaining mechanisms of eating disorder psychopathology (Dalle Grave & Calugi, 2020; Fairburn, 2008), might be more appropriate for older adolescents in whom these processes are operating. Moreover, an "adult" form of treatment may be more acceptable for older adolescents than a family-style approach. These hypotheses will be tested through the CogFam non-inferiority randomized trial, which will compare FBT and CBT-E in patients referred to eight participating local outpatient clinics in Norway for eating disorders between the ages of 12 and 18 years; the project period is 2023–2027, and inclusion of participants is started in 2024 (https://cogfam.no).

Further evaluation of the relative effects of the broad and focused forms of CBT-E is warranted, including the exploration of whether incorporating specific modules to address comorbidities (e.g., clinical obesity, post-traumatic stress disorder) or making adaptations for specific populations (e.g., neurodivergent individuals, LGBTQ individuals) could enhance treatment effectiveness in some patient subgroups.

Another possible way to increase the effectiveness of CBT-E might be to study the reasons for non-response and modify the treatment accordingly, as well as the mediators of the effects of the treatment, to make the intervention more effective and efficient. Additionally, studying the mediators of treatment effects is important for addressing the controversial issue of the optimum duration of CBT-E for eating disorders. While a fixed and brief treatment duration offers advantages such as cost-effectiveness and facilitating patient initiation and conclusion without fostering dependence, it may lack personalization and sufficient duration for individuals with varying severity of psychopathology and eating disorder features.

Last, efforts to maximize the availability of CBT-E are underway through two key strategies. First, exploring the most effective means of training more therapists (face-to-face with workshops or digital training), and, as in our experience, it is crucial to implement the treatment well to overcome the obstacles to offering supervision by experts to a group of clinicians during the CBT-E training. Second, investigating innovative forms of digital treatment to enhance the scalability of CBT-E (Fairburn & Patel, 2014). It is also important to strengthen the promotion of CBT-E through social networks and other contemporary communication strategies. To this purpose, a dedicated website (www.cbte.co) has recently been established to provide information for the general public, therapists, and patients.

References

Byrne, S., Wade, T., Hay, P., Touyz, S., Fairburn, C. G., Treasure, J., et al. (2017). A randomised controlled trial of three psychological treatments for anorexia nervosa. *Psychological Medicine, 47*(16), 1–11. https://doi.org/10.1017/s0033291717001349

Calugi, S., Dalle Grave, R., Sartirana, M., & Fairburn, C. G. (2015). Time to restore body weight in adults and adolescents receiving cognitive behaviour therapy for anorexia nervosa. *Journal of Eating Disorders, 3*, 21. https://doi.org/10.1186/s40337-015-0057-z

Calugi, S., El Ghoch, M., & Dalle Grave, R. (2017). Intensive enhanced cognitive behavioural therapy for severe and enduring anorexia nervosa: A longitudinal outcome study. *Behaviour Research and Therapy, 89*, 41–48. https://doi.org/10.1016/j.brat.2016.11.006

Calugi, S., Sartirana, M., Frostad, S., & Dalle Grave, R. (2021). Enhanced cognitive behavior therapy for severe and extreme anorexia nervosa: An outpatient case series. *The International Journal of Eating Disorders, 54*(3), 305–312. https://doi.org/10.1002/eat.23428

Cole, T. J., Flegal, K. M., Nicholls, D., & Jackson, A. A. (2007). Body mass index cut offs to define thinness in children and adolescents: International survey. *BMJ, 335*(7612), 194. https://doi.org/10.1136/bmj.39238.399444.55

Cooper, Z., & Dalle Grave, R. (2017). Eating disorders: Transdiagnostic theory and treatment. In S. G. Hofmann & G. J. G. Asmundson (Eds.), *The science of cognitive behavioral therapy* (pp. 337–357). Academic Press.

Dakanalis, A., Timko, C. A., Clerici, M., Zanetti, M. A., & Riva, G. (2014). Comprehensive examination of the trans-diagnostic cognitive behavioral model of eating disorders in males. *Eating Behaviors, 15*(1), 63–67. https://doi.org/10.1016/j.eatbeh.2013.10.003

Dakanalis, A., Carrà, G., Calogero, R., Zanetti, M. A., Gaudio, S., Caccialanza, R., et al. (2015). Testing the cognitive-behavioural maintenance models across DSM-5 bulimic-type eating disorder diagnostic groups: A multi-centre study. *European Archives of Psychiatry and Clinical Neuroscience, 265*(8), 663–676. https://doi.org/10.1007/s00406-014-0560-2

Dalle Grave, R. (2012). *Intensive cognitive behavior therapy for eating disorders*. Nova.

Dalle Grave, R. (2013). *Multistep cognitive behavioral therapy for eating disorders: Theory, practice, and clinical cases*. Jason Aronson.

Dalle Grave, R. (2022). Enhanced cognitive behavior therapy for eating disorders. In V. Patel & V. Preedy (Eds.), *Eat Disord* (pp. 1–21). Springer International Publishing.

Dalle Grave, R. (2023). The implications of the disease model and psychological model on eating disorder treatment. *Eating and Weight Disorders - Studies on Anorexia, Bulimia and Obesity., 28*(1), 7. https://doi.org/10.1007/s40519-023-01527-6

Dalle Grave, R., & Calugi, S. (2018). Transdiagnostic cognitive behavioural theory and treatment of body image disturbance in eating disorders: A guide to assessment, treatment, and prevention. In M. Cuzzolaro & S. Fassino (Eds.), *Body image, eating, and weight* (pp. 309–321). Springer.

Dalle Grave, R., & Calugi, S. (2020). *Cognitive behavior therapy for adolescents with eating disorders*. Guilford Press.

Dalle Grave, R., & Calugi, S. (2024). *A young person's guide to cognitive behaviour therapy for eating disorders*. Routledge.

Dalle Grave, R., & Cooper, Z. (2016). Enhanced cognitive behavior treatment adapted for younger patients. In T. Wade (Ed.), *Encyclopedia of feeding and eating disorders* (pp. 1–8). Springer Singapore.

Dalle Grave, R., & el Khazen, C. (2022). *Cognitive behaviour therapy for eating disorders in young people: A parents' guide*. Routledge.

Dalle Grave, R., & Pike, K. M. (2023). Cognitive behavioral therapy and eating disorders. In P. Robinson et al. (Eds.), *Eating Disorders*, 1–15. Springer.

Dalle Grave, R., Di Pauli, D., Sartirana, M., Calugi, S., & Shafran, R. (2007). The interpretation of symptoms of starvation/severe dietary restraint in eating disorder patients. *Eating and Weight Disorders, 12*(3), 108–113. https://doi.org/10.1007/BF03327637

Dalle Grave, R., Bohn, K., Hawker, D., & Fairburn, C. G. (2008a). Inpatient, day patient and two forms of outpatient CBT-E. In C. G. Fairburn (Ed.), *Cognitive behavior therapy and eating disorders* (pp. 231–244). Guilford Press.

Dalle Grave, R., Pasqualoni, E., & Calugi, S. (2008b). Intensive outpatient cognitive behaviour therapy for eating disorder. *Psychological Topics, 17*(2), 313–327.

Dalle Grave, R., Pasqualoni, E., & Marchesini, G. (2011). Symptoms of starvation in eating disorder patients. In V. R. Preedy (Ed.), *Handbook of behavior, food and nutrition* (pp. 2259–2269). Springer Science+Business Media.

Dalle Grave, R., Calugi, S., Conti, M., Doll, H., & Fairburn, C. G. (2013a). Inpatient cognitive behaviour therapy for anorexia nervosa: A randomized controlled trial. *Psychotherapy and Psychosomatics, 82*(6), 390–398. https://doi.org/10.1159/000350058

Dalle Grave, R., Calugi, S., Doll, H. A., & Fairburn, C. G. (2013b). Enhanced cognitive behaviour therapy for adolescents with anorexia nervosa: An alternative to family therapy? *Behaviour Research and Therapy, 51*(1), R9–R12. https://doi.org/10.1016/j.brat.2012.09.008

Dalle Grave, R., Calugi, S., El Ghoch, M., Conti, M., & Fairburn, C. G. (2014). Inpatient cognitive behavior therapy for adolescents with anorexia nervosa: Immediate and longer-term effects. *Frontiers in Psychiatry, 5*, 14. https://doi.org/10.3389/fpsyt.2014.00014

Dalle Grave, R., Sartirana, M., & Calugi, S. (2019a). Enhanced cognitive behavioral therapy for adolescents with anorexia nervosa: Outcomes and predictors of change in a real-world setting. *The International Journal of Eating Disorders, 52*(9), 1042–1046. https://doi.org/10.1002/eat.23122

Dalle Grave, R., Eckhardt, S., Calugi, S., & Le Grange, D. (2019b). A conceptual comparison of family-based treatment and enhanced cognitive behavior therapy in the treatment of adolescents with eating disorders. *Journal of Eating Disorders, 7*(1), 42. https://doi.org/10.1186/s40337-019-0275-x

Dalle Grave, R., Conti, M., & Calugi, S. (2020). Effectiveness of intensive cognitive behavioral therapy in adolescents and adults with anorexia nervosa. *The International Journal of Eating Disorders, 53*(9), 1428–1438. https://doi.org/10.1002/eat.23337

Dalle Grave, R., Sartirana, M., & Calugi, S. (2021). *Complex cases and comorbidity in eating disorders. Assessment and management*. Springer Nature.

Dalle Grave, R., Chignola, E., Franchini, C., Macrì, L., Manganotti, A., Monti, V., et al. (2022a). Number and characteristics of patients seeking treatment for eating disorders at a CBT-E clinical service before and during the COVID-19 pandemic. *IJEDO., 4*, 4. https://doi.org/10.32044/ijedo.2022.06

Dalle Grave, R., Dametti, L., Conti, M., Bersan, C., Dalle Grave, A., & Calugi, S. (2022b). Day-hospital enhanced cognitive behavior therapy for adults with eating disorders: Immediate and follow-up effects. *The International Journal of Eating Disorders, 55*(1), 125–130. https://doi.org/10.1002/eat.23632

Dalle Grave, R., Sartirana, M., Dalle Grave, A., & Calugi, S. (2023). Effectiveness of enhanced cognitive behaviour therapy for patients aged 14 to 25: A promising treatment for anorexia nervosa in transition-age youth. *European Eating Disorders Review*. https://doi.org/10.1002/erv.3019

Fairburn, C. G. (1981). A cognitive behavioural approach to the treatment of bulimia. *Psychological Medicine, 11*(4), 707–711.

Fairburn, C. G. (2008). *Cognitive behavior therapy and eating disorders*. Guilford Press.

Fairburn, C. G. (2013). *Overcoming binge eating* (2nd ed.). Guilford Press.

Fairburn, C. G., & Patel, V. (2014). The global dissemination of psychological treatments: A road map for research and practice. *The American Journal of Psychiatry, 171*(5), 495–498. https://doi.org/10.1176/appi.ajp.2013.13111546

Fairburn, C. G., Cooper, Z., & Shafran, R. (2003a). Cognitive behaviour therapy for eating disorders: A "transdiagnostic" theory and treatment. *Behaviour Research and Therapy, 41*(5), 509–528. https://doi.org/10.1016/s0005-7967(02)00088-8

Fairburn, C. G., Stice, E., Cooper, Z., Doll, H. A., Norman, P. A., & O'Connor, M. E. (2003b). Understanding persistence in bulimia nervosa: A 5-year naturalistic study. *Journal of Consulting and Clinical Psychology, 71*(1), 103–109.

Fairburn, C. G., Bailey-Straebler, S., Basden, S., Doll, H. A., Jones, R., Murphy, R., et al. (2015). A transdiagnostic comparison of enhanced cognitive behaviour therapy (CBT-E) and interpersonal psychotherapy in the treatment of eating disorders. *Behaviour Research and Therapy, 70*, 64–71. https://doi.org/10.1016/j.brat.2015.04.010

Grilo, C. M. (2013). Why no cognitive body image feature such as overvaluation of shape/weight in the binge eating disorder diagnosis? *The International Journal of Eating Disorders, 46*(3), 208–211. https://doi.org/10.1002/eat.22082

Hoiles, K. J., Egan, S. J., & Kane, R. T. (2012). The validity of the transdiagnostic cognitive behavioural model of eating disorders in predicting dietary restraint. *Eating Behaviors, 13*(2), 123–126. https://doi.org/10.1016/j.eatbeh.2011.11.007

Kaye, W. H., Weltzin, T. E., Hsu, L. K., McConaha, C. W., & Bolton, B. (1993). Amount of calories retained after binge eating and vomiting. *The American Journal of Psychiatry, 150*(6), 969–971. https://doi.org/10.1176/ajp.150.6.969

Lampard, A. M., Byrne, S. M., McLean, N., & Fursland, A. (2011). An evaluation of the enhanced cognitive-behavioural model of bulimia nervosa. *Behaviour Research and Therapy, 49*(9), 529–535. https://doi.org/10.1016/j.brat.2011.06.002

Le Grange, D., Eckhardt, S., Dalle Grave, R., Crosby, R. D., Peterson, C. B., Keery, H., et al. (2020). Enhanced cognitive-behavior therapy and family-based treatment for adolescents with an eating disorder: A non-randomized effectiveness trial. *Psychological Medicine, 52*, 1–11. https://doi.org/10.1017/s0033291720004407

Lock, J., & Le Grange, D. (2013). *Treatment manual for anorexia nervosa: A family-based approach* (2nd ed.). Guilford Press.

Lowe, M. R., Witt, A. A., & Grossman, S. L. (2013). Dieting in bulimia nervosa is associated with increased food restriction and psychopathology but decreased binge eating. *Eating Behaviors, 14*(3), 342–347. https://doi.org/10.1016/j.eatbeh.2013.06.011

National Guideline Alliance. (2017). *Eating disorders: Recognition and treatment.* National Institute for Health and Care Excellence (UK); 2017 May. (NICE Guideline, No. 69.).

Poulsen, S., Lunn, S., Daniel, S. I., Folke, S., Mathiesen, B. B., Katznelson, H., & Fairburn, C. G. (2014). A randomized controlled trial of psychoanalytic psychotherapy or cognitive-behavioral therapy for bulimia nervosa. *The American Journal of Psychiatry, 171*(1), 109–116. https://doi.org/10.1176/appi.ajp.2013.12121511

Radden, J. (2018). Rethinking disease in psychiatry: Disease models and the medical imaginary. *Journal of Evaluation in Clinical Practice, 24*(5), 1087–1092. https://doi.org/10.1111/jep.12982

Shafran, R., Lee, M., Payne, E., & Fairburn, C. G. (2007a). An experimental analysis of body checking. *Behaviour Research and Therapy, 45*(1), 113–121. https://doi.org/10.1016/j.brat.2006.01.015

Shafran, R., Lee, M., Cooper, Z., Palmer, R. L., & Fairburn, C. G. (2007b). Attentional bias in eating disorders. *The International Journal of Eating Disorders, 40*(4), 369–380. https://doi.org/10.1002/eat.20375

Spangler, D. L., Baldwin, S. A., & Agras, W. S. (2004). An examination of the mechanisms of action in cognitive behavioral therapy for bulimia nervosa. *Behavior Therapy, 35*(3), 537–560. https://doi.org/10.1016/S0005-7894(04)80031-5

Tabri, N., Murray, H. B., Thomas, J. J., Franko, D. L., Herzog, D. B., & Eddy, K. T. (2015). Overvaluation of body shape/weight and engagement in non-compensatory weight-control behaviors in eating disorders: Is there a reciprocal relationship? *Psychological Medicine, 45*(14), 2951–2958. https://doi.org/10.1017/s0033291715000896

Tasca, G. A., Presniak, M. D., Demidenko, N., Balfour, L., Krysanski, V., Trinneer, A., & Bissada, H. (2011). Testing a maintenance model for eating disorders in a sample seeking treatment at a tertiary care center: A structural equation modeling approach. *Comprehensive Psychiatry, 52*(6), 678–687. https://doi.org/10.1016/j.comppsych.2010.12.010

Tobin, D. L., Banker, J. D., Weisberg, L., & Bowers, W. (2007). I know what you did last summer (and it was not CBT): A factor analytic model of international psychotherapeutic practice in the eating disorders. *The International Journal of Eating Disorders, 40*(8), 754–757. https://doi.org/10.1002/eat.20426

Turner, H., Tatham, M., Lant, M., Mountford, V. A., & Waller, G. (2014). Clinicians' concerns about delivering cognitive-behavioural therapy for eating disorders. *Behaviour Research and Therapy, 57*, 38–42. https://doi.org/10.1016/j.brat.2014.04.003

von Ranson, K. M., Wallace, L. M., & Stevenson, A. (2013). Psychotherapies provided for eating disorders by community clinicians: Infrequent use of evidence-based treatment. *Psychotherapy Research, 23*(3), 333–343. https://doi.org/10.1080/10503307.2012.735377

Waller, G., Mountford, V. A., Tatham, M., Turner, H., Gabriel, C., & Webber, R. (2013). Attitudes towards psychotherapy manuals among clinicians treating eating disorders. *Behaviour Research and Therapy, 51*(12), 840–844. https://doi.org/10.1016/j.brat.2013.10.004

Watson, H. J., Raykos, B. C., Street, H., Fursland, A., & Nathan, P. R. (2011). Mediators between perfectionism and eating disorder psychopathology: Shape and weight overvaluation and conditional goal-setting. *The International Journal of Eating Disorders, 44*(2), 142–149. https://doi.org/10.1002/eat.20788

Wilson, G. T., Fairburn, C. C., Agras, W. S., Walsh, B. T., & Kraemer, H. (2002). Cognitive-behavioral therapy for bulimia nervosa: Time course and mechanisms of change. *Journal of Consulting and Clinical Psychology, 70*(2), 267–274.

Zunker, C., Peterson, C. B., Crosby, R. D., Cao, L., Engel, S. G., Mitchell, J. E., & Wonderlich, S. A. (2011). Ecological momentary assessment of bulimia nervosa: Does dietary restriction predict binge eating? *Behaviour Research and Therapy, 49*(10), 714–717. https://doi.org/10.1016/j.brat.2011.06.006

Dynamic-Relational Treatment of Pernicious Personality: Working with Perfectionism

Paul L. Hewitt, Anna Kristen, Samuel F. Mikail, and Gordon L. Flett

1 Dynamic-Relational Treatment of a Pernicious Personality: Perfectionism

Recently there has been an increasing emphasis on clinical work and research that goes beyond symptom reduction by addressing transdiagnostic and core vulnerability factors that are foundational to the development of various forms of psychopathology and maladaptation. These vulnerabilities function as causal and maintenance factors in various forms of distress, dysfunction, and disorder. Although there have been various factors proposed as transdiagnostic, much attention has been given to personality styles that are pernicious both in their links with severe forms of clinical distress and psychological disorders and also in that these personality styles interfere with the psychotherapy process and compromise effective treatment outcomes. Perfectionism is one such pernicious personality style, and there is substantial evidence from over three decades of research of the deleterious outcomes of this multidimensional and multilevel personality style.

This chapter is aimed at providing an overview of perfectionism and a psychodynamic-interpersonally informed treatment approach, known as dynamic-relational therapy (DRT), based on conceptual models and empirical research developed and led by Hewitt and colleagues over the past 35 years (see Hewitt, 2020; Hewitt et al., 2017, 2020a, b, c). We will briefly describe the conceptualization of

P. L. Hewitt (✉) · A. Kristen
University of British Columbia, Vancouver, BC, Canada
e-mail: phewitt@psych.ubc.ca; anna.kristen@ubc.ca

S. F. Mikail
University of Waterloo, Waterloo, ON, Canada

G. L. Flett
York University, North York, ON, Canada
e-mail: gflett@yorku.ca

perfectionism and discuss its clinical relevance as well as details of the DRT treatment approach and techniques. Finally, we present an overview of the empirical support for the treatment and directions for future work to refine and extend DRT to enhance clinicians' work with patients presenting with a perfectionistic personality style.

2 Defining Perfectionism

Although several definitions of perfectionism have been proposed, such as viewing perfectionism solely from a cognitive/attitudinal perspective, one of the most commonly utilized conceptualization and operationalization of perfectionism derives from a psychodynamic-interpersonal perspective (see Hewitt, 2020; Hewitt et al., 2017) known as the Comprehensive Model of Perfectionistic Behavior (CMPB). This perspective views perfectionism as a multifarious personality style that reflects a deeply ingrained "way of being in the world" (see Hewitt, 2020; Hewitt et al., 2017) capturing the interplay of relational, motivational, affective, cognitive, and defensive underpinnings of this pernicious personality style (see Greenspon, 2008; Horney, 1939, 1950; Hewitt et al., 2017). We describe this conceptualization below.

3 A Dynamic-Relational Perspective

In our work over the past 35 years, we have conceptualized and demonstrated that perfectionism is a broad, ingrained, and multidimensional personality style involving the requirement for, and both the interpersonal and intrapersonal expression of, perfection of the self or others (Hewitt et al., 2017). Perfectionism is driven by longstanding thwarted needs for belongingness, self-cohesion, self/other worth, and a deep sense of never being "good enough." Thus, perfectionism represents a pernicious, rigid, and fundamentally maladaptive approach to living, leaving people vulnerable to many forms of distress, dysfunction, and disorder.

Based on the clinical work of the first author and the ensuing research (e.g., Flett et al., 1998; Hewitt & Flett, 1991a, b; Hewitt et al., 2003), we developed the Comprehensive Model of Perfectionistic Behavior (CMPB; see Hewitt et al., 2017 for an overview), to conceptualize and define perfectionism. According to the CMPB, perfectionism is composed of stable and enduring trait dimensions that drive and energize perfectionistic behavior. Hewitt and Flett (1991a, b) identified three trait perfectionism dimensions: *self-oriented perfectionism* (i.e., the requirement of perfection for oneself), *other-oriented perfectionism* (i.e., the requirement of perfection for others), and *socially prescribed perfectionism* (i.e., the perception that others require perfection of oneself). In addition to the trait perfectionism component, Hewitt et al. (2003) proposed that the expression of perfectionism in both the interpersonal and intrapersonal domains is crucial for a complete understanding of this personality style. Thus, in the interpersonal domain, we proposed another component of the CMPB, namely, perfectionistic self-presentation (PSP) styles that capture the interpersonal expression and communication of one's purported perfection to others. PSP includes three facets: *perfectionistic self-promotion* (i.e., promoting and proclaiming oneself as perfect), the *nondisplay of imperfection* (i.e., concealing overt displays of one's own imperfect behavior), and the *nondisclosure of imperfection* (i.e., not disclosing or verbally revealing any imperfection). Finally, Hewitt et al. (2017) discussed an intrapersonal or self-relational component of perfectionism that is reflected, in part, by an individual's internal dialogue with the self. This component involves not only automatic perfectionistic self-statements (Flett et al., 1998), but also automatic harshly critical self-recriminations and condemnations (Hewitt et al., 2024) and excessive concerns over shortfalls and perceived errors (see Frost et al., 1990). Moreover, we have indicated that this component also reflects a behavioral element involving neglect of the self in terms of limited self-care, self-denial, and, in extreme forms, self-harm and self-destructiveness. Finally, we and others have demonstrated the independence and the extensive pernicious nature of these perfectionism components for adults, adolescents, and children (see Flett & Hewitt, 2002; Hewitt et al., 2017; Sirois & Molnar, 2016).

With substantial and high-quality empirical evidence of the perniciousness of the elements of the CMPB, we developed a model known as the Perfectionistic Social Disconnection Model (PSDM; Hewitt et al., 2017) to attempt to explain both the development of perfectionism and the processes involved in how and why perfectionism produces and maintains the myriad of difficulties experienced. This model is built upon an integration of psychodynamic and interpersonal theories, and there is substantial research evidence supporting the influence of intra- and interpersonal elements in the development of perfectionism.

4 The Perfectionism Social Disconnection Model

4.1 Development of Perfectionism

The first portion of the PSDM places a particular emphasis on interpersonal/relational dynamics and draws on the empirically supported insights of attachment theory (Bowlby, 1988; Eagle, 2017) and self-psychology (Kohut, 1971) proposing that perfectionism develops within an early relational context. In this portion of the model, failures or poor fit between the child's needs and the caregiver's responses—which we refer to as "asynchrony"—creates the conditions for perfectionism to develop as a means of being seen and gaining acceptance. Although needs for relational safety are fundamental, the unmet need to belong or fit with others and the unmet need for self-worth and esteem are particularly central to developing perfectionism. As children generally view their experiences through an egocentric lens, experiences of pervasive asynchrony in response to a child's need for relatedness and affirmation contribute to viewing the self as fundamentally flawed with the pursuit of perfectionism emerging as the path that holds the promise of repair and connection.

For the emerging perfectionist then, the needs for safety, belonging, and esteem are thwarted or tenuous in early development and remain frustrated throughout the person's life, often in response to the perfectionistic behavior—the very solution that is intended to garner emotional security and connection. Thus, the need to be or appear perfect develops to attempt to prevent wounding experiences of rejection and abandonment and promote acceptance, connection, and belonging in the world. In addition, perfectionism develops as an avenue to repair or mitigate a deep sense of defectiveness and never being good enough by bolstering self-cohesion and self-worth. Ultimately, perfectionism emerges as the path to the promise of being good enough and acceptable to others and the self.

As discussed in Hewitt (2020) and Hewitt et al. (2017), the development of perfectionism involves the experience of asynchrony in the caregiver relationship (e.g., difficulties in the child's expressive abilities, the caregivers' receptive capacity and responsiveness, or both) creating attachment anxiety that is moderated by constitutional factors (e.g., an anxious temperament) and other environmental contingencies. This shapes the child's internal working model of others to be rigidly represented as unavailable, critical, or incapable. Similarly, asynchrony disturbs the child's internal working model of the self to be rigidly represented as fragile, fragmented, defective, or loathsome. These internal models are associated with painful affective states such as shame, anxiety, depression, or anger—connected to the anticipation of or perceived or actual experience of humiliation, rejection, or abandonment in interaction with others. Consequently, the individual faces the world with this distorted perceptual lens, experiencing current and anticipated interpersonal encounters as inevitably wounding and rejecting, despite the wishing and longing for acceptance and affirmation.

Perfectionism represents a defensive position that unfolds in the person to navigate this situation, with the aim of repairing the damaged self through attempts to become or to appear perfect, in hopes of garnering acceptance, affirmation, and mattering (Hewitt et al., 2017). The individual lives his or her life in accord with the motivation: "If I am perfect, there will be nothing to criticize, to judge or to reject—nothing to be ashamed of—and I will be accepted, I will be whole, and I will have worth" (Hewitt et al., 2017, p. 101). In short, perfection offers the promise of satisfying the unrequited needs of belonging and self-cohesion and esteem. Unfortunately, this solution, to be or appear perfect, reinforces an insecure attachment style that involves guarded, inflexible, rebarbative, and evasive interpersonal interactions that distances, alienates, and, at times, agitates others, producing the disconnection and rejection that the perfectionist was working so hard to avoid (Hewitt et al., 2006, 2018a, b). The development of perfectionism can further be reinforced throughout individuals' lives in subsequent relational experiences colored by their internal working models of self and others. Thus, relationships shape internal working models, and internal working models shape relationships.

4.2 Maintenance and Cause

The second portion of the PSDM posits that perfectionism generates subjective and objective social disconnection, which in turn confers a vulnerability for adverse mental and physical health outcomes as well as relationship and achievement problems. Subjective social disconnection reflects the perception that others are not interested in connecting or do not care enough, and involves heightened rejection sensitivity, the view of others as harshly judgmental, and a view of the self as irrelevant and unimportant to others (Cha, 2016; Chen et al., 2015; Flett et al., 2014, 1996). Objective social disconnection reflects the veridical reality that other people often avoid and reject perfectionists due to their sometimes subtle and sometimes overt off-putting behaviors such as coldness, self-concealment, passive-aggressiveness, hostility, and excessive reassurance-seeking (Haring et al., 2003; Hewitt et al., 2003; Kawamura & Frost, 2004). Also, the PSDM asserts both subjective and objective social disconnection contribute to intense feelings of alienation and this rejection, whether real or perceived, reinforces the person's sense of being flawed, defective, and not good enough.

In these interpersonal patterns of perfectionism, individuals use relationships (both with self and with others) to attempt to fulfill their unmet needs. However, these interpersonal styles inevitably produce the opposite effect, creating disconnection and distress (Chen et al., 2012; Hewitt et al., 2006, 2017), a perfect example of the neurotic paradox! Consequently, perfectionism's allure to solving unmet needs for belonging and self-esteem is a false promise that often ends in a self-generated disaster.

Moreover, the social disconnection arising from perfectionistic behavior may serve an additional, unconscious motive: to protect the individual from intimate connections perceived to result in rejection. The perfectionist longs for connection and mattering, believing that perfection will deliver it, yet at the same time fears that being truly known by another—flaws included—would risk exposure to contempt and eventual abandonment (Hewitt, 2020). It is thus clinically useful to consider the degree to which an individual's perfectionistic features may represent an unconscious compromise formation between the seeking of acceptance and connection and an effort to avoid dreaded yet anticipated rejection.

The social disconnection and alienation arising from perfectionism not only occurs in personal, professional, and intimate relationships, but Hewitt et al. (2018a) also indicated that the PSDM mechanisms are relevant for the clinical context. As alluded to earlier, perfectionistic behavior seems to create problems with clinicians and with the clinical process and PSDM has been extended to help understand this process. In describing the PSDM in a clinical context, we theorized that the subjective and objective social disconnection generated by perfectionism interferes with the establishment and maintenance of the therapeutic alliance, which subsequently stifles treatment progress. Indeed, perfectionistic patients project emotions and relational expectations stemming from social disconnection onto the therapist. For instance, patients with elevated socially prescribed perfectionism are hypervigilant to perceived signs of rejection and, as such, are often hesitant to disclose information they believe will cause the therapist to rebuff them. Likewise, the rebarbative interpersonal behavior generated by trait perfectionism dimensions can cause therapists to disconnect from patients (Hewitt et al., 2021).

Evidence in support of this portion of the PSDM is accumulating. For example, Hewitt et al. (1995) reported that pain patients rated other-oriented perfectionistic spouses as less supportive, and both Dunkley et al. (2000) and Sherry et al. (2008) found that low perceived social support mediated the relationship between socially prescribed perfectionism and depression symptoms. Furthermore, Nepon et al. (2011) reported that undergraduates with elevated socially prescribed perfectionism had higher rejection sensitivity, and that rejection sensitivity, in turn, mediated the effects of socially prescribed perfectionism on depression symptoms and social anxiety. Likewise, Roxborough et al. (2012) demonstrated that social hopelessness mediated the relationship between socially prescribed perfectionism and suicide potential in child and adolescent outpatients. Finally, Smith et al. (2017) found self-oriented and socially prescribed perfectionism in daughters, as well as other-oriented perfectionism in mothers, predicted increased depression symptoms in daughters through a negative relationship with daughters' social self-esteem.

5 The Clinical Relevance of Perfectionism

There are several reasons perfectionistic behavior should be a key therapeutic focus in clinical assessment and treatment. First, perfectionistic behavior can act as a core vulnerability factor (Hewitt & Flett, 2002), influencing the cause, maintenance, and symptom expression of a variety of dysfunction and disorders. For example, there is compelling clinical evidence that the trait components of perfectionism act as vulnerability factors for mood and anxiety disorders, eating disorders, and interpersonal dysfunctions (Enns & Cox, 1999; Hewitt & Flett, 1993; Hewitt et al., 1996). Moreover, certain trait and self-presentational components of perfectionism are robustly associated with suicide ideation and suicide attempts in both adolescents and adults (see Hewitt et al., 2006, 2017; for a review, see Smith et al., 2018). Second, perfectionism interferes with the therapeutic process and outcomes (e.g., Blatt et al., 1995; Hewitt et al., 2008, 2021; Hewitt et al., 2020; Shahar et al., 2004). Third, although treatments focusing on symptoms or disorders associated with perfectionism (e.g., anxiety or depressive disorders) have been found to reduce symptoms, such treatments typically yield limited to no clinically significant reductions of core perfectionistic features, and thus the putative vulnerability factor (i.e., perfectionism) remains as a predisposing and perpetuating factor in distress and symptom development (e.g., Ashbaugh et al., 2007; Bastiani et al., 1995; Blatt et al., 2010; Radhu et al., 2012; Riley et al., 2007). Importantly, even treatments from a cognitive behavioral orientation that purportedly do target perfectionism itself (e.g., Egan et al., 2016) appear very limited in their clinical utility. Meta-analytic research has shown that these treatments do not effect change in the most pernicious elements of perfectionism, they are not tolerated well (i.e., dropout rates are high), and posttreatment gains are not sustained beyond treatment termination (see Smith et al., 2023). These findings lend support for targeting the developmental and relational underpinnings of perfectionism in clinical treatment.

6 Dynamic-Relational Therapy of Perfectionism

Just as our conceptualization of perfectionism and our research is integrative, our treatment model also integrates psychodynamic (e.g., Bowlby, 1988; Kohut, 1971; Horney, 1939; Strupp & Binder, 1984) and interpersonal (Benjamin, 1996; Kiesler, 1983; Sullivan, 1953) principles (see Hewitt et al., 2017) to target the underlying relational patterns of perfectionism. As described in Mikail et al. (2022), we use the developmental relational elements as treatment aims first to develop awareness of the relational dynamics and unique patterns underlying a patient's need for perfection and then work with the patient to move toward more adaptive, flexible, and healthy ways of securing these needs of safety, belonging, self-worth, and self-esteem. Treatment begins with an extensive psychodiagnostic assessment, including an initial clinical interview and psychometric testing, to develop an initial clinical formulation describing the individual's unique and idiosyncratic model of how their perfectionism manifests and how and why perfectionism evolved as a strategy to attempt to meet their needs for belonging and self-esteem (see Hewitt et al., 2020b). The formulation also identifies the effects of perfectionism, including disconnection, distress, and dysfunctions that arise from the patient's perfectionistic and associated behavior. Clinicians are guided in the development and the refinement of the formulation throughout treatment, with the use of the Triangle of Adaptation and the Triangle of Object Relations (see Hewitt et al., 2017). The Triangle of Adaptation reflects the internal dynamics of the individual with the focus on the specific nature of the underlying unmet relational needs, the painful affects that arise from the unmet needs, and the defensive responses to mitigate the affect and the defensive behaviors engaged in to attempt to meet the unrequited needs (see left panel of Fig. 1 with prototypic examples of the elements). The Triangle of Object Relations reflects the nature and quality of interpersonal and intrapersonal relational patterns from past and current relationships, and, importantly, in the therapeutic relationship (see right panel of Fig. 1 with prototypic examples). The object relational patterns arise from attempts to meet the relational needs and reflect the behaviors engaged in as a way to meet the needs in past, current, and the therapeutic relationship (Fig. 2).

These heuristics aid the clinician in understanding the specific and idiosyncratic nature of the relational needs, affective reactions, and defenses. Moreover, they also reflect the inter- and intrapersonal behaviors and patterns used in the real world to attempt to fulfill those needs (see Cheek et al., 2018; Hewitt et al., 2017 for details). In addition to the triangles, the formulation includes the cyclical relational pattern (CRP) that derives from the work of Strupp and Binder (1984) that captures the

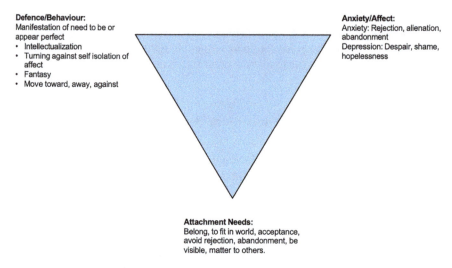

Fig. 1 Generic Triangle of Adaption for perfectionistic person

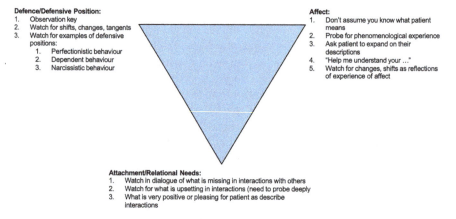

Fig. 2 Triangle of Adaption: how to gather data

behaviors, expectations, and affects that serve to perpetuate self-limiting patterns of relating to self and others.

Specifically, the CRP is aims to articulate the patient's specific behaviors, wishes, or expectations of others' behavior in response to the patient's behaviors, the actual behaviors of others in response to the patient's behaviors, and, finally, how the patient relates and integrates the responses of others in their self-concept. The CRP can provide a concise example of the workings of the two triangles for a patient. The clinician shares the initial or working formulation with the patient, encouraging collaboration to ensure accuracy and engagement and establishing a safe and secure therapeutic alliance with the patient.

In targeting elements of the formulation (e.g., examples of the triangles in the person's life) over the course of treatment, especially in the here and now of the therapeutic relationship, the patient builds a deeper experiential connection to the self-limiting dimensions of their relational patterns with the aim of gaining appreciation of the intended aim of perfectionistic behavior and how it actually forestalls meeting their relational needs while ultimately producing painful affects and dysfunctions. This allows for the consideration and shift toward more flexible and adaptive patterns of relating to self and others. Importantly, the treatment not only focuses on relational patterns in the past, present, and therapeutic context, it also focuses on the patient's relationship with the self—the self-directed esteem, self-acceptance, trust of the self, and self-caring that is so antithetical for perfectionistic individuals.

As treatment progresses, the patient is guided toward experiences and behaviors more aligned with their needs and wishes while learning to tolerate accompanying anxiety and reduce deeper emotional states such as shame. Through this work, the patient internalizes new ways of relating to the therapist and others and develops healthier internal working models and a more realistic appreciation of others' capacity to meet the patient's needs. Ultimately, the realization of this therapeutic objective aids the patient in relinquishing maladaptive patterns of defending and relating.[1] It is our experience over the years that patients will "discover themselves" engaging in behavior with others and with the self that they have not heretofore been able to engage in. We underscore that the treatment does not involve practicing specific techniques but rather focuses on acknowledging the pain and long-standing attempts to invite others to meet those needs who may not currently or ever have been able to provide the need fulfillment.

In sum, our dynamic-relational treatment is formulation-driven and attempts to make changes in the relational elements that underlie perfectionism. That is, rather than focusing on symptoms per se or even specific perfectionism behaviors directly, we effect change by focusing on shifting the relational underpinnings (both self-relational and interpersonal) that produce perfectionistic behavior. A reduction in perfectionism will, in turn, reduce the psychological pain, distress, and symptoms experienced (see Hewitt et al., 2015, 2020, 2023) and increase the nature and quality of relationships with others and quality of life (see Hewitt et al., 2023).

---

[1] Parenthetically, perfectionistic individuals often prefer information over emotional experiences. Hence, within this process-oriented treatment, it is imperative the clinician ensures learning that occurs during therapy does not remain exclusively at an intellectual level but also occurs at the experiential level. Indeed, learning experientially through the therapeutic relationship promotes real and sustained growth through reduction of limiting and punishing components of perfectionism.

6.1 Stages of Treatment

Although we present the specific details of goals of the treatment process in early, middle, and late stages the treatment process is iterative. That is, movement of the treatment process is not linear but rather there is a repetition and revisiting that is ongoing in the process. We present the stages and tasks as illustrative. In Table 1, we provide a list of many of the specific tasks and goals of the various stages throughout treatment.

6.2 Early Phases of Treatment

In the early phase of DRT, as well as throughout the treatment process, establishing and maintaining a strong therapeutic alliance is of the utmost importance. This begins with the first contact with the patient and is maintained throughout the entire assessment and the treatment process. There can be significant ambivalence in patients with perfectionism as they navigate the assessment and treatment process with demands to reveal the self to the therapist and their own need to protect the self, as they have done throughout their life, by creating and keeping a distance from others and not revealing the damaged, flawed, and "not good enough" self. Moreover, patients with perfectionism experience significant anxiety and a sensitivity, vigilance, and wariness of clinicians (Hewitt et al., 2008, 2021). Creating an atmosphere of safety and a connection with the patient that emphasizes safety, genuine concern, honoring the dignity of the patient's plight, and professionalism is fundamental to the process.

In this phase, patients may offer an account of their difficulties by drawing on well-rehearsed narratives that have defined significant aspects of their lives. While it is important to attend to this content, it represents only a small fraction of the relevant clinical material. A considerable degree of salient material—including history, adverse or stressful events, affect, relationships with others, and interpersonal patterns—may not be verbalized, owing to the patient's defensive responses to a perceived lack of safety. Thus, process information from the clinical interview is crucial to the formulation. For example, critical information is gleaned from the patient's affective tone and the level of detail offered when describing significant relationships or events in their lives. The therapist must remain alert to the possibility of suppressed or repressed affects and experiences, paying attention to subtle shifts in the patient's expressions, contradictions in the patient's account, and defenses such as idealization, isolation of affect, or turning against the self, when describing important attachment figures. For example, vague descriptions of significant others that lack detail, an absence of a nuanced appreciation of the other's humanness, or limited memories of significant milestones can be suggestive of fractured attachment bonds. These may provide clues that can inform inferences about the patient's relational needs and adaptations, shaping the focus of intervention.

Table 1 Tasks of DRT for early, middle, and late phases of treatment

Early phase
Establishing the therapeutic alliance
Create safety, connection, and sense that patient matters
Allow the person to tell their story. Assume a stance of receptivity and curiosity as you explore the person's narrative
Be aware of exquisite tension between the person's longing to connect and seek validation vs. fear of being rejected that gives rise of caution and selective sharing
Norm setting (here and now focus, affect exploration, looking at relational elements, alliance checks)
Using therapeutic alliance as a source of information
Observation of content and process as well as transference and countertransference reactions: Be aware of early countertransference reactions and their implications for refinement of case conceptualization but refrain from commenting on them
Watch self for pulls from patient
Developing the working formulation
Investigate and develop elements of the triangles so to begin to establish a working formulation (Triangles and CRP)
Chase affect and attempt to get deeper emotional content which often leads to attachment/relational needs being described and, potentially, experienced
Identify predominant defenses and defensive positions and the underlying anxiety and/or perceived threat
Tentatively connect and work with vertices of T of A
Extending and working with the formulation
Continue developing the working formulation with triangles and CRP
Chase affect, chase affect, and chase affect. This gets you to unfulfilled relational needs and painful dimensions of the person's self-concept
Look for stylistic aspects of relationships with past, current, and therapeutic relationship
Watching for asynchrony in past, current, and therapeutic relationship
Continue to work with T of A connecting vertices
Middle phase
Deeper exploration of T of A with an emphasis on affect
Use of therapeutic relationship to further explore relational styles, defenses, and affect
More depth to emotions, needs, and defenses, especially deeper affect as other components become clearer
Get at deeper relational needs from the needs through affect
Connecting vertices more frequently and more deeply
Gently challenge defenses and associated distortions, particularly in the person's view of self/introject
Work in the here and now
Help person to experience the affect in the here and now, with emphasis on their reaction to expressions of compassion, support, empathy, and acceptance by the therapist and similar responses by others in the person's life
Exploration of past relationships and current relationships, and therapeutic relationship in the here and now

(continued)

Table 1 (continued)

Deeper exploration of T or OR
Working more with T of OR, CRP by connecting vertices or components
Connecting vertices more frequently and more deeply
Genesis of PH perfectionism in childhood and how it served relational purpose
Explore and bring to awareness purpose of the perfectionism for person
Appraisals of past and current relationships in terms of invitations for them to provide something or be different
Evaluation of others' ability to meet these needs (where appropriate viewing others as human, limited, or wounded rather than intentionally hurtful; asynchrony)
Limits of relationships with others
Exploration of current and past asynchrony in all relationships and role in it (including especially the therapeutic relationship—with some emphasis on the person's experience of the therapist's errors, limitations, failures in empathy, or understanding of the person's pain)
Exploring and gently challenging the person's desire/expectation to have others be something they are not
Emphasize helping the individual to recognize their interpersonal impact on others in various contexts and the resulting on self
Exploration with relationship with self
Nature of relationship with self—uncovering parts of self with air of discovery and not evaluation
Reflect/point out recurrent relational patterns that perpetuate and reaffirm person's negative view of self—may include identifying projections
Explore limits with self and differences in how to treat self and how one can treat others
Process of discovering what person is truly like (i.e., not defective nor not good enough)
Support of intrinsic interests, desires, needs, wishes (these have been shameful and denigrated in past)
Late phase
Experiencing grief
Grief of the asynchrony
Grief of inability of others to meet all of one's needs and wishes
Grief over lost time, energy of attempts to be perfect
Stronger focus on T of OR
Focus on autonomy
Support for standing apart from others, autonomy, and more realistic relationships
Trust in intrinsic interests, needs, desires, drives as worthy and acceptable
Self-acceptance focus
Support and strengthen the person's capacity to tolerate frustration of unmet needs, including the ability to express them in intimate relationships without blame or lashing out
Termination
Discussion and ending with the therapist including disappointments, missed opportunities, wished for relationship and its meaning and implication for the person's unfulfilled needs

The emphasis during the early phase of treatment is first on exploring the ways patients have adapted to their circumstances and formative relationships. The clinician's focus is identifying and exploring the patient's predominant affective states, defenses, and relational needs (i.e., Triangle of Adaptation) and underscoring and sharing with the patient the connections among these elements. The aim is to help the patient recognize that unfulfilled and frustrated attachment needs have given rise to understandable aversive emotions that have contributed to the formation of defenses that were once an essential means of coping but are now actually self-limiting and inflexible (in this case, perfectionistic behavior and ways of viewing self and/or others). Sharing with the patient the connections among these unfulfilled needs, affects, and defenses fosters the insight that perfectionistic defenses do not, in fact, solve the problem of unfulfilled relational needs (e.g., to fit, belong, be accepted or to repair a sense of being flawed and defective). It is our experience that initially focusing on the expressed affect, and helping the person articulate and experience the deeper levels of that affect, as well as what they are feeling in the here and now, provides a pathway for deeper understanding and demonstrates the therapist's empathic attunement.

6.3 Middle Phase of Treatment

Interventions during the middle phase of treatment expand upon the earlier focus on affect, defense, and underlying relational needs (i.e., Triangle of Adaptation) and introduce relational themes and patterns in current relationships and past relationships that illustrate the working of the Triangle of Adaptation in these various contexts. As these patterns between past and current relationships emerge, the clinician begins to comment on the unfolding of the needs, affects, and defenses within the here and now of the therapeutic relationship (i.e., Triangle of Object Relations). Thus, the clinician is targeting both triangles at this time. Specifically, maladaptive patterns of relating stemming from unmet attachment needs are identified, explored, and challenged. As dimensions of the individual that have been neglected, dismissed, or shamed are brought into full view, the patient's defenses may intensify in response to the perceived psychological risks of vulnerability and exposure. It is at this juncture that interventions become increasingly penetrating and intent on deepening affective expression and experience. The overriding objective during the middle phase of treatment is to facilitate the patient's ability to achieve greater congruence and authenticity. Often, the latter part of this phase of treatment involves working through feelings of anger, resentment, and loneliness (Fig. 3).

Exploration of past relationships, most often early childhood relationship with family members, is more extensive in this phase, and the clinician aids the patients in undercovering the needs and expressing the affects associated with these early and painful experiences. It is important to begin to address the idea that the development of perfectionism for the patient was an elegant solution to the problem of not feeling good enough or of mattering. And though it offered the promise of being loved by others and of creating a sense of being no longer flawed and unlovable, the requirement of perfection was ultimately ineffective and destructive (Fig. 4).

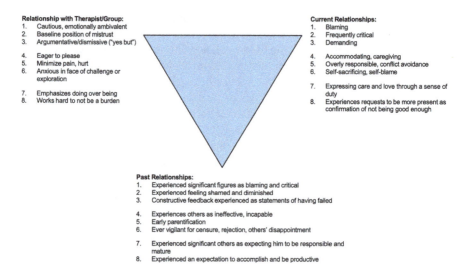

Fig. 3 Generic Triangle of Object Relations with examples of nature and quality of relational patterns

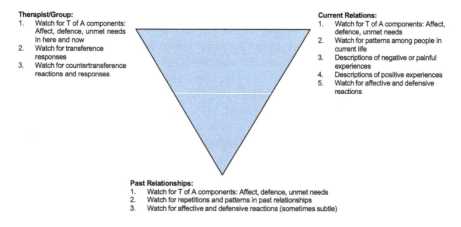

Fig. 4 Triangle of Object Relations: how to gather data

6.4 Late Phase of Treatment

As treatment enters the final phase, the predominant affective tone shifts to one of loss and mourning, as well as sadness, but a sadness devoid of despair. A primary task at this point is acknowledging and attending to the patient's grief as they embrace the realization that long-held hopes and wishes for a better past cannot be realized. Meaningful and sustainable change is signaled by the patient's capacity to relinquish blame and resentment toward significant figures who, due to their own psychological wounds, were unable to respond optimally to the patient's attachment needs. Some patients may equate this process with one of forgiveness, which they may not ever be ready to do. Our emphasis is not on forgiveness but on helping patients recognize that harboring blame and resentment, and the accompanying shame and despair, holds them to a pattern of unhealthy attachment that constricts their capacity to embrace a sense of self that is free of the distorted responses of early attachment figures. This can take the form of helping patients set boundaries within significant relationships and to have realistic appraisals of the imperfection of others and evaluation of others in terms of relational safety, and their ability to provide need fulfillment. The patient essentially learns to start the process of developing an individuated sense of self-worth that reflects the ability to consider both interpersonal feedback and responses as well as the patient's intrinsic needs, desires, and wishes. We also focus closely on the development of self-acceptance of one's own limits and strengths and attempt to focus on discovery of aspects of the self with a sense of curiosity rather than a reflexive negative evaluation. Thus, our focus during this phase is almost exclusively on the consolidation of individuated, realistic relationships with oneself and others (i.e., Triangle of Object Relations). The central therapeutic task is to help patients embrace their awareness that humanness (their own, the therapist's, and others) includes a mixture of vulnerability and strength, wounds and resilience, limitations and gifts; all falling short of perfection.

7 Individual Versus Group Dynamic-Relational Therapy

Although the phases described above were originally designed for Individual DRT (I-DRT), the general goals of each of the phases are also appropriate for DRT delivered in a group format (G-DRT). There are, however, several substantial differences between the use of I-DRT and G-DRT. First, in G-DRT the role of the therapist or therapist (typically we use two therapists), also known as group facilitators, is not to provide individual treatment for each participant in the group, but rather to facilitate the group itself as the therapeutic agent. This means that the therapists facilitate a cohesion in the group and provide guidance so the group itself becomes the primary source of therapeutic interventions. This is done through the careful facilitation of connectedness among members and experiential understanding of the relational underpinnings of perfectionism and how the perfectionism is an ineffective and damaging way of being in the world. Second, the group takes part in a preparatory session to learn about the group therapy process, for example how to benefit from group treatment, rules and procedures of the group, and how perfectionism and needs show up in a group context. Third, the groups are often time-limited with an established end point prior to commencement of the group. Typically, this is 16 sessions; however, research is required to determine if there is an optimal treatment length. Fourth, the unfolding of the therapeutic processes in the group context diverges from that of individual therapy, and four phases of group development throughout treatment have been identified. These four phases, as described in detail in Mikail et al. (2022), with specific interventions and tasks for the group therapists are provided below.

The first phase of G-DRT, referred to as *engagement and pseudo attachment*, is marked by heightened anxiety and feelings of uncertainty of group members who are expressing the need for safety, connection, and acceptance and vigilance for any hint of judgment or disapproval, whether real or perceived. The predominant emphasis during phase one is on the encouragement of and support for patients telling their story and to hear the stories and experiences of others. The therapists aim to encourage members to be curious about each other, note when members identify with what another member has shared, and normalize signs of ambivalence and caution that members may be feeling. The therapists need to manage both the hesitation and reticence of some individuals and the demanding and controlling nature of others. The primary tasks of the therapists include establishing norms for the tasks of the group, building cohesion by highlighting themes and struggles that are common among group members, and, of course, creating a safe environment that makes it possible for members to begin to disclose and take risks necessary to achieve growth. Group-as-a-whole interventions are employed when offering observations, interpretations, and summary statements as a means of underscoring the shared and common experiences of group members.

During phase two, known as *pattern interruption*, the major emphasis is on disrupting or challenging perfectionistic defenses and the self-limiting aspects of the individual's relational pattern in a manner that is supportive and encouraging. This involves working within the group on the interactions among group members. Much of the interpersonal behavior of perfectionistic individuals involves defenses and positions reflecting an internalized means of garnering acceptance, belonging, and self-worth that are intended to make one tolerable or acceptable to others and to oneself. Therapists focus on supporting members in the uncovering of the needs for acceptance and worth and encourages the group to aid in members relinquishing established ways of relating to both self and others that have been considered essential to guarding against aloneness and sense of being flawed. Interventions are often employed to encourage member-to-member interactions and deepen affective experience of these interactions. The former serves as a vehicle for making available the feedback necessary to expand group members' awareness of their interpersonal impact on others, whereas the latter is a means of uncovering unmet attachment needs. Moreover, identification of ruptures in interconnectedness and the encouragement of repairing those ruptures are crucial.

Phase three, known as *self-redefinition/painful authenticity*, involves efforts to establish new ways of relating which can feel awkward, confusing, and threatening from patients' perspectives. During this phase, patients can be confronting and become aware of disavowed parts of the self that have contributed to the development of defensive positions including perfectionism. In the past, patients have tended to externalize blame and/or engage in self-condemnation and now, at this point in the treatment, they begin to shift toward expressions of longing for intimacy, authenticity, and acceptance of self. Therapist interventions are more heavily weighted toward here-and-now interactions that target dynamics on the vertex of current relationships in the Triangle of Object Relations and also to connect to past ways of relating to important others. Most interventions by the therapists will involve some form of metacommunication, be it a group-as-a-whole statement identifying the interpersonal dynamic being enacted, making overt the implied meaning that members have drawn from another's comments, underscoring the relational intention and longing reflected in a member's comments to another member, or highlighting a member's subtle ways of devaluing the self and guarding against intimacy. In the treatment of perfectionism, therapists' readiness to acknowledge their mistakes and limitations while inviting group members to express their reactions to those errors can be a powerful source of modeling that offers a corrective albeit unsettling experience for many individuals who struggle with perfectionism.

In time-limited groups, preparing members for the final phase of *termination* is part of every session from the moment treatment begins. The patients are reminded throughout the treatment of the time-limited nature of the group. It is our experience that the groups do tend to become cohesive, close, and express the uniqueness of the group experience in terms of acceptance and of having a voice that is heard. In the final few weeks of group sessions, memories of previous unresolved endings and experiences of loss are often expressed by members. The therapists must achieve a balance between allowing members to share their accounts of these experiences while placing emphasis on ending their time in the group without simply repeating the ways past losses were dealt with. Consolidating change for patients is facilitated by having them reflect on critical moments and interactions both within and outside the group as well as identifying regrets and missed opportunities. Final reflections by the therapists for members and the group as a whole can aid patients in understanding that the therapy had, as its goal, removal of impediments to personal growth, involving self-acceptance and meeting of relational needs that have, in the past, been so elusive.

8 Empirical Support for Dynamic-Relational Therapy

In this section, we provide a brief review of the research supporting the effectiveness and efficacy of DRT designed specifically for perfectionism and associated dysfunctions.

8.1 Dynamic-Relational Group Psychotherapy

Outcome research for our dynamic-relational treatment is steadily accumulating and has primarily focused on group psychotherapy. We first demonstrated the effectiveness of DRT for perfectionism by assessing the changes in CMPB components (i.e., traits, self-presentational facets, and self-relational components) and psychological symptoms and interpersonal problems, in a group psychotherapy format in the University of British Columbia's Treatment of Perfectionism Study (UBC-TPS). In the first evaluation of DRT, Hewitt et al. (2015) utilized a sample of 60 patients who were initially screened for extreme scores on the CMPB-based measures of trait components of perfectionism, perfectionistic self-presentation, and automatic perfectionistic self-statements and also completed a clinical interview, extensive psychometric testing, and met specific inclusion and exclusion criteria for acceptance into the treatment study. DRT was provided by senior clinical psychology students under the direct supervision of the first and third author to ensure fidelity and adherence. The first report from this study involved patients' self-reports and showed that following 10 sessions of group DRT for perfectionism all trait, self-presentational, and self-relational cognitive elements of perfectionism significantly improved posttreatment (with 92% showing clinically significant improvements, based on the Reliable Change Index (RCI; Jacobson & Truax, 1991) on at least one perfectionism measure and 82% reporting clinically significant improvements on two or more perfectionism measures). Clinically significant improvements were also observed in depression, anxiety, and interpersonal problems (Hewitt et al., 2015). Moreover, at the 4-month follow-up period, perfectionism, and associated symptoms, continued to improve, a result often found with psychodynamic psychotherapies (see Shedler, 2010). Finally, in comparison to a wait-list control group, the group receiving treatment experienced reduced levels of self-oriented perfectionism, socially prescribed perfectionism, perfectionistic cognitions, and all three PSPS facets, as well as reductions in severity of depression and interpersonal problems indicating changes in perfectionism were due to DRT.

In a second report (Hewitt et al., 2020c), we addressed whether DRT for perfectionism produced changes in perfectionism as rated by close informant reports (e.g., spouse). Significant or close others provided ratings of the three perfectionism traits and three perfectionistic self-presentational styles at pre- and posttreatment as well as at the 4-month follow-up (self-relational components are not as evident to others and thus were not measured). Our results showed that close other ratings of levels of patients' self-oriented and other-oriented perfectionism and all three facets of perfectionistic self-presentation were significantly reduced at posttreatment and further reductions were observed at the 4-month follow-up (Hewitt et al., 2020c). Close other measures of patients' socially prescribed perfectionism did not show change over treatment and follow-up, possibly due to socially prescribed perfectionism being less observable to others than other trait elements of perfectionism. In this study, we also calculated RCI scores and found that 67% of participants showed clinical improvement on at least one perfectionism subscale measure. Overall, the reports of close others support the effectiveness of DRT and corroborate results using self-reports of patients (Hewitt et al., 2015).

Taken together, the UBC-TPS demonstrated that DRT enacted significant and clinically meaningful improvements in all elements of perfectionism posttreatment, and further improvements were observed at the 4-month follow-up as reported by patients and their close others. Importantly, DRT showed that large and clinically significant changes occurred not only in cognitive elements of perfectionism, but also in the deeply ingrained trait and interpersonal style variables. This is important as trait and self-presentational components of perfectionism are extremely pernicious vulnerability factors and associated broadly with various serious forms of pathology (see Cascale et al., 2024). These findings are particularly noteworthy as some researchers have suggested that the trait features of perfectionism are immutable and not amenable to change (see Shafran et al., 2002) and numerous studies show that these CBT treatments do not produce change in trait or self-presentational elements of perfectionism in comparison to list controls (e.g., Riley et al., 2007; Radhu et al., 2012; see Smith et al., 2023 for meta-analytic review). The results of the UBC-TPS stand to counter such notions that trait features of perfectionism (much like other personality dysfunctions) are fixed, a discourse that can be potentially stigmatizing and harmful to individuals with perfectionism leaving them feeling hopeless and with the sense that they are in fact defective. Overall, the UBC-TPS provides very promising support for the effectiveness of DRT for treating perfectionism.

Extending this work, we recently completed a randomized controlled trial (RCT) evaluating DRT in comparison to a supportive psychodynamic psychotherapy (PST) control (Hewitt et al., 2023). Again, we used well-trained senior clinical psychology graduate students under the direct supervision of the first and third author for DRT (Hewitt et al., 2017) or Dr. David Kealy, an expert in psychodynamic supportive treatment (e.g., see Kealy & Ogrodniczuk 2019; Rasmussen & Kealy, 2019) for the PST, to ensure fidelity and adherence in both treatment approaches. In this study, we had a sample of extremely perfectionistic patients randomly assigned to 12 group therapy sessions of either the DRT (initially $n = 41$, with 37 completers) or the PST (initially $n = 39$, with 33 completers). Analyses revealed significant improvements in all elements of perfectionism, psychiatric symptoms, and both life satisfaction and work and social adjustment for both patients receiving dynamic-relational treatment and for patients receiving supportive treatment and further improvements were observed 6 months later (Hewitt et al., 2023). Moreover, of the 37 individuals who completed the DRT, 36 individuals (97%) showed clinically significant improvement (i.e., RCI > 1.96) on at least one perfectionism measure, and of the 33 individuals completing the PST, 28 (90%) individuals showed clinically significant improvement on two or more perfectionism measures. Also, DRT produced significantly greater improvement on self-oriented perfectionism, all PSPS facets, as well as work and social adjustment in comparison to PST.

In a second set of analyses from this RCT study, we examined changes in various attitudinal measures of perfectionism, self-esteem, self-criticism, and self-reassurance and we found improvements on all measures in both DRT and PST. In terms of clinically significant change in concern over mistakes, in the DRT, 22 of 37 (60%) patients showed clinically significant change and, in the PST, 16 of 33 (49%) showed clinically significant change. Also, using the DAS perfectionism subscale, in the DRT, 26 of the 37 (71%) participants showed clinically significant change compared to 18 of 33 (55%) in PST. Finally, DRT showed superior effects on measures of dysfunctional attitudes and self-reassurance in comparison to PST.

Finally, in an evidence-based case report, Hewitt et al. (2020b) published a case study of DRT treatment of perfectionism that detailed specifics of the assessment, formulation, treatment, and outcome of a 27-year-old female patient. In this case study, the patient completed an initial assessment and a clinical formulation according to our model was developed (see Hewitt et al., 2017). The patient completed 12 group therapy sessions of DRT. Perfectionism measures as well as symptom measures were administered pre-, mid-, and posttreatment as well as at a 6-month follow-up. It was shown that the patient showed clinically significant changes in trait, self-presentational, and cognitive self-relational elements of perfectionism as well as depression, anxiety, and overall psychiatric symptoms as measured by the Brief Symptom Inventory (Derogatis, 1993). This case study adds to the evidence base of the effectiveness and efficacy of DRT in the treatment of perfectionism.

Overall, there is accumulating evidence for effectiveness and efficacy of DRT for perfectionism. Moreover, the psychodynamic treatments included in our research (DRT and PST) that focus on the relational underpinnings and use relational interventions (Hewitt et al., 2015, 2020c, 2023) appear to not only reduce symptoms of clinical disorders (e.g., depression) but, importantly, reduce perfectionism, a putative vulnerability for many dysfunctions and disorders. DRT, in particular, appears to offer significant benefit to individuals with perfectionism by effecting changes not only in the more ingrained and pernicious elements of perfectionism traits, self-presentation, self-relational, but also in the cognitive and attitudinal elements in contrast to other forms of perfectionism treatment (see Smith et al., 2023).

9 Future Directions and Refinements

We envision several central future directions as DRT for perfectionism continues to be developed, refined, and researched. One key direction of research is the evaluation of the effectiveness and efficacy of DRT in an individual psychotherapy context. Based on decades of experience treating individuals with perfectionistic behavior, we expect that the results of these evaluations will yield highly comparable results to the extant evidence supporting DRT in a group psychotherapy context. Even so, research in the individual context is not only an important next step in the continued accumulation of empirical support for DRT, but this research could also open the door for the exploration of potential mechanisms of change in DRT across both group and individual contexts. Such process research could eventually shed light on the most salient components for particular groups of perfectionistic patients and, in turn, provide insight into how to best leverage the different psychotherapy contexts (i.e., group and individual) to support patients in achieving the most successful outcomes.

Another important line of DRT research will be the continued exploration of the relationship between treatment length and clinical outcomes. Thus far, we have only examined the impacts of short-term group DRT (10-sessions and 12-sessions), yet there is some evidence that suggests true clinically relevant change does not begin until after the 30th session, regardless of treatment type (Morrison et al., 2003). Future research evaluating longer-term DRT is thereby necessary for a comprehensive understanding of the effectiveness and efficacy of DRT. This kind of research could also allow for the examination of patterns and predictors of differential patient trajectories of treatment response over the course of treatment and beyond. Relatedly, future research should also test the effects of DRT using longer follow-up assessments to examine durability of observed treatment gains over longer periods of time (i.e., years). Extended treatment and follow-up assessments will also allow for further longitudinal research to assess whether reducing perfectionism leads to the reduction in, or prevention of future, episodes of depression, anxiety, and other psychopathologies over time. Nevertheless, the extant research demonstrating that short-term group DRT enacts clinically meaningful and enduring improvements is very promising. These results are especially optimistic considering growing criticisms surrounding manualized CBT programs for various pathologies and the observed evaporation of treatment gains at follow-up timepoints (Shelder, 2018; Westen et al., 2004). This has certainly been the case with CBT for perfectionism (Smith et al., 2023). It is our belief that formulation-driven and person-centered treatments such as DRT are essential for enacting meaningful and enduring changes.

And finally, an essential next step for DRT treatment development and research is the extension of DRT for children and adolescents. Perfectionism is highly prevalent among the youth population. Recent studies have estimated at least one in four children and adolescents experience some element of perfectionism, and some research has indicated that perfectionistic tendencies and behaviors may emerge as early as 3-4 years old (see Flett & Hewitt, 2022). Concerningly, several studies have revealed that rates of perfectionism among children and adolescents are on the rise (Curran & Hill 2019), and the destructive effects of youth perfectionism are evident in its consistent associations with poor outcomes such as depression and anxiety (Guignard et al., 2012; Hewitt et al., 2002, 2011; Huggins et al., 2008; Ko et al., 2019; Sironic & Reeve, 2015; Stornæs et al., 2019; Tang et al., 2020), eating and personality disorders (Castro et al., 2004; Duan et al., 2019; Farrell & Vaillancourt, 2019; Hewitt et al., 2011; Livet et al., 2023; Vacca et al., 2020), and a myriad of relational and achievement problems (see Flett & Hewitt, 2023; Morris & Lomax, 2014). As noted earlier, perfectionism is robustly associated with heightened risk for suicidal ideation and suicide attempts among adolescents (Hewitt et al., 2014; Jacobs et al., 2009; Roxbourough et al., 2012), and perfectionistic youth rarely disclose struggles or seek help, often suffering in silence in service of presenting a "perfect" self (Flett & Hewitt, 2022).

Although the devasting effects of perfectionism among the youth population are well documented, there is relatively limited research identifying empirically robust and developmentally appropriate treatments for youth perfectionism. Intervention research in the field of child and adolescent perfectionism has primarily focused on developing and evaluating school-based prevention programs for perfectionism. While prevention programs are essential and some do appear to be effective in reducing elements of perfectionism among community samples of youth (Essau et al., 2012; Vekas & Wade, 2017; Wilksch et al., 2008), minimal work has focused on the development of treatments for youth experiencing clinically elevated levels of perfectionism or with psychiatric disorders. Few treatments have been proposed in the literature (e.g., Adlerian play therapy, CBT) but it is not yet clear whether these approaches are truly effective in producing changes, most especially changes in the most detrimental elements of perfectionism (see Flett & Hewitt, 2022 for a brief review).

With that, it is our belief that DRT has the potential to be a developmentally appropriate and beneficial treatment for children and adolescents with perfectionism. The emphasis DRT has on targeting and shifting developmental and relational patterns underpinnings of perfectionism, rather than an exclusive focus on symptom reduction may be particularly well suited for young people, given the profound developmental sequences and processes occurring (and the malleability and plasticity of the developing brain) throughout childhood and adolescence. In addition, like other psychodynamic psychotherapies, the emphasis on broadly supporting developmental processes and fostering positive psychological capacities and resources during key developmental stages across childhood and adolescence could help mitigate enduring or future psychological problems (Shelder, 2010). In fact, there is substantial evidence supporting the effectiveness of psychodynamic psychotherapies in treating a range of personality and mental health vulnerabilities in children and adolescents (Abbass et al., 2013; see Midgley et al., 2021 for a review). Ultimately, developing developmentally aligned versions of DRT with children and adolescents experiencing perfectionism may be a fruitful endeavor, and we are now taking some steps with preliminary work focused on adapting and evaluating DRT for adolescents.

10 Concluding Remarks

Decades of research supports perfectionism as a key therapeutic target. We have presented our model of perfectionism in the context of this personality style reflecting a core vulnerability factor for many disorders and dysfunctions. We argued that targeting foundational elements of functioning that contribute to the increased vulnerability for various forms of distress and dysfunction, such as perfectionism, is crucial to effect long-standing change. We described how we believe perfectionism develops and how it is maintained and outlined our model of treatment that has evolved and been informed by over 35 years of treating individuals with perfectionistic behavior. Moreover, we have shown that there is significant promise for a psychodynamic-interpersonal treatment, known as the dynamic-relational treatment of perfectionism, by describing several outcome studies suggesting that this treatment can reduce the more deeply ingrained personality and relational elements as well as the cognitive/attitudinal features of perfectionism.

References

Abbass, A. A., Rabung, S., Leichsenring, F., Refseth, J. S., & Midgley, N. (2013). Psychodynamic psychotherapy for children and adolescents: A meta-analysis of short-term psychodynamic models. *Journal of the American Academy of Child and Adolescent Psychiatry, 52*(8), 863–875. https://doi.org/10.1016/j.jaac.2013.05.014

Ashbaugh, A., Antony, M. M., Liss, A., Summerfeldt, L. J., McCabe, R. E., & Swinson, R. P. (2007). Changes in perfectionism following cognitive-behavioral treatment for social phobia. *Depression and Anxiety, 24*(3), 169–177. https://doi.org/10.1002/da.20219

Bastiani, A. M., Rao, R., Weltzin, T., & Kaye, W. H. (1995). Perfectionism in anorexia nervosa. *International Journal of Eating Disorders, 17*(2), 147–152. https://doi.org/10.1002/1098-108x(199503)17:2<147::aid-eat2260170207>3.0.co;2-x

Benjamin, L. S. (1996). *Interpersonal diagnosis and treatment of personality disorders* (2nd ed.). Guilford Press.

Blatt, S. J., Quinlan, D. M., Pilkonis, P. A., & Shea, M. T. (1995). Impact of perfectionism and need for approval on the brief treatment of depression: The national institute of mental health treatment of depression collaborative research program revisited. *Journal of Consulting and Clinical Psychology, 63*(1), 125–132. https://doi.org/10.1037/0022-006x.63.3.494

Blatt, S. J., Zuroff, D. C., Hawley, L. L., & Auerbach, J. S. (2010). Predictors of sustained therapeutic change. *Psychotherapy Research: Journal of the Society for Psychotherapy Research, 20*(1), 37–54. https://doi.org/10.1080/10503300903121080

Bowlby, J. (1988). *A secure base: Parent-child attachment and healthy human development*. Basic Books.

Casale, S., Svicher, A., Fioravanti, G., Hewitt, P. L., Flett, G. L., & Pozza, A. (2024). Perfectionistic self-presentation and psychopathology: A systematic review and meta-analysis. *Clinical Psychology & Psychotherapy, 31*(2), e2966. https://doi.org/10.1002/cpp.2966

Castro, J., Gila, A., Gual, P., Lahortiga, F., Saura, B., & Toro, J. (2004). Perfectionism dimensions in children and adolescents with anorexia nervosa. *Journal of Adolescent Health, 35*(5), 392–398. https://doi.org/10.1016/j.jadohealth.2003.11.094

Cha, M. (2016). The mediation effect of mattering and self-esteem in the relationship between socially prescribed perfectionism and depression: Based on the social disconnection model. *Personality and Individual Differences, 88*, 148–159. https://doi.org/10.1016/j.paid.2015.09.008

Cheek, J., Kealy, D., Hewitt, P. L., Mikail, S. F., Flett, G. L., Ko, A., & Jia, M. (2018). Addressing the complexity of perfectionism in clinical practice. *Psychodynamic Psychiatry, 46*(4), 457–489. https://doi.org/10.1521/pdps.2018.46.4.457

Chen, C., Hewitt, P. L., Flett, G. L., Cassels, T. G., Birch, S., & Blasberg, J. S. (2012). Insecure attachment, perfectionistic self-presentation, and social disconnection in adolescents. *Personality and Individual Differences, 52*(8), 936–941. https://doi.org/10.1016/j.paid.2012.02.009

Chen, C., Hewitt, P. L., & Flett, G. L. (2015). Preoccupied attachment, need to belong, shame, and interpersonal perfectionism: An investigation of the perfectionism social disconnection model. *Personality and Individual Differences, 76*, 177–182. https://doi.org/10.1016/j.paid.2014.12.001

Curran, T., & Hill, A. P. (2019). Perfectionism is increasing over time: A meta-analysis of birth cohort differences from 1989 to 2016. *Psychological Bulletin, 145*(4), 410–429. https://doi.org/10.1037/bul0000138200

Derogatis, L. R. (1993). *Brief Symptom Inventory: Administration, scoring and procedures manual* (4th ed.). National Computer Systems, Pearson, Inc.

Duan, W., He, C., Huang, L., & Sheng, J. (2019). The 12-item big three perfectionism scale for adolescents. *Personality and Individual Differences, 151*, Article e109536. https://doi.org/10.1016/j.paid.2019.109536

Dunkley, D. M., Blankstein, K. R., Halsall, J., Williams, M., & Winkworth, G. (2000). The relation between perfectionism and distress: Hassles, coping, and perceived social support as mediators and moderators. *Journal of Counseling Psychology, 47*(4), 437–453. https://doi.org/10.1037/0022-0167.47.4.437

Eagle, M. N. (2017). Attachment theory and research and clinical work. *Psychoanalytic Inquiry, 37*(5), 284–297. https://doi.org/10.1080/07351690.2017.1322420

Egan, S. J., Wade, T. D., Shafran, R., & Antony, M. M. (2016). *Cognitive-behavioral treatment of perfectionism*. Guilford Publications.

Enns, M. W., & Cox, B. J. (1999). Perfectionism and depression symptom severity in major depressive disorder. *Behaviour Research and Therapy, 37*(8), 783–794. https://doi.org/10.1016/s0005-7967(98)00188-0

Essau, C. A., Conradt, J., Sasagawa, S., & Ollendick, T. H. (2012). Prevention of anxiety symptoms in children: Results from a universal school-based trial. *Behavior Therapy, 43*(2), 450–464. https://doi.org/10.1016/j.beth.2011.08.003

Farrell, A. H., & Vaillancourt, T. (2019). Developmental pathways of perfectionism: Associations with bullying perpetration, peer victimization, and narcissism. *Journal of Applied Developmental Psychology, 65*, Article e101065. https://doi.org/10.1016/j.appdev.2019.101065

Flett, G. L., & Hewitt, P. L. (2002). *Perfectionism: Theory, research, and treatment*. American Psychological Association. https://doi.org/10.1037/10458-000

Flett, G. L., & Hewitt, P. L. (2022). *Perfectionism in childhood and adolescence: A developmental approach*. American Psychological Association. https://doi.org/10.1037/0000289-000

Flett, G. L., & Hewitt, P. L. (2023). Reflections on the costs of rigid perfectionism and perfectionistic reactivity: The core significance of the failure to adapt in sports and in life. In A. P. Hill (Ed.), *The psychology of perfectionism in sport, dance, and exercise* (2nd ed., pp. 399–420). Routledge. https://doi.org/10.4324/9781003288015-20

Flett, G. L., Hewitt, P. L., & De Rosa, T. (1996). Dimensions of perfectionism, psychosocial adjustment, and social skills. *Personality and Individual Differences, 20*(2), 143–150. https://doi.org/10.1016/0191-8869(95)00170-0

Flett, G. L., Hewitt, P. L., Blankstein, K. R., & Gray, L. (1998). Psychological distress and the frequency of perfectionistic thinking. *Journal of Personality and Social Psychology, 75*(5), 1363–1381. https://doi.org/10.1037/0022-3514.75.5.1363

Flett, G. L., Besser, A., & Hewitt, P. L. (2014). Perfectionism and interpersonal orientations in depression: An analysis of validation seeking and rejection sensitivity in a community sample of young adults. *Psychiatry, 77*(1), 67–85. https://doi.org/10.1521/psyc.2014.77.1.67

Frost, R. O., Marten, P., Lahart, C., & Rosenblate, R. (1990). The dimensions of perfectionism. *Cognitive Therapy and Research, 14*(5), 449–468. https://doi.org/10.1007/BF01172967

Greenspon, T. S. (2008). Making sense of error: A view of the origins and treatment of perfectionism. *American Journal of Psychotherapy, 62*(3), 263–282. https://doi.org/10.1176/appi.psychotherapy.2008.62.3.263

Guignard, J. H., Jacquet, A.-Y., & Lubart, T. I. (2012). Perfectionism and anxiety: A paradox in intellectual giftedness? *PLoS One, 7*(7), e41043. https://doi.org/10.1371/journal.pone.0041043

Haring, M., Hewitt, P. L., & Flett, G. L. (2003). Perfectionism, coping, and quality of intimate relationships. *Journal of Marriage and Family, 65*(1), 143–158. https://doi.org/10.1111/j.1741-3737.2003.00143.x

Hewitt, P. L. (2020). Perfecting, belonging, and repairing: A dynamic-relational approach to perfectionism. *Canadian Psychology/Psychologie canadienne, 61*(2), 101–110. https://doi.org/10.1037/cap0000209

Hewitt, P. L., & Flett, G. L. (1991a). Perfectionism in the self and social contexts: Conceptualization, assessment, and association with psychopathology. *Journal of Personality and Social Psychology, 60*(3), 456–470. https://doi.org/10.1037/0022-3514.60.3.456

Hewitt, P. L., & Flett, G. L. (1991b). Dimensions of perfectionism in unipolar depression. *Journal of Abnormal Psychology, 100*(1), 98–101. https://doi.org/10.1037/0021-843x.100.1.98

Hewitt, P. L., & Flett, G. L. (1993). Dimensions of perfectionism, daily stress, and depression: A test of the specific vulnerability hypothesis. *Journal of Abnormal Psychology, 102*(1), 58–65. https://doi.org/10.1037/0021-843x.102.1.58

Hewitt, P. L., & Flett, G. L. (2002). Perfectionism and stress processes in psychopathology. In *Perfectionism: Theory, research, and treatment* (pp. 255–284). https://doi.org/10.1037/10458-011

Hewitt, P. L., Flett, G. L., & Mikail, S. F. (1995). Perfectionism and relationship adjustment in pain patients and their spouses. *Journal of Family Psychology, 9*(3), 335–347. https://doi.org/10.1037/0893-3200.9.3.335

Hewitt, P. L., Flett, G. L., & Ediger, E. (1996). Perfectionism and depression: Longitudinal assessment of a specific vulnerability hypothesis. *Journal of Abnormal Psychology, 105*(2), 276–280. https://doi.org/10.1037/0021-843x.105.2.276

Hewitt, P. L., Caelian, C. F., Flett, G. L., Sherry, S. B., Collins, L., & Flynn, C. A. (2002). Perfectionism in children: Associations with depression, anxiety, and anger. *Personality and Individual Differences, 32*(6), 1049–1061. https://doi.org/10.1016/S0191-8869(01)00109-X

Hewitt, P. L., Flett, G. L., Sherry, S. B., Habke, M., Parkin, M., Lam, R. W., McMurty, B., Ediger, E., Fairlie, P., & Stein, M. B. (2003). The interpersonal expression of perfection: Perfectionistic self-presentation and psychological distress. *Journal of Personality and Social Psychology, 84*(6), 1303–1325. https://doi.org/10.1037/0022-3514.84.6.1303

Hewitt, P. L., Flett, G. L., Sherry, S. B., & Caelian, C. (2006). Trait perfectionism dimensions and suicidal behavior. In T. E. Ellis (Ed.), *Cognition and suicide: Theory, research, and therapy* (pp. 215–235). American Psychological Association.

Hewitt, P. L., Habke, A. M., Lee-Baggley, D. L., Sherry, S. B., & Flett, G. L. (2008). The impact of perfectionistic self-presentation on the cognitive, affective, and physiological experience of a clinical interview. *Psychiatry: Interpersonal and Biological Processes, 71*(2), 93–122. https://doi.org/10.1521/psyc.2008.71.2.93

Hewitt, P. L., Blasberg, J. S., Flett, G. L., Besser, A., Sherry, S. B., Caelian, C., Papsdorf, M., Cassels, T. G., & Birch, S. (2011). Perfectionistic self-presentation in children and adolescents: Development and validation of the perfectionistic self-presentation scale—junior form. *Psychological Assessment, 23*(1), 125–142. https://doi.org/10.1037/a0021147

Hewitt, P. L., Caelian, C. F., Chen, C., & Flett, G. L. (2014). Perfectionism, stress, daily hassles, hopelessness, and suicide potential in depressed psychiatric adolescents. *Journal of Psychopathology and Behavioral Assessment, 36*(4), 663–674. https://doi.org/10.1007/s10862-014-9427-0

Hewitt, P. L., Mikail, S. F., Flett, G. L., Tasca, G. A., Flynn, C. A., Deng, X., Kaldas, J., & Chen, C. (2015). Psychodynamic/interpersonal group psychotherapy for perfectionism: Evaluating the effectiveness of a short-term treatment. *Psychotherapy, 52*(2), 205–217. https://doi.org/10.1037/pst0000016

Hewitt, P. L., Flett, G. L., & Mikail, S. F. (2017). *Perfectionism: A relational approach to conceptualization, assessment, and treatment*. The Guilford Press.

Hewitt, P. L., Flett, G. L., Mikail, S. F., Kealy, D., & Zhang, L. (2018a). Perfectionism in the therapeutic context: The perfectionism social disconnection model and clinical process and outcome. In J. Stoeber (Ed.), *The psychology of perfectionism: Theory, research, applications*. Routledge.

Hewitt, P. L., Mikail, S. F., Flett, G. L., & Dang, S. (2018b). Specific formulation feedback in dynamic-relational group psychotherapy of perfectionism. *Psychotherapy, 55*(2), 179–185. https://doi.org/10.1037/pst0000137

Hewitt, P. L., Smith, M. M., Deng, X., Chen, C., Ko, A., Flett, G. L., & Paterson, R. J. (2020). The perniciousness of perfectionism in group therapy for depression: A test of the perfectionism social disconnection model. *Psychotherapy, 57*(2), 206–218. https://doi.org/10.1037/pst0000281

Hewitt, P. L., Flett, G. L., & Mikail, S. F. (2020a). *Perfectionism: A relational approach to conceptualization, assessment, and treatment*. (V. Cavelletti & S. Cheli Trans.) The Guilford Press.

Hewitt, P. L., Mikail, S. F., Dang, S. S., Kealy, D., & Flett, G. L. (2020b). Dynamic-relational treatment of perfectionism: An illustrative case study. *Journal of Clinical Psychology, 76*(11), 2028–2040. https://doi.org/10.1002/jclp.23040

Hewitt, P. L., Qiu, T., Flynn, C. A., Flett, G. L., Wiebe, S. A., Tasca, G. A., & Mikail, S. F. (2020c). Dynamic-relational group treatment for perfectionism: Informant ratings of patient change. *Psychotherapy, 57*(2), 197–205. https://doi.org/10.1037/pst0000229

Hewitt, P. L., Chen, C., Smith, M. M., Zhang, L., Habke, M., Flett, G. L., & Mikail, S. F. (2021). Patient perfectionism and clinician impression formation during an initial interview. *Psychology and Psychotherapy: Theory, Research and Practice, 94*(1), 45–62. https://doi.org/10.1111/papt.12266

Hewitt, P. L., Kealy, D., Mikail, S. F., Smith, M. M., Ge, S., Chen, C., Sochting, I., Tasca, G. A., Flett, G. L., & Ko, A. (2023). The efficacy of group psychotherapy for adults with perfectionism: A randomized controlled trial of dynamic-relational therapy versus psychodynamic supportive therapy. *Journal of Consulting and Clinical Psychology, 91*(1), 29–42. https://doi.org/10.1037/ccp0000787

Hewitt, P. L., Ge, S., Smith, M. M., Flett, G. L., Cheli, S., Molnar, D. S., Ko, A., Mikail, S. F., & Lang, T. (2024). Automatic self recriminations: Development and validation of a measure of self-condemnatory internal dialogue. *Journal of Personality Assessment, 106*, 1–13. https://doi.org/10.1080/00223891.2024.2303429

Horney, K. (1939). *New ways in psychoanalysis* (1st ed.). Routledge. https://doi.org/10.4324/9781315010540

Horney, K. (1950). *Neurosis and human growth: The struggle towards self-realization*. W. W. Norton.

Huggins, L., Davis, M. C., Rooney, R., & Kane, R. (2008). Socially prescribed and self-oriented perfectionism as predictors of depressive diagnosis in preadolescents. *Australian Journal of Guidance and Counselling, 18*(2), 182–194. https://doi.org/10.1375/ajgc.18.2.182

Jacobs, R. H., Silva, S. G., Reinecke, M. A., Curry, J. F., Ginsburg, G. S., Kratochvil, C. J., & March, J. S. (2009). Dysfunctional attitudes scale perfectionism: A predictor and partial mediator of acute treatment outcome among clinically depressed adolescents. *Journal of Clinical Child and Adolescent Psychology, 38*(6), 803–813. https://doi.org/10.1080/15374410903259031

Jacobson, N. S., & Truax, P. (1991). Clinical significance: A statistical approach to defining meaningful change in psychotherapy research. *Journal of Consulting and Clinical Psychology, 59*(1), 12–19. https://doi.org/10.1037/0022-006X.59.1.12

Kawamura, K. Y., & Frost, R. O. (2004). Self-concealment as a mediator in the relationship between perfectionism and psychological distress. *Cognitive Therapy and Research, 28*(2), 183–191. https://doi.org/10.1023/b:cotr.0000021539.48926.c1

Kealy, D., & Ogrodniczuk, J. S. (2019). *Contemporary psychodynamic psychotherapy: Evolving clinical practice*. Academic Press.

Kiesler, D. J. (1983). The 1982 Interpersonal Circle: A taxonomy for complementarity in human transactions. *Psychological Review, 90*(3), 185–214. https://doi.org/10.1037/0033-295X.90.3.185

Ko, A., Hewitt, P. L., Chen, C., & Flett, G. (2019). Perfectionism as a mediator between attachment and depression in children and adolescents. *Perspectives, 4*(2), 181–200.

Kohut, H. (1971). *The analysis of the self*. International Universities Press.

Livet, A., Navarri, X., Pomerleau, P. P., Champagne, S., Yunus, F. M., Chadi, N., McVey, G., & Conrod, P. (2023). Perfectionism in children and adolescents with eating-related symptoms: A systematic review and a meta-analysis of effect estimates. *Adolescents, 3*(2), 305–329. https://doi.org/10.3390/adolescents3020022

Midgley, N., Mortimer, R., Cirasola, A., Batra, P., & Kennedy, E. (2021). The evidence-base for psychodynamic psychotherapy with children and adolescents: A narrative synthesis. *Frontiers in Psychology, 12*, Article e662671. https://doi.org/10.3389/fpsyg.2021.662671

Mikail, S. F., Hewitt, P. L., Flett, G. L., & Ge, S. (2022). Group dynamic-relational therapy for perfectionism. *Research in Psychotherapy: Psychopathology, Process, and Outcome, 25*(3), 249–257. https://doi.org/10.4081/ripppo.2022.635

Morris, L., & Lomax, C. (2014). Review: Assessment, development, and treatment of childhood perfectionism: A systematic review. *Child and Adolescent Mental Health, 19*(4), 225–234. https://doi.org/10.1111/camh.12067

Morrison, K. H., Bradley, R., & Westen, D. (2003). The external validity of controlled clinical trials of psychotherapy for depression and anxiety: A naturalistic study. *Psychology and Psychotherapy: Theory, Research and Practice, 76*(2), 109–132. https://doi.org/10.1348/147608303765951168

Nepon, T., Flett, G. L., Hewitt, P. L., & Molnar, D. S. (2011). Perfectionism, negative social feedback, and interpersonal rumination in depression and social anxiety. *Canadian Journal of Behavioural Science/Revue Canadienne Des Sciences Du Comportement, 43*(4), 297–308. https://doi.org/10.1037/a0025032

Radhu, N., Daskalakis, Z. J., Arpin-Cribbie, C. A., Irvine, J., & Ritvo, P. (2012). Evaluating a web-based cognitive-behavioral therapy for maladaptive perfectionism in university students. *Journal of American College Health, 60*(5), 357–366. https://doi.org/10.1080/07448481.2011.630703

Rasmussen, B., & Kealy, D. (2019). Reflections on supportive psychotherapy in the 21st century. *Journal of Social Work Practice, 34*(3), 281–295. https://doi.org/10.1080/02650533.2019.1648245

Riley, C., Lee, M., Cooper, Z., Fairburn, C. G., & Shafran, R. (2007). A randomised controlled trial of cognitive-behaviour therapy for clinical perfectionism: A preliminary study. *Behaviour Research and Therapy, 45*(9), 2221–2231. https://doi.org/10.1016/j.brat.2006.12.003

Roxborough, H. M., Hewitt, P. L., Kaldas, J., Flett, G. L., Caelian, C. M., Sherry, S. B., & Sherry, D. L. (2012). Perfectionistic self-presentation, socially prescribed perfectionism, and suicide in youth: A test of the Perfectionism Social Disconnection Model. *Suicide and Life-threatening Behavior, 42*(2), 217–233. https://doi.org/10.1111/j.1943-278X.2012.00084.x

Shafran, R., Cooper, Z., & Fairburn, C. G. (2002). Clinical perfectionism: A cognitive–behavioural analysis. *Behaviour Research and Therapy, 40*(7), 773–791. https://doi.org/10.1016/s0005-7967(01)00059-6

Shahar, G., Blatt, S. J., Zuroff, D. C., Krupnick, J. L., & Sotsky, S. M. (2004). Perfectionism impedes social relations and response to brief treatment for depression. *Journal of Social and Clinical Psychology, 23*(2), 140–154. https://doi.org/10.1521/jscp.23.2.140.31017

Shedler, J. (2010). The efficacy of psychodynamic psychotherapy. *American Psychologist, 65*(2), 98–109. https://doi.org/10.1037/a0018378

Shedler, J. (2018). Where is the evidence for "evidence-based" therapy? *Psychiatric Clinics of North America, 41*(2), 319–329. https://doi.org/10.1016/j.psc.2018.02.001

Sherry, S. B., Law, A., Hewitt, P. L., Flett, G. L., & Besser, A. (2008). Social support as a mediator of the relationship between perfectionism and depression: A preliminary test of the social disconnection model. *Personality and Individual Differences, 45*(5), 339–344. https://doi.org/10.1016/j.paid.2008.05.001

Sirois, F. M., & Molnar, D. S. (2016). *Perfectionism, health, and well-being*. Springer.

Sironic, A., & Reeve, R. A. (2015). A combined analysis of the Frost Multidimensional Perfectionism Scale (FMPS), Child and Adolescent Perfectionism Scale (CAPS), and Almost Perfect Scale—Revised (APS-R): Different perfectionist profiles in adolescent high school students. *Psychological Assessment, 27*(4), 1471–1483. https://doi.org/10.1037/pas0000137

Smith, M. M., Sherry, S. B., Gautreau, C. M., Mushquash, A. R., Saklofske, D. H., & Snow, S. L. (2017). The intergenerational transmission of perfectionism: Fathers' other-oriented perfectionism and daughters' perceived psychological control uniquely predict daughters' self-critical and personal standards perfectionism. *Personality and Individual Differences, 119*, 242–248. https://doi.org/10.1016/j.paid.2017.07.030

Smith, M. M., Sherry, S. B., Chen, S., Saklofske, D. H., Mushquash, C., Flett, G. L., & Hewitt, P. L. (2018). The perniciousness of perfectionism: A meta-analytic review of the perfectionism-suicide relationship. *Journal of Personality, 86*(3), 522–542. https://doi.org/10.1111/jopy.12333

Smith, M. M., Hewitt, P. L., Sherry, S. B., Flett, G. L., Kealy, D., Tasca, G. A., Ge, S., Ying, F., & Bakken, K. (2023). A meta-analytic test of the efficacy of cognitive behavioural therapy for perfectionism: A replication and extension. *Canadian Psychology/Psychologie Canadienne, 64*(4), 355–376. https://doi.org/10.1037/cap0000360

Stornæs, A. V., Rosenvinge, J. H., Sundgot-Borgen, J., Pettersen, G., & Friborg, O. (2019). Profiles of perfectionism among adolescents attending specialized elite- and ordinary lower secondary schools: A norwegian cross-sectional comparative study. *Frontiers in Psychology, 10*, Article e2039. https://doi.org/10.3389/fpsyg.2019.02039

Strupp, H. H., & Binder, J. L. (1984). *Psychotherapy in a new key: A guide to time-limited dynamic psychotherapy*. Basic Books.

Sullivan, H. S. (1953). *The interpersonal theory of psychiatry*. W W Norton.

Tang, X., Tang, S., Ren, Z., & Wong, D. F. (2020). Psychological risk and protective factors associated with depressive symptoms among adolescents in secondary schools in China: A systematic review and meta-analysis. *Children and Youth Services Review, 108*, Article e104680. https://doi.org/10.1016/j.childyouth.2019.104680

Vacca, M., Ballesio, A., & Lombardo, C. (2020). The relationship between perfectionism and eating-related symptoms in adolescents: A systematic review. *European Eating Disorders Review, 29*(1), 32–51. https://doi.org/10.1002/erv.2793

Vekas, E. J., & Wade, T. D. (2017). The impact of a universal intervention targeting perfectionism in children: An exploratory controlled trial. *British Journal of Clinical Psychology, 56*(4), 458–473. https://doi.org/10.1111/bjc.12152

Westen, D., Novotny, C. M., & Thompson-Brenner, H. (2004). The empirical status of empirically supported psychotherapies: Assumptions, findings, and reporting in controlled clinical trials. *Psychological Bulletin, 130*(4), 631–663. https://doi.org/10.1037/0033-2909.130.4.631

Wilksch, S. M., Durbridge, M. R., & Wade, T. D. (2008). A preliminary controlled comparison of programs designed to reduce risk of eating disorders targeting perfectionism and media literacy. *Journal of the American Academy of Child & Adolescent Psychiatry, 47*(8), 939–947. https://doi.org/10.1097/chi.0b013e3181799f4a

ACT and SchemaTherapy

Luca Altieri, Valeria Monaco, and Stefano Stefanini

1 ACT

From a historical perspective, behavioural therapies have evolved from their inception—around the end of the 1950s—to the present day. It is possible to identify three waves or generations, each characterised by a dominant set of assumptions as well as specific methods and goals underlying theory and clinical practice.

A first wave with a purely behaviourist preponderance was followed by a second wave, in which a cognitivist view was grafted in, broadening the horizon and methods of intervention. Finally, there is a third wave that does not focus exclusively on changing cognitive content or problematic behaviour, but is characterised by the fact that it also emphasises the way in which the patient relates to his internal experiences, accepting them and integrating them into his life. Acceptance and commitment therapy (ACT; Hayes, Strosahl & Wilson) and schema therapy (ST; Young) are part of this latest generation of approaches.[1]

---

[1] Without claiming to be exhaustive, third-generation therapies include dialectical behaviour therapy (DBT; Linehan), functional analytic psychotherapy (FAP; Kohlenberg and Tsai), integrative behavioural couples therapy (IBCT; Jacobson, Christensen, Price, Cordova and Eldridge), mindfulness-based cognitive therapy (MBCT; Segal, Williams and Teasdale), behavioural activation (BA; Ferster), metacognitive approaches (MT; Wells), compassion-focused therapy (CFT; Gilbert), and emotion-focused therapy (EFT; Johnson and Greenberg).

L. Altieri
Department of Clinical and Experimental Sciences, University of Brescia, Brescia, Italy

V. Monaco
Centro di Psicologia e Psicoterapia Liberamente, Bergamo, Italy

S. Stefanini (✉)
Department of Mental Health (DSMD), ASST Spedali Civili di Brescia, Brescia, Italy

European Biomedical Research Foundation, Bergamo, Italy

1.1 The Roots of Acceptance and Commitment Therapy

First-generation behaviourism,[2] whose fathers are John B. Watson and B. F. Skinner, is based on the concepts of classical conditioning and operant conditioning,[3] of a pragmatist kind..[4]

The assumption behind early behaviourism was that through laboratory observation of the animal world, and in particular the principles of learning, it would also be possible to explain human behaviour.

By resorting to a rigorous scientific methodology that relied exclusively on directly observable variables, it was able to increase the possibility of *predicting* what organisms would do in particular circumstances, and of *controlling* or modifying these behaviours using operant principles. At the same time, however, the explanation of human behaviour was limited to what could be measured, and was unable to capture either its complexity or its multiplicity.

For this reason, in his article 'A review of B. F. Skinner's Verbal Behavior', the linguist Noam Chomsky fiercely criticised the dominant idea of Skinner's behaviourism, according to which human behaviour could only be explained through quantifiable and verifiable data, arguing that knowledge of internal mental processes was instead essential to understanding human behaviour.

Chomsky observed that the same stimulus could be followed by at least two different verbal responses. This asymmetry in verbal behaviour helped to challenge the

---

[2] This movement was officially born in America in 1913, when John B. Watson (1878–1858) published an article entitled Psychology as the Behaviorist View It.

[3] For further discussion, see Moderato P, Presti P, Dell'Orco F (2023) ACT: Acceptance and Commitment Therapy. Hogrefe: Florence. p. 231.

Classical conditioning: experimental paradigm for the study of learning developed by Ivan Pavlov (1849–1936). It consists of a process of stimulus function transfer whereby a previously neutral stimulus acquires the ability to produce the response that was originally elicited by another stimulus. The experimental procedure is based on the repeated pairing of a conditioned stimulus (e.g. the ringing of a bell) with an unconditioned stimulus (e.g. food); this pairing results in a conditioned response to the conditioned stimulus (bell) similar to the unconditioned response (salivation) elicited previously by the unconditioned stimulus (food).

Operant conditioning: experimental paradigm for the study of learning developed by Burrhus F. Skinner (1904–1990), in which spontaneously emitted behaviour is modelled, according to the reinforcement process, by the consequences it produces. If the behaviour produces the appearance of a positive reinforcer or the removal of a negative one, it will be reinforced and will tend to recur, when on the other hand it no longer produces consequences that reinforce it, its recurrence will become progressively less frequent.

[4] Pragmatism is a philosophical current that developed in the United States in the late nineteenth and early twentieth century. According to this conception, the truth and validity of a theory are entrusted to its practical verification. In other words, pragmatism maintains that the effectiveness and applicability of an idea or concept must be tested through concrete experience and observation of the results obtained. This attitude privileges concrete results and practical applications over abstract principles. It is a perspective that emphasises action and the solution of real problems, rather than purely theoretical considerations. Its founders include Charles Sanders Pierce and William James.

assumption that human behaviour could be reduced to simple 'stimuli' and 'responses', paving the way for new disciplines such as cognitive science.

In an attempt to overcome these critical issues, the second generation, termed cognitive-behavioural therapy (CBT), emerged in the early 1970s. CBT is based on a deeper understanding of cognitive processes and aims to create significant changes in the relationship between thoughts, emotions and behaviour.

The second generation of behavioural therapies focused more on the patient's thought processes and beliefs, that is, those cognitive processes, explicit or implicit, that often underlie psychopathological manifestations. Concepts such as negative automatic thoughts, dysfunctional beliefs and maladaptive patterns were identified and used as the basis for therapy, with the aim of understanding and modifying the cognitive distortions that influence behaviour and emotions.

Whereas the first wave of behavioural therapies produced, through repeated and rigorous laboratory investigations, specific procedures in the service of sound clinical practice, the second generation focused primarily on how the brain processes information. There have, however, been no experimental demonstrations of how thoughts actually control behaviour, nor has basic cognition research provided a clear methodological example of how thoughts should be systematically modified in order to induce behavioural change.

Without an understanding of these processes, any attempt to develop therapeutic strategies, aimed at impacting the relationship between thoughts and behaviour, is merely conjecture, however refined (Woods & Kanter, 2016).

This created a divide among behavioural psychologists. One group stuck to the use and implementation of first-generation interventions, downplaying the importance or usefulness of cognitive interventions as change agents. A second group, led by Steven Hayes of the University of Nevada, Reno, revised the primitive approach to behaviour analysis and implemented it.

The elaboration of a new research programme on language and human cognition led to the development of relational frame theory (Hayes et al., 2001), a post-Skinnerian behavioural theory in which acceptance and commitment therapy (Hayes et al., 1999) has its roots, representing its empirical implication.

In particular, the project envisaged the need to overcome radical behaviourism,[5] redefining the underlying philosophical framework of behaviour analysis in terms of functional contextualism.[6]

This expression, coined by Hayes and Wilson (1993), refers to two fundamental elements of behaviourism: the first is that behaviour must always be considered in

---

[5] Radical behaviourism is defined by Woods and Kanter (2007) as *'the philosophy of a science of behaviour treated as a discipline in its own right, independent of internal, mental or physiological explanations'*.

[6] Functional contextualism seeks to bring empirically based concepts and rules to life, as is the case in the natural sciences. This approach adopts a pragmatic truth criterion, according to which what makes it possible to predict and influence events is true. Despite its pragmatic character, the knowledge that contextual behavioural science aims for is general, abstract and applicable to most organisms.

relation to the context (setting) in which it is carried out; the second is that in order to understand and influence behaviour, we need to study what it is aimed at (its function) (Törneke, 2017).

RFT is a behavioural theory of human language and cognition that aims to predict and *influence* (no longer control!) behaviour, including verbal behaviour, with precision, breadth and depth.[7]

RFT is based on the idea that linking one concept to another underlies all human language: all human cognition is based on the ability to create relational connections (frames) between stimuli.

A frame is defined as a set of relationships that frame events, symbols, images, gestures and sounds in the world in an immediate, abstract and arbitrary way.[8] These relationships enable us to learn without the need for direct experience.

For example, a cat will not touch a hot cooker twice but needs to touch it at least once to learn not to do so again. A child, on the other hand, does not need to touch a hot cooker to learn that it is hot because it has been taught verbally that it can burn itself (Hayes & Smith, 2005).

Human beings think relationally, that is, they are able to arbitrarily relate objects from the environment, thoughts, feelings, impulses, actions (basically anything) to other objects from the environment, thoughts, feelings, etc., in every possible way.[9]

This ability, which animals apparently do not possess, is our key evolutionary resource, but it can also be a source of suffering and psychological distress. For example, if one event is associated with something frightening and unpleasant, all other events that for whatever reason, or even arbitrarily, we relate to it may themselves become frightening or unpleasant.

Whereas Skinner (1957) considered verbal behaviour in the same way as any other operant behaviour, Hayes defines language as *generalised operant* conditioning[10] characterised by three peculiar properties, which allow stimuli or events to be related: reciprocal implication, combinatorial implication and transformation of the stimulus function.

The first describes the relationship between two stimuli or events: if 'A = B then B = A'. For example, if Marco is slower than Luca, Luca will be faster than Marco.

Combinatorial implication describes the relationship between three or more stimuli: if 'A is more than B and B is more than C', then 'A is more than C and C is less than A'. Continuing in the example, if we add that Carlo is faster than Luca, a

---

[7] For a more in-depth analysis, see Moderato P and Presti G (2019) Thoughts, Words, Emotions. CBT and third generation ABA: experimental and clinical bases. Franco Angeli Editions, Milan.

[8] There are coordination frames: 'the same as', 'similar to', 'like'; temporal and causal frames: 'before and after', 'if/then', 'because of'; comparative and evaluative frames: 'better than', 'bigger than', 'faster than'; deictic frames: 'I/you', 'here/there'; and spatial frames: 'near/far', and so on.

[9] This relating is referred to in the RFT as relational framing, or, in a more technical term, arbitrarily applicable relational response.

[10] Whereas an operant produces very similar responses, that is, behaviours that, in the same context, have the same effect, in the case of a generalised operant the shape of individual responses, while the context remains unchanged, varies considerably.

new relationship between Carlo and Marco arises spontaneously, according to which the former is the faster of the two.

Finally, the third property of language is the transformation of the stimulus function. Given the A-B-C relationship, partly taught (between Marco and Luca and between Carlo and Luca), and partly born spontaneously (between Carlo and Marco), we could hypothesise that in a three-way competition Carlo would win, even though no one has ever observed him running!

So a man who experiences his first panic attack in the shop downstairs might develop the rule 'if I feel panic in one little shop, who knows what will happen to me in bigger shopping centres'. This man might feel great discomfort at the mere thought of entering Harrods in London, even if he has never set foot in there before (Woods & Kanter, 2016).

If relational frame theory has the merit of highlighting the problems that a dysfunctional use of language creates, acceptance and commitment therapy (Hayes et al., 1999) applies its principles in clinical practice with the aim of promoting psychological well-being and behavioural change in the patient.

1.2 *Acceptance and Commitment Therapy (ACT)*

Within its hexagonal treatment model (Fig. 1), ACT analyses concepts such as acceptance, defusion, the self as context, values, committed actions and adherence to the present moment, which are six key processes for achieving *psychological flexibility*,[11] a term by which we refer to the ability to be fully in touch with the present moment as conscious human beings.

This therapeutic approach also involves the use of mindfulness, metaphors, logical paradoxes and experiential exercises, which aim to mitigate the excessive rigidity of language.

ACT does not aim at the modification of the content of thoughts or emotions (anxiety, anger, frustration, etc.) nor at their reduction, but aims at their acceptance.

The concept of *acceptance is* intrinsically linked to that of readiness and non-resignation, and its opposite is experiential avoidance.

In one of his famous fables, Aesop[12] tells of a hungry fox, who, seeing bunches of grapes hanging from a vine, longs to grab them, but, being unable to do so, says to himself 'so unripe are they'. 'They are unripe' represents avoidance.

This experience of defeat, common to every living being, if accepted, would allow them to learn new strategies for interacting with their living context.

To clarify the concept of acceptance, ACT makes use of many experiential exercises. Let us examine one of them. Take an ice cube from the freezer and hold it in

---

[11] Psychological flexibility is understood as the acceptance, without intermediation and in the present moment, of the aversive stimulus functions conveyed by language (Hayes et al., 1999).

[12] Aesopus (Ancient Greek: Αἴσωπος, Áisōpos; Menebria, c. 620 BC–Delphi, 564 BC), The Fox and the Grapes.

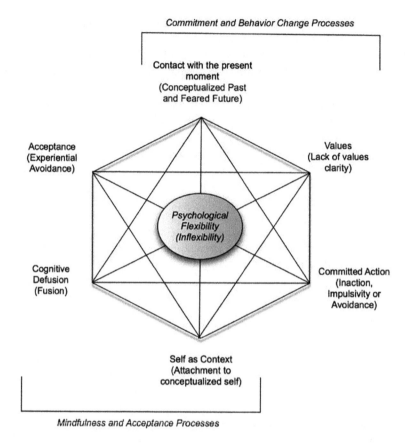

Fig. 1 Flexible and inflexible hexaflex

your hand, running it between your fingers and across your palm to maximise exposure. Now, if you are willing, hold the cube until it has melted.

There are two possible attitudes when faced with increasing cold: stiffen up and move your hand away from your body, or gently rest your arm on your leg. Try this second position. When you become distracted, gently bring your attention back to your hand, whenever needed (Flaxman et al., 2011).

This exercise illustrates that we can sometimes encounter pain, discomfort or psychological suffering. If we are not willing to experience this pain, to accept it and make room for it, we will not have taken even the first step on the road to overcoming it.

Experiential avoidance refers to the deliberate attempt to change the form and frequency of words, traumatic memories, thoughts, feelings, etc., experienced as aversive (Hayes et al., 1996). Experiential avoidance produces only a temporary reduction in the anxiety associated with the averted stimulus, resulting in an increase in the frequency of precisely that with which we struggle (Heffner & Eifert, 2003; Levitt et al., 2004).

Such a persistent attitude leads to a rigid control by the verbal context in which we are immersed, associated with poorly adaptive and stereotyped behaviour.

To promote awareness of the negative effects of avoidance, ACT suggests the metaphor of quicksand. If you are trapped in quicksand, the immediate impulse is to fight your way out, but this is exactly what does not work, because the more you struggle, the more you sink. The only way to save yourself is to distribute your body weight over as large an area as possible.

So why do we tend to avoid thoughts, feelings, memories, etc., if this behaviour is counterproductive? Sometimes human beings do not simply acknowledge that aversive stimuli exist, and accept them, but develop maladaptive responses, which are, however, highly consistent in their eyes with their idea of reality. They have an idea of reality that is as distorted as it is inflexible. In essence, they tell themselves a story, and live in the story they are telling themselves, convinced that it is the only true and possible story.

ACT assumes that language and human cognition distort, and often augment, highly emotional experiences, and that an effort is needed to defuse language-based processes when they prove problematic. Thus, acceptance work is usually associated with cognitive defusion work and work on the self as context.

Cognitive fusion occurs when we merge with our thoughts, take them literally and identify with them. For example, firmly believing a negative thought such as 'I am worthless'.

Instead of merging with thoughts, *defusion* allows us to distance ourselves from them. We do not take our thoughts literally, but observe them as temporary mental events.

Imagine that our mind is like a radio that never stops broadcasting stories. These stories are our thoughts. They can be images, memories or 'silly little sentences' that we say to ourselves. Some thoughts are positive, others negative. It is normal to have thoughts of both types.

The ability to distance ourselves from our thoughts allows us not to be overly influenced by the unpleasant ones, and to avoid dwelling on them (Hayes et al., 2004).

The process of defusion makes it possible to reduce the aversive-avoidance function of negative stimuli. Placing our behaviour under the control of all that flows, that is, in terms of operant, direct and derived contingencies based on value choices, rather than under strict verbal control, allows the use of new adaptive strategies and the achievement of psychological flexibility.

Defusion techniques seek to alter the undesirable functions of thoughts or other intimate events, rather than altering their form or frequency (Hayes et al., 2006).

As for the *conceptualised self,* it represents the idea we have of ourselves.

For example, if I were to meet someone for the first time, I could describe myself as follows: male sex, six feet tall, wearing a pair of jeans and a T-shirt. These are factual descriptors.

Instead, if we consider assertions such as I am a loser, I am a failure, I am lacking in willpower, we make evaluative descriptors that would not help anyone to immediately identify me. These are evaluative descriptors.

The conceptualised self is the result of a fusion of factual and evaluative descriptors, with the result that for those describing themselves 'I am a loser' may seem just as true as 'I am six feet tall'.

When we tightly cling to a negative concept we have of ourselves, preventing other more functional thoughts, feelings or behaviour from making room for themselves, psychological distress increases, creating alienation.

The alternative is to get in touch more deeply with a *self as a perspective*, that is, to be able to observe, assist or simply be aware.

This sense of self allows us to see that we are more than the unpleasant or negative thoughts we have of ourselves. Once this self as perspective is developed, thanks to cognitive defusion, human beings can get in touch with the present moment, and act in a committed manner, even in the presence of difficult or interfering private events.

The term 'committed action' refers to the choice to engage in behaviour that pursues one's life values, even at the cost of encountering unpleasant or painful experiences.

In practice, *committed actions* may include everyday behaviour, decisions, relationships and work activities that reflect what a person considers important and meaningful. The goal is to live consistently with one's values, rather than being driven by fears, anxieties or a desire to avoid pain.

In the ACT context, *values* are defined as freely chosen qualities of being or acting. They are fundamental in guiding behaviour so that it is in line with what the person really wants to be and do, representing what is most important in his or her life.

Values in ACT are not specific goals to be achieved, but rather directions in which one is committed to move. They are freely chosen and cannot be evaluated in terms of success or failure.

ACT encourages people to identify their values and to use these values as a guide for action, even when encountering difficult thoughts and feelings. This approach aims to increase psychological flexibility, enabling people to live richer, more meaningful lives in line with what they consider important.

This short story[13] provides a good example of what value is:

> In the street above the station there was a lady who couldn't park. She kept getting out of the parking space at the side of the road and trying again, she would miss her manoeuvre because she was not steering enough. Behind her, a queue of about ten cars blocked by her attempts, including mine. People started honking after not even five seconds, impatient, some waving their hands out of the window, increasing the tension. Since I too was in a hurry and was in danger of missing the train, I put on my four blinkers, got out of my car and walked towards the lady's car. I knocked on the window, the lady looked at me at first frightened, then lowered it halfway. I asked her if I could help her park. She was all red in the face, tight in her black coat and visibly flustered, she nodded her head twice. She sat me down in the driver's seat, I engaged reverse gear and parked in one manoeuvre. The lady said a half-voiced thank you, almost embarrassed, I told her not to worry and got out very quickly. As I climbed back into my car, ready to drive off again, people in cars started

---

[13] Matteo Bussola. (2018) La vita fino a te, Giulio Einaudi editore, Torino (pp 34–35).

honking at me. A guy in a white Mercedes pulled up next to me and invading the other lane expressed all his Venetian politeness, disturbing God, a few saints and even my mother. He sped off but was forced to nail the red light fifty metres ahead. My vein closed and someone inside me thought: I'm going to go over there, pull him out of the Mercedes by the ear and give him the opportunity to offer me a spontaneous apology. It was at that moment that I saw the lady from the car park walking away with brisk steps towards the station steps, dragging a pink trolley. She turned for a moment, realised I was looking at her, waved to me, I waved back, she smiled and a blue Panda honked at me, then I closed the door, started the car and turned off the four blinkers. When I drove off I had a fuck in my ears and a smile in my eyes and I thought that, in the end, the quality of each of your days only depends on which one is more valuable to you.

Problems of clinical interest usually arise when impulsive choices, aimed at immediate anxiety reduction, significantly outweigh committed, value-based actions.

Thus, a surgeon who pursued a medical career in order to please his father's wishes, failed to make contact with two values: an autonomous choice of career path and the possibility of maturing a more intimate and equal relationship with his father (Barnes-Holmes et al., 2004).

Clarifying these values and talking honestly with the father, despite the discomfort that would follow, would have required a lot of effort, not so much to get around the obstacle, but to accept it.

The problem, in this case, is the rule: I must not let him down, which, on the one hand, has the function of eliminating anxiety linked to taking responsibility for a personal choice, but, on the other hand, induces those who adhere to it to live someone else's life.

Finally, the practice of *mindfulness*, which is one of the cornerstones of third-generation therapies and is used in ACT to foster contact with direct contingencies, distancing from the literal content of internal states, and contact with a broader and more flexible sense of self, has proved very useful in clinical practice.

Mindfulness, which has been used for thousands of years for religious purposes by followers of Buddhism,[14] is now known in the West as the 'awareness that emerges through paying non-judgmental attention, moment by moment, to the succession of each experience' (Kabat-Zinn, 2003). Mindfulness is a muscle that benefits from regular training and in its essence involves these three steps:

1. Be present: intentionally bring your attention to the here-and-now experience with a dual quality of concentration and flexibility. Involve your senses (sight, hearing, touch, taste, smell) as a way of *anchoring* yourself *in the present* and centring yourself.

---

[14] Buddhism, which arose in the fifth-sixth centuries BC as a spiritual discipline, took on the character of a philosophical doctrine in the following centuries. Starting in India, it spread over the following centuries mainly in South-East Asia and the Far East, reaching the West from the nineteenth century onwards.

2. Open up: cultivate an attitude of curiosity and dispassionate receptivity, making space for whatever arises in your experience, allowing it to come and go freely without merging with it or trying to avoid it.
3. Return: gently bring your attention back to the here and now each time you wander, noticing and naming in a non-judgmental way what hooks you (e.g. 'there is a thought'). If your mind gets hooked a hundred times, you will have a hundred opportunities to practise mindfulness.

In conclusion, through the six cornerstones illustrated in the hexaflex model, ACT aims at achieving psychological flexibility. Success in therapy can be said to be achieved when patients develop this awareness: 'you alone have the right to judge your own behaviour, thoughts and emotions, and to take responsibility for them and accept the consequences'.[15]

1.3 Scientific Evidence and Application Contexts of ACT

As is well known, acceptance and commitment therapy (ACT) is a therapeutic approach supported by a solid scientific basis (Anchisi et al., 2017).

With the aim of developing a theory based on empirically effective techniques, since the publication of the first book *Acceptance and Commitment Therapy: An Experiential Approach to Behaviour Change* (Hayes et al., 1999), numerous studies have been conducted to investigate and prove the validity of the therapeutic model.

Since ACT postulates that pain arises from the maladaptive solutions employed to solve a given problem and that underlying psychopathology are mechanisms such as experiential avoidance and cognitive fusion, many of these studies have focused on exploring the specific components of ACT that contribute to psychological flexibility (defusion, acceptance, contact with the present moment, mindfulness and the value aspect).

Research has particularly focused on the effects ACT treatment can have on certain clinical and sub-clinical conditions, and on comparing ACT outcomes with other known and scientifically supported therapeutic interventions (Hayes & Smith, 2010).

Currently, the American Psychological Association [APA] lists ACT as a research-supported treatment, considering it effective for disorders such as mixed anxiety conditions, depression, obsessive-compulsive disorder, chronic or persistent pain in general, and psychosis.[16]

---

[15] First right of assertiveness (Anchisi & Gambotto Dessy, 2013).

[16] Cf. Div. 12 of the American Psychological Association [APA] (Society of Clinical Psychology: https://div12.org/treatments/). Again, consulting the website of the Association for Contextual Behavioral Science [ACBS] gives an idea of the breadth of research on the subject. The site provides a list of No. 494 meta-analyses, systematic, scoping or narrative reviews of the ACT evidence base; No. 1,099 Randomized Controlled Trials (RCTs) on ACT, conducted worldwide and pub-

Among the many clinical conditions that can be treated with ACT, the following studies aim to offer, without claiming to be exhaustive, an overview of the results identified through empirical research.

In *anxiety disorders,* the efficacy of ACT tools is well known, and how they have proven to be comparable or slightly more useful than cognitive-behavioural theory cognitive-behavioural therapy (CBT) (Hayes, 2020).

The ACT model does not necessarily aim to reduce or eliminate anxious inner experiences, but rather to help patients to manage them, that is, to function as well as possible despite anxiety, by means of increased psychological flexibility. It would seem, in fact, that there is a good correlation between psychological flexibility and anxiety and depression (Twohig & Levin, 2017).[17]

In *depressive disorders,* the cornerstones of psychological flexibility on which ACT is based act positively on rumination, a major contributor to depression, when used as a coping strategy to avoid difficult emotional experiences.

In fact, ACT tools make it possible to intervene on the relationship the patient has with thoughts, instead of acting on the literal content by trying to change it. By working on the value aspect, moreover, the patient feels engaged in pursuing more useful and functional actions, at the expense of maladaptive behaviours that often maintain or exacerbate symptoms (Hayes, 2020).[18]

---

lished in scientific journals; as well as a partial list of research examining mediation and moderation, and studies with negative or conflicting results (www.Contextualpsychology.org)

[17] In a meta-analysis conducted by Bluett et al. (2014), the authors examined precisely the relationship between psychological flexibility and anxiety dimensions. The results obtained from the research demonstrated a correlation between Hayes et al.'s AAQ scale (Hayes et al., 2004, cited by Bluett et al., 2014) and Bond et al.'s AAQ-II (Bond et al., 2011, cited by Bluett et al.. 2014), through which psychological flexibility was measured and general and specific measures of anxiety disorder. While emphasising the importance of conducting further studies and expanding the field of research, the authors pointed out that several randomised clinical trials (RCTs) conducted on ACT reveal the effectiveness of the treatment in anxiety disorders and depression. In particular, the results of the meta-analysis show modest support of the ACT protocol in mixed anxiety disorders, generalised anxiety disorder (GAD) and social phobia (SAD), obsessive compulsive disorder (OCD) and some obsessive compulsive spectrum disorders (Bluett et al., 2014). A similar result was reached by Landy et al. (2015) in their review of existing RCTs on ACT in the treatment of anxiety disorders, acknowledging the effectiveness of the ACT method in the treatment of anxiety disorders in adults, and further suggesting that this approach is to be considered effective on par with other treatments, such as CBT for SAD and mixed anxiety disorders, and relaxation techniques in GAD.

[18] In their randomised controlled trial, Bohlmeijer et al. (2011) investigated the effects of early ACT treatment on a sample of subjects with mild to moderate depressive symptoms. While highlighting the limitations of the study, the results showed a significant reduction in symptoms post-treatment and at 3-month follow-up compared to the wait list, used as a control group. Again, Heydari et al. (2018) conducted a study to explore the effectiveness of ACT treatment on anxiety and depressive symptoms. The quasi-experimental research conducted on the staff of the Razi Psychiatric Centre shows results in line with the initial hypothesis, showing a significant difference between the results obtained at post-test and follow-up of the experimental group compared to the control group. Therefore, despite the lack of a larger representative sample, which limits the possibility of generalisation, the authors suggest that ACT therapy has utility in reducing anxiety and depression. Finally, Ferreira et al. (2022) analysed 48 RCTs with a meta-analytic method. The results show

Another part of the research focused on the effects of ACT in the treatment of *chronic pain*, showing that the way a person avoids or copes with painful experiences can have an impact on the perception and ability to manage pain. Scientific evidence demonstrates the effectiveness of ACT: neurophysiological brain correlates associated with clinical improvement in chronic pain following the use of ACT tools have been traced (Galvez-Sánchez et al., 2021).[19]

Several studies have analysed the potential of ACT in the management of *obsessive-compulsive disorder* (OCD), with the aim of investigating its effectiveness, its ability to mitigate symptoms and improve cognitive flexibility in patients.[20]

In spite of the need for a larger number of randomised clinical trials, the results obtained legitimise the authors to consider acceptance and commitment therapy as a possible intervention for OCD, especially when used in conjunction with other valid therapies, such as SSRI (selective serotonin reuptake inhibitors) drugs, CBT or ERP (exposure and response prevention) therapy.

---

that group ACT treatment on a sample of adults had a significant outcome on both anxiety symptoms (with a medium to large effect, according to Cohen's standards) and depressive symptoms (with an impact that can be considered small to medium, according to the same standards) compared to the non-active groups, and active only in the case of depressive symptoms. The study therefore seems to confirm the usefulness of the approach in reducing the symptoms examined. However, it should be pointed out that in view of the considerable heterogeneity in the RCTs examined, the authors recommend caution when assessing the overall estimates.

[19] An example is provided by the study by Trindade et al. (2021), who, by means of the first systematic review and meta-analysis conducted on the topic, probed the effects of online ACT treatment on adults with chronic pain, whereas the more florid literature has focused on the benefits of in-person therapy. Using the analysis of five RCTs, the experimental groups undergoing online treatment were compared with control groups (TAU—treatment as usual, waiting list or non-ACT active control), and then compared the results obtained at post-treatment follow-up and at 6 months. The study showed that the online ACT intervention has significantly positive effects, with an average overall effect size at post-treatment follow-up and at 6 months with respect to pain acceptance and interference, and with overall reduced significance of pain intensity only at the 6-month follow-up. Reduced effects at both follow-ups were also found in the secondary outcomes (psychological flexibility, mindfulness and depressive symptoms), but only in the 6-month follow-up for anxiety symptoms. On the other hand, no significance emerged in favour of ACT treatment over value-based action. Of course, as the authors point out, the study's limitations include the small number of RCTs included, which represent a cross section of the research conducted on ACT treatment online so far.

[20] An example is the RCT by Twohig et al. (2010). In this study, which used a sample of 76 diagnosed adults, the authors compared the effect of ACT therapy without in-session exposure versus progressive relaxation techniques (PRTs), which were found to be significantly effective for OCD. The results, obtained through assessments with questionnaires administered pre- and post-treatment and at 3-month follow-up, showed improvements in both conditions. However, ACT treatment was significantly more effective in reducing OCD (at post-treatment and follow-up), in reducing depressive symptoms (where present and mild before treatment) and in improving quality of life-post-treatment. Equally favourable were the outcomes inherent in the psychological constructs associated with cognitive flexibility, which were greater, at least initially, in the ACT group. Soondrum et al. (2022) also addressed ACT in obsessive-compulsive disorder through a systematic review and meta-analysis. The authors compared ACT treatment, also in combination with other therapies, with active (medication, PRT, exposure-response prevention) and inactive control conditions, showing that ACT treatment had overall significant post-treatment improvements.

ACT and SchemaTherapy 457

In *psychotic disorders*, ACT aims to change the way the subject interacts with delusions and hallucinations. By promoting awareness and acceptance of psychotic experiences, the patient's propensity to avoid them, suppress them or believe their content to be true is reduced.

This more open and non-judgmental attitude towards symptoms leads to positive results in the treatment of the disorder, as shown by the research of Bach and Hayes (2002)[21] and Gaudiano et al. (2023).[22]

Although the authors emphasised the need to extend the scope of the studies, with reference to the duration of ACT treatment and the size of the sample analysed, respectively, the results obtained, although subject to cautious evaluation, legitimately lead one to believe that the combined delivery of ACT, administered by routine hospital staff, may be considered acceptable and feasible for this clinical population.

In addition to the aforementioned clinical conditions, the countless studies conducted show the effectiveness of ACT therapy in further areas, for example, smoking and substance addiction, burnout, stress-related problems, the management of diseases such as diabetes, cancer, epilepsy (Hayes & Smith, 2010; Harris, 2011), borderline personality disorder (Harris, 2011), weight control and the relationship with body image (Harris, 2011; Dufrene & Sandoz, 2019).

Improvements have also been observed in patients treated with ACT in *issues not strictly clinical*, related to various aspects of life, from work or school, to the relational and interpersonal sphere; from learning new skills and procedures, to coping with stigma and prejudice (Hayes & Smith, 2010; Dufrene & Sandoz, 2019).

The reason why such vast clinical and non-clinical areas respond positively to the use of this therapeutic approach is essentially due to the fact that ACT aims to

---

[21] In a randomised controlled trial, Bach and Hayes (2002) examined a sample of psychotic subjects with positive symptoms in an acute hospital to whom they administered brief ACT therapy (ACT+TAU) and evaluated whether or not this intervention produced significant changes according to the number of re-hospitalisations during the 4-month follow-up period. The data collected from the study showed a significant reduction in the rate of hospitalisation in the ACT condition compared to the active control group (TAU). They also showed that there were no significant differences between the two groups with respect to the presence of symptoms, their frequency and associated discomfort. On the other hand, in the ACT condition, the number of symptom reports was higher, suggesting a greater acceptance of the symptoms, attributable to a lower credibility of the symptoms than in the control group.

[22] In a recent RCT, Gaudiano et al. (2023) investigated the possibility of implementing acceptance and commitment therapy in hospital settings for schizophrenia spectrum disorders, by frontline clinicians, who are not experts in ACT, but are trained for the purpose. Specifically, the authors aimed to verify both patient satisfaction with the treatment and any changes in symptoms, functioning and re-hospitalisation during the 4-month follow-up. Patients in the experimental condition were treated with an ACT intervention combined with a classical intervention (TAU) and compared with a control group treated with TAU and TAM (time/attention support). The results showed that both treatments were deemed credible and satisfactory, improved the magnitude of symptoms and psychosocial functioning during follow-up, but not quality or value of life or psychological flexibility. The ACT condition proved significantly more satisfactory for patients in reducing psychological distress, and also significantly reduced the incidence of re-hospitalisation.

intervene on processes that are common to all human beings, since they are language-based.

Indeed, the main goal of acceptance and commitment therapy is to ensure that the patient achieves psychological flexibility, understood as the ability to respond adaptively to difficult feelings and situations (Dufrene & Sandoz, 2019).

The ACT approach does not aim to change the subject's internal states, but rather the way he or she relates to that experience, through the path of acceptance and awareness (Hayes & Smith, 2010). It is for this reason that it aims at cognitive defusion, strengthening contact with the present moment, reducing the suffering that results from this fusion, and taking committed actions that allow one to live a life in line with one's values (Harris, 2011).

To give an *example*, in *depersonalisation disorder* (DPD), acceptance and commitment therapy proves to be particularly useful in both reducing psychological distress and facilitating improved quality of life (Donnelly & Neziroglu, 2016).

In DPD, symptom-related experiences of anxiety and distress not only exacerbate the disorder, but also exacerbate the suffering experienced. This happens both because the processes of rumination and self-focusing prompt experiences of depersonalisation, and because the sufferer, driven by worry and the desire to get rid of it, often engages in an exhausting struggle with the disorder, with attempts at resolution or avoidance. Although understandable, these strategies do not prove useful in the long run, as they leave the person with little time, space and energy for anything else.

DPD's use of ACT, on the other hand, aims to increase the subject's psychological flexibility. This allows one to deflect from one's internal experiences by decreasing rumination and distress, and to stabilise on the present moment.

It also allows one to expose oneself more favourably to negative feelings, reduce experiential avoidance and proactively engage in achieving goals in line with one's values.

Again, the cardinal principle of psychological flexibility also proves useful in the treatment of *dysmorphic disorders*, where people experience negative feelings about their body image and the way they experience their physicality (Dufrene & Sandoz, 2019).

As is well known, acceptance and commitment therapy considers the influence that thoughts and emotions have on the subject's choices to be possibly problematic, rather than the internal states per se.

Consistent with this view, the ACT approach postulates that, beyond negative impressions of one's appearance, what generates pain is that these perceptions, experienced as real, significantly influence a person's life.

Indeed, in those who suffer from eating disorders and related body image problems, there is a high presence of avoidance and suppression strategies for painful emotional states, as well as dysfunctional behaviour that exacerbates psychic distress. Moreover, those who engage in a battle against their bodies, immersed in obsessive thoughts, worries and control efforts, miss out on opportunities to engage in other rewarding and stimulating experiences.

The authors illustrate how through ACT it is possible to break free from this struggle and focus on the flexibility of the body image (Dufrene & Sandoz, 2019).

Also in the area of *substance abuse,* research is favourable towards acceptance and commitment therapy, showing positive results both during and after treatment (Hayes, 2020). Particular emphasis is placed on the key role that acceptance and flexibility have in reducing avoidance strategies, typical in addiction, in managing craving and in recognising triggers and compulsive thoughts that drive use.

Defusion practices also help people distance themselves from self-critical and judgmental thoughts and internalised stigmatising ones, while working on one's values supports a commitment to pursue healthier life goals, as well as a determination to face challenges, relapses and difficult times.[23]

To close this overview, it should be noted that a considerable amount of research has investigated the effectiveness of ACT interventions in the treatment of children and adolescents: at the end of 2010, ACT for Kids, a Special Interest Group (SIG) affiliated with ACT-Italy, was established, specifically dedicated to childhood and adolescence (Anchisi et al., 2017).

Several studies have also looked at topics such as parenting, the management of child-parent conflict and the prevention of problematic behaviour and the couple relationship.[24]

Although the high heterogeneity makes any generalisations risky, the outlook is optimistic, as the results suggest that ACT, together with the other third-generation interventions analysed, can be considered a useful transdiagnostic intervention in

---

[23] In the randomised controlled trial conducted by Shorey et al. (2017), the authors examined the possibility of successfully integrating a group treatment based on ACT and MBRP (Mindfulness-Based Relapse Prevention) with usual treatment in a residential substance addiction programme. The aim was to assess, by means of pre- and post-treatment questionnaires, the desire to use substances, psychological flexibility and innate propensity for mindfulness at the end of therapy, and to explore the possibility of benefits in residential settings. Indeed, previous research has indicated that mindfulness-based interventions can reduce desire to use and increase dispositional (innate) awareness, which in turn is negatively correlated with substance use. They also show that there is a negative correlation between the latter and psychological flexibility (focus of ACT). The results of the study showed that there were no significant differences between the two groups, but there was a small difference in the post-treatment effect size with regard to substance craving and increased psychological flexibility in the experimental group. In addition, a higher importance was found for the ACT group, which was negatively associated with drug craving and positively with psychological flexibility.

[24] In their meta-analysis, Perkins et al. (2023) analysed 50 RCTs in order to determine whether the third-generation therapies examined (ACT, compassion-focused therapy, mindfulness-based cognitive therapy, and metacognitive therapy) could be considered effective for young users (children and adolescents) with respect to emotional symptoms/internalised problems, behavioural difficulties/externalising problems, interference from difficulties (emotional or physical), third-wave processes (e.g. acceptance, awareness, self-compassion), well-being, quality of life and physical problems (health/pain). Significant differences were found from the control groups (active and inactive) regarding emotional symptoms/internalising problems, interference from difficulties, third-wave processes, well-being and quality of life, but not for behavioural difficulties/externalising problems and physical health/pain.

the treatment of young people, not least by virtue of the long-term benefits on the emotional sphere and internalised problems.

2 Schema Therapy

Schema therapy belongs to the group of third-generation psychotherapies, that is, the set of psychotherapeutic approaches that have developed since the 1990s, in continuity with earlier behavioural and cognitive therapies.

Its founder is Jeffrey Young, a cognitive psychologist who sought to expand the boundaries of Aaron Beck's (the father of cognitive therapy) model by integrating elements of behavioural, cognitive, gestalt, psychodynamic and attachment theory therapies to achieve a therapeutic model initially designed to more effectively treat personality disorders resistant to standard CBT treatment (Arntz & Jacob, 2013).

It should be emphasised that schema therapy is not intended to replace other approaches (such as CBT), but rather as a possible supplement or enhancement where treatment of those pathological aspects of personality that underlie the disorder or keep it active is needed (Young et al., 2007).

Moreover, it has been noted that the main features of ACT, with the six foundational points of hexaflex, are entirely consistent with schema therapy, and therefore the latter can also be considered a contextual therapy[25].

First, in the TS, the centrality given to needs implies that there is no intrinsic truth concerning schemas: a schema can be adaptive or maladaptive, depending on the context and its ability to help the person experience the satisfaction of his or her needs in that context.

The schema approach is therefore a functional-contextual model in which the fulfilment of needs is the medium of context.

The following implications, important for the therapist, derive from this contextual perspective:

1. Patterns and patterns of behaviour are functional (i.e. they ultimately fulfil some function) and it is necessary to get to know them.
2. Context is to be understood in a very broad sense, extending from the present situational causes to the developmental antecedents of the patterns (e.g. childhood trauma).
3. Changing certain aspects of the context, either in the therapist's office (e.g. by favouring defusion), or in the patient's personal life (by getting needs met) can lead to therapeutic change and is therefore an important aspect of treatment.

---

[25] Roedinger E., Stevens B.A., Brockman R. (2018), Contextual Schema Therapy: a third generation integrated approach for the treatment of personality disorders, Edizioni Centro Studi Erickson, Trento.

4. The therapist's ultimate goal is to build a healthy and flexible self, which aims at the fulfilment of one's needs, taking into account a long-term time perspective and the nature of one's values.

2.1 Theoretical Foundations of Schema Therapy: Core Needs; Early Maladaptive Schemas and Their Domains; Coping Styles and Modes

The central theoretical core of schema therapy is the belief that every human being, from childhood onwards, has basic needs to be met (*core needs*):

(a) The need for security, stability, care and acceptance
(b) The need for autonomy, skills and a sense of identity
(c) The need to be free to express one's needs and emotions
(d) The need for spontaneity and play
(e) The need for realistic limits that foster the emergence of self-control

This therapeutic approach argues that mental health depends on the ability to meet one's needs effectively. If basic needs are not adequately met during childhood, so-called *early maladaptive schemas* (EMS) develop.

A 'schema' is a cognitive model that organises information about ourselves, others and the world, based on childhood experiences and influencing emotions, behaviour and relationships. It develops during childhood or adolescence and evolves throughout life.

Despite being a source of discomfort, these maladaptive patterns are maintained because they represent what is known and familiar, from which we do not want to separate ourselves. Consequently, we are attracted to situations that reinforce the patterns, because after all, they are what we know best and are used to.

These patterns can be triggered by specific situations that somehow evoke painful events from the past and can be relived several times throughout life, causing intense suffering and leading to dysfunctional behaviour. Young specifically identified 18 EMS pertaining to five domains:

1. *Disconnection and Rejection*: the expectation that one's needs for security, protection, stability, nurturing, empathy, shared feelings, acceptance and respect will not be met in a predictable manner.
2. *Impaired Autonomy and Performance*: this domain concerns the perception of not being able to survive or function independently.
3. *Impaired Limits*: this domain concerns the perception that rules and restrictions are not important.
4. *Other Directedness*: this domain concerns the tendency to put others before oneself.
5. *Over-vigilance and Inhibition*: this domain concerns the tendency to suppress one's feelings and needs, often to avoid making mistakes or being criticised (Young et al., 2007).

Summary table of early maladaptive schemas

Domain	EMS	Main features	Experiences
Disconnection and rejection	Abandonment	Those with this pattern have the perception that others will never be able to continuously provide for their emotional needs or support as they may suddenly disappear from their lives or may abandon them in favour of someone better.	An experience of unpredictability/unreliability of emotional relationships is present. The person experiences a continuous state of anxiety, sadness, anger or is emotionally cold and detached.
	Mistrust/abuse	One who has this pattern has the belief that others will hurt, exploit, humiliate, cheat or manipulate him/her. They believe that pain is caused intentionally or is the result of unjustified and extreme neglect.	The typical attitude is one of being constantly on the defensive, in constant tension.
	Emotional deprivation	Applying this pattern involves believing that one's emotional needs will never be met (or at least not adequately) by others. There are three forms of emotional deprivation: due to lack of care (lack of affection, attention, warmth); due to lack of empathy (lack of listening and understanding, intimacy); due to lack of protection (lack of guidance).	Chronic feelings of sadness, isolation and loneliness are often present.
	Defectiveness/shame	The person with this pattern has the feeling of being wrong, inferior, bad, lacking in some fundamental area of life. She fears that, on the basis of this inadequacy, she will be rejected.	He experiences a deep sense of shame with respect to his own faults and often does not allow himself to be approached by others. Tends to be hypersensitive to criticism, reproach or rejection.
	Social isolation	There is a feeling of being isolated from the rest of the world, of being different from others and/or not being part of any group or community.	These people experience a chronic sense of alienation.

Impaired autonomy and Performance	Dependence/ incompetence	The person has the feeling of being unable to handle daily responsibilities adequately without considerable help from others.	These people have an experience of helplessness and ineptitude. They cannot be independent or make decisions.
	Vulnerability to harm/ illness	These people have an exaggerated fear that something imminent and catastrophic (medically, emotionally or from external events such as accidents or natural disasters) may occur at any time and that it is impossible to prevent it.	They present a chronic fear in anticipation of something catastrophic.
	Enmeshment/ undeveloped self	There is excessive emotional involvement in significant relationships (especially with family members of origin or partners). There is a lack of social development and a clear personal identity.	There may be a chronic feeling of emptiness and disorientation, of feeling merged with others or of not having a sufficient individual identity.
	Failure	This pattern leads to the feeling of failure and of not being able to achieve one's goals, of having fewer capabilities than the peer group.	It implies a chronic feeling of being unintelligent, inept or untalented.
Impaired limits	Entitlement/grandiosity	Those with this pattern feel superior to others, endowed with special rights, privileges, not bound by normal social rules. They tend to have unrealistic or unreasonable demands or intentions that do not take into account the needs of others.	He often has an overly competitive or controlling attitude in order to satisfy his own desires; it is difficult for him to feel empathy and understand the wishes and needs of others.
	Insufficient self-control/self-discipline	People with this pattern lack sufficient self-control, handle frustrations ineffectively, and do not contain excessive manifestations of impulses.	Tendency to avoid conflictual, painful situations, confrontations or responsibilities at the expense of personal fulfilment, dedication or moral integrity

(continued)

(continued)

Domain	EMS	Main features	Experiences
Other directedness	Subjugation	Excessive tendency to repress one's preferences, needs, desires and emotions by submitting. These behaviours are enacted to avoid all possible negative consequences.	People with this pattern are overly complacent and leave control of their lives to others
	Self-sacrifice	Excessive dedication to satisfying the needs of others and renunciation of one's own gratifications. To avoid feelings of guilt they take care of the suffering of others whom they tend to consider weaker than they really are.	Sometimes the feeling of dissatisfaction with one's own needs can lead to developing resentment or irritation towards those they care for.
	Approval-seeking / recognition-seeking	Excessive importance is given to the approval of others, economic and social status, outward appearance and success, sacrificing the development of a stable and authentic sense of identity.	Frequently, this leads to making important life decisions in a way that is inauthentic, unsatisfactory or hypersensitive to rejection.
Over-vigilance and inhibition	Negativity/pessimism	Pervasive tendency to focus on the negative aspects of life, minimising the positive ones. Exaggeratedly pessimistic expectations are often present in many areas.	Lives in a state of hyper-alertness, indecision and chronic fear of making mistakes
	Emotional inhibition	Excessive inhibition of spontaneous actions and feelings, usually with the aim of avoiding the disapproval of others, feeling ashamed or losing control of one's impulses.	The person has difficulty freely expressing their needs, feelings and emotions (especially anger). There is a lack of spontaneity and an excessive tendency to rely on rationality.
	Unrelenting standards	People with this pattern strive to meet high internalised standards while feeling under pressure. They tend to be hypercritical of themselves, perfectionists, follow strict moral rules and need to work and achieve more and more.	Very often there is significant deprivation of pleasure, recreation, a sense of self-worth and satisfying interpersonal relationships.
	Punitiveness	There is a feeling that people should be severely punished when they make mistakes. There is often a reluctance to consider extenuating circumstances, accept human imperfections or empathise with the feelings of others.	These people tend to be angry, intolerant, punitive and impatient even with themselves.

An individual's maladaptive behavioural responses triggered by the activation of a dysfunctional pattern are called *'coping styles'*. These behaviours, although initially adaptive during childhood (they can be considered functional survival mechanisms), tend to become maladaptive over time, maintaining the dysfunctional patterns (Basile & Calzoni, 2013).

Young groups coping styles into three categories: surrender, avoidance (escape) and counterattack (overcompensation):

1. *Surrender*: the individual surrenders to the pattern, accepting it as true and submitting to it. For example, an individual with the dependency pattern might seek out strong people to depend on.
2. *Avoidance (escape)*: this coping style leads to avoidance of schema activation. For example, an individual with the distrust/abuse schema might avoid interpersonal relationships altogether in order not to get in touch with his or her schema.
3. *Counterattack* (overcompensation): in this case, the individual reacts to the activation of the schema by opposing it and behaving as if the opposite were true. For example, an individual with the pattern of inadequacy might behave infallibly and perfectly.

Schema therapy involves the possibility of transforming a maladaptive schema into a more functional one by working towards cognitive, emotional and behavioural change through learning new adaptive strategies and more functional coping styles (Young et al., 2007).

The concept of 'schema' was later joined by that of *'mode'*. Observing that, especially in severe personality disorders, simultaneous activation or rapid alternation of patterns could occur, Young defined mode as 'the set of patterns or manifestations of patterns—adaptive and maladaptive—that are activated in an individual at a given time'.

If schemas can be interpreted as the person's underlying 'traits', then modes would represent their manifestation (i.e. state) at a given time and context.

The modes are classified as 'child modes' (which may be vulnerable or angry or unruly), parent modes (punitive, critical or demanding), 'coping modes' (of submission, avoidance or overcompensation/attack) and 'functional modes' (those of the healthy adult or happy child) (Basile & Calzoni, 2013).

2.2 Therapeutic Goals of Schema Therapy

Schema therapy aims at enhancing the modes of the healthy adult and the happy child in us, who cares for and values our vulnerable side, protects us from self-criticism or unrealistic demands, modifies dysfunctional behaviour and is oriented towards our own values in order to experience healthy activities and relationships and realise our goals.

TS aims to identify with the patient their patterns and dysfunctional modes and, where these originated in childhood, to recognise their effects in adult life, in order to actively find functional ways to modify them (Taylor et al., 2017).

In fact, schema therapy emphasises people's emotions and needs, trying to identify which experiences are activated at a given moment, and assists the patient in finding adaptive and healthy ways to satisfy their needs. It provides an understanding of current difficulties through episodes and dynamics from childhood and adolescence, reworking and transcribing painful experiences of the past to foster new and corrective experiences in the present.

To achieve this, this approach uses cognitive, behavioural and emotional activation techniques adapted, calibrated or created specifically for TS.

In schema therapy, the cognitive and behavioural techniques of standard cognitive-behavioural therapy are also integrated, which have proven highly effective in reducing symptoms and changing fundamental beliefs, for example, identifying and changing one's beliefs, reducing perfectionism or self-criticism, analysing pros and cons, examining techniques to improve social skills and increasing positive activities or relaxation techniques.

A key element in the therapeutic process is the setting up of the *therapeutic relationship*, which is seen as a secure basis and a fundamental factor for change.

The therapist, in schema therapy, presents himself/herself as a person capable of warmth and affection, willing to satisfy the patient's basic needs for security, stability, acceptance and autonomy not met in childhood, in terms of 'limited reparenting'.

In a gentle and clear way, the therapist confronts the person with his or her suffering and coping strategies. Through empathic confrontation, he tries to relate to all parts of the patient: his most vulnerable part (the so-called vulnerable child) and his different coping strategies; his severe, criticising and devaluing part (the so-called internalised parental part); and his healthy parts (the so-called happy child and healthy adult), with the aim of building a healing dialogue with each of them.

As in other cognitive approaches, in schema therapy one works with specific goals, and the therapist plays an active role in assisting the individual in achieving them.

The patient and the therapist, for example, agree together on which experiential exercises to carry out outside the sessions, in order to replace maladaptive coping strategies with more functional responses.

These exercises help patients recognise how life decisions influence their behavioural patterns and experience more functional choices.

During the sessions, the therapist prepares the patient to overcome possible obstacles through imaginative and role-playing techniques. After the execution of a task, the results are analysed together (Young et al., 2007).

2.3 The Phases of Schema Therapy

Schema therapy is a highly structured type of psychotherapy that develops through three distinct phases: assessment and psycho-education, treatment and change, and autonomy.

The *first phase, assessment and psycho-education,* focuses on assisting the patient in analysing the main problems. This phase helps to identify patterns and 'modes', understand their origins and make connections between them and current problems in the patient's life.

The therapist works to create a therapeutic relationship in which the patient feels understood, respected and safe. Together, the therapist and the patient construct an individual template that collects and explains the main problems and provides guidance for the second phase of treatment. In some cases, during the assessment phase, various questionnaires can be used, for example, the Young Schema Questionnaire (Young & Brown, 2005) or the Young Parenting Inventory (Young et al., 2003) to elaborate with the patient a diagnosis and a personal conceptualisation of his or her distress.

In the *second phase, treatment and change*, various techniques and strategies are activated in a structured and integrated manner. These include experiential/emotional techniques, cognitive techniques, behavioural techniques and relational techniques.

Their common goal is to correct patterns and replace maladaptive coping styles with more functional patterns of behaviour. This allows the patient to develop and strengthen his part as a 'healthy adult' and to satisfy his needs in a healthy and rewarding way, following his own life values.

During the *third, autonomy phase,* the patient assumes more and more responsibility, develops healthy relationships outside the therapeutic context and increases social and work integration. In this phase, contacts between the patient and the therapist gradually decrease (Young et al., 2007).

2.4 Scientific Evidence and Application Contexts of Schema Therapy

The first specific interventions of schema therapy concerned the treatment of *personality disorders*, especially in those cases found to be particularly resistant to treatment with standard CBT, concerning people with severe borderline and narcissistic personality disorders (Arntz & van Genderen, 2009; Young et al., 2007). The treatment of such disorders is currently the one most supported by scientific evidence, and is widely supported in the literature, both in terms of individual and group therapy (Farrell et al., 2009[26]; Giesen-Bloo et al., 2006[27]).

The use of schema therapy appears to lead to a significant reduction in symptoms and an increase in patients' quality of life (Zhang et al., 2023[28]). The technique has also been used with positive results on symptom reduction in specific populations such as criminals with personality disorder (Bernstein et al., 2023[29]).

In *borderline personality disorder*, treatment is long and complex. Those who treat this type of disorder face a turbulent path, and often have to deal with the activation of their own patterns.

Affected patients are often seen as manipulative and selfish, although such a view is deleterious, as it risks reinforcing the patient's dysfunctional modes and patterns. Instead, the more constructive view is that of the patient understood, according to the model, as a 'vulnerable child'. These persons would in fact assume

---

[26] The authors conducted a multicentre, randomised study that set out to compare the effectiveness of schema therapy (ST) and transference-focused psychotherapy (TFP) in patients with borderline personality disorder. Eighty-eight patients were recruited and subsequently divided into the two groups ST and TFP. Patient assessments were carried out prior to randomisation and then every 3 months for 3 years. The study concluded that at 3 years, ST and TFP were effective in reducing the psychopathological dysfunction specific to borderline personality disorder and generally improving quality of life.

[27] The authors tested the efficacy of adding group schema therapy (ST) for a duration of 8 months and a total of 30 sessions to routine individual psychotherapy (TAU) for borderline personality disorder (BPD). Patients ($N = 32$) were randomly assigned to the ST-TAU group or to TAU alone. Dropout was 0% in the ST group and 25% in the TAU group. Significant reductions in BPD symptoms and overall severity of psychiatric symptoms were observed in the ST-TAU group, as well as an improvement in global function with large treatment effects. At the end of treatment, 94% of the ST-TAU group compared to 16% of the TAU group no longer met the diagnostic criteria for BPD ($p < .001$). This study supports the efficacy of ST group therapy as an effective treatment for BPD leading to recovery and overall improvement of function.

[28] In this meta-analysis, a literature search was conducted using PubMed, Embase, Web of Science, CENTRAL, Psycinfo and Ovid Medline. Eight randomised controlled trials with a total of 587 participants and seven single-group trials with a total of 163 participants were identified. The study revealed that compared to the control, the use of schema therapy had a moderate effect in reducing personality disorder symptoms. Analysing the secondary outcomes showed that compared to the control, there was also a moderate effect on increased quality of life and that there was indeed a reduction in early maladaptive patterns. In conclusion, this study expresses itself favourably on the use of this model in the treatment of personality disorders.

[29] In this recent randomised controlled trial, a population of violent offenders with personality disorder was examined. The aim was to test the effectiveness of a long-term psychotherapeutic intervention as a rehabilitation strategy for these patients. A schema therapy approach was compared with TAU (treatment as usual) at eight forensic hospitals in the Netherlands. The sample included 103 male offenders with antisocial, narcissistic, borderline, paranoid or Cluster B personality disorder not otherwise specified. The duration of treatment was 3 years, and an evaluation was carried out every 6 months. The primary outcome was rehabilitation that included gradual reintegration into the community and improvement of personality disorder symptoms. Significant improvements occurred in both the schema therapy group and the TAU group, although the former was superior in both primary outcomes. The results of the study contradict the pessimistic view regarding the treatment of offenders with personality disorder and support the effectiveness of long-term rehabilitation therapy aimed at their reintegration into the community.

inappropriate behaviour not out of selfishness, but out of desperation, as they are in need and lack someone to look after their safety.

In general, active participation on the part of the therapist is necessary, who must encourage the patient to express his or her emotions and needs. An approach based on silence and reflection seems not to be indicated, as silence is often interpreted as disinterest or lack of support.

The effectiveness of schema therapy applied to the treatment of *narcissistic personality disorder* has been well described in the literature (Arntz & Jacob, 2013; Zhang et al., 2023; Bamelis et al., 2014[30]), although the treatment presents considerable difficulties.

Narcissistic patients are incapable of having authentic affective experiences, so it is common for maladaptive patterns to persist throughout their lives, unless they begin therapy or experience a constructive relationship with a person capable of counteracting these patterns.

The therapist will have to build an alliance with the patient's functional modes and at the same time counteract the maladaptive ones. It will be crucial to show empathy and compassion for these patients, who must feel that sincere understanding and deep sorrow is felt for them.

Even outside the context of personality disorders, it is worth emphasising that numerous studies are emerging that show an objective benefit in the use of schema therapy.

For example, it has found application in the treatment of depressive symptoms, particularly chronic *depression* (Carter et al., 2013[31]).

---

[30] A multicentre randomised controlled trial with a single-blind parallel design was conducted between 2006 and 2011 in 12 Dutch mental health institutions. A total of 323 patients with personality disorder were randomly assigned (TS, $N = 147$; usual treatment, $N = 135$; clarification-oriented psychotherapy, $N = 41$). The primary outcome was recovery from the personality disorder 3 years after the start of treatment (assessed by blinded interviewers). Secondary outcomes were dropout rates and measures of personality disorder traits, depressive and anxiety disorders, general psychological complaints, general and social functioning, discrepancy between self and ideal, and quality of life. Schema therapy was superior to usual treatment with regard to recovery, other interview-based outcomes and dropouts.

[31] In this randomised clinical trial, the comparative effectiveness of CBT and TS for depression was examined. One hundred participants with major depression received weekly sessions of cognitive-behavioural therapy or schema therapy for 6 months, followed by monthly therapy sessions for 6 months. Key outcomes were comparisons over the course of the weekly and monthly therapy sessions together with remission and recovery rates. Further analysis looked at the outcome for those with chronic depression and personality disorders in comorbidity. TS was not significantly better (nor worse) than CBT for the treatment of depression. The therapies had comparable efficacy on all key outcomes. There were no differential treatment effects for those with chronic depression or personality disorders. This preliminary research indicates that TS may provide an effective alternative therapy for depression, although it is not the therapy of narrow choice.

Huibers and Renner (2016)[32] are the first to have developed a specific treatment model for this disorder, identifying avoidance modes and coping styles as a key aspect in maintaining the depressive picture.

Indeed, a strong correlation seems to emerge between the pervasiveness and severity of the patterns, on the one hand, and the severity of depressive symptoms, on the other (Basile et al., 2018).[33]

In *obsessive-compulsive disorder* (OCD), the patient would aim to prevent an emotion of guilt for one's own responsibility, evaluated as severe or unacceptable.

The literature shows that early experiences can sensitise individuals to emotions of guilt and disgust, acquiring maladaptive patterns that can be overcome through possible therapeutic intervention.

Schema therapy in this context aims to reduce the vicious circles underlying the maintenance of symptoms by decreasing the sensitivity to guilt (Basile et al., 2017[34]).

Preliminary research suggests that schema therapy can be successfully extended to *mood and anxiety disorders* (Hawke & Provenker 2011; Peeters et al., 2021[35]). Studies, which undoubtedly need further investigation, have shown that people with

---

[32] The aim of this study was to test the effects of individualised schema therapy (ST) in patients with chronic depression. The sample included 25 patients with major depressive disorder. When comparing the treatment period with the control period without treatment, the therapeutic intervention had a significant and large effect on depressive symptoms. However, this study has limitations, such as the small sample size and the lack of a control group. These results provide evidence that TS could be an effective treatment for patients with chronic depression.

[33] The aim of this study was to corroborate Renner's ST model for depression by investigating maladaptive schemas, dysfunctional modes and avoidant coping styles in a large non-clinical sample and in two subgroups of subjects with high and low rates of depression. Within the total sample, a positive correlation was observed between depression levels and most maladaptive patterns, dysfunctional modes and intrapsychic avoidant coping strategies. Significant differences emerged between the two subgroups. Despite some important reservations, such as the recruitment of a non-clinical sample, the authors argue that the data obtained further support Renner's schema model for depression, adding some new evidence on the role of specific maladaptive modes and avoidant coping strategies, which seem to play a role in this psychopathological condition.

[34] The objective of this study was to explore coping patterns, modes and styles in outpatients with obsessive-compulsive disorder (OCD). Thirty-four patients with OCD were recruited. Patterns, modalities and coping styles were measured. Indices of OCD symptoms, levels of guilt and disgust were also collected. Descriptive, correlation and multiple regression analyses were performed. The work reports that the severity of OCD symptoms was significantly associated with patterns of social isolation, failure, subordination and punishment, and the punitive parent mode. A positive relationship was also found between OCD severity, avoidance and intrapsychic coping styles and disgust intensity. An important limitation of the study is the lack of a control group.

[35] This systematic review examined the evidence regarding the effectiveness of schema therapy for anxiety disorders, obsessive-compulsive disorder (OCD) and post-traumatic stress disorder (PTSD). A database search (PsycINFO, MEDLINE, EMBASE, WEB OF SCIENCE and Academic Search Ultimate) was conducted to identify eligible studies until 2 April 2021. A total of 41 studies were identified as eligible according to topic. However, only six (comprising 316 patients with anxiety, OCD and PTSD) were eligible for inclusion. The results showed that schema therapy can lead to beneficial effects in disorder-specific symptoms and early maladaptive patterns. However, the authors point out several methodological limitations observed in the analysed studies. Thus, TS appears to be a promising treatment for anxiety, OCD and PTSD. The review concludes by sug-

these disorders exhibit high levels of early maladaptive schemas, some of which seem to reflect the characteristics of specific disorders.

Still, positive preliminary results on the effectiveness of the schema therapy model applied to the treatment of *post-traumatic stress disorder* (PTSD) emerge from the literature (Peeters et al., 2021). Indeed, recent studies have suggested that schemas play a key role in the development and maintenance of this condition (Boterhoven de Haan et al., 2019[36]).

Schema therapy has been identified as a potentially valid treatment option in *eating disorders*. Conducted with group sessions, the research has produced positive results especially for binge eating disorder (Simpson et al., 2010[37]; McIntosh et al., 2016[38]), although the study needs to be expanded.

The treatment of eating disorders is a difficult undertaking because only a relatively small proportion of patients respond to and complete standard cognitive-behavioural therapy (CBT), given the prevalence of comorbidities and complex personality traits in this population.

Regarding the use of schema therapy in *substance use disorders,* data in the literature are still limited and focus more on the study regarding the types of schemas that are activated in these conditions (Knapík & Slancová, 2020; Straver, 2017; Kersten, 2012).

To conclude this brief overview, let us look at the *timing.*

Schema therapy is generally not considered a short form of psychotherapy: the duration of treatment may depend on various factors, including the severity of the

---

gesting the need for future research that will be crucial to build a solid evidence base for the efficacy of schema therapy in chronic anxiety, OCD and PTSD.

[36] The article describes some key components of TS and how these can be applied to the treatment of patients with more chronic or complex forms of PTSD. These components include the formulation of a patient's symptom presentation in terms of their early maladaptive patterns (SMP) and modes.

[37] This time-limited pilot study aimed to evaluate the effectiveness of group schema therapy on a sample of eight participants with eating disorders. The results suggested that most participants achieved clinically significant improvements in terms of pattern severity, eating disorder symptoms, anxiety levels and quality of life. However, the results must be viewed with caution due to the small sample size and lack of long-term follow-up. Unfortunately, due to practical constraints, it was not possible to include a face-to-face comparative control group in the study. Therefore, it is not possible to determine to what extent these results are due to the participants' response to therapy in general, group TS in particular, or other factors. However, the initial results suggest that group-based schema therapy may be beneficial for patients with eating disorders.

[38] The current study compared traditional CBT with two enhanced versions of CBT: schema therapy and appetite-focused CBT. A total of 112 women with binge eating transdiagnosed DSM-IV were involved and randomly assigned to the three types of therapy. Treatment consisted of weekly sessions for 6 months, followed by monthly sessions for a further 6 months. The primary outcome was the frequency of binge eating episodes. Secondary and tertiary outcomes included other behavioural and psychological aspects of the eating disorder and other areas of functioning. No significant differences were found between the three therapy groups for primary or other outcomes. In all groups, large improvements in binge eating frequency, symptoms of other eating disorders and general functioning were observed. Schema therapy and appetite-focused CBT appear to be suitable alternative treatments to traditional CBT for binge eating.

patient's problems, the frequency of sessions and the effectiveness of the coping strategies the patient develops during treatment (Young et al., 2007). For example, for the treatment of borderline personality disorder, 2–3 years of therapy are required in most cases, sometimes even longer.

Bibliography

ACBS-Association for Contextual Behavioral Science. (2024). State of the ACT evidence. https://contextualscience.org. Ultimo accesso 13 Feb 2024.

Anchisi, R., & Gambotto Dessy, M. (2013). *Manuale di assertività. Teoria e pratica delle abilità relazionali: alla scoperta di sé e degli altri*. FrancoAngeli.

Anchisi, R., Moderato, P., & Pergolizzi, F. (a cura di). (2017). *Roots and Leaves. Radici e sviluppi contestualisti in terapia comportamentale e cognitiva*. Franco Angeli.

Arntz, A., & Jacob, G. (2013). *Schema therapy in practice: An introductory guide to the schema mode approach*. Wiley Blackwell.

Arntz, A., & van Genderen, H. (2009). *Schema therapy for borderline personality disorder*. Wiley Blackwell.

Bach, P., & Hayes, S. C. (2002). The use of acceptance and commitment therapy to prevent the rehospitalization of psychotic patients: A randomized controlled trial. *Journal of Consulting and Clinical Psychology, 70*(5), 1129–1139. https://doi.org/10.1037/0022-006X.70.5.1129

Bamelis, L. L., Evers, S. M., Spinhoven, P., & Arntz, A. (2014). Results of a multicenter randomized controlled trial of the clinical effectiveness of schema therapy for personality disorders. *American Journal of Psychiatry, 171*(3), 305–322. https://doi.org/10.1176/appi.ajp.2013.12040518. PMID: 24322378.

Barnes-Holmes, Y., Barnes-Holmes, D., McHugh, L., & Hayes, S. C. (2004). Relational Frame Theory: Some implication for understanding and treating human psychopatology. *International Journal of Psychology and Psychological Therapy, 4*, 355–375.

Basile, B., & Calzoni, R. (2013). *La Schema Therapy: Un approccio cognitivo orientato alle emozioni e ai ricordi infantili*. Rivista ordine psicologi Puglia.

Basile, B., Tenore, K., Luppino, O., & Mancini, F. (2017). Schema therapy mode model applied to OCD. *Clinical Neuropsychiatry, 14*, 407–414.

Basile, B., Tenore, K., & Mancini, F. (2018). Investigating schema therapy constructs in individuals with depression. *Journal of Psychology and Clinical Psychiatry, 9*(2), 214–221.

Bernstein, D. P., Keulen-de Vos, M., Clercx, M., de Vogel, V., Kersten, G. C. M., Lancel, M., Jonkers, P. P., Bogaerts, S., Slaats, M., Broers, N. J., Deenen, T. A. M., & Arntz, A. (2023). Schema therapy for violent PD offenders: A randomized clinical trial. *Psychological Medicine, 53*(1), 88–102. https://doi.org/10.1017/S0033291721001161. Epub 2021 Jun 15. PMID: 34127158; PMCID: PMC9874993.

Bluett, E. J., Homan, K. J., Morrison, K. L., Levin, M. E., & Twohig, M. P. (2014). Acceptance and commitment therapy for anxiety and OCD spectrum disorders: An empirical review. *Journal of Anxiety Disorders, 28*(6), 612–624. https://doi.org/10.1016/j.janxdis.2014.06.008

Bohlmeijer, E. T., Fledderus, M., Rokx, T. A. J. J., & Pieterse, M. E. (2011). Efficacy of an early intervention based on acceptance and commitment therapy for adults with depressive symptomatology: Evaluation in a randomized controlled trial. *Behaviour Research and Therapy, 49*(1), 62–67. https://doi.org/10.1016/j.brat.2010.10.003

Bond, F. W., Hayes, S. C., Baer, R. A., Carpenter, K. M., Guenole, N., Orcutt, H. K., Waltz, T., & Zettle, R. D. (2011). *Acceptance and Action Questionnaire II* (AAQ-II) [Database record]. APA PsycTests. https://doi.org/10.1037/t11921-000

Boterhoven de Haan, K. L., Fassbinder, E., Hayes, C., & Lee, C. W. (2019). A schema therapy approach to the treatment of posttraumatic stress disorder. *Journal of Psychotherapy Integration, 29*(1), 54–64. https://doi.org/10.1037/int0000120

Bussola, M. (2018). *La vita fino a te*. Giulio Einaudi editore.

Calvert, F., Smith, E., Brockman, R., et al. (2018). Group schema therapy for eating disorders: Study protocol. *Journal of Eating Disorders, 6*, 1. https://doi.org/10.1186/s40337-017-0185-8

Carter, J. D., McIntosh, V. V., Jordan, J., Porter, R. J., Frampton, C. M., & Joyce, P. R. (2013). Psychotherapy for depression: A randomized clinical trial comparing schema therapy and cognitive behavior therapy. *Journal of Affective Disorders, 151*(2), 500–505. https://doi.org/10.1016/j.jad.2013.06.034. Epub 2013 Jul 17. PMID: 23870427.

Chomsky, N. (1959). A review of B.F. Skinner's verbal behaviour. Language, 26–58.

Donnelly, K., & Neziroglu, F. (2010). *Overcoming depersonalization disorder: A mindfulness and acceptance guide to conquering feelings of numbness and unreality*. New Harbinger Publications, Inc./Edizione italiana.

Donnelly, K., & Neziroglu, F. (2016). *Fuori da me. Superare il disturbo di depersonalizzazione*. (trad: Sanavio F). Erickson.

Dufrene, T., & Sandoz, E. K. (2013). *Living with your body and other things you hate*. New Harbinger Publications, Inc./Edizione italiana.

Dufrene, T., & Sandoz, E. K. (2019). *Stare bene con se stessi e con il proprio corpo. Ritrovarsi con l'Acceptance and Commitment Therapy*. (trad: Campanini E). Franco Angeli.

Farrell, J. M., Shaw, I. A., & Webber, M. A. (2009). A schema-focused approach to group psychotherapy for outpatients with borderline personality disorder: A randomized controlled trial. *Journal of Behavior Therapy and Experimental Psychiatry, 40*(2), 317–328. https://doi.org/10.1016/j.jbtep.2009.01.002. Epub 2009 Jan 14. Erratum in: J Behav Ther Exp Psychiatry. 2018 Apr 18;: PMID: 19176222.

Ferreira, M. G., Mariano, L. I., de Rezende, J. V., Caramelli, P., & Kishita, N. (2022). Effects of group Acceptance and Commitment Therapy (ACT) on anxiety and depressive symptoms in adults: A meta-analysis. *Journal of Affective Disorders, 309*, 297–308. https://doi.org/10.1016/j.jad.2022.04.134

Flaxman, P. E., Blackledge, J. T., & Bond, F. W. (2011). *Acceptance and commitment therapy. The CBT Distictive Features Series*. Taylor & Francis Group/Edizione Italiana.

Flaxman, P. E., Blackledge, J. T., & Bond, F. W. (2012). *L'Acceptance and commitment therapy (a cura di Tenore K.)*. FrancoAngeli.

Fox, E. (2013). https://foxylearning.com. Tratto da https://foxylearning.com/tutorials/rft.

Galvez-Sánchez, C. M., Montoro, C. I., Moreno-Padilla, M., Reyes Del Paso, G. A., & de la Coba, P. (2021). Effectiveness of acceptance and commitment therapy in central pain sensitization syndromes: A systematic review. *Journal of Clinical Medicine, 10*(12), 2706. https://doi.org/10.3390/jcm10122706

Gaudiano, B. A., Ellenberg, S., Johnson, J. E., Mueser, K. T., & Miller, I. W. (2023). Effectiveness of acceptance and commitment therapy for inpatients with psychosis: Implementation feasibility and acceptability from a pilot randomized controlled trial. *Schizophrenia Research, 261*, 72–79. https://doi.org/10.1016/j.schres.2023.09.017

Giesen-Bloo, J., van Dyck, R., Spinhoven, P., van Tilburg, W., Dirksen, C., van Asselt, T., Kremers, I., Nadort, M., & Arntz, A. (2006). Outpatient psychotherapy for borderline personality disorder: Randomized trial of schema-focused therapy vs transference-focused psychotherapy. *Archives of General Psychiatry, 63*(6), 649–658. https://doi.org/10.1001/archpsyc.63.6.649. Erratum in: Arch Gen Psychiatry. Sep;63(9):1008. PMID: 16754838.

Harris, R. (2009). *ACT made simple*. New Harbinger Publications, Inc./Edizione italiana.

Harris, R. (2011). *Fare ACT. Una guida pratica per professionisti all'Acceptance and Commitment Therapy*. (trad: Miselli G, Zucchi G). Franco Angeli.

Hawke, L., & Provencher, M. (2011). Schema theory and schema therapy in mood and anxiety disorders: A review. *Journal of Cognitive Psychotherapy, 25*, 257–276. https://doi.org/10.1891/0889-8391.25.4.257

Hayes, S. C. (2019). *A liberated mind: How to pivot toward what matters*. Avery, an imprint of Penguin Random House/Edizione italiana.

Hayes, S. C. (2020). *La mente liberata. Come trasformare il tuo pensiero e affrancarti da stress, ansia e dipendenze* (trad: Pezzica E, Hall KMR). Giunti, Firenze.

Hayes, S. C., & Smith, S. (2005). *Get out of your mind and into your life*. New Harbinger Publications, Oakland. Edizione italiana.

Hayes, S. C., & Smith, S. (2010). *Smetti di soffrire, inizia a vivere. Impara a superare il dolore emotivo, a liberarti dai pensieri negativi e vivi una vita che vale la pena di vivere (a cura di: P Moderato)*. Franco Angeli.

Hayes, S. C., & Wilson, K. (1993). Some applied implications of a contemporary behavior-analytic account of verbal events. *The Behavior Analyst, 16*, 283–301.

Hayes, S. C., Wilson, K. G., Gifford, E. V., Follette, V. M., & Stroshal, K. (1996). Emotional avoidance and behavioral disorders: A functional dimensional approach to diagnosis and treatment. *Journal of Consulting and Clinical Psychology, 64*, 1152–1168.

Hayes, S. C., Strosahl, K. D., & Wilson, K. G. (1999). *Acceptance and commitment therapy: An experiential approach to behavior change*. Guilford Press. Edizione italiana.

Hayes, S. C., Barnes-Holmes, D., & Roche, B. (2001). *Rational frame theory*. Kluwer Academic Publishers.

Hayes, S. C., Masuda, A., Bisset, R., Louma, J., & Guerrero, L. F. (2004). DBT, FAP, and ACT: How empirically oriented are the new behavior therapy technologies? *Behavior Therapy, 35*, 35–54.

Hayes, S. C., Luoma, J. B., Bond, F. W., Masuda, A., & Lillis, J. (2006). Acceptance and commitment therapy: Model, processes and outcomes. *Behaviour Research and Therapy, 44*(1), 1–25. https://doi.org/10.1016/j.brat.2005.06.006. PMID: 16300724.

Hayes, S. C., Strosahl, K. D., & Wilson, K. G. (2013). *ACT Teoria e pratica dell'Acceptance and Commitment Therapy (a cura di: C Maffei)*. Raffaello Cortina.

Heffner, M., & Eifert, G. (2003). The effects of acceptance versus control context on avoidance of pain-related symptoms. *Journal of Behavior Therapy and Experimental Psychiatry, 34*, 293–312.

Heydari, M., Masafi, S., Jafari, M., Saadat, S. H., & Shahyad, S. (2018). Effectiveness of acceptance and commitment therapy on anxiety and depression of Razi Psychiatric Center Staff. *Open Access Macedonian Journal of Medical Sciences, 6*(2), 410–415. https://doi.org/10.3889/oamjms.2018.064

Kabat-Zinn, J. (2003). Mindfulness based interventions in context: Past, present. *Clinical Psychology: Science and Practice, 10*, 144–156.

Kersten, T. (2012). Schema therapy for personality disorders and addiction. In *The Wiley-Blackwell handbook of schema therapy: Theory, research, and practice* (pp. 415–424). https://doi.org/10.1002/9781119962830.ch31

Knapík, P., & Slancová, K. (2020). Core beliefs – Schemas and coping styles in addictions. *Cognitive Remediation Journal [online], 9*(3), 9–19. Available on WWW: https://cognitive-remediation-journal.com/artkey/crj-202003-0001_core-beliefs-8211-schemas-and-coping-styles-in addictions.php. ISSN 1805-7225.

Landy, L. N., Schneider, R. L., & Arch, J. J. (2015). Acceptance and commitment therapy for the treatment of anxiety disorders: A concise review. *Current Opinion in Psychology, 2*, 70–74. https://doi.org/10.1016/j.copsyc.2014.11.004

Levitt, J. T., Brown, T. A., Orsillo, S., & Barlow, D. H. (2004). The effects of acceptance versus suppression of emotion on subjective and psychophysiological response to carbon dioxide challenge in patients with panic disorder. *Behavior Therapy, 35*, 747–766.

McIntosh, V. V. W., Jordan, J., Carter, J. D., Frampton, C. M. A., McKenzie, J. M., Latner, J. D., & Joyce, P. R. (2016). Psychotherapy for transdiagnostic binge eating: A randomized controlled trial of cognitive-behavioural therapy, appetite-focused cognitive-behavioural therapy, and schema therapy. *Psychiatry Research, 240*, 412–420. https://doi.org/10.1016/j.psychres.2016.04.080. Epub 2016 Apr 25. PMID: 27149410.

Moderato, P., & Presti, G. (2019). Pensieri, parole, emozioni. *CBT e ABA di terza generazione: basi sperimentali e cliniche.* FrancoAngeli, Milano

Moderato, P., Presti, P., & Dell'Orco, F. (2023). *ACT: Acceptance and commitment therapy.* Hogrefe.

Peeters, N., van Passel, B., & Krans, J. (2021). The effectiveness of schema therapy for patients with anxiety disorders, OCD, or PTSD: A systematic review and research agenda. *The British Journal of Clinical Psychology, 61,* 579–597. https://doi.org/10.1111/bjc.12324

Perkins, A. M., Meiser-Stedman, R., Spaul, S. W., Bowers, G., Perkins, A. G., & Pass, L. (2023). The effectiveness of third wave cognitive behavioural therapies for children and adolescents: A systematic review and meta-analysis. *The British Journal of Clinical Psychology, 62*(1), 209–227. https://doi.org/10.1111/bjc.12404

Polk, K. L., & Schoendorff, B. (2014). *The ACT matrix. A new approach to building psychological flexibility actoss settings & population.* New Harbinger Pubblications.

Renner, F., Arntz, A., Peeters, F. P. M. L., Lobbestael, J., & Huibers, M. J. H. (2016). Schema therapy for chronic depression: Results of a multiple single case series. *Journal of Behavior Therapy and Experimental Psychiatry, 51,* 66–73. ISSN 0005-7916. https://doi.org/10.1016/j.jbtep.2015.12.001

Roedinger, E., Stevens, B. A., & Brockman, R. (2018). *Contextual schema therapy: An integrative approach to personality disorders, emotional dysregulation, and interpersonal functioning.* Edizione italiana.

Roedinger, E., Stevens, B. A., & Brockman, R. (2021). *Contextual schema therapy.* Un approccio integrato di terza generazione per il trattamento dei disturbi di personalità (a cura di D Baroni e N Marsigli) Edizioni Centro Studi Erickson, Trento.

Shorey, R. C., Elmquist, J., Gawrysiak, M. J., Strauss, C., Haynes, E., Anderson, S., & Stuart, G. L. (2017). A randomized controlled trial of a mindfulness and acceptance group therapy for residential substance use patients. *Substance Use & Misuse, 52*(11), 1400–1410. https://doi.org/10.1080/10826084.2017.1284232

Simpson, S. G., Morrow, E., van Vreeswijk, M., & Reid, C. (2010). Group schema therapy for eating disorders: A pilot study. *Frontiers in Psychology, 1,* 182. https://doi.org/10.3389/fpsyg.2010.00182. PMID: 21833243; PMCID: PMC3153792.

Skinner, B. F. (1957). *Verbal behavior.* New York: Appleton.

Society of Clinical Psychology, American Psychological Association (Division 12). (2024). Psychological Treatments. https://div12.org. Ultimo accesso 13 Feb 2024.

Soondrum, T., Wang, X., Gao, F., Liu, Q., Fan, J., & Zhu, X. (2022). The applicability of acceptance and commitment therapy for obsessive-compulsive disorder: A systematic review and meta-analysis. *Brain Sciences, 12*(5), 656. https://doi.org/10.3390/brainsci12050656

Straver, F. R. (2017). *A theoretical model of substance use based on schema therapy concepts.*

Taylor, C. D. J., Bee, P., & Haddock, G. (2017). Does schema therapy change schemas and symptoms? A systematic review across mental health disorders. *Psychology and Psychotherapy: Theory, Research and Practice, 90,* 456–479. https://doi.org/10.1111/papt.12112

Törneke, N. (2010). *Laerning RFT. An introduction to relational frame theory and its clinical applications.* New Harbinger Publications/Edizione italiana.

Törneke, N. (2017). *Fondamenti di RFT. Un'introduzione alla Relational Frame Theory e alle sue applicazioni cliniche.* (trad di E. Rossi et al) Giovanni Fioriti Editore.

Trindade, I. A., Guiomar, R., Carvalho, S. A., Duarte, J., Lapa, T., Menezes, P., Nogueira, M. R., Patrão, B., Pinto-Gouveia, J., & Castilho, P. (2021). Efficacy of online-based acceptance and commitment therapy for chronic pain: A systematic review and meta-analysis. *The Journal of Pain, 22*(11), 1328–1342. https://doi.org/10.1016/j.jpain.2021.04.003

Twohig, M. P., & Levin, M. E. (2017). Acceptance and commitment therapy as a treatment for anxiety and depression: A review. *The Psychiatric Clinics of North America, 40*(4), 751–770. https://doi.org/10.1016/j.psc.2017.08.009

Twohig, M. P., Hayes, S. C., Plumb, J. C., Pruitt, L. D., Collins, A. B., Hazlett-Stevens, H., & Woidneck, M. R. (2010). A randomized clinical trial of acceptance and commitment therapy versus progressive relaxation training for obsessive-compulsive disorder. *Journal of Consulting and Clinical Psychology, 78*(5), 705–716. https://doi.org/10.1037/a0020508

Woods, D., & Kanter, J. (2007). *Understanding behavior disorders.* Context Press/Edizione italiana.

Woods, D., & Kanter, J. (2016). *Disturbi psicologici e terapia cognitivo-comportamentale. Modelli e interventi clinici di terza generazione.* (trad e cura di R. Anchisi, & S. Stefanini) FrancoAngeli, Milano.

Young, J. E., Brown, G. (2005). Young schema questionnaire-short form; Version 3 (YSQ-S3, YSQ) [Database record]. APA PsycTests. https://doi.org/10.1037/t67023-000

Young, J. E., Klosko, J. S., & Weishaar, M. E. (2003). *Schema therapy: A practitioner's guide.* Guilford Press. Edizione italiana.

Young, J. E., Klosko, J. S., & Weishaar, M. E. (2007). *Schema therapy.* La terapia cognitivo-comportamentale integrata per i disturbi della personalità (a cura di A. Carrozza, N. Marsigli, G. Melli) Eclipsi.

Zhang, K., Hu, X., Ma, L., Xie, Q., Wang, Z., Fan, C., & Li, X. (2023). The efficacy of schema therapy for personality disorders: A systematic review and meta-analysis. *Nordic Journal of Psychiatry, 77*(7), 641–650. https://doi.org/10.1080/08039488.2023.2228304. Epub 2023 Jul 4. PMID: 37402124.

Integrating Sexology into Evidence-Based Psychotherapy Practice

Francesca Cavallo, Gianpaolo Salvatore, and Andrea Lenzi

1 Introduction

One of the primary objectives of psychotherapy is to reduce patient's shame, increase their sense of security, and enhance their ability to access and reprocess pathogenic beliefs. These are defined as cognitive distortions that negatively influence behavior and psychological well-being. Psychotherapy can facilitate the process of differentiation between idealized self-projections and the authentic self. The enhancement of self-awareness, a consequence of psychotherapy, contributes to self-acceptance. These objectives include the necessity to assist patients in becoming more aware and confident regarding their affectivity, as well as their needs and desires, including those related to the sexual sphere. The sexual area, which has been relatively under-explored in psychotherapy sessions, provides useful elements for understanding the functioning of our patients, just like all other areas of life. Consequently, it is imperative that every psychotherapist, at the very least during the diagnostic phase, be proficient in conducting an adequate *sexological assessment* (Tripodi, 2021). In this context, psychotherapy should also accord importance to *sexual dysfunctions*, which are not infrequently present in our lives. For example, sexual difficulties may arise with the onset of menopause or andropause, decreased libido due to pharmacological treatments, illnesses, bereavement, or work-related stress (DSM-5, 2013).

F. Cavallo (✉)
Scuola di Psicoterapia Integrata, Centro Clinico Integrato, Bergamo, Italy

G. Salvatore
Department of Social Sciences, University of Foggia, Foggia, Italy

A. Lenzi
Department of Experimental Medicine, Endocrinology and Food Sciences,
University of Rome La Sapienza, Rome, Italy

© The Author(s), under exclusive license to Springer Nature Switzerland AG 2024
B. Poletti et al. (eds.), *Training in Integrated Relational Psychotherapy*,
https://doi.org/10.1007/978-3-031-71904-2_21

Despite the typically confidential and nonjudgmental context of a therapeutic relationship, patients often have trouble in opening up about sexual topics. This phenomenon, known as *sexual taboo*, is characterized by a reluctance to express thoughts and feelings about sex. Patients may openly discuss private aspects of their work and love lives, recount traumatic episodes from their childhood, and reveal negative thoughts, but they may display significant reluctance to speak openly about what sexually excites or inhibits them. This reluctance is partly attributable to the shame and repression that pervade sexual discourse in our culture. Despite the massive exposure to sexual images through the media, and despite decades of sexual education and literature promoting sexual evolution, most individuals still consider the details of their sexual lives as private and not shareable, even with a therapist. This perception is linked to a view of the body as a source of shame and its desires as taboo (Bader, 2003).

The purpose of this chapter is to provide clinicians with essential knowledge to facilitate their understanding of the theoretical and clinical relevance of sexuality in the context of psychotherapy, and to integrate diagnostic and therapeutic interventions into clinical practice. We will commence with general scientific concepts related to sexuality, such as biological sex, gender identity, sexual orientation, and current scientific evidence on intersexuality and homosexuality. We will then illustrate the complexity and multidimensionality of human sexuality through the tripartite brain model and the motivational systems related to the sexual sphere, and how these dimensions can assist psychotherapists in understanding not only the sexual functioning of their patients but also their overall functioning. Furthermore, fundamental concepts of *evidence-based psychotherapies*, such as attachment, metacognition, and the importance of the therapeutic relationship and alliance, will be described to provide the reader with an overview of these dimensions in relation to sexuality. In the final section, we will revisit the importance of exploring the sexual dimension in psychotherapy to understand our patients' functioning. The text will also provide practical advice on how to integrate sexological assessment into *case formulation* and will illustrate the integration of therapeutic techniques in both sexological and psychotherapeutic contexts through the presentation of a clinical case.

2 Essential Elements of Sexuality and General Concepts

The role of sexuality in evolution remains largely unknown, and its functioning presents numerous paradoxes. While sexuality is not merely an effective means for reproduction, its hedonistic component, sexual pleasure, represents a fundamental element of personal well-being and plays a significant role in existence. Even nonhuman animals exhibit remarkable creativity in terms of pleasure and reproduction, with strategies of seduction, courtship displays, couple conflicts, fidelity and infidelity, masturbation, and homosexuality. This suggests that sexual pleasure is not merely a simple by-product of evolution but a factor that fosters original interactions and contributes to animal biodiversity (Lodé, 2023).

Sexuality is a primary need, representing an active motivational system throughout the entire lifespan, including the prenatal period. The first sexual reflexes can be observed several months before birth. Sexuality encompasses various aspects, including biological sex, gender identities and roles, sexual orientation, eroticism, pleasure, intimacy, and reproduction. Sexuality is experienced and expressed in a multitude of ways, including thoughts, fantasies, desires, beliefs, attitudes, values, behaviors, practices, roles, and relationships. The interaction of biological, psychological, social, economic, political, ethical, legal, historical, religious, and spiritual factors influences sexuality (WHO, 2006). When discussing the biological dimension of sexuality, the male/female dichotomy is often referenced. It is noteworthy to point out that the *biological sex* encompasses three distinct categories:

1. *Chromosomal Sex*: Typically, humans are dichromatic, exhibiting two distinct sex chromosomes: XX for females and XY for males. Nevertheless, variations, such as XXY (Klinefelter syndrome), XO (Turner syndrome), XXYY, and others, can result in the manifestation of intersex characteristics. The term "intersexuality" is used to describe a range of conditions in which a person is born with sexual characteristics that do not align with the typical definitions of male or female. Such characteristics may include variations in genitalia, gonads (ovaries and testes), sex chromosomes, and hormone levels (Hughes et al., 2006).
2. *Gonadal Sex*: Regardless of chromosomal configuration (XX or XY), the human embryo is initially sexually undifferentiated. Embryonic gonads are bipotential structures that have the potential to develop into either ovaries or testes. In the context of an embryo with an XY chromosomal configuration, sexual differentiation is triggered around the sixth week of gestation by the activation of the SRY gene (Sex-determining Region Y), located on the Y chromosome. The SRY gene encodes a single transcription factor, which initiates a cascade of molecular events leading to the differentiation of bipotential gonads into testes. In the absence of the SRY gene or a block in the subsequent endocrine cascade, as in the case of an XX embryo or an XY embryo with androgen receptor pathology, gonadal differentiation proceeds toward ovarian development. This process is regulated by a series of other genes and molecular factors that promote female differentiation. Consequently, depending on the genetic and molecular programs that are activated, bipotential embryonic gonads differentiate into ovaries or testes (Brennan & Capel, 2004). Individuals with intersex traits may exhibit gonads that are not easily distinguishable as testes or ovaries, such as ovotestes, or gonads that do not align with their chromosomal sex configuration.
3. *Phenotypic Sex*: The phenotypic sex of an individual is determined by the hormonal secretions of the gonads, which influence the development of external genitalia. In an embryo with an XY chromosomal configuration, once the embryonic gonad differentiates into a testis, it begins to produce male hormones. These hormones facilitate the differentiation of the genitalia in a male direction. In the absence of these hormones, or if the target organs do not respond adequately, the resulting sexual phenotype is female. This occurs because female sexual development does not require the production of specific hormones and proceeds by

default in the absence of "male" signals. The development of sexual morphology is characterized by an intricate orchestration of specific events during embryonic development, which culminates in the appearance of secondary sexual characteristics during puberty. It is possible for each phase of sexual differentiation to vary, resulting in outcomes that differ from typical configurations. The genitalia may be ambiguous or deviate from the expectations based on the sex chromosomes. An individual with XY chromosomes may be born with genitalia that appear female. For instance, hormonal imbalances during fetal development can influence sexual differentiation. Alternatively, androgen insensitivity can result in an individual with XY chromosomes developing female physical characteristics (Capel, 2000).

Biological sex describes the physical dimension and the set of primary and secondary physical characteristics that define us as male or female. This includes all intersex variations, as previously discussed. When we refer to feelings of being a woman or a man, we enter the realm of subjective perceptions of identity, which may be considered a sort of psychological sex that reflects a mental construct (Money et al., 1957).

Gender identity is a complex concept, pertaining to an individual's self-perception as belonging to a specific gender, which may or may not correspond to their biological sex. It is an essential component of personal identity and can influence numerous aspects of an individual's life. Gender identity is an internal and profound sensation regarding one's own gender, which can be stable over time or fluid (Egan & Perry, 2001). A person's gender identity may diverge from their biological sex. For example, an individual may self-identify as male despite having female genitalia, or vice versa. This phenomenon is observed in *gender dysphoria*, a condition of significant distress due to the discrepancy between gender identity and biological sex, as defined by the Diagnostic and Statistical Manual of Mental Disorders, Fifth Edition (DSM-V, 2013). The World Health Organization (2019) has renamed this condition as *gender incongruence* and has moved it from the section of mental disorders to a more neutral section to remove the pathologizing stigma associated with the condition (ICD-11, 2019).

Studies have indicated that genetic and hormonal factors can influence gender identity (biology), while personal experiences during childhood and adolescence can also impact the development of gender identity (psychology). Additionally, cultural and social norms regarding gender can affect how a person perceives and expresses their gender identity (sociology). Furthermore, the degree of support from family and community can significantly impact one's experience of gender identity (Tobin et al., 2010). Gender identity is expressed through behaviors, adornments, clothing, voice, hairstyles, and other gender expressions and roles considered "masculine or feminine" (Shively & De Cecco, 1977). In western culture, women who exhibit masculine expressions, such as "being able to drive," "working like a man," or "cheering for a football team," are often considered women "with attributes." In contrast, men's feminine gender expressions, such as "sensitivity," "being nurturing," or "being fragile and vulnerable," tend to be less socially accepted. In some cultural and familial contexts, the inability to express emotions can be associated with *gender violence*, where men suppress feelings of inadequacy and exhibit emotional dysregulation as anger dysregulation (Graglia, 2022).

The complex construction of *sexual identity,* which comprises biological sex, gender identity, gender roles, and gender expressions, encompasses various dimensions, including sexual attraction, sexual behavior, romantic attraction, sexual fantasies, and self-identification. *Sexual orientation*, like other constructs of sexual identity, is not dichotomous, exclusively heterosexual, and/or homosexual. Rather, it is a continuum with intermediate positions, including bisexuality (Kinsey et al., 1950). It can change over time, be fluid, or be inhibited due to stigma. Many behaviors that are considered "nonheterosexual" are also inhibited by stigma, such as anal sexuality. Human anatomy teaches us that the anus, along with the entire pelvic floor, perineum, vagina, vulva, and clitoris, is traversed by the pudendal nerve, which is rich in nerve endings capable of sending pleasurable sensations to the brain. When stimulated in an appropriate manner and under conditions of muscle relaxation, it lubricates and can contribute to achieving orgasm. Men who are heterosexual, comfortable with their bodies, and free from homophobic prejudices allow their partners to stimulate the anus, which enhances erectile capacity and amplifies ejaculatory climax (Waldinger & Venema, 1998).

None of us can choose whom we are attracted to. A neuroimaging study on *sexual desire* investigated the time it takes for the brain to categorize stimuli as sexually desirable or not. The results indicated that this process occurs within 200 milliseconds of the presentation of a given stimulus. The brain can identify individuals with whom we are sexually attracted even before we become consciously aware of this attraction (Ortigue & Bianchi-Demicheli, 2008). In accordance with evolutionary theories, during the prehistoric era, the role of hunters was predominantly assumed by men. This task required the utilization of advanced visuospatial skills, which were essential for the tracking of prey, the navigation of unknown territories, and the utilization of hunting tools. The emphasis on visuospatial abilities may have conditioned men to be more responsive to visual stimuli. The sight of potential sexual partners could have provided immediate signals of fertility and health, crucial elements for mate selection. For example, the preference for younger partners ensures healthy offspring (Hamann et al., 2004).

Neuroscientific and psychological studies have demonstrated that males tend to respond more intensely to erotic images than females. This may be indicative of an evolutionary adaptation where mate selection based on visual cues was important. During the same prehistoric era, women were primarily responsible for the care and upbringing of offspring and the maintenance of the community. This necessitated the development of sophisticated social and communication abilities to sustain interpersonal connections and foster collaboration within the collective. The use of storytelling, language, and emotional expression may have been instrumental in the formation and sustenance of interpersonal relationships (Fisher, 1992). Verbal expressions of desire and appreciation could have signaled security and commitment from the partner. It has been observed that women tend to respond more intensely to verbal and emotional stimuli, such as romantic stories, declarations of love, as well as narratives of erotic fantasies and expressions of desire from their partner. This may reflect an evolutionary adaptation to assess the quality of a partner in terms of emotional support and commitment. In general, women are attracted to older and/or socially stronger partners who could guarantee protection for offspring and the family unit. It is crucial to acknowledge that these theories provide generalized explanations that do not account for individual variations. It is important to note that not all individuals respond to stimuli in the same way.

Finally, it is necessary to mention recent scientific evidence regarding *homosexuality* in order to better understand the current theoretical-scientific-clinical paradigm. As evidenced by the esteemed meta-analysis on social and nonsocial mammals published in Nature in August 2023 (Gomez et al., 2023), homosexuality is becoming more increasingly represented in nature. From an evolutionary perspective, it emerged relatively recently. One important function would be the regulation of aggression. Indeed, it is more prevalent in species where adulticide occurs by males (although it also occurs by females, but the correlation is less significant). This implies that in species where adulticide is present, homosexual behaviors are more likely to emerge, thereby moderating these tendencies (Gomez et al., 2023). The regulatory function of homosexuality can be observed in the context of intrasexual competition. In such a setting, the shift from fighting to seduction allows for the calming of aggression. Furthermore, in certain species, it serves to pacify conflicts with rivals initially and subsequently ensures heterosexual mating. In practice, it is part of a bisexual function. Furthermore, it helps regulate the population size of a given species. The prevalence of homosexuality in each species is known to fluctuate during periods of elevated population density. A similar phenomenon is observed in Atlantic octopuses.

Moreover, data from genetic research and studies on birth order are of relevance. Studies on monozygotic twins (especially male) indicate a higher concordance rate of sexual orientation compared to dizygotic twins. This is observed in twin pairs raised together as well as (more importantly) in those raised apart. Regarding transgender individuals, the limited existing studies indicate that the heritability rate for male-to-female (MtF) individuals is between 33% and 50%, while that for female-to-male (FtM) individuals is between 23% and 40%. The correlation coefficients for transgender individuals are slightly higher, indicating that gender expression variance is manifested to a greater extent and to a lesser degree of intensity. A portion of the X chromosome (the distal portion of Xq28) has been identified as genetically linked to a matrilineal genetic marker of male homosexuality. About *transsexualism*, some studies have identified different genetic markers for MtF and FtM, which may be indicative of a genetic basis for this condition. However, these markers do not represent the final identification of the genes involved in transsexualism. With regard to birth order, numerous studies have demonstrated that homosexual men, and only they, exhibit a significant tendency to be born later in the sibling series and to have a higher number of older male siblings. This phenomenon may be attributed to a maternal immune response, which is triggered exclusively by male fetuses. This response intensifies with each subsequent pregnancy, as the maternal immune system is the sole biological system capable of "remembering" the number of male (and not female) fetuses. This results in an antibody response that could potentially alter fetal androgenization (D'Ettore, 2021).

3 Intrinsic Multidimensionality of Sexuality: Tripartite Brain and Systems

Sexuality is a complex and multidimensional component of our identity. It affects our decisions, actions, and relationships at the biological, psychological, and social levels. It is linked to various aspects, including the biological substrate, emotional functioning, cognitive motivations, and the social and cultural context in which we live (Bancroft, 2009).

Among the primary drives that can be used to interpret sexuality are the drive for reproduction, play, perceiving oneself as a couple within a group, self-knowledge through the other, sharing a story, and procreation. These drives can be traced back to a very remote past and constitute various dimensions through which to view the complexity of sexuality. The dimensions of sexuality can thus be employed as a framework for investigating the sexual history of everyone. LeVay and Baldwin (2012) posit that while these dimensions are universal, they manifest uniquely in each individual. Indeed, everyone expresses these dimensions in a distinctive manner, akin to a work of art that reflects their unique identity.

The phylogenesis and ontogenesis of the human being are based on a complex biological structure comprising a set of motivational and behavioral systems. These systems, selected over millions of years, guide our behaviors in both innate and learned ways (Hinde, 1974; Liotti, 2001; Veglia, 2004). In his 1984 work, MacLean proposed a triune brain model, which has since been revisited considering neuroscientific advances (Panksepp & Biven, 2012). This model posits that the triune brain is composed of three interconnected and communicating parts. Each of these components is associated with distinct mandates and/or interpersonal motivational systems (IM (IMS[1]). The *reptilian brain* (R-complex), the most archaic nucleus of the human brain, is composed of a group of neurons inherited from amphibians and placed at the level of the brainstem. It is the source of our instinctual behaviors aimed at survival, such as the regulation of body temperature, and of dorso-vagal (*feigned death*) and ortho-sympathetic (*fight or flight*) activations (Porges, 2001). Here, sexuality is understood in its reproductive dimension, namely, as the primary need to reproduce for the preservation of the species. The initial layer of the reptilian brain, known as the limbic brain (K complex), serves as the foundation for subsequent cognitive processes. This evolved subsequently from the reptilian, as some animal species, namely, mammals, began to organize themselves into groups.

---

[1] SMI, are composed of an emotional, cognitive, and motor dimension, regulating interaction with our conspecifics through action patterns aimed at satisfying our needs within relationships (Liotti,2001).

The *limbic system*, also known as the emotional brain, is responsible for regulating emotions.[2] Furthermore, it oversees social motivation, which in turn affects learning and memory. The limbic brain plays a pivotal role in the experience of pleasure and sexual desire. This is evident in the pursuit of immediate gratification, autoeroticism, and the exploration of the other's body. This aspect of sexuality thus intersects with the need for social play and relates to the *playful dimension*. The limbic system also plays a role in the formation of emotional bonds, particularly in the context of the *attachment/care dimension*. This system regulates the construction and maintenance of a special bond with another person, as evidenced by the desire for bonding and the pleasure derived from sharing. The present discussion concerns the *social dimension* of sexuality. Continuing our examination of the phylogenetic development of sexuality, we reach the pinnacle of this evolutionary journey, which begins to decline in conjunction with the advent of the erect posture, a defining characteristic of *Homo erectus*. This evolutionary transition also marks the elongation of the spinal cord. This stage of evolution is associated with the development of the cerebral neocortex, which can be traced back approximately 200 million years. The neocortex is the site of higher functions, including language, rational thought, planning, and metacognition.[3] It facilitates reflection on sexual experiences (Perkins & Grover, 2010), the processing of complex emotions related to sexuality, and the regulation and integration of sexual behavior in accordance with one's own values and social norms. The *neocortex* allows for the differentiation of three dimensions: the first is the semantic dimension, in which the need to share with the other transcends the physicality of the gesture and becomes a generator of meaning and significance; the second is the *narrative dimension*, in which the need to construct one's identity has to do with the sense of self, attributions of meaning, and projectability; the third is the *procreative dimension*, in which the need to reproduce flows into a more complex need to procreate, marked by the desire for motherhood and fatherhood (Bonicelli et al., 2018).

The dimensions of sexuality—reproductive, playful, social, semantic, narrative, and procreative—represent different yet interconnected aspects of the human sexual experience. Each dimension provides a distinctive perspective through which to examine and comprehend sexual behavior and relationships.

---

[2] The higher emotions are those that develop through complex cognitive processes and are often closely linked to our capacity for reflection, consciousness, and social interactions. These emotions go beyond basic emotional responses such as fear, joy, or anger, and include feelings such as empathy, gratitude, pride, and shame (LeDoux, 1996).

[3] Metacognition is the ability to reflect on one's thoughts, emotions, and behavior. It is the ability to reflect on one's mental states, understand and monitor one's cognitive and emotional processes, and use this information to guide behavior and emotional regulation. It also includes the ability to understand the thoughts and emotions of others and to use these understandings to improve social interactions and interpersonal relationships (Flavell, 1979; Semerari et al., 2003; Dimaggio et al., 2013). Different regions of the neocortex, including the prefrontal cortex, are involved in metacognitive processes such as monitoring and regulating one's own actions and thoughts (Fleming & Dolan, 2012).

Integrating the various dimensions of sexuality into psychotherapeutic practice allows for a deeper understanding and greater effectiveness in understanding sexual functioning and treating sexual problems (Levine, 2003). For the psychotherapist, an understanding of these dimensions allows for a comprehensive and nuanced reconstruction of the patient's life history, sexual and otherwise. This is of great importance for the identification of sources of sexual distress or dysfunction, as well as for the improvement of the understanding of couple dynamics. For instance, a patient may exhibit sexual anxiety due to physical issues (reproductive dimension), negative cultural connotations associated with sex (semantic dimension), or traumatic past experiences (narrative dimension). With a comprehensive grasp of the various dimensions, the psychotherapist is better positioned to construct a more comprehensive and accurate case formulation. This enables the identification of the factors contributing to the problem and the development of a more targeted treatment plan. If a patient has trouble in experiencing sexual pleasure, the therapist can explore how the patient's social relationships and past experiences influence this difficulty. An understanding of the multidimensionality of sexuality enables the development of more personalized and effective interventions. For instance, cognitive-behavioral therapy techniques (Wincze & Weisberg, 2015) can be augmented with dimension-specific sex therapy interventions. The social dimension may be addressed by enhancing sexual communication skills within the couple, whereas the semantic dimension may necessitate an intervention to restructure dysfunctional beliefs about sex. Moreover, a focus on different dimensions allows for a more comprehensive and engaging psychoeducation on sex. In this context, psychoeducation is not merely the provision of information; rather, it entails an active involvement of the patient in comprehending the manner in which the various dimensions influence their sexual experience. During psychoeducation, the therapist may guide the patient in exploring the ways in which his social experiences (social dimension) and the meanings he attributes to sexuality (semantic dimension) influence his perception of pleasure (playful dimension).

4 Essential Concepts of Evidence-Based Psychotherapy: Attachment, Metacognition, Therapeutic Relationship, and Therapeutic Alliance

In order to facilitate comprehension, we will limit our discussion to the fundamental concepts of metacognition, attachment, and the relationship/therapeutic alliance. These aspects are considered further dimensions of sexuality. These modalities represent how sexual and relational experiences are lived, interpreted, and managed. They provide a lens through which sexual and relational dynamics can be understood and intervened upon, thereby enabling an integrated and comprehensive therapeutic approach.

Attachment is defined as a deep and enduring emotional bond that a child develops with their primary caregiver. This bond is characterized by behaviors that promote proximity and contact, such as crying, smiling, and clinging. This bond is of critical importance for a child's emotional security and has a profound impact on their future development (Bowlby, 1969). The *attachment dimension* concerns the influence of attachment experiences and patterns formed during childhood on intimate and sexual relationships in adulthood. The type of attachment (*secure, anxious, avoidant, disorganized*) constitutes a relational model that influences how a person approaches intimacy and sexuality (Ainsworth et al., 1978). The type of attachment affects the emotional experiences related to sexuality. For instance, an individual with a secure attachment style may experience sexuality and bonding with another in a more tranquil and trusting manner than someone with an anxious or avoidant attachment style. The modalities of sexual interaction, such as the ability to communicate desires and needs or the management of rejection and acceptance, are influenced by the type of attachment. An understanding of the patient's attachment style enables the therapist to comprehend their relational patterns, expectations, and dynamics that may emerge in intimate and social relationships. The identification of an anxious or avoidant attachment style can explain behaviors such as jealousy, fear of rejection, or difficulty establishing intimacy. Furthermore, attachment styles also influence how a person manages their emotions. Secure attachment is typically associated with superior emotional regulation, whereas anxious or avoidant attachment, which is often accompanied by *negative self and other representation*, can result in difficulties in managing stress and intense emotions. The ability to identify a patient's attachment style allows for the development of personalized interventions that aim to improve emotional regulation and modify dysfunctional beliefs and behaviors (Mikulincer et al., 2013). A secure attachment fosters a therapeutic relationship based on trust, whereas disorganized attachments, as in complex post-traumatic disorder (C-PTSD, ICD-11), may necessitate more intensive work to build and maintain a robust therapeutic alliance.

In this context, the *metacognitive dimension*, as defined by Semerari et al. (2003) and Dimaggio et al. (2013), refers to the ability to recognize and understand one's own thoughts and feelings regarding sexuality. This encompasses sexual awareness, which can be demonstrated by a person reflecting on their sexual fantasies and understanding how these influence their behavior (Perkins & Grover, 2010). Furthermore, effective sexual metacognition enables individuals to achieve a balance between satisfying their own needs and respecting their partner (*self-regulation*), and it facilitates the comprehension of another's mind, in this case, their partner's sexual experiences and needs, thereby enhancing empathy and communication within the relationship. Metacognition, as a dimension of sexuality, refers to the awareness and regulation of sexual thoughts, emotions, and behavior. The functioning of these aspects facilitates a more conscious and respectful management of one's own and one's partner's sexuality. By fostering improvements in our patients' metacognition, we facilitate the development of greater self-awareness and a more nuanced understanding of their emotional and behavioral reactions. Metacognitive difficulties can result in difficulties with self-control and impulse management.

Intervening on these skills can assist the patient in developing more effective strategies to manage dysfunctional behavior and improve self-regulatory capacity (Dimaggio et al., 2013; Garofalo et al., 2018). The capacity to comprehend the emotions and thoughts of others is of paramount importance for the establishment of healthy interpersonal relationships. Enhancing metacognition can facilitate a more nuanced comprehension of relational dynamics, thereby enhancing the patient's social and empathic abilities.

Safran and Muran (2000) dedicated a substantial portion of their work to the study of the *therapeutic relationship.* They underscored that the therapeutic relationship is a dynamic and interactive process, characterized by a continuous exchange between therapist and patient. The quality of the therapeutic relationship is often more decisive for the outcome of therapy than any specific technique used. It is essential that the therapist be receptive to feedback from the patient and engage in open dialogue about relational dynamics. Meta-communication, or the capacity to discuss the relationship itself, can facilitate the resolution of difficulties or misunderstandings that may arise during therapy. It is inevitable that breakdowns in the *therapeutic alliance* will occur, but the subsequent opportunity for growth can be significant. Safran and Muran underscore the significance of recognizing and addressing these ruptures in a collaborative manner, with the objective of attaining a genuinely cooperative level of alliance and authentic, profound communication. Involving the patient actively in the therapeutic process has been demonstrated to increase their motivation and commitment to treatment. The therapist's capacity to comprehend and corroborate the patient's experience is of paramount importance in the establishment of a robust therapeutic alliance (Safran & Muran, 2000; Semerari et al., 2003; Norcross, 2011). Validation serves to reassure the patient that their experiences are understood and accepted, in a nonjudgmental environment where any issue can be addressed without excessive inhibition. The therapist's empathic understanding enables the patient to explore their experiences and fosters trust. A robust therapeutic alliance is predicated upon an active and collaborative relationship between therapist and patient. It is essential that the patient feels an integral part of the therapeutic process and has a voice in treatment decisions.

Investigating attachment styles, metacognitive skills, and consistently striving to create a therapeutic environment conducive to growth and healing is fundamental in psychotherapy. These aspects have been shown to profoundly impact patients' emotional well-being, interpersonal relationships, and capacity to self-regulate. A multitude of studies have demonstrated the crucial role of addressing these factors in determining the efficacy of psychotherapy. For instance, the studies by Mallinckrodt et al. (2005) examine how exploring attachment styles and the client's attachment to the therapist positively influence psychotherapy outcomes. Similarly, the studies by Levy et al. (2011) confirm how different attachment styles influence the process and outcomes of psychotherapy, offering a detailed perspective on how attachment dynamics between client and therapist can contribute to effectiveness. Lysaker et al. (2011), provide a comprehensive overview of the research on metacognition and its role in the treatment of mental disorders is provided, along with an examination of how working on and improving a patient's metacognitive skills can lead to positive outcomes in psychotherapy. In the meta-analysis by Martin et al. (2000), the correlation between therapeutic alliance and psychotherapy outcomes is investigated, demonstrating that a robust therapeutic alliance is positively correlated with therapeutic outcomes, as corroborated by studies by Norcross (2011) and Wampold (2015). When considered in conjunction with the exploration of the patient's sexual sphere, these factors provide further valuable insights for *case formulation*.

5 The Importance of Integrating Sexuality into Clinical Practice

Sexual health is a fundamental aspect of an individual's overall health and well-being. The World Health Organization (WHO) defines sexual health as a state of physical, emotional, mental, and social well-being related to sexuality. It is not merely the absence of disease, dysfunction, or infirmity. It necessitates a constructive and respectful approach to sexuality and sexual relationships, as well as the capacity to engage in pleasurable and secure sexual experiences, free from coercion, discrimination, and violence. In order to achieve and maintain sexual health, it is essential that the sexual rights of every human being are respected, protected, and fulfilled.

The study of sexuality is a convergence of biological, psychological, and sociological phenomena. Consequently, the study of sexuality necessitates an *interdisciplinary approach* that integrates diverse perspectives, including those of medicine, psychology, neuroscience, and cultural anthropology, to achieve a holistic vision. In the field of psychology, reference approaches and models include evolutionism (Symons, 1979), constructivism (Kelly, 1955), social constructionism (Foucault, 1978), psychotraumatology (van der Kolk, 2014), and attachment theory (Bowlby, 1969).

In the field of sexology, psychotherapeutic treatments have historically placed a significant emphasis on *body-based approaches*. The field of sexological psychotherapy can be traced back to the work of Wilhelm Reich and Alexander Lowen, who were among the first to explore the potential of body-based approaches. Reich (1942) is renowned for his contributions to the field of orgasmology, which include the introduction of concepts such as orgone energy.[4] He held the view that sexual energy was of fundamental importance to both psychological and physical health and developed techniques designed to facilitate the release of accumulated bodily tensions.

---

[4] Every single unit of a vital energy with which the whole of nature would be pervaded, according to the theory developed by the Austrian psychiatrist and psychoanalyst W. Reich, and which in humans would manifest itself in the form of sexual energy and libido. Orgonomics is said to be the theory and therapeutic practice proposed by Reich, aimed at releasing repressed sexual energy in patients and which should lead to the resolution of psychophysical tensions resulting in the healing of numerous illnesses.

Lowen (1975), his student, developed bioenergetic therapy, which combines psychotherapy and bodywork. Bioenergetics is a therapeutic approach that aims to release physical and emotional tensions through exercises that stimulate body awareness and emotional expression. The significance of addressing the body in the context of clinical sexology is a fundamental tenet of psychotherapy (Geuter et al., 2010). This is evident in the work of Masters and Johnson (1970), who developed sensate focus therapy with the aim of reducing anxiety and enhancing body awareness. Similarly, integrated task-oriented therapy (Panzeri, 2023) represents one of the most established therapies in this field, employing a holistic, integrated, and multifactorial approach. In addition, contemporary clinical sexology employs the integration of bodily techniques, such as mindfulness (Kabat-Zinn et al., 2007), which helps to reduce anxiety and enhance the satisfaction of the pleasure experience. Sensorimotor therapy (Ogden et al., 2006) is another technique that trains patients in the management of emotional arousal. Polyvagal theory (Porges, 2001) is a particularly useful framework for understanding and managing physical and emotional reactions in sexual difficulties. Finally, eye movement desensitization and reprocessing, EMDR, (Shapiro & Forrest, 2017) is a valuable tool for processing and overcoming any sexual trauma. The borderline between the psychological and medical fields is characterized by the most up-to-date approaches that emphasize the relevance of variables such as the therapeutic relationship, couples therapy, and the social context. These variables are relevant in the narrative approach (Freedman & Combs, 1996) and in relational psychodynamics (Stern, 2010). It is important to note that in the DSM (DSM-V TR, 2022), sexual disorders are divided into three categories: *gender dysphoria, paraphilic disorders*, and *sexual dysfunction*. Treatment, which is reserved for psychotherapists with specific training in clinical sexology, includes, in addition to the aforementioned therapies, evidence-based techniques such as cognitive-behavioral therapy to modify dysfunctional thoughts (Dèttore, 2004), couple therapy, which is effective in improving communication and relationship (Wincze & Weisberg, 2015), and finally, pharmacotherapy and psychoeducational interventions, which can complete the treatment (Jannini et al., 2017).

Investigating the sexual life area of patients is important for a psychotherapist, even if he or she is not strictly a clinical sexologist (to whom patients should be referred for specific treatment of sexual disorder). Sexual health is a fundamental aspect of general well-being, and problems in this area can significantly impact a person's quality of life and emotional well-being (Levine, 2003). Moreover, sexual difficulties may be indicative of underlying psychological issues such as anxiety, depression, stress, trauma, or relationship problems. An investigation of this area can facilitate the identification and treatment of these conditions. Sexuality is often intricately linked with the quality of interpersonal relationships and constitutes a pivotal element of personal identity and self-esteem. Such difficulties may give rise to feelings of inadequacy, shame, or low self-esteem, which may in turn fuel other psychological and interpersonal problems (APA, 2020).

Bancroft et al. (2009) posit that sexuality is an integral component of human life that interacts with numerous other areas of mental health and well-being. A holistic approach, as proposed by the authors, which encompasses the investigation of the sexual area, can facilitate a more comprehensive understanding of the patient and support more effective treatment.

5.1 Practical Tips for Integration into Case Formulation: Assessment of Sexual Function and Correlation with Other Aspects of Functioning

The "rules" concerning the therapeutic setting and assessment in clinical sexology are similar to those of any psychotherapeutic approach. In the initial sessions with patients, when investigating all areas of life and functioning (DSM-V TR, 2022), it is crucial to also investigate sexuality. However, it is important to avoid limiting the inquiry to brief and superficial responses that may indicate avoidance on the part of the patient or the therapist. Exploring sexual areas within the therapeutic setting can also often facilitate the development of more effective, uninhibited, and clear communication. It can assist in the normalization of patients' experiences and concerns, thereby reducing the sense of isolation and shame that may be experienced.

In order to ensure the efficacy of therapeutic interventions in the field of sexology, it is essential that the setting be meticulously designed to foster comfort, security, and transparency. A climate of trust must be established from the outset, with empathy and active listening being practiced from the first meeting onward. It is important to acknowledge and welcome emotions of shame, modesty, and distress, without judgment. The therapist's language must be accessible, with the avoidance of complex technical terms unless they are adequately explained. Additionally, the use of overly popular and/or "vulgar" language must be avoided (Kaplan, 1974; D'Ettore, 2021). In the active listening technique, it is necessary to provide rephrasing, to repeat what the patient has said to confirm understanding, to use open-ended questions to deepen the topics discussed, and to use silence strategically to allow the patient to reflect.

It is of the utmost importance to cultivate a therapeutic relationship that is respectful of the patient's experiences and feelings, and to avoid judgment. In the case of patients who are more inhibited, it may be necessary to anticipate the topics that will be discussed or to provide psychoeducation on the importance of sexual intimacy in a person's well-being. Ensuring confidentiality, nonjudgment, and cooperation with the patient allows to develop trust and security in the therapeutic relationship, which are often novel experiences for patients. Furthermore, defining the rules of the therapeutic contract helps to establish an alliance and to define the goals of therapy, whether individual or couple (Fenelli & Lorenzini, 1991).

In general, during the sexological assessment, the first step is to collect personal data, which includes fundamental information such as the person's age, residence, educational background, work experience, and sociocultural substratum. These data are of critical importance for contextualizing the patient's sexual life area. It is also necessary to ascertain from whom the patient received the referral. This may be a colleague, a medical professional, or another relevant figure. Upon receipt of the referral, it is imperative to proceed with the analysis of the question, clearly identifying the problem or symptoms that led the patient to seek assistance. Once the problem has been analyzed, it is imperative to provide the patient with a summary of the observations and indications. This may also include an initial invitation to observe oneself, reflect on one's own behavior and thoughts, and question them.

To ascertain a correct sexual history, the onset of the sexual problem is examined in detail by exploring the patient's sexual life history. This may include information on past and present relationships, sexual satisfaction, and possible dysfunction. The areas to be investigated regarding the sexual history of the patient are as follows: the biological area, which encompasses any present or past medical conditions; the psychological area, which includes any previous psychotherapies, the use of psychotropic drugs, psychological difficulties, traumas experienced, and childhood experiences; the relational area, which concerns the attachment style and any interpersonal difficulties; the family area, which examines ideas, beliefs, taboos, and prejudices present in the family of origin; finally, the social area, which examines the patient's social, economic, and work resources (Binik & Hall, 2014). The anamnesis phase in a sexological pathway may necessitate multiple interviews. The diagnosis is formulated at the conclusion of the anamnestic process, which also involves the use of psychometric diagnostic tools. This is because it is assumed that the intervention can be totally personalized, based on careful reflection on the relational and intrapsychic mechanisms that usually underlie the sexual disorder. The diagnosis is not a static entity; rather, it is a dynamic process that can result in progressive reformulations of the problem and the formulation of a therapeutic work plan to be discussed with the patient. This process ultimately leads to the establishment of a therapeutic contract that opens the way to the actual therapy and treatment deemed most appropriate to the situation. The transition from diagnosis to treatment plan is shaped by an in-depth analysis and integration of the information in the patient's narrative. The concept of functional diagnosis in sexology provides substantial support for the hypothesis that each symptom has a unique narrative. Functional diagnosis entails an examination of dysfunction at two levels: the analysis of the critical sequence of the symptom and the placement of the critical sequence within the historical context (Bonicelli et al., 2018).

It is noteworthy that in clinical sexology, as well as in cognitive and third-wave psychotherapy, a tool analogous to the ABC is employed (Ellis, 1962). CESPA is a useful tool for reconstructing the critical sequence of the symptom in imaginative terms, thus enabling the visualization of the details. CESPA, an acronym that stands for context, emotions, soma, thought, and action, is a tool used in sexology to zoom in on the patient's experience using episodic memory. The examination of single episodes allows for the exploration of the patient's inner world, encompassing thoughts, beliefs, SMI of Attachment, Cooperation, Sexuality, Agonism, Belonging, and Play. These innate tendencies to action that have interpersonal "purposes" and that "produce" different and multiple emotions have been identified as key factors in the development of emotional responses (Kayatekin & Plakun, 2009).

The sexual area of our patients is often overlooked, yet as we have seen, it is an essential dimension. Sexuality is not merely a biological function; it is also a profound reflection of our identity, fears, desires, and relationships. To consider this topic in psychotherapy is to venture into the core of human experience, where emotions and thoughts intertwine in complex and fascinating ways. It is an invitation to explore the human being in its totality, recognizing that sexuality is a fundamental melody that accompanies us throughout our lives. During the initial sessions, the exploration of sexuality can facilitate the disclosure of previously concealed aspects of the patient's identity. For instance, the use of sexual fantasies in therapy can provide valuable insights into a patient's history and pathogenic beliefs (Bader, 2003).

A competent clinician should be able to contextualize the sexual sphere within the broader framework of their patient's psychological functioning. Integrating this area into the assessment and case formulation of psychotherapy is not only useful but also essential for comprehensive treatment. The various elements of this approach collectively provide invaluable tools for a more comprehensive understanding of the patient and the development of effective and targeted therapeutic interventions. This integrated approach, which encompasses an understanding of the patient's mind and life history, including sexual aspects, facilitates the conceptualization of the case and subsequent treatment planning. This approach ensures a more accurate and tailored approach to case conceptualization and treatment planning. The objective of this integrated approach is to enhance the patient's emotional well-being, interpersonal relationships, and self-regulatory capacity, thereby facilitating positive and enduring change (Norcross, 2011).

5.2 The Case of Viola

This clinical example demonstrates the significance of addressing sexuality in the context of treating a complex patient. In this case, it was crucial to conduct a comprehensive assessment of the patient's sexual history. This allowed us to gain insight into her experiences and idiosyncratic processes of attributing meaning. This understanding was instrumental in developing a more comprehensive case formulation. Moreover, the psychoeducational interventions, which were based on the case formulation, had a positive impact on the patient's sexual functioning, metacognitive abilities, and self-perception. These improvements also influenced the quality of the patient's interpersonal relationships and her overall sense of well-being. Similarly, the patient's ability to overcome dysfunctional behaviors and replace them with actions aligned with her genuine goals and desires was facilitated by the integration of trauma-focused EMDR, episodic memory exploration with ABC, and the promotion of metacognitive skills.

Clinical Case
Viola, a 34-year-old woman, comes to therapy because of recurring episodes of panic attacks and loss of interest in activities that she used to find enjoyable, such as

painting and teaching (the patient is a teacher at the primary school in her village). Her request for help is to "stop feeling anxiety." Growing up in a large family, the fourth of five children, Viola had a childhood marked by the presence of a rigid and authoritarian father, who was short-tempered and not very affectionate. Her mother, submissive and, like her father, rather cold in her displays of affection, tried to keep the peace in the house, often at the expense of her own needs. Viola remembers a childhood devoid of physical affection and emotional expressions. "My mother was always tired and worried about not upsetting my father. He, on the other hand, rarely spoke to us except to scold us." One incident Viola vividly remembers is when, at the age of 10, she had brought home a bad grade. Her father, furious, yelled at her and forbade her to leave the house for a month, thus, according to him, forcing her to study harder. "I felt humiliated and powerless," says Viola, "my mother did nothing to defend me, she just watched in silence." Viola also reports that she was sexually abused by a neighbor when she was about 8 years old. At that time, she started to eat poorly and had several gastrointestinal problems. This traumatic event was never adequately processed, the patient claims to have "come to terms with it," and was never told to her family, who at the time, did not notice anything. Meaningful relationships are few and she tends to isolate herself socially, reporting feelings of distrust in relationships with others and themes of judgment. At work, although Viola has been a "model student," and today a highly competent and scrupulous teacher, she often feels insecure in her role and overwhelmed by relationships with colleagues, where she reports a difficulty in being assertive with respect to tasks, but also to social "exchange" during breaks. She reacts with avoidance behavior and perfectionism, where she finds herself fulfilling each other's demands even at weekends. When exploring the sexual sphere, he reveals that he suffers from anorgasmia and vaginismus. She has difficulty lubricating herself during sexual intercourse and experiences pain during penetration. Despite her love for her husband, she describes sex as a duty rather than a pleasure, often accompanied by anxiety and frustration. "I cannot feel pleasure during sexual intercourse," she says, "and I feel blocked. My husband says I am the problem." The patient is frightened about the possibility of her husband getting fed up with her and reveals that she would like to be able to solve her sexual problems. When investigating sexual history, we also trace the absence of masturbation and self-exploration of the body.

From the point of view of psychological functioning, Viola shows signs of insecure-avoidant attachment, characterized by a strong desire for closeness and security, but also a "due distance" to feel safe. Her intense fears about being unlovable cause her to engage in anxious behavior, such as brooding and interpersonal control, perfectionism, and complacency in interpersonal relationships. Her capacity for metacognition is limited; she has difficulty reflecting on her mental states and recognizing her emotions; and she is unable to look inside herself and explain her psychosomatic symptoms. In the therapeutic relationship, Viola tends to maintain an emotional distance and has initially shown resistance to exploring painful themes from the past.

The therapist, through an empathic and nonjudgmental approach, validation, and self-revelation interventions, managed to encourage Viola to explore her experiences and feelings in a safe and supportive environment. During diagnostic restitution, she helps the patient move from her explicit request for help with anxiety and panic attacks to a broader awareness of her psychological functioning. It is explained how her perfectionism, a strategy to feel "lovable," has been established since her early childhood episodes of criticism and invalidation and also how traumatic experiences contribute to the maintenance of her symptoms. By collecting the ABCs of life history, Viola was able to identify dysfunctional thoughts, emotions, and behavior. Specific metacognitive interventions developed in the patient a greater awareness and understanding of her own mental states, putting her in touch with her pathogenic self-image and beliefs about it, and all the strategies she put in place to resolve the resulting suffering. With EMDR (desensitization and reprocessing through eye movement) therapy, the deepest traumas were addressed and processed. This work allowed Viola to process her childhood experiences and begin to build a more positive and integrated narrative of herself. Through a series of psychoeducation sessions, Viola was able to better understand the mechanisms of her body and mind. This included explanations of the female sexual response and how stress and anxiety can interfere with it. We discussed how her alexithymia, the inability to recognize and verbalize emotions, may contribute to her physical symptoms, such as lack of lubrication and vaginismus. Psychoeducational interventions showed the patient that ortho-sympathetic activations, such as brooding, tension, anxiety, and control, could affect a hypertonus of the pelvic floor and vaginal musculature, probable contributors to her pain on penetration.

Viola, after a few months, became more aware of her mind and body functioning and reactions, reducing brooding, perfectionism, control, and avoidance, also related to sexual intercourse. Viola reported a reduction in anxiety and an increase in the ability to live in the present moment, increasing levels of intimacy and trust with each other and improving emotional connection with her husband. As therapy progressed, Viola noticed a significant improvement in her sex life. She reported feeling more relaxed and being able to enjoy more intimate moments with her husband. Episodes of vaginismus and anorgasmia decreased, and Viola experienced an increase in natural lubrication, resulting in less pain during sexual intercourse. Viola learned to see sex no longer as a duty, but as an opportunity for mutual connection and pleasure.

At the end of the therapy course, Viola no longer had panic attacks, returned to painting and took up yoga and Pilates, suggested in therapy. She also gave herself the opportunity, outside the work environment, to meet a couple of colleagues with whom she made new friendships. She expressed gratitude for the work done and manifested a new confidence in her own abilities, in terms of security and self-efficacy. Viola now recognizes the importance of continuing to take care of herself and maintaining open and authentic communication with herself and others.

References

American Psychiatric Association. (2013). *Diagnostic and statistical manual of mental disorders* (5th ed.). American Psychiatric Association.

American Psychiatric Association. (2022). *Diagnostic and statistical manual of mental disorders* (5th ed., text rev.). American Psychiatric Association. https://doi.org/10.1176/appi.books.9780890425787

American Psychological Association. (2020). *Guidelines for psychological practice with sexual minority persons*. American Psychiatric Association.

Ainsworth, M. D. S., Blehar, M. C., Waters, E., & Wall, S. (1978). *Patterns of attachment: A psychological study of the strange situation*. Erlbaum.

Bader, M. (2003). *Arousal: The secret logic of sexual fantasies*. Virgin Books.

Bancroft, J. (2009). *Human sexuality and its problems* (3rd ed.). Elsevier Health Sciences.

Bancroft, J., Janssen, E., Strong, D. R., & Vukadinovic, Z. (2009). Sexuality and the human condition. *The Journal of Sexual Medicine, 6*(4), 888–896.

Binik, Y. M., & Hall, K. S. K. (Eds.). (2014). *Principles and practice of sex therapy* (5th ed.). The Guilford Press.

Brennan, J., & Capel, B. (2004). One tissue, two fates: Molecular genetic events that underlie testis versus ovary development. *Nature Reviews Genetics, 5*(7), 509–521.

Bonicelli, C., Rossetto, V., & Veglia, F. (2018). *Sessuologia clinica: Modelli di intervento, diagnosi e terapie integrate*. Erikson.

Bowlby, J. (1969). *Attachment and loss: Vol. 1. Attachment*. Basic Books.

Capel, B. (2000). The battle of the sexes. *Mechanisms of Development, 92*(1), 89–103.

D'Ettore, D. (2021). *Trattato di psicologia e psicopatologia del comportamento sessuale*. Giunti.

Dèttore, D. (2004). La terapia sessuale. In A. Galeazzi & P. Meazzini (Eds.), *Mente e comportamento. Trattato italiano di psicoterapia cognitivo-comportamentale*. Giunti Editore.

Dimaggio, G., Montano, A., Popolo, R., & Salvatore, G. (2013). *Terapia metacognitiva interpersonale*. Raffaello Cortina.

Egan, S. K., & Perry, D. G. (2001). Gender identity: A multidimensional analysis with implications for psychosocial adjustment. *Developmental Psychology, 37*(4), 451–463.

Ellis, A. (1962). *Reason and emotion in psychotherapy*. Citadel.

Fenelli, A., & Lorenzini, R. (1991). *Clinica delle disfunzioni sessuali*. La Nuova Italia Scientifica.

Fisher, H. E. (1992). *Anatomy of love: A natural history of mating, marriage, and why we stray*. W.W. Norton & Company.

Flavell, J. H. (1979). Metacognition and cognitive monitoring: A new area of cognitive–developmental inquiry. *American Psychologist, 34*(10), 906–911.

Fleming, S. M., & Dolan, R. J. (2012). The neural basis of metacognitive ability. *Philosophical Transactions of the Royal Society B: Biological Sciences, 367*(1594), 1338–1349.

Foucault, M. (1978). *The history of sexuality, volume 1: An introduction*. Pantheon Books.

Freedman, J., & Combs, G. (1996). *Narrative therapy: The social construction of preferred realities*. Norton & Company.

Garofalo, C., Velotti, P., Callea, A., Popolo, R., Salvatore, G., Cavallo, F., & Dimaggio, G. (2018). Emotion dysregulation, impulsivity and personality disorder traits: A community sample study. *Psychiatry Research*. https://doi.org/10.1016/j.psychres.2018.05.067

Geuter, U., Heller, M. C., & Weaver, J. O. (2010). Handbook of body psychotherapy. *International Body Psychotherapy Journal, 9*(2), 75–83.

Gómez, J. M., González-Megías, A., & Verdú, M. (2023). The evolution of same-sex sexual behaviour in mammals. *Nature Communications, 14*(1), 5719. https://doi.org/10.1038/s41467-023-41290-x

Graglia, M. (2022). *Sex, gender, and orientation: Best practices for inclusion*. Carocci.

Hamann, S., Herman, R. A., Nolan, C. L., & Wallen, K. (2004). Men and women differ in amygdala response to visual sexual stimuli. *Nature Neuroscience, 7*(4), 411–416.

Hinde, R. A. (1974). *Biological bases of human social behavior*. McGraw-Hill.

Hughes, I. A., Houk, C., Ahmed, S. F., & Lee, P. A. (2006). Consensus statement on management of intersex disorders. *Archives of Disease in Childhood, 91*(7), 554–563. https://doi.org/10.1136/adc.2006.098319

Jannini, E. A., Lenzi, A., & Maggi, M. (2017). *Medical sexology: Treatise on psychosexology, sexual medicine, and couple's health*. Edra.

Kabat-Zinn, J., Segal, Z., Teasdale, J., & e Williams M. (2007). *Ritrovare la serenità*. Raffaello Cortina.

Kaplan, H. S. (1974). *The new sex therapy: Active treatment of sexual dysfunctions*. Brunner/Mazel.

Kayatekin, M. S., & Plakun, E. M. (2009). A view from Riggs: Treatment resistance and patient authority–X: From acting out to enactment in treatment resistant disorders. *The Journal of the American Academy of Psychoanalysis and Dynamic Psychiatry, 37*(2), 365–381. https://doi.org/10.1521/jaap.2009.37.2.365. PMID: 19591566.

Kelly, G. A. (1955). *The psychology of personal constructs* (Vol. 2). Norton.

Kinsey, A. C., Pomeroy, W. B., & Martin, C. E. (1950). *Sexual behavior in the human male*. Bompiani.

LeDoux, J. (1996). *The emotional brain: The mysterious underpinnings of emotional life*. Simon & Schuster.

LeVay, S., & Baldwin, J. (2012). *Discovering human sexuality* (2nd ed.). Sinauer Associates.

Levine, S. B. (2003). *Handbook of clinical sexuality for mental health professionals*. Routledge.

Levy, K. N., Ellison, W. D., Scott, L. N., & Bernecker, S. L. (2011). Attachment style. *Journal of Clinical Psychology, 67*(2), 193–203. https://doi.org/10.1002/jclp.20756

Liotti, G. (2001). *Le opere della coscienza*. Raffaello Cortina.

Lodé, T. (2023). *Beastly mating*. Carocci.

Lowen, A. (1975). *Bioenergetics*. Penguin Books.

Lysaker, P. H., Olesek, K. L., Warman, D. M., Martin, J. M., Salzman, A. K., Nicolò, G., Salvatore, G., & Dimaggio, G. (2011). Metacognition in schizophrenia: Correlates and stability of deficits in theory of mind and self-reflectivity. *Psychiatry Research, 190*(1), 18–22. https://doi.org/10.1016/j.psychres.2010.07.016

Martin, D. J., Garske, J. P., & Davis, M. K. (2000). Relation of the therapeutic alliance with outcome and other variables: A meta-analytic review. *Journal of Consulting and Clinical Psychology, 68*(3), 438–450. https://doi.org/10.1037/0022-006X.68.3.438

Masters, W. H., & Johnson, V. E. (1970). *Human sexual inadequacy*. Bantam Books.

MacLean, P. (1984). Brain evolution. The origins of social and cognitive behaviors. *Journal of Children in Contemporary Society, 16*, 9–21.

Mallinckrodt, B., Porter, M. J., & Kivlighan, D. M. (2005). Client attachment to therapist, depth of in-session exploration, and object relations in brief psychotherapy. *Psychotherapy: Theory, Research, Practice, Training, 42*(1), 85–100. https://doi.org/10.1037/0033-3204.42.1.85

Mikulincer, M., Shaver, P. R., & Berant, E. (2013). An attachment perspective on therapeutic processes and outcomes. *Journal of Personality, 81*(6), 606–616. https://doi.org/10.1111/j.1467-6494.2012.00806.x

Money, J., Hampson, J. G., & Hampson, J. L. (1957). Imprinting and the establishment of gender role. *Archives of Neurology and Psychiatry, 77*(3), 333–336. https://doi.org/10.1001/archneurpsyc.1957.02330330119019

Norcross, J. C. (Ed.). (2011). *Psychotherapy relationships that work: Evidence-based responsiveness* (2nd ed.). Oxford University Press.

Ogden, P., Minton, K., & Pain, C. (2006). *Trauma and the body: A sensorimotor approach to psychotherapy*. W. W. Norton & Company.

Ortigue, S., & Bianchi-Demicheli, F. (2008). The chronoarchitecture of human sexual desire: A high-density electrical mapping study. *NeuroImage, 43*(2), 337–345.

Panksepp, J., & Biven, E. (2012). A meditation on the affective neuroscientific view of human and animalian MindBrains. In A. Fotopoulou, D. Pfaffe, & M. A. Conway (Eds.), *From the couch to the lab. Trends in psychodynamic neuroscience* (pp. 145–175).

Panzeri, M. (2023). *Terapia mansionale sessuale. Un approccio integrato*. Il Mulino.

Perkins, R. H., & Grover, K. W. (2010). The role of metacognitive beliefs in sexual dysfunction: Implications for cognitive-behavioral therapy. *Sexual and Relationship Therapy, 25*(2), 123–138.
Porges, S. W. (2001). The polyvagal theory: Phylogenetic substrates of a social nervous system. *International Journal of Psychophysiology, 42*, 123–146.
Reich, W. (1942). *The function of the orgasm: Sex-economic problems of biological energy*. Farrar, Straus and Giroux.
Safran, J. D., & Muran, J. C. (2000). *Negotiating the therapeutic Alliance: A relational treatment guide*. Guilford Press.
Semerari, A., Carcione, A., Dimaggio, G., Falcone, M., Nicolò, G., Procacci, M., & Alleva, G. (2003). How to evaluate metacognitive functioning in psychotherapy? The metacognition assessment scale and its applications. *Clinical Psychology & Psychotherapy, 10*(4), 238–261.
Shapiro, F., & Forrest, M. S. (2017). EMDR therapy and sexual health: The role of eye movement desensitization and reprocessing in the treatment of sexual dysfunctions and trauma-related sexual disorders. *Journal of EMDR Practice and Research, 11*(2), 84–95. https://doi.org/10.1891/1933-3196.11.2.84
Symons, D. (1979). *The evolution of human sexuality*. Oxford University Press.
Shively, M. G., & De Cecco, J. P. (1977). Components of sexual identity. *Journal of Homosexuality, 3*(1), 41–48. https://doi.org/10.1300/J082v03n01_04
Stern, D. B. (2010). *Partners in thought: Working with unformulated experience, dissociation, and enactment*. Routledge.
Tobin, D. D., Menon, M., Menon, M., Spatta, B. C., Hodges, E. V. E., & Perry, D. G. (2010). The intrapsychics of gender: A model of self-socialization. *Psychological Review, 117*(2), 601–622. https://doi.org/10.1037/a0018936
Tripodi, F. (2021). Counselling and psychotherapy in sexual medicine. In M. Lew-Starowicz, A. Giraldi, & T. Krüger (Eds.), *Psychiatry and sexual medicine* (pp. 187–207). Springer. https://doi.org/10.1007/978-3-030-52298-8_12
van der Kolk, B. A. (2014). *The body keeps the score: Brain, mind, and body in the healing of trauma*. Viking.
Veglia, F. (2004). *Manuale di educazione sessale – volume 1. Teoria e metodologia*. Erickson.
Waldinger, M. D., & Venema, P. L. (1998). The neurobiological approach to premature ejaculation: Implications for treatment. *Journal of Sexual Therapy, 24*(2), 231–242.
Wampold, B. E. (2015). How important are the common factors in psychotherapy? An update. *World Psychiatry, 14*(3), 270–277. https://doi.org/10.1002/wps.20238
Wincze, J. P., & Weisberg, R. B. (2015). *Sex therapy: Innovations and advances*. The Guilford Press.
World Health Organization. (2019). *International classification of diseases for mortality and morbidity statistics* (11th Rev.). Retrieved from https://icd.who.int/en
World Health Organization. (2006). *Sexual and reproductive health: Defining sexual health*. World Health Organization.

Part VII
Personalization of the Treatment

Stepped Care Model in Integrated Evidence-Based Practice Relational Psychotherapy

Angelo Compare, Barbara Poletti, Luca Pievani, Jacopo Stringo, and Antonino La Tona

1 Introduction

Mental health disorders are a major public health problem worldwide, affecting approximately one in eight individuals (World Health Organisation [WHO], 2022). Despite this high prevalence, access to appropriate mental health treatment remains a significant challenge globally. Epidemiological research consistently indicates that the proportion of individuals with mental disorders receiving minimally effective treatment is alarmingly low, particularly in low- and middle-income countries (Alonso et al., 2018; Thornicroft et al., 2017). For example, a multinational study revealed that only 13.8% of individuals with anxiety disorders and 22.4% of those with depressive disorders in high-income countries receive at least minimally adequate treatment (Alonso et al., 2018). The situation is even more critical in low- and middle-income countries, where only 2.3% of individuals with anxiety disorders and 3.7% of those with depression received adequate treatment (Thornicroft et al., 2017).

This significant treatment gap is not only due to the scarcity of mental health services, but also to low rates of help-seeking behaviour among those in need. The World Mental Health Survey revealed that 41.3% of people with anxiety disorders

---

A. Compare · J. Stringo · A. La Tona (✉)
Department of Human and Social Sciences, University of Bergamo, Bergamo, Italy
e-mail: antonino.latona@unibg.it

B. Poletti
Department of Oncology and Hemato-Oncology, University of Milan, Milano, Italy

Department of Neurology and Laboratory of Neuroscience, IRCCS Istituto Auxologico Italiano, Milan, Italy

L. Pievani
Scuola di Psicoterapia Integrata, Bergamo, Italy

© The Author(s), under exclusive license to Springer Nature Switzerland AG 2024
B. Poletti et al. (eds.), *Training in Integrated Relational Psychotherapy*,
https://doi.org/10.1007/978-3-031-71904-2_22

and 56.7% of those with depression said they did not need any treatment (Clement et al., 2015). These findings indicate that, in addition to improving the availability of mental health services, it is crucial to address the factors that deter the general population from seeking psychological care. Several factors can hinder access to mental healthcare, including stigma, financial constraints, and lack of awareness about mental health problems and available services (Thornicroft et al., 2016; World Bank, 2016). Economic barriers, such as the high cost of psychological services and limited insurance coverage, contribute to exacerbating existing inequalities in access to mental healthcare, and those from lower socioeconomic backgrounds are particularly affected (Knapp & Wong, 2020; World Bank, 2016).

The principal issue pertains to identifying disorders and formulating treatment plans. Various studies, as referenced, indicate that a significant number of patients with these disorders goes untreated or does not receive proper care. One of the reasons for the lack of or insufficient treatment is the challenge in recognising these disorders early or at the onset. High economic costs (e.g., insurance policies not covering private treatments), difficulties in accessing healthcare, lack of time on the part of adult workers, stigma, and other factors could explain these low percentages; however, untreated mental disorders lead to lower wages and employment rates and have other negative social and economic consequences (Golberstein et al., 2016; Smit et al., 2006). For example, Smit et al. (2006) found that the costs of mental disorders are similar to those of physical illnesses. As such, healthcare systems are actively searching for better ways to (i) deliver evidence-based treatments in a cost-effective manner and (ii) reach as many patients as possible.

A solution could be the adoption of stepped-care approaches. The term refers to a model of healthcare delivery that aims to increase the efficiency of welfare services by adopting briefer minimal interventions, within stepped care models (Bower & Gilbody, 2005). If the first treatment is ineffective, then the programme moves incrementally to more intensive therapies; as such, stepped care approaches could help in reaching and treating a larger percentage of patients, improving the efficacy of welfare services, and reducing overall healthcare costs.

1.1 The Stepped Care Model

The stepped care model is an evidence-based approach that involves a series of treatments that start from the least intensive treatment possible and increase in intensity as the severity of the illness increases (Loeb et al., 2000; Ho et al., 2016; Tasca et al., 2019). This model's structure allows for various types of interventions: not just individual psychotherapy sessions, but also medical therapy management treatments, psychoeducational interventions, guided self-help (such as bibliotherapy), group therapies, and brief interventions, among others (Liuzzi, 2016). This working method also simplifies the decision-making process regarding the intensification of treatment to maximise the benefit to the patient while simultaneously addressing their needs and prioritises low-intensity interventions whenever feasible to avoid unnecessary treatments (Meeuwissen et al., 2019).

Two fundamental concepts that pertain to the stepped care approach are those of least restrictive and self-correcting (Bower & Gilbody, 2005). 'Least restrictive' does not refer exclusively to the impact the interventions have on the patient's life, but, in a public health context, to the use of resources and professionals dedicated to the individual case as well. Since both time and cost resources are extremely limited, it is expected that the stepped care model will provide the treatment that is both most effective and least expensive in terms of resources. In this way, only those patients who have not responded positively to previous interventions will progress to more intense and demanding treatments.

Providing the lowest-intensity and most effective treatment available is only possible through the second mechanism, namely, that of 'self-correcting'. In fact, each treatment delivered is constantly monitored, and if improvements are not detected, a change in level results. This process, called 'stepping up', sees the treatment increase in terms of both intensity and the level of resources invested. The aim is clearly to keep track of the progress of the intervention in terms of progression, improvement, and possible challenges. This may resonate as a way of working already familiar to many professionals, who apply it daily in their clinical practice. The main difference introduced by the stepped care model concerns the standardisation of procedures and transitions in accordance with the specific needs and placements of each individual case (Bower & Gilbody, 2005).

The clinical effectiveness of this model has been validated by several studies, demonstrating its efficiency in general medicine, addiction care, and mental health. The treatment evolves in tandem with the course of symptoms, which are monitored both periodically and in response to therapy (Bower & Gilbody, 2005; Meeuwissen et al., 2019). The true novelty of this model lies in its goal of making the therapeutic process entirely effective and efficient through the systematic standardisation of the monitoring process of successive interventions. Such standardisation allows for therapy outcomes to be evaluated and decisions to be made about how treatment should develop; these decisions are also influenced by factors such as the disorder's characteristics and the patient's functioning (Liuzzi, 2016).

1.2 Key Features and Benefits

As mentioned, intensity modulation is an essential requirement in the stepped care model, allowing for the use of short, structured interventions, such as brief therapy or self-help interventions with minimal professional assistance. Recent studies confirm that this approach effectively balances treatment intensity with patient needs, enhancing therapeutic outcomes in various settings (Richards et al., 2020). Further fundamental characteristics of the stepped care model are listed below:

1. *Least Restrictive First-Line Treatment*: The fundamental principle of the stepped care model is to begin with the least restrictive treatment that is likely to provide significant health gains. This could mean starting with interventions that require minimal therapist input, such as bibliotherapy or computerised therapy (Newman, 2000; Liuzzi, 2016). Evidence suggests that starting with less intensive treatments is effective for mild to moderate conditions and can prevent unnecessary escalation to more intensive interventions (Huxley et al., 2019).
2. *Self-Correcting Mechanism*: The model includes systematic monitoring of treatment outcomes and patient progress. If initial interventions do not yield significant health gains, patients are 'stepped up' to more intensive treatments (Sobell & Sobell, 2000). This ensures that the therapeutic approach is responsive to individual patient needs.
3. *Efficiency in Resource Utilisation*: By starting with less intensive treatments, the stepped care model maximises the use of the available resources. This is particularly beneficial in publicly funded healthcare systems where therapist time and financial resources are limited (Haaga, 2000). Studies have shown that stepped care can reduce overall treatment costs while maintaining or improving patient outcomes (Yan et al., 2019).
4. *Clinical Effectiveness*: Various studies have validated the clinical effectiveness of the stepped care model. For instance, it has shown efficiency in managing depression, anxiety, and other mental health conditions by tailoring the intensity of the intervention to the patient's needs and monitoring progress closely (Bower & Gilbody, 2005).
5. *Cost-Effectiveness*: Stepped care can be more cost-effective than traditional models of care by reducing the average amount of therapist input per patient while maintaining clinical effectiveness. This approach allows for broader access to mental health services (Lovell & Richards, 2000; Anderson et al., 2019).

The stepped care approach, recommended by the National Institute for Health and Clinical Excellence (NICE), is widely used in England within the '*Improving Access to Psychological Therapies*' (IAPT) service. The goal of IAPT is to increase access to psychological therapies for the most common mental disorders (Boyd et al., 2019). As mentioned earlier, the preference is for the least intrusive intervention possible. However, if the patient presents a more complex condition or severe disorder, such as post-traumatic stress disorder, a more intensive treatment is recommended from the outset, shifting towards a stratified model. This stratified model is a form of stepped care in which the therapist evaluates the intervention's intensity and does not necessarily start with low-intensity treatments (Boyd et al., 2019).

An example of a disorder that can be effectively treated within a stepped care model is binge-eating disorder (BED). Research by Tasca et al. (2019) shows that individuals with BED do not always require specialised treatments but can achieve the same results with a stepped care approach starting with self-help activities. However, long-term outcomes are not the same if only low-intensity treatments are used for issues such as anxiety and depression. For these conditions, it is necessary to proceed to subsequent phases with more intensive treatments (Ali et al., 2017;

Tasca et al., 2019). Indeed, the guidelines for treating depression through stepped care emphasise how to develop the intervention by monitoring the positive or negative responses to therapy in the preceding, less intensive phases (Meeuwissen et al., 2019; NICE, 2018; Spijker et al., 2013; Richards et al., 2002). This makes it a valid intervention method for disorders that commonly present chronicity and relapses, as it supports the patient throughout the entire necessary period for their recovery.

Liuzzi (2016) proposes an example of the stepped care model's structure that could be articulated into four levels. The first level involves a self-help intervention, such as bibliotherapy, deliberately devoid of operator intervention to promote the patient's natural recovery and avoid pathologizing them. The second level includes mental health professionals' participation, still within a guided self-help intervention, with a maximum of two sessions to direct the person to the most suitable therapeutic path. The intensity increases at the third level, where up to six sessions of brief intervention are offered, while the fourth level involves up to 16 sessions, constituting a long-term treatment.

The implementation of stepped care in psychological therapies, according to Liuzzi (2016), can be illustrated through various structured levels:

1. *First Level*: Self-help interventions such as bibliotherapy or online self-help programmes without therapist involvement. These promote natural recovery and avoid the unnecessary pathologizing of mild conditions (Liuzzi, 2016). Digital self-help interventions have shown promising results, especially when integrated into general practices, providing high levels of acceptability and feasibility among patients (Haugh et al., 2019).
2. *Second Level*: Guided self-help with minimal therapist input, such as one or two sessions to guide the patient through self-help materials. This step often involves mental health professionals such as practice nurses or primary care mental health workers (Richards et al., 2002).
3. *Third Level*: Brief individual or group therapy sessions (up to six sessions) for patients who need a more structured but still lower-intensity intervention (Lovell & Richards, 2000). Recent implementations have shown that these sessions are particularly effective for managing moderate conditions, improving clinical outcomes while maintaining cost-effectiveness (Meuldijk et al., 2021).
4. *Fourth Level*: More intensive and longer-term therapy (up to 16 sessions) for patients with more severe or persistent conditions (Bower & Gilbody, 2005).

1.3 *Challenges and Considerations*

While the stepped care model offers significant advantages, there are also challenges and considerations to address:

- *Patient Acceptance*: Ensuring that patients find minimal interventions acceptable and are willing to engage with these treatments is crucial for the success of the model. Studies have shown mixed results in patient acceptance, with some patients preferring more direct therapist involvement (Scogin et al., 2003). Recent studies have shown that patient acceptance of the stepped care model is generally positive, especially in primary care settings where patients often prefer self-help interventions over other treatment options (Haugh et al., 2019). However, some studies indicate that patient engagement can be improved with better integration of technology and personalised feedback mechanisms (Anderson et al., 2019).

- *Professional Acceptance*: Therapists and mental health professionals need to be comfortable with the theoretical underpinnings of stepped care and the changes in practice it entails. Recent evaluations highlight that professionals generally find the model acceptable, particularly when it integrates seamlessly into their workflow and offers practical benefits, such as better patient management tools and real-time feedback (Anderson et al., 2019). Yet, continuous training and support are essential for maintaining high levels of professional acceptance.
- *Research and Validation*: Continued research is needed to validate the assumptions underlying stepped care, such as its clinical equivalence to traditional therapy and cost-effectiveness. Modelling and controlled trials can help in understanding the long-term outcomes and optimising the model. Recent studies have supported the clinical effectiveness and cost-effectiveness of stepped care models, particularly in mental health and addiction treatment contexts (Brettschneider et al., 2020). However, challenges remain in generalising findings due to variability in implementation and patient populations across different studies.

1.4 Stepped Care Model: Recent Evidence

A recent study (Meuldijk et al., 2021) demonstrated the effectiveness of the stepped care model in treating older adults with anxiety and depression. Conducted across multiple sites, the study initially gave participants low-intensity cognitive behavioural therapy (CBT) programmes, accessible online or through a workbook with brief phone support. If necessary, treatment was intensified to face-to-face CBT sessions, stepping up to higher-intensity face-to-face CBT if needed. This approach showed improvements in symptom severity and quality of life compared to treatment as usual (TAU).

In the treatment of panic disorder, a comparison between the stepped care model and guideline-based treatment revealed similar remission rates and symptom reduction. However, the stepped care model required significantly less therapist contact time, suggesting its efficiency despite higher dropout rates (Kampman et al., 2020). For insomnia, the use of a stepped care model starting with digital CBT (dCBT) and, if necessary, moving to face-to-face CBT was shown to be effective. This approach not only reduced insomnia symptoms but also maintained treatment gains over time, with effects lasting for up to 2 years after the initial treatment (Bayoneto et al., 2023). Another significant example is the treatment of anorexia nervosa (AN) in adolescents. A stepped care model, based on family preferences and clinical needs, achieved remission rates of 45.1% at 24 weeks and 52.4% at 48 weeks (Le Grange et al., 2021). During the COVID-19 pandemic, a stepped care programme involving internet-based psychological interventions for healthcare workers proved effective in reducing anxiety and depression symptoms and provided scalable support during a period of high mental health demand (Mediavilla et al., 2022). In a recent study (Do et al., 2022), adapting the stepped care model to manage depression showed substantial reductions in depression severity and improvements in life satisfaction and anxiety levels. This model combined group psychotherapy and community-based activities, demonstrating its effectiveness in low-resource settings.

These examples highlight how the stepped care model can be successfully applied in various contexts and populations, improving accessibility and efficiency in psychological therapies. Cunningham et al. (2021) provide another example of the stepped care model's applicability, demonstrating its effectiveness in treating functional abdominal pain disorders (FAPD) in children. These are common issues that often persist for years with sometimes debilitating effects, causing psychological discomfort in affected youths (Campo et al., 2001, 2004; King et al., 2011). The study shows that psychoeducation and basic relaxation strategies improve pain management and fit perfectly into the basic medical treatment. For patients requiring more intensive intervention, CBTs can be implemented, yielding positive outcomes for both physical and mental health (Cunningham et al., 2021).

1.5 Strategic Use of the Stepped Care Model in Integrated Relational Psychotherapy

This model can be applied to psychotherapeutic interventions in many forms. The first stage involves identifying possible interventions that meet the stepped care level of intensity. One possible modelling would see a links between the steps of the model and the possible levels of finalised intervention to be implemented at different stages and moments in therapy. As mentioned earlier, the first step represents the lowest level of intervention intensity, followed by the second. Applied to a psychotherapeutic model, we might hypothesise placing the interventions of *history-gathering*, *patient acquaintance* (PA), and *context analysis*—in short, the constituent elements of the first interviews—within the first two steps of the stepped care model. By extension, all interventions that aim to explore the patient and their instances can fall under the first two steps and return several times during the course of therapy, even at more advanced stages (e.g., the ABC technique, genogram, clarification, and so on) (Ellis, 1955; McGoldrick & Gerson, 1985; McGoldrick et al., 2020). At this stage, treatment planning is organised, building on the *working alliance.*

Immediately thereafter, in the third step, once a wealth of information has been gathered about the patient's problem or reasons for coming to therapy, *symptom management* (SM) and interventions aimed at this can be carried out. Some examples may be Mindfulness-Based Stress Reduction (MBSR) (Kabat-Zinn, 1990), the ERP protocol, or the EMDR protocol (Shapiro, 1989, 1995) applied to intrusive thoughts and non-complex trauma. The fourth step, on the other hand, will be devoted to questions about the symptom, why it was there, and what factors serve to maintain it.

Another very important psychotherapeutic task is to make the patient aware of their own functioning (*awareness of functioning*, AF). This, which can be the fifth step, can be performed with techniques that work specifically to make it evident to the patient, as is the case in some of the steps in, for example, Attachment-Based Family Therapy (ABFT) (Diamond et al., 2014), working on mentalisation, applying Guidano's moviola technique (Guidano, 1988, 1992), or the two-chair technique.

Reaching the sixth step, we go on to work with the *transformation of the patient's functioning* (TF). Therapeutic techniques and acts are put in place that change the content of the functioning that the patient learnt to understand in the previous step. Examples of interventions may be cognitive restructuring, acceptance, and commitment therapy (ACT) (Hayes, 2016; Hayes et al., 2012) and Schematherapy (Young et al., 2006; Zeigler-Hill & Shackelford, 2020).

Finally, the last step applies in cases where intervention is needed for *complex trauma processing* (CTP). It is the highest level of intensity, and the therapeutic work is on a greater level of severity. It requires specific techniques and great clinical expertise. Possible interventions could be EMDR, Sensorimotor psychotherapy (Ogden & Fisher, 2015) or trauma-focused CBT (TF-CBT) (Cohen et al., 2006; Mannarino et al., 2014). From the third step to the seventh, one of the most important objectives in therapy is to enhance and strengthen the therapeutic alliance by monitoring it throughout. This aim derives from the perspective that a good-quality therapeutic alliance not only strengthens treatment adherence and the sharing of goals and tasks, but can also lead to a more positive and stable outcome over time.

As can be seen in Table 1, the layers of the stepped care model lend themselves to complementing and clarifying other types of modelling as well. For example, one based on the types of interventions that can point toward some specific techniques and approaches. Clearly, this is a simplification: many of the classified techniques or theorising actually have a much greater scope and act on multiple levels. The ultimate goal is to arrive at a case formulation and prepare a treatment plan that can be submitted to the patient. By thus agreeing on goals and objectives and sharing the various steps in the treatment process, it is possible to work in a way that preserves the alliance, improves adherence to treatment, and monitors any ruptures that may arise.

The nexus that this approach aims to create is between taking charge of the patient, understanding the symptom, and managing it so work can be carried out on the patient's functioning. When reference is made in this chapter to the term *functioning*, it specifically means modelling based on three main theories: those of *attachment* (Bowlby, 1969, 1973, 1980; Crittenden, 1990, 1992, 2016), those of interpersonal motivational systems (*IMS*) (Liotti et al., 2017; Liotti & Monticelli, 2008, 2014), and that of personal meaning organisations (*PMO*) (Guidano, 1988,

Table 1 Application scheme of stepped care applied to techniques

Stepped care	Typology of interventions	Techniques	Alliance
First level	PA	Clarification, ABC, CESPA, Self-observation, Emotional Validation, Genogram, Joint Family Drawing, Film Narrative, Autobiography, Alliance Building Techniques	Working alliance
Second level			
Third level	SM	Behavioural Homework, MBSR, Autogenic Training, Progressive Muscle Relaxation – Jacobson, ERP, Imagery (and rescripting), Decomposition of Attention Space, Stabilisation, Grounding, Orientation, Breathing Techniques	Therapeutic alliance
Fourth level	SM/AF	[Mainly working on the causing and maintaining factors of symptoms, building a bridge between SM and AF]	
Fifth level	AF	Psychoeducation, Reformulation, Metacommunication, Two-chair Technique, Empty Chair Technique, Focusing, Metaphor, Motto, Moviola/Replay, Crystallisation, Tests and Interviews	
Sixth level	TF	MIT, Demonstration/Modelling, Enactment, ACT, ABFT, DBT, CT-ED, Schematherapy, Cognitive Restructuring	
Seventh level	CTP	EMDR, TF-CBT, Sensorimotor Psychotherapy	

For the typology of interventions, the acronyms stand for: Patient Acquaintance (AP), Symptoms Management (SM), Acknowledgement of Functioning (AF), Transformation of Functioning (TF) and Complex Trauma Processing (CTP); for the techniques, ABC stands for Antecedents, Behavior, Consequences, CESPA stands for Context, Emotion, Somatic Sensation, Thought (Pensiero), Action, MBSR is Mindfulness-Based Stress Reduction, ERP stands for Exposure and Response Prevention, MIT is Metacognitive Interpersonal Therapy, ACT stands for Acceptance and Commitment Therapy, ABFT for Attachment-Based Family Therapy, EMDR stands for Eye Movement Desensitization and Reprocessing, and TF-CBT stands for Trauma-Focused Cognitive-Behavioural Therapy

1992). Each of these topics is explored in depth in this manual and is contextualised in the clinical process. From the fourth level to the seventh and final stepped care level, it is possible to delve into and explore these different perspectives related to functioning, which helps the clinician understand how the patient moves through their living environment—physical and relational.

2 The Steps Explained

As we can see in Fig. 1, a correspondence can be detected between the levels of stepped care and the performance delivered in terms of techniques and protocols. In detail:

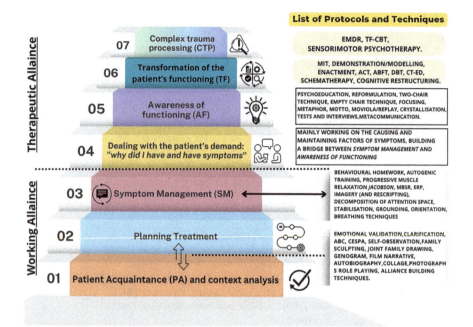

Fig. 1 Schematic overview of stepped care model in integrated evidence-based practice relational psychotherapy. (Please see the section "Strategic use of the Stepped Care model in integrated relational psychotherapy" for application details)

1. *First and Second Level, Patient Acquaintance (PA)*:

   - **Emotional Validation**, in which the therapist recognises and accepts the patient's emotions as valid, confirming their importance and normalizing them. The aim is to promote self-acceptance, increase self-esteem, and reduce emotional reactivity.
   - **Clarification** is a technique that aims to help the patient clearly express their thoughts and feelings, facilitating mutual understanding. It improves communication and mutual understanding, reducing misunderstandings.
   - **Antecedents Behaviour Consequences (ABC)** (Ellis, 1955) is a cognitive-behavioural technique that analyses the sequence between Antecedent, Behavior, and Consequence to identify and modify dysfunctional patterns, thoughts and behaviours, promoting positive behavioural changes.
   - **Context, Emotion, Somatic Sensation, Thought (Pensiero), Action, (CESPA)** (Liotti & Monticelli, 2008, 2014) is a cognitive technique that in cognitive psychotherapy is used to zoom in on what is the patient's experience, using episodic memory. It is applied by trying to work on single episodes and acts on two fronts: helping the patient to formulate connections and leading them to greater awareness.
   - **Self-observation**, in which the patient is encouraged to monitor and reflect on one's thoughts, emotions, and behaviours, to increase personal awareness, identify dysfunctional patterns, and promote self-regulation.

- **Family Sculpting** is a spatial representation of family relationships, aimed to explore dynamics and roles within the family unit. It increases awareness of family dynamics, promotes change and conflict resolution.
- **Joint Family Drawing** is a technique where drawing together is aimed to explore family dynamics and promote communication and mutual understanding. It improves family communication, increases mutual understanding, and may resolve conflicts.
- **Genogram** (McGoldrick & Gerson, 1985; McGoldrick et al., 2020) is a visual map of family relationships across generations, useful for identifying patterns, transgenerational influences and promoting awareness of family dynamics.
- **Film Narrative** is a way of using films or videos to explore therapeutic themes, facilitating identification and reflection. It promotes empathy, facilitates emotional exploration, and stimulates reflection on relevant themes.
- **Autobiography** consists of writing one's life story or a part of it as a therapeutic tool to explore and integrate personal experiences. It's useful to increase self-awareness, integrate past experiences, and promote personal growth.
- **Collage** is a graphic technique using cut-out images to express emotions, thoughts, or tell stories, facilitating creative exploration. It facilitates emotional expression, stimulates creativity, and promotes personal reflection.
- **Photographs** can help the patients to explore emotions and memories, facilitating communication and reflection, stimulating memory, and promoting personal insight.
- **Role-playing**, in which the patient is encouraged in acting out situations to practice responses and behaviours, improving social skills and conflict management.
- **Alliance Building Techniques** are strategies to create a positive and collaborative therapeutic relationship between patient and therapist, improving the therapeutic relationship, increasing trust, and promoting collaboration in the therapeutic process.

2. *Third Level, Symptoms Management (SM)*:

- **Behavioural Homework** consisting in exercises to be done at home to reinforce techniques learned in therapy and promote behavioural change. The aim is to generalize skills learned in therapy to everyday life, promote change and personal growth.
- **Autogenic Training** is a relaxation technique based on self-suggestion that induces a state of calm through mental exercises. It reduces anxiety and stress, promotes deep relaxation, and improves psychophysical well-being.
- **Progressive Muscle RelaxationJacobson** is a relaxation technique that alternates between muscle tension and relaxation to reduce anxiety. It reduces muscle tension, decreases anxiety, and improves body awareness.
- **Mindfulness-Based Stress Reduction (MBSR)** (Kabat-Zinn, 1990) is an evidenced-based model aiming to alleviate symptoms via meditation and

self-compassion. Initially designed to treat chronic pain and associated conditions, it is effective in treating anxiety and depression symptoms, and improving general wellbeing.
- **Exposure and Response Prevention (ERP)** is a behavioural therapy that gradually exposes people to situations designed to provoke a person's reaction to distressful situations in a safe environment. The aim of the ERP is to provide a patient with coping skills for when a triggering situation presents itself in everyday life, allowing them to then use the skills to prevent their compulsion from taking over. It's mainly used to treat anxiety and obsessive-compulsive disorders.
- **Decomposition of Attention Space** is a technique to improve concentration and attention by reducing mental dispersion; in doing so, it increases attention effectiveness.
- **Imagery (and Rescripting)** is a guided visualization to modify negative memories and create new positive associations. It reduces emotional distress related to negative memories, promotes positive change, and improves emotional well-being.
- **Stabilization** is a technique that helps patients feel safe and in control, especially in crisis or trauma situations. It promotes safety and emotional stability, reduces the risk of crisis, and facilitates trauma symptom management.
- **Grounding** is a technique to stay anchored in the present, often used for managing trauma and reducing anxiety. It addresses dissociative symptoms, improves present-moment awareness, and promotes emotional stability.
- **Orientation** is a technique to orient oneself in time and space, useful for managing anxiety and trauma. It improves temporal and spatial orientation, reduces anxiety, and facilitates trauma symptom management.
- **Breathing Techniques** are methods to control breathing and reduce anxiety, improving relaxation and well-being. It reduces anxiety, promotes relaxation, and improves body awareness.

3. *The Fourth Level* will be devoted to questions about the symptom(s), *why it was there, and what factors serve to maintain it.* The aim is to build a bridge between SM and AF.

4. *The Fifth Level, Awareness of Functioning (AF)*:

    - **Reformulation** consists in repeating what the patient has said in different words to confirm understanding and stimulate reflection. That aims to increase awareness and understanding of one's thoughts and feelings, and foster introspection.
    - **Psychoeducation** is a procedure where the professional informs the patient about psychological topics relevant to their problem, increasing awareness and skills. It provides useful knowledge for managing symptoms, and promotes patient autonomy and empowerment.
    - **Metaphor**, in which it is possible to use stories or analogies to explain complex psychological concepts in an understandable and relatable way. In that

way, it facilitates the understanding of complex concepts, promotes insight, and stimulates reflection.
- **Motto**, in which a phrase or statement is used to guide behaviour or thoughts, providing motivation and direction. Doing so provides behavioural guidance, increases motivation, and supports positive change.
- **Metacommunication** consists in talking about communication itself, in order to improve mutual understanding and resolve misunderstandings. The aim is to improve communication quality, resolve conflicts, and promote mutual understanding.
- **Two-Chair Technique**, is a Gestalt method for exploring internal conflicts through dialogue between two parts of oneself. It aims to resolve internal conflicts, increase self-awareness, and promote integration of the self.
- **Empty Chair Technique**, is an imaginary dialogue with a significant person to process emotions and resolve unresolved conflicts. It helps processing unresolved emotions, resolving interpersonal conflicts, and promoting personal growth.
- **Focusing** is a technique for exploring physical sensations and their emotional meaning, facilitating introspection. It increases emotional awareness and facilitates internal problem-solving.
- **Replay/Zooming (Moviola)** is a technique to revisit past experiences in detail, facilitating understanding and reprocessing. The aim is to increase awareness of past experiences, facilitate understanding, and promote problem resolution.
- **Crystallisation** is a process of clarifying and defining thoughts, helping to achieve greater awareness. It promotes mental clarity, increases self-awareness, and facilitates internal problem-solving.
- **Assessment Tools and Instruments**, consisting of various psychological evaluation techniques to better understand the patient's problems and characteristics and to diagnose psychological disorders, assess patient characteristics, and guide therapeutic intervention. Examples are *Adult Attachment Interview* (AAI; Hesse, 2016), *Coping Orientation to Problems Experienced* (COPE; Carver et al., 1989), *Profile of Mood States* (POMS; McNair et al., 1971), *State-Trait Anxiety Inventory* (STAI; Spielberger et al., 1983), *Structured Clinical Interview for DSM-5- Clinical Version* (SCID-5-CV; First et al., 2017) or Minnesota Multiphasic Personality Inventory-2 (MMPI-2; Butcher et al., 2004).

5. *The Sixth Level, Transformation of Functioning (TF)*:
    - **Metacognitive Interpersonal Therapy (MIT)** is a therapy that integrates metacognitive and interpersonal aspects to treat personality disorders, focusing on understanding and modifying dysfunctional mental representations. It aims at improving understanding of one's mental states, enhancing interpersonal relationships, and reducing symptoms of personality disorders.

- **Demonstration/Modelling** consists in showing a desired behaviour to teach it through imitation and observational learning. That aims to teach new behaviours and skills, provide positive role models.
- **Enactment**, in which acting out real-life situations to explore relational dynamics and promote behavioural change. It then makes it possible to modify relational dynamics, promote awareness, and facilitate behavioural change.
- **ABFT (Attachment-Based Family Therapy)** (Diamond et al., 2014) is a family therapy based on the theory of attachment, focused on improving family relationships and emotional support. It is divided into five tasks, aimed at different objectives. It broadly works on improving family relationships, increasing emotional support, and promoting attachment security.
- **ACT (Acceptance and Commitment Therapy)** (Hayes, 2016; Hayes et al., 2012) is a therapy based on accepting one's thoughts and emotions and committing to personal values. Increase psychological flexibility, promote acceptance, and engage in behaviours consistent with personal values.
- **Cognitive Therapy for Eating Disorders (CT-ED)** is a specific cognitive therapy for eating disorders aimed at identifying and modifying dysfunctional thoughts related to food, body, and weight.
- **Dialectical Behaviour Therapy (DBT)** (Linehan, 1981, 1993; Linehan & Wiks, 2015) is a therapy that combines cognitive and behavioural techniques with mindfulness practices. Originally developed for the application of cognitive-behavioural therapy to high-suicidal individuals, it is evidence-based approach to treat borderline personality disorder. It is particularly effective in reducing self-harm behaviours, improving emotional regulation, increasing distress tolerance, and enhancing interpersonal skills.
- **Schematherapy** (Young et al., 2006; Zeigler-Hill & Shackelford, 2020) is an integrative therapy that combines elements of cognitive, behavioural, psychodynamic, and Gestalt therapies to treat personality disorders, focusing on early maladaptive schemas.
- **Cognitive Restructuring** is a technique that works on modifying dysfunctional or distorted thoughts, replacing them with more realistic and adaptive thoughts. It reduces emotional distress, improves psychological well-being, and promotes positive behavioural changes.

6. *The Seventh Level, Complex Trauma Processing (CTP)*:

- **Eye Movement Desensitization and Reprocessing (EMDR)** (Shapiro, 1989, 1995) is a broad therapy for treating trauma and stress symptoms using guided eye movements to reprocess traumatic or distressful memories. It's aimed to reduce distress related to traumatic memories, facilitate reprocessing of traumatic experiences, and promote psychological well-being.
- **Trauma-Focused Cognitive-Behavioural Therapy (TF-CBT)** (Cohen et al., 2006; Mannarino et al., 2014), is a short-term, structured intervention model that effectively improves trauma-related symptomatology in 8–25 sessions with the child/adolescent and caregiver, even if a diagnosis of PTSD is not necessary to receive this treatment. TF-CBT also effectively addresses

- **Sensorimotor Psychotherapy (SP)** (Ogden & Fisher, 2015) is a body-centred approach that aims to treat the somatic symptoms of unresolved trauma. SP welcomes the body as an integral source of information that can guide resourcing and the accessing and processing of challenging, traumatic, and developmental experience. SP is a holistic approach that includes somatic, emotional, and cognitive processing and integration.

3 Conclusion

The stepped care model in psychological therapies holds promise for improving access, effectiveness, and efficiency in mental healthcare. By providing a structured approach that starts with the least intensive treatment, it ensures that resources are used efficiently and patients receive the level of care that is appropriate to their condition. In addition, the application of the epistemological insights that come from the stepped care model to psychotherapeutic clinical practice shows extremely interesting implications for producing interventions that are tailored and calibrated to the specific needs of the patient. At the same time, the application of this model is of concrete aid in enabling services to deliver interventions that are viable and sustainable.

However, further research and careful implementation are necessary to fully realise the potential of this model in diverse healthcare settings. While the stepped care model offers significant advantages in terms of efficiency and effectiveness, addressing patient and professional acceptance through continuous feedback and support, as well as ongoing research to validate its broad applicability, remains essential for its successful implementation and sustainability.

References

Ali, S., Rhodes, L., Moreea, O., McMillan, D., Gilbody, S., Leach, C., Lucock, M., Lutz, W., & Delgadillo, J. (2017). How durable is the effect of low intensity CBT for depression and anxiety? Remission and relapse in a longitudinal cohort study. *Behaviour Research and Therapy, 94*, 1–8.

Alonso, J., Liu, Z., Evans-Lacko, S., Sadikova, E., Sampson, N., Chatterji, S., Abdulmalik, J., Aguilar-Gaxiola, S., Al-Hamzawi, A., Andrade, L. H., Bruffaerts, R., Cardoso, G., Cia, A., Florescu, S., de Girolamo, G., Gureje, O., Haro, J. M., He, Y., de Jonge, P., et al. (2018). Treatment gap for anxiety disorders is global: Results of the World Mental Health Surveys in 21 countries. *Depression and Anxiety, 35*(3), 195–208. https://doi.org/10.1002/da.22711

Anderson, J., Proudfoot, J., Gale, N., Christensen, H., Reeves, P., & O'Moore, K. (2019). Implementation and cost effectiveness evaluation of an integrated mental health stepped care service for adults in primary care. *International Journal of Integrated Care, 19*(4), 446. https://doi.org/10.5334/ijic.s3446

Bayoneto, A., Cheng, P., Iqal, J., Kalmbach, D., & Drake, C. (2023). Durability of treatment effects for a stepped-care model integrating digital therapy for insomnia. *Sleep, 46*(Supplement_1), A174. https://doi.org/10.1093/sleep/zsad077.0393

Bower, P., & Gilbody, S. (2005). Stepped care in psychological therapies: Access, effectiveness and efficiency. Narrative literature review. *British Journal of Psychiatry, 186*(Jan), 11–17. https://doi.org/10.1192/bjp.186.1.11

Bowlby, J. (1969). *Attaccamento e perdita* (Vol. I). Bollati Boringhieri.

Bowlby, J. (1973). *Attaccamento e perdita* (Vol. II). Bollati Boringhieri.

Bowlby, J. (1980). *Attaccamento e perdita* (Vol. III). Bollati Boringhieri.

Boyd, L., Baker, E., & Reilly, J. (2019). Impact of a progressive stepped care approach in improving access to psychological therapies service: An observational study. *PLoS One, 14*(4), E0214715.

Brettschneider, C., Heddaeus, D., Steinmann, M., et al. (2020). Cost-effectiveness of guideline-based stepped and collaborative care versus treatment as usual for patients with depression – A cluster-randomized trial. *BMC Psychiatry, 20*, 427. https://doi.org/10.1186/s12888-020-02829-0

Butcher, J. N., Atlis, M. M., & Hahn, J. (2004). The Minnesota multiphasic personality Inventory-2 (MMPI-2). In M. J. Hilsenroth & D. L. Segal (Eds.), *Comprehensive handbook of psychological assessment, Vol. 2. Personality assessment* (pp. 30–38). Wiley.

Campo, J. V., Di Lorenzo, C., Chiappetta, L., Bridge, J., Colborn, D. K., Gartner, J. C., Jr., et al. (2001). Adult outcomes of pediatric recurrent abdominal pain: Do they just grow out of it? *Pediatrics, 108*, E1.

Campo, J. V., Bridge, J., Ehmann, M., Altman, S., Lucas, A., Birmaher, B., Di Lorenzo, C., Iyengar, S., & Brent, D. A. (2004). Recurrent abdominal pain, anxiety, and depression in primary care. *JAMA Pediatrics, 113*, 817–824.

Carver, C. S., Scheier, M. F., & Weintraub, J. K. (1989). Assessing coping strategies: A theoretically based approach. *Journal of Personality and Social Psychology, 56*, 267–283.

Clement, S., Schauman, O., Graham, T., Maggioni, F., Evans-Lacko, S., Bezborodovs, N., Morgan, C., Rüsch, N., Brown, J. S., & Thornicroft, G. (2015). What is the impact of mental health-related stigma on help-seeking? A systematic review of quantitative and qualitative studies. *Psychological Medicine, 45*(1), 11–27. https://doi.org/10.1017/S0033291714000129

Cohen, J. A., Mannarino, A. P., & Deblinger, E. (2006). *Treating trauma and traumatic grief in children and adolescents*. Guilford Press.

Crittenden, P. M. (1990). Internal representational models of attachment relationships. *Infant Mental Health Journal, 11*(3), 259–277.

Crittenden, P. M. (1992). Quality of attachment in the preschool years. *Development and Psychopathology, 4*, 209–241.

Crittenden, P. M. (2016). *Raising parents: Attachment, representation, and treatment*. Routledge.

Cunningham, N., Kalomiris, A., Peugh, J., Farrell, M., Pentiuk, S., Mallon, D., Le, C., Moorman, E., Fussner, L., Dutta, R. A., & Kashikar-Zuck, S. (2021). Cognitive behavior therapy tailored to anxiety symptoms improves pediatric functional abdominal pain outcomes: A randomized clinical trial. *The Journal of Pediatrics, 230*(62–70), e3. https://doi.org/10.1016/j.jpeds.2020.10.060

Diamond, G. S., Diamond, G. M., & Levy, S. A. (2014). *Attachment-based family therapy for depressed adolescents*. American Psychological Association Press.

Do, M. T., Nguyen, T. T., & Tran, H. T. T. (2022). Preliminary results of adapting the stepped care model for depression management in Vietnam. *Frontiers in Psychiatry, 13*, 922911. https://doi.org/10.3389/fpsyt.2022.922911

Ellis, A. (1955). New approaches to psychotherapy techniques. *Journal of Clinical Psychology, 11*(3), 207–260. https://doi.org/10.1002/1097-4679(195507)11:3%3C207::AID-JCLP2270110302%3E3.0.CO;2-1

First, M., Williams, J., Karg, R., & Spitzer, R. (2017). *Structured clinical interview for DSM-5 (SCID-5 for DSM-5) Arlington*. American Psychiatric Association.

Golberstein, E., Eisenberg, D., & Downs, M. F. (2016). Spillover effects in health service use: Evidence from mental health care using first-year college housing assignments. *Health Economics, 25*(1), 40–55.

Guidano, V. F. (1988). *La complessità del Sé*. Bollati Boringhieri.

Guidano, V. F. (1992). *Il Sé nel suo divenire*. Bollati Boringhieri.

Haaga, D. (2000). Introduction to the special section on stepped care models in psychology. *Journal of Consulting Journal of Consulting and Clinical Psychology and Clinical Psychology, 68*, 547–548.

Haugh, J. A., Herbert, K., Choi, S., Petrides, J., Vermeulen, M. W., & D'Onofrio, J. (2019). Acceptability of the stepped care model of depression treatment in primary care patients and providers. *Journal of Clinical Psychology in Medical Settings, 26*, 402–410. https://doi.org/10.1007/s10880-019-09599-2

Hayes, S. (2016). Acceptance and commitment therapy, relational frame theory, and the third wave of behavioral and cognitive therapies – Republished article. *Behavior Therapy, 47*(6), 869–885. https://doi.org/10.1016/j.beth.2016.11.006

Hayes, S., Strosahl, K., & Wilson, K. (2012). *Acceptance and commitment therapy: The process and practice of mindful change*. Guilford Press.

Hesse, E. (2016). The adult attachment interview protocol, method of analysis and selected empirical studies: 1985–2015. In J. Cassidy & P. J. Shaver (Eds.), *Handbook of attachment. Theory, research and clinical applications* (3rd ed., pp. 553–597). The Guilford Press.

Ho, F. Y., Yeung, W. F., Ng, T. H., & Chan, C. S. (2016). The efficacy and cost-effectiveness of stepped care prevention and treatment for depressive and/or anxiety disorders: A systematic review and meta-analysis. *Scientific Reports, 6*, 29281. https://doi.org/10.1038/srep29281

Huxley, E., Lewis, K. L., Coates, A. D., Borg, W. M., Miller, C. E., Townsend, M. L., & Grenyer, B. F. S. (2019). Evaluation of a brief intervention within a stepped care whole of service model for personality disorder. *BMC Psychiatry, 19*(1), 341. https://doi.org/10.1186/s12888-019-2308-z

Kabat-Zinn, J. (1990). *Full catastrophe living*. Delta.

Kampman, M., van Balkom, A. J. L. M., Broekman, T., Verbraak, M., & Hendriks, G. J. (2020). Stepped-care versus treatment as usual in panic disorder: A randomized controlled trial. *PLoS One, 15*(8), e0237061. https://doi.org/10.1371/journal.pone.0237061

King, S., Chambers, C. T., Huguet, A., MacNevin, R. C., McGrath, P. J., Parker, L., & MacDonald, A. J. (2011). The epidemiology of chronic pain in children and adolescents revisited: A systematic review. *Pain, 152*(12), 2729–2738. https://doi.org/10.1016/j.pain.2011.07.016

Knapp, M., & Wong, G. (2020). Economics and mental health: The current scenario. *World Psychiatry, 19*(1), 3–14. https://doi.org/10.1002/wps.20692

Le Grange, D., Pradel, M., Pogos, D., Yeo, M., Hughes, E. K., Tompson, A., Court, A., Crosby, R. D., & Sawyer, S. M. (2021). Family-based treatment for adolescent anorexia nervosa: Outcomes of a stepped-care model. *International Journal of Eating Disorders, 54*(11), 1989–1997. https://doi.org/10.1002/eat.23629

Linehan, M. M. (1981). A social-behavioral analysis of suicide and parasuicide: Implications for clinical assessment and treatment. In H. Glazer & J. F. Clarkin (Eds.), *Depression, behavioral and directive intervention strategies* (pp. 229–294). Garland Press.

Linehan, M. M. (1993). *Skills training manual for treating borderline personality disorder*. Guilford Press.

Linehan, M. M., & Wilks, C. R. (2015). The course and evolution of dialectical behavior therapy. *American Journal of Psychotherapy, 69*(2), 97–110. https://doi.org/10.1176/appi.psychotherapy.2015.69.2.97

Liotti, G., & Monticelli, F. (2008). *I sistemi motivazionali nel dialogo clinico*. Raffaello Cortina.

Liotti, G., & Monticelli, F. (2014). *Teoria e clinica dell'alleanza terapeutica. Una prospettiva cognitivo-evoluzionista*. Raffaello Cortina.

Liotti, G., Fassone, G., & Monticelli, F. (2017). *L'evoluzione delle emozioni e dei sistemi motivazionali*. Raffaello Cortina.

Liuzzi, M. (2016). *La psicologia nelle cure primarie. Clinica, modelli di intervento e buone pratiche.* Il Mulino.

Loeb, K. L., Wilson, G. T., Gilbert, J. S., & Labouvie, E. (2000). Guided and unguided self-help for binge eating. *Behaviour Research and Therapy, 38*, 259–272.

Lovell, K., & Richards, D. (2000). Multiple access points and levels of entry (MAPLE): Ensuring choice, accessibility and equity for CBT services. *Behavioral and Cognitive Psychotherapy, 28*(4), 379–391.

Mannarino, A. P., Cohen, J. A., & Deblinger, E. (2014). Trauma-focused cognitive-behavioral therapy. In S. Timmer & A. Urquiza (Eds.), *Evidence-based approaches for the treatment of maltreated children. Child maltreatment* (Vol. 3, pp. 165–185). Springer. https://doi.org/10.1007/978-94-007-7404-9_10

McGoldrick, M., & Gerson, R. (1985). *Genograms in family assessment.* Norton & Company.

McGoldrick, M., Gerson, R., & Petry, S. (2020). *Genograms: Assessment and treatment.* Norton & Company.

McNair, D., Lorr, M., & Droppleman, L. (1971). *Manual for the profile of mood states.* Educational and Industrial Testing Service.

Mediavilla, R., McGreevy, K. R., Felez-Nobrega, M., Monistrol-Mula, A., Bravo-Ortiz, M. F., Bayón, C., Rodríguez-Vega, B., Nicaise, P., Delaire, A., Sijbrandij, M., Witteveen, A. B., Purgato, M., Barbui, C., Tedeschi, F., Melchior, M., van der Waerden, J., McDaid, D., Park, A., Kalisch, R., Petri-Romão, P., et al. (2022). Effectiveness of a stepped-care programme of internet-based psychological interventions for healthcare workers with psychological distress: Study protocol for the RESPOND healthcare workers randomised controlled trial. *Digital Health, 8*, 20552076221129084. https://doi.org/10.1177/20552076221129084

Meeuwissen, J., Feenstra, T., Smit, F., Blankers, M., Spijker, J., Bockting, C., van Balkom, A. J. L. M., & Buskens, E. (2019). The cost-utility of stepped-care algorithms according to depression guideline recommendations – Results of a state-transition model analysis. *Journal of Affective Disorders, 242*, 244–254. https://doi.org/10.1016/j.jad.2018.08.024

Meuldijk, D., Wuthrich, V. M., Rapee, R. M., Draper, B., Brodaty, H., Cuijpers, P., Cutler, H., Hobbs, M., Johnco, C., Jones, M., Chen, J. T. H., Partington, A., & Wijeratne, C. (2021). Translating evidence-based psychological interventions for older adults with depression and anxiety into public and private mental health settings using a stepped care framework: Study protocol. *Contemporary Clinical Trials, 104*, 106360. https://doi.org/10.1016/j.cct.2021.106360

Newman, M. (2000). Recommendations for a cost-offset model of psychotherapy allocation using generalized anxiety disorder as an example. *Journal of Consulting and Clinical Psychology, 68*, 549–555.

NICE/National Institute for Health and Care Excellence. (2018). *Depression in adults: Recognition and management: Clinical Guideline* [CG90]. NICE/National Institute for Health and Care Excellence. https://www.nice.org.uk/guidance/cg90

Ogden, P., & Fisher, J. (2015). *Sensorimotor psychotherapy.* Norton & Company.

Richards, D., Richards, A., Barkham, M., Cahill, J., & Williams, C. (2002). PHASE: A 'health technology' approach to psychological treatment in primary mental health care. *Primary Health Care Research & Development., 3*(3), 159–168. https://doi.org/10.1191/1463423602pc103oa

Richards, D., Enrique, A., Eilert, N., Franklin, M., Palacios, J., Duffy, D., Earley, C., Chapman, J., Jell, G., Sollesse, S., & Timulak, L. (2020). A pragmatic randomized waitlist-controlled effectiveness and cost-effectiveness trial of digital interventions for depression and anxiety. *npj Digital Medicine, 3*(1), 85. https://doi.org/10.1038/s41746-020-0293-8

Scogin, F., Hanson, A., & Welsh, D. (2003). Selfadministered treatment in stepped-care models of administered treatment in stepped-care models of depression treatment. Depression treatment. *Journal of Clinical Psychology, 59*, 341–349.

Shapiro, F. (1989). Efficacy of the eye movement desensitization procedure in the treatment of the traumatic memories. *Journal of Traumatic Stress, 2*(2), 199–223. https://doi.org/10.1002/jts.2490020207

Shapiro, F. (1995). *Eye movement desensitization and reprocessing: Basic principles, protocols, and procedures*. Guilford Press.

Smit, F., Cuijpers, P., Oostenbrink, J., Batelaan, N., de Graaf, R., & Beekman, A. (2006). Costs of nine common mental disorders: Implications for curative and preventive psychiatry. *Journal of Mental Health Policy and Economics, 9*(4), 193–200.

Sobell, M. B., & Sobell, L. C. (2000). Stepped care as a heuristic approach to the treatment of alcohol problems. *Journal of Consulting and Clinical Psychology, 68*(4), 573.

Spielberger, C. D., Gorsuch, R. L., Lushene, R., Vagg, P. R., & Jacobs, G. A. (1983). *Manual for the state-trait anxiety inventory*. Consulting Psychologists Press.

Spijker, J., van Straten, A., Bockting, C. L., Meeuwissen, J. A., & van Balkom, A. J. (2013). Psychotherapy, antidepressants, and their combination for chronic major depressive disorder: A systematic review. *Canadian Journal of Psychiatry. Revue Canadienne de Psychiatrie, 58*(7), 386–392. https://doi.org/10.1177/070674371305800703

Tasca, G., Koszycki, D., Brugnera, A., Chyurlia, L., Hammond, N., Francis, K., Ritchie, K., Ivanova, I., Proulx, G., Wilson, B., Beaulac, J., Bissada, H., Beasley, E., Mcquaid, N., Grenon, R., Fortin-Langelier, B., Compare, A., & Balfour, L. (2019). Testing a stepped care model for binge-eating disorder: A two-step randomized controlled trial. *Psychological Medicine, 49*(4), 598–606. https://doi.org/10.1017/S0033291718001277

Thornicroft, G., Mehta, N., Clement, S., Evans-Lacko, S., Doherty, M., Rose, D., Koschorke, M., Shidhaye, R., O'Reilly, C., & Henderson, C. (2016). Evidence for effective interventions to reduce mental-health-related stigma and discrimination. *The Lancet, 387*(10023), 1123–1132.

Thornicroft, G., Chatterji, S., Evans-Lacko, S., Gruber, M., Sampson, N., Aguilar-Gaxiola, S., Al-Hamzawi, A., Alonso, J., Andrade, L., Borges, G., Bruffaerts, R., Bunting, B., de Almeida, J. M., Florescu, S., de Girolamo, G., Gureje, O., Haro, J. M., He, Y., Hinkov, H., et al. (2017). Undertreatment of people with major depressive disorder in 21 countries. *The British Journal of Psychiatry, 210*(2), 119–124. https://doi.org/10.1192/bjp.bp.116.188078

World Bank. (2016). *Out of the shadows: Making mental health a global development priority*. International Bank for Reconstruction and Development / The World Bank.

World Health Organisation. (2022). *Mental disorders*. https://www.who.int/news-room/fact-sheets/detail/mental-disorders

Yan, C., Rittenbach, K., Souri, S., & Silverstone, P. H. (2019). Cost-effectiveness analysis of a randomized study of depression treatment options in primary care suggests stepped-care treatment may have economic benefits. *BMC Psychiatry, 19*(1), 240. https://doi.org/10.1186/s12888-019-2223-3

Young, J. E., Klosko, J. S., & Weishaar, M. E. (2006). *Schema therapy: A practitioner's guide*. Guilford Press.

Zeigler-Hill, V., & Shackelford, T. K. (2020). Schema-focused therapy. In *Encyclopedia of personality and individual differences* (p. 4564). Springer. https://doi.org/10.1007/978-3-319-24612-3_302302

Using Patient Feedback in Psychotherapy and Training

Katie Aafjes-van Doorn

1 Introduction

Several terms have been used to describe the practice of using patient-reported standardized outcome measures to monitor progress throughout the course of treatment, including routine outcome monitoring (ROM), clinical feedback, patient feedback, progress monitoring, and measurement-based care. Importantly, the measurement is followed by immediate, frequent, and systematic feedback of the patient's scores to the therapist. Numerous research teams have developed measures and computerized systems to help collect and make sense of the data by providing normative feedback on patient progress. Some PM tools only provide raw scores to therapists, whereas others benchmark the patients' scores against expected recovery trajectories or have added clinical support tools that assess the therapy processes after a patient is identified as not on track. By monitoring the patient's progress, the therapist can potentially adjust the treatment when a lack of progress occurs, so that poor outcomes might be prevented.

To emphasize the continual monitoring as opposed to treatment outcomes, and to avoid aligning with one specific measure in this chapter, we will refer to the broad term of "Progress Monitoring (PM)" tools. Though various definitions appear in the literature, implementation of PM commonly includes three core elements: (1) routine monitoring of relevant outcomes (e.g., symptoms, functioning) using repeated administration of psychometrically sound symptom and/or alliance measures; (2) using the data to inform treatment decisions; and (3) sharing symptom measurement data with patients and/or supervisors.

The purpose of this chapter is to introduce the reader to the framework of PM in its broadest definition and to discuss some of the frequently used tools to help

K. Aafjes-van Doorn (✉)
Department of Social Sciences, NYU Shanghai, Shanghai, China
e-mail: kav9239@nyu.edu

© The Author(s), under exclusive license to Springer Nature Switzerland AG 2024
B. Poletti et al. (eds.), *Training in Integrated Relational Psychotherapy*,
https://doi.org/10.1007/978-3-031-71904-2_23

therapists monitor the therapeutic process and progress. As we illustrate later, PM provides a context to view and understand the clinical situation and form a tool in the toolbox of evidence-based practice.

2 Rationale for Patient Monitoring

2.1 Empirical Findings

Gaining feedback from patients about how the therapy is progressing is important, not only because they are the 'customer' and their opinion matters, but also because we as therapists can't really trust our own clinical intuition. Trainees and seasoned therapists alike tend to think their patients are progressing relatively well in treatment and are notoriously bad at predicting therapeutic change in our patients. They tend to be unaware of cases that are not improving or are deteriorating over the course of therapy. Research suggests that therapists who gain regular feedback using PM show reduced rates of deterioration and improved treatment outcomes, especially for those patients who aren't on track. Interestingly, treatments appear to have better outcomes when therapists implement PM, regardless of how they respond to the provided information. Detecting problems in a patient's response to treatment as it evolves thereby reduces treatment failures and premature dropout.

PM has the greatest utility when patients are not on track (Shimokawa et al., 2010). For patients who are doing fine, there is no significant impact (e.g., If your patient is doing fine, getting back a score from a PM system that tells you your patient is doing fine doesn't really make any difference on your patient's outcomes). But for patients who are not doing fine—i.e., NOT (not on track) patients—who comprise about 30% of treated individuals, feedback helps in that far fewer patients deteriorated and many more had positive treatment outcomes. This has shown to be the case for seasoned therapists as well as for junior therapists in training.

Engaging in the tracking process itself appears to make the therapist more attentive and more deliberate in the session-by-session processes of change, which might be enough in milder cases. For more severe cases, it has been shown to be helpful to compare the measurements over time to expected trajectories based on collected data of similar types of patients. Moreover, direct clinical support (as provided by some PM tools such as the OQ-Analyst) might be helpful in interpreting the measurements. These clinical support tools offer concrete suggestions for alternative strategies based on the assessment of the treatment process, which may help the therapist adjust their treatment more specifically. Most recently, a meta-analysis of all 58 empirical studies reported that there is a significant positive effect of PM on treatment outcome as well as on treatment dropout rates. While the effect sizes were relatively small, the authors conclude that PM is a relatively small and simple intervention within the full context of psychotherapy and can be viewed as an add-on intervention for enhancing treatment outcomes in routine practice. Gaining feedback from the patient about their experienced alliance as well as symptoms is more effective than feedback on symptom severity alone (de Jong et al., 2021).

Overall, the many empirical studies, reviews, and meta-analyses conducted around the use of PM in different clinical and training settings highlight that the question today is not if patient progress should be monitored, but the question is how. And perhaps more importantly, how the information obtained should be interpreted.

2.2 Reported Clinical Benefits of PM

The benefits of PM might be explained in two ways; supporting the therapist, as well as facilitating the therapy process. First, PM may enhance therapists' clinical skills by raising their awareness about patients' needs and progression in therapy, improving identification of patients at risk for treatment failure, and providing therapists with reliable and valid information to adjust their approach and improve their interventions. It may also reduce therapists' stress and burnout because it can provide actionable guidance to therapists, particularly for their most challenging cases in which patient symptoms have not improved or have gotten worse.

Second, according to the American Psychological Association's (APA) Division 28 Task Force on Empirically Supported Relationships, PM may also lead to an improvement in the therapeutic alliance because it encourages collaboration between patients and therapists, thus promoting engagement, dialogue, and exploration of therapeutic issues, needs, and preferences (Solstad et al., 2021). In other words, the use of PM can facilitate the therapeutic process in that it can be used as a helpful conversational tool (Sundet, 2012). Specifically, it has shown to be helpful in prompting: (a) patient agency and greater influence over the treatment; (b) conversations about feedback, progress, and change; (c) conversations about experiences, meanings, and perspectives about the therapeutic work. For example, using a self-report measure allows patients to express concerns, without having to explicitly state this in the session. Many symptoms and experiences might be discussed in session automatically, but a feedback system also flags risk items, including suicidal thoughts/behavior, and use of substances, known to be trickier for patients to bring up and for therapists to ask about.

2.3 PM Aligns with Current Practice Guidelines & Research

Aside from the stated empirical findings and reported benefits, the implementation PM fits very well with current directions of psychotherapy training and research that emphasize evidence-based practice, transtheoretical models of change, and research-practice networks of therapists in naturalistic settings. First, there has been a clear and consistent move towards the use of evidence-based practices (EBPs) in psychotherapy over the past four decades. Evidence-based practice is often described as a three-legged stool that rests on seeking empirical evidence to support the use of specific treatments in combination with clinical judgment and expertise, and patient values and preferences. In essence, EBP holds that treatments, of whatever theoretical persuasion, need to be based on objective and scientifically credible evidence (Ollendick, 2014). More specifically, one could argue that the concept of PM fits with all three areas of EBP (i.e., empirical evidence, clinical experience, and patient characteristics); the effectiveness of using patient feedback itself has been shown in research; the algorithms that help us make sense of our patients' ratings are based on scores from thousands of previous patients who completed these measures; and by asking the patient to complete a self-report measure, we emphasize the importance of the patients' perspective on how they are doing. This means that rather than simply seeing patients' progress in black and white (or color-coded, as we'll describe later), we can use our patients' feedback to deliberately integrate what you know is most likely to be helpful for this patient at this stage in treatment. In other words, in the context of many subjective experiences in the therapy session (e.g., transference/countertransference, supervisor opinion, and theoretical framework expected to practice in), self-report measures completed by patients provide an additional objective datapoint of the alliance/outcome.

Moreover, the use of PM itself is an evidence-based practice that cuts across theoretical orientations and interventions. Of course, therapists with different theoretical, training, and therapeutic backgrounds might prefer to use different process or outcome tools, might differ in the frequency of routine monitoring, and might differ in the way they discuss the patient self-report data in the sessions and/or supervision. Similarly, the measurements and trajectories of change might be interpreted differently depending on the aims, length, and theoretical understanding of the case and treatment change more broadly. PM systems are designed to be atheoretical, permitting their use with a variety of theoretical perspectives. Just like other types of evidence-based practice, PM is not wedded to any one theoretical position or orientation but reflects an approach to knowledge and a strategy for improving the outcomes of treatment that uses research evidence to improve patient care (see American Psychological Association Presidential Task Force on Evidence-Based Practice, 2006.

Besides its fit with EBP and transtheoretical thinking, the implementation of PM also bridges the gap between therapists and researchers. It makes each therapist a researcher of their own cases, and by the collation of treatment data across patients and therapists, it can be used for research on psychotherapy effectiveness in naturalistic settings. Such studies could easily meet key components of practice-oriented research (POR; Castonguay et al., 2013), which has been promoted as a way to expand the empirical knowledge base of psychotherapy (Barkham et al., 2010). Rather than being guided primarily by the theoretical interests of researchers and conducted in controlled settings, the design of these studies would require the expertise and collaboration of different stakeholders and would most likely take in clinical routine. Conducted within such a collaborative context and naturalistic settings, the results of these studies may well provide clinically relevant and actionable information.

2.4 Being Well Prepared for the Future

Although PM was initially driven by managed care pressures for accountability, PM is now used almost universally in routine clinical services and has recently become the norm in most training clinics (Peterson & Fagan, 2021). Measuring outcomes on a routine basis is likely important to ensure the viability of our field, in which we will need to show what we do is effective, and it is no longer enough to say that it *feels* effective to us. That said, collecting session-by-session feedback from your patients can seem daunting. Graduate training is thus a perfect time to start to experiment with different routine PM measurements and ways in which you can use them clinically. Once you have some experience collecting feedback and using feedback clinically, it will make it easier to apply PM to different work settings after graduation. Practicing PM in graduate training may also facilitate more effective use of PM in usual care settings, as psychologists trained in PM may be in an ideal position to subsequently educate colleagues and supervisees from other disciplines on the value of these practices.

3 PM Measurement Tools

A plethora of specialized systems for PM have been developed and studied, such as the COMPASS outpatient tracking system (Howard et al., 1993), the Outcome Questionnaire System (OQ-System; Lambert, 2015), the Partners for Change Outcome Management System (PCOMS; Duncan & Reese, 2015), Clinical Outcomes in Routine Evaluation (CORE) System (Barkham et al., 2015), Systemic Therapy Inventory of Change (STIC; Pinsof & Chambers, 2009), Treatment Outcome Package (TOP; Boswell et al., 2015), the Counseling Center Assessment of Psychological Symptoms (CCAPS; Youn et al., 2015), Behavioral Health Measure-20 (BHM-20; Kopta et al., 2015), and A Collaborative Outcome Resource Network (ACORN) Brown et al., 2015). These PM systems differ in many respects: Some track only a single outcome domain (e.g., symptoms of a particular disorder), whereas others track multiple domains; some are administered digitally, whereas others still allow for paper-and pencil administration; some provide additional therapist- and service-level performance feedback and benchmarks, whereas some monitor relevant processes, such as alliance; and some provide recommendations about therapist actions. Depending on the type of PM system, the feedback is either based on clinical significance, clinical cut-offs, or expected treatment response for people starting at the same level of symptoms. What all the PM systems have in common is that they all monitor patient progress in psychotherapy with the aim of notifying the therapist of the possible need for making changes in the intervention, thereby potentially preventing patient non-improvement, deterioration, or dropout. In this chapter we will briefly discuss four of these PM systems, the two most researched PM systems (OQ & PCOMS) as well as the ones that are freely available (CORE-OM) and that are the most advanced in adapting to individual patients' needs (NORSE).

3.1 Outcome Questionnaire System (OQ Analyst)

Before therapy sessions, patients complete the Outcome Questionnaire 45 (OQ-45, a 45-item self-report), which comprises questions about symptomatic distress, interpersonal problems, and social role difficulties (i.e., work/school or in other daily activities). The OQ system helps to assess the attainment of expected progress during therapy by providing feedback to therapists on whether the patients are staying on track toward positive treatment outcomes. The online platform that charts your patients' responses on the OQ-45 provides a color-coded alert status to help you make sense of the data for this patient (based on computer algorithms of scores from a previously collected large sample of patients who started at the same baseline). The color codings are the following: White (patient functions in the normal range, no more change expected); Blue (change from intake is so positive that the patient will probably have good outcome and maintain the change for at least 1 year); Green (patient is following the expected progress trajectory over time); Yellow (patient is not making expected progress); Red (patient is doing very different from what is expected, is not on track, and may have a negative outcome or drop out). In addition, to these color-codings, the OQ-Analyst also provides decision support to the therapist to maximize the likelihood of a positive outcome for the patient. Versions of the scales are available for adults, adolescents, and children in many different languages.

A drawback of the OQ-45 is that the use of this measure requires a license fee per user (even if you wouldn't use the OQ-Analyst feedback metrics), and that the OQ-45 does not provide feedback on the therapeutic alliance. The tracking of the alliance requires an additional step of using the Assessment for Signal Patients (ASC; Lambert, 2015), which can be used to assess factors that may be contributing to a patient's lack of progress. The ASC, which can also be tracked on the OQ system, measures therapeutic alliance, motivation for change, life events, and level of social support. Using the CST alongside the OQ-45 may help to further clarify how patients are experiencing the therapeutic process and has been shown to result in better treatment outcomes than when patients only provide OQ-45 feedback. Another drawback is the length of the OQ-45. It is sometimes a lot to ask a patient to complete 45 items each session, which takes approximately 10 minutes. Several shorter versions of the OQ-45 have been developed (30-item and 10-item versions), but the 45-item version is deemed most valid and has the most research behind it.

3.2 PCOMPS

The PCOMS is comprised of two four-item measures: (1) the Outcome Rating Scale (ORS; Miller et al., 2003) and (2) the Session Rating Scale (SRS; Miller et al., 2006). The ORS is a brief 4-item visual analogue scale that consists of four different lines (10 cm each), each representing a different domain of functioning: individual, interpersonal, social, and overall well-being (Miller & Bargmann, 2012). Different from the color codings provided by the OQ-Analyst, the PCOMPS categorizes patients in every session as on-track (OT) or not-on-track (NOT) of a good treatment outcome (Bertolino & Miller, 2012). The SRS (Miller et al., 2006) measures the therapeutic alliance. The SRS is comprised of four items assessing the relationship (how much patients feel heard by the therapist), goals and topics (how much patients feel they were able to work on goals and topics they wanted to work on), approach or method (match between therapist's approach and patients), and overall fit of the session (general quality of the session). The SRS is designed to be scored and discussed with patients before they leave so that any concerns or problems can be addressed.

Both measures take about a minute to complete are designed for administration every session: the ORS at the beginning and the SRS at the end of the session. Versions of the scales are available for all ages, in several different languages, and are free for individual therapists (at https://goo.gl/GqRwQT.In). The measures are also much shorter than the OQ-45 and retain the clinical utility of the OQ-Analyst System. Whereas the discussion of the OQ-45 results with a patient is described as optional, the measures are specifically designed to encourage discussions about the scores together with patients. A number of computer- based applications are available that can simplify and expedite the process of administering, scoring, interpreting, and aggregating data from the scales. Such programs include web-based outcome management systems and smartphone apps (e.g., fit-outcomes. Com, myoutcomes.com, pragmatictracker.com) as well as web services designed for integration into electronic health records (e.g., OpenFIT),

Although the OQ System and PCOMS are the two PM systems with the most research support, two other PM systems are worthwhile mentioning (Lyon et al., 2016). For example, the CORE-Outcome Measure (OM) has been adopted nationwide in the United Kingdom. It is a 34-item measure of global psychological distress across four domains that include well-being, symptoms, functioning, and risk. Several shorter measures can be used for routine monitoring or with special populations, such as students, adolescents, and those with learning disorders. The CORE-OM ROM system also has a goal attainment form as well as a therapeutic alliance measure available for use. A benefit of this system is that it is free and is available in several translations. More information on the CORE-OM system can be found at http://www.coreims.co.uk/index.html.

Another example is the Norse Feedback (NF), a relatively novel clinical feedback system developed by the Førde Hospital Trust and standardized for the Norwegian population (McAleavey et al., 2021). Different from other feedback system, the NF aims to combine the advantages of standardized measures with idiographic approaches to create a person-adapted system for clinical feedback (Jensen-Doss et al., 2018). Therefore, the set of items that are included in the measure evolves throughout therapy, based on an algorithm that adapts the number of items to individual patients' responses. As therapy progresses, patients will receive fewer items on domains where their scores are low but continue to receive the full set of items on domains where scores are high.

3.3 Technological Advancement in PM

Traditionally, PM has been conducted with self-report paper-and-pencil questionnaires that patients complete before (symptoms) or after therapy sessions (alliance). In the current day and age most therapists use tablets, computers, or phones to collect their measurements for each session, and to review the graphs of the trajectories over time. Most recently, this session-by-session monitoring has been complemented by additional sources of feedback data by using novel technologies such as the use of momentary ecological assessment (e.g., collected on a mobile phone in between sessions), continuous monitoring during the session (e.g., tracking of physiological markers of sweat and heartrate with a wearable watch or sensor) and review of videorecorded sessions and their transcripts. These technologies allow therapists to evaluate and receive patient progress feedback in real time, thus minimizing patient self-report bias (e.g., recall & response bias). Additionally, this type of data collection outside the session allows for obtaining objective data of patient changes in natural settings, for example, using sensors (accelerometers, positioning systems, or pedometers, among others). It is thus expected that the use of handheld technology devices such as smartphones, tablets, or laptops might increase the effectiveness of PM by facilitating measurements before, during, and after treatment, providing the information immediately to therapists and researchers, and making it easier to combine collection of objective and subjective patient data (Hegland et al., 2018).

4 How and When to Use PM?

4.1 Collecting Feedback and Sharing Results

No patient is the same. Some patients may need direct and frequent discussions about the rationale for using PM, or the meaning of their results, for example, to direct and structure sessions, or initiate conversations about difficult topics. Other patients may prefer less frequent and more subtle uses, such as discussing status or current events in their lives or providing feedback about therapeutic needs and preferences.

Examining details of the results may not be necessary. Some patients prefer to use the PM primarily as a safeguard in case of sudden or rapid deterioration, or as a way of getting progress monitoring out of the way, so that sessions may focus on more complex therapeutic topics. A required minimum for successful use seems to be informing patients of the purposes of PM and, at some point, reviewing and acknowledging their feedback. Each unique patient and therapist dyad should thus explore and negotiate how and when best to use PM (Solstad et al., 2021).

Introducing PM to your patients by providing a rationale.

> Therapist: *"It gives us a snapshot of how you are doing. It's hard sometimes to see incremental progress when you're always living your life as yourself. It gives us a good jumping off point to sort of get at what you might be feeling, even if that is hard to bring up in sessions We then together can look at a graph and make*

sense of the changes or lack of changes we see. In my experience, it really does help to kind of inform my interventions or my techniques."

4.2 Making Sense of PM Results Requires Hard Work and Integration

Tracking outcomes doesn't miraculously make you an expert therapist. It (unfortunately) doesn't tell you exactly what you did well, what you should do differently, and how to improve from experience. More hard work and deliberate practice is needed, where we set therapeutic goals for ourselves and use feedback to benchmark and practice our therapeutic skills (Miller et al., 2018). If a patient is deteriorating, therapists may check in about how the patient experiences treatment, therapeutic relationships, or motivation for therapy. Those steps might include sitting down with a supervisor to review recordings of the sessions to determine what to attend to in subsequent work with that patient and also having conversations with the patient to modify the course of treatment in order to help the patient get back on track toward a positive treatment outcome trajectory.

As we said earlier, PM can never replace clinical judgment; at best if offers an additional source of reliable information. The PM is a source of data to inform your clinical work and training and must be interpreted within the context of all the other data at hand. Let's take the interpretation of the OQ-Analyst's color codings as an example. We can make sense of these color codings in different ways depending on the patient and clinical context. The "Red" alert could be a sign that something isn't working, and that's likely something to think about and discuss with your supervisor. At the same time, in some cases, it could actually be a sign that a previously underreporting patient is now finally comfortable enough to disclose how they are really doing, which would be a marker of progress. Similarly, when you get a "White" alert, your patient might indeed be doing well, but when you get a white alert for a patient who is doing very poorly, it might be possible that the patient is underreporting—which is, in itself, another important piece of data. Thus, you should still consider your other sources of data—other measures, your own experiences with the patient, your supervisor's input, etc. The PM feedback tells you if/when your patient is not on track, and you can then consider whether you need to change anything about your approach. Of course, what it is that needs to change (e.g., patient's expectations/therapist's techniques/alliance building, or referring to a different therapist) will be a clinical decision that needs some thought from you and your supervisor.

In the section below, we will explore six clinical situations that might occur when using PM with your patient.

1. Patient is on track
2. High alliance scores every session
3. Patient does not make progress
4. Patient not on track
5. Risk item
6. Inconsistencies

4.3 On Track

When your patient is improving throughout the treatment as is expected in a successful therapy, the PM can be used to empower the patient by highlighting the progress made.

Therapist: *"Are these scores reflective of how you feel? You're showing me that you've gotten this much better. Is that reflected?' 'Do you understand how much work you've done to do that?"*

Also, it might be worthwhile to examine the items/subscales in more detail, to understand relative areas of concern that might otherwise be overlooked (Box 1).

Therapist: *"It seems that the scores overall are improving, but this item on XXX seems to be an exception. Did you notice that too? Maybe it is helpful to talk a little more about your experiences with XX."*

> **Box 1: Example: Patient on Track**
>
> Steven was referred to therapy by his wife after his father passed away. Steven's wife was concerned that Steven was grieving for his father but did not have a way to express his emotions. Steven's baseline ORS scores were relatively mild, but the therapist noticed that he reported the most difficulties on the interpersonal functioning item. Steven revealed that while he was grieving over his father's death, he was not as affected by his death as his wife believed he was. Steven's mother and father had been divorced, and Steven had had a distant relationship with his father. Steven was frustrated his wife and children were making assumptions about how he felt, and the ORS allowed him to define for himself the struggles he was having. By the tenth session, Steven achieved reliably significant clinical change. The therapist pointed out the improvement in ORS scores to Steven and asked him about his perceptions of his sense of well-being over the course of therapy. The therapist and Steven explored how being able to express his unspoken conflicted feelings for his father, and his tense relationship with his father's side of the family, had allowed him to process his guilt over his father's death. The therapist also asked Steven what was unhelpful and helpful in therapy. Steven informed the therapist that it had been helpful for him to hear his feelings and thoughts reflected back to him by the therapist and to feel that he was heard. Steven then initiated the conversation of having therapy once every 2 weeks before terminating therapy. Meanwhile throughout therapy, Steven's SRS scores had been between very high, indicating that he experienced a positive therapeutic alliance which was maintained across the course of treatment. The ORS scores also provided a tool to help support discussions around clinical decision making, including frequency of sessions and termination, given his progress.

4.4 High Alliance

If the patient reports a high alliance for each session, the therapist might wonder how meaningful these scores are.

Therapist: *I can see that you rate the alliance high again today, I wonder about that, if I am honest, I felt that maybe we were a little less in tune today. I am wondering if we somehow were a bit off topic today, not working on what you hoped we would."*

Therapist: *"I see that you tend to report us having a very good working relationship, it seems to be the case for every session we have. On the one hand that is nice to hear, on the other hand that means that we are not learning a lot from these scores. What would I need to do more of to get this score lower, make you feel less heard understood and respected".*

5 No Progress

There might be other times where patients don't report much change at all, and the therapist feels a bit stuck. The therapist might then wonder if a new technique/approach could be warranted.

Therapist: *"Looking at your responses, we've kind of been here for a while, maybe would you be willing to try something different to see if we can get your symptoms even more in control based on what we're receiving from the data."*

Therapist: *"It seems to me that we are both working really hard in the sessions, and I hope that our work is helping you feel better, but that that isn't really reflected in these measures. I wonder if we somehow need to rethink what we are focusing on in our time together."*

5.1 NOT on Track

If the patient is not on track and shows a stagnation or deterioration over time, it is especially important to discuss treatment progress. The therapist can communicate concern about the patient's wellbeing and facilitate a discussion around the patient's perspective of the sessions and achieved lack of change. It also alerts the therapist to a need to change the way treatment is being provided. The therapist might, for example, begin thinking about other referrals, such as an evaluation for medication, group therapy, support groups, or other avenues in which the patient may benefit in addition to/instead of psychotherapy.

Therapist: *"I see from your progress graph that your symptom scores are about the same or even higher than when you came in, and I feel concerned you are not getting what you hoped for when you came into therapy. I imagine that feels frustrating. I see on your scores that every area rated feels unmanageable right now. Is there an area that you think we could focus on that would help you to begin to work toward feeling improved? Or are there things about our relationship or the way we are working on your goals that could go differently for you so that our time together would be more beneficial to you? I want to help you, and if I am not the right person for the job, I also want us to be honest about that".*

5.2 Risk

Regardless of the overall trajectories of change over time, it is always worthwhile to check the patient's responses on risk items (suicide/self-harm) etc.

Therapist: *I noticed your score on the item about suicidal ideation. I am grateful you let me know. It might not be easy, but would it be helpful to make some time today to talk about what you are experiencing?*

Therapist: *"I realize that we have not spoken much about your drug use in our sessions, so I am very glad you are completing these measures and reminding me that that might play a role in how you are feeling lately. Would it be okay for us to talk a bit more about it?"*

5.3 Inconsistencies

Any potential discrepancies between what is reported on the measure and what is discussed in session are relevant clinical information in itself. In most instances, when patients know that these measures are being used to help them get better and that the therapists are sincerely interested in the scores, patients will be honest about their progress. That said, a discrepancy between what the patient reports on the measures and what is discussed in the session can lead to a very meaningful interaction. For example, a patient's symptom score today may be higher than last week's score, but the patient says, "I actually feel better than last time. It could be that in the early stages of treatment a patient may not have been as truthful in their answers or maybe not as self-aware, or they now trust you more to be open with you. Alternatively, it could also be that the patient knows that progress is important and does not want to disappoint the therapist, or the patient wants to stop coming to therapy and wants a reason. Without talking to the patient, a therapist will not know what might be explaining the discrepancy in reported experiences. A therapist might bring up the discrepancy in the session in different ways.

Therapist: *"This is what you reported this morning as opposed to two weeks ago. Does that feel accurate?"*

Therapist: *This discrepancy makes me wonder how you see your own concerns and well-being and if you have a tendency to minimize or deny difficult experiences.*

Therapist: *I am thinking about what you said about your family, and how you tend to be people pleaser. Is it possible that you are also trying to please me by not wanting to criticize the session? I know it can be tricky to see it as an opportunity to provide constructive feedback.*

6 Discussing PM in Supervision

Supervisors can play an important role in helping trainees contextualize data from measures and from clinical observations, address trainee anxiety about negative feedback, and model appropriate use of PM feedback. This sharing process with supervisors requires a supportive supervision climate, a growth mindset, and the guts to be open-minded and willing to discuss a lack of patient improvement.

Some training programs teach and/or require their trainees to use patient feedback systems in their work and incorporate them into supervision. Some students are, for example, required to present OQ progress graphs in their formal group supervision presentations. These data provide an important complement to those provided through video and case reports to evaluate treatment progress. Students can also be trained to look for patient outcomes and alliance scores that indicate patients who are not progressing as expected. The graph of your patients, particularly those who were not making progress as expected, could be regular inclusions during supervision meetings. Telling you immediately whom to prioritize in supervision and in case conferences to get feedback on how to help these patients improve the next week, given their feedback.

Supervisors can then help trainees learn to initiate different kinds of clinical conversations that come up when using PM with patients. Such a practice is consistent with deliberate practice, in that not only are therapists reflecting on their effectiveness, but supervisors also are supporting this formal time to help them improve their effectiveness with individual patients in a way that will best support patient outcomes in treatment. PM might be easier to use in supervision than video recordings because PM provides a brief way of evaluating the global trajectory of treatment, whereas watching an entire therapy video is unpractical every session. Certainly, videos and case reports provide more depth and context to the nuanced processes that are captured in the graph, but the graph provides an opportunity for supervisors to gain a quick understanding of the patient's perception of the outcome and alliance (Box 2).

> **Box 2: Example Supervision Example**
>
> A supervisee wanted help with a 'tricky patient' and showed the patient's PM graph to her supervisor, which displayed a line representing scores that had not changed much. In essence, there had been no change from the patient's perspective. The patient's alliance score was lower than the optimal. The supervisee reflected that she and the patient seemed to have a good

> **Box 2** (continued)
> relationship, but they "always seemed to run out of time to talk about the alliance measure." Given the patient's scores, the supervisor suggested pushing pause on the treatment techniques and going back to building rapport and gaining an understanding of the patient's view of the alliance. The supervisor also encouraged the supervisee to try to end the session a few minutes early to make it a priority to process the alliance scores at the end of session to further monitor the alliance. Evaluating both the alliance and outcome scores on the graph allowed the supervisor to be clued into the potential for a lack of a therapeutic relationship before even seeing the video or reading a case report. The graph generated discussion about how the supervisee felt in the room with the patient and about in what ways the patient might be interacting with the supervisee or others in his life, and got the ball rolling, so to speak, as to uncovering part of what might be the reason the supervisee felt stuck.

Notably, it is important to highlight that PM is not a method of evaluating trainees' competence. Despite some studies on development of clinical expertise that wrongly adopted observed patient change on PM systems, as an indication of therapist expertise, patient progress CANNOT be used as a proxy of therapist skill. Many additional variables are at play, including the patients' characteristics, external events, current and previous treatment, and clinic context, that could explain who a patient is or isn't improving. And to put it more bluntly, it is fully possible to—unintentionally—provide harmful interventions that will remain undetected by these systems, providing patients, therapists, and service providers with a false sense of security (Langkaas et al., 2018). This is also true for positive outcomes. We might like to think that we are the reason for their improvement in symptoms, but just because we track the progress of our patients, doesn't mean that we can be sure that their improvement is due to our treatment. Some have calculated that a therapist would need to have at least 60 completed treatment cases to get a good estimate of how well the therapist is doing. Luckily, we don't have to wait for that. We can improve our responsiveness to individual patients immediately by attending to the graphs of the trajectories of change for our patient.

As you might have gathered by now, the usefulness of PM seems connected to the therapist's openness to integrating the information with other ongoing processes in therapy and making it meaningful and helpful for patients. Whether that means that you review, practice, and revise your therapeutic skills on your own volition, track the feedback with your supervisor, and/or discuss each score with your patient, it offers an additional datapoint that helps you reflect on the treatment process and progress thus far. In that sense, you might see the clinical use of PM in treatment as a facilitative interpersonal skill, for example, as part of alliance work, which needs to be taught and practiced to realize its potential.

Chapter Review Exercises

1. Read the following statements and indicate if these are true or false.
   (a) FM is only useful if the feedback is discussed with the patient.
   (b) FM is only useful if a patient deteriorates or is likely to dropout.
   (c) FM is only useful if my patient' scores are compared to expected trajectories of similar patients.
   (d) FM is a method to assess the therapist's competency.

2. In the case below, how might the process and progress monitoring impact the therapeutic process with this patient?
   Therapist: *"I know you are saying that you are doing fine, but I the outcome score that you just completed indicates that you are not doing so well really."*
   Patient: *"Well yes, but I don't really want to bother you, you are a therapist in training, I am sure I will feel better soon."*
   Therapist: *"I hope so too, and I am here to support you, but if it doesn't improve that is also important for us to know."*

3. In the case described in Exercise 2, how might the process and progress monitoring impact the supervision process?

4. In the case described below, what clinical challenges might arise when implementing FM.
   XX
   Therapist: *"You know, at the beginning of the session today your outcome score suggested that you were feeling better than you were last week. The way you are describing the changes in the past week do not seem to fit what you shared on your outcome measure."*
   Patient: *"Well yes, because the measure only asks these standard questions, and it doesn't really fit with what I am feeling."*
   Therapist: *"Ahh, right, so it feels a little off, from what is relevant for you. I am glad we are talking about it. What would be helpful to track over time, would it be more helpful to indicate how you are feeling more generally? Listening to you I wonder if it actually would be helpful to check in regularly about the therapy process to make sure we are working towards the same goal"*

5. In the case described in Exercise 4, which alliance or progress monitoring tools would you choose to implement and explain why.
   (answer 1 = a, b, c, d are false)
   (answer 5 = PCOMPS & Norse Feedback)

References

Barkham, M., Hardy, G. E., & Mellor-Clark, J. (Eds.). (2010). *Developing and delivering practice-based evidence: A guide for the psychological therapies*. (pp. xxv, 379). Wiley-Blackwell. https://doi.org/10.1002/9780470687994

Barkham, M., Mellor-Clark, J., & Stiles, W. B. (2015). A CORE approach to progress monitoring and feedback: Enhancing evidence and improving practice. *Psychotherapy, 52*(4), 402.

Boswell, J. F., Kraus, D. R., Castonguay, L. G., & Youn, S. J. (2015). Treatment outcome package: Measuring and facilitating multidimensional change. *Psychotherapy, 52*(4), 422.

Brown, G. S. J., Simon, A., Cameron, J., & Minami, T. (2015). A collaborative outcome resource network (ACORN): Tools for increasing the value of psychotherapy. *Psychotherapy, 52*(4), 412.

Castonguay, L., Barkham, M., Lutz, W., & McAleavey, A. (2013). Practice-oriented research: Approaches and applications. In M. J. Lambert (Ed.), *Bergin and Garfield's handbook of psychotherapy and behaviour change* (pp. 85–133). Wiley.

de Jong, K., Conijn, J. M., Gallagher, R. A. V., Reshetnikova, A. S., Heij, M., & Lutz, M. C. (2021). Using progress feedback to improve outcomes and reduce drop-out, treatment duration, and deterioration: A multilevel meta-analysis. *Clinical Psychology Review, 85*, 102002. https://doi.org/10.1016/j.cpr.2021.102002

Duncan, B. L., & Reese, R. J. (2015). The Partners for Change Outcome Management System (PCOMS) revisiting the client's frame of reference. *Psychotherapy, 52*(4), 391.

Force, A. T. (2006). APA presidential task force on evidence based practice. *American Psychologist, 61*, 271–285.

Hegland, P. A., Aasprang, A., Hjelle Øygard, S., Nordberg, S., Kolotkin, R., Moltu, C., Tell, G. S., & Andersen, J. R. (2018). A review of systematic reviews on the effects of patient-reported outcome monitoring with clinical feedback systems on health-related quality of life—Implications for a novel technology in obesity treatment. *Clinical Obesity, 8*(6), 452–464.

Howard, K. I., Brill, P., Lueger, R. J., O'Mahoney, M. T., & Grissom, G. (1993). *The COMPASS outpatient tracking system*. COMPASS. Inc.

Jensen-Doss, A., Smith, A. M., Becker-Haimes, E. M., Ringle, V. M., Walsh, L. M., Nanda, M., Walsh, S. L., Maxwell, C. A., & Lyon, A. R. (2018). Individualized progress measures are more acceptable to clinicians than standardized measures: Results of a national survey. *Administration and Policy in Mental Health and Mental Health Services Research, 45*(3), 392–403.

Kopta, M., Owen, J., & Budge, S. (2015). Measuring psychotherapy outcomes with the Behavioral Health Measure–20: Efficient and comprehensive. *Psychotherapy, 52*(4), 442.

Lambert, M. J. (2015). Progress feedback and the OQ-system: The past and the future. *Psychotherapy, 52*(4), 381.

Langkaas, T. F., Wampold, B. E., & Hoffart, A. (2018). Five types of clinical difference to monitor in practice. *Psychotherapy, 55*(3), 241–254. https://doi.org/10.1037/pst0000194

McAleavey, A. A., Nordberg, S. S., & Moltu, C. (2021). Initial quantitative development of the Norse Feedback system: A novel clinical feedback system for routine mental healthcare. *Quality of Life Research, 30*, 1–19.

Miller, S. D., Hubble, M. A., & Chow, D. (2018). The question of expertise in psychotherapy. *Journal of Expertise, 1*(2), 121–129.

Ollendick, T. H. (2014). Advances toward evidence-based practice: Where to from here? *Behavior Therapy, 45*(1), 51–55. https://doi.org/10.1016/j.beth.2013.08.004

Peterson, A. P., & Fagan, C. (2021). Improving measurement feedback systems for measurement-based care. *Psychotherapy Research, 31*(2), 184–199. https://doi.org/10.1080/10503307.2020.1823031

Pinsof, W. M., & Chambers, A. L. (2009). Empirically informed systemic psychotherapy: Tracking client change and therapist behavior during therapy. In J. H. Bray & M. Stanton (Eds.), *The Wiley-Blackwell handbook of family psychology* (pp. 431–446). Wiley Blackwell.

Shimokawa, K., Lambert, M. J., & Smart, D. W. (2010). Enhancing treatment outcome of patients at risk of treatment failure: Meta-analytic and mega-analytic review of a psychotherapy quality assurance system. *Journal of Consulting and Clinical Psychology, 78*(3), 298–311. http://psycnet.apa.org/journals/ccp/78/3/298/

Solstad, S. M., Kleiven, G. S., Castonguay, L. G., & Moltu, C. (2021). Clinical dilemmas of routine outcome monitoring and clinical feedback: A qualitative study of patient experiences. *Psychotherapy Research, 31*(2), 200–210. https://doi.org/10.1080/10503307.2020.1788741

Sundet, R. (2012). Therapist perspectives on the use of feedback on process and outcome: Patient-focused research in practice. *Canadian Psychology/Psychologie Canadienne, 53*(2), 122–130. https://doi.org/10.1037/a0027776

Youn, S. J., Castonguay, L. G., Xiao, H., Janis, R., McAleavey, A. A., Lockard, A. J., Locke, B. D., & Hayes, J. A. (2015). The counseling center assessment of psychological symptoms (CCAPS): Merging clinical practice, training, and research. *Psychotherapy, 52*(4), 432.

Using Patient Preferences to Customise Therapy

Antonino La Tona, Agostino Brugnera, Jacopo Stringo, and Mick Cooper

> *It is much more important to know what sort of a patient has a disease than what sort of disease a patient has.*
>
> William Osler, 1906, from Norcross & Cooper, 2021

1 Introduction

Over the last decade, research on patients' preferences in psychotherapy and their impact on treatment efficacy has grown considerably. The literature suggests that assessing and, if possible, accommodating patients' preferences in therapy can have a highly beneficial effect on outcomes, with meta-analyses demonstrating that personalising psychotherapy to client preferences results in lower dropout rates, improved working alliances and greater psychological well-being at the end of treatment (Swift et al., 2019; Windle et al., 2020). From a purely ethical point of view, psychotherapy is a step that, in the light of a patient's needs, should be considered—rendering it an 'ethical imperative' of the therapeutic pathway (Norcross & Cooper, 2021). Making patient's preferences an embedded element of the therapeutic act becomes, therefore, not only clinical but also formally aimed at well-being towards truly integrated care. In fact, this approach is part of a healthcare perspective that is moving towards *personalised medicine* (Cooper et al., 2021; Norcross & Cooper, 2021).

Each of us—regardless of whether we are a therapist or a layperson—has preferences, expectations and desires towards the therapy. However, our own preferences may differ greatly from what is then offered to the patient. Taking this awareness

---

A. La Tona (✉) · A. Brugnera · J. Stringo
Department of Human and Social Sciences, University of Bergamo, Bergamo, Italy
e-mail: antonino.latona@unibg.it

M. Cooper
School of Psychology, University of Roehampton, London, UK

and humanity into one's work as a therapist could benefit clinical practice, especially when one is confronted with the inevitable individuality that each patient understandably brings to the table. However, to further emphasise how much this issue at least deserves to be weighed properly as part of the delicate balance constituted by the relationship of the therapeutic dyad, it is important to consider that at stake are not only the preferences of the patient/client but also the human and the understandable subjective preferences of the individual therapist. As stated by Cooper et al. (2019), mental health professionals practice psychotherapy largely on the basis of their own unique and personal preferences, which include theoretical orientations, clinical expertise and personal therapy. It then becomes very simple to acknowledge how recognising the same legitimate stance in the Other can only benefit the course and quality of the relationship and clinical practice itself, since it is an ineradicable element, even in the therapists themselves. In doing so, it is possible to take the Other into consideration in its wholeness, recognising the patient as an even more active member of the therapeutic process.

The relevance of including clients' preferences in clinical practice was highlighted by the Presidential Task Force on Evidence-Based Practice of the American Psychological Association (2006), which aimed 'to promote effective psychological practice and enhance public health by applying empirically supported principles of psychological assessment, case formulation, therapeutic relationship, and intervention' (p. 280).

This chapter introduces the concept of preferences in therapy, attempting to make tangible the reasons why it could be a rich perspective and seeks to provide a description of the benefits and limitations of this approach. In addition, this chapter explores the role of patient preferences in customising therapy and methods for assessing these preferences, integrating them into treatment, addressing challenges and considering cultural and individual differences.

1.1 *Understanding Patient Preferences*

Clients' preferences in psychotherapy can be defined as the environmental and relational conditions that clients desire during a therapeutic process (Tompkins et al., 2013). These preferences influence various aspects of therapy, including the type of therapeutic approach, the characteristics of the therapist, the frequency and duration of the sessions and the specific goals of treatment. Understanding and incorporating these preferences is crucial for several reasons. Enhancing therapeutic outcomes is a primary benefit. Research has consistently shown that when patients feel that their preferences are acknowledged and respected, they are more likely to engage in therapy, adhere to treatment plans and achieve better outcomes (Cooper et al., 2019; Swift et al., 2011). Several meta-analyses have verified that considering these factors within therapy has a tangible impact not only on the therapeutic relationship in general but also on satisfaction levels and outcomes in general (Lindhiem et al., 2014; Swift et al., 2019; Windle et al., 2020).

Building a strong therapeutic alliance is another key factor. The therapeutic alliance, or the collaborative relationship between therapist and patient, is a critical predictor of therapy success. Incorporating patient preferences helps strengthen this alliance by demonstrating respect and empathy, fundamental components of a positive therapeutic relationship (Cooper et al., 2023; Norcross & Wampold, 2011). Swift et al. (2019) describe three distinct types of preferences: (a) *activity preferences*, which is the expectation of what will actually be done in the course of therapy; (b) *preferences about the therapist*, which may refer to all those characteristics that belong to each client's ideal professional; and (c) *treatment preferences*, which are related to predispositions regarding the type of approach (e.g. cognitive–behavioural or systemic therapy) (Cooper et al., 2023; Norcross & Cooper, 2021). Keeping in mind these three dimensionalities, in which the possibility and differentiation of the subject's individual predispositions unfolds, represents a first step in making the therapeutic intervention integrated and personalised—centring it on the patient's most specific needs. In fact, in order to answer the question 'why should we care about our patients' preferences?', we need to carefully consider what actually happens in clinical practice on a daily basis. Most research, and understandably so, establishes the efficacy of specific treatments applied to equally specific disorders, and to do that they statistically compact a large population of people carrying the same diagnosis into a homogeneous whole. However, even patients with similar symptomatic conditions are unlikely to resemble each other sufficiently to overlap as individuals. As stated by Norcross and Cooper (2021), 'Perhaps the patients are diagnostically homogeneous, but nondiagnostic variability is the rule […]. It is precisely the unique individual and the singular context that many psychotherapists attempt to treat' (p. 5). However, even recognising the major role of the individual differences in every patient, often a specific training to acknowledge them is absent in the clinical courses (Norcross & Cooper, 2021).

While the *traditional* approach to medicine sees a unidirectional, hierarchically orientated relationship in which the patient is a passive receptor of treatments to which they must simply adhere, the *psychosocial model* advocates a bidirectional relationship between the two instances involved and instead sees the individual actively engaged in sharing preferences, idiographies and cultural aspects (Norcross & Cooper, 2021). In doing so, both the therapy and the relationship with the treating professional can hopefully take due account of them. Increasing patient satisfaction is, in fact, also important. When therapy is tailored to meet patients' individual needs and preferences, patients are more likely to be satisfied with their treatment, leading to higher levels of motivation and commitment to the therapeutic process (Norcross & Cooper, 2021). Making the patient feel that they are an active part of the path and that they can exercise their individuality in choosing also makes the level of satisfaction higher, rather than experiencing it as an intervention dropped from above. Thus, considering preferences is not only clinically significant but also an ethical matter encompassing respect for autonomy and informed decision-making.

1.2 Assessing Patient Preferences

Although client preferences may be explored in an unstructured manner during initial therapeutic sessions, some authors have recommended using patient self-report instruments to situate client preferences along dimensional continua (Norcross & Cooper, 2021; Swift et al., 2018). Such processes also allow for the monitoring of these preferences over time. The advantages of administering self-report measures compared to unstructured interviews are similar to those associated with any normed and reliable psychological scale. Standardised measures provide a more comprehensive assessment, greater consistency of measurement and the ability to estimate the strength of expressed preferences relative to the general population and therapists' typical practices.

Several questionnaires are used to assess clients' preferences in therapy, including the Psychotherapy Preferences and Experience Questionnaire (PEX; Frövenholt et al., 2007), the Preference for College Counseling Inventory (PCCI; Hatchett, 2015) and the Counseling Preference Form (CPF; Goates-Jones & Hill, 2008). However, many of these instruments were developed and validated among non-clinical samples and for different roles related to helping professions in general, which can limit their applicability in clinical settings. In contrast, the Therapy Personalisation Form (TPF; Bowens & Cooper, 2012) was specifically developed and validated for clinical settings, although its considerable length can discourage clients from completing it (McHorney, 1996). In 2016, Cooper and Norcross developed the Cooper–Norcross Inventory of Preferences (C-NIP) to balance reliable measurements with clinical utility. The C-NIP, derived from the TPF, a literature review and clinical experience, consists of 18 items and yields four bipolar scales (see Fig. 1). The C-NIP demonstrated satisfactory internal consistency in the original validation study (coefficient alpha ranged from .60 to .85) carried out on a sample of 860 clients treated by psychologists, psychotherapists and counsellors (Cooper & Norcross, 2016). It should be noted that the original four-factor model did not work well in non-English translations (Řiháček et al., 2023). Consequently, Řiháček et al. (2023) proposed a new five-factor model that split the original emotional intensity factor into two new factors: (emotional intensity vs. emotional reserve and immediacy-non-immediacy) that was tested and validated on cross-cultural samples. C-NIP has been translated into over 10 languages, including German (Heinze et al., 2022), Portuguese (Malosso, 2019), Chinese (She et al., 2023) and Italian (La Tona et al., 2024, paper submitted), with an estimated 12,000 clients having used this measure since its inception in 2015.

About the C-NIP

The C-NIP can be used in an initial assessment or an early session of psychotherapy to facilitate an initial dialogue with clients about their therapy preferences. It can also be used in further sessions at regular intervals (e.g. sessions 5 and 10) and is

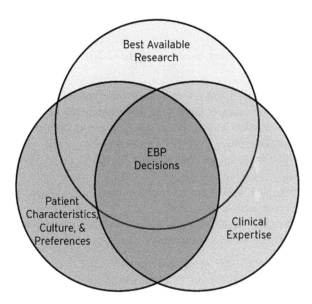

Fig. 1 Evidence-based practice components demonstrating major convergence: adopt. (*Source:* Norcross & Cooper, 2021. Copyright 2017 by J. C. Norcross, T. P. Hogan, G. P. Koocher and L. A. Maggio. Adapted with permission from Norcross et al., 2017)

particularly useful during a review session or routine outcome monitoring. The C-NIP consists of two parts. Over 18 items, the first part invites clients to indicate their preferences for how they would like a psychotherapist/counsellor to work with them. The items are grouped into four bipolar scales: therapist directiveness vs. client directiveness, emotional intensity vs. emotional reserve, past orientation vs. present orientation and warm support vs. focused challenge. At the end of each scale is a scoring key that calculates if any strong preferences exist in either direction. The second part asks multiple open-ended questions about client preferences. For instance, clients are asked if they have strong preferences concerning the number of therapy sessions, the type of therapy format/modality or anything they would particularly dislike. Completion and scoring of the C-NIP typically takes 5 min. The length of the subsequent discussion and treatment planning varies considerably. The C-NIP measure is free to use and is licenced under the Creative Commons Attribution-NoDerivs 4.0 international licence. No permission is required. However, you are asked not to alter the form and to use the latest version (currently 1.1). Several studies have provided evidence of the instrument's reliability and clinical validity (Cooper & Norcross, 2016; Řiháček et al., 2023; She et al., 2023). For more information, see https://www.c-nip.net/.

The Initial Invitation

Clients can be verbally invited to complete the C-NIP in a variety of ways. For example:

- 'I have been conducting and researching psychotherapy for XX years, and we have learned the importance of tailoring or personalising psychotherapy specifically to you. Here is a brief instrument that can help us do just that.'
- 'We really want counselling to be as suited as possible to what you want. So we'd be grateful if you could spend a few minutes completing this questionnaire to tell us what that is.'
- 'Let's determine your strong preferences for this therapy. Would you kindly take a few minutes to complete this form?'
- 'Research attests that psychotherapy works best when it matches clients' preferences. Here's a brief, efficient way that we can begin that discussion.'

Consistent with the C-NIP's emphasis on honouring client preferences, we do not require clients to complete the C-NIP. If a client indicates that they are not willing, interested or ready to complete the form, then we respect that decision. The form can be completed either later in the psychotherapy/counselling or not at all.

Scoring

Scoring the C-NIP is straightforward. Sum/total the five items constituting each scale (three items for the past/present orientation scale), and then determine whether that scale score indicates a strong preference in either direction or no strong preference. Scores marked with a minus should be subtracted from the total. For instance, if a client scores 3, 0 and -2, the total would be 1; if they score -2, -3 and 2, the total would be -3. For each scale, circle in the coloured scoring box whether the client has indicated a strong preference (in either direction) or no strong preference. The C-NIP was normed so that approximately a quarter of client scores would fall into a strong preference on one side of the scale, another quarter into a strong preference on the other side and the remaining one-half of scores would fall into the average or no strong preference range.

The subsequent dialogue with clients about any identified strong preferences is generally the most important part of the C-NIP process. Remember that the C-NIP scores provide the starting point for a genuine exchange about how clients can get the most out of their psychotherapy. When strong preferences are identified, the clinician can reflect this back to the client and enquire further into its meaning. For instance:

- 'I can see here that you desire quite an emotionally intense therapy. Can you say more about that?'
- 'Your responses suggest that you want me to challenge you. Is that right? What sort of challenge do you think might be helpful?'

- 'You're keen to meet every two weeks. Do you have a sense of how that would be helpful to you?'

It may also prove helpful to enquire into the origins of clients' preferences. This typically generates more context and meaning for their treatment desires. For instance:

Clinician: You indicated here that you want quite a directive approach with lots of guidance and structure. Do you have a sense of why that is?
Client: Yes. The last counsellor I had was really nice, but she didn't say too much, and I found it all a bit ... aimless and meandering. So I think this time I'd like someone who focused me more.
Clinician: So, it's about, maybe, having someone to focus you. Is that right? [Client: Mm]. For instance, would it be helpful if I asked you what you'd like to work on at the start of each session?

Of course, there may be times when it is appropriate for clinicians to bring their own knowledge and experience to the exchange. For example, if a client has been saying that they frequently defer responsibility to others, then indicates on the C-NIP that they have a strong preference for therapist directiveness, the therapist may enquire about potential parallels here. For instance:

Clinician: I can see here that you are asking for a directive approach.
Client: Yes, I feel like I just don't know my own mind.
Clinician: OK. I'm aware that you were talking earlier about being deferential to others and that that's a real problem for you. I'm OK about being quite directive here; at the same time, I'm wondering if that's necessarily the best thing for you. Do you know what I mean? I wonder if it's going to end up being like the thing you said was really unhelpful.
Client: Uh ... I—I get so lost. Particularly when I feel under pressure.
Clinician: I totally get that. Maybe there'll be something here about your own authority—taking more decisions by yourself. And that might include here in therapy, too.

On occasion, the clinician may also bring in research evidence. For instance, when clients indicate a strong preference for emotional intensity, the psychotherapist may note that emotional processing tends to be associated with improved outcomes (Pascual-Leone et al., 2016; Peluso & Freund, 2018). This discussion presents a valuable opportunity, particularly during an assessment session, for clinicians to indicate whether they believe they can accommodate the client's strong preferences. When a client expresses a strong preference for therapist directiveness, for example, and the counsellor is committed to classical person-centred therapy, the clinician might reply as follows: 'I can see you strongly desire a psychotherapist who is going to structure and lead. That's not what I offer in my practice. My approach tends to be much more about allowing the client to take the lead. Is this something you would like to try, or should we talk about other options that better suit you?' It is essential that the therapist does not convey judgments about the client's therapeutic preferences. Clients should feel that their preferences are valued, whatever they have indicated.

Using the C-NIP in Supervision

The client's C-NIP scores can be brought into supervision to inform a discussion about treatment planning and selection—that is, the best way of working with that particular client. Although patients' preferences represent a single consideration, an awareness of what the client wants can provide valuable insights into the best way forward. For instance:

Clinician: I think, with Annie, she's finding it hard to connect with her emotions and a lot of what we do feels very 'heady'.
Supervisor: Mm. Any sense of what might help her connect more emotionally?
Clinician: I did think about two-chair work. Just—I'm not sure whether she'd go for that or not.
Supervisor: What did she put on her C-NIP about emotional intensity?
Clinician: [Checks the C-NIP]. Yes, she did say she wanted something emotionally intense.
Supervisor: So, she's mentioning that that is something she might be up for.

1.3   *Integrating Patient Preferences into Treatment*

Integrating patient preferences into therapy involves a nuanced approach, summarised by the 'four As': *Adopt, Adapt, Alternative* and *Another*.

Adopting patient preferences means fully integrating them into the treatment plan. This approach is straightforward when patient preferences align with clinical expertise, ethical standards and evidence-based practices. For example, if a patient prefers a cognitive–behavioural approach for anxiety, and this method is supported by research, the therapist can seamlessly adopt this preference (Norcross & Cooper, 2021). When patient preferences cannot be fully adopted, they can often be adapted. This involves modifying the preferences to fit within the constraints of clinical practice while still honouring the patient's desires. For instance, a patient may prefer a specific therapy technique that is not entirely supported by evidence. The therapist might adapt by incorporating elements of the preferred technique into a broader, evidence-based approach (Norcross & Cooper, 2021). Adoption obviously brings many positive advantages to the success of therapy: it improves the relationship of trust between patient and practitioner, limits the chances of premature drop out of therapy, increases the likelihood of successful therapy, and puts the patient at ease. Adopting clients' demands into one's therapy, however, should not mean losing one's sense of authenticity as a professional. Meeting clients' needs is important, and doing so requires resilience, but as in everything, it is crucial to find a healthy middle ground so that one's work does not lose its meaning.

The second choice to consider is to *adapt*. In cases where the client's preferences cannot be adopted, an attempt can be made to offer the client an adapted version of what they have requested. Tailoring a request to one's own method is, therefore, a good middle ground, since the client's preference may not be most helpful to them. In this case, one tries to keep what one can of the above request but contextualises it in the therapy. This strategy could be, in some cases, the solution for convincing a sceptical patient to continue therapy and not stop it prematurely. Adaptation, of course, is not always possible, but in cases where it is, it should be seen by the therapist as an ethical obligation to increase the client's autonomy and involvement.

As discussed earlier, the therapist has a duty to accommodate patients' requests, but only as long as they do not clash with ethical issues and scientific evidence. The *third* choice, to offer an *alternative*, tends to be taken when strong client preferences may not lead to effective outcomes or, when they go against ethical codes. It should be emphasised that this process, in which an alternative is offered to patients, is very delicate and could at times be misunderstood. For this reason, caution should be employed so that we can properly place ourselves in the patient's position when they are offered the alternative, we propose instead of the preferences they have explicitly requested. These arrangements are referred to by the authors as the '*three Es*': *Explain, Empathise* and *Educate* (Norcross & Cooper, 2021).

Explain is the part in which the professional explains to the person in front of them why their requests could not be put into practice, arguing in a concrete way and showing that there are valid reasons behind this choice. Before a course of therapy begins, there may already be several aspects due to which it is impossible to adopt or adapt patients' preferences, such as if one were faced with ethical conflicts, a lack of expertise of the practitioner in a particular area and a non-progressive patient. All of these cases require an alternative. For example, a patient might have solid preferences regarding the therapist's background, gender or experience. Empathise is about expecting emotional reactions from the patient receiving the news and handle them together with him, without assuming that it will not be easy to accept this choice on the part of the client. What is at stake here is the trust between patient and therapist, so empathy must be at the forefront in dealing with this phase.

Educate means explaining to the patient what the techniques will consist of in therapy, what results they should achieve and what activities will be conducted as well as, most importantly, emphasising the benefits or rationale over the techniques the client would have preferred.

On the ethical side, there are cases in which the therapist has to set boundaries. An example might be a patient who seeks physical contact or a client who expressly says they want to take their own life; in the latter case, the family and therapists must be notified about it, even if this goes against the patient's wishes. In such cases, using empathy and open dialogue, and even expressly stating one's intentions, can be effective ways to encourage the patient to stay safe without ruining the loyalty pact between the two parties. By doing so, despite the fact that you are not following the wishes of the person in front of you, who is opening up by revealing something sensitive about themselves, you can respect your own ethicality and at the same time not impose yourself on the other person but patiently and calmly explain the reasons for making certain decisions for their safety. However, in the case where one is faced with a patient who is not making progress, there are several actionable strategies (Norcross & Cooper, 2021). First of all, one has to understand the reasons why the work with the client is not working: talk again about the strong preferences and see whether they have been enough space to be able to check whether they are indeed not working. The therapist can also use evidence-based research to find other methods applicable to the specific situation, try to understand the degree to which the patient is willing and whether they are ready to accept the change, make sure not to create ruptures in the trust pact between therapist and patient, and request supervision of the case and possibly send the person to another therapist. When, on the other hand, the demands of the person can be followed, accepted and implemented but are beyond the scope of the therapist's expertise, the solution is to recommend an *alternative* therapist who may be suitable for the patient's needs. The other choices that the therapist can make (adapt, adopt or offer an alternative) can be implemented by the therapist themselves. However, in this case, the therapist should step aside so that a more suitable person can take their place and follow up with the patient. To be able to understand whether you are the right person to engage in a course of therapy with a patient, the first thing to do is to understand what the patient wants, but that is not all. A patient who is approaching treatment for the first time might rely on the first person they find without knowing that there are different paths of treatment and different therapists who offer completely different services, who investigate different things and who propose different solutions depending on the problem, the way one wants to deal with it and the results one would like to achieve. Unfortunately, few studies have addressed how to approach a patient in recommending another therapist. The following are some strategies that can be implemented in such cases (Cooper & McLeod, 2011).

First, one must understand one's own methods and goals as a therapist. Knowing one's skills and accepting one's own limitations are the basis for being able to figure out whether to agree to start a course with a patient. That is, one must accept one's limitations, obviously referring to purely work-related ones, which certainly does not mean admitting defeat but simply realising that one cannot offer just anything to anyone; one must always take into account one's skills and understand when they may be inefficient in a given context.

Another important aspect is the way one approaches the patient. One must show understanding and make it clear that any decision will be made in mutual agreement between the two parties working together for a common goal: the patient's well-being. In this way, the choice is more likely to seem reasoned and will not sound like an imposition on the client. To do this, one must always try to make it clear to the other person that the advice to be followed by another therapist is not due to the client but rather to a lack of the therapist itself. It is also useful to have advice to offer and contact therapists suitable for the client's situation—of course, after also

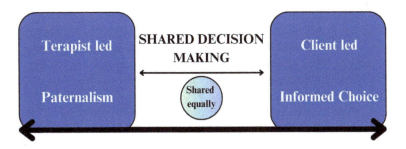

Fig. 2 The spectrum of shared decision-making. (*Source:* Norcross & Cooper, 2021. Readapted from the original Gibson (2020). Copyright 2017 by J. C. Norcross, T. P. Hogan, G. P. Koocher, and L. A. Maggio. Adapted with permission from Norcross et al. 2017)

consulting the other party and being sure that the figure to whom the patient is referred is the right one and can actually take charge of them.

Three possible mechanisms underlie the positive effect of preference integration. The first is *matching effects*: that patients have some knowledge of what works for them, such that providing this is more likely to be helpful. The second mechanism is *choice effects*—that is, the positive impact and empowerment that having different treatment choices offered may give. The final mechanism concerns *alliance effects*: offering choice and dialogue on the nature of therapy can have positive effects on the alliance and adherence to agreed-upon goals and tasks (Cooper et al., 2023; Norcross & Cooper, 2021).

Working with patient preferences has many parallels to *shared decision-making* (SDM) in the medical field (Norcross & Cooper, 2021). Although applied mainly to single interventions of medicine and surgery, at the conceptual level, SDM can offer several insights that can also be applied to psychotherapy (see Fig. 2). We can define SDM as a way of working contrasted with the *paternalistic* model at one extreme and with *informed patient choice* at the other. Shared decision-making falls within the middle three points, where it can be more therapist led or more client led, or more equal (Gibson et al., 2020). SDM is commonly defined as a process through which therapists and patients work together to find treatments, management or support packages based on clinical evidence and the patient's preferences. This process needs evidence-based information about options and outcomes, together with support counselling and a system for recording and indulging patients' informed preferences.

2 Challenges and Ethical Considerations

Therapists often face ethical dilemmas when accommodating patient preferences. Balancing patient autonomy with clinical judgement requires careful consideration of several factors. Patients have the right to make informed decisions about their treatment. However, therapists must use their clinical judgement to guide these decisions, especially when patient preferences conflict with evidence-based practices (Beauchamp & Childress, 2019). When patient preferences are not supported by research, therapists must decide whether to honour these preferences or to guide patients towards more effective treatments. This decision-making process should involve transparent communication and collaboration with patients (Norcross et al., 2017).

It is important to value patients' preferences, while still making sure to allow for adequate understanding of the risks and benefits. In doing so, presenting reasonable alternatives to one's services and providing integrated care can be seen as a professional act in accordance with the General Principles of the APA's Ethical Principles of Psychologists and Code of Conduct (APA, 2017). Although, upon explicit reference to the code itself, the 'General Principles, in contrast to Ethical Standards, do not represent obligations and should not form the basis for imposing sanctions' (APA, 2017, p. 3), it is nevertheless an ennobling interpretation of the practice by adhering to ethics and deontology, since it honours its principles of beneficence and non-maleficence, integrity, respect for the person, their dignity and self-determination.

Disagreements between patients and therapists can arise when preferences are not aligned. Effective management of these disagreements involves open communication, encouraging open and honest dialogue about preferences and concerns, engaging patients in the decision-making process to ensure that their voices are heard and respected and finding a middle ground that respects patient preferences while adhering to clinical guidelines (Norcross & Cooper, 2021). Positive management of such disagreements also requires a strong therapeutic alliance and preventing its rupture, possibly in two ways: *withdrawal* and *confrontation*. Consistent with the definition of rupture in Bordin's (1979) transtheoretical alliance paradigm, an alliance can be defined as a combination of purposeful collaboration and affective bonding within a framework of emotional attunement between the two individuals involved in treatment. Research on alliances has provided acknowledged empirical support for the concept that a strong alliance is vital for effective treatment (Flückiger et al., 2018). Interestingly, again based on Bordin's (1979) tripartite conceptualisation of alliance, ruptures can be characterised as disagreements between patients and therapists inherent in treatment goals, a lack of cooperation on treatment tasks and/or tension in emotional bonding. It is significant to see how, within nonetheless different theoretical perspectives, it is possible to trace meaningful resonances. However, further research is needed in this regard to understand the impact with greater accuracy.

As previously stated, cultural background significantly influences patient preferences in therapy. Culturally sensitive care involves recognising the cultural factors that shape patient preferences and behaviours and adapting therapeutic approaches to align with the cultural values and expectations of patients (Sue et al., 2019). More importantly, it is essential to adopt an accepting attitude that can welcome the idiographies of each person, whether they are part of a cultural, social, gender or nationality background. It may happen, as Sue et al. (2019) pointed out to us, that therapists and counsellors do not pay attention to specific characteristics or do not respect them as part of the person's history and identity, and they end up committing microaggressions that are often unintentional but damage the relationship with the patient.

3 Conclusion

Incorporating patient preferences into psychotherapy is a dynamic and complex process that requires ongoing assessment, flexibility and collaboration. By understanding and integrating patient preferences, therapists can enhance therapeutic alliances, improve treatment outcomes and provide more personalised and effective care. For example, the use of the C-NIP in combination with other routine outcome-monitoring instruments may have the potential to amplify the benefits of therapy (Mahon, 2021). In this regard, Cooper et al. (2021) hypothesised that diverse preferences may suit different therapeutic moments or stages of treatment. The use of the C-NIP within various psychotherapeutic approaches and for different client characteristics deserves deeper investigation (Mahon, 2021; Tait et al., 2022). This chapter has outlined the key concepts, methods and challenges involved in customising therapy based on patient preferences, highlighting the importance of patient-centred care in contemporary psychotherapy.

References

American Psychological Association. (2006). Evidence-based practice in psychology. *The American Psychologist, 61*(4), 271–285. https://doi.org/10.1037/0003-066X.61.4.271
American Psychological Association. (2017). *Ethical principles of psychologists and code of conduct*. American Psychological Association.
Beauchamp, T. L., & Childress, J. F. (2019). *Principles of biomedical ethics*. Oxford University Press.
Bordin, E. S. (1979). The generalizability of the psychoanalytic concept of the working alliance. *Psychotherapy: Theory, Research & Practice, 16*(3), 252–260. https://doi.org/10.1037/h0085885
Bowens, M., & Cooper, M. (2012). Development of a client feedback tool: A qualitative study of therapists' experiences of using the Therapy Personalisation Forms. *European Journal of Psychotherapy and Counselling, 14*(1), 47–62. https://doi.org/10.1080/13642537.2012.652392
Bragesjö, M., Clinton, D., & Sandell, R. (2004). The credibility of psychodynamic, cognitive and cognitive-behavioural psychotherapy in a randomly selected sample of the general public. *Psychology and Psychotherapy: Theory Research and Practice, 77*, 297–307. https://doi.org/10.1348/1476083041839358
Cole, B. P., Petronzi, G. J., Singley, D. B., & Baglieri, M. (2018). Predictors of men's psychotherapy preferences. *Counselling and Psychotherapy Research*. https://doi.org/10.1002/capr.12201
Cooper, M., & McLeod, J. (2011). Person-centered therapy: A pluralistic perspective. *Person-Centered and Experiential Psychotherapies, 10*(3), 210–223. https://doi.org/10.1080/14779757.2011.599517
Cooper, M., & Norcross, J. C. (2016). A brief, multidimensional measure of clients' therapy preferences: The Cooper-Norcross Inventory of Preferences (C-NIP). *International Journal of Clinical and Health Psychology, 16*(1), 87–98. https://doi.org/10.1016/j.ijchp.2015.08.003

Cooper, M., Norcross, J. C., Raymond-Barker, B., & Hogan, T. P. (2019). Psychotherapy preferences of laypersons and mental health professionals: Whose therapy is it? *Psychotherapy, 56*(2), 205–216. https://doi.org/10.1037/pst0000226

Cooper, M., van Rijn, B., Chryssafidou, E., & Stiles, W. B. (2021). Activity preferences in psychotherapy: What do patients want and how does this relate to outcomes and alliance? *Counselling Psychology Quarterly, 35*(3), 503–526. https://doi.org/10.1080/09515070.2021.1877620

Cooper, M., Di Malta, G., Knox, S., Weie Oddli, H., & Swift, J. K. (2023). Patient perspectives on working with preferences in psychotherapy: A consensual qualitative research study. *Psychotherapy Research, 33*(8), 1117–1131. https://doi.org/10.1080/10503307.2022.2161967

Flückiger, C., Del Re, A. C., Wampold, B. E., & Horvath, A. O. (2018). The alliance in adult psychotherapy: A meta-analytic synthesis. *Psychotherapy, 55*, 316–340. https://doi.org/10.1037/pst0000172

Frövenholt, J., Bragesjö, M., Clinton, D., & Sandell, R. (2007). How do experiences of psychiatric care affect the perceived credibility of different forms of psychotherapy? *Psychology and Psychotherapy: Theory Research and Practice, 80*, 205–215. https://doi.org/10.1348/147608306X116098

Gibson, A., Cooper, M., Rae, J., & Hayes, J. (2020). Clients' experiences of shared decision making in an integrative psychotherapy for depression. *Journal of Evaluation in Clinical Practice, 26*(2), 559–568. https://doi.org/10.1111/jep.13320

Goates-Jones, M., & Hill, C. E. (2008). Treatment preference, treatment-preference match, and psychotherapist credibility: Influence on session outcome and preference shift. *Psychotherapy: Theory, Research, Practice, Training, 45*(1), 61–74. https://doi.org/10.1037/0033-3204.45.1.61

Hatchett, G. T. (2015). Development of the preferences for college counseling inventory. *Journal of College Counseling, 18*(1), 37–48. https://doi.org/10.1002/j.2161-1882.2015.00067.x

Heinze, P. E., Weck, F., & Kühne, F. (2022). Assessing patient preferences: Examination of the German Cooper-Norcross Inventory of Preferences. *Frontiers in Psychology, 12*, 795776. https://doi.org/10.3389/fpsyg.2021.795776

Horvath, A. O., & Symonds, B. D. (1991). Relation between working alliance and outcome in psychotherapy: A meta-analysis. *Journal of Counseling Psychology, 38*(2), 139–149. https://doi.org/10.1037/0022-0167.38.2.139

King, M., Sibbald, B., Ward, E., Bower, P., Lloyd, M., Gabbay, M., & Byford, S. (2000). Randomised controlled trial of non-directive counselling, cognitive-behaviour therapy and usual general practitioner care in the management of depression as well as mixed anxiety and depression in primary care. *Health Technology Assessment, 4*(19), 1–83.

Lindhiem, O., Bennett, C. B., Trentacosta, C. J., & McLear, C. (2014). Client preferences affect treatment satisfaction, completion, and clinical outcome: A meta-analysis. *Clinical Psychology Review, 34*(6), 506–517. https://doi.org/10.1016/j.cpr.2014.06.002

La Tona, A., Brugnera, A., Salerno, S., Tasca, G. A., Carrara, S.,Lo Coco, G., Cooper, M., Norcross, J., & Compare, A. (2024). *Factorial Structure and Measurement Invariance of the Italian Version of the Cooper – Norcross Inventory of Preferences (C-NIP)*. Manuscript Submitted for Publication.

Mahon, D. (2021). Choice, voice and collaboration: Using preference accommodation and feedback in trauma therapy. *Mental Health and Social Inclusion, 25*(4), 396–406. https://doi.org/10.1108/mhsi-06-2021-0032

Malosso, M. (2019). *Adaptção transcultural para o português e validação de duas ferramentas de avaliação das preferências do cliente em psicoterapia: C-NIP e PEX.P1*. ISPA.

McHorney, C. A. (1996). Measuring and monitoring general health status in elderly persons: Practical and methodological issues in using the SF-36 Health Survey. *The Gerontologist, 36*(5), 571–583.

Norcross, J. C. (2005). The psychotherapist's own psychotherapy: Educating and developing psychologists. *American Psychologist, 60*(8), 840–850. https://doi.org/10.1037/0003-066X.60.8.840

Norcross, J. C., & Wampold, B. E. (2011). Evidence-based therapy relationships: research conclusions and clinical practices. *Psychotherapy (Chicago, Ill.), 48*(1), 98–102. https://doi.org/10.1037/a0022161

Norcross, J. C., & Cooper, M. (2021). *Personalizing psychotherapy: Assessing and accommodating patient preferences*. American Psychological Association.

Norcross, J. C., & Lambert, M. J. (2018). Evidence-based therapy relationships. In J. C. Norcross & M. J. Lambert (Eds.), *Psychotherapy relationships that work* (3rd ed., pp. 3–21). Oxford University Press.

Norcross, J. C., Hogan, T. P., Koocher, G. P., & Maggio, L. A. (2017). *Clinician's guide to evidence-based practices: Behavioral health and addictions* (2nd ed.). Oxford University Press.

Pascual-Leone, A., Paivio, S., & Harrington, S. (2016). Emotion in psychotherapy: An experiential-humanistic perspective. In D. Cain, K. Keenan, & S. Rubin (Eds.), *Humanistic psychotherapies* (2nd ed., pp. 147–181). American Psychological Association.

Peluso, P. R., & Freund, R. R. (2018). Therapist and client emotional expression and psychotherapy outcomes: A meta-analysis. *Psychotherapy, 55*(4), 461–472. https://doi.org/10.1037/pst0000165

Petronzi, G. J., & Masciale, J. N. (2015). Using personality traits and attachment styles to predict people's preference of psychotherapeutic orientation. *Counselling and Psychotherapy Research, 15*(4), 298–308. https://doi.org/10.1002/capr.12036

Řiháček, T., Cooper, M., Cígler, H., She, Z., Di Malta, G., & Norcross, J. C. (2023). The Cooper-Norcross Inventory of Preferences: Measurement invariance across & international datasets and languages. *Psychotherapy Research*, 1–13. https://doi.org/10.1080/10503307.2023.2255371

Řiháček, T., Cooper, M., Cígler, H., She, Z., Di Malta, G., & Norcross, J. C. (2023). The Cooper-Norcross Inventory of Preferences: Measurement invariance across international datasets and languages. *Psychotherapy Research, 34*(6), 804–816. https://doi.org/10.1080/10503307.2023.2255371

She, Z., Xi, J., Cooper, M., Norcross, J. C., & Di Malta, G. (2023). Validation of the Cooper-Norcross Inventory of Preferences in Chinese lay clients and mental health professionals: Factor structure, measurement invariance, and scale differences. *Journal of Counseling Psychology, 70*(4), 436–447. https://doi.org/10.1037/cou0000661

Sue, D. W., Sue, D., Neville, H. A., & Smith, L. (2019). *Counseling the culturally diverse: Theory and practice*. Wiley.

Swift, J. K., & Greenberg, R. P. (2012). Premature discontinuation in adult psychotherapy: A meta-analysis. *Journal of Consulting and Clinical Psychology, 82*(3), 520–531. https://doi.org/10.1037/a0028226

Swift, J. K., Callahan, J. L., & Vollmer, B. M. (2011). Preferences. In J. C. Norcross (Ed.), *Psychotherapy relationships that work* (2nd ed., pp. 301–315). Oxford University Press.

Swift, J. K., Callahan, J. L., Ivanovic, M., & Kominiak, N. (2013). Further examination of the psychotherapy preference effect: A meta-regression analysis. *Journal of Psychotherapy Integration, 23*(2), 134–145. https://doi.org/10.1037/a0031423

Swift, J. K., Callahan, J. L., Cooper, M., & Parkin, S. R. (2018). The impact of accommodating client preference in psychotherapy: A meta-analysis. *Journal of clinical psychology, 74*(11), 1924–1937. https://doi.org/10.1002/jclp.22680

Swift, J. K., Callahan, J. L., Cooper, M., & Parkin, S. R. (2019). Preferences. In J. C. Norcross (Ed.), *Psychotherapy relationships that work* (3rd ed., pp. 157–187). Oxford University Press.

Tait, J., Edmeade, L., & Delgadillo, J. (2022). Are depressed patients' coping strategies associated with psychotherapy treatment outcomes? *Psychology and Psychotherapy, 95*(1), 98–112. https://doi.org/10.1111/papt.12368

Tompkins, K. A., Swift, J. K., & Callahan, J. L. (2013). Working with clients by incorporating their preferences. *Psychotherapy (Chicago, Ill.), 50*(3), 279–283. https://doi.org/10.1037/a0032031

Windle, E., Tee, H., Sabitova, A., Jovanovic, N., Priebe, S., & Carr, C. (2020). Association of patient treatment preference with dropout and clinical outcomes in adult psychosocial mental health interventions: A systematic review and meta-analysis. *JAMA Psychiatry, 77*(3), 294–302. https://doi.org/10.1001/jamapsychiatry.2019.3750

Index

A
Acceptance and commitment therapy (ACT), 445–460, 508, 509, 514
Alliance ruptures, 13, 39, 143–144, 148, 151, 154, 155, 180, 181, 183–187, 189, 237, 239, 271, 307, 313, 323
Anorexia nervosa (AN), 216, 222, 363, 400, 401, 403, 407, 410, 411, 506
Attachment, 12, 25, 49, 76, 105, 142, 167, 179, 200, 235, 263, 280, 310, 330, 350, 391, 419, 460, 478, 508
Attachment assessment, 112, 113, 116, 119, 120, 122–133
Attachment-based family therapy (ABFT), 330–334, 337–341, 508, 509, 514
Attachment relationships, 13, 27, 58, 120, 168–172, 175, 185, 283
Attachment theory, 26–29, 49, 56, 167–169, 172, 174, 218, 263, 265, 280, 282–286, 288, 300, 330, 338, 419, 460, 488
Awareness, 5, 34, 50, 85–86, 107, 149, 187, 206, 249, 262, 281–282, 313, 363, 423, 453, 486, 502, 523, 537

B
Binge-eating disorder (BED), 400, 403, 504
Biosocial theory, 380–381, 383–386
Borderline personality disorder (BPD), 181, 188, 216, 217, 223, 380–383, 388–391, 457, 468, 472, 514
Bowlby, J., 26, 49, 53, 56, 63, 168–170, 172, 176, 182, 200, 263, 265, 283, 288, 296, 310, 330, 365, 488, 508

Bulimia nervosa, 398–401, 403, 407, 410

C
Caregiving system, 49, 51, 53, 61, 201
Case formulation, 25, 26, 31–41, 122–133, 182, 273, 312, 318–319, 383, 392, 478, 485, 488, 490–492, 508, 538
Clinical outcomes, 436, 505, 525
Cognitive behaviour therapy (CBT), 210, 212, 215, 330, 345, 347, 352–355, 359, 366, 392, 404, 435, 437, 438, 447, 455, 456, 460, 467, 471, 506, 508
Common Factors in Psychotherapy, 3–7, 181
Competitive system, 54, 56–59
Cooper-Norcross Inventory of Preferences (C-NIP), 540–544, 549
Co-trainer, 264–266, 269, 272–275, 279–301

D
Deliberate practice, 156, 157, 234, 239–241, 529, 533
Depression, 12, 37, 39, 58, 59, 119, 141, 144, 171, 191, 203, 221, 318, 334, 344, 356, 359–361, 365, 384, 389, 409, 420, 422, 434, 436, 437, 454, 455, 469, 489, 501, 502, 504–507, 512, 515
Dialectical behavior therapy (DBT), 308, 330, 379–392, 509, 514
Dialectics, 72, 73, 89, 144–146, 379, 380
Dynamic-maturational model (DMM), 105, 107–109, 112, 114, 117, 119–123, 125, 132, 134, 135

Dynamic-relational therapy (DRT), 417, 418, 423–438

E
Eating disorders, 58–59, 75–77, 90, 132, 222–223, 357, 363, 364, 389, 390, 397–411, 422, 458, 471, 514
Emotional processing, 210, 353, 543
Emotional regulation, 89, 209, 338, 350, 358, 363, 387, 484, 486, 514
Epistemic trust, 171–174, 177, 179–182, 190
Evolutionary psychology, 47
Experiential avoidance, 388, 449, 450, 454, 458
Experiential learning, 183, 273, 289, 294–295
Experiential techniques, 219, 268, 308, 312–314, 316, 317, 320, 323, 324
Experiential training, 262, 272, 285, 294
Eye movement desensitization and reprocessing (EMDR), 130, 210–215, 217, 218, 308, 320, 343–367, 489, 492, 494, 508, 509, 514

F
Facilitative interpersonal skill (FIS), 237–241, 534
Functional Family Formulation (FFF), 122–124, 127, 130, 132, 135

I
iCAST, 245–255
Individual psychotherapy, 381, 383–386, 436, 502
Integrated psychotherapy, 9–11, 16, 18, 261–275, 280, 290, 352–355
Integration of evidence-based practices, 3–18, 501–515
Integrative therapy, 514
Interpersonal skills, 13, 208, 233–241, 514

M
Maladaptive behaviors, 104–105, 110, 111, 380, 386
Mentalizing, 26–29, 35, 36, 39, 40, 174, 179–181, 183–192, 273
Metacognition, 75, 281, 286, 298, 300, 309, 312, 315, 316, 324, 478, 484–488, 493
Metacommunication, 152, 154, 155, 157, 180, 181, 188, 286, 315, 325, 433, 509, 513

Motivational systems, 47–61, 200, 201, 204, 206, 224, 265, 266, 272, 280, 282–286, 295, 296, 298, 300, 319, 478, 479, 483, 508

N
Nonverbal behavior, 245–248, 250, 251, 255
Nonverbal synchrony, 249, 253, 254

O
Outcome monitoring, 15, 521, 541, 549
Outcomes, 10, 29, 53, 144, 168, 179, 202, 234, 261, 308, 343, 410, 436, 456, 480, 503, 521

P
Patient feedback, 15, 521, 524, 533
Patient preferences, 16–17, 538–549
Perfectionism, 58, 65, 77, 296, 312, 313, 400, 404, 406, 417–438, 466, 493, 494
Pernicious personality, 417, 418
Personality disorders, 8, 57, 181, 198, 290, 308, 366, 437, 460, 513
Personalization of treatment, 5, 18, 294
Personal meaning organisations (PMOs), 73–93, 96, 97, 99, 265, 295, 300, 508
Postrationalist approach, 75, 99
Post-traumatic stress disorder (PTSD), 196–197, 202, 203, 210–224, 344, 345, 347, 349, 352–356, 358–362, 366, 391, 411, 470, 471, 504, 514
Preconscious processes, 123
Progress monitoring (PM), 521–531, 533–535
Psychodynamic psychotherapy (PST), 218, 435, 436
Psychological disorders, 114, 167, 358, 417, 513
Psychological flexibility, 449, 451, 452, 454, 455, 458, 514
Psychological interventions, 4, 14, 15, 17, 362, 507
Psychopathologies, 9, 15, 29, 32, 54–61, 74, 89–90, 104, 105, 114, 167, 172, 213, 216, 221–224, 254, 290, 308, 309, 311, 324, 350, 358, 362, 398, 399, 402–404, 406, 411, 417, 437, 454
Psychotherapeutic application, 290
Psychotherapy, 3, 25, 53, 73, 131, 141, 168, 181, 202, 233, 262, 279, 307, 343, 381, 398, 417, 467, 477, 502, 522

Psychotherapy training, 10, 279, 281, 287, 523

R
Rupture repair strategies, 183

S
Schema therapy, 219, 308, 445, 460–472
Self-awareness, 71, 85, 92, 94, 97, 267, 269, 271, 281–282, 287, 291, 295, 296, 300, 477, 486, 511, 513
Sexology, 284, 488–491
Sexual health, 488, 489
Stepped care models, 502–510, 515
Supervision and training, 10, 145, 155
Supervisions, 10, 15, 142, 143, 145–152, 154–157, 161, 162, 236, 251, 264–266, 269, 272–274, 280, 281, 290, 293, 295, 298, 299, 337–340, 408, 411, 434, 435, 524, 533–535, 544, 546

T
Therapeutic alliances, 10–14, 29, 39, 40, 55–61, 64–66, 142, 143, 150, 174–175, 179, 181–185, 187, 188, 190, 202, 205, 208–209, 215, 216, 263, 271, 288, 297, 309, 323, 333, 421, 424, 426, 427, 485–488, 508, 509, 523, 526, 527, 530, 539, 548, 549
Therapeutic effectiveness, 350
Therapeutic relationships, 4, 5, 7–9, 11, 12, 15, 30, 31, 39, 157, 168–170, 173, 174, 181, 190, 200–209, 221, 246, 255, 261, 264, 266, 267, 271, 273, 280, 281, 291–295, 308–312, 314–318, 324, 325, 382, 423, 425, 427–429, 466, 467, 478, 485–490, 493, 511, 529, 534, 538, 539
Therapeutic tasks, 169, 271
Therapist's task, 351
Therapist training, 340
Therapy, 5, 26, 56, 74, 130, 142, 173, 181, 202, 233, 262, 280, 308, 329, 343, 379, 417, 445, 485, 502, 521
Trauma, 27, 57, 109, 167, 179, 195, 284, 308, 331, 344, 391, 460, 489, 508
Trauma resolution, 338
Treatment, 3, 25, 93, 103, 143, 167, 181, 205, 233, 253, 266, 294, 308, 332, 343, 380, 397, 417, 449, 477, 501, 521
Treatment intensity, 408, 503
Triangle of Adaptation, 31–33, 35–41, 423, 429

Printed in the USA
CPSIA information can be obtained
at www.ICGtesting.com
CBHW061147231124
17726CB00009B/17

9 783031 719035